HISTORY
of
BLOUNT COUNTY TENNESSEE

From War Trail to Landing Strip

1795–1955

Inez E. Burns

Originally Sponsored by
MARY BLOUNT CHAPTER DAUGHTERS OF THE
AMERICAN REVOLUTION
THE TENNESSEE HISTORICAL COMMISSION
1957

HERITAGE BOOKS
2011

HERITAGE BOOKS
AN IMPRINT OF HERITAGE BOOKS, INC.

Books, CDs, and more—Worldwide

For our listing of thousands of titles see our website
at
www.HeritageBooks.com

A Facsimile Reprint
Published 2011 by
HERITAGE BOOKS, INC.
Publishing Division
100 Railroad Ave. #104
Westminster, Maryland 21157

Copyright © 1957 Inez E. Burns

— Publisher's Notice —
In reprints such as this, it is often not possible to remove blemishes from the original. We feel the contents of this book warrant its reissue despite these blemishes and hope you will agree and read it with pleasure.

International Standard Book Numbers
Paperbound: 978-0-7884-3779-3
Clothbound: 978-0-7884-8950-1

1749–1800

William Blount was appointed in 1790 to serve as Governor of the "Territory South of the River Ohio"—now Tennessee. He served in this position until the state of Tennessee was established in 1796. A part of Knox County was cut off in 1795 to form a new county which was called Blount in honor of the territorial governor. The county seat was called Maryville in honor of William Blount's wife, Mary Grainger Blount.

Mr. Parham

DEDICATED

To

Mr. William E. Parham

Mrs. Louise Langstroth Messler

Mrs. India Patton Broady

Mrs. Messler

Mrs. Broady

FOREWORD

To assemble the data necessary to write a history of Blount County has required every variety of search and research that is customary in a work of this sort, besides the many "wild goose chases." It would be impossible to enumerate the many sources of information which have been investigated during the past ten years.

Those who expect a genealogical work will be disappointed in this volume. Family history is not a subject to be treated hurriedly nor lightly, and family data have been used only incidentally and where they were pertinent to the subject under discussion. Many stories have been left untold for various reasons, and others could have been better phrased by someone else. This volume does not purport to be a complete story of Blount County, it is merely the pioneer volume which will establish certain hitherto inaccessible facts.

Primarily, I am indebted to the work of the late William E. Parham in abstracting the early Blount County records and organizing them in usable form. This work alone has saved me from many hours of tiresome and fruitless research. Mr. Parham also wrote a great number of historical sketches and collected voluminous files of family data which have furnished many valuable leads. Members of the Mary Blount Chapter Daughters of the American Revolution helped to organize these materials and furnished a typist for Mr. Parham and in return were given a copy of the materials for their historical collection. These materials have been made available for my use at any time, and thus materially speeded up certain phases of work. Mrs. Louise Langstroth Messler worked with Mr. Parham some and encouraged him to carry his abstracts through to a conclusion. In her capacity as Regent and Historian of the D.A.R. (and Daughters of 1812) she encouraged him to write historical sketches which incorporated many interesting bits of information. Copies of all these, published and unpublished, and many scrapbooks of clippings were kept by Mrs. Messler. The Messler family recently presented this collection to me. The third person to whom I owe much is Mrs. India Patton Broady who spent her entire lifetime collecting data which has proven invaluable to me. She had an insatiable interest in such data and collected and kept every type of materials that was available. Since files of the early newspapers are rather sketchy, her choice numbers have been "gold mines" of information. Since she also worked with Mr. Parham, she, too, had a rather full collection of his sketches. The McClung Room at Lawson McGhee Library in Knoxville has the Parham Papers, especially the complete family files. However, none of the four named sources of Mr. Parham's sketches has all that he wrote. There is one or two in practically every collection which is not in the others.

For positive and accurate information from primary sources, I am greatly indebted to Mr. Robert T. Quarles of the Tennessee State Archives. His help and guidance during my early research helped me to definitely decide that I would finish this work. His interest and suggestions as the work has progressed has been most encouraging. Mrs. Gertrude Parsley of the Tennessee State Library has been very kind in promptly locating odd bits of information for me.

The final word in regard to Blount County history is, of course, her own original records which are found in the local offices. I have had the full cooperation of every county official whom I have approached in my research. Mr. Joe L. Marshall, and Mrs. Frances Harris, in the County Court Clerk's office, have been consistently cooperative and helpful beyond the call of duty. Mr. Runa S. White and Mrs. Mildred M. Watson and their personnel, in the Register's office, have been most cordial and willing to lend assistance in my search for materials.

I am indebted to the Joint Universities Library in Nashville; the Lawson McGhee and the University of Tennessee libraries in Knoxville; and to the Maryville College and A. K. Harper Memorial libraries of Maryville for the loan of materials and for the use of non-circulating materials in their collections. I am also indebted to the Maryville *Times* and the Maryville *Enterprise* for the use of their files and for the fine cooperation of their personnel.

Several people have very graciously opened their private libraries to me, especially Mrs. Charles F. Wayland, Mrs. L. W. McCown, Miss Mary U. Rothrock and the Broady-McKenzie family. The many churches and organizations whose officials have cooperated by furnishing records are too numerous to mention here, but they are acknowledged in their proper place.

I am particularly indebted to Mr. H. S. Garner and Mr. Thomas F. Broady for their help in locating places and identifying people, and to Mr. and Mrs. Boyd McKenzie for the use of the Broady Collection which have been a veritable gold mine of data. Lastly, I am deeply indebted to Mrs. Adele McKenzie, Mrs. Elizabeth Baugh and Mrs. Elizabeth Timmons for their help in locating old photographs and to Mrs. Spears of Spears Studio for her fine work in copying old photographs.

This volume would have not been possible without the help of Mr. and Mrs. Eugene Little in revising and typing. Many changes and additions have had to be made in the process of assembling materials which necessitated much re-typing. Mrs. Fred C. Mynatt has assisted in the final editing and Miss Betty Boone has been a ready and willing typist during the final stages.

Lastly, I would like to respectfully tender my appreciation to those members of the Tennessee Historical Commission, who have been deeply interested in the progress of this volume, and have given their consistent moral support to these efforts, and to the Mary Blount Chapter of the Daughters of the American Revolution, which has seen fit to accept this volume as worthy of their sponsorship.

INEZ BURNS

Maryville, Tennessee

DEDICATION

✦

To WILLIAM E. PARHAM, a genealogist of note, whose prodigious labors in abstracting, and compiling Blount County records of all sorts have saved endless hours of research for historical data;

To MRS. LOUISE LANGSTROTH MESSLER, who keenly appreciated the ever-increasing value of such materials, and who guided and aided Mr. Parham in organizing his materials into usable form;

To MRS. INDIA PATTON BROADY, who had a "grass-roots" knowledge of Blount County families and history, and spent her life delving into records and collecting a wide variety of materials which have been invaluable in the preparation of this volume;

To these three individually, and to the three as a group who often worked together on historical projects, this volume is humbly and gratefully dedicated as a permanent reminder of their contribution to Blount County history.

Maryville, Tennessee
October 24, 1956

CONTENTS

Chapter		Page
I.	The Pre-settlement Period	1
II.	The Settlement Period	13
III.	The County Government	31
IV.	The County's Role in the Wars	53
V.	Early Inns and Watering Places	71
VI.	The Churches of Blount County	95
VII.	Education	133
VIII.	Medical Men and Institutions	181
IX.	Courts, Public Offices and Men of Law	197
X.	Industries and Occupations	217
XI.	Communities	255
	Appendix	288
	Index	332

ILLUSTRATIONS

WILLIAM BLOUNT	*Facing Page* II
MR. PARHAM, MRS. BROADY, AND MRS. MESSLER	*Facing Page* III
PARKINS AND GILLESPIE STONE HOUSES	*Facing Page* 26
PLOT OF CITY OF MARYVILLE (1821)	*Facing Page* 27
MAP OF BLOUNT COUNTY FORTS	*Pages* 22 & 23
FOUNDERS AND BUILDERS OF BLOUNT COUNTY	*Facing Page* 44
MAP OF BLOUNT COUNTY ABOUT 1824	*Facing Page* 45
MAJOR JAMES HOUSTON'S EXPENSE ACCOUNT, 1788	*Page* 54
SAM HOUSTON AS AN ARMY OFFICER	*Facing Page* 60
SOME MILITARY MEN OF NOTE	*Facing Page* 61
MAP OF MONTVALE AND VICINITY	*Page* 82
MONTVALE SPRINGS HOTEL	*Facing Page* 84
MARYVILLE COLLEGE, 1879	*Page* 132
WOMEN OF NOTE	*Facing Page* 148
MASONIC INSTITUTE AND FRIENDS SCHOOL	*Facing Page* 149
EDUCATIONAL LEADERS	*Facing Page* 164
PORTER ACADEMY AND COLUMBIAN HALL	*Facing Page* 165
MEN OF MEDICINE	*Facing Page* 196
MEN TO REMEMBER	*Facing Page* 197

CHAPTER I

The Pre-Settlement Period

WHENEVER an artist paints a picture, certain objects stand out sharply against a background of fathomless depth. The background is not a hodge-podge of purposeless strokes, but each line in the perspective contributes to the perfect unity of the finished work. A Tennessee history cannot begin with the erection of William Bean's cabin on Watauga in 1769, nor can a history of Blount County begin with the first influx of settlers into Blount County in 1785. It is necessary to reach back a hundred years into the misty shadows of history to show why events developed as they did.

In 1609, King James I issued a patent for the land between 34° and 36° "from sea to sea." Thus, until Charles I issued a grant in 1629 for the land between 31° and 36° to another party, what is now Tennessee was Virginia. After 1629, it was, roughly speaking, a part of Carolina, although the boundaries of Carolina were not permanently fixed for a good many years. In 1719 when Carolina was divided, the Tennessee Country fell to North Carolina and so remained until after the Revolutionary War.[1]

Two hundred years ago, the region now known as East Tennessee was an unbroken wilderness with few signs of human occupancy. The only breaks in the thick undergrowth were the buffalo trails. The buffalo was a large, heavy animal capable of breaking a trail where he chose, and he, unerringly, chose the easiest path and the shortest distance where practicable. There is no question as to his ability as an engineer, because modern highways today follow the paths of the old buffalo trails or traces in Tennessee.

The main trails, used for years, were deep-cut and about three feet wide—just right for travel with pack animals. Buffaloes, like men, were seeking clear springs, salt licks, and green fields, so the paths led always further on toward the "beyond." [2]

During the years prior to English Settlement, the Spanish may have passed over the southern boundary of the state; and the French may have paused briefly on the bluffs of the Mississippi, but they left no permanent mark, and the final settlement of what is now Tennessee was not due to the concerted action of any agency but to the American pioneer. Goodpasture defines the pioneer as the "first person to explore or visit the country, especially the one who makes the first permanent settlement." The Tennessee Country was known only to the Indians,

---

[1] John Haywood, *Civil and Political History of the State of Tennessee to 1796*, (Nashville, 1915), 16. Hereinafter cited, *Haywood*.

[2] Gilbert Imlay, *A Topographical Description of the Western Territory of North America*, 3rd ed. (London, 1797) 323; Passim. Hereinafter cited *Imlay*.

1

prior to 1673. That portion of the Tennessee Valley north of the Little Tennessee River, along whose banks dwelt the Overhill Cherokees, was, up to that time, an unoccupied hunting ground with few signs that it ever had been occupied.

In 1646 Fort Henry, a trading post, had been established by Abraham Woods near present-day Petersburg, Virginia, from which traders went out and established trading paths. Each year they ventured further and further, until they reached from Virginia into the Carolinas and Georgia among the Indians. Thus it is, that the paths were first made in the hope of personal gain, but other men later followed these beaten paths for different reasons.[3]

At first, the traders were afraid to venture off the main path, but they finally yielded to the urge to explore and began to prowl up and down the small coves and water courses. The traders then began to tell each other what they had seen and each vied with the other in daring. So, they finally reached the top of the Allegheny Mountain range and looked into the "Promised Land." The occasional Indian that they met was questioned closely about this land over the mountains.

Early in the year 1673, James Needham, recently arrived from South Carolina, and Gabriel Arthur, an indentured servant of Woods, and eight Indians came to the top of the Allegheny Mountain range and ventured over into the unknown. They followed the buffalo trails as best they could and endured many hardships. They related how they crossed five rivers and finally, Needham, Arthur and one Indian came to a sixth, and on the south bank of the sixth river this side of the mountains, they found an Indian village. They were well received and later placed on a platform where all the people could look at them. Needham returned to Virginia to report to Woods, leaving Arthur to learn the Indian language. On his way back to the villages, Needham was killed by his Indian guide. Arthur was kept a virtual prisoner by the Indians for many years. He went on hunting expeditions with the Indians and was finally captured by hostile Indians north of the Ohio and after a while escaped and made his way to Virginia by way of Cumberland Gap to tell his experiences. The story was recorded in a letter from Woods to John Richards in London, August 22, 1674.[4]

It is significant that the year of this first recorded excursion of the white man into the wilderness which is now East Tennessee was the same year that the French explorers, Marquette and Joliet, explored the Mississippi River Valley and paused at the western extremity of the state.

It is possible that there were casual visitors, traders or hunters in this territory before 1673 but the fact is not recorded. Certainly during the next few decades there were dozens of them, but most of them doubtless came over the well-defined path from Charleston which led through

---

[3] Alvord, Clarence Walworth and Lee Bidgood, *The First Explorations of the Trans-Allegheny Region by the Virginians 1650-1674*, (Cleveland, 1912), 29-114. Passim.
[4] *Ibid.*, 80 ff; 210 ff.

the Lower and Middle Cherokee towns to the Overhill towns on the Little Tennessee and neighboring streams to the south. It also stands to reason that these curious ones reached out and explored the surrounding country on hunting expeditions, but they left no records. And, of course, there were always the white renegades who became savage and forgot their own civilization. These left no record of their doings and for our purpose we are mainly interested in those people who came from the northeast and crossed into what is now Blount County.[5]

In 1690 Cornelius Doherty, a trader from Virginia, visited the Indian villages east of the mountains and introduced horses among them, and of course, horse-stealing followed. Doherty did not appear among the Overhill Indians as a trader until 1719, when Virginia was trying to establish trade relations.

Charleston was settled in 1670 and by 1690 South Carolina traders were beginning to reach across the mountains into the Tennessee Country. The famous James Adair arrived among them by 1730 or 1735 where he spent the next forty years studying the Indians and writing about them. Trading was well established and regulated by now.

In 1740 a packman named Vaughn, from Amelia County, Virginia, recorded the route he followed from Virginia to the Indian villages. When he reached the French Broad at the island, he went up Little Pigeon; crossed over some small mountains to the Tuckaleechee towns and followed Little River to the main path. Near the Tuckaleechee towns the path branched off into Cades Cove and through Ekaneetlee Gap to the Upper Cherokee towns. Vaughn said these trails were old when he first saw them. He continued to use them until about 1754.[6]

Dissension among the traders and infiltration of French propaganda as well as the change of governors in Virginia and South Carolina caused a withdrawal of trade about this time.

The Cherokees were afraid of attack from the North and began to beg the respective governors of Virginia and the Carolinas to build a fort for their protection from the Northern tribes and their French allies. The colonies, in turn, wanted the Cherokees to furnish warriors for the French and Indian War. A coolness developed between the governors of Virginia and South Carolina over this project, caused mostly by choosing unsuitable messengers to the Cherokees. Governor Glen of South Carolina did not feel that Virginia had furnished her quota of troops at Fort Necessity and demanded the return of South Carolina troops. Some Cherokees did go with the Virginia troops against the French. After a most strenuous campaign, the Indians started home on foot. They stole some horses in Virginia on their way home

---

[5] J. G. M. Ramsey, *The Annals of Tennessee to the Eighteenth Century* (Reprinted Kingsport, Tenn., 1926), 38, 64. Hereinafter cited Ramsey, *Annals*.
[6] Ramsey, *Annals*, 63; Haywood, 40–41

Samuel Cole Williams, *Adair's History of the American Indian* (Johnson City, 1930), 394 ff. The path evidently came through Wears Cove into Tuckaleechee Cove and down Little River.

and were followed by the owners and part of the Indians were killed by the whites. So the relations between the colonists and the Cherokees, in 1756 were tense.[7]

Both the Virginia and South Carolina governors had been asked by the Cherokees at the Treaty of Saluda in 1756 to build a fort to protect their women and children while their warriors were away from home assisting the Colonial troops against the French. Funds of ten thousand pounds were sent to Governor Dinwiddie of Virginia from England for the purpose of building a fort. Governor Glen of South Carolina was piqued because the funds were not sent to him and he wrote for money to build his own fort. Governor Dinwiddie sent Governor Glen one thousand pounds and put off doing anything for a while. Finally, Major Andrew Lewis was commissioned to enlist sixty artisans and proceed to Chota and confer with the chiefs as to the location of a fort. He was to be as frugal as possible in this project. It was expected that troops from South Carolina would meet and join with them in this work and that the fort would be garrisoned by South Carolina men.

The fort was to have walls four feet thick, nine feet high, with a seven foot stockade on top of the wall and was to be 105 feet square. It was to be finished in as little time as possible. The Cherokees would not hear of the South Carolinians garrisoning the fort. The Virginia fort was situated on the north side of the Little Tennessee River about a mile from Chota, the Cherokee City of Refuge. The site of this fort was within the bounds of Blount County after the Treaty of 1819, when the Little Tennessee River became the southern boundary.

Major Lewis was cognizant of the fact that much undercover interchange with the French was on foot, while he was in the Indian towns, but he still hoped that the Indians would give him troops when he returned to Virginia. Only seven warriors and three women returned with him when he left the ungarrisoned fort in the fall, after waiting all summer for someone from South Carolina to appear. However, some groups of Indians from the other Indian towns arrived in Virginia in November.

The fort was never named nor used. Since it was a threat to the Indians, ungarrisoned, it was soon destroyed and even its story is now almost lost. Very few historians even mention it.

Early in 1756, there was a plan suggested in Virginia to erect a **trading house** or "factory" on the Holston, perhaps, at Long Island. The plan progressed far enough to appoint trustees and order goods, but rumors of war were rife and the plan never materialized.

Under constant demand of Indians, and pressure from traders, Fort Prince George, at the Lower Towns in South Carolina finally had been built in 1753. But this did not satisfy the Cherokees. They still wanted a fort west of the mountains to protect the Overhill tribes against the French and Northern Indians. Under threat, South Carolina, after three

---

[7] *Haywood*, 42

years' dalliance finally voted a loan to King George to build a fort, and sent an agent over the mountain to select a location.[8]

A new governor arrived before plans were put into motion and caused some delay and dissatisfaction. Finally, in September 1756, Capt. Raymond Demeré, with supplies and artisans set out from Fort Prince George. This was after the Virginia fort had been finished and the Virginians, tired of waiting for the South Carolinians, had gone back to Virginia. The trader, John Elliot, contracted to carry the twelve swivel guns by pack horse across the mountain trail.

The engineer, J. W. Debrahm, had planned the fort very elaborately and was supposed to supervise the building but was unable to get along with the men and left in December. The fort was not built so elaborately as the plans which are now in existence. There had been disagreement about the site when Debrahm arrived, and by dramatic means he tried to get the site he preferred; but eventually agreed on the higher ground first chosen on a narrow ridge in the fork of the Little Tennessee and Tellico rivers near a small Indian town, Tuskeegee. Capt. Raymond Demeré was replaced by Capt. Paul Demeré in August 1757.

The fort was surrounded by a deep ditch with thorn locusts planted in the bottom. It was built of heavy square logs with blockhouses and bastions connected by palisades, which were trunks of trees embedded in the earth touching each other and sharpened at the top, with loopholes at proper places. The twelve guns were mounted on the four bastions.

The fort was named for John, Earl of Loudoun, who had recently arrived in America to take command of all British forces on the continent. Even before the completion of the fort, a few families had settled in the neighborhood; traders and blacksmiths were most common and always welcome in the Indian towns.

By this time the French and Indian War had been going on long enough for the French to try every possibility of turning support in their favor. This was partly the cause of a change of command at Fort Loudoun. Several hundred Indians had gone to Virginia and borne the brunt of battle under Washington. Incidents had happened in their passing through the country which led to violence on the part of both Indians and whites. It is impossible to place the blame, but the bounties offered by the Virginia Legislature for scalps seems to have aggravated the outrages.[9]

A state of strained relations continued and Governor Lyttleton refused to talk to the Indian chiefs who went to Charleston or to send them to London where they wanted to go. He also added insult to injury by virtually holding the chiefs as prisoners at Fort Prince George on their way home. This, together with uncalculated demands, precipi-

---

[8] Samuel Cole Williams, *Dawn of Tennessee Valley and Tennessee History*, (Johnson City, 1937), 70 ff. Hereinafter cited Williams, *Dawn*

Phillip M. Hamer, *Tennessee, A History, 1673-1932* (New York, 1935) 33 ff. Hereinafter cited *Hamer*

[9] Williams, *Dawn*, 189-201

tated war with the Cherokees. An urgent call to North Carolina netted no help. The call to Virginia for help to Fort Loudoun resulted in a vote to send 1,000 men under Col. Wm. Byrd. Byrd asked to be released from the assignment. When he was not released, he was slow in moving. The South Carolina troops attacked and laid waste to the Lower Towns. They were not successful with the Middle Towns and by their failure only succeeded in sealing the fate of Fort Loudoun. The English still refused to release their imprisoned chiefs, so in January 1760, the Cherokees laid siege to Fort Loudoun. A state of siege existed all spring and summer. Chief Atta-Culla-Culla remained friendly and favored the English whenever he could.

The last communication that Capt. Demeré had from either Virginia or South Carolina was in June. Hope of relief was very indefinite. By August they were facing starvation. Four men made their way to Byrd in Virginia, but he made no move to assist the unfortunate group. A formal surrender was made August 7, 1760, whereby the garrison was guaranteed safe conduct wherever the commanding officers decided to go. Part of the party was treacherously massacred at the first night's camp on Cane Creek.

The French were invited to take over the fort, and the inability to get their boats through the "Suck" (on the Tennessee River) is probably all that kept them from taking over. Fort Loudoun was soon destroyed. By one account Chief Oconastota had it burned, another says it was destroyed by order of the English.[10]

By the last years of the French and Indian War, "tourists" with more serious intentions were beginning to make brief and more extended excursions into the valleys and over the hills of East Tennessee. Among those who left their mark was Daniel Boone on the famous "beech tree." However this was probably not his first hunting trip over the mountain.[11]

The news of the fall of Fort Loudoun struck the Virginians with horror, and no doubt caused them some soul-searching moments. The Seaboard governors all agreed that retaliation must be dealt. A plan was formed whereby the Indian towns were to be crushed between simultaneous attacks from Virginia and the Carolinas. The Virginians should have reached the field first, but instead they marched to the headwaters of the Holston and enforted. The Carolinians had been on the scene, burning and killing for thirty days, and still Col. Byrd dallied (he finally resigned the command).

Major Lewis led an advance guard in July, 1761, down the middle fork of the Holston to Long Island. A fort was built there called Fort Robinson. Col. Adam Stephen was now in command. Among the men were Ensign Henry Timberlake and Dr. Thomas Walker, men who later made themselves immortal by recording their explorations and observations in the wilderness. The Virginia troops were joined at Long

---

[10] *Ibid.*, 233–49; Ramsey, *Annals*, 57–60.
[11] Ramsey, *Annals*, 67 ff

Island by a North Carolina force under Col. Hugh Waddell. They made no attempt to march against the Cherokees. To this fort, in November, came a group of four hundred Indians suing for peace.[12]

After the peace treaty at Long Island was signed in November 1761, Chief Standing Turkey asked that an officer be sent home with them to cement the peace. Ensign Henry Timberlake and Sgt. Thomas Sumter volunteered to go. The Indians wanted them to go overland but Timberlake was determined to go by water. He kept memoranda of the river and thus made the first survey of the Holston River. The trip downstream took twenty-three days. The men were royally received in the villages. Timberlake read and interpreted the articles of peace to the Indians at the Town House in Chota. During the winter he spent among them, Timberlake made a study of their government, religion and way of life. He recorded his observations in his memoirs, first published in London in 1765, which is almost the only extant early authority on the Cherokees. He studied the ruins of Fort Loudoun and learned from observation that the Indians were still inclined toward the French, but allied themselves to the British for the purposes of trade.

On his return to Virginia the following May, Timberlake followed the Great War Trail, which passed near the present site of Maryville. They camped at the mouth of Ellejoy Creek at Little River. He recorded that it was the former site of an Indian town "Elajay." He was surprised that it was abandoned and stated that it would make as fine a seat for an estate as he had ever seen. They met a large herd of buffaloes further on and had to run for safety. They found Fort Robinson abandoned, when they reached Long Island, but a plentiful supply of flour among the stores made the Indians happy.[13]

Chief Ostenaco and a few Indians accompanied Timberlake to Williamsburg, where the chief begged Gov. Fauquier to send him to England (because Chief Atta-Culla-Culla had been there). It was agreed, and Ostenaco and two warriors made the trip. They were received at court and feted extensively for two months. Lt. Timberlake, who with Sgt. Sumter had accompanied the Indians, did not return with the Indians to America, but returned in November 1762.[14]

As soon as peace was signed between England and France in 1763, every plan for settlement that had been thought of formerly, and several new ones, were considered for the Mississippi and Tennessee valleys but nothing came of any of them, partly because of the "Royal Proclamation" which forbade the granting or settling of these lands. Nevertheless, settlers kept crowding the frontier line and the Indians began getting restless and quarrelsome.

---

[12] Williams, *Dawn*, 260 ff (differs with Haywood and Ramsey as to date of building the fort) Ramsey, *Annals*, 53 ff

[13] Lt. Henry Timberlake, *Memoirs*. (London, 1765) Reprint annotated and with Index by Samuel Cole Williams (1927). 38 ff

[14] Williams, *Dawn*, 275 ff; Carolyn Thomas Foreman in *Indians Abroad* (Univ. of Oklahoma, 1943) quotes in great detail the contemporary news accounts of the entertainment and activities of this party while in England; 78 ff

In October 1767, the Cherokees met with John Stuart at Hard Labor, South Carolina and fixed a southern boundary line. November 5th, Sir William Johnson met with the Six Nations at Fort Stanwix for the same purpose. The boundaries were fixed at each treaty without any apparent consultation between the authorities and there was ever after a question of overlapping territory.[15]

The question of a "factory" on the Holston came up again in 1766 but the Cherokees would not agree to its being established and the scheme fell through.

The period between the fall of Fort Loudoun in 1760 and the building of the first permanent home on Watauga in 1769 was a time of exploration. Especially notable is the expedition lasting 18 months of a group from Halifax and Pittsylvania counties, Virginia, into present-day Sullivan County and Carter's Valley. This party named Walden's Ridge, Cumberland Gap, Cumberland Mountain and river, the Clinch and Powell rivers. The same party is reputed to have returned and explored further naming other streams and geographic points. Numerous recorded expeditions were made into the Middle Tennessee regions at this time.

When the treaty of Fort Stanwix, in 1767, was noised abroad, a party of four who had been at Long Island with Col. Stephen in 1767, set out on an exploration tour. One of them was Gilbert Christian, the future founder of Kingsport. They went down the Holston Valley as far as the junction of the Tennessee and Clinch rivers where they met a party of Indians who relieved them of their supplies of flour and ammunition. This dulled their zest for settling and they returned home.[16]

It is worthy of more than passing note that although the Tennessee Country was legally North Carolina, no reference is found to show that North Carolina was aware of the fact, or cared what happened over the mountain. All early interest and action was from Virginia or South Carolina. The flood of migration by 1768, when the news of Stanwix became known, began to trickle with a slowly gathering force up the valleys of Virginia toward the headwaters of the Holston. Many soldiers who had been at Long Island in 1760 remembered the country they had seen and had heard about from traders and "long-hunters." So by 1768, many Virginians were looking further up the valley with longing eyes, but fear of the Cherokees who were in a foul mood at this time, held them and they came no closer than the headwaters of the Holston.

In view of this fact, it is not surprising, that in 1769, William Bean from Pittsylvania County, Virginia, built his cabin at the mouth of Boone's Creek at Watauga River and became the first settler to remain permanently in the State of Tennessee. Tradition says he had hunted

---

[15] Ramsey, *Annals*, 71–75.
[16] *Haywood*, 45 ff.

with Boone and that was why he chose Boone's camp site to build his cabin. The site of Boone's Camp was judiciously located against a hillside near the mouth of Boone's Creek which had its entrance guarded by a waterfall. It was a well-screened spot not calculated to catch the eye of a casual passerby.

The year following Bean's settlement, John Honeycut was on the Watauga. James Robertson followed in 1771 on a tour of inspection. He made a crop and laid out estates for several of his friends and neighbors, and went back after his family in the fall. A settlement and store in Carter's Valley had appeared in 1770. Settlers' cabins sprang up like mushrooms in every cove up and down the streams.[17]

John Ryan came from North Carolina to Nolachucky some time before 1771, when he sold his pre-emption claim to Jacob Brown. Evan Shelby appeared on the scene in 1771, and by 1772 had a store at Sapling Grove. John Sevier first appeared in 1771 but did not settle until 1773.

The first settlers may have thought they were in Virginia but soon learned they were in North Carolina. It was impossible to get a title to the land since Lord Granville's land offices were closed. The Watauga settlers decided to negotiate a lease with the Cherokees for a safety measure. Jacob Brown, on Nolachucky, soon negotiated a similar trade.[18]

New settlers came in hordes and among them a lawless element. Some form of organization seemed necessary. Since the Watauga settlers were outside of the jurisdiction of Virginia and beyond the protection of North Carolina, the Watauga Association was formed in 1772. This association became the first independent governmental body organized by native Americans in America as well as the first such organization west of the Alleghanies.

The wave of immigration moved steadily in ever widening circles mostly from Virginia, but partly from North Carolina and about half of all settlers were Scotch-Irish. A road was laid out and cleared by Fincastle County, Virginia, into the new country. The Saltville mines were close to this road and supplied an urgent need. Mills appeared and traders began to bring in goods from the Valley of Virginia. The new settlements appeared to be really established.

In 1773 Boone's party, on its way to Kentucky, was waylaid by the Indians, thus causing a general alarm over the countryside. The uneasiness increased in 1776 and the ambushing of a single Cherokee almost precipitated open war, but that was postponed through the efforts of James Robertson. Immediately after this happening, a group of Wataugans engaged in Lord Dunmore's War with great credit.

Late in 1774, John Logan, a renegade white chief, appeared in the Tennessee Country at the head of an army of some Northern Indians

---

[17] Ramsey, *Annals*, 94; *Haywood*, 52–55; Williams, *Dawn*, 338 ff
[18] *Imlay*, 343 ff; Ramsey, *Annals*, 112–16; *Haywood*, 55.

and began to make scattered forays. The frightened population enforted wherever possible and some fled back to civilization. Rangers were on patrol, and a plea was sent out to the Cherokee chiefs to intercede for peace, before Logan finally withdrew.[19]

Early in 1775, Richard Henderson and his associates finally organized under the title Transylvania Company and met with the Cherokees at the Sycamore Shoals of Watauga. After much haranguing, in which Chief Dragging Canoe bitterly opposed the transaction, a deed was signed on March 17, 1775, conveying all the lands between the waters of the Kentucky and the Cumberland rivers. Then after this agreement the famous "Path" deed was executed, giving Henderson and his association a path over the Indian lands to their holdings. Following this the Watauga Association on March 19th purchased the lands they had formerly leased. A land office was immediately opened and rights of pre-emption recognized in issuing grants. Jacob Brown, on Nolachucky, followed suit and on March 25th made two purchases for himself which joined the Watauga Purchase.[20]

Neither Governor Dunmore of Virginia nor Governor Martin of North Carolina approved of these purchases; in fact, they both issued orders against it to both parties concerned.

About this time in England, Edward Burke was making his famous speech on "Conciliation with the Colonies," and Cartwright was publishing his plan for a division of the trans-Alleghany region into territories later to become states.

After the treaty of Sycamore Shoals, affairs settled down to normal and news of the coming struggle with England did not reach the back country until late in the year. All was quiet on the western front until news came that two Virginians had been murdered. Andrew Greer, on a trip to the Indians' territory, had become suspicious of the actions of another trader while in the Indian Towns and when he reached the French Broad River he turned off on another trail and so escaped the fate of two others who were following close behind but kept to the main trail.[21]

This summer of 1775 also marks the date that Rev. Joseph Rhea came from Maryland into the Tennessee Country north of Holston with a view of locating. He preached at several meeting-houses, among them Hopewell, one of Cummings' churches (now Gunnings Chapel) and Weavers' (Old Concord) also a Cummings church. Rev. Charles Cummings had located at Wolf Hills, now Abingdon, Virginia, in 1772.

When news of the war with Great Britain reached the Tennessee Country, late in 1775, the settlements formed themselves into Washington District, the first geographic division to be named for George Washington, July 5th, 1776. They appointed their Committee of Safe-

---

[19] Williams, *Dawn*, 396 ff
[20] *Imlay*, 309; Ramsey, *Annals*, 117; *Haywood*, 30.
[21] Ramsey, *Annals*, 143. One of these men named Boyd carried a watch engraved with his name and since the body was sunk in the creek, that creek was named Boyd's Creek.

ty composed of thirteen members. Immediately after the Declaration of Independence, in 1776, Washington District petitioned to be annexed to North Carolina, and was recognized November 1776, when four delegates were admitted to the North Carolina Legislature. However, it was not until a year later that Washington County was established and the actual exercise of jurisdiction begun.[22]

The British could not reach the back country but they were able to incite the Indians to hostilities and supplied them with ammunition, arms and stores. Early in the summer of 1776, Isaac Thomas and William Falling brought word given by Nancy Ward, the Cherokee Pocahontas, that the Indians were gathering for an invasion of the Watauga settlements. Word came from other sources to the same intent.

Forts were scarcely built and garrisoned when the Indians were upon them. Some families had chosen not to enfort, and were subjected to attacks, scalpings, and captivity. One force, about four hundred strong, was under Chief Dragging Canoe who had opposed the sale of lands to the whites at Sycamore Shoals. As they approached Heaton's Station, the settlers marched out, and routed the Indians at the battle of Island Flats.

Another band of three hundred Indians under Old Abraham of Chilhowee attacked the Fort on Watauga at sunrise of the same day and was driven off in full retreat. During this battle the thrilling rescue of "Bonny Kate" Sherrill was effected by John Sevier. Two other armies of Redskins, learning of the defeat at Island Flats, turned aside to plunder and lay waste isolated settlements before returning home.

The British plan seemed to be, to wipe out the western settlements so as to give them free entrance into the southern colonies from the west. The Wataugans determined to make a movement in force to invade the Indian towns. Col. William Christian with a Virginia force, reinforced by two companies of North Carolina troops, moved against the Middle Towns and Col. Williamson in South Carolina against the Lower Towns, while a Georgia force invaded the Lower Overhill villages.

The campaign was highly successful and the strength of the Indians was crushed for the time and they sued for peace. The result was Avery's Treaty or the Treaty of Long Island in 1777. A very important part of this campaign is the fact that Christian's soldiers got a look at new lands, which they did not forget. However, Chief Dragging Canoe had taken no part in the treaties and having organized a renegade band of a thousand Indians, continued depredations on a large scale. In 1779, Col. Evan Shelby headed an expedition against this band. The campaign was highly successful. He succeeded in capturing the British stores, burning eleven villages, and destroying the Indians' crops. Many of Shelby's men made exploratory "detours" on their way home and

---

[22] Williams, *Dawn*, 427; Ramsey, *Annals*, 159

staked claims on land which they later entered when it was opened for settlement.[23]

Among the settlers who came to Tennessee from North Carolina in 1779, was an entire Baptist congregation which migrated west after the Battle of Alamance. This group of people was organized by Elder Tidence Lane into the Buffalo Ridge Baptist Church which was the first Baptist church organized in Tennessee.[24]

Early in 1780, with the fall of Charleston, the way seemed to be open for an invasion of the back country by the British, but they met unexpected strength and resistance from the Over-Mountain men and were handed a humiliating defeat at King's Mountain. This is one of the most thrilling chapters in the story of the Revolution and the part played by the men of Watauga is well known. John Sevier and Isaac Shelby were voted swords by North Carolina for their part in the battle.

John Sevier had no time to rest from his labors on his return from King's Mountain. He found the Cherokees on the war path and reportedly on their way to attack the settlements. He moved immediately with what troops he could muster on his way and met the Indians at Long Creek in Greene County. The Indians retreated after a skirmish. Sevier overtook them at Boyd's Creek and completely routed them and thus saved the settlements from attack. This battle is one of the most brilliant of Sevier's thirty-five always-victorious Indian battles. Sevier paused long enough for the main body of soldiers to catch up with him and proceeded against the Indian Towns. Practically all the villages from the head of the Tennessee to the Hiwassee were burned and the fields laid waste. A treaty was made, and Sevier returned home. However, stealthy depredations continued and Sevier made another foray into the Middle Towns before returning to South Carolina to assist Marion against the British until January 1782.[25]

With the peace with Great Britain, Indian hostilities ceased. Greene County was erected from Washington County and with Sullivan County made three counties in the Western Country. The Rev. Samuel Doak built his log schoolhouse at Salem Church, which was organized in 1780, in Washington County, and Martin Academy (now Washington College) was chartered in 1783 as the first literary institution west of the Alleghanies. A very important happening of this same year was the opening of a land office for the sale of lands to pay off the Revolutionary soldiers in Hillsboro, North Carolina.[26]

The end of the war and the opening of the Armstrong land office paved the way for new settlements and the beginning of a new era.

---

[23] *Haywood*, 65–67; Ramsey, *Annals*, 151–169; 187 ff
[24] Ramsey, *Annals*, 182; A petition in 1829 stated that Buffalo Ridge was organized fifty years before. Tennessee, State Archives, Nashville, Tennessee.
[25] Ramsey, *Annals*, 230–249; 261–273
[26] *Ibid.*, 277, 294, 642.

CHAPTER II

The Settlement Period

IN NOVEMBER 1777, Washington District became Washington County, North Carolina, with approximately the same boundaries as the present state of Tennessee. A land office was set up at forty shillings per hundred acres with John Carter as entry taker. Each head of family was allowed to enter 640 acres and 100 acres for his wife and each child. Among the entries made in 1778, at least two are recognizable as Blount County locations: one for 640 acres surveyed for Andrew Greer in 1790 on Four Mile Creek entered by William Randolph for Daniel Shine; another for 200 acres surveyed in 1792 for Archibald Sloan "at the Blue Spring in the center between Little River and the Tennessee River," entered by John Clinkenbeard. None of Blount County was open, by Indian consent, for entry by any pretext until after the Treaty of Dumplin Creek, which was made in 1785. It will be noticed that these grants were not surveyed before 1790.[1]

In April 1778, all entries of land inside the Indian Boundaries were declared void, and monies ordered refunded. Sullivan County was erected from Washington County in 1779 and Jonesboro, the oldest town in Tennessee, was laid out. Greene County was erected from Washington in 1783 and included what is now Blount County. In the same year a land office was opened for the sale of lands for the purpose of paying off Revolutionary War soldiers. For this purpose, John Armstrong's office in Hillsboro was opened in May 1783. The land was to be issued in tracts of 5,000 acres or less.[2]

By the next year, the settlements extended as far as the Big Island in the French Broad River thirty miles above Knoxville. There were also a few settlements on Boyd's Creek south of the French Broad. At this time no grants were yet supposed to be issued for land south of the French Broad River.

The Blount County considered in the settlement period is bounded on the south and west by the Little Tennessee River, along whose banks lived the Cherokees from whom the land was wrested. On the Northwest was the Holston, from its junction with the Little Tennessee to its junction with Little River. From thence the line followed the established lines of Knox and Sevier counties to the North Carolina line and back to the Little Tennessee River. Occupation of at least half of this territory was disputed by the Indians, and was contrary to Treaty

---

[1] Ramsey, *Annals*, 175; *Haywood*, 70; John Carter's *Entry Book*, Tennessee State Archives, Nashville, Tennessee.
[2] *Haywood*, 73, 121 ff.

agreements. This led to the incidents related in this chapter. If the territory outlined seems exaggerated, bear in mind that parts of Blount County were used in the formation of Monroe and Loudon counties, and that certain large landowners preferred to pay their taxes in Monroe County at one time and petitioned the Legislature to accommodate them. At the time settlement began in 1785, Blount County was a part of Greene County. After Knox County was erected in 1792, it was part of Knox County until Blount County was formed in 1795.

The states were much in debt as a result of the Revolutionary War and Congress had proposed that the states should give their western lands to the Federal Government and that Congress should sell these lands and pay all the debts. The states agreed to this plan, and in 1784, North Carolina ceded the twenty-nine million acres lying between the Alleghanies and the Mississippi River to the United States and gave Congress two years to accept or reject the grant. Congress needed money, but that was not the main reason for the cession of the territory. Much of the best part had already been granted to settlers. Up to that time the people of the ceded territory had presented many claims for compensation for military services in campaigns against the Cherokees which North Carolina did not altogether believe just. On the score of poverty, North Carolina had also refused to establish a Superior Court or to appoint a prosecuting officer.[3]

The people of the Tennessee Country were alarmed because they had no Brigadier-General who could legally call out the militia in cases of Indian attacks. There was no Judge who could legally try criminal cases. After much berating of the mother state, the leaders decided to take care of themselves in their own way, without leave from anyone. Each military company elected two representatives to form county committees. They called a general convention which met at Jonesboro in August 1784, and elected John Sevier, president, and Landon Carter, secretary.[4]

This convention resolved to form a new state and called another convention for the purpose of drawing up a constitution and starting a new government. The first constitution which was drafted provided that no lawyer, doctor, or preacher could ever serve in the Legislature. The Rev. Sam Houston advocated this document which was not too popular. The Constitution of North Carolina was finally adopted with modifications, and the name Franklin was chosen for the new state.

John Sevier was elected governor of the new state and David Campbell, Judge of the Superior Court. Greeneville was capital of the new state. As soon as Governor Martin of North Carolina heard what was going on over the mountains, he sent an Address to the people of the

---

[3] John Preston Arthur, *A History of Watauga County*, North Carolina, (Richmond, 1915), 117; *Haywood*, 149

[4] Ramsey, *Annals*, 285; James Phelan, *History of Tennessee*, (Boston, 1889), 70 ff

new state, ordering them to disband their government and return their allegiance to the State of North Carolina. The North Carolina Legislature repealed the Act of Cession to the United States; John Sevier was appointed Brigadier-General of the militia; and David Campbell was appointed Judge of the Superior Court of the District. Sevier advised the people to drop the Franklin Movement since North Carolina had provided all the civil institutions that were necessary. Since he could not persuade the people to follow his advice, he then put forth every effort to establish and maintain the State of Franklin. County Courts, as well as Superior Courts were established and Justices of the Peace were appointed. Three new counties were erected: Spencer, which occupied what is now Hawkins County; Caswell, which corresponded to present Jefferson County; and Sevier County which was as now, and included part of Blount. The State of Franklin also included Wayne County, North Carolina. Taxes were levied, and monetary value placed on staple products for tax-paying purposes.[5]

The most important act of the State of Franklin, as far as Blount County is concerned was the treaty with the Cherokees at Henry's Station on Dumplin Creek, May 31, 1785. The Indians agreed that all the lands on the south side of French Broad and Holston rivers as far as the dividing ridge between Little River and Great Tennessee might be open to white people. This treaty was followed in the summer of 1786 by the Treaty of Coyatee which made the agreement stronger.

It is highly possible that there were some people already in what is now Blount County before the spring of 1785; but just as soon as the bars were let down we know that the people flocked down the Great War Path—McTeer, Craig, Houston, Gamble, and others who later had forts went straight to the claims they had no doubt marked in 1776 or in 1779 when they marched against the Cherokees with Col. Christian and Col. Shelby.[6]

The earliest reference to a permanent location in Blount County is the gathering of troops at Houston's Station in 1786. By this time settlement was enough to warrant the establishment of two Presbyterian churches—Eusebia, near McTeer's and New Providence near Fort Craig.[7]

The State of Franklin was becoming weaker each day and when Sevier's term of office expired in March 1788, the state was dead and North Carolina was in full control. Courts were held at Greeneville in May under North Carolina jurisdiction without any interruption, or perceptible change in form.[8]

The Cherokees began to show a strong desire for war early in 1788.

---

[5] Ramsey, *Annals*, 323 ff; *Haywood*, 150–165
[6] Ramsey, *Annals*, 298
[7] *Haywood*, 176; Ramsey, *Annals*, 341.
[8] Ramsey, *Annals*, 519–20

One May morning John Kirk and his son John left home on Nine Mile Creek. While they were gone, Slim Tom, an Indian, who was known to the family, came to the door and asked for food. When he got the food, he left but soon returned with a party of Indians who fell on the unsuspecting family and massacred all eleven of them. When Kirk came home he found their bodies and gave the alarm. Several hundred militiamen under Col. Sevier, met at David Craig's Station on Nine Mile Creek. From here they marched to the Hiwassee River. Some Indians were killed and some prisoners were taken. The militia returned to Hunter's Station. The next day they marched up the river and burned Tallassee town. On their way back they stopped at Chilhowee and called Old Abraham, a friendly chief, who lived across the river to bring the "Tassel" (another chief), and come over and talk to them. They were put in a house to await Sevier who was absent at the time. Major Hubbard, an Indian hater, allowed young Kirk, the son of the man whose family was killed, to go into the house where the Indians were saying: "take the vengeance to which you are entitled." Young Kirk tomahawked the whole group of unarmed Indians who were there under a flag of truce. Although Sevier was not in the camp at the time this happened, he was severely criticized for allowing it to happen, especially by Major David Craig.⁹

After the Kirk Massacre, people were compelled to live in forts. A deposition made by James W. Lackey in September 1823 in support of Major James Houston's claim for $702.50 for rations and ammunition furnished volunteers in 1788, summarized the happenings at Houston's Station. It furnished one of the few first-hand accounts of early happenings: Lackey stated that Col. Daniel Kennedy of Greene County, in answer to Houston's call for help, told Houston that the safety of the settlements east of the Cumberlands were dependent on his holding out and to go ahead and furnish whatever was necessary to support the station and that he would use his influence to have him repaid by North Carolina. Lackey said he, himself, rode 220 miles and got only twenty pounds of powder for which he paid 75 cents per pound. The fort, manned by eleven men was attacked at daybreak by four hundred Indians but the settlers withstood the attack since Lackey had arrived with the powder only the night before. The livestock was all killed or driven away, and the settlers stripped of support. At one time a company of thirty-two men under Lackey was stationed there for ninety days. Capt. Fain and thirty-five men were stationed there for ninety days; a detachment from Gen. Martin's army for twenty days; and a detachment of volunteers for ninety days. All were furnished rations

---

⁹ *Ibid.*, 149; *Haywood*, 194; John P. Brown, *Old Frontiers*, (Kingsport, 1938), 277; Hereinafter cited *Brown*. References to most of the Indian depredations may also be found in American State Papers, *Indian Affairs*, Vol. 1, Passim, and in the *Draper Manuscripts*.

by Major Houston. Cession of this territory to the United States was made by North Carolina shortly afterward and when Houston applied for payment, North Carolina refused, saying the western part of the state must pay that debt.[10]

General Martin in 1788, sent a party under Major Thomas Stewart to Houston's Station to garrison it and protect the inhabitants. Captain John Fain with some enlisted men who composed part of the guard, and some of the settlers were sent out to scout and reconnoiter. The following newspaper account related what happened: [11]

On Friday the 8th of August last a party of armed men consisting of 31 under command of Capt. John Fain left Houston's Station on Nine Mile Creek and crossed the Tennessee River about eight or nine miles distant in order to gather apples in the vicinity of an Indian town called Citico, lately abandoned by the Indians. The Indians suffered them to pass the river unmolested and immediately unperceived by our people took possession of the ford they had crossed, likewise another at a small distance above. By this time some of our people were in the orchard and some in the trees gathering fruit, when they were suddenly attacked by a body of the savages on all quarters. This sudden and unexpected alarm threw them into the utmost confusion, so that every man who did not immediately fall endeavored to make a retreat but the savages being in possession of the fording places, a number took to the river and whilst endeavoring to escape by swimming were killed or wounded. The latter were pursued and most of them fell as sacrifice to savage barbarity.

The following is a list of the unfortunate men who were killed or wounded. Killed: John Fain, Capt.; Caleb Jones, Joseph Alexander, Van Percefield, William Long, Jonathan Dean, John Branam, William English, John Medlock, Robert Housem, George Mathews, Isaac Anderson, Chas. Payne, Luther Johnson, Herman Gregg, George Buly. Wounded: Elisha Haddon, John Kirk, Thomas Brown, and Bullock.[12]

Haywood says sixteen were killed, four wounded, and one taken prisoner. Captain Nathaniel Evans raised thirty men and reached the scene on the evening of the third day. They buried the dead on the north bank of the river and camped about a mile from the river on high ground. Major Stewart joined Capt. Evans and next morning they crossed the river and buried the mutilated remains they found there.

The Indians who had pursued the survivors of the Citico Massacre resolved to attack Houston's Station but were beaten off by the garrison. Sevier was marching to the defense of Houston's, and had not heard of the attack, when he unexpectedly met up with a band of a hundred savages and forced them to give way. Joined by Capt. John Craig and other Captains' companies the army marched through the

---

[10] Photostat of deposition of James W. Lackey, Tennessee State Archives. In the same file is also one by John Houston, and the itemized bill for supplies filed by Major James Houston.
[11] *Haywood*, 197; *North Carolina State Gazette*, Edenton, October 6, 1788.
[12] *Brown*, 279 says Kirk was wounded, but hid in a hollow log and later escaped to Houston's Fort.

Indian Villages. At Citico, Capt. Evans and John Ish, who were riding guard, discovered two Indians hiding in a house, and killed them. At Chilhowee the party killed thirteen Indians in a skirmish and returned home.[13]

In a few weeks Sevier headed a larger expedition South and returned home to be arrested for treason by North Carolina officers. He was carried to Morganton, North Carolina for trial. He was dramatically carried away by friends and the matter ended. General Martin made another foray into the Indian towns but neither expedition did much to quell the Indians.

The troops had no more than reached home when two or three hundred Indians under John Watts came to Gillespy's Station on the waters of Pistol Creek near Little River a little after sunrise, October 17th. Most of the men were absent at the time and the few remaining made the best resistance they could. When ammunition ran out, the Indians swarmed over the roofs of the cabins into the fort and a horrible scene ensued. Ramsey says "our loss is twenty-eight persons, mostly women and children." Breazeale said the Indians killed Gillespy and nine others, burned the station and took thirty-one or thirty-two prisoners. On their march back they killed Ephraim McDowell and Jacob Rife, McDowell's son-in-law. Sevier immediately followed them into their town and took an equal number of prisoners which were exchanged in the spring.[14]

The fall of the State of Franklin and the resumption of relations with North Carolina were effected without much commotion. The laws were the same, and in most cases the officers were the same. However in one section of Franklin, that south of French Broad and Holston, the State of Franklin officials remained in power under their "Articles of Association" and popular will. Elsewhere the jurisdiction of North Carolina was acknowledged and her authority obeyed. The reluctance of the mother state to pay off service-claims for the military services necessary to protect the western frontier caused a revival of the complaints and discontents of the western people and more especially the late Franklin counties. North Carolina began to realize that her western counties were an inconvenient, expensive and troublesome appendage and those who had formerly opposed the Franklin separation were now ready to agree to a separation. The assembly accordingly passed an act to cede certain western lands to the United States.

On February 25, 1790, the senators from North Carolina executed a deed to the United States. On April 2nd Congress accepted the deed and what is now Tennessee ceased to be a part of North Carolina. On May 25, 1790, Congress passed an act setting up the government of the Territory South of the River Ohio. For the purpose of temporary gov-

[13] *Haywood*, 198 (Ish was later killed by Indians while working in his field. The trial and hanging of the Indian is related elsewhere.)
[14] Ramsey, *Annals*, 518, *Haywood*, 202 ff

ernment, it was to be one district. The conditions, benefits, and privileges were to be the same as for the Northwest Territory.

President Washington appointed William Blount of North Carolina, governor of the territory, and David Campbell and Joseph Anderson, judges. Governor Blount arrived in the Territory South of the River Ohio, as it was termed, on October 10, 1790 and proceeded to appoint and commission Civil and Military officers for Washington District in East Tennessee and Mero District in Middle Tennessee. By February, 1791, he had made the rounds of the territory and had sent Major King to the Cherokees with proposals to hold a treaty in the ensuing May to make peace if possible. Indications seemed favorable for effecting peace at this time.[15]

Three million acres of land had been sold in John Armstrong's office. This land was all in territory allotted to the Indians by the treaty of Hopewell. There were also settlers south of the French Broad, in violation of the law of North Carolina in 1785 which made the French Broad and Holston the boundary, as well as in violation of the Treaty of Hopewell. Their numbers amounted to twelve hundred militiamen and they were extended over the ridge that divides the waters of Little River from those that flow into the Tennessee as low as Nine Mile Creek, a branch of the Tennessee, within five miles of Chota. The people south of the French Broad had settled there in opposition to these laws, and although the people had petitioned to be formed into a county, the Assembly of North Carolina refused to accede to their request. They had commenced their settlements under the assumed authority of the State of Franklin. These settlers expected the right of pre-emption to be granted them. The Assembly of North Carolina had provided that the people living in this section should not be precluded from entering their pre-emption in that tract of country should an office be opened for that purpose under an act of that legislature.[16]

The only outbreak recorded in what is now Blount County in 1790 was at Houston's Station. The fort contained, at the time of the attack, several families but only seven gunmen. The fort is described as being a single one-story cabin with portholes. Two or three hundred Indians approached the place to attack and destroy it. The men withheld their fire until the assailants were near enough for certain aim. All fired at once and repeated as soon as possible giving the effect of a much larger force. The Indians thought that it was defended by a large force, and picking up their dead, retired.

The time arrived for Governor Blount's meeting with the Cherokees at Knoxville. On the 2nd of July the conference was ended and the Treaty agreed to and signed. All prisoners in the nation were to be returned and the boundary was officially fixed as the ridge dividing the

---

[15] *Haywood*, 206–215; 262 ff; Ramsey, *Annals*, 542–54
[16] *Haywood*, 263–4

waters of Little River from the Tennessee (which is about the middle of present Blount County). Other provisions were made for the settling of disputes and the general preservation of peace between the contracting parties. Immediately following the treaty, the Secretary of War wrote to Governor Blount, directing him not to call out the militia of the Territory except in cases of real danger, and pointing out the importance of having the boundary line run.[17]

On the 6th of September 1792, John Cochrane returning from Pistol Creek to his father's house on Little River was met by a white man, a stranger, who engaged him in conversation. Three Indians lying in ambush fired on him. Two or three bullets passed through his hat and clothes without doing him any harm. He and his father's family escaped down the creek and alarmed the neighborhood who began to build a fort. A few days later Gillespy and two sons went home after some corn. The Indians killed Gillespy and the oldest boy, but the younger they took prisoner. A white man in the company of the Indians (Lashley) excused the murder of the older brother by stating they had fired at, and missed a paleface and killed his (Gillespy's) brother for satisfaction of their lost powder.[18]

On the 3rd of October, Black's Blockhouse on the head of Crooked Creek, a branch of Little River, there was a Sergeant's command. It was attacked by surprise just after dark by a party commanded by a Cherokee of Wills Town, called the "Tail." The party consisted of three other Cherokees and five Creeks. James Paul was killed inside the house; George Morse and Robert Sharp were killed at the fire on the outside; and John Shockland was wounded. Three horses were killed and seven taken.

Later in October young Gillespy was conducted in safety to Major David Craig's Station on Nine Mile Creek by John Christian and two young Cherokees from Estanaula. He had been purchased from the eight Indians who captured him, by James Carey and the Upper Cherokee Chiefs, for the sum of $150.00.[19]

The forts in what is now Blount County were reinforced and guarded by men from Knox County Militia. Some were left at Henry's, Craig's and Ish's stations and afterwards at Tellico Blockhouse. This blockhouse was a strong fort of considerable size with a projection on each square, furnished with portholes, and calculated to stand a siege by an enemy provided with small arms only. Colonel James Scott commanded the troops of this frontier in the absence of Sevier.[20]

[17] Ramsey, *Annals*, 552; Clarence Edwin Carter, ed.; *The Territorial Papers of the United States*, V. 14, *Territory South of the River Ohio*, 1700–96, (Washington, 1936) 60, (Text of Treaty) Hereinafter cited *Carter*.
[18] Ramsey, *Annals*, 563; *Knoxville Gazette*, November 11, 1792.
[19] *Haywood*, 277; *Carter*, 185
[20] Ramsey, *Annals*, 568. (Blount County was formed from Knox three years from this date). What is now Blount County was included in Knox County when Knox was erected in 1792.

Governor Blount informed the Secretary of War that the five Lower Towns under John Watts had formally declared war and had set out on some expeditions. The local militia was ordered out, but nearly all disbanded when the scare died down. The following is a list of the Blount County stations and their strength on December 22, 1792:

> Gambel's Station—William Ragan, Lieutenant; Men—Thirteen; on furlough—five.
> Black's Station—Joel Wallace, Ensign; Men—four.
> Henry's Station—George Huffacre, Corporal; men—six.
> Well's Station—Richard De Armond, Corporal; men—six.
> Ish's Station—Matthew Karr, Sergeant; men—eight.

It can be seen from this listing that the man-power in these stations was very weak in case of attack.

On the night of the 5th of November, five Creeks headed by young Lashley, son of a Scotsman in the Creek Nation (the same who headed the party that killed and captured Gillespy's son in September) came in upon the waters of Little River and stole and took off eight horses. They were traced toward Chilhowee, the nearest Cherokee town. This gave reason to suspect the Chilhowee Indians of the theft. Whereupon as many as fifty-two of the neighboring people including the sufferers, assembled together in arms and resolved to go and destroy Chilhowee, and Tallassee too. They actually did march but Gen. Sevier learned of their intentions and dispatched orders to them to disperse and return home, which order they reluctantly obeyed and trouble was averted.[21]

On Tuesday the 22nd of January, 1793, the Indians killed and scalped John Pate on Crooked Creek. On the 29th they returned to the same neighborhood and stole three of William Davidson's horses from Gamble's Station on Little River.[22]

These aggressions prompted the spontaneous assemblage of the people again at Gamble's Station for the purpose of marching to the nearest Indian towns and retaliating upon them the injuries they were suffering. Governor Blount immediately ordered Col. Alex. Kelly, with militia, to go to the dissatisfied and incensed citizens on the frontier and endeavor to restrain them from going with arms across the Tennessee River or entering any of the Indian towns. The governor finally found it necessary to issue a proclamation requiring the citizens to desist from an invasion of the Indian Territory, which was now contemplated by a party of eighty men who had assembled at Gamble's for that purpose. He attended them himself to aid by his personal and official influence, in the preservation of peace. In this he was assisted by Col. White and others. To reassure the population and to further allay the rising storm of retaliation, a company of cavalry was ordered to range from the Holston to Little River and quiet was restored for the time being.

[21] *Ibid.*, 565, 571
[22] *Haywood*, 293-5

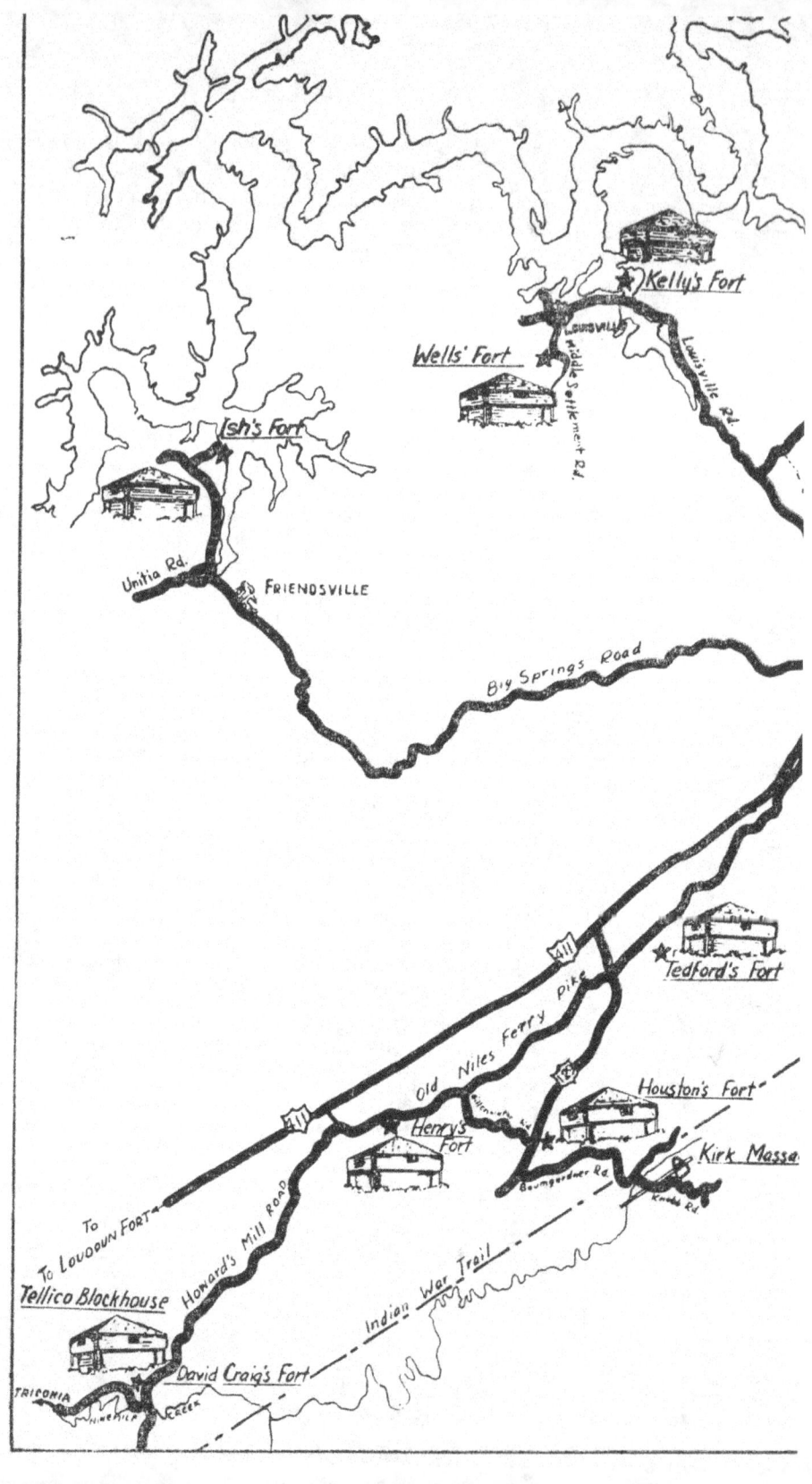

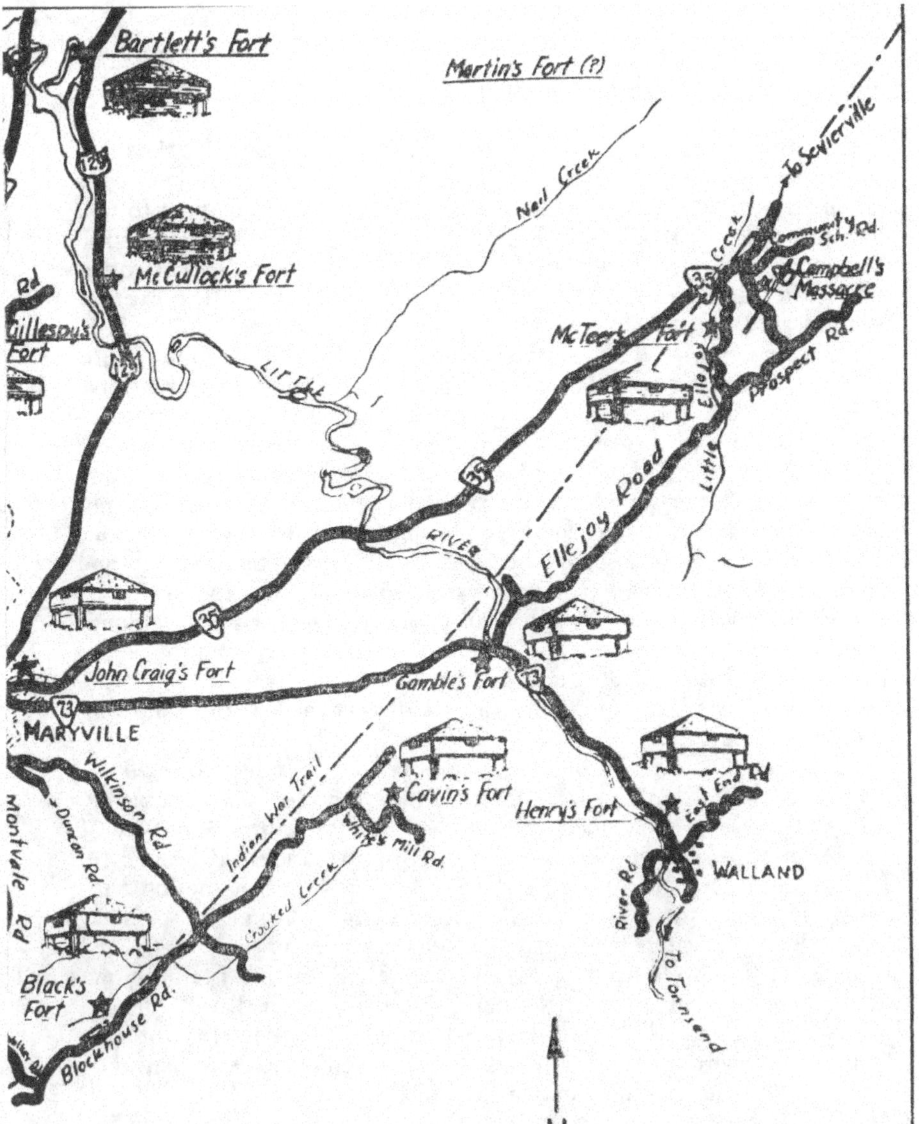

BLOUNT COUNTY FORTS

By Mrs. Jeff Breazeale

Governor Blount in an Address to the Cherokees about this time told them that he had ordered out the Rangers to keep bad Cherokees from coming to the white settlements and that their people in coming to visit him must come to David Craig's Station, as no one had been killed in that neighborhood. The people there were not so irate as in other places. In a letter to the Secretary of War, April 9th, 1793, Governor Blount said that John Watts sent him a message from the Maw in February that he wanted to come to Knoxville but if he couldn't come there in safety he would meet him elsewhere. They met at Samuel Henry's Station (now Brick Mill) with the Maw and about sixty Indians. The gist of information gained in the conference was that the Creeks were bent on war, chiefly directed against the Cumberland settlements. Blount stated that he had ordered out some additional militia in Knox and Jefferson counties. He said further that the conference lasted two days; the last day being devoted to drinking, eating, and light conversation (which Watts was fond of). The expense of the conference was slightly over $100.00, mostly for whisky. (Blount thought the United States could be as liberal with the liquor as the Indians were thirsty!) He reported that Watts was friendly but made no promises. Evidently nothing came of this meeting as the following events will indicate.[23]

In April, 1793, a party of Creeks led by young Lashley burned the house of James Gallaher on the south side of the Holston. Fortunately the family was at an adjacent station. The Indians returned by way of Coyatee and asked the "Hanging Maw" for provisions. When he refused them, they shot his dog and left. A detachment of mounted infantry followed them over the Tennessee without being able to overtake them. The waters having risen suddenly, the company was obliged to swim their horses back across the Tennessee. In this attempt John McCulloch, a young man of the company, was drowned.

The same party of Indians hovered about the settlements three or four days. A party of Lt. Tedford's Rangers fired on some Indians they saw at a distance and killed one of the Indians who proved to be "Noon Day" of Toqua, a Cherokee, and not the Creeks they were looking for.

The people on the frontier, in general, were greatly alarmed and crowded into forts. Governor Blount reported that he had visited John Craig's Station (now Maryville) and found 280 men, women, and children living in a miserable manner in small huts.[24]

This was evidently the period referred to in Major McTeer's story of an attack by a large party of Indians. The women and children were hidden in a dense thicket along the creek about a mile west of the fort. The fort was successfully defended and the Indians withdrew.

Another story related by Major McTeer is a story handed down in the McGinley family about a mare which was taken from Colonel James McGinley's stable by the Indians. A remaining mare raised a

---
[23] *Carter*, 236, 249, 282
[24] *Haywood*, 294–300; *Carter*, 251; *Knoxville Gazette*, April 20, 1793.

disturbance and the loss was discovered. The Colonel followed swiftly and the thief was overtaken as he was crossing the river near Tellico Blockhouse. The colonel dismounted and took aim. The shot found its mark and, thus released, the mare swam back to her master and her mate.[25]

The state of unrest continued all spring and in June the Indians twice stole horses on Little River near Gamble's Station. Some of the white men pursued until they could see the town of Chilhowee from the point of a mountain on the west side of the Tennessee which they could not cross by orders of the U. S. Government.[26]

On the 30th of June, after sunset, as four of Lt. Tedford's party of Rangers were returning from reconnoitering the woods in search of Indians, they were fired on near Well's Station by a party of Indians. John McAlister and James Gillespy were slightly wounded but escaped under cover of darkness.

Nuisances and depredations became a daily occurence. July 1st, the Indians burned two houses on a Mr. Hogg's plantation on Baker's Creek including all his household goods and a quantity of corn belonging to a Mr. Logan. The next day they burned a Mr. Logan's house on Nine Mile Creek and destroyed his flax crop in addition to part of his corn crop. They also fired at a man on Pistol Creek this same day.

They stole seven horses from Bird's Station and the clothes of four families which were washed and hanging on the line. Near Kelly's Station the Indians cut up a plow belonging to a Mr. Conner and carried off the irons, and the following day six Indians fired on Ensign Joel Wallace at the head of Pistol Creek. He was uninjured except for cuts from a shattered knife handle.[27]

Activities continued in August. On the 11th, Indians fired on a Mr. Black and another man belonging to Tedford's Rangers as they were returning from a cornfield at Well's Station.

On the 20th, the Indians burned James Tedford's house, all his flax and other property. They cut down Capt. Joseph Tedford's corn crop, killed all his hogs, and threw down the fences. The tracks which they left indicated a large party of Indians.

The Indian activities at this time seemed to have been directed chiefly against those people who were settled south of the dividing ridge between the Little Tennessee and Little River contrary to the terms of the Treaty of Holston. This period of warfare seems to have been chiefly acts of aggravation toward these illegal settlers, and what few acts of retaliation that the whites did against the Indians seemed to have no effect.

About August 22nd, the Indians killed Abraham Wells near his house

---

[25] Will A. McTeer, *History of New Providence Presbyterian Church*, (Maryville, 1921)
[26] *Haywood*, 310; *Knoxville Gazette*, June 29, 1793
[27] *Haywood*, 302. (Hogg's is the farm later bought by Major Sam Houston and where General Sam Houston, of Texas fame, spent his boyhood and youth)

and burned three houses which were deserted. The situation was becoming desperate. The threat of attack was heavier each day. General Sevier was advised to call out one-third of the militia of the three upper counties but they could not reach Knoxville before the first of September. All personal communications with the Indians were at an end. Letters were fastened to posts on the banks of the river.[28]

At daylight on the 29th day of August, a party of one to three hundred Indians made an attack on Henry's Station. Lt. Tedford and a man named Jackson had gone to the corn field when the firing commenced, and when they attempted to run to the station they were unexpectedly cut off by the Indians. Lt. Tedford was taken prisoner and carried about one hundred and fifty yards and put to death. A man by the name of Henderson was also killed. Jackson, who was outside the fort, fortunately made his escape and ran to John Craig's Station ten or twelve miles in distance and spread the alarm to the adjacent frontiers. Jackson was so closely pursued by the Indians that he stripped himself so as to prevent the Indians from seizing him.[29]

The militia was gathering at Sevier's headquarters at Ish's Station south of the Holston. Scouts were patrolling the approaches to Knoxville to prevent an expected attack on that place. On the evening of the twenty-fourth of September, one thousand Indians, three hundred Cherokees and seven hundred Creeks, evaded discovery and marched by night across what is now Blount County, and arrived in sight of Knoxville by sunrise. The firing of the sunrise guns made them believe they were discovered and they fled west from Knoxville.

When they stopped to rest about eight miles west of Knoxville, they were in sight of Cavet's Station. They attacked the station and treacherously made surrender terms which they did not keep. Only the youngest of Cavet's sons was spared, only to be killed later in the Indian towns. The station was plundered and burned. The firing at Cavet's was heard and reported to Sevier who lay at Ish's, not more than six miles distant. A troop was sent under Captain Harrison, which followed the Indians to the Clinch River and then returned to Ish's.[30]

This attack by Watts went far to convince the authorities that it was no longer wise or safe to limit their activities to defensive warfare. The frontier had known this all along and had protested loudly against the decision of the executives.

Governor Blount was absent at this time and Secretary Smith authorized an expedition into the heart of the Cherokee Nation. The army was already at Ish's under Sevier and was joined by additional troops under Col. Blair and Col. Christian; in all, about seven hundred men. They crossed the Tennessee and marched to Estinaula, and Etowah (now

---

[28] *Haywood*, 304; *Knoxville Gazette*, August 27, 1793.
[29] *Haywood*, 306; J. W. M. Breazeale, *Life As It Is* . . . , (Knoxville, 1842), 77. Hereinafter cited *Breazeale*.
[30] *Haywood*, 308; *Knoxville Gazette*, February 13, 1794; October 11, 1794.

The Parkins Stone House

The Gillespie Stone House

PLOT OF TOWN OF MARYVILLE—as laid out in 1795 and re-surveyed in 1819, by John Wilkinson, Surveyor. The double black lines represent the bounds as laid out by the order of Court of 1798—the dotted lines represent the bounds as laid out by the order of Court of 1815.

Rome, Georgia). After laying waste the crops and burning the towns, Sevier returned without having encountered many Indians. He made his report to Governor Blount from "Ish's Mill" (near Friendsville). This was the last military service rendered by Sevier. He is credited with having been the first to introduce the war whoop as a battle cry among white troops in his battles with the Indians and the British.[31]

After this there were stronger indications of peace on both sides. A conference was held at Tellico Blockhouse between Governor William Blount and Colonel John Watts. This conference was attended by four hundred warriors, Col. Abithia Thomas, Major John Sevier, Major David Craig, Captain Samuel Henry and Ensign Samuel Davidson among others.[32]

Late in December, Roger Oats and Nicholas Ball were killed by Indians near Well's Station in Blount County as they were transporting a load of corn to the blockhouse for the support of their families. This party was made up of at least ten men. The Indians took four horses from the wagon and a mulatto boy fourteen years old. They left beside Mr. Oats' body a speckled-stock trading gun of the type furnished to the Creeks by the Spanish. The gun had been broken over his head. Several small bands of supposed spies were discovered within the Knox County boundaries about this time, supposedly checking on the state of defenses on the frontier.

A number of frontiersmen gathered and followed the murderers of Oats and Ball to Hanging Maw's camp and here they killed three men and seven women.

On the 10th of January, 1794, Capt. Evans of the Knox County Cavalry was on a patrol assignment from Eagle Ford on Clinch River when he ran across a trail of shod horses. He supposed these to be those taken when Oats and Ball were killed and followed the trail. It led him through the Tellico Plains to a camp on the mountain. The Indians discovered their approach and all escaped except two children. A stolen horse was recovered and several scalps were found. Among them was the scalp of Mr. Oats, identified by the bald crown.[33]

In February, Assembly in session, recommended better defenses on the frontier for the protection of inhabitants. A committee was appointed to draft an Address in which they demanded a declaration of war against the Creeks and Cherokees. They recited the various acts committed on the frontier since the Treaty of Holston, viz., "two hun-

---

[31] Ramsey, *Annals*, 584-89; *Carter*, 235. It appears that the Secretary of War wrote a letter to Governor Blount censuring him because of the expense of maintaining the militia at this time. Blount in his reply said that the people of the Territory had been confided to his care and that since Watts had raised a force and openly declared war that he could do no less than he had done. He further stated that if he had discharged the militia and the unprotected people had been attacked that he would have received the heaviest censure of the Federal Government and the people.

[32] American State Papers, *Indian Affairs*, I, 536-38 (Minutes and Correspondence); *Knoxville Gazette*, November 10, 1794

[33] *Haywood*, 311-16; *Breazeale*, 81; *Knoxville Gazette*, January 2, 1794.

dred people dead, one thousand horses stolen valued at $100,000 besides malicious destruction of property and livestock." They further recited the miserable existence the settlers had endured while enforted on the frontiers for more than a year past. They noted the measures which had been taken for their protection, but lamented that it was of too little avail. They averred that they loved peace but that self-preservation would force them to enter into unauthorized warfare in the event that the Federal Government did nothing to relieve the situation. The Indians continued to prowl around the frontier forts.[34]

On the 7th of February, Peter Bowerman, a soldier in Captain Singleton's company of militia was fired on by three Indians, near Well's Station. One ball struck his hunting shirt. Sunday, March 10th, Samuel Martin was killed near Henry's Station on the path to his father's house. About sunset the same day, James Ferguson, his sister and David Craig's son were fired on from ambush as they were passing from David Craig's on Nine Mile Creek to John Craig's on Pistol Creek. When the Indian fired on them they killed Ferguson who was leading. An Indian rushed into the road with uplifted tomahawk and seized the young lady's horse by the bridle. She gave the bridle a sudden jerk and broke loose from the Indian. Young Craig had halted to help her if he could, and when she got loose they made off as fast as their horses could take them. The road forked near the place and came together again within a hundred yards. Miss Ferguson took one fork and young Craig the other, and where the roads came together their horses met with such force that Craig's knocked the young lady's horse down and she was thrown off. Craig jumped off his horse and helped her remount and they fortunately made their escape although the Indians were close behind them.[35]

The first of April, 1794, a party of thirty or forty Indians ambushed a path near Cavin's Blockhouse on Crooked Creek and fired on Samuel Wear, his two sons and William McMurray as they were going out from the blockhouse to work on their farm. One bullet passed through McMurray's clothes. On their retreat to the blockhouse another party of Indians fired on them but did no injury.

At this time "Hanging Maw" wrote to Governor Blount that the Cherokees were now willing and determined to "take the United States by the hand" and not listen to Spanish talk any more.

Notwithstanding this avowal, on July 24th, a party of Indians killed John Ish at his plow in the field, within one hundred-eighty yards of his own blockhouse, and scalped him. He left a wife and eight children, the oldest not more than eleven years old. Major King and Lt. Cunning-

---

[34] *Knoxville Gazette*, March 13, 1794; Assembly in session recommended a chain of blockhouses to be built. One in Tuckaleechee on Little River, one at the head of Crooked Creek, known as Blacks', one at Mr. Slone's on Nine Mile Creek, one on the North of the Tennessee River (Tellico Blockhouse) and one at Coyatee Ford.

[35] *Haywood*, 313; *Breazeale*, 83; *Knoxville Gazette*, February 13, 1794, March 13, 1794

ham and a detachment of Cherokees went by Hanging Maw's and followed their trail to Hiwassee. Being informed of the murderer's whereabouts, they captured him, and delivered him to the Indian agent, Mr. McKee, at the Tellico Blockhouse July 28, 1794.[36]

The governor issued a commission of Oyer and Terminer for this Indian's trial. A court was held by Judge Joseph Anderson and an indictment was found by the grand jury against Obongphohego of Toocauscaugee (or Punk Knot) on Oakfuskee.

On the first day of August, the grand jury composed of: Foreman John Patterson, Andrew Hanna, Samuel Hindman, George Stout, Oliver Wallace, Moses Brooks, Wm. Trimble, William and Thomas Richie, George Walker, Jeremiah Jeffrey, John Steele, William Lee, Robt. Kirkpatrick, Thomas Millican, George Hays and George Cuningham, returned a true bill that Obongphohego, a Creek, . . . with a certain gun of the value of one dollar, charged with powder and leaden bullet . . . did shoot . . . the said John Ish . . . so that he instantly died . . . contrary to the laws of the United States . . . and against the Treaties of Peace made with the Creek Nation of Indians and against the peace and dignity of the United States.

Obongphohego was found guilty by the following jury: Andrew McCammel, Thomas Robinson, Martin Priest, James Walker, William Sharp, Joseph Brooks, James Milliken, John Kerr, Nicholas Neal, Alexander Cole, Thomas Inglis, and Thomas Bounds.

The sentence was that he should be hanged; which execution was effected on Monday the 4th of August, 1794. A contemporary account says that the Indian was taken on horseback to the place and since he was so tall they were afraid his feet would touch the ground, they asked the Indian to stand on the horse while they secured the rope. While the sheriff was fastening the rope after passing it over the limb, the Indian lost his balance and the executioner hanged him by holding onto the other end of the rope. The total cost of the trial was $68.00.

A penciled note on the margin of the original paper says "Alexander Ish said he had been informed by John McCarty that Obongphohego was not the Indian that killed his father, John Ish, but that it was an Indian by the name of Will I Omough, that upon consultation, it was thought best to surrender Obongphohego as he was rather simple than otherwise." [37]

Two days afterwards, eight Creeks were seen twenty-five miles below Hiwassee on their way to the settlements south of the French Broad. They were pursued by the Cherokees and a few Federal troops from "Hanging Maw's" village. Their trail crossed the Tennessee and on the 10th of August, they came up with the Creeks in sight of Major

---

[36] *Haywood*, 319–22; *Knoxville Gazette*, April 10, 1794; July 3, 1794.
[37] Original papers in Hamilton District Court Records, Knox County Courthouse. Also related in above news account. (Said to be the first hanging in Knox County)

Craig's Station (on Nine Mile Creek). They killed and scalped one and wounded another and captured a few goods. The war party celebrated that night with a scalp-dance. The Cherokees had joined friendly hands with the whites and were now engaged in warfare with the Creeks.[38]

Late in 1794, the Territorial Legislature saw fit to divide Jefferson County into two counties. The new county was called Sevier. The first court was held at the house of Isaac Thomas. The county seat, Sevierville, was laid out in 1795.

Early in 1795, Indians, in a last spasm of hostilities, came into Blount County and committed numerous depredations. Colonel Alexander Kelly raised forty or fifty men and marched across Chilhowee Mountain to Tallassee Old Town. When he reached the river he saw smoke on the opposite side and sent a detachment across to attack from the rear. They succeeded in routing the Indians from the bluffs, and killed eight in all with no injury to his party. Suspension of hostilities now took place, but garrisons were maintained all along the frontier.[39]

The Territorial Assembly met on the last Monday in June, 1795, to discuss the possibility of forming the Territory into a state and to take the proper steps to effect it. They rejoiced that a general peace had been achieved and that the calamities of Indian warfare had ceased. They passed a law to enumerate the inhabitants to see if they amounted to sixty thousand or not, and last, but most important to this narrative, Blount County was erected out of that part of Knox County, south of the Holston River, and west of Stock Creek.[40]

On August 2nd, 1795, the following appointments were made for Blount County: Alexander Kelly, Lt. Col. Commandant; John McKee, Lt. Col.; Samuel Glass, 1st Major; James Woods Lackey, 2nd Major; George Ewing, Capt.; William Ragan, Lt.; John Ragan, John Singleton, Robert Rhea, Samuel Houston, Henry Ragan, John Cochran, James Scott, James Houston, Robert Boyd, George Tedford, Joseph Tedford, Joel Wallace, and Samuel Bogle, all Ensigns. Calvary officers were: James Cunningham, Capt.; John Lowry, 1st Lt.; John Alexander, Cornet. Civil appointments: Littlepage Sims, Sheriff; John McKee, Clerk; William Wallace, Register; Robert Rhea, Coroner. Justices of the Peace: David Craig, William Wallace, John Trimble, Samuel Houston, George Ewing, James Greenway, Mathew Wallace, James Scott, Andrew Bogle, Thomas McCulloch, William Lowry.[41]

By these appointments the machinery of Blount County was ready to set into motion in September, 1795.

---

[38] *Haywood*, 324; a conference was held on the 7th and 8th of November at Tellico Blockhouse between Governor Blount and John Watts. *Knoxville Gazette*, November 18, 1794.
[39] Ramsey, *Annals*, 637; *Breazeale*, 90
[40] *Haywood*, 484
[41] *Carter*, 469

CHAPTER III

County Government*

BY TERMS of the short-lived Treaty of Dumplin Creek executed between the State of Franklin and the Cherokees in 1785, settlers had swarmed over the hills south of the French Broad. The collapse of the State of Franklin brought about six years of serious frontier warfare with the Indians, relieved somewhat by the Treaty of Holston which again set the boundary at the watershed between Little River and the Little Tennessee. What is now Blount County became an extension of Greene County, until the erection of Knox County in 1792.[1]

The Cherokees were dissatisfied with the terms of the Holston Treaty in 1791 and protested the delay in running the boundary line and the removal of the whites who were over the line. For this reason depredations continued and only strong conciliatory efforts prevented open warfare.

John Sevier finally organized the Campaign of 1793 against the Cherokees and effectively squelched them. The first territorial assembly met at Knoxville in 1794 and among other acts chartered Blount College, now the University of Tennessee.

In 1795 two acts important to this story were passed: one, to take a census to determine whether the territory had sufficient population to become a state, and another act to form Blount County from a part of Knox County.

In July 1795, the General Assembly of the Territory South of the Ohio River erected a new county from Knox to be called Blount in honor of Governor William Blount. Joseph Black, David Craig, Samuel Glass, Samuel Henry, John Trimble and William Wallace were appointed commissioners to select the site for the county seat. They chose fifty acres belonging to Capt. John Craig near Craig's Fort and laid out 120 lots and necessary streets.[2]

They were empowered to sell the lots and erect a building for the Courts of Pleas and Quarter Sessions. They laid out the town and named it Maryville in honor of Mary Grainger, wife of Governor Blount. The town as first laid out was from present Cates Street to Norwood Street and from creek to creek. The present Bank of Maryville corner was reserved as the court square, and the first jail was where the present jail stands and the courthouse on the next lot west. These buildings were not ready for the first session of court.[3]

---

* Information, not otherwise accounted for, is from the Blount County Court Minutes. Hereinafter cited *Minutes.*
[1] This was the same boundary set at the Treaty of Dumplin.
[2] Ramsey, *Annals*, 643 ff (Craig had bought 343 acres from Stockley Donelson's grant of 5,000 acres.)
[3] Map from re-survey made in 1819. Copy in author's collection: *Minutes*, Passim

On the second Monday in September 1795, the Blount County Court of Pleas and Quarter Sessions held its first meeting at the house of Abraham Wear. William Wallace,* William Lowry,* Oliver Alexander and James Scott were present with commissions from Governor Blount with certificates thereon that they had taken the oath of office and the oath to support the Constitution of the United States. David Craig* and George Ewing presented their commissions and took the required oaths. William Wallace was appointed chairman.[4]

The following men produced commissions from Governor Blount: John McKee, clerk; Littlepage Sims, sheriff; William Wallace, register; and Robert Rhea, coroner. Each made oath and entered into bond with securities for their respective offices.

John McKee was appointed Trustee for the County and made the required bond. James Gaily, James Blair and Gray Sims presented commissions as constables and qualified.

Tuesday morning, Thomas McCullock* and William Hamilton* presented proof of their qualifications as justices and sat with the court. Archibald Cowan was appointed deputy clerk and took the oath of office.

James Greenaway also qualified as justice. At this first session of court three permits were issued for building mills: to John Craig on Pistol Creek, to John Walker in Tuckaleechee, to Samuel Thompson on Crooked Creek; a power of attorney was registered; a lunacy hearing was held; two wills were registered, and papers of administration issued; two brands were registered; an overseer was appointed for one road; and a committee was appointed to view a road to Tuckaleechee.[5]

The Court of Pleas and Quarter Sessions was a carry-over from the North Carolina setup. As a Court of Pleas, it was a judicial body similar to our present-day Circuit Courts. It was usually composed of three justices and could empanel a jury. It heard civil and criminal cases, bound apprentices, probated wills, partitioned land, etc. As a Court of Quarter Sessions, it met four times a year and was the legislative, and chief executive body of the county for a good many decades and was consequently the most powerful agent in county affairs.

Until the State of Tennessee was formed the justices and county officials were appointed by the Territorial Governor. After statehood, justices were appointed by the governor (during good behaviour) and

---

* These were Commissioned as Justices when Knox County was formed in 1792 and were already serving as justices. (Ramsey, *Annals*, 568)

[4] From 1795 until 1856, when the county had a county judge under a general law which was repealed in 1858 and from 1858 until 1920 when the office of county judge was created, the presiding officer of the court was the chairman. He was elected from the body each year. Since 1875, the chairman has differed only in minor aspects from a county judge. Moreover the chairman could act independently as a justice of the peace.

[5] Several permits for mills had already been granted by Knox County before Blount County was erected. Robert McTeer on Ellejoy, John Slone on Nine Mile Creek, Thomas McCullock on Pistol Creek, John Ish on Gallaher Creek, Alexander Kelly on Lackey's Creek, Nicholas Bartlett on Stock Creek and perhaps others.

it was not until 1836 that they were elected by the people. After statehood, county officials were elected by the County Court until the 1834 Constitution went into effect.[6]

The court had the power to levy taxes. The method of collection was quite different from present-day procedures. The county was not divided into districts as now. The only organized unit was the Militia Company. Every able-bodied man between the ages of 21 and 50 belonged to the organization. Each county was allowed one constable and two justices for each militia company with an extra justice for each of the "town" companies. After the tax had been determined by the court and levied, a justice was named to "list" the property liable to taxation in each militia company. Taxes were levied according to the number of slaves, number of acres, or number of town lots with no distinction as to the value. Assessment according to value of property did not come until 1836. The list, when made, was turned over to the Sheriff for collection.

The first taxes were levied on units of hundred acres of land and black and white polls only. Later taxes for jail, courthouse, poor, jury, billiard tables, studs, town lots, etc. were levied.

The County Court laid out and supervised roads, and issued permits for operation of ferries and set toll rates; but spent no money on layout nor up-keep until much later, except in a few rare cases where sledges (heavy hammers for breaking rocks) were bought by certain overseers and later paid for by order of the County Court.

The second term of court met at John Craig's, December 14th, 1795. Justices Wallace, Lowry, McCulloch, Craig, Hamilton, and Ewing were present. William Wallace was appointed chairman. John Trimble, Samuel Houston and Andrew Bogle presented commissions as justices and took the prescribed oaths. Ephriam Dunlap and Luke Boyer qualified before the court as lawyers. James Sims qualified as constable. The first jury was empaneled and the first trial resulted in an acquittal.

Three permits for mills were issued as well as Bills of Sale, and marks of ownership registered. The following roads were ordered to be viewed by various committees, from Maryville to: the forks of the Tennessee and Holston rivers; Tellico Blockhouse; the Sevier County line; Colville's Ford; McCullock's Ford; Bartlett's Mill and Kelly's Mill. The committees were to report at the next session.

Andrew Bogle, James Houston, Jr., and William Gillespie were appointed judges for election of delegates to the State Constitutional Convention and John Lowry, Alexander McCullock and Archibald Cowan were elected clerks for the same.[7]

---

[6] There is a collection of petitions and depositions in the State Archives relative to the removal of Matthew Wallace from office for mal-practice as justice. No case was made and the matter was dropped. (*Petitions*, Box #3.)

[7] David Craig, James Greenway, Joseph Black, Samuel Glass, and James Houston were elected to the convention which met January 11, 1796 at Knoxville. Craig and Black were appointed to the committee to draft the constitution. Ramsey, *Annals*, 650 ff.

The March term of court met at the courthouse in Maryville. Justices Wallace, McCullock, Hamilton, Lowry, Ewing, and Bogle were present and Matthew Wallace qualified as justice.

It was ordered that the following justices make a return of the taxable property in Blount County: Samuel Houston for Capt. Tedford's Company, John Trimble and William Hamilton for Capt. Singleton's Company, William Lowry for Capt. Ewing's Company, Andrew Bogle for Capt. Boyd's Company, and David Craig for Capt. Scott's Company. The tax rate was to be: .12½ on all free males between 21 and 50 years of age and .12½ on all slaves, male and female, between the ages of ten and fifty in this county.

At the June term, 1796, commissions were produced from John Sevier, governor of Tennessee, appointing the following Justices of the Peace: Andrew Bogle, Joseph Black, William Davidson, Andrew Miller, William Lowry, George Ewing, William Wallace, John Wallace, Samuel Houston, James Greenway, and Matthew Wallace. All except John Wallace (who qualified later) took the oaths prescribed.

The court elected James Houston clerk for the court, and Archibald Cowan, his deputy, and Joseph Colville, sheriff. James Blair was sworn as constable to attend the court and William Lowry was elected Presiding Justice of the court. Andrew Bogle was elected coroner; William Wallace, register; Oliver Alexander, woodranger; James Gayley, Zachariah Goforth, Erastus Tippet, John Caldwell and John Morris were appointed constables and installed.[8]

The following rates were set for Ordinary-Keepers in this county:

Breakfast	16⅔
Dinner	25
Supper	12½
Lodging	8⅓
Good Whisky ½ pt.	8⅓
Rum	16⅔
Good Beer qt.	8⅓
Good Brandy ½ pt.	12½

William Wallace, and Samuel Houston were appointed to contract with workmen to build a pair of stocks for the county.

William Burk, Josiah Danforth and John Wallace each got leave to keep a Public House.

Luke Boyer was appointed the first County Solicitor.

At the September term, 1796, John Trimble got leave to operate a ferry on the Holstein, (sic) just above the fork. Rates: .19 for a man and horse or pack horse, $1 for wagon and team, .13 for cattle, hogs, and sheep; .14½ for a single horse. William Stockton was also given leave to operate a ferry on the Holston.

At the December term, 1796, Andrew Bogle, John Cochran and Samuel Houston were commissioned by the court to contract for building Stocks and Pillory. Andrew Thompson was appointed stand-

---

[8] Houston had been appointed justice but resigned in order to be clerk, *(Minutes)*.

ard-bearer (to check weights and measures) by this court. New tavern rates were adopted and license issued to John Woods and David Taylor to keep Public House.⁹

At the March 1797 session, Major George Farragut was granted leave to operate a ferry at Stony Point and it was also ordered that a road be viewed from said ferry by Matthew Wallace's Mill (Jena) to Tellico Blockhouse. New rates were issued for Farragut's and Stockton's ferries.¹⁰

At the April term, 1797, it was ordered that the "county tax rate be equal to the government tax and as high as the law allows." Justices to make returns were appointed: Capt. Bogle's Company, George Ewing; Capt. Alexander's, William Wallace; Capt. Moor's, William Davidson; Capt. Colville's, Andrew Bogle; Capt. Rhea's, John Cochran; Capt. Scott's, Matthew Wallace; Capt. Lackey's, Thomas Gallahar.

The court ordered in December that Daniel Boterite be allowed two dollars for putting one round on the gaol (jail) more than his first contract; five dollars for cutting down and planking the corners; six dollars for erecting a compleat (sic) door to the upper story and five dollars for erecting a ladder and platform for the upper story.

There is no mention in the county records to show that there was any concern about the dozens of families who were removed by force from the Indian lands late in 1797. There was great dissatisfaction on the part of the Indians because the whites had encroached on their lands and because the line as agreed on at the Holston Treaty (1791) had not been run until 1797, and dissatisfaction among the whites because they claimed that the line as finally run by Winchester, Pickens and Hawkins had given the Secretary of War incorrect information. They reported that instead of sixty-eight families who had already settled over the Indian Line prior to cession by North Carolina that there were three times that number.¹¹

An exploratory line was run by Campbell, McKee, and McClung in 1792, but so many settlers were found south of the line that it was abandoned. The Hawkins line was run in 1797. The surveyors noted that from the Holston River to Chilhowee Mountains there were many intruders on Indian lands. In Murphy's Cove they found four intruders and in Tuckaleechee Cove, two were found. After the Treaty of 1798, the line of survey coincided with the Hawkins line east of the Chilhowees but lay to the south between the Chilhowees and Southwest Point.¹²

A petition sent to Congress stated that 2,500 to 3,000 men, women,

---

⁹ Andrew Thompson was allowed $5.50 for building stocks in March, 1797.
¹⁰ Later Lowe's Ferry. Major Farragut was the father of Admiral David Glasgow Farragut.
¹¹ American State Papers, *Indian Affairs*, V. 1, p. 206, 545, 637; Hereinafter cited *ASP*. Knox Treaties of 1792 and 1794 had attempted to appease the Cherokees; Robert H. White, ed., *Messages of the Governors*, (Nashville, 1952), V. 1 p. 33, Hereinafter cited White, *Messages*.
¹² *ASP*, 623 ff; *Carter*, 62, (The map and report of this survey appear to be lost)

and children were removed from Cherokee lands by October 25, 1797, many of whom held bonafide grants from the State of North Carolina.

There was great concern registered in the State Senate about the affair. They protested the removal until the people had time to secure their crops and look for new country. Their committee also reported that the line of Treaty, if properly run, would relieve a great many of the unfortunate.

Later in the year they protested strongly against Lt. Col. Thomas Butler removing up to 3,000 men, women, and children on short notice during very inclement weather.[13]

One list of names of people living over the line has been found dated November 8, 1796, and headed Tellico Blockhouse: John Cowan, Hance Russell, and Joseph Ore were on Baker's Creek, one-half mile from the mouth; James Gayley, James Hazen and Ezekiel Henry were near Cowan's; Diarmond was living near the mouth of Baker's Creek on the banks of the Tennessee River; David Montgomery was living near Diarmond; Bell at the Big Spring; Townsley at Cedar Creek on the road to Knoxville; John Taylor, John Hannah, Samuel Hannah, Gailbraith, Robinson, John and Enoch Williams, John and James Wallace were on Nine Mile Creek and its waters. The informant added, "There are many others but I have not been able to obtain their names." [14]

It is not known how long these people were actually off the land. There is a great deal of correspondence from Joseph Anderson, Andrew Jackson, and W. C. C. Claiborne, Members of Congress from Tennessee, to the Secretary of War James W. Henry, regarding the plight of these distressed people, should they not be permitted to return to their land in time to make their summer crops "since they derive their support from the pursuit of agriculture alone."

There are dozens of passports on file of people who were removed and who sought to return and gather crops and take care of livestock during 1798. At least eighty separate names are found among them, some of them more than once.[15]

The President and Congress were finally prevailed on to settle this matter with the Indians and another Treaty was effected in October 1798. The successful consummation of this matter was due entirely to the groundwork laid by Governor John Sevier during the summer months.[16]

The Treaty of Tellico specified that the line should be run from the Militia Spring to the Chilhowee Mountain so as to leave all farms to the north and east of this line. This was not done in all cases as attested by various petitions later.[17]

---

[13] Senate *Journal*, 1st Session 1797, pp 18, 73, 98, 118.
[14] Tennessee State Archives, *Sevier Papers*.
[15] *Petitions* Box #1, Tennessee State Archives, Nashville, Tenn.
[16] White, *Messages*, 50-70; *ASP*, 637.
[17] Petition of Henry Logan says that the line left him only five acres north of the line and that the Regulars took over his buildings as barracks and that surveyors refused to survey it for him in accordance with the act of 1819.

COUNTY GOVERNMENT   37

A letter from George Walton and Thomas Butler who acted for the government at the Tellico Treaty, to Andrew Thompson and John Wallace representing the citizens of Maryville, indicates that they have been addressed with approval by the citizens for their efforts in the late treaty. They stated that in the discharge of their duty they were urged by a knowledge of the suffering of the victims and were happy to have been an instrument of their relief. "They can now return to the settlements they have made and continue their occupancy upon the same terms as at the time of their removal. Their claims upon the soil being neither diminished nor increased by the events that have taken place." [18]

The county was scarcely organized before Andrew Thompson, Barclay McGhee, William Lowry, John Cochran, and John Woods were appointed in August 1799, to let the contract for a new courthouse and to rent a temporary courthouse if necessary. A committee had been appointed in August 1798, to repair the old courthouse. The following May they paid Joseph Weir $8 for the use of his house and wood for two courts. The next year they paid John Wallace for three sessions, and Weir was paid for his house and fires for the November session.[19]

The court allowed notes for $513.50 to Josiah Danforth on the courthouse contract in 1800 and later settled for a total of $571.33 1/3 in 1804. John Lowry had paid $50 for the old courthouse lot in the meantime.

The "jail bounds" were laid out, up and down Main Street, with the jail as center, to contain fifteen acres. This was increased to twenty acres in 1803.[20]

In September 1803, the Assembly passed an act allowing Blount County the privilege of holding two fairs each year at the town of Maryville for the purpose of selling all kinds of goods, wares and merchandise, free to every citizen of the state. This fair was to be held the last Wednesday in March and October and could continue for two days. At first the fairs were probably held at the camp ground near "Calamity Corner." Later the fairs were held at the Watkins farm near the City Spring on the Sandy Springs Road.[21]

The new courthouse on the Bank of Maryville lot was not finished until 1804. Town lots were sold from time to time to apply on the cost of building the courthouse. This fact is mentioned several different times. The key was turned over to John Lowry, merchant, in May 1804. He was not to permit abuse of the building. He was also commissioned to sink a cistern six feet square and report the cost to the court.

---

[18] *Knoxville Register*, October 23, 1798.
[19] It is of interest that the court adjourned Wed. August 3, 1798, from 12 p.m. to 3 p.m. to attend services of the Presbyterian Churches in America: "Clerk to present Mr. Blackburn a copy of this order."
[20] Prisoners not charged with felony or treason could move at large. Some even had to provide their own food. Public houses were generally included in the bounds. They were, of course, under bond to keep within bounds.
[21] *Acts, 1803*, ch. 94, sec. 2.

A poor tax was first levied in 1801: three cents per hundred acres, and on white polls; six cents on black polls, and twelve cents on stud horses. In 1805, merchants were assessed a $5.00 county tax, which is the first privilege tax on record in the county.

Until after the compact of 1806 between North Carolina, Tennessee, and the Federal government, the most of the settlers of Blount County had no legal title to their land. Some few had North Carolina landgrants which had been registered, but most settlers held their land only by right of pre-emption and occupancy. Surveyors were busy from 1806 to 1810 surveying the holdings of these people; and courts were busy settling overlapping claims.

In 1807, by an act of legislature a Board of Commissioners for the City of Maryville was appointed composed of: John Montgomery, John Wilkinson, John Lowry, merchant, John Lowry, attorney, Andrew Thompson, Samuel Love, hatter, and David Russell. They were to have lots surveyed and the corners set according to the original plan. The Cedar Spring was never to be sold but reserved for the use of the town.[22]

They were to keep the streets in repair, tax property, prevent damage by fire, suppress horse-running and collect fines.

By the Compact of 1806, it was now possible for land-holders to get title to their lands. It appears that the commissioners of Maryville did not get title to the plot as a unit, but that it became an individual matter. That was the reason for the above-named survey of the town.

In 1809, it appears from a further act that the Register of East Tennessee had refused to issue a grant for the town of Maryville because the "exterior boundary will include a greater territory than called for by certificate." He was directed to issue grants for as much as was not separately surveyed by the respective claimants, without expressing exterior lines, merely using lot numbers. A part of this act designated July 4th, every year, as the date on which the townsmen should meet at the courthouse and elect seven commissioners acccording to the act of 1807.[23]

The map or plan of the town was lost and in 1821, John Wilkinson, surveyor and lawyer, made a new map and swore to its accuracy (he having surveyed over sixty of the lots for the purchasers). This map was found in the files of the Supreme Court of Tennessee in Knoxville and in December 1922, a copy was placed in the archives of the City of Maryville. The original plot contained 120 lots of one-quarter acre each, making a total of thirty acres. Twenty acres were used for streets and alleys. Maps and surveys of many lots are in an old book in the Register's office of Knox County.[24]

In 1807, $100.00 was appropriated for the town commissioners of

---

[22] *Acts, 1807*, ch. 84, "An act to regulate the City of Maryville," (ten sections)
[23] *Acts, 1809*, ch. 3.
[24] Parham Papers, *Maryville*. Copy of map in writer's collection.

Maryville, to convey water into the town. Nothing is recorded as to what was done.

The same year at least five cotton gin owners reported their cotton gins for taxation which indicates that cotton was an important crop at this period. The tax on cotton gins was according to the terms of an agreement by the state with the inventors of the machine.

The first Circuit Court was organized February 2, 1810, by James Trimble, who appointed Robert Houston, clerk.[25]

About this time Sam Houston of future Texas fame was in town and he and Capt. John B. Cusick disturbed the court with a drum to the extent that they fined Houston $5 and Cusick $10 (the fine was suspended next day). This was, of course, leading up to the time that Captains McKamy, Duncan, Tedford, Trimble, Tipton, Walker, Buchanan, Gillespie, and others recruited men locally and went to the battles of the Horseshoe and New Orleans.

Morganton, which became in the 1820's and 30's a very important county town was established by act of legislature in 1813. The petition of Hugh and Charles Kelso and others, asked to lay out the town of Portsville, since public inspection was established there by act of legislature. The plan, of the town submitted, contained nineteen lots at the junction of Baker's Creek and the Tennessee River. William Lowry, James J. Greene, John Eakin, Richard Dearmond, Matthew Wallace, James Wyley, John Lambert, Sr., and Joseph Dunkin are named as commissioners to have the power to fill all vacancies. The town was established as Morganton, probably named so in honor of Gideon Morgan who was a prominent citizen of this period.[26]

At this place was probably the first ferry authorized by the Blount County Court. Hugh Kelso operated a saw and grist mill here prior to the establishing of Morganton. The ferry has been called Wear's and Tipton's as well as Morganton.

Amos Barnett and John Lambert were both issued permits to operate ordinaries in Morganton in 1817. A post office was established here in 1818. In the 1823 county election, Morganton is reported as one of the three voting places in Blount County.[27]

Among interesting acts of June 1815, was the emancipation of George Erskine by request of Abel Pearson and Isaac Anderson; Dr. Isaac Wright's permit to build a warehouse on Holston River; Major James Houston resigned as clerk of the court, and was succeeded by Jacob F. Foute.[28]

---

[25] Only son of Major James Houston, who later died in Bermuda.

[26] Tennessee State Archives, *Petitions* Box #12; *Acts, 1810*, ch. 5, sec. 24; *Acts, 1803*, p. 233. Inspectors were appointed to prevent exportation of unmerchantable goods. "In Blount County, to be stationed at the mouth of Baker's Creek and the fork of Holston on Tennessee."

[27] Tennessee State Archives. *Petitions*, Box #33. (Maryville, Morganton and Tuckaleechee are named as voting places.)

[28] George Erskine was ordained by the Presbytery of Union as a traveling evangelist for the colored race. He eventually went to Liberia where he superintended church and school work; James Houston's resignation was not officially accepted until some years later.

In 1817, the Sheriff objected to keeping prisoners for debt in jail because of its insufficiency. A commission was appointed and empowered to buy a lot, make plans and let the contract for a new jail in December, to be built "anywhere except the public square." The tax to build a new jail and to repair the courthouse was ordered laid to the full extent.

This second jail was built in 1818 on lot No. 11 back of Blount Laundry on McCammon Street. This frame jail was replaced by a brick building on the same lot in 1848 which still stands.

The details of what took place in the county between 1818 and 1834 are not available in court records since these records are missing and no doubt many interesting things have been lost from the local records.

In 1819 Calhoun's Treaty released, unconditionally, all Indian claims to what is now Blount County. Prior to this date, the line had been extended as far east as the Chilhowee Mountains and south of the Hawkins line in 1798. Now, when Monroe, McMinn, and Hamilton counties were erected from this newly acquired territory in 1819, the line between Blount and Monroe was set at the Tennessee River from the state line to its junction with the Holston.[29]

The line did not remain thus, very long, because in 1823 the line was moved so as to include certain tax payers in Monroe County. The line has been changed by private acts several times since 1823 to accommodate various citizens who found it more convenient to pay taxes in Monroe County.[30]

In 1823 a mass meeting of citizens reputedly met in Maryville to discuss a matter which was destined to work a complete revolution in the American system of choosing a presidential candidate.

The meeting advanced the idea that the people had a right to choose their own candidates by the simple process of voting, without having to be schooled in political maneuvers. Up to this time electors for presidents had been chosen by the Legislature and not by popular vote. The election of 1824 was the first presidential year in which a record of popular votes was kept. This was the beginning of the agitation that led to the election of presidential electors by popular vote rather than by legislators. This change was probably responsible for Jackson's election in 1828.

By 1825 Blount County had thirty-two acting justices and sixteen companies of militia. In the 1825 enumeration report, Blount County had 1,774 voters as compared with Sevier's 898 and Monroe's 1,707.[31]

In 1820 the Unicoi Turnpike had already been opened in Monroe County through the mountains to North Carolina and Georgia, and the Calloway Turnpike was being constructed in Monroe County to Tallassee Ford (now Calderwood). The Houstons, John Sr., and Jr., James Jr., and Robert petitioned in 1821 for a charter to build a turnpike

[29] *ASP*, V. 1, p. 637; V. 2, p. 187; *Acts, 1798*, Ch. 6, Sec. 1; *Acts, 1801*, Ch. 52
[30] *Acts, 1823*, Ch. 256; *Acts, 1836*, Ch. 143; *Acts, 1838*, Ch. 270; *Acts, 1877*, Ch. 130
[31] Tennessee State Archives, *Petitions*, Box 39, 43.

from Maryville to the Tuckaseegee River in North Carolina, for a "nigher cut" to Augusta, Georgia. The charter was granted in 1822 from Abram's Creek to the North Carolina Line. In 1825, Joshua Parsons and John Isbill were granted a new charter for this same road, which was built.[32]

In 1830, Daniel D. Foute was granted a charter for a road through the mountains to intersect a road opened by Parsons and Calloway. This road from Maryville to Chilhowee by Montvale was used for some fifty years, although its existence is known to very few in this generation.[33]

Another very ambitious engineering project of the 1830's was the attempt of the McCampbells, Caldwells, Andersons and others to build a road from Tuckaleechee Cove across Smoky Mountains near Briar Knob. This road was under the supervision of Isaac Anderson, the founder of Maryville College, and was built through School House Gap as far as the ridge now known as Defeat Ridge. The work was done mostly by Indian labor. The above-named ridge tells the results of this project.[34]

In accordance with the newly adopted constitution, William McTeer, Samuel Tullock, Spencer Henry, John Hackney, and William Wallace were delegated to lay off the territory of Blount County into districts for the purpose of electing justices of the peace and constables. They proceeded in 1836 to lay off seventeen civil districts in Blount County and filed their minute descriptions of the boundaries together with a sketch of the districts. Samuel Henry's Mill (Brick Mill) was the starting point which served as a corner for the 1st, 2nd, 6th and 7th districts, while other corners named were: Big Spring, Shank's Spring, William Toole's "well place," and the "pole bridge" on the Tuckaleechee road.[35]

Each district voting place was named. The first five in order were: Samuel Tullock's, Alexander McCollum's, Jesse Robertson's, Captain John Walker's home and Esq. Bowerman's Mill. Clover Hill was the voting place for the sixth district, and the muster ground, at James M. Kerr's was named for the seventh.[36]

Andrew L. Anderson's home was the election place for the eighth and the Courthouse for the ninth, or town district. Louisville was to serve as polling place for the tenth district and Stephens' Mill (Rockford) for the eleventh. Peter Wheeler's home, McTeer's Mill, Peter

[32] *Acts, 1825*, ch. 312; *Acts 1822*, ch. 212.
[33] *Acts, 1830*, ch. 178; In 1852 Foute built another road to intersect Parson's Turnpike to North Carolina, through Cades Cove by way of Chestnut Flats. Part of this road is still in use as a fire road by park rangers.
[34] *Acts, 1838*, ch. 34. (Joseph Estabrook, John Anderson and others); *Acts, 1833*, ch. 276 (John, Robert and James McCampbell, Samuel, Isaac and Robert M. Anderson, Richard G. Dunlap, Wm. Maurey, Joseph Estabrook, and James Gruett to begin in Tuckaleechee Cove).
[35] *Acts, 1835–36*, ch. 1, sec. 1; Resolution 3.
[36] Tennessee State Archives, Nashville, Tenn.; McTeer's Mill was changed to the school house in 1840 *(Minutes)*.

Snider's store in Tuckaleechee and Capt. Jacob Tipton's home in Cades Cove were named as voting places for the twelfth, thirteenth, fourteenth, fifteenth, sixteenth districts respectively while Lewis Smith's home was named for the seventeenth.

This district setup was unaltered except for minor changes until 1870 when Loudon County was erected mainly from portions of Blount, Knox, and Roane counties. All of the third district was taken, and most of the second from Blount. There was not enough acreage to re-create two districts in the vicinity. After much disagreement and protest a new second district was formed by taking part from the fifth and fourth districts and the third was re-erected in 1880 from part of the eighth beyond the top of the Chilhowee Mountain. The fifteenth was divided and Miller's Cove became the eighteenth district and Tuckaleechee Cove the fifteenth. In 1891, the ninth was divided to form the ninth and nineteenth. From time to time, district boundaries were altered to accommodate various citizens. There was also an attempt, or trial, of a twentieth district at Calderwood about 1915. This did not work out because there was not enough territory.

Just as in the Militia setup, two justices and one constable are still elected in each civil district with an extra justice for each incorporated town.

In 1837, an act was passed to incorporate the town of Maryville which provided that seven Aldermen should be elected each year. This plan did not differ from the commission setup already in use, except in name.[37]

In the same year the Maryville-Knoxville Turnpike was chartered and seventeen commissioners named from Knox and Blount counties.[38]

There is on file in the State Archives a very interesting petition from sundry citizens of Blount County dated December 1837. The narrative stated that the courthouse in convening either the Circuit or County Court was too small for comfort and that its condition was so dilapidated as to make it entirely unfit for the purposes for which it was designed. The jury was crowded into a narrow compass, there were no accommodations for the Bar and the citizens and litigants were almost excluded from witnessing the proceedings.

It was further represented that the roof and walls were rotten, the underpinnings fallen out, and it was without windows and doors. There was no jury's or clerk's rooms. This condition was being endured because of the oppression it would occasion to tax the people to build one unassisted.[39]

Also the jail was represented as "unsufficient" for the prisoners, three having escaped recently. The state was requested to appropriate the state tax for five years or whatever part of it the Legislature saw fit to

---

[37] *Acts, 1837*, ch. 246.

[38] *Ibid.*, ch. 117, sec. 17.

[39] Photostat of original which is filed with *Petitions*, Tennessee State Archives, Nashville, Tenn., in author's collection.

apportion. Needless to say the proposal was tabled and that ended the matter.

In March 1838, a committee was appointed to receive plans and proposals for building a courthouse and to give the plans publicity in the *Knoxville Register*. Inspectors were also appointed to report on the jail conditions.

In April 1838, Jesse Thompson, A. C. Montgomery, Henry Hannum, William Toole, Samuel Pride, Henry Hamil, and James Trundle were appointed to contract and superintend the building of a new courthouse.

In May 1838, a committee was appointed by the court to examine and inquire on what terms the public square could be enlarged for the purposes of erecting a new courthouse. They were also to ascertain the best terms on which another site could be obtained within the limits of the town and report to the next term of court. The vote was eleven to nine for the same site when the report was made.

A new lock was bought for the jail and a courthouse tax was levied which was double the amount of the jury and county taxes in 1839.

The courthouse contract was awarded to Thomas Crutchfield in May 1840. He had built several other county courthouses and was considered an expert.

During the months that the courthouse was being built (1839–42) court was held at Henry Sesler's and at Dr. James H. Gillespy's Tavern House.

In 1844, an attempt was made to establish a new county to be called Jones, in honor of Governor James C. Jones, from portions of Blount and Monroe counties lying along the Little Tennessee River. The seat of justice was to be Joseph Ashley's (Chilhowee). John Hardin, Samuel Glen, and Andrew Cowan of Blount County and Arthur Henry and Joseph S. Milligan of Monroe were to have a survey made and find if there was sufficient population and territory without running closer than twelve miles to the county seat of either county. They were then to hold an election and find whether the majority of the voters were in favor of Ashley's for the county seat.[40]

The act was passed a second time in 1845 for a re-survey to remove constitutional objections but nothing came of the attempt to set up the new county because, evidently, objections could not be removed.

By April 1847, the courthouse debt was evidently taken care of and James Henry, Edward George, Benjamin D. Brabson, Stephen J. McReynolds, and Sam Pride were appointed to contract for and erect a new jail house, and a jail tax was levied by the court.

In November, there appeared in the *Knoxville Register* a notice to brick masons and carpenters that bids would be received. The building was to be 48 x 20 feet with a passage through the center. The first floor was to be nine feet high and the second floor eight feet high. The walls at the jail end were to be twenty-two inches thick and the rest of the

---

[40] *Acts, 1844*, ch. 196; *Acts, 1845*, ch. 12.

building eighteen inches thick. There was to be an ell, 16 x 30 feet, with thirteen-inch walls for a dining room and kitchen with a fireplace in each. There were two nine-light 8 x 10 windows in each prison room and two separate iron grates to each window.[41]

The prison site was to remain the same and the contractor was to take the old building at its value.

Pride and Barnes was awarded the contract, and an entry in the Trustee's report for 1849 indicates that the total bill to date was $1718.18¼ with $1151.38 paid on the account. The total cost was $1950.00 and was all paid by 1852.

In 1852, Henry Sesler was given permission to use the room between the Circuit Court Clerk's office and the Grand Jury room for one year as Post Office, provided that he put glass in the window. The same year, four locks costing $20.50 were bought in Charleston, S. C. and put on the courthouse doors.

In 1848, an act was passed allowing the mayor and aldermen to extend the corporate limits of Maryville with the consent of the property owners. According to Mr. Parham, the first slate of city fathers was: Dr. Sam Pride, mayor; and Aldermen: Julius Caesar Fagg, merchant; William McTeer, tailor and innkeeper; John E. Toole, lawyer; Sam T. Bicknell, planter, lawyer, and politician; Andrew McClain, tanner; and Reuben Cates, saddler.[42]

The Railroad Movement which had been periodically active for more than twenty years was strongly revived, locally, in 1856. William Wallace, William A. Spencer and Dr. James H. Gillespy had been commissioners in the Hiwassee Railroad Movement which was suspended in 1839 due largely to: the panic of 1837; too liberal state aid; inefficiency of methods; and poor management.

The company was re-organized in 1848 as the East Tennessee and Virginia Railroad. J. Allison, Dr. J. H. Gillespy, B. D. Brabson, R. Porter, Dr. Sam Pride, John E. Toole, and William Wallace were elected commissioners from Blount County.

H. T. Cox, Jabez Coulson, James Donaldson and William Wallace were commissioners of the Junction Railroad in 1852.

In January 1852, Blount County Court through the chairman, Dr. Sam Pride, bought stock in the East Tennessee and Georgia Railroad. They had previously bought seven shares of stock in the Hiwassee Railroad.

In April 1854, at the request of Gen. William Wallace the court voted to subscribe 120,000 shares of stock in the Knoxville and Charleston Railroad. John E. Toole, B. D. Brabson, R. I. Wilson, Sam Pride, and William Wallace were elected commissioners at a meeting of stockholders May 25, 1854. This movement was, at first, very staunchly supported in Blount County but after the first enthusiasm wore off,

---

[41] *Knoxville Register,* November 3, 1847.

[42] *Acts, 1848,* ch. 139. No record of election of city officers is recorded prior to this date, although the first act of incorporation was passed in 1837.

REV. GIDEON BLACKBURN
First pastor of New Providence and Eusebia Presbyterian Churches, 1794-1810. Photo Courtesy of the *Knoxville News Sentinel*.

MAJOR JAMES HOUSTON
In charge of Houston's Station, 1788; First Clerk of Blount County Court, 1796-1818. From painting in Blount County Courthouse.

FOUNDERS AND BUILDERS

REV. ISAAC ANDERSON, D.D.
Pastor of New Providence Presbyterian Church, 1812-1857; Founder of Southern and Western Theological Seminary—; Maryville College after 1844.

DANIEL D. FOUTE
Circuit Court Clerk, 1822-1836; Operated Montvale Springs Hotel, 1832-1850.

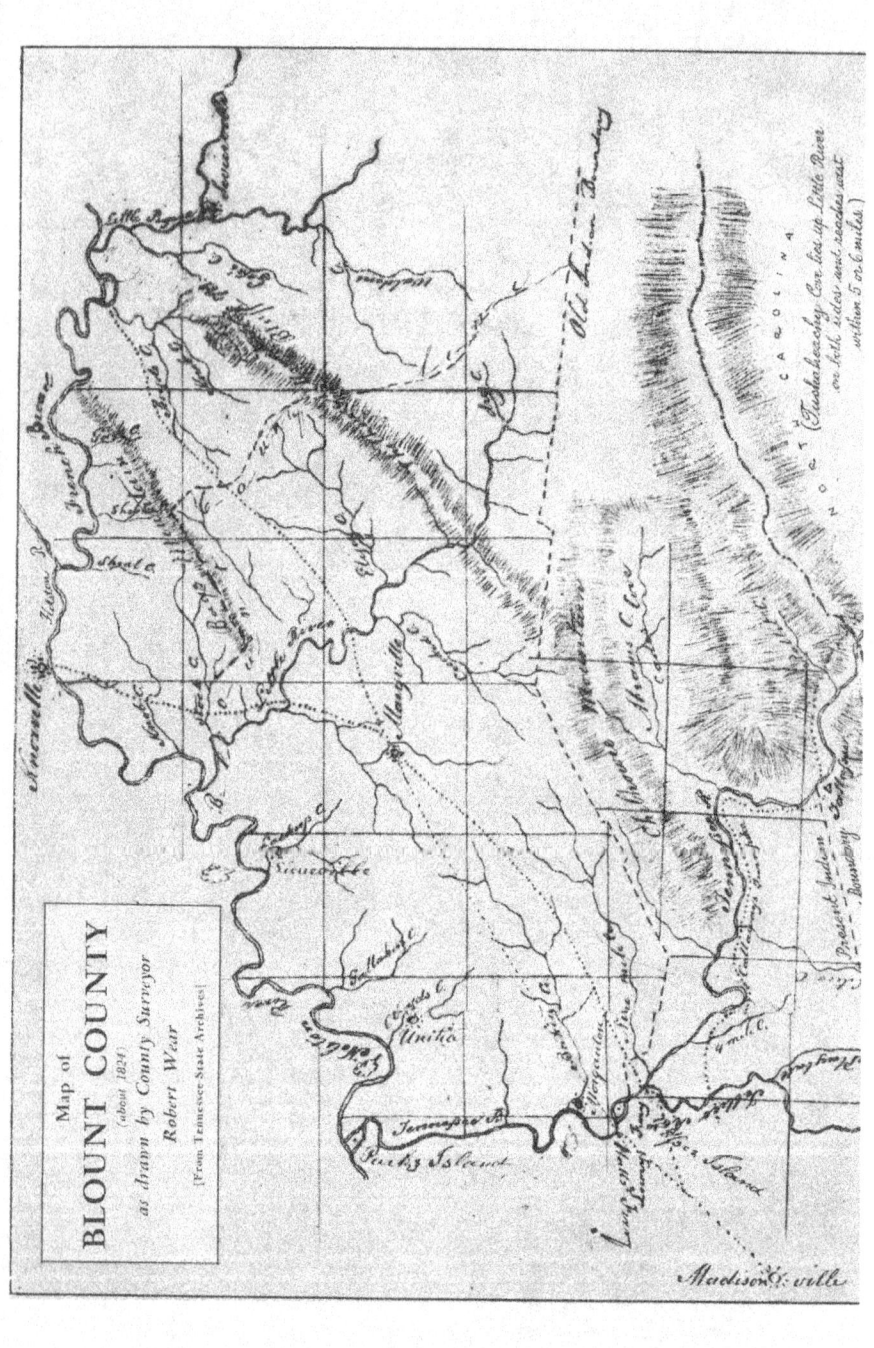

they applied to Chancellor Van Dyke for an injunction to restrain collection of the railroad tax.[43]

A bill to repudiate the county subscription was introduced in the Legislature but was defeated in the Senate. The fact that the above named steps had been taken, left a moral bar against collection of the railroad tax.[44]

In July 1856, the K. & C. stockholders met in Maryville and elected directors: William G. Swan, Sam Pride, William Wallace, John E. Toole, Edward George, James Porter, R. I. Wilson, John J. Craig, and William McTeer. Swan was elected president and Toole, secretary-treasurer. Contracts were let for only sixteen of the advertised thirty miles on account of the litigations pending in relation to Blount County Bonds.[45]

July 18, 1857, the stockholders met at Maryville and elected substantially the same directors, with Wallace, president and Toole, secretary-treasurer. At a called meeting of the County Court, August 4, 1857, the chairman appointed seventy-five citizens to attend a meeting in Knoxville on the 10th. This roster is the most inclusive list of prominent citizens of this period.

In 1858, Spencer Henry, tax collector, was allowed more time to collect the railroad tax for Blount County.[46]

In 1865, a private act reviewed the situation thusly: "by act of January 27, 1854, the county was authorized to subscribe the stock to the K. & C. Railroad and levy a railroad tax. Eight or ten thousands were collected and paid into the county treasury. The railroad failed to carry out the provisions of the act, so they loaned out the money and part of it was lost. By this act, the Railroad Fund was changed to the General County Fund. This act was to apply only to that part of the fund which was collected from 1855 to 1858. A collector was appointed to collect the fund, who was to receive six per cent of the fund.[47]

The bonds, as issued in 1854, were payable in thirty years. The war prevented collection of the tax. The K. & C. work was revived and a payment was demanded from the county in 1867, and the court ordered the bonds to be issued.[48]

Loudon County was formed from a portion of Blount County in 1870; but those citizens of that fraction were obligated to pay their proportionate share on the bonds of the railroad. The railroad collector was authorized in 1876 to file suit against the Blount fraction of Loudon County to enforce collection of the assessment against those citizens. The decision in this case was that they should pay their share. In 1883, the Loudon County merchants rebelled and refused to pay their taxes

---

[43] *Knoxville Register*, February 28, 1856.
[44] *Ibid.*, March 13, 1856.
[45] *Ibid.*, July 17, 1856; July 24, 1856.
[46] *Acts, 1858*, ch. 40, sec. 1.
[47] *Acts, 1865*, ch. 11.
[48] *Minutes*, 1867.

to Blount. When assessed double by court order, they petitioned for relief and were allowed to pay the original tax plus costs in the case.

Blount County Court refused to levy a railroad tax during the years that the courthouse tax was levied. The railroad bonds were not all redeemed until 1901, when a remainder of $123.29 was paid back to Loudon County as its share of the surplus.

The only indication in the court minutes that a war was in progress was a discussion of the salt problem. In May 1862, Dr. Sam Pride appeared before the County Court and reported that he had been to the salt works in Virginia and had contracted with Stewart Buchanan Company for the delivery of 5,000 bushels of salt. On account of the condition of public affairs and the blockade of ports of entry to the South, the people of the county were in need of salt; and the situation was steadily growing worse. In view of the uncertain conditions of the times, the court voted to assume responsibility for the contract, so that Dr. Pride stood to lose nothing financially. He was to make delivery and use prudence in the sale and distribution of the salt.[49]

In December the situation had grown so serious that Alexander McClain was sent to Virginia to act as agent for the county with authority to issue warrants up to $15,000. The salt was to be prorated to the justices for distribution and to be divided as equally as possible. No private funds were to be expended by the agent in procuring salt.

The town and the courthouse had suffered rather heavy damages during the skirmishes and changes of occupation prior to the end of the siege of Knoxville late in 1863. By the latter part of 1864, the court ordered the purchase of a new water bucket and dipper, six chairs, eighteen tax assessment books, a county seal, a deed book, and three Codes of Tennessee.

In August 1865, four new padlocks were ordered for the jail and the gratings at the jail windows were repaired. The jail and courthouse were both to be repaired and restored where they required, and a fence was to be built around the jail lot.

A smallpox epidemic in 1866 necessitated the replacement of all jail guards by those who had had smallpox. A committee was appointed with guards to enforce quarantine, in an effort to control an epidemic raging in the vicinity of Cook's Mill (Mint).

In October 1867, the court ordered that poorhouse inmates be given coffee twice daily. Committees were very busy investigating conditions of roads, and more especially bridges, in the county.

By 1868, they were ready to replace the broken furniture and the two-story porch on the courthouse. The contract for the latter was let to Martin Christopher Best and Henry Blevins for $465.

In October $50.00 was appropriated for road tools which were to be kept in charge of the Trustee. The Clerk of the court was ordered to record the wills. (Prior to this they had been kept loose in files and not recorded.) He was to be allowed five cents per hundred words.

---

[49] An itemized account of the distribution of salt in the 7th Civil District by James M. Henry, Esq. belongs to Mrs. Bessie Henry Olin.

In January 1870, a school tax was levied for the first time but it was annulled in October. An election was called for electing school commissioners.

The erection of Loudon County created a problem because of the fact that the entire third district of Blount and parts of the third and fourth districts, were taken away. The first plan was to reconstruct the original districts from neighboring districts. This would not work because there was not enough territory. It was finally ascertained by survey that only two districts could be formed in place of the original three. A new map of the county, completely re-numbered, was presented and accepted in October 1871, but was rescinded in July 1872. The original numbering still stands, there being no third district until 1880.[50]

The difficulties of collecting the almost twenty thousand dollars due from Loudon County made the justices wonder seriously about the financial status of the county in general. They accordingly ordered an audit of the various funds for the years since the war, which showed $6,000 due the county by collecting officers, apart from the school fund and the County Court clerk.

The school tax was voted down by the court and submitted to the people and rejected each year until 1875, when a tax of ten cents per hundred plus twenty-five cents poll tax was levied.

In 1875, in compliance with the new constitution, Hugh L. McNutt became the first tax assessor. He was to work on a commission basis. The Dog Tax of 1876 was not at all satisfactory since owners could claim they had killed the dog and be forgiven the tax. ($1.00; $5.00 for bitches.)

In the appropriations for 1876–79, appears an interesting item first noted in July, 1876. (There is no preliminary explanation.) "Polly Toole $5.00." Later the item is clarified by adding "for saving court records during the late war." In October 1878, the court increased her allowance from $20.00 per year to $40.00 to be issued quarterly. In April 1879, the court voted to pay the funeral expenses of Polly Toole out of her allowance and to pay the remainder, if any, to her son, Marshall Pope.[51]

In 1877 Thomas P. Cowan was given the contract at 2½ cents (later says .10 cents) per hundred words to copy the Register's Record.

"On the 8th of February, 1879, the courthouse burned down." The county records all seem to have been saved except for some loose records which were in boxes and were dropped in the hasty removal.

County Court met the following week and made arrangements for offices for each of the county officials. A committee was appointed to make arrangements for a definite meeting place for the County Court.

In April the court met in "Presbyterian Hall" over E. Tedford's Drugstore. The committee reported that in view of the fact that public

---

[50] *Acts, 1870*, Ch. 2.
[51] Marshall Pope was a one-legged Negro, who worked for the Duncan Family during the Civil War. Sometime after 1879, he is listed as an inmate of the Poor Asylum and John D. Headrick was made an allowance for him in 1893.

school funds would be short the ensuing year, and it would not be possible to have school, the school directors of the public school building known as the New Providence Female Institute had offered their building for the use of the court. The court was to be responsible for natural and unnatural damages to furniture, property and fixtures for the sum of $150.00 until September 1880. It was decided to accept the offer. S. L. Greer, H. S. Catlett, S. F. Bell, A. R. McBath, and James Waters were appointed a courthouse committee. A tax rate of 35 cents per hundred plus a 50 cents poll tax was levied for the courthouse fund.

It was decided to rebuild on the same lot. In the middle of April 1879, the building committee visited the Loudon County Courthouse and decided to employ an architect. They hired J. F. Bauman of Knoxville and paid him a $250.00 fee for the plans and specifications. Bids were closed in August. David Jones was low bidder on the stone and brick work. Mount and Hooper got the carpentry contract. On account of the slope of the lot, which had not been taken into account, the steps at the northeast corner made the contract cost $90.00 additional.

This was the only mistake in the contract. The total cost of building, furniture, and fixtures was $12,779.01. A furnace was installed the following year. In 1883, the justices of peace first discussed buying a rock crusher for the county but no report was made. Dr. John P. Blankenship had been acting in the capacity of county health officer under the County Court, but after the enactment of the state law in 1884, Dr. Blankenship became county health officer and physician officially and continued until 1900. One of his first official acts was to supervise the installment of a sanitary sewer system at the jail.

An iron fence was built around the front and sides of the courthouse lot and a rock wall across the back. As soon as the courthouse was paid for, a county-wide bridge program was launched. Among them was the footbridge across Pistol Creek to the depot.

One of the perennial water works companies was granted a right-of-way through the streets in 1884. The Health Department put on a sixty-day drive to clean up the city streets and alleys.

It was decided, in January 1889, to build a new poor house since the old one was in a very dilapidated condition. Bauman Bros. submitted the plans and specifications. The contract was let to McKinney, Irwin, and Cowan for $1485.83. About this time, it was decided to place children who were county charges in the State Industrial Home if they could be accommodated. Since there were more than the county's quota, it was necessary to pay for the expenses of some.

The Maryville Electric Light and Power Company was granted a county right of way in 1892. In 1893, $700 was invested in a county rock crusher and a wagon for moving it.

In 1894, the court was invited to visit the Blount Industrial Home and was very pleased with the institution. They recommended that allowance should be made for those children transferred from the Poor Asylum.

In 1925, it was decided that it was necessary to appoint certain members of the court to serve on that Board. The Poor Commission was appointed. This has been continuous since 1925.[52]

In July, Hon. Will A. McTeer presented to the court a copy of *Laws of the State of North Carolina* by James Iredell, with the following inscription: "Knoxville, September 10th, 1795. Presented to the court by your obt. servt. Wm. Blount." The book had been bought from the estate of W. D. McGinley, who wrote in the front, "W. D. McGinley took this book and mended it up on the 15th day of February, 1848." Major McTeer presented the book to the court on its Centennial meeting with the suggestion that it be preserved under glass in the vault.

The People's Telephone was granted right of way to erect their lines in Blount County in 1896.

In 1900, Dr. Gamble replaced Dr. Blankenship who had served as county physician since 1866. A committee was appointed to investigate the cost of a new jail. At this time the Freedman's Institute approached the County Court with a proposal to operate a Negro industrial home and school on the same basis as the Industrial Home and it was voted to allow them to do so, provided that they would sign a contract. A year later the act was rescinded without any explanation.

In October 1899, the Tennessee Lumber and Canal Co. was released from paying taxes for five years. In April 1900, the act was rescinded and the county part of the tax on the K. & C. Railroad from Maryville to Chilhowee Gap (Walland) was to be paid to England and Bryan of Philadelphia to reimburse them for right of ways.

The jail committee reported at the July term that the site of the Ferrary Saloon directly back of the courthouse was the most likely location. The property was to be sold through a court order. The committee was directed to purchase the lots and pay not more than $1100. The plans were to build a fire-proof jail and jailer's residence not to cost more than $10,000. G. W. Walker, F. H. Lamon, J. L. Clemens, W. E. Parham, and J. T. Sams served on the building committee.

In January 1901, the committee reported that bids and plans were not satisfactory. Pauley and Company of St. Louis submitted three sets of plans, one of which was accepted. When the bids were taken for the plans, the Pauley Company was awarded the contract at $14,021.54.

The first plan was to build the jail on the lower side of the lot. The citizens objected and after several hundreds of dollars had been expended on excavation, the company and the public in general agreed that the building would look much better on the upper side of the lot and the change was made.

When the foundation was finished, it was found that the quality of

---

[52] *Charters*, 102. The Charter was issued July 9, 1894 to Lizzie K. Burger, Martha A. Lamar, Sarah Stanley, Elizabeth Huddleston, and Phrona Small, for the Blount County Industrial Home as a house of refuge or house of correction for women and destitute children.

brick contracted for could only be obtained locally from David Jones and that this would cause a delay of two months in the building, because he could not immediately furnish the bricks. After conference and investigation, it was decided to get the bricks from Powell's Station in Knox County, although this would add $225 to the original bid.

When the building was finished the committee found that swinging doors had been installed to the cells instead of the sliding doors contracted for. The building was finished and accepted in the fall of 1901.

There are appropriations listed at practically every session of Quarterly Court from 1898 to 1908 for small pox. In 1898, Dr. Blankenship was allowed $75 for services and $50 for supplies. In 1901 the appropriations were over $350 for small pox. In January 1902, Dr. Gamble reported that 107 cases were in the county during the past year.

The Board of Health was ordered not to audit any smallpox accounts where the family was able to pay for services. They had built a pesthouse and detention camp for whites and maintained guards in the Home Avenue section and at the Freedman's Institute for the Negroes of Maryville, and at Louisville and Cades Cove. The total expenditures for this epidemic was over $1,000 (itemized) besides $387.50 allowed to Drs. McTeer and Gamble. In July 1902, Dr. Gamble was allowed $780 and over $1200 was paid for guards and supplies. This was the worst epidemic recorded, but every year the smallpox item was heavy in the appropriations varying from $500 in 1901; $400 in 1905; $40 in 1906, and $26 in 1908.

While the new jail was being built, a committee was investigating costs of a water system for the jail and courthouse. They were finally limited to one thousand dollars. This project was finally finished in 1907 at a cost of $850.

In 1903 it was decided by the court that the old jail building could be used as an industrial school for indigent children, if repairs could be made without cost to the county. In 1905, a committee checked the condition of the building and rooms, and painted the roof. The building is referred to as the "Neighborhood House." In March 1906, the Board of Managers of the "Neighborhood House" asked for a fence to be built around the lot.[53]

In January 1905, the L. & N. Railroad was granted leave to bring a line into Maryville. In April, the first typewriter was bought for the Clerk's office (it had been in use for four years), and in July it was voted to install vaults in the offices of the clerk and master, the Circuit Court clerk and the trustee's office as soon as possible.

The ink on the above order was hardly dry when the courthouse burned (July 28, 1906). A special term of court met at Columbian Hall August 6, 1906 to provide the means and to authorize the building of a courthouse and to buy and sell such property as necessary to construct same. J. L. Clark, W. L. Russell, Sam Everett, E. B. Waller, and

---

[53] Mrs. Eliza Blackburn, who had been engaged in mission work in Utah, and her daughter Nellie (later Summers-Cowan) are credited with the community work. Mr. R. S. Kithcart and Linnaeus Hasting are also believed to have assisted in Sunday School work in connection with their community work.

Charles T. Cates, Sr., were appointed to investigate and report at the October term of the most suitable place to build a courthouse; to take opinions and bids on the old courthouse and jail property and make recommendations. Arrangements were made for all offices. A tax of 25 cents per hundred was levied for the courthouse.

On account of the noises of traffic on Main Street, the committee recommended that the location be moved. Six locations were presented for consideration in October 1906, among them the West Side School lot, the Fort Craig School lot and the present courthouse property. After three ballots, the West Side lot was chosen, then they reconsidered, and the Cates property was chosen. The price was $10,000.

W. B. Townsend, W. B. Howard, Ben Cunningham, Will A. McTeer, and R. P. McReynolds were appointed a building committee to secure plans and bids not to exceed $500,000. Bauman Bros. were employed to draw plans. A bond issue was voted for $40,000 in April 1907. Seven thousand dollars were set aside for furniture and fixtures.[54]

The final report, in April 1908, summarized the entire building story. In digging for the foundation, pockets of soft lime made it necessary to dig to great depths. This caused the foundation to cost $1,335 extra. The total cost of the architects, lot and building was almost $61,000. The sum realized from insurance on the old courthouse, from the old jail, courthouse lots and the old Cates residence was about $14,000.

Comments were made in the minutes on each of the three previous courthouses. The first was wooden with a cellar underneath. The second was clumsily and awkwardly built of poorly burned brick. The contractors lost heavily on the third building.

As soon as the offices were moved from the old residence on the courthouse grounds, it was removed. The grounds were graded and six telephones were installed in the courthouse as well as a public booth in the hall. A hitch-lot was laid off to run around the courthouse grounds, concrete walks were laid around the courthouse and in front of the jail. The new street in front of the courthouse was macadamized.

After four years of considering the question, in 1909, it was decided to build bridges at Rockford, across Little River at Brabson's Ford (changed to Kennedy's Mill), Snider's Ford, Ellejoy, and Pistol Creek at George's Mill. In 1910 a bridge at Abram's Creek was voted. In 1911, a $300,000 bond issue was finally voted for roads and bridges.

In 1907, an act was passed to incorporate the town of Maryville. The city was originally chartered in 1837. The charter had been given up in 1879 in order to control liquor-selling within the town.[55]

In 1934, when it became necessary for Knoxville to relocate McGhee Tyson Airport, no suitable location could be found in Knox County and it was finally decided to locate it on the old Kidd farm, a very short distance north of Alcoa in Blount County. Work began in March, 1934. The first runway was 600 feet wide and 2700 feet long and was for

[54] *Acts, 1907*, Ch. 553.
[55] *Acts, 1907*, ch. 116.

emergency landings only. In the first development, $35,000 Federal funds were used, in addition to $5,000 appropriated by Blount County, $11,000 by the Aluminum Company of America, and several thousand by Knox County. No buildings were erected at first. The Administration building was finished in 1937 at which date the airport property was deeded to the City of Knoxville.[56]

In 1941 the administration building was enlarged and the field regraded and expanded in cooperation with the U. S. Navy and the Civil Aeronautics Administration.

In 1945 a new master plan was evolved which was comprehensive enough to provide for requirements far in advance of new developments, and flexible enough to meet changes and adaptations necessary to incorporate new trends in airport building. A million dollar enlarging and modernizing of the administration building and airport facilities was completed in 1956. The field now has two 5,000-foot runways and a 7,000-foot runway of concrete. This expansion program was entirely apart from the adjoining Air Defense Base and landing facilities which occupy 850 of the 1500 acres of McGhee Tyson Air Field.[57]

American Airlines began serving the public from McGhee Tyson Airport in 1937. Capital Airlines began in 1940, Delta C. & S. in 1941, and Piedmont Airlines in 1952. The local airport at present handles approximately 150,000 enplaned passengers per year.

Perhaps the most important item of road building undertaken by the county within the past thirty years was the Deal's Gap road which when opened in 1931 gave a large section of North Carolina access to Tennessee markets. The Maryville-Knoxville Highway by Rockford had been finished in the late Twenties. The Niles Ferry Highway was built in the Thirties, and the new highway to Knoxville was made necessary in the late Thirties by the location of the Knoxville Municipal Airport just north of Alcoa (in Blount County) in 1934.

The relocation of many roads have been made necessary by the formation of Loudon Lake and the Smoky Mountains National Park. Since times are continually changing, the highway pattern changes with them and improvements are a constant necessity. State and Federal funds however have been available for most of these projects.

In 1945 County Court appropriated $5,000 to be used to erect a memorial to those who had given their lives in World War I and World War II. Soon after this it was learned that Federal funds might be secured to help build a hospital which the county needed desperately. It was decided to combine the two ideas and with the help of the public-spirited people who made personal donations, the Aluminum Company of America and Federal funds, Blount County was able to build Blount Memorial Hospital. The hospital was occupied in 1947, and in 1948 another wing was added to the building. A second addition was already under way late in 1955.

[56] McGhee Tyson Airport was named in honor of Charles McGhee Tyson, son of Gen. L. D. Tyson, who was killed over the North Sea, October 11, 1918.
[57] Information from the office of the Airport Manager, Alan Atkin.

CHAPTER IV

The County's Role in the Wars

The Revolutionary War predates the settlement of Blount County but many of the first settlers had seen service in the Revolution, either from Virginia, North Carolina, Pennsylvania or Upper East Tennessee. Many of the first wave of settlers moved further west as new lands were opened for settlement, but a goodly number remained and helped to tame the wilderness and establish the heritage which is ours today.

Whether the first settlers had been under fire or not, all who were here before 1794 became veterans of Cherokee warfare. Most of the early militia officers had seen service in the Revolution. From 1792 until 1797, what is now Blount County had five companies of militia and one of cavalry. The five captains and the ten justices which were allowed to the area, represented the law-making and policy-making body of the region. When Blount County was formed in 1795, one year before the formation of Tennessee in 1796, this group, of course, became more localized in function.[1]

By 1810, Blount County had eleven companies of militia, and the cream of these companies took an active part in the War of 1812. It is impossible to estimate even approximately, how many local men took part in this war, because the volunteer companies were not strictly local in character. The fact that the enlistments were for three and six months, made for a great deal of change in personnel on the field and en route, due to re-enlistments. Very few descriptive muster rolls are available, which is another reason why origin of personnel is hard to trace. There was also a general shift of population directly after 1815 toward the new territories and new people from the upper counties replaced them here. At least eighteen different captains were either commissioned from Blount County, or part of their men enlisted from Blount County during the 1812-15 period. This statement is supported by information from pension files and other sources.[2]

In October 1812, Governor Blount was asked to send fifteen hundred men to New Orleans. He appointed Andrew Jackson as major general of the Volunteers. They got as far as Natchez before an official order came to disband. Jackson refused to do so until they returned to Tennessee soil. East Tennesseans had been ignored in this call for Volunteers, but they knew that there had been trouble instigated with the Seminole Indians on the Florida border by the British agents. Some of the well-informed men thought it expedient to arm themselves and go to the aid of their fellow citizens in Georgia. Two hundred forty men

---

[1] *Minutes*, Passim; Annual Reports in Tennessee State Archives.
[2] One of the descriptive muster rolls extant is that of Captain Ruben Tipton of Knox County; 20 per cent of his company were from Blount County including four of his brothers.

53

The Public Dr.
To James Houston for
Rations furnished for the
Support of volunteers in 1788

To 16 Men	90 days	10¢	$144.00
" 35 do	90 "	10	315.00
" 12 "	30	10	36.00
20	90	10¢	180.00
20ᵗʰ Powder		75¢	15.00
100ᵗʰ Lead		12½¢	12.50
			$702.50
			$702.50

An expense account rendered to the State of Tennessee in 1823 for rations furnished the troops who helped to defend Houston's Station against the Indians in 1788.

enrolled under Col. John Williams. They equipped and supplied themselves and agreed to pay their own expenses. Early in December 1812, they marched to the Georgia frontier and offered their services to the U.S. regular army detachment stationed there. They were accepted and helped in an expedition against the Seminoles, and returned home at the end of three months. This expedition is described as equivalent to knights-errant, having no parallel in modern history. One of the companies that went on this expedition was Captain William Walker's company. Captain Walker was a major in the Blount County militia at this time. In his company were: Alexander Outlaw, Enoch Parsons, Pleasant M. Miller, Gideon Morgan, and Richard G. Waterhouse. In other companies there were highranking army officers such as Major John Cocke serving as privates.[3]

No sooner had these volunteers gotten settled at home than the Fort Mims Massacre took place in the Mississippi Territory, August 30, 1813. General Jackson ordered a mobilization of troops to move against the Creeks. Captains James Tedford, William Wallace, James Gillespy, and William Walker each led a company of volunteers in this campaign. Col. John Williams had been commissioned to raise the 39th Regiment U. S. Infantry. This regiment of six hundred men was organized at Knoxville. From there they proceeded to Fort Deposit near Huntsville, Alabama. From Fort Deposit, they went by boat to Fort Strother, and then to Fort Williams. From Fort Williams, they went to Tallapoosa. The narrator was wounded at the Battle of the Horseshoe and he mentioned the death of Major Lemuel P. Montgomery. From Tallapoosa, they returned to Fort Williams and from thence went to the "Hickory Grounds" at the fork of the Coosa and the Tallapoosa rivers. They remained here a month before going to Mount Vernon and on to Scaba Bay; then back to Mount Vernon and on to Fort Minnis. They built Fort Montgomery one mile from Fort Minnis and from there marched to Pensacola. The narrator was discharged at Fort Montgomery December 22, 1814. According to the story of another local narrator, they were "too late for the Battle of the Horseshoe, but in time for the Battle of the Hillobees."

After the Battle of Talladega in November, there was near-mutiny at Fort Strother which was caused by the end of three-month enlistments and short provisions. Some of the men remained, or transferred to other companies, while others are recorded as "deserted." In January 1814, three new companies from Blount County, under Captains Edwin Allen, Edward Buchanan and Joseph Duncan were formed for six months. After his near-defeat in March, General Jackson had rallied

---

[3] *Messages of the Governors*, 390 ff; Photostats of various Muster Rolls, National Archives, Washington, D. C.; Loudon County had not yet been formed. Blount County men are found with Sevier, Knox, and Roane County companies. S. C. Williams, *A Forgotten Campaign*, in Tenn. Hist. Magazine, vol. VIII, No. 4, p. 266; ASP, 1812, "well-equipped, well-mounted. Not only the most respectable citizens but the finest-looking body of men ever seen in the section." (All were dressed in black hats, hunting shorts and pantaloons.)

his men and reinforced by these new recruits, located Fort Williams and arrived at the Horseshoe by the 27th.

It was at the Battle of the Horseshoe that Major Lemuel P. Montgomery of the 39th Regulars was killed while leading a charge over the breastworks and was replaced by one ensign, Sam Houston, who successfully led the charge over the barricade. Houston was twice wounded that day.[4]

When a treaty was effected with the Creeks in August 1814, General Jackson asked for a Brigade of volunteers under Col. Coffee to make an expedition along the Gulf Coast to dislodge the Spanish governor. After this task was finished, Jackson started to assemble his army to march on New Orleans.

When Jackson arrived at New Orleans to reconnoiter, December 2, 1814, he found that no preparations for defense had been made, and that only two thousand men were available. New recruits from Blount County were on their way down the river, among them, companies under Captains Alexander Biggs and Samuel Thompson. Along with them came a boat load of gunpowder manufactured by Andrew Kennedy, a Revolutionary soldier, who operated a saw and grist mill on Little River. New recruits also were enroute from Pensacola with Col. Coffee. Jackson was becoming desperate. It was the evening of December 17th that Col. Coffee finally got Jackson's urgent message to neither rest nor sleep until he was within striking distance of New Orleans. When Coffee got this message he was 129 miles away. His horse was exhausted and he had three hundred sick men. He pushed on with eight hundred picked men and reached New Orleans in three days—as motley a crew of ununiformed men as ever faced an enemy, but among them were Captain Ruben Tipton's Company from Knox and Blount counties, Jehu Stephens' company, David McKamy's and John Trimble's companies from Blount County. General Jackson is reputed to have said if he had an entire company of Tiptons he could lick the whole British army![5]

The first skirmish occured on December 23rd, the second on January 1st, and the third, generally referred to as the "Battle of New Orleans," was on January 8th.

---

[4] John Trotwood Moore, ed., *Tennessee, The Volunteer State*, (Nashville, Tennessee), 353 ff. Hereinafter cited Moore, *Tennessee*; Pension file of George Grace; *Petition* of Robert Rhea who had served in the Revolution and against the Seminoles, says that he was wounded at the Horseshoe and was carried back to Blount County on his bier but recovered and fought with General Taylor in the *Southern Wars*. (He was Major under Col. Ewen Allison), Tennessee State Archives, Nashville, Tennessee; this is the same Sam Houston, who grew up in Blount County, was later Governor of Tennessee and held all the high offices in the Republic of Texas and the State of Texas.

[5] Captain Samuel Thompson was a Revolutionary soldier and was really too old to go on this expedition, but insisted because he was such an ardent admirer of Gen. Jackson. There are many petitions in the Archives at Nashville asking the Legislature to pay for "borrowed" guns and guns lost in the war of 1812. This is because men got guns wherever they could, to use in this war. Jehu Stephens was a brother-in-law of the five Tiptons in Ruben Tipton's Company. Stephens' company was all from Blount County. (see note 2).

Some authorities claim that the Battle of New Orleans was pointless since the treaty had already been signed, but others point out that the Louisiana Purchase could have been repudiated by the English if they had captured New Orleans at this time.

When the Seminole trouble arose in 1817, Jackson took 1,000 volunteers from Tennessee. Jackson captured Pensacola, deported the Spanish governor, set up a new government and executed the English emissaries. In 1819 Florida became a Territory of the United States, as a direct result of this campaign.[6]

In 1836, when trouble again arose with the Seminoles, Tennessee was asked to furnish 2,000 mounted volunteers for this purpose, and 4,000 volunteered. It was necessary to designate which companies should go. Two companies of volunteers were accepted from Blount County; Captain James Tedford with fifty-three men and Captain Ben Cunningham with sixty-nine men. These two companies with Captains Morrow of Knox County and Ellis and West of Sevier, made up the Fifth Brigade of the First Division which rendezvoused at Athens, July 7, 1836, for six months' service.

Immediately following this campaign, the Cherokee Removal became imminent. Quite a few Tennessee troops were already enrolled with the troops stationed in Georgia, and it appears that Captain Robert A. Tedford's company also served an enlistment and re-enlisted at Camp Cass in 1838. Captain Thomas J. Caldwell enlisted a company in Madisonville, Tennessee, for this second campaign, which had a good per cent of men from Blount County.

These men under General Winfield Scott conducted the march, generally referred to as the "Trail of Tears," which began in October 1838 and ended in March 1839 when they reached the Indian Territory in what is now Oklahoma.[7]

Just a few years after the Indian removals, came the annexation of Texas in 1846. Tennessesans had thrilled to the stories of bravery of fellow Tennesseans at the Alamo and a good many had emigrated to Texas seeking excitement and new land. Consequently Tennesseans were very anxious to get into the war with Mexico when it developed.

When Governor Brown called for one regiment of cavalry and two regiments of infantry, 30,000 men volunteered and it became necessary to draw lots in the four military divisions of the state to decide which companies should go. Among the three companies chosen to form the

---

[6] Jackson was severely criticized for his high-handed action during this campaign.
[7] Ben Cunningham, Capt.; William Dever, 1st Lt.; William Headrick, 2nd Lt.; Jacob T. Tipton, Ensign. James Tedford, Captain, John Strutton, 1st Lt.; Barkly Russell, 2nd Lt.; James Hendron, Ensign. Drs. Robert Hodson and Barclay McGhee served as surgeons in the removal. Newton Cannon, *Military Papers,* Tennessee State Archives, Nashville, Tennessee, (a full roster of Captain Tedford's company is given, but only the officers of Captain Cunningham's company. The 1838 enlistments are taken from an alphabetical file in the Tennessee State Archives. General John Wool had been in command of these troops in 1836 against the Seminoles. He did not approve of the treatment of the Cherokees and resigned.)

First Tennessee Regiment of Mounted Volunteers was Captain William Caswell's company from Knoxville. The regiment was organized and mustered in at Camp Carroll near Memphis, June 15, 1846. They left Camp Carroll, July 18th, marching across country and reached the Rio Grande, November the 5th. This company was present at the Battles of Vera Cruz, Cerro Gordo, and Mexico City.[8]

The Fifth Regiment was composed of Captain Newman's company from Knox, Capt. Bounds' of Hawkins, Thomason's from Grainger, Reese's of Jefferson, Dill's of McMinn, Vaughn's of Monroe, McKenzie's of Meigs, Stuart's of Rhea, Fagg's of Blount, and McClelland's of Sullivan County.[9]

Company F of Fifth Regiment of Tennessee Foot Volunteers was organized by Captain Julius C. Fagg at Maryville, Tennessee, November 11, 1847. This regiment was in command of Col. George R. McClelland, and Dr. Barclay McGhee was assistant surgeon. This regiment was stationed for a while at National Bridge (Mexico). They did not reach Mexico City until after it had been taken. Tipton in his journal said that the cavalrymen who had lost their horses had to drop back with the foot soldiers. Quite a number of sick men were left behind at Vera Cruz, some with fever and some with measles and mumps.[10]

Among the Blount Countians who served with the regular army in this war was Lt. John Y. Bicknell of the Second Regiment, U. S. Dragoons. He was a West Point graduate, who served with General Scott for five years. He died at his home in Maryville in 1849.

While Texas was wresting her lands from Mexico and her boundaries were being settled by the Mexican War, certain internal movements in the United States had been growing and gaining momentum. Slavery, and the political and social aspects which had grown out of it, had become a problem which could no longer be ignored.

The first definite anti-slavery society in East Tennessee was formed in 1814 and the state organization was formed in 1815. The Quakers and Covenanters were foremost in this movement, and the Rev. John Rankin of Jefferson County was the Martin Luther of the cause. There was a county organization in Blount County by 1822.[11]

The State Archives of Tennessee has many petitions dated in the 1830's and 40's relating to Manumission (liberation from slavery) and

---

[8] J. W. H. Tipton of Tuckaleechee Cove was a private in this company and kept a journal from the beginning of their march from Memphis through the Battle of Cerro Gordo. His minute description of the route taken and the incidents of the march and battles is good. (Copy of the journal in writer's collection). Other officers of this company were: Samuel W. Bell, Calvin Gossett and James Anderson, 1st, 2nd, and 3rd Lts. respectively; *Goodspeed*, 940.

[9] *Knoxville Tribune*, February 2, 1848; March 15, 1848.

[10] The bid to transport troops to Memphis was given to James M. Anderson at $4.98 per head. (Knoxville, *Tribune*, November 10, 1847; March 15, 1848; October 10, 1849). Photostats of Muster Rolls, National Archives, Washington, D. C.

[11] Delegates to the 1822 Convention from Blount County were: David Delzell, Aaron Hackney, William Lee, John Coulson, Andrew Cowan. Other members belonging: Andrew Creswell, Alexander Logan, James Houston, Ephriam Lee.

related problems from Blount County as well as surrounding counties. James Jones, a Quaker, of Unitia was especially active in promoting these memorials through correspondence.

Ezekiel Birdseye tells about meeting the Rev. John S. Craig from Maryville College at Mr. Robert Bogle's in Blount County and discussing Abolition. The Rev. Mr. Craig told him that of thirty ministerial students, twelve were Abolitionists. Richard Williams (Quaker), the Rev. Thomas S. Kendall of the Seceder Church (Big Springs) and the Rev. Elijah Eagleton (Presbyterian) were very active in discussing Abolition and Colonization in their churches and also in disciplining their slave-holding members.[12]

Before 1820, Union Presbytery had freed, educated, and licensed two of the Negro race to preach at Maryville. When the Colonization movement was instituted one of these, the Rev. George Erskine, went to Liberia and took charge of the schools. Interest in these movements decreased in the Forties and secession became the chief topic of conversation.

Late in 1860, when secession seemed inevitable, the loyal people of East Tennessee at once selected delegates to represent them at a convention. John F. Henry was chosen from Blount County. Mass meetings were held over the county and feeling ran high. A home guard was organized which met regularly until feeling became too tense.

The Secessionists sent "outside" speakers into East Tennessee to try to convert the Unionists, and while they were at work, the Unionists were also holding rallies. On Ellejoy in May 1860, Horace Maynard spoke for two hours and a half to six or seven hundred people.

When secession became the issue, an East Tennessee Convention was called to meet in Knoxville, May 30, 1861 to which every county was invited to send delegates. Leaders held forth their views for two days and then adjourned to meet again after the state vote was cast on June 8th. Blount County voted 1,766 to 414 against separation from the Union. The Convention re-assembled at Greeneville, June 17th. The Rev. W. T. Dowell of the Methodist church was the outstanding delegate from Blount County. The committee formulated a series of defiant resolutions which were debated for four days and much modified before their adoption.[13]

After the state voted for separation, East Tennessee was surrounded by the Confederacy, and forces of five to ten thousand were stationed here to keep the section under control, and to collect whatever firearms could be found. About this time a Union rally was held at the muster grounds above the Walland gap. A flag had been made and was raised on a tall flag pole at a ceremony attended by perhaps fifteen hundred

---

[12] Tennessee Historical Magazine, V. 1, #4, December 1915, p. 261; East Tennessee Historical Society, Publications #3, 1931, p. 146; Liberia in West Africa was established in 1822 as a home for slaves. It became an independent state in 1847. Financial control and internal administration is still assumed by the United States.

[13] Oliver P. Temple, *East Tennessee and the Civil War*. (Cincinnati, 1899), 191-98. Hereinafter cited *Temple*.

people. A Confederate cavalry unit was stationed in the county to collect firearms at this time. Judge Jesse Wallace advised them, when they started to Tuckaleechee Cove, not to touch the flag flying at the Muster grounds at the Gap. When they reached the spot, some of the men raised their rifles. Lt. White (brother of Capt. White) in charge of the detail made them a speech telling them, that it was the flag under which they were born, etc. They then filed into a circle around the flag and saluted it and rode on. The news went ahead of them and they were treated kindly in the Coves that day, but they had stood in a trap which would have "sprung," had they behaved differently at the gap of the mountain into the Coves. However, the natives did not bring out their guns, nor could they be found! [14]

By late in 1861, every pass in the mountains along the Kentucky line was occupied and guarded by the Confederate Army of Tennessee. After the bridge-burning episode the military patrols were considerably tighter, and it began to be evident that Unionists must either escape the net or be drafted into the Confederate Army. Major McTeer tells of the wounding and later killing of one McClanahan and the wounding of William Elledge (Confederate enlistees) from ambush in the Ellejoy section because of their "loud talk." The report was carried to Knoxville that three hundred Yankee soldiers were hiding in the Ellejoy section and Col. John H. Morgan and a company of Confederate soldiers brought an ambulance to get the wounded men. Three men—Adam Farmer, Jonathan Houser and William Jeffries fired on them from the hill and caused quite a bit of excitement, but of course they easily made their escape.[15]

Professional guides began conducting parties over the border to the Union Camps at Cumberland Gap. In July 1862, a group of eighteen men, among them Major Will A. McTeer arrived at Camp Morgan and became part of the Sixth Tennessee Infantry, but later transferred to the cavalry when it was organized. They were piloted by Thomas Burkhart, a one-armed man from Knox County. Company G of the Third Tennessee Infantry; Company H of the Fifth and most of Companies I, and K of the Fifth; and Company A of the Sixth Tennessee

---

[14] Will A. McTeer, *Autobiography*. (220 pages typed); Knoxville *Journal*, December 15, 1946. (Cavalcade section); Will A. McTeer, *Among Loyal Mountaineers*. (pamphlet). When the men went to the home of one Frederick Emert in Tuckaleechee Cove, he loudly protested that he didn't have a gun on the top side of the green earth. (He had buried the gun).

[15] The plan was to burn nine bridges on the same night between Stevenson, Alabama and Bristol, Tennessee. Five bridges were burned and six arrests were made. Five of the six men were executed by the Confederates. It was at this time that Parson Brownlow had to hide out in the mountains of Wear's and Tuckaleechee coves. The Rev. J. D. Lawson was probably their guide. (He later guided Federal troops by a back route into Gatlinburg, when they took the fort). In Parson Brownlow's book, he identifies the place he hid as on the East Fork of Little River. It could be reached through only one gap (through Wear's Cove). It seems that it would be the same cave, near the "Sinks" which was used as a hide-out by Henry King, a Federal soldier, when he came home on leave to make his family an outfit of shoes during the war.

Sam Houston, as he appeared as an officer in the Army.
(Photo courtesy of Sam Houston Memorial Museum, Huntsville, Texas)

H. L. MATTHEWS

C. B. MATTHEWS

MILITARY MEN OF NOTE

GENERAL HUGH L. MATTHEWS
U. S. Marine Corps
Distinguished Service Medal, 1918; Navy Cross.

BRIG. GEN. CALVIN B. MATTHEWS
U. S. Marine Corps
Distinguished Service Cross, Nicaraugua, 1932.

COLONEL JOSEPH BENJAMIN PATE
U. S. Army
Distinguished Service Cross, 1918; Distinguished Service Medal, 1941.

2ND LIEUT. WILEY J. BRICKEY
U. S. Army
Posthumous Distinguished Service Cross; Philippine Islands, 1900.

PRIVATE SAM HATCHER
U. S. Army
Distinguished Service Cross; World War I, 1918.

J. B. PATE

W. J. BRICKEY

SAM HATCHER

Infantry under Captain A. M. Gamble (later Major) were mostly of men from Blount County.[16]

Those who arrived at Cumberland Gap in the early fall were organized into cavalry units. Col. William C. Pickens of Sevier County and Col. R. M. Edwards of McMinn County were commissioned to organize a regiment of cavalry. A feud developed between the two colonels which resulted in the organization of the Third Regiment. The Second Regiment was organized in September 1862, under Col. D. M. Ray of Sevier County and was composed of men from Knox, Sevier and Blount counties. George Hutsell and Rhad Dunn from Blount County were promoted from captains to majors. Captains James H. Walker of Company F; Samuel P. Rowan of Company H; James M. Henry of Company L; also Captains M. L. McConnell, T. F. Wallace, and Robert N. Hood and probably others, were from Blount County. William T. Dowell was chaplain and John P. Blankenship was surgeon.

In the Third Tennessee Cavalry were Col. W. C. Pickens, Majors Sam W. Pickens and Ben Cunningham; Adj. Will A. McTeer, Captains Sam Pickens of Company A, William Farmer of Company H, John H. Morton of Company K, Oliver McCammon of Company L, and Captain Elias Goddard. This Regiment was composed mostly of men from Blount and Sevier counties. The regiment surgeon was Dr. J. A. Souers and quartermaster was A. B. McTeer.[17]

Most of the Blount County men who served in the Confederate Army (C.S.A.) were in the Third, 31st and 37th Tennessee Infantry. In Company E of the Third Tennessee was Captain James A. McKamey (later Colonel) and Sam Toole who later became captain. In Company B of the 31st Tennessee Infantry, was Capt. John E. Toole, who later served as provost marshall of East Tennessee. Company G of the 37th, under Captain A. R. Wiggs (later J. M. Kidd) and Company I, under Captain William Wallace of the First Tennessee Cavalry (C.S.A.) were composed of local men. Captain William Holland enrolled a local company of cavalry. Dr. John W. Cates, B. W. Thompson, John S. Davis and William C. McCampbell were the officers.[18]

Captain W. H. Henry was in command of Company L, Fourth Tennessee. Captain W. Y. C. Hannum of Maryville was a cadet at Virginia Military Institute at the outbreak of the war and enlisted as

---

[16] Will A. McTeer, *Autobiography*. Of the eighteen men, only five returned home. William Jeffries, Jonathan Houser and Joshua Patty were lost on the Sultana. Major McTeer said that in the section between Little River and the Sevier County line between Bays Mountain and Chilhowee, 125 Union soldiers and ten Confederates served throughout the war. Forty-three Union men never returned and four died en route or shortly thereafter. Six of the Confederates were lost.

[17] According to Major McTeer, Col. Pickens called out at the height of an argument: "all who are with Pickens follow me" and that the majority of the regiment went with Pickens and left Edwards in charge of the First Regiment. McTeer says that he was the first man sworn into Co. A of the Third and the last man mustered out.

[18] Twenty-six men are listed in a registered agreement for the C. S. A. to pay for their horses which gives the names of the people who furnished the horses. This company became Company E, Fifth Tennessee Cavalry.

1st Lt. of Company B, 48th Infantry. He was elected Captain in 1862, and served with "Stonewall" Jackson. Captain Hannum lost a leg in action and resigned in 1863. The local chapter of United Daughters of the Confederacy was named in his honor. Sam T. Bicknell was assistant quartermaster general with General Caswell, and John Love was brigade surgeon on the staff of Stewart's Corps. These are by no means all who participated in the struggle. They are merely those that are definitely known.[19]

Woolford's Cavalrymen were the first Federal soldiers to be stationed in Blount County. They arrived September 2, 1863. Their quite orderly behavior gave the citizens, even the "Rebels," a rather good opinion of the Federal soldiers. Wheeler made his first raid into the county on the morning of November 14, 1863. One regiment of Woolford's Kentucky Cavalry was in Maryville, encamped near the railroad water tank and were taken by surprise and put to flight after a pretty lively fight. One hundred men were missing after this encounter. Woolford was at Rockford and came to meet them but retreated to Knoxville. Twenty-five men were wounded in this skirmish. Wheeler and his cavalry ranged the county for some time and had detachments stationed at Maryville and Louisville, keeping watch on the road and river traffic. The Federal troops under Woolford had not occupied Louisville, but the 6th Illinois Cavalry occupied the town November 28th.

December 4th, 1863, Sherman came as far as Maryville to the relief of Burnside with 25 or 30 thousand men. Maryville and all the surrounding county was alive with camps and campfires. Sherman made his headquarters at Dr. Pride's residence, later the Quaker School. General O. O. Howard had his headquarters at the Kerr (Kyker) house near Thompson's bridge. His division spread out over the county toward Louisville. All accounts remark on the nice behavior of these troops, and their liberality with "shin plasters" in paying for foodstuffs and exchanging commodities. Nevertheless, no countryside could support that many soldiers for any length of time and not suffer from destruction of fences and other property. Sherman withdrew after conferring with General Burnside and left General Beatty with a brigade of infantry in charge of the town. His headquarters were at the George Toole house where the Post Office now is. Most of the time during the winter of 1863–64, Maryville was disputed ground. Scouting parties from both sides frequently came to town the same day.[20]

Lieutenant, later Captain James M. Dorton and a provost guard of 28 men from the Second Tennessee Infantry was stationed in Maryville for quite a while. Dorton's men enforted in the courthouse on

---
[19] *Goodspeed*, 940; Thomas J. Taylor, *Confederate Military History*, Vol. VIII (Atlanta, 1899), 522.
[20] *Maryville Times*, March 5, 1880; February 24, 1886; A. H. Love, *History of Louisville; The Medical and Surgical History of the War of the Rebellion*, Part 1, Vol. 2, XCII (official reports).

August 1864, when a detachment of Wheelers' men in command of Major Lewis entered town by the Clover Hill Road. Lewis was drinking and consequently not in too good condition to command. He thought he could smoke them out, but only succeeded in burning everything around the courthouse square except the courthouse and two houses. About 11 P.M., they sent for a piece of artillery and set it up at the corner of Love Street and Broadway and passed several cannon balls through the courthouse walls, before Lt. Dorton surrendered.

Two incidents of the war merit mention. The first is the bravery of Miss Mary Love in helping to carry a message to Burnside from Grant during the siege of Knoxville. (Five couriers were sent and this is the only message that got through.) She was captured but was released because she told them she was a sister of Dr. John Love who was serving in the Confederate army, and was on her way to Louisville to wait on his sick wife, which was partly true. Traveling 35 miles from Kingston through bitter cold over treacherous roads, she reached the home of her brother-in-law, Horace Foster, in Louisville. A thirteen-year-old boy, John T. Brown, slipped through Wheeler's men that night, crossed Little River, and delivered the message the next day.[21]

The other story is that of the "Loyal Ladies Home Guard" of the Sixth District, who rode out to meet Sherman's men on the hill above Brick Mill and tell them that Longstreet had retired from Knoxville. The story was related by Lt. (later Capt.) John T. Gunn who had charge of the advance guard of Kentucky troops that day. This band of six young ladies under Captain Cynthia Dunn were so active in their work that Lt. Harriet McTeer was once arrested for spying, and Dora Jackson Birdwell's husband lost his life because he was suspected of spying. Other members were Eva Jackson, Samantha and Adalia Miller. The flag they carried that day had been made in 1860 for the local Home Guard commanded by Cynthia's brother Rhad Dunn (now Major) and kept hidden until then at the home of Montgomery McTeer. Captain James M. Henry's Co. L had been sworn in under this flag. Lieutenant Gunn was deeply impressed by the spectacle made that day, and they were cheered by line after line of soldiers as they marched past the girls beside the road.[22]

It would also be unfitting to forget the part that the Quakers played in this conflict locally. They, as a sect, are opposed to fighting, but William J. Hackney of Friendsville did not think that men, whether Friends (Quakers) or not, should be forced to fight for a cause which they did not approve. Across the road from the Friends Church in

---

[21] *Temple*, 522–4.
[22] Knoxville *Sentinel*, November 4, 1923; Nashville *Tennessean*, October 5, 1952; ("Soldiers in Hoopskirts"). This story was first told in a letter from Lt. Gunn to Major McTeer in 1910. McTeer checked the story and it was first published in detail in the *National Tribune*, (Washington, D. C.) July 18, 1912. The story that the materials in the flag were from articles of clothing in war-time is not true. A collection was taken and materials were bought by Montgomery McTeer in Knoxville to make a flag for the Home Guard according to an account in the papers of Mrs. John F. Henry (Harriet McTeer).

Friendsville was a large cave known to but a few and not easily found. During the war years, he helped more than two thousand men to hide and "get out of the country," most of them to join the Union Army. He was not concerned with their reasons if they were sincere in their sentiments. He acted as conductor for the people when the time was right.

He was suspected but nothing was ever proven. When Burnside came to Knoxville, Mr. Hackney was sent for and offered a place on Burnside's staff for his work, but, of course, refused. The story "Cudjo's Cave" is based on his work and that of another Friend in Greene County.

Wheeler's Cavalry made raids into Friendsville vicinity taking most of the horses and grain. Frank and George Hackney, Hart Boring and others lost all they had. Soon after this, the Ish sons and thirty others made a raid from North Carolina and when they found grain, and all the horses gone except one horse at Lee's, they took pocketbooks, watches etc. Wayne Lee followed them to Ish's and made Ben Ish get his horse back and got to keep the two left in its place.[23]

The little church at Friendsville lost by confiscation, $165,000 in gold value; 76 of 96 horses they had owned; 2,853 bushels of corn; and 1,586 bushels of oats. This will serve as a sort of index to what was taking place elsewhere in the county.[24]

There was numerous tales of depredations and wanton destruction on both sides. Joseph Smith was murdered by a band of raiders, who claimed to be affiliated with the Southern Army, but were not. John Gourley, while on furlough, was shot by Jeff Hinton who claimed to be with Union forces. No one was prosecuted for either crime.

A prominent Sevier Countian was killed when a group of "Young Bucks" raided smokehouses on Crooked Creek, and no questions were ever asked. Numerous things of this sort happened continually during the war. "Raiders" visited the coves and looted unprotected citizens.

During the Civil War two Texas Rangers in the Confederate Army retreating out of Knoxville came to Rockford Cotton Mills and demanded to know if they had arms and why they were not in the army. Richard I. Wilson, the proprietor, told them that all men were assigned there by order of the Confederate Military authorities. In the controversy Charles Coffin, a nephew of Wilson, was shot between the eyes. One soldier was killed and the other escaped to Louisville and was treated by Dr. Madison Cox. The dead soldier was buried near the Russell-Walker line fence and marked "Samuel Grover." The grave is now lost.

---

[23] Maryville *Enterprise*, March 3, 1932 (a letter from Riley Lee to his Uncle, Jepthah Morgan in Warren County, Ia., September 21, 1864. (Ben Ish killed a man by the name of Whetsell on one of these raids.) The Bowermans kept their horses from being stolen by drawing a horse hair through their hocks to make them lame.
[24] Fernando G. Cartland, *Southern Heroes, or the Friends in Wartime*, (Cambridge, 1895) p. 299–315. The *Republican*, July 18, 1882, (a list of fifty Blount County citizens were paid about $7,500 for damages and supplies furnished Federal troops during occupation. This is only one of dozens of such lists.)

At the close of the war one marked instance of injustice was the dragging from his sick-bed in Cades Cove of Daniel D. Foute. He was carried to Knoxville and thrown in jail. Later he was paroled to the home of his daughter, Mrs. Hamilton, under guard, where he died.[25]

Cades Cove seems to have been the scene of more raids than any other section of the county and feeling "ran high" even after the war. The fifteenth and sixteenth districts had a strongly organized Home Guard which had to be active in protecting property. Several skirmishes took place between the Home Guard and conscripting or raiding parties. One of the best known of these raids was the one in which Captain DeWitt Ghormley's horse was shot from under him by Green Dunn of the Guards. The gun is now treasured by a great-grandson of both parties.[26]

In one of these raids Henry Shields was wounded and lost the use of his arm, and Russell Gregory was killed. The grave of a Federal soldier named Shaw, who was killed by raiders from North Carolina is still a landmark near Deal's Gap on the U.S. Highway 129.

Practically every family in the Coves has stories to tell of how the raiders were foiled. One of the cleverest stories is that of "Jacky" Stephenson, of Tuckaleechee Cove, who hid his meat under an upturned log watering-trough and sat on the log all night whittling and swapping tales with the raiders. He also was successful in hiding his horses on the mountainside (he was especially known for his fine horses).

After the Civil War was ended there seems to have been a very strong Radical tendency on the part of some of the citizenry. Four Negroes and three white men were elected to the Board of Aldermen for Maryville. Brownlow was still spending his vacations at Montvale. The Union League, or the Loyal League of America organized January 2, 1867, had a very active local branch in Maryville. The expressed purpose (the promotion of the Union cause, the election of all without reference to race, color or creed) was to make sure that the Negro stayed within bounds and cast his vote for the Republican Party! Those men who were officers in the organization were the Reverend W. T. Dowell, R. J. Allen, James A. Goddard, R. C. Tucker, W. T. Parham, Dr. John Blankenship, John W. Hamil and Edward Sanderson. This organization was active until 1869. The death of Dowell, a bosom pal of Brownlow, and the chief promoter of the League, as well as the changing times caused its disbandment.[27]

---

[25] Excerpts from a Journal of the Foute family, owned by a granddaughter, Miss Ethie Eagleton of McCamey, Texas. Several "bushwhackings" are told by oldtimers —Elijah Hatcher was killed in Miller's Cove, Shimmon Crye, Lawson Fields, and Larkin Anderson near Centenary. Daniel Best was ambushed at Tomotley Ford.

[26] A muster roll of the Home Guard for the 15th district in 1865 was recently found by Mrs. Virginia Coleman among some papers acquired by Sutton's Transfer and Storage Company. A partial roll of the 7th district was furnished to Mr. Parham by Chris Hannah.

[27] Minutes of the *Union League of Maryville, Tennessee, 1867-69* are in the McClung Historical Collection, Lawson McGhee Library, Knoxville, Tennessee.

One hundred prominent men were enrolled as members and the minutes speak of other leagues in the county. Negro members held offices and were very active. In April, 1867, a committee was appointed to warn the Southern Methodist Minister Haynes to leave the county and two weeks later another group was appointed to thrash him if he didn't "get out." Otherwise they occupied their time debating.

That part of Blount County, east of the Maryville-Knoxville road was not occupied at any time during the war. Cavalry ranged over the county occasionally, and Conscript agents made a few visits, but desisted after an agent was killed in an altercation. Federal Cavalry made one trip through the Coves guided by the Rev. J. D. Lawson ("Black Jim") when they went through Wear's Cove and across Fighting Creek Gap to capture Gatlinburg. "Raiders" made more than one trip to the Coves about which stories have been handed down.[28]

When the blowing-up of the Battleship *Maine*, February 15, 1898, precipitated the Spanish-American War, four regiments were accepted from Tennessee. The First was the only one to see active duty. The Fourth commanded by Col. Leroy Brown and Lt. Col. Harvey Hannah served in Cuba, but arrived too late to meet the enemy in battle. Company B of the Fourth under Captain John J. Blair (later Judge Blair) was composed mostly of Loudon and Blount County men. Leonard S. Goddard was 1st Lieutenant and Hugh Matthews was 1st Sergeant. The regiment was organized August 1898, trained at Camp Bob Taylor at Fountain City, and mustered out at Savannah, Georgia one year later. There was only one casualty, George Riddle, musician, who died from measles and tuberculosis while Company B was stationed in the vicinity of Sancti Spiritus on occupation duty in Cuba.[29]

Company G of the Third Regiment was organized at Sherman Heights, May 1898, and mustered in at Camp Dewey at Nashville. A small per cent of this company was Blount County men, who had volunteered at Knoxville, but they did not see any active service. Some of these men reenlisted for Philippine service.

In August 1899, Lt. Goddard and thirty-six men from Blount County left Maryville for Camp Meade, Pennsylvania to join Company H of the 47th Volunteer Infantry (three of the thirty-six were named Charles Russell). They reached the Philippines by the way of the Suez Canal, and had their first engagement in January 1900. The men from Blount County gave an excellent account of themselves. It was the custom to put the largest men in front of the columns in marching. Both sets of four were from Blount County. Frank Burns was Corporal of the squad composed of Perry and William Weagley, D. L. (Fate) Brickey, Roscoe Cochran, Richard Burns, Charles Childress, and Tom

---

[28] Major McTeer tells the story of the death of the Conscripter, Farmer, who was killed by Franklin Cummings, when they met on the road. After this no other Conscription agent visited Ellejoy.

[29] Moore, *Tennessee*, 590; Maryville *Times*, August 28, 1898. Lt. Goddard and Sgt. Matthews both made careers of the service, Goddard in the Army and Matthews in the Marines.

Jenkins. The Blount contingent furnished the "crack" scouts. Eagle Rose, Perry Weagley, Frank Burns, Richard Burns, Fate Brickey and Charles Childress are often mentioned in scouting reports.[30]

Of the thirty-six men who went from Blount County to the Philippines, two were killed (Sgt. Wiley J. Brickey and Sgt. Frank W. Burns), and eight were wounded. It is interesting to note that Hugh Matthews who served as sergeant under Lieutenant L. S. Goddard in Cuba was awarded the Distinguished Service Medal for action in France in 1918, and Wiley J. Brickey who served as sergeant under Lieutenant Goddard in the Philippines was awarded a posthumous Distinguished Service Cross in 1933.*

Three Negro soldiers from Blount County—Doc Tate, King Coffin, Alonzo Hodsden and perhaps others, enlisted in the 48th Regiment at Fort Thomas, Kentucky, for Philippine service.

Captain Goddard and several of the 47th Regiment remained in the Philippines with the Regular Army at the end of their enlistment, and were joined later by volunteers, among them Joseph Benjamin Pate who only recently retired from the Army as Colonel and was awarded the Distinguished Service Cross for action in the Argonne in 1918. He was also awarded a Distinguished Service Medal for his work in effecting a boundary settlement between Ecuador and Peru.

The story of Blount County's Men in World War I will be confined to those men who fought in the 117th Infantry and the Thirtieth Division, because they were the first in the field and their behavior under fire and the record they made, is representative of Blount County military men.

The National Guard organization was known as the Third Infantry when they were called into Federal service. The regiment had spent nine months on the Mexican border, patrolling our southern boundary. They were mustered out March 20, 1917 only to be recalled a few weeks later by the State and then the Federal service.

The regiment was under command of General Lawrence D. Tyson, and Colonel Cary F. Spence of Knoxville during its entire service in the First Battalion. Under Major Charles W. Dyer, was Captain Emerson J. Lones' Company B, composed of men from Maryville and Knoxville.

---

[30] The files of the *Maryville Times* from August 1898 until the return of these men, has a full account of the activities of this group in the letters to the editor from Lt. Goddard and Sgt. W. J. Brickey.

* Major General Hugh Matthews (1876–1943) retired from the Marine Corps in the early 1940's. He was holder of the U.S. Navy Cross, and the Distinguished Service Medal as well as the French Croix de Guerre. He served 8 years as quartermaster general of the Marine Corps. Brigadier General Calvin B. Matthews (1883–1939) was president of the Marine Examining Board at the time of his death. He was holder of the Distinguished Service Cross which was awarded for his work in directing rescue work while serving as chief of the Nicaraguan National Guard in 1932. He was a gunnery expert and the Calvin Matthews Rifle Range at San Diego, California is named for him. The Matthews brothers are both buried in Arlington National Cemetery.

The regiment left Knoxville for Camp Sevier, South Carolina, in September where it became the 117th Infantry of the 49th Brigade of the Thirtieth, or "Old Hickory" Division. Some changes in personnel took place during the next eight months.[31]

In May 1918, they embarked from New York for England where they trained several weeks under British officers before moving up to the front in Belgium. After twenty-four days of supervision, on the front lines at Ypres, they were left in charge. They were withdrawn from the front line after two weeks under fire and given two weeks of intensive training with tanks. On September 26th, the 59th Brigade relieved the Australian troops on the front lines, and on September 26th launched the famous offensive against the Hindenburg Line. Casualties were heavy but they gained their objective. During the Somme offensive Captain Lones and 27 enlisted men were killed.

October 8th, 1918, the 117th engaged in another major offensive which netted the heaviest casualties of any one day at the front. October 7th, 8th, and 9th the Regiment lost thirty-four officers and 1,051 men. October 16th, they went back into battle. When they were relieved, they expected to go back to the front November 15th but due to the Armistice November 11th, they did not.

The 117th remained at Le Mans until March 10, 1919, when they entrained for St. Nazaire, from which point, they sailed for Charleston March 16, 1919, and were mustered out at Camp Oglethorpe in April.

The Regiment participated in three major engagements between July 16 and October 20, 1918. It shared in ten citations conferred on the Thirtieth Division by the British and Australian High Command. Colonel Spence was cited by General Pershing for his distinguished leadership in action. Private Sam Hatcher of Walland was awarded the Distinguished Service Cross for action with this group. (Sergeant W. C. Taylor of Sullivan County now of Tuckaleechee Village was also awarded a Distinguished Service Cross.)[32]

One of the Blount County men who enlisted in the Aviation Corps, which was then in its infancy, was Lieutenant Claude O. Lowe. After completing his training at Mineola, New York in August 1916, he was instructor at Dayton, Ohio, March 1918. He was transferred to Arcadia, Florida, where he was killed when his plane crashed in the summer of 1918. An aviation field there was named in his honor.[33]

Those officers from Blount County who were killed in action were Captain Emerson J. Lones, Lieutenant Thomas W. Goddard and Lieutenant Milton L. Harper. Thirty-eight other local men are known to

---

[31] *Knox County in the World War*, 1917-18-19 (Knoxville, 1919) 87, 95, 99 ff.

[32] Moore, *Tennessee*, 642-3, (General Pershing's Mother was Elizabeth Thompson of Blount County. Her birthplace was marked jointly in 1924 by the American Legion and the State Historical Commission. The site is near Hubbard on the Atchley farm.)

[33] *Ibid.*, 639; *Knox County in the World War*, 1917-18-19 (Knoxville, 1919), 123.

have been killed in action or died while in the service. There are without doubt, several others.³⁴

The local American Legion Post is named in honor of Captain Emerson J. Lones who was killed in action.

The pattern of behavior and the fine record of Blount County has been repeated in the later wars, but space will not allow any discussion of later wars in this work.

Sergeant William T. Hembree, Lieutenant Vernon V. Ferguson, Lieutenant Ray Tipton, Major Leslie Boyd, and Glenn Morton were awarded a Distinguished Flying Cross for bravery in action in World War II. Other decorations may have been awarded but the recipients are not known.

The 178th Field Artillery of the National Guard was organized in May 1924, by Lieutenant Colonel J. G. Sims and Major M. B. Crum. The original muster included one battery of fifty men, a headquarters company and a combat train of twenty men. The headquarters especially built for the group in 1928 is the building next to the Baptist church on Ellis Avenue. The present Armory building on Methodist Hill was occupied in 1941.

Battery C 191st AFA Battalion (105 FT Howitzer) is composed of 59 men. The Medical Detachment has 8 men. Battery A 114th AAA (Gun Battalion 90-mm) was organized October 17, 1951 and is composed of 65 men. Headquarters and Headquarters Battery 191st AFA Battalion (105 FT Howitzer) is composed of 75 men.

June 20, 1955 ground was broken for an Air National Guard Armory on a 12-acre tract adjoining the northwest edge of McGhee Tyson airport. It is intended that it shall be used more as a permanent radar site than an armory. It will be headquarters for the 119th Aircraft Control and Warning Flight which to date has been located in Knoxville. This is the only Air National Guard Unit in the state. The unit, under command of Lieutenant Colonel John R. Douglas contains approximately 200 men. 50 per cent of the officers and 20 per cent of the men are from the Blount area.

When Air Defense Command was established in the fall of 1950, the 105th Fighter Squadron was assigned to ADC to protect the industrial area of East Tennessee.³⁵

November 1, 1951, a flight of the 105th Fighter-Interceptor Squadron began standing alert at McGhee Tyson Municipal Airport in Republic F-47's. In April 1952, the entire squadron was moved to McGhee Tyson under Lieutenant Colonel John L. Elder, Jr.

In February 1952, the 105th Fighter-Interceptor Squadron was divided into the 74th Air Base Squadron under Lieutenant Colonel William H. Powell, Jr., and the 469th Fighter- Squadron, under Lieutenant

---

[34] Moore, *Tennessee*, 652 ff.
[35] The 105th Aero Squadron was organized August 24, 1917 at Kelly Field, San Antonio, Texas. In 1919, World War I pilots in the vicinity of Nashville organized into a squadron of National Guard at Berry Field. The 105th Fighter Squadron was ordered to Federal duty in 1940 and returned to inactive status in September 1946.

Colonel Elder. Both units had been moved to McGhee Tyson by the spring and summer of 1952.[36]

The 74th Air Base Squadron was superseded by the 516th Air Defense Group which was activated in February 1953 and consisted of: 516th Air Base Squadron, 516th Materiel Squadron, 516 USAF Infirmary and 469th Fighter-Interceptor Squadron. At this time the transition from F-47's to F-86A's was initiated.

The mission of the 516th Air Defense Group was to support and maintain facilities under Air Force control at McGhee Tyson and to provide cover for the industries of the area: TVA, Oak Ridge, and ALCOA (Aluminum Company of America).

In the spring of 1953 the first assigned Sabre Jet landed at McGhee Tyson Air Base during Armed Forces Day celebration (May 16th).

In the spring of 1954 the 469th was converted from Day-Fighter to All-Weather aircraft and the second Fighter-Interceptor Squadron was activated within the 516th Air Defense Group. This group was designated as the 460th Fighter-Interceptor Squadron. They were equipped with F-86A's and early in October 1954 the 460th began sharing responsibility with the 469th flying alert duty. There are now approximately 1,500 men stationed at the air base.

In July 1953 the Base-Community Welfare Council was organized for the purpose of establishing stronger and better relationships between the Air Base and nearby towns. At the present time Base-Community relations at McGhee Tyson are considered about the best to be found in the Services.

McGhee Tyson Rest Camp was officially opened near Friendsville in July 1954. This is a recreational area for the use of personnel and their families. On the air base there is a library, post office, movies, athletic facilities of all sorts, clubs for the various groups from the nursery up. A swimming pool, a 9-hole golf course and a new post exchange was finished in 1955. The base hospital takes care of all military personnel and their families, except for fitting glasses.

There are four or five ambulances on call. The Knoxville Garden Clubs have been carrying out a beautification project on the base which has done much for appearances.[37]

---

[36] The National Guard unit was de-activated December 1, 1952 and the 105th was redesignated as the 469th Fighter-Interceptor Squadron. McGhee Tyson Air Base was officially opened August 9, 1952.

[37] Information from: *History of the 516th Air Defense Group* (typed) in the office of Information at McGhee Tyson Air Base, and an interview with A.2.C. Ballas June 20, 1955.

CHAPTER V

Early Inns and Watering Places

From time immemorial man has had to travel into far countries and as a result inns have sprung up along the main-traveled roads to furnish the necessary food and shelter for the traveler. At first man had to carry his own provisions and shift for himself, but just as soon as a semblance of civilization developed, the inn appeared.

The story of Inns and Taverns in Blount County probably predates the county formation but we have no information about the fact. David Russell, Nicholas Byers and Arthur H. Henley had an early agreement with the Cherokees whereby they were to have one or more tavern sites in connection with their Unicoi Turnpike since they were to operate a mill on Four Mile Creek for the benefit of the Indians. One of these may have been in what is now Blount County. According to an act of Legislature later, they had the use of one acre of ground, including their ferry landing. Certainly David Russell seems to have been no novice as an innkeeper when he came to Maryville in 1803 to operate the Wood Tavern.[1]

The innkeeper was bound to keep good rule and order in his house. The local citizens liked to gather in and hear what news the traveler carried and of course the Inn was the social center for the neighborhood. Competition always seems to stimulate better service and it seems there has always been at least two hostelries in Maryville from the first to the present.

A Federal Road had already been laid to Tellico Blockhouse even before the county was formed and Maryville was laid out. The fact that Maryville was the county seat made it imperative to provide some place for justices to lodge during "court week."

The ordinary rates as prescribed by the County Court in 1796 were: Breakfast 16⅔, dinner 25, supper 12½, lodging 8⅓, ½ pt. good whisky or beer 8⅓, good rum 16⅔, ½ pt. good brandy 12½.[2]

John Wallace was given leave to give tavern service at his house in 1796. David Taylor and John Wood also were given permits in 1796 to operate ordinaries.

John Lowry had been trading with the Indians for several years before the formation of the county, and he soon got permission to operate

---

[1] *Goodspeed*, 102 ff; *Acts, 1820*, ch. 118; *Acts, 1817*, ch. 7, authorized Russell and others to open a road from Samuel Thompson's on Nine Mile Creek (Thompson's Bridge) "to intersect a road already open."

[2] *Minutes*, 1796.

71

a Public House. Lowry and Waugh were also permitted to sell spirituous liquors in 1805 (in Maryville where they operated a store).[3]

Many important men, of necessity, passed through Maryville whether they tarried or not. Among the early celebrities who traveled through the county were Louis Phillipe of France and his two brothers in 1797 who may have stopped at one of the local taverns or inns.[4]

John Trimble, Archibald Cowan, Richard Cast, Joseph Hannah, and Josiah Danforth all had tavern and inn permits in 1797 and 1798. Alexander Boyd, Oliver Wallace, and William Craig had liquor permits only.

In 1798 new rates were listed:

Breakfast and dinner 1/6, supper 1, cold meal 0/9, horse at hay, or fodder for night 0/6, pt. whisky bearing 33⅓% proof 0/9, lodging per night 0/6, pasture 0/6, good beer qt. 0/6, good rum ½ pt. 0/6, ½ pt. wine 1, ½ pt. imported gin 0/6, ½ pt. country made gin 1/6, ½ pt. good French brandy, 0/6, ½ pt. peach brandy 1.

In 1799, Thomas Berry, distiller, was allowed to sell liquor at home at tavern rates. Captain Butler, of Tellico Blockhouse, appeared before the court at the same session to prevent William Stuart from being licensed as Public House keeper. David Miller in 1800 was allowed to sell liquors at his house at Militia Springs at tavern rates. (This was very near Tellico Blockhouse.) William Logan had been granted permission in 1797 to sell whisky on Nine Mile Creek, in the same neighborhood, at tavern rates for six months.[5]

John Wood and Josiah Danforth were first licensed to operate a public house in 1796. Wood was assisted by David Taylor in 1797. The location of this tavern is known to be lot No. 59 between Proffitt's and the old Bank of Maryville building. It was an eight-room, two-storied, shuttered frame building with a two-story porch on the front. The entrance hall extended through the building to the back porch ell. From the rear porch was the stairway to the upstairs porch. The bedrooms contained four beds in each room.

In 1801, David Cunningham was again licensed to operate a tavern. His inn was on lot No. 63 where the J. C. Penney Store now stands. This inn was built similar to the one just described.[6]

In 1803, David Cunningham and David Russell were both licensed. The tax list for 1803 names three Public House keepers in the county who paid the five dollars privilege license fee. David Russell, David Cunningham, and Stanfield and (James) Smith. We do not know where the latter was located.[7]

Innkeepers other than those already mentioned elsewhere are: Jacob Thomas, and William Floyd—1809; William Long, David DeArmond,

---

[3] *Carter*, 461, 463.
[4] *Knoxville Gazette*, May 1, 1797.
[5] *Minutes*, 1797; 1798.
[6] Location and description from a paper on *Inns*, by Mrs. India Patton Broady (Broady Collection). Also from *Parham Papers*.
[7] *Minutes, 1803; Tax List*, Tennessee State Archives, Nashville, Tennessee.

and John Wilkinson—1814; and Samuel Bogle, Major Beavers and Jesse DeLozier—1817.

The Wood Tavern was operated by David Russell for about fifteen years. In 1817, John Norwood of Sullivan County became the proprietor, under the name of the "Green Tree" and pledged himself to keep the best materials for his table and bar. He soon changed the name to "General Jackson." In 1827, Robert Caldwell was the proprietor under the "Eagle" sign, and the following year John Freeman operated it. Michael Smith operated it from 1832 to 1838, when Mrs. Jane Owens advertised under the sign of "Green Tree." William Toole bought this inn and lived there until his death in 1860 and his widow continued there for some years. John Currier was living there when it burned in 1867.[8]

Miles and David Cunningham operated Cunningham Tavern House from 1801 to 1812. Jesse Wallace then took over and operated for fifteen years under the sign "General Washington." He pledged himself to be as "reasonable as any in his charges if not more so and to keep a stable of the best quality."[9]

In 1827, Campbell Wallace announced that he had taken over the business, and after making some "comfortable improvements" was operating the "Village Hotel" and with his father's help he hoped to give satisfactory service. He especially noted that his bar was well-furnished with liquors for travelers but none for "retail."

Early in 1829, Captain John Freeman bought the property from Campbell Wallace. Freeman sold to James Carson in 1832.[10]

In 1832, Mrs. Jane Owens announced that she had taken the "long-known and commodious tavern house" in Maryville formerly occupied by Captain John Freeman.[11]

In 1832, James and Campbell Gillespy bought the property of Carson and in 1839 we find that the County Court met at Dr. James H. Gillespy's Tavern two or three times as there was no courthouse. In 1854, the Gillespys sold the property to the Rev. John S. Craig, and he in turn sold to Roderick McKenzie in 1855. McKenzie sold lots 82 and 63 to Alexander Kennedy in 1856. Alexander Kennedy and Jeremiah Hudson operated it as the "Maryville Hotel." By November Roderick McKenzie advertised as running it and no doubt continued until it burned in 1863 during the siege of the courthouse.[12]

From 1846 to 1852 we find William Gault operated Gault House and maybe longer at the northeast corner of Harper and Love streets.[13]

---

[8] *Minutes*, Passim; May 16, 1827; October 17, 1827; March 14 and 26, 1832; *Knoxville Register*, May 28, 1832. Smith was evidently operating the Inn as a stage stop since he advertised for several years as operating a stage line from Knoxville to Huntsville, Alabama, through Maryville; Mrs. Owens in 1842 married James P. H. Porter of Sevier County, formerly a member of the State Legislature.
[9] *Knoxville Gazette*, August 16, 1813.
[10] *Knoxville Register*, October 17, 1827; February 18, 1829; Deeds, Book 4, p. 223.
[11] *Knoxville Register*, March 14, 1832.
[12] Deeds, 4, p. 224; *Minutes*, 1839; Deeds, X, 646; Y, 214.
[13] Deeds, Y 565.

Samuel Love advertised the "Rising Sun Tavern" in 1837 at the northeast corner of Broadway and Love streets where Royal Jewelers is now.[14]

The next mention of this hostelry is in a transfer made by the Love heirs to John E. Toole of "Love's Tavern" in 1851. Toole transferred the property to William Goddard in 1865. In the last two transfers it is not described as a tavern but merely identified by lot numbers. What happened to the property for the next few years is not clear.[15]

In 1876, the Rev. George Coleman was living upstairs and operating his printing office downstairs. In 1875, he had bought the *Daily News* from Charles F. Brause of Kingston and moved it to Maryville and changed the name to *The Independent*.[16]

In 1887, Claudius B. Lord bought the Love Tavern property from John P. Duncan which he described in a trust deed made in 1892 as a two-story frame hotel building known as "Eureka House." [17]

In 1890 or 1891, the Rev. B. C. Taylor, a Methodist minister, who had been operating a store at Clover Hill which had burned, moved his family to Maryville and operated the Eureka Hotel for one or two years. W. H. Tullock, of Black Sulphur, had been manager immediately prior to this time.[18]

In January 1894, the newly renovated "Sam Houston" Inn officially opened with a "gathering of friends." In June 1895, Mr. and Mrs. W. P. Barnhill who had been operating Sam Houston Inn took over management of Wildwood Springs Hotel and Miss Anna Lord, assisted by Arthur Greer took charge of Samuel Houston Inn. Special mention is made of catering to "Knights of the Grip" (traveling men). This arrangement continued for some years. Miss Lord was operating a photographic gallery in the adjoining building at that time.

In 1899 J. L. Porter was proprietor and hacks were meeting all trains. J. H. Greer and Co. were proprietors in 1903. In 1904, Mrs. Josie Marcum was proprietor followed in August by the W. A. Lanes who continued for a year or two. In 1907 Bowman Smith was proprietor. The hotel was under a varied management for the next several years.[19]

In 1902 the elder Lord deeded the property to his daughter, Miss Helen M. Lord. She held title to the property until May 1917, when she sold the property to W. C. Penn, Sam E. and Robert S. Young. Later G. M. Bassell bought an interest in the property.[20]

In September 1937, Bassell, Penn and Young sold the property to

---

[14] *Knoxville Register* May 31, 1837.
[15] *Deeds*, W, 205 (from our father and mother, Samuel and Mary Love) *Deeds*, A A, 220, A A, 529.
[16] Emma Middleton Wells, *The History of Roane County* (Chattanooga 1927). Some copies of the *Independent* are on file in the McClung Room, Lawson McGhee Library, Knoxville, Tennessee.
[17] *Deeds*, MM, 317; *Trusts*, 4, p. 67.
[18] Information from Mrs. Alice Taylor Rumbley of Ridgewood, N. J., Daughter of B. C. Taylor. She has both Tullock and Taylor permits.
[19] *Maryville Times*, January 24, 1894; June 6, 1895; September 10, 1896; 1896-1907 Passim.
[20] *Deeds*, 57, p. 476; 81, p. 80; 82, p. 467; 83, p. 310; 97, p. 310.

Dr. A. M. Gamble. Sam Houston Inn continued operations until 1939 when it was razed to make way for the Gamble building. M. D. Baker was the last proprietor.

Captain John Freeman said he had rented the McGhee House in 1832 which he stated was well suited for public entertainment. He claimed a well-furnished stable. The location of this place is not fixed.[21]

In 1842, William McTeer built the "College Inn," a fourteen-room two-story frame hotel on lots No. 52 and No. 53. It was flush with the sidewalk. On the first floor was the reception room, office, and parlor. The harness room was at one end and some bedrooms at the other. There were five entrances from the street on two levels. The bar, a large dining room, the kitchen and storerooms were in the basement. It was advertised shortly after its opening as the "The Citizen's Hotel."[22]

The Citizen's Hotel was newer and larger and enjoyed a more choice trade than its competitors. Ten years later Montgomery McTeer asked the Mayor and Aldermen for permission to build a porch over the sidewalk with massive white pillars, three feet in diameter, which lent an aristocratic air to the establishment. Thus it became the "Verandah Hotel" in 1852 and was the official stage stop during the years that Montvale Springs was entertaining the aristocracy of the South. Many political speeches were made from the second-story porch. Frank Marion Hood, McTeer's brother-in-law was manager in 1854 and his ad stated that all coaches to and from Montvale stopped there for "Dinner." In 1855 McTeer sold the property to Alexander Kennedy.[23]

The parlor was tastefully furnished and was the setting for many genteel community gatherings of a social nature until the war, when it became a rendezvous for the military leaders of whichever side was in possession at the moment.

In 1860, Alexander Kennedy sold the "Verandah Hotel" to Roderick McKenzie and it was known as the "McKenzie House" for the next fifteen years or so.[24]

In 1880, H. C. Austin operated the hotel as "Austin House." In 1883, Juliett C. Gass of Sevier County bought the property from H. S. Catlett and the following year leased the building to Jesse Richardson, photographer, and Foster Clark.[25]

Shops then filled up the space opening on Broadway and Post's Wagon Works occupied the basement until 1894 when the building was cleared for the erection of the Broadway Methodist Church.[26]

---

[21] *Deeds*, 124, p. 157; *Knoxville Register*, June 27, 1832.
[22] *Parham Papers*; D.A.R. Collection; *Inns*, Broady Collection; *Knoxville Argus*, May 18, 1842; and for years thereafter—"For the reception and entertainment of travelers and boarders." Main Street near the college. "No efforts spared to give satisfaction"; *Knoxville Gazette*, May 18, 1842.
[23] *Maryville Enterprise*, April 5, 1912; *Deeds*, Y, 142.
[24] *Deeds*, Z, 619.
[25] Austin was named one of stockholders in Montvale Turnpike Company; *Deeds*, H H, 572; *Deeds*, B B, 579; Foster Clark was an English lawyer who was interested in mineral developments around Montvale, and also engaged in land speculation.
[26] *Maryville Record*, July 22, 1904, (feature story) says church was organized 1865; first church was built 1870.

In 1868, F. G. Wayland built a two-story frame building on the corner of Washington and Depot (now Ellis Avenue) streets, opposite the Southern Depot on a lot purchased from the William Wallace heirs.

In 1869, he described the property as a large painted dwelling with some rooms behind and having stables on the back corner. It is further described as being opposite the depot and running with the railroad on the south, "where I am transacting business." He sold the property in 1871 to W. Y. C. Hannum. The property was always referred to as "Wayland House."

W. W. Everett operated a hack line to Mount Nebo Hotel for a good many years from this stand and people waiting for trains used the house for a waiting place. W. W. Everett and wife transferred the property to Mary Everett, who in turn sold to S. T. Post. The property was described as Wayland House (including the barns), when the property was bought in 1913 by J. C. Bittle. Bittle dismantled the old house and built a brick building from street to alley fronting the depot. A rooming-house was operated upstairs until the building was renovated in the late Forties.[27]

In 1886, George C. Jackson bought lot No. 54 on the corner of College and Broadway from Alexander Henry and built a three-story brick hotel. This hotel was operated as Jackson House until 1914. W. R. Teeguarden was the first proprietor. J. H. Magill advertised a "first class hotel" in 1894. Wiley Lasseter advertised a thorough overhaul job in 1902.

In 1914, the property passed from the Jacksons to Robert B. Roberts of Knoxville who sold in 1918 to Johnson and Law. In 1919, Dr. A. M. Gamble became the owner and the name was changed to Blount Hotel. At Dr. Gamble's death the property passed to Miss Mary Gamble. The hotel has been managed since 1937 by T. A., and later Frank, Roylston.[28]

In 1874, the Rev. William Bowman remodeled the Rev. John S. Craig's residence into a hotel which was operated by Lyle Anderson and his sisters as Central House and later by Roylston and last by Mr. Baily. This building was condemned and torn down in 1939. This building occupied the lot opposite McCammon and Ammons on Broadway with a veranda which extended over the sidewalk, and along each side.[29]

The latest hostelry in point of origin is the Fort Craig Hotel. This building was originally the Sam George residence on Washington Street and East Main Avenue near the site of Fort Craig. This property was bought by Dr. J. E. Carson and made into a private hospital in

---

[27] *Deeds*, K K, 399; C C, 109; D D 125; 74, p. 144. The Wayland House was operated in 1887 by William H. Love (Tennessee State Gazeteer and Business Directory (Nashville, 1887).

[28] *Deeds*, 43, p. 402 (on which Jackson House is being built); *Maryville Times*, January 3, 1894; June 21, 1902; *Deeds*, 75, p. 50. (It was known as Ingleside Hotel from 1914–18); Book 153, p. 337.

[29] *Parham Papers*; *Maryville Times*, January 3, 1894; June 1902, August 29, 1903.

1928 and was operated until about 1944 as Fort Craig Hospital. The building was then remodeled as a tourist hotel and opened in 1948 as Fort Craig Hotel.[30]

Besides the inns in Maryville, there have been others of note within the bounds of the county. A H. Love in his history of Louisville says that the Nathaniel Cox home was at one time a stage-stop. (He said that it was the second house built in Louisville.) He said also that Doctor George Hunt Chaffin was innkeeper in Louisville later on as well as the Heartsills (Hiram and Abraham). The accommodation of a public house was made necessary on account of the volume of river traffic, the ferries, and the extensive warehouses located in Louisville and vicinity.[31]

In Morganton, two inns were licensed by the County Court in 1817 and again in 1818 to Amos Barnett, and John and James Lambert. Morganton was another shipping point for steamboats and also a ferry-point. The stationing of a shipping inspector here in the early 1800's led to the founding of the town of Morganton.[32]

It was necessary to have stopping-places at various "stages" along the main roads. The main stage route No. 10 through Blount County came from Knoxville through Maryville and Tellico Blockhouse south to Huntsville, Alabama. Another route (No. 17) came from Hot Springs, North Carolina, Newport, and Sevierville by way of Brabson's Ford to Maryville and to Morganton and Kingston or Southwest Point as well as points south.[33]

The McCulloch place at Little River, now McTeer's was the first stage stop in Blount County on the way from Knoxville (Stock Creek at the county line was a stopping place). The spring at this place was most welcome to the weary traveler. Sam Houston is reputed to have made a special stop here on his last trip to Tennessee. The next stop was the John Ambrister house in Springfield, less than two miles from Maryville, near the spring and pumping station on the old Knoxville highway. This house was built before 1830 and was used as a stage stop until the advent of the railroad in 1868. It carries the tradition that all three of the native son Presidents are supposed to have stopped here in their travels.

Below Maryville at the Byerly (now Pate) place was the next stop. William Yearout, who died in 1888, drove a stage from Knoxville to Athens for Jake Sessler and said that there was not a switch nor a drink of water to be had along the road from Maryville to Brick Mill except at the Maxwell place where there was a well. "Maxwell kept an inn and we changed horses there."[34]

[30] *Deeds*, 100, p. 481.
[31] A. H. Love, *History of Louisville*, unpublished manuscript. Copy in author's collection. (Doctor Chaffin married Cox's widow).
[32] *Minutes*, 1817–18.
[33] Eastin Morris, *Tennessee Gazeteer*, Appendix.
[34] This Inn was first built and operated by George Henry; *Parham Papers*, Yearout family. *Nashville Business Directory*, 1857, gives Fagg, Bushnell and Sessler, proprietors of a stage line from Maryville to Knoxville.

The next stopping-place was the Norwood Inn on the crest of a hill west of Greenback Industries. Here in 1820, John Norwood built a long two-story Inn, with an ell at the back flanked by porches, reached by a long drive lined with black locusts. Mr. Norwood had operated an Inn in Maryville for several years but he had seen the need for a stage stop on this long stretch of the old Federal Road, from Maryville to the south.

The Norwood Inn was an eight-room affair, commodious and pretentious for its day. The hand-made brick chimneys at each end of the main building and two on the ell furnished heat for the establishment. The floors, weatherboarding, and paneling were all of heart pine. There were two entrances at the front, and ten windows. One entrance was into the reception hall and the other into the Master's room. The walls were plastered. From the reception hall, one entered the long thirty-foot summer dining room, which opened on the right into another dining room with a large fireplace and built-in cupboards. Back of the dining room was the kitchen with its large six-foot fireplace and swinging crane with the usual array of copper and iron pots, pans, and ovens. A storeroom off the kitchen completed these quarters.

Some of the furniture bought for the inn is still in the possession of the family; four-poster beds with trundle beds beneath, chests, bureaus, and tables.

A small taproom, or bar in one corner of the reception room furnished refreshments for the thirsty traveler. The stairway led to the small upper hall which gave access to the two large end-rooms with fireplaces and the smaller middle one which was generally used for storage, and the attic storeroom over the ell.

The business prospered for six years and John Norwood died. His son John III continued as innkeeper until his death in 1840. At this time John's brother, Wesley Norwood became the proprietor of the Norwood Inn and continued to carry on the family traditions of hospitality. He enlarged the plantation to 1200 acres and built up quite an establishment.

In 1850 the first circus that we have record of in Blount County presented an exhibition at Norwood's. It was described as the "largest company in the world. Four magicians and an Imperial chariot drawn by thirty elegant horses." Admission was fifty cents, and children and Negroes paid half price.[35]

In time, the inn was not sufficient to house Norwood's growing family and clientele and so three more rooms were added. The inn was now five rooms long, each room having its own entrance. Business continued to flourish until the Civil War when bad times were succeeded by worse. Unpleasant happenings caused the Norwoods to flee to Indiana for safety during the days when the lawless element took advantage of the general confusion attendant on war times.

---

[35] Knoxville *Register*, May 1, 1850; Broady Collection, *Inns* (Mrs. Broady was a Norwood granddaughter.)

After the war and the coming of the railroad to the county, innkeeping ceased to be profitable and Wesley Norwood devoted his time to his plantation and in his latter days retired to Maryville where he lived to the ripe age of ninety-five. The Norwood Inn was abandoned as a habitation many years ago and fell into decay and was eventually torn down. Traces of the old lane, the spring, and a few locust trees still remain as a reminder of former grandeur and hospitality. Henry Lunsford killed a man there, named Thompson, by shooting into the main room through a hole in the chimney (left for ventilation). Lunsford was tried and sentenced to be hung. This accounts in part for the "haunted house legend." [36]

On reaching Maryville when one took the route to Sevierville the first stop was the old William McCamy house built before 1811 at Brabson's Ford, (then McCamy's Ford). This route was used extensively by traders from upper East Tennessee in driving livestock to market in Atlanta. So a large lot for corralling stock was part of the regular provision at McCamy's. The next stop was over the line in Sevier County. This is the same general route now followed by U.S. Highway 411 from Upper East Tennessee to Atlanta.[37]

MONTVALE SPRINGS

The Montvale of today gives no idea of the prestige it once enjoyed as the "Saratoga of the South." Prior to 1830 the Chilhowee Mountain was an unclaimed virgin wilderness and mineral springs were regularly patronized by the wild animals, who no doubt valued the waters as highly as men did later. Certainly it was the patronage of the animals which first led men to the springs as hunters.

There are two or three traditions as to how the name Montvale originated. The accepted one is that Jesse Wallace and Jesse Thompson discovered the springs, while searching for lost cattle and applied the name. In any case, Daniel D. Foute entered the surrounding mountain lands in 1832. When he made a trust deed for the debts in 1837, he included the "Montvale tract where I live." [38]

There are two fine springs within a few steps of the hotel site and another called "Black Sulphur" two or three miles away, which Foute acquired from David Delzell in 1834 shortly after he had built his log hotel. Foute also built a road by way of Murray Gap through Rhea Valley (now Happy Valley), to intersect the Calloway and Parson's Turnpike which was a short cut for travel to Georgia by way of the

---

[36] The inn was known locally as the "haunted house." People declared they saw light in the deserted house at night. Knoxville *Register*, July 22, 1829; "sentenced and hung near Maryville yesterday." (Newspaper account says Thompson was killed, but tradition says Murphy).

[37] *Maryville Enterprise*, August 18, 1911. Paper read by James McKamy at Logan's Chapel Decoration.

[38] *Parham Papers; Inns*, Broady Collection; *Deeds*, S, 252 (It appears from a quitclaim deed made by John Norwood to Foute in 1831 that James Berry and Norwood had entered the "Spring tract" previous to this.

Uncoi Turnpike. Tradition says this road was built with Indian labor. Foute also planted a large vineyard and orchard on the mountainside at this time. He owned several thousand acres of land extending along the Chilhowees and reaching across into Cades Cove. The "Foute Trail," which he no doubt sponsored in order to reach his holdings more easily, is still in use. This path led from the hotel to "Look Rock" and from thence along the ridge to what was later called the "Cooper Road" into Cades Cove.[39]

Foute operated a resort hotel from 1832 to 1850, and his log hotel according to a drawing based on the description of J. Gray Smith, an English neighbor, was a somewhat pretentious rustic affair. It was a two-story log hotel about ten rooms in length with a two-story veranda extending the whole length. A kitchen and dining room ell extended to the rear.

Foute secured a post office in 1837 which would indicate that his patronage was demanding such service. Foute was succeeded as postmaster by Robert H. Anderson in 1847, who had been managing the hotel. Foute seems to have become involved in a suit brought by the Common Schools Commissioners about 1840 and during the next years made four or five trust deeds involving the Montvale and Black Sulphur tracts. In 1841 a local ad described Montvale as the "fountain of youth and health," and accommodations as the "best within our means." Wiley Smith became postmaster in 1848 which may indicate that he was hotel manager at this time.[40]

In 1850 Daniel D. Foute and Alexander B. Gamble, Andrew C. Montgomery, administrators of Jesse Thompson and James M. Toole, transferred 3,840 acres including the Sulphur Springs tract to Asa Watson of Mississippi.

In 1853, William C. Lillard bought from James Bell his lease of the Montvale Springs Hotel. Later in the year Asa Watson paid Lillard $1,000 for the old furniture and took over the lease on the property.[41]

Asa Watson replaced Foute's two-story log hotel in 1853 with a three-story, seven-gabled frame building which was described as the largest and best to be found at any place in all the Southwest. It was two hundred feet long, with a hundred and fifty-foot ell. Porches ran

---

[39] *Acts, 1829*, 178. A charter to Daniel D. Foute to open a road through the mountains to intersect the Calloway-Parson's Turnpike (Rights secured for fifty years); *Knoxville Register*, June 27, 1832 said road was finished. *Acts, 1851–52*, 241. Charter for a four-foot road from Six Mile through Cades Cove to the North Carolina line by Ekanetelee Gap. (This is, no doubt, the Cooper Road); *Minutes;* September 3, 1838 said road was finished except one mile.

[40] All Post Office data is taken from photostats of the Post Office records in the National Archives, Washington, D. C.; *Knoxville Register*, June 8, 1839; March 17, 1840; *Deeds*, T, 388; Q, 296; S, 17; S, 1; S, 252; *Argus*, June 30, 1841; The *Post*, June 28, 1841; In February, 1954 Miss Ethie Eagleton of McCamie, Texas, sent an ad for "Montvale or Modern Bethesda Springs" in the handwriting of Daniel D. Foute written June 28, 1832. (D. D. Foute was Miss Eagleton's grandfather.) Miss Eagleton has furnished other data including a photograph of D. D. Foute.

[41] *Estates*, 1853.

the whole length of each floor. In addition there were about sixty cottages and at the height of the season which was from June 1st to October 1st, there were generally three to four hundred guests. Rates were $2.00 per day, $12.00 per week; and $40.00 per month (children half price).[42]

Besides enlarging the facilities, Watson also did extensive landscaping on the ten to twenty-acre lawn. Today there are cypress, gingko trees, Scotch broom, Paulonia and other trees not indigenous to this section scattered over the slopes of the hotel lawn which bear witness to the work of Asa Watson.

The hotel and springs were snug against the foot of the Chilhowee Mountains and is still reached by a long picturesque drive through a dense woods along a rhododendron-bordered stream which still does an excellent build-up for the rustic setting of the resort. (In early days there was a choice between the "upper" or "lower" road.)

William McTeer, who was at times an innkeeper in Maryville, was postmaster in 1851 which may mean that Watson did not immediately take charge himself. In fact, there was no post office from the fall of 1851 until 1854 which indicates that the hotel may not have been in active operation for the next three years while building was in process. Watson was a very successful press agent and succeeded in spreading its fame abroad. He does not appear to have been at Montvale in 1856 as Hardy Cunningham was named the postmaster there. Guests who came to Montvale prior to the Civil War arrived by stage from Knoxville. The line of "No. 1, Troy Coaches" left Knoxville at 6:30 A.M. and reached the hotel in time for the noon meal. Fare was $2.25 each way; headquarters were at some hotel, generally the Lamar House. Mail arrived at Montvale on Tuesday, Thursday, and Saturday at 3 P.M. and left the following morning at 8 A.M.[43]

The best contemporary description of Montvale of that period is from the pen of John Mitchell while he was hibernating in Tuckaleechee Cove in 1856. "Montvale Springs is one of the great watering places of the South. It is a vast wooden house with accommodations for three or four hundred boarders. Many families from Georgia, Alabama, and Louisiana spend some time in summer and drink the sulphurous waters." He later wrote his sister Mary that most of the 250 guests were from Georgia. There was a brass band and dancing every night. He added that he had never seen such gorgeous dressing in America nor any other place.[44]

In 1857, Sterling Lanier was postmaster and hotel manager. Lanier had come to Tennessee from Georgia the previous October to join his brother Sampson in operating a hotel in Knoxville, the Lamar House. In December or January, Sterling and his son-in-law, Abram P. Watt, undertook the management of Montvale Springs.

---

[42] *Deeds*, W, 76; *Knoxville Whig*, August 27, 1853.
[43] *Whig*, July 17, 1858; *Knoxville Register*, May 13, 1858.
[44] William Dillon, *Life of John Mitchell*, (London, 1888). V. 2, p. 76 (1856); *Knoxville Register*, May 24, 1855.

In February 1860, Abram P. Watt, Sterling Lanier, Sidney and William B. Lanier (sons of Sterling) incorporated themselves into Montvale Company, and September 29, 1860, bought the Montvale Springs Property from Asa and Tennessee Watson of Monroe County, Mississippi for $25,674. (The deed is to Watt and Lanier.)

The elder Laniers spent the next three years at Montvale while the sons alternated between Montvale and Montgomery, Alabama, where the firm owned another hotel. They had intended this for a permanent location until the War between the States changed their minds. Young Sidney Lanier had roamed the paths and rested in the pleasant shade of the forest trees while absorbing the inspiring scenes of the rustic beauty which he afterward wove into his poetry. The setting of the novel "Tiger Lilies" is undoubtedly at Montvale.

When Tennessee did not immediately secede and East Tennessee became the scene of guerrila warfare, Lanier, due to his age, lost his taste for mountain seclusion and began to make arrangements to go to Alabama where his sons and son-in-law had already gone.

In March 1863, Lanier and Watt sold their property to Joseph L. King of Knoxville for $40,000. Sterling Lanier signed the deed for the company and shook the dust of East Tennessee from his feet forever.

The ante-bellum Montvale enjoyed a hey-day never equalled after; Watson and Lanier advertised widely at a period when people had leisure and the yen for resort society and the great and near-great

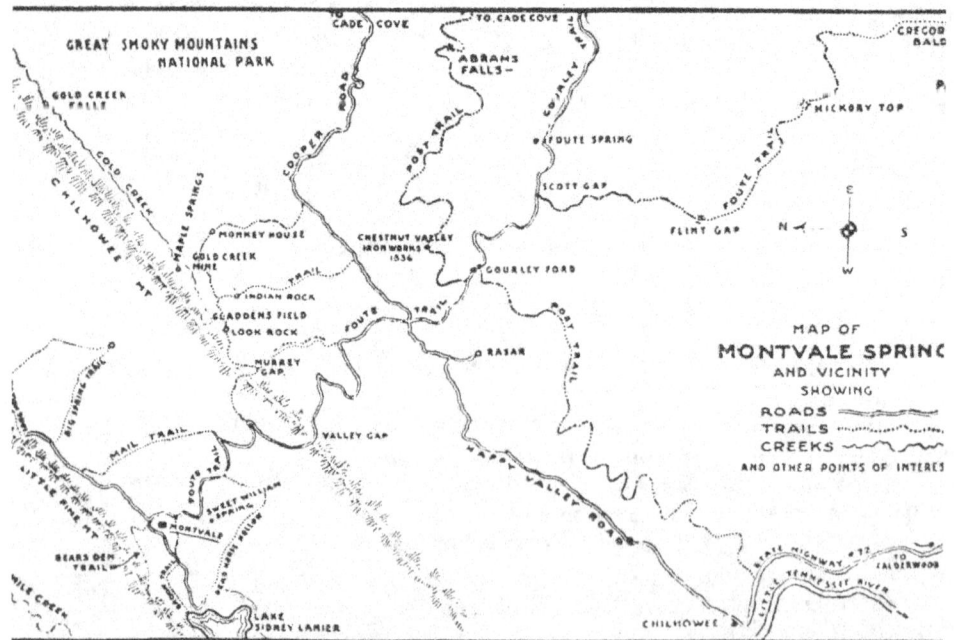

flocked to Montvale. This was due of course to the newly opened East Tennessee and Georgia Railroad. Such guests as Parson Brownlow were close enough to make an overnight trip to check on their business affairs if need be. The "Parson" became a self-appointed press agent always comparing any other resort he visited to Montvale's advantage. Brownlow said that Montvale was the fairest place he knew of on the green earth.[45]

Arnold Guyot, the Swiss geologist, was a guest at Montvale in 1859. Clingman's Dome was named for a relative of the Laniers, Thomas Lanier Clingman of North Carolina. Joseph LeConte for whom Mount LeConte was named was a friend of the Lanier family.[46]

All was not frivolity however, because about this time Bishop Otey of the Episcopal Church in his Journal tells about spending a night at Montvale on his way from Maryville to Mr. James' at Chilhowee and says that he preached to the guests.[47]

After the close of the war, a new postmaster, John C. Flanders, was appointed in June 1866. In 1868, King and two associates incorporated their business under the same title that the Laniers had used. During this year the Knoxville and Charleston Railroad laid a line to Maryville. Montvale Station was later at Carpenter's Campground, but the railroad was not extended to this point until 1907. The proprietors had provided a billiard hall, a shooting gallery, a separate ballroom, a ten-pin alley, a bar and croquet grounds, and business boomed for a while until the reaction to the war years wore off.[48]

Joseph L. King had executed a trust deed to Spencer Munson of Knoxville in favor of David Engel of Baltimore and the property eventually went to Engel. At Engel's death, the executors sold the property to Charles S. King of Blount County in 1875. In 1878 three hundred guests were reported at the hotel about equally divided between cabins and the hotel.[49]

In 1879 James Anderson, a native of Carter County, leased Montvale expecting to make money, but his letter to Jordan C. Hardin of Johnson City, Tennessee, in August 1879 said: "The yellow fever epidemic in Memphis just about ruined this summer's business . . . our Georgia and Alabama guests are afraid of exposure." The letterhead reads:

---

[45] *Maryville Times*, June 6, 1895; April 16, 1898; July 22, 1898.

[46] Nathalia Wright, *Montvale* in East Tennessee Historical Publications No. 19 (1947), p 56ff.

[47] *Deeds*, 49, p. 314; *Maryville Times*, May 20, 1899; June 9, 1900; August 9, 1900; June 9, 1905.

[48] John C. Flanders was listed as manager of Lea Springs Hotel in 1868 (*Whig*, August 8, 1868), In 1871, he was at Lamar House in Knoxville; *Tri-Weekly Whig*, May 8, 1868; *Daily Chronicle*, June 23, 1871.

[49] *Deeds*, B B, 796 (has a detailed inventory of furnishings; 100 beds, 12 large dining tables, 12 dozen sets of table silver, 175 water pitchers, 60 spittoons, 3 billiard tables, 4 parlor sofas, 15 parlor chairs, are a few of the items listed; *Ibid.*, F F, 575, (has David Engel's will attached); *Maryville Times*, July 24, 1878.

Montvale Springs Hotel

"Montvale Springs, Blount County, East Tennessee, Wilson and Anderson, Proprietors, J. E. Black, of Memphis, resident physician." [50]

Daniel F. Goodhue, Robert N. Hood, and Franklin G. Martindale were all appointed postmasters within six months in 1881 when the post office was re-instated. (The first two are named in the charter for the Montvale Turnpike Company.)

Joseph P. Lawrence may have managed the hotel when he was postmaster in 1886 because he later was manager of Montvale and also Alleghany Springs, a nearby resort hotel. A local news item stated that they had 150 guests and more coming.

The property reverted to J. C. Engel, who acted as postmaster and proprietor. Engel advertised special rates for families and servants. He stated in 1888 that they could accommodate 500 guests in the elegantly furnished hotel. Engel sold the property in June, 1889, to D. H. Sims and James Birks who failed to meet their payments. When it was sold at auction in August 1893, Frederick Bonner of New York was the highest bidder.[51]

In 1893 James Stephenson and company were proprietors. They advertised cabins for rent and stated that McKenzie's hack was furnishing transportation. May 13, 1896, the hotel burned and the property was finally sold through Chancery Court to Andrew Gamble, November 21, 1899.[52]

Some sort of accommodations were evidently furnished in 1898 because D. B. Baldwin ran a regular ad throughout the regular season stating that Dr. Gothard of Virtue, and Dr. Brock of Unitia were at Montvale for the season and that boarders were taken for $3.50 per week. They also spoke of trips to "Sweet William," the Iron Spring, and to "Look Rock." [53]

In 1901 Gamble built a smaller hotel a little further away from the springs. The hotel was in charge of Will and Joseph Lawrence. Guests from twelve states were reported.

In 1904 the property passed from Gamble to Thomas F. Cooper, who had formerly owned an interest in the property but had sold it on account of poor health. He planned to enlarge facilities because the place was usually crowded. The second week in June 1904, seventy-two guests were registered at Montvale; forty of these were campers. In May the proprietor had advertised as being able to take care of 125 guests and that Mr. and Mrs. W. A. Lane would assist.[54]

In 1911 Cooper sold the property to Ludwig Pflanze who was the

---

[50] Mary H. McCown Collection, Johnson City, Tennessee. Photostat in author's collection.
[51] *Maryville Times*, August 2, 1886; May 29, 1889; *Deeds*, 41, p. 484; 45, p. 528.
[52] *Maryville Times*, July 19, 1893 (meals were fifty cents); *Deeds*, 52, p. 185.
[53] *Maryville Times*, May 7, 1898; August 6, 1898.
[54] *Ibid.*, August 9, 1902; January 25, 1902; May 24, 1904; June 17, 1904; *Maryville Record*, May 20, 1904.

last to operate a hotel at Montvale. Mr. Pflanze built a dam and formed a lake on the property which covered the "lower" road to Montvale and left only one entrance to the property. He gave the name Lake Sidney Lanier to this small body of water. The walk around this lake became popular, along with the longer walk to Look Rock for the hardier folks and the shorter walk to the "Sweet William Spring."

On November 21, 1933 this famous old hotel burned. The day of the watering-place had long since passed into the "lavender and old lace" category and the Montvale tract since 1949 is the setting for a boys' camp and great minds are still laying big plans on the lawns at Montvale. The forests have been mutilated and have lost their pristine beauty and the glory has departed from the lovely lawns. However, anyone who has the capacity to daydream can still recapture some of the lost grandeur of a day which has long since departed.[55]

MOUNT NEBO SPRINGS HOTEL

According to the story as read from the deeds, the Mount Nebo tract was granted by the State of Tennessee in 1826 to Abijah Conger (who planted the Clover Hill) and James Williams. The tract was deeded by Conger to D. D. Foute by his agent in 1848 and called the Yellow Springs Place. Foute in 1856 sold the Yellow Spring tract to William C. Gillespy who mortgaged the property in 1865. How the property changed hands next is not known, but some sort of transfer was evidently made.

October 26, 1876, a charter was issued to Alexander Kennedy, R. I. Wilson, R. F. Chandler, J. M. Greer, W. W. Lawrence and R. N. Hood to be known as Mount Nebo Springs Company. They were to erect, furnish and keep a hotel for the entertainment of guests and invalids near a mineral spring known as Mount Nebo in the 14th district, "formerly known as the Walker Spring and entered by Abijah Conger and James Williams in the entry taker's office of Blount County."[56]

Kennedy built the hotel and a handbill announced the opening of Mount Nebo Springs June 20, 1877 as a watering-place. Board was $27.00 per month. A. Kennedy, Sr. was proprietor for several years. Then the property was sold to David Jones. John and Susan Miller came from Illinois and operated the hotel. The building contained about sixteen rooms. The Millers built an extension of eight rooms. There were at least six cottages about the grounds. A large croquet court, croquinole and cards furnished recreation by day and the dance pavilion by night. There were generally two dances each week. Dick and Charley Lane "made music" for the dances. The Millers built and operated Melrose Springs hotel after they left Mount Nebo.[57]

[55] Deeds, 72, p. 142.
[56] Blount County Entry Taker's Book, #240, November 6, 1826; Deeds, V, 78; Y, 355; A A, 1; 564; F F, 368.
[57] Information from the various members of the Miller family, Walland, Tennessee. Handbill in the Kennedy (C. M.) Collection. Photostat in author's collection.

In 1887 David and Mary J. Jones sold the property to Mrs. Mary A. Wilson of Knox County (Husband, Abner A. Wilson). The property is described as 200 acres on the north side of Chilhowee Mountain one mile west of Little River, known as Mt. Nebo Springs, formerly Gillespy Mineral Springs. The deal included all furniture in, and belonging to the hotel.

Mrs. Wilson operated the hotel on a large scale. At this period people flocked to resorts for the summer from the coastal towns where epidemics of yellow fever and cholera were general. Many local families and their "city cousins" made it an annual custom to spend their summers together at "the springs," especially the McTeer connections. Mrs. Wilson operated the boarding club at Maryville College during the school year and Mt. Nebo during the summer. Mrs. Wilson sponsored a Sunday school for the local children at the hotel. Later Monroe Harding organized a Sunday school at Rocky Branch School. Rev. Isaac Emory, a Presbyterian Sunday school missionary, gave the bell which was used by the Sunday school and the day school. Will Everett drove the hack from Maryville with guests who came on the train. Someone always watched with the "spy glass" to see how many guests to set the table for. Sam Williams drove the hack from Maryville part of the time. Mrs. Wilson's husband and son Clem died before she did and she left the property to the Foreign Mission Board of the Presbyterian Church.[58]

Will A. McTeer acting for the board of Foreign Missions of the Presbyterian Church, in 1908 sold the property to J. W. Fisher and wife of Cocke County, Tennessee.

The Fishers in 1912 sold the property to Sue S. Calloway of Knox County, Tennessee. Miss Calloway sold building lots to J. Pike Powers and Mrs. Martha G. Guilford, and cottages sprung up along the road to the hotel. The addition built by the Millers in 1877 was torn down, the main building remodeled and water was installed. Old-timers remember that she once served a banquet to a group of 65 persons from the University of Tennessee in great style. When Miss Calloway took over, Bill White drove the hack for guests, to and from the station.

Miss Calloway transferred the property to S. H. Ogle in January, 1925. The Ogles sold to Fannie C. Carson of Knox County; F. A. Elmore of Blount; and R. W. Cox of Fulton County, Georgia, in 1937.[59] Since that time the hotel was open during one season. Such resorts are not as popular as they once were and the hotel is used only by these families now. However, Mount Nebo Hotel enjoys the unique distinction of being the only old resort hotel standing in Blount County today.

---

[58] *Deeds*, M M, 274; the ad featured: 2500 feet above sea level—iron water—telephone and daily mail, *Maryville Times*, June 21, 1902. Interviews with several different families who lived in the community and worked at the hotel; *Deeds*, 63, p. 416.

[59] *Deeds*, 73, p. 42; 97, p. 183; 119, p. 111.

ALLEGHANY SPRINGS HOTEL

In 1837, a 186-acre tract of mountain land was granted to William Gault and Jable Park in the 17th district extending along the Chilhowee Mountains. In 1850 Gault sold the tract to Hugh O. Taylor and Israel Woolsey of Greene County. Taylor, in 1851, sold his interest to Woolsey, who in turn sold the property to William M. Neal in 1854. In 1858, C. B. Neal, W. W. Neal, William L. Eakin, Esq., John Minnis and others were granted a charter as the Yellow Springs Company to erect at the Yellow Springs a public hotel and such other buildings and improvements as necessary to promote the property and usefulness of the springs as a watering-place and a summer resort. For some reason this project did not get under way and Neal made a deed to Jesse Kerr, Jr., in 1859. In the following year, whether before or after the sale of the property, it is not known, a group of men obtained a charter for a road. Daniel P. Carmichael, C. W. Norwood and their associates were chartered as the Yellow Springs and Montvale Springs Turnpike Company, to begin near Yellow Springs, and go to the top of the Chilhowee Mountain to join Foute's road to Montvale Springs. These also were ambitious plans which never materialized. Each transaction of the above named tract stated that it included the "Chilhowee Medical Spring" and the "Yellow Sulphur Spring." The last named transaction stated that the tract was unencumbered except by a camp or cabin built and occupied by Mistress Mary K. McGhee. Neal signed the deed in Giles County, Virginia.[60]

Kerr built a hotel of some sort at the Yellow Sulphur Spring which was more readily accessible than the Chilhowee Medical Spring. In 1861, the Yellow Sulphur post office was established and it is thought that guests were in the house when it was fired by slaves late in 1861. The post office was re-established in 1866 and it is thought that Kerr may have continued some sort of resort accommodations. It is not known if the property was a total loss or not. The idea that it was not, is supported by the fact that he made a trust deed to Hiram Walker stating in 1866, in the deed, that he did so in order to have time to repair his "springs" property. G. C. Kerr sold the tract to Nathan McCoy in 1885 and the Yellow Sulphur post office was replaced by Alleghany Springs in 1886.[61]

Nathan McCoy was a Civil War veteran from Camden, Jay County, Indiana, who came to Blount County and purchased several tracts of mountain land and by dint of much hard labor, hollowed a flat out on the mountainside above the Yellow Sulphur Spring, and built a pretentious three-story, sixty-room resort hotel at a cost of more than $50,000.

---

[60] *Deeds*, W, 151; Y, 51; Y, 59; Z, p. 439; *Acts, 1857–58*, 71; *Acts, 1859–60*; ch. 89, Sec. 25; (Mrs. Mary K. McGhee was the mother of Mrs. Charles Jones, Sr. and Mrs. Josh R. Jones, of Monroe County, Tennessee).

[61] Any Post Office information used is from Photostats of early records from National Archives, Washington, D. C.; *Deeds*, A A, 593; M M, 24.

June 1, 1886, Alleghany Springs Hotel opened for business. As was the custom of that period, a lookout tower and flagpole topped the building. There were accommodations for three to four hundred guests. Gas lights and electric call-bells gave a touch of luxury. There was water on each floor and the bathhouse afforded hot and cold baths.[62]

Provisions were made for croquet, tennis, bowling, dancing, fishing, boating and driving. A wide two-story veranda extended the full length of the building and furnished a lovely panorama of the countryside for the rocking chair brigade and card players. Daily mail connections were provided, which also furnished a passenger service to Maryville. Medical services were furnished by a resident physician as was common in resort hotels. Rates were listed first as two dollars per day and later as $5.00 a week. A. A. Shoaff was manager during the first season and Nathan McCoy, proprietor. Shoaff was the first postmaster of Alleghany Springs Post Office. James F. McCoy (brother of Nathan) followed Shoaff in 1887; Joseph C. Greer in 1889; Charles C. Smith in 1890; and Nathan McCoy in 1892.

The parlor was on the second floor and was luxuriously furnished in golden brown plush upholstered love-seats, divans and chairs, and a rosewood piano. Crystal chandeliers reflected rainbow colors over the Brussels carpets and rich brocade drapes. Marble-top dressers, washstands and tables of walnut were used throughout the hotel. The sumptuous Bridal Chamber was furnished in cherry. In fact everything about the hotel's appointments was of the very best for that day. The ballroom in the basement would accommodate a hundred dancers at once and had comfortable accommodations for orchestra and spectators.

In the office was a large safe that old-timers remember which required seven yokes of oxen to haul it up the mountainside. It was used in off-seasons to store valuables, which among others, included several dozen sets of table silver, a large silver pitcher and dozens of silver goblets as well as other large service pieces.[63]

The guests had their choice of iron, sulphur, or freestone water. The Yellow Sulphur Spring was around the mountain from the hotel. The Chilhowee Medical (arsenic) Spring was in the ravine to the left below the hotel and was called the "Eye," or the "Beauty Spring," and a small sulphur spring was at the foot of the steps to the hotel. Freestone water was piped from the mountainside above the hotel.

A news item stated that Jones Brothers Orchestra (composed of Charles Sr., and sons, Ole Bull, and Moultrie Jones) had been engaged to furnish music for the dances. They continued to play for the dances

---

[62] McCoy had some sort of partnership with J. C. Greer. At least one tract was bought by them (*Deeds*, J J, p. 56) Photostats of Hotel Register, 1888, said McCoy and Greer; *Maryville Times*, August 2, 1886, (full page ad with picture).

[63] The safe is still lying at the hotel site. Description and information by Mrs. Diva Jones Moroney, whose grandmother, Mrs. Mary K. McGhee was named above and Bob Hannah who was a later manager.

for ten or fifteen years. They were specifically mentioned again in a news item in 1898.

When Alleghany Springs Hotel was opened, R. L. Belt and Josh R. Jones operated a store, or commissary at the Springs. The store and bathhouse were between the hotel and the Yellow Sulphur Springs. There were three cabin units there and another group of three double-cabins and a couple of singles near the Yellow Sulphur Spring.

Business was good, and all went well for a few years, but the investment was too heavy and the appointments of the hostelry too luxurious for the isolated setting. In 1895, we find the property in the hands of a receiver pending sale in Chancery Court. The Bank of Maryville took the property over and owned it for a short while.

Alleghany Springs Hotel enjoyed a wide popularity under various managers as long as watering-places were the style. The cream of Knoxville society were regular patrons as well as many from afar. Alleghany Station (Greenback) on the L. & N. Railroad was established for the convenience of hotel guests coming by train. The cabins were reported full in 1898 under the managership of Dr. J. L. Kerr.[64]

John T. Hanlin and wife, of Jay County, Indiana, bought and operated the hotel in 1899. Mr. and Mrs. J. P. Lawrence advertised as managers in 1900; "along with the same old rates and plentiful fare," and again in 1904. John Van Kirk of Indiana was manager in 1905.[65]

McCoy had planted two fine vineyards nearby and after he lost the hotel property and returned to Indiana, he came back after a few years and bought another tract and became well known for his excellent wines until revenue men objected.[66]

Hanlin did not find business too profitable, it seems, because he soon mortgaged the property. The Mortgagee transferred the property to Dr. James H. Martin who turned the property over to Mrs. Lydia E. Hanlin in 1907.[67]

In 1910, Ben Young was manager. In 1911 and 1912, J. R. Hannah operated the hotel, followed by Miss Lena Henley in 1913. In 1914 and 1915, Luther A. Williams of Knoxville was in charge. This was the last season that the hotel was officially opened for guests.

The hotel burned December 6, 1932, and in 1933 the County Clerk of Knox County, transferred the property to Dr. Joe E. Hall of Loudon County and it is now the property of his heirs.[68]

---

[64] *Maryville Times*, June 6, 1895; April 16, 1898; July 22, 1898.
[65] John T. Hanlin's and the Nathan McCoy's biographies, in an undated *Gazeteer* were found in the basement of the deserted hotel and preserved. A History of Jay County, Indiana, is in the back of the book. (Courtesy of Mrs. Ova Belt Lindsay.)
[66] *Deeds*, 49, p. 314; *Maryville Times*, May 20, 1899; June 9, 1900; August 9, 1900; June 9, 1905.
[67] *Trust Deeds*, 2, p. 84; p. 463 (7/8 interest); *Deeds*, 66, p. 584; *Maryville Times*, June 22, 1906.
[68] *Deeds*, 111, p. 173. It had been proposed earlier in that year that the Blount County Medical Association buy the property.

MELROSE SPRINGS

John H. Morton, in 1884, sold to John and Susan Miller 50 acres known as the McGinley or Millsaps Spring tract; it being part of a tract entered by John Everett and Isaac White, later owned by John White. This tract is about three miles west of Mount Nebo Springs at the foot of Chilhowee Mountain.

In 1891 Susan Miller, then a widow, deeded the tract to Joe L. Miller, a son. The Millers built a 24-room hotel of the traditional resort hotel type, with a large living room and dining room.[69]

According to a family anecdote, when the hotel was ready for its opening, Mr. Miller was writing his ad for the newspaper and the hotel was as yet unnamed. His eye was attracted to a label on a shoe box on the table before him, and the hotel was thus christened "Melrose." The railroad station later took its name from the hotel.[70]

John Martin brought guests by hack from the train which came to Maryville daily. One of the favorite pastimes at Melrose was to walk up to the "Cloudland Spring," which was just under the brow of the mountain. A tall flagpole added the customary patriotic touch to the spring location which became a traditional "Lover's Nook."

Melrose was famous for its good food. (The Millers had made a name for themselves at Mt. Nebo while they were managing this resort.) Mary and Eliza Rorex (Negroes) are still remembered for the good food which they prepared at Melrose. When the Millers died, the hotel ceased to operate (before 1920). A son-in-law, Hugh Millsaps bought out the Miller heirs.[71]

The buildings were torn down about 1924 to build a small house which later burned, and there are very few signs remaining to show that such a place ever existed and even the memory is almost erased. After 1937, the land was parceled out in small tracts and lost its identity.

KINZEL SPRINGS AND SUNSHINE [72]

In 1894, E. J. Kinzel paid a visit to Tuckaleechee Cove and was so impressed by the tranquil beauty of its wooded slopes and peaceful valley that he purchased a tract from Colonel J. W. H. Tipton at the western entrance to the Cove, which included two mineral springs and a long hollow filled with a tumbling branch bordered by lush ferns and laurel on each side of the river. Here, on the south side of the river near the springs, Kinzel built a summer home.

Many of the Kinzels' friends paid protracted visits, and enjoyed the spot so much that the idea of a small resort grew. The Little River

---

[69] *Deeds*, K K, 181; 43, p. 426.
[70] Interview with Mrs. Nola Millsaps, July 1952.
[71] The hotel tract adjoined the Millsaps tanyard which was operated before the Civil War and after by James Millsaps, Sr., (signs of the dye pits are still visible.)
[72] Unless otherwise identified, information is from Miss Sophie Kinzel or personal knowledge.

Railroad had been in operation since 1902 and furnished easy access to the place.

In 1914, a 28-room hotel and 10 cottages were built by the Kinzels, which became known as Kinzel Springs and was also the name of the railroad station. In 1907 Kinzel donated a site on the north side of the river to the International Sunshine Society, for a vacation hotel for working girls. The earliest name for this hotel was "Sunshine Rest Cottage" which was later known by other names and last as Smoky Mountain Inn, when it burned in 1952.[73]

Kinzel Springs was incorporated from 1928 to 1935. The post office was established April 1925, with Bluford S. Newman, postmaster. The post office was discontinued in 1945 when the hotel ceased to operate. As is usual, a great number of land speculators rushed in and bought tracts of land and laid great plans for development. A hotel was actually begun on Mount Luke, one of the four peaks above Kinzel Springs bearing the Biblical names of Matthew, Mark, Luke and John. This project was a fantastic dream of Mr. John Dupes, Sr., of Knoxville, Tennessee. It was abandoned, partly because there was no way of getting water to the top of the mountain. The trace of the long winding road leading up to the site is still plain, as is the foundation of the building. A sizable colony of summer homes sprung up and have continued over a quarter century. Since Tuckaleechee is the "stepping off" point into the Smoky Mountains National Park, Kinzel Springs or Sunshine is likely to continue to be a semi-resort community due to its easily accessible location from large centers of population. The proximity of Laurel Lake, Tuckaleechee Caverns, and Cades Cove, (which was publicized three-quarters of a century ago as the "Switzerland of America") all tend to keep alive a semblance of resort life here.[74]

COWAN SPRINGS AND CURE-ALL SPRING [75]

A watering-place which falls into a slightly different category is Cowan Springs. Here clustered about the two springs of iron water, one large and one small, was maintained for two or three generations a small private summer resort within the family circle of Cowans and Gambles.

Cowan Springs is located at the foot of Chilhowee Mountain on the north side of Little River off the Cold Springs road. A very delightful account of a camping trip there is recorded in a newspaper of fifty some years ago.[76]

---

[73] *Deeds*, 46, p. 325; 63, p. 300. E. J. Kinzel and wife, Catherine to Mrs. Mary J. Williams, trustee of Sunshine Society and Nellie Leonard Hall, Susie Young, Fannie Newman, and Emma Ragsdale, Trustees of the Mary J. Williams Sunshine Club of Knoxville. (Post Office records from National Archives in Washington, D. C.).

[74] Dr. William Clark of Franklin, Tennessee, who accompanied General Wilder into this section when he was making a geological expedition just after the close of the Civil War, wrote a series of articles such as: "The Switzerland of America" and "Tennessee Paradise," in praise of the scenery of this section: Dr. Clark was Editor of the forerunner of the Nashville *Banner*.

[75] Information on Cowan Springs given by Mrs. Nina Gamble Murphy.

[76] *Maryville Times*, June 9, 1900. "*Ten days at Cowan's Springs.*"

There were five cabins built in the 20's and 30's when the springs were last patronized; the Mose Gambles, the Joe Gambles, the Dr. A. M. Gambles, the Gamble Sisters, and the Bob Cowans. The cabins have fallen into decay but an air of another generation hovers over the picturesque landscape, and the site almost seems haunted by the past.

The Cure-all Spring has been patronized for three generations of Kagleys, Baumgardners and Taylors. This spring is located to the left of the power line below the Morton Bluff on the side of Chilhowee Mountain between Alleghany and Montvale springs.

There were formerly two or three cabins at the spring but only the rock foundations and a tumble-down chimney remain now. This is a fine, cold mineral spring with only a hint of sulphur.

WILDWOOD SPRINGS HOTEL

Late in 1870, the Rev. Claudius B. Lord came from New York to East Tennessee and purchased the Dr. Jefferson Stone tract from the executors of the estate of Joseph Hodgson: Thomas Sanderson, and James Davis, a stonemason. The tract contained 262 acres and included a log house at the Sulphur Spring. According to Joe Waters who tore the building down in 1949, the lower part of the log house was most substantially built of 24-inch hewn logs 24 x 28 feet, laid close together as if for a fort. The upper story was built with an overhang and a good stone chimney. The two-story addition built by Dr. Stone was built of extra heavy timbers, 24 x 24, in a style not peculiar to this section (probably influenced by New England architecture). The chimney of this part of the house was brick which did not survive weathering too well and was rapidly disintegrating when razed after 102 years. The document which will be referred to later was found sealed in this chimney, when it was torn down.[77]

The Rev. Lord had also studied medicine, according to Mr. C. M. Kennedy, who told a story of falling off a two-story porch when he was quite a small child. Dr. Lord came by at the time, and stopping, made a cast of clay for the shoulder. Mr. Kennedy said that Lord was a small, thin, gray-haired man who wore "good clothing" and always drove a two-horse buckboard. (The 1887 *Gazette* lists his son Claude Lord as a "painter.")

Caroline Lord (Mrs. Follette) is said to have given the name "Wildwood" to the estate. This period was an era of "watering-places" and about 1886 an annex was built onto the original log and frame building and paying guests were received. "Uncle Johnny" Walker and his sons, Bob and Tom, were in charge of the hotel during the first years. The log cottage on the grounds was probably built prior to this date. Three other cottages were later built. One section of the hotel ran west toward the spring and the main section containing twelve or thirteen rooms ran south from the old kitchen wing.[78]

---

[77] *Deeds*, F F, 160 (January 5, 1871).
[78] Mrs. Otis Waters. Also Mr. C. M. Kennedy. A mortgage described the hotel in 1902 as a large frame and log hotel building (*Trusts*, 8, p. 89).

The Rev. Lord had daughters: Caroline (Mrs. Follette), Helen M. (Nellie), Anna M. (who had a photographic gallery on the grounds first, and later in Maryville), and Mary T.; and sons John and Claude. John had daughters Henrietta and Cecilia who were very popular young ladies. In 1902, when the Rev. Lord disposed of his property, only Helen, Carrie, and Claude are named.[79]

From 1891 to 1902 the hotel is variously advertised as: "Lithia Springs"; "Wildwood Sulphur Springs," and "Wildwood Mineral Springs"; under the managership of Mr. and Mrs. W. P. (Pete) Barnhill. During this period Mr. Barnhill's parents, Mr. and Mrs. Bond lived in the log cottage and Mrs. Barnhill ("Aunt Jennie") was primary teacher at Porter Academy part of this time. The hotel afforded dormitory accommodations for students and teachers who wished to board themselves during the "off-season."

Newspaper ads for this ten-year period describe the resort as 12½ miles from Knoxville and seven miles from Maryville with hack connections from both places on Mondays, Wednesdays, and Saturdays, and "subject to order." Board was $1 per day.

In 1902, sixty guests were mentioned as being present at the Hotel and Dr. and Miss Lord were named as the well-beloved hosts.[80]

A news item of 1904 said Dr. J. G. Harrill had leased the hotel for five years.[81]

Wildwood continued to enjoy popularity under various managers until 1912, although from all reports, there was considerable decline after the Barnhills left. The Haggard family took over the management in 1912 and continued until 1925. The average number of guests during the season was twenty-five during the week and fifty for the weekends. Automobiles had become fairly common by this time and had begun to make a big difference in "resort trade."[82]

The A. O. Goddards were there in 1925 which was the last season that Wildwood was open as a resort.[83]

At various times Dr. Lord had sold thirty-five acres of the original tract, but he still held 228 acres when he deeded the property to Helen M. Lord, Carrie Lord Follette and Claude Lord in 1902. Claude Lord sold his interest to Charles D. Blair, who soon transferred his share to Miss Lord and Mrs. Follette.

In 1927 Lord and Follette sold the hotel property to W. M. and Mae R. Condry, including all furniture and equipment (with some exceptions). In a short while the Condrys sold the property to W. W. Mullendore and wife Cora S. They formed a partnership early in 1931 with

---

[79] *Deeds*, F F, 160 (January 5, 1871). Dr. Stone had in 1854 given 18 acres to Logan's Chapel church from this tract; *Deeds*, F F, 336, registered 1876. Will of Joseph Hodgson (1867); *Deeds*, 57, p. 478.
[80] *Maryville Times*, 1891–1902, Passim.
[81] *Maryville Record*, June 3, 1904.
[82] Letter from Miss Una Haggard, Knoxville, Tennessee, June 29, 1953.
[83] Miss Gladys Goddard.

John P. Blankenship and Cyrus Cullen to subdivide the tract and dispose of the property. In June 1931, the tract containing the springs and hotel buildings were bought by Albert Hill.[84]

Mr. Hill died in 1936 (October) and in the settlement of the estate Owen Hill was given title to the property. Hill sold the property to P. A. Waters and he sold the tract in 1941 to J. D. and Carl Waters.

When the old log and timber hotel was torn down in 1949 the following document was found sealed in a bottle and built into the chimney:

Jefferson Stone was born in Litchfield County, Connecticut, December the 5th, 1806. Moved to Tennessee, March, 1839. Bought this farm 1845. Built this chimney 1847. Was a graduate of Yale College 1827. Practiced medicine in Washington, New Preston Society, Ct. 10 years. In Knoxville, Tennessee, 5 years. My first wif was daughter of Col. Wm. Belden. Henrietta brought me tow sons, Charles and Frank. My seckond wif, Sophronia White, I married in Blount County. Have two children Olivia, and Henrietta. November 3rd, 1847. Jefferson Stone.

This chimney was built by Wm. Davis & son James.

(signed)
Wm. Davis, Mason
James D.
November the 4th 1847[85]

OTHER INNS

Perhaps we should not completely ignore the inns necessitated by the introduction of industry into Blount County. Townsend Inn was operated under the sponsorship of Little River Lumber Company and patronized largely by teachers and traveling salesmen. It had served its purpose by the time the lumbering operations ceased in 1938 and closed soon after.

Chilhowee Inn, built and put into operation by Schlosser Leather Company had always enjoyed a reputation for fine foods and has continued to be a popular eating place since commercial operations closed at Walland in 1931. The property passed to private ownership soon after.

Babcock Lumber Company had its "Club House" in Alcoa which has long since been forgotten.

The "Club House" at Calderwood continues operation for the benefit of the employes who do not maintain homes at Calderwood.

---

[84] *Deeds*, 57, p. 478; 66, p. 96; 67, p. 203; 100, p. 102; 104, p. 304; *Contracts* 4, p. 63; *Deeds*, 109, p. 390.

[85] *Deeds*, 121, p. 197; 125, p. 387; 129, p. 98; Document found by and in the hands of Joe D. Waters, July, 1953.

CHAPTER VI

The Churches of Blount County

The first consideration of the Pioneer was, of necessity, to establish a home in the wilderness and to provide for the physical needs of his family. Immediately after the physical needs were satisfied, he built a church to take care of his spiritual needs. The Scotch-Irish who made up the main strength of the first settlements in Blount County came from the old established Presbyterian communities in Virginia and brought a strong regard for the church with them. Therefore it follows as a matter of course that within a year after the first communities were settled (1786), we find two Presbyterian churches established in what is now Blount County. Ramsey described the Rev. Samuel Carrick as being bound for Houston's Station beyond Little River when he first preached at "Lebanon in the Forks" in the fall of 1790.[1]

The Methodists were here in strength in 1792. William Burke tells of having appointments at that time but Methodist records are not very generous of local details and nothing tangible is extant on their activities before 1810. However, there seems to have been two strong congregations: Middlesettlements and Little River.[2]

The Baptists mark their beginning with the establishment of Tuckaleechee church in 1802.

These three denominations seem to have held the field until near mid-century when schisms, divisions and separations gave birth to new churches and a growing population introduced other denominations.

THE PRESBYTERIAN CHURCH U.S.A.

It is recorded that the Rev. Charles Cummings and Rev. Joseph Rhea, who accompanied Col. William Christian's men when they made their expedition against the Cherokees in 1776, had already organized two churches by 1772 in upper East Tennessee. Ten years later, in the late summer of 1786, the Rev. Archibald Scott from Augusta County, Virginia, made a visit to the Tennessee Country, south of the French Broad and here in the wilderness among his former neighbors, in their new homes, he organized two congregations: Eusebia, near McTeer's Fort and New Providence, near Craig's Fort.[3]

Eusebia ("Reverence toward God") was located at the camping ground near the War Path used by the first travelers in passing through the wilderness. It was a clearing underneath a wide-spreading beech tree near a large spring just over the Boyd's Creek-Ellejoy divide. Ac-

---

[1] Dr. J. G. M. Ramsey, *History of Lebanon Presbyterian Church*, (1875).
[2] McFerrin, John B., *History of Methodism in Tenn.*, (1888), v. 1, 1783–1804, p. 91. Hereinafter cited *McFerrin*.
[3] Ramsey, *Annals*, 159, 169.

cording to tradition, a woman of one of the early emigrant parties died and was buried here in a rude coffin made from wagon boards. We know from records and a tombstone inscription that Joseph Bogle was buried here in 1790. From this we know that there were at least two burials by 1790 and it was natural that this spot should be chosen for the Eusebia Presbyterian Church site.

It is not known when the first building was erected, but probably not until there were prospects of a regular pastor. It is thought that Eusebia Church was probably built before New Providence but the camp site east of the church site was probably used before a church was built. From description it seems to have been a more elaborate campground than any other in the county. In 1792, Gideon Blackburn marched with a company of militia from Jefferson County to Fort Craig and stayed to build a church. He was duly installed as pastor of Eusebia and New Providence churches in 1794. The church represented 40 families in 1797 and was judged able to pay a pastor $130.00 per year. The Rev. Blackburn served as pastor until 1810. The first church building of logs may have served as a school too, for a while. Later the schoolhouse was a separate building near the church, but most certainly under the supervision of the church. In 1810, a larger building was necessary and an addition was built to the old log building. A little later a large frame building with two aisles from front to back and a cross-aisle in the center from side doors was built. The pulpit was about four feet high with steps from each side guarded by elaborate railings.[4]

This building was used until 1874, when a small brick house was built. The latter was replaced in 1930 by the present building. The records of Eusebia begin with a roll of members, as of October 1822. Names appearing include: Bogle, Creswell, McCroskey, McCallie, McMurry, Malcom, Sims, Boyd, Kirkpatrick, Shadden, and Dunlap. The first elders were: William Malcom, David Ashmon, John Simms, James Upton, and James Dunlap.[5]

Eusebia was without a regular pastor from 1810 until April 1824 when Dr. Alexander McGhee, who is described in Union Presbytery records as a converted atheist, was ordained and installed as pastor and served until 1827. The Rev. Fielding Pope served from 1838 to 1856; the Rev. John M. Alexander served from 1894–1909; the Rev. E. W. Hall from 1910–1937. Other pastors served only one or two years and were mostly from the then current Maryville College faculty.[6]

The church roll of Eusebia today will show many of the same family names as the first roll and has consistently carried them through the years more faithfully than any other church in this locality.

New Providence took its name from the Houstons' church in Virginia. A goodly number of Houstons and their relations should have

---

[4] Will A. McTeer, *Eusebia Church History*. 1924 (a pamphlet); *Report of Presbytery of Abingdon to General Assembly*, March 1797.
[5] Eusebia, *Session Bk. 2, 1822–1858*. In church vault, copy in author's collection.
[6] *Union Presbytery Minutes*, (In Maryville College vault).

been among the charter members. The Rev. Sam Houston, the first Presbyterian minister to be ordained on Tennessee soil, was active in the organization of the State of Franklin, and later served as a justice of the peace in Blount County when it was organized. He was probably instrumental in the organization of these first churches. January 1, 1799, he resigned as justice and returned to Virginia.[7]

The Rev. Gideon Blackburn was the first pastor of New Providence and Eusebia churches. Traveling under the protection of a company of militia from Jefferson County, Blackburn arrived at Fort Craig in 1792 with his rifle and Bible. He built a cabin for himself and a log church to house New Providence congregation. Blackburn was duly installed as pastor of the two congregations in 1794. He served both churches until 1810, often conducting joint meetings at a common campground on an island in Little River near Brabson's Ford.[8]

The Rev. J. J. Robinson in his *Memoir of Dr. Anderson* says that the charter membership of New Providence was eighteen. Robert McNutt, Arthur Beatty, John Hannah, and William Hannah were elders. Joseph Hart was the first clerk of the session. The membership in 1811 was 217 according to Joseph Hart, who didn't keep full records until 1840.

The 1797 report to General Assembly says New Providence congregation had 60 families and was able to pay $170.00 per year. Gideon Blackburn became, in 1802, the first missionary from General Assembly to the Cherokees and established schools at Hiwassee and Sale Creek. He resigned as pastor of New Providence and Eusebia churches in 1810.

Isaac Anderson was installed as pastor in 1812 and served until his death, in 1857. Although he was never the organizer and builder that Blackburn was, the church continued to grow. The log church was replaced in 1829 by a fine stone building with galleries on three sides. It was small and on special occasions it was necessary to use the campground, which was at the corner of Harper and Aluminum avenues.[9]

No specific description has been preserved of this campground such as we have of Eusebia and others, but Parson Brownlow and others relate incidents while attending meetings there.[10]

The membership of New Providence grew steadily until the 1840's when records show more than six hundred members. Soon after, with-

---

[7] *Hanover Presbytery Minutes* August 20, 1783 at Providence on Nolachucky. (Abstract of minutes in author's collection); *Journals of Senate and House of 2nd General Assembly of the State of Tenn.* (Kingsport, 1933).

[8] Rev. J. E. Alexander *Brief History of the Synod of Tennessee 1817–1877* (Phila. 1888); *Report of Presbytery of Abingdon to General Assembly* 1797; *Union Presbytery Minutes* 1799–1810 Passim.

[9] McTeer, Will A., *History of New Providence Presbyterian Church* (1921) 23, 28. Hereinafter cited *McTeer*.

[10] Wm. G. Brownlow, *Helps to the Study of Presbyterianism*. (Knoxville, 1834) 247, (1827). "My appointment in Maryville happened on the Sabbath of the Hopkinsian Sacrament held at their campground near the village; and as I had previously arranged my appointments to be in the after part of the day, I attended and heard them preach two or three sermons." He speaks of "an inflated little priest by the name of Minnes who talked pretty much through his nose"; and also relates of rising during the sermon to make a remark about something the minister said.

out any explanations, the record simply and tersely states "after the purge—three hundred members." About this time there were unsuccessful attempts to organize Mt. Vernon and Louisville churches. Doctrinal and political dissensions were rife at this period also, and perhaps these three reasons would explain the serious drop in membership. However, the session record is silent on any explanation of the drop in membership.[11]

The stone church was torn down in 1852 and the stones are still to be seen around the old church cemetery site at Cates and Broadway where the first three church buildings stood.

The third building was brick. The materials and construction were poor and the congregation was never satisfied with it. The War Between the States found it unfinished and the soldiers who occupied the town for a time left it in bad condition. The struggle to make it fit for use during the "straitened years" of the Reconstruction Period was accomplished with the help of the National Board.

In 1882, agitation was begun to build a new church. In 1890 the contract was let for a new church to be built on the old seminary—or college lot down-town at College and Broadway, formerly Main. The old building, known as Columbian Hall was used as a community gathering place until 1911 when it was removed.[12]

After the death of Dr. Anderson, Dr. Fielding Pope acted as pastor until 1865. All ministers who were not loyal to the Union were disqualified by presbytery and only four ministers were left in Union Presbytery in 1864: the Reverends William Harrison, Ralph E. Tedford, T. J. Lamar and W. A. Smith. From 1865 to the turn of the century various supply pastors, mostly Maryville College professors, served from one to four year terms. Since that time William F. Graham, William H. Crothers, John A. McAfee and Thomas E. Graham have served longer periods.[13]

In 1913 a Sunday school annex was built to the church which sufficed until the new Gothic structure of native stone on West Broadway was occupied early in 1953.

In 1796 the Tennessee Congregation was established, composed of Baker's Creek and Gallaher's Creek. These two congregations had 65 families and were able to pay $200.00 (which was larger by five families than New Providence). This charge was not settled until 1806 although Presbytery Minutes record several calls to various ministers.[14]

The Baker's Creek church was built on Samuel Henry's land. No deed was registered by Henry but his grant from the State of Tennessee included "the church lot." In 1821, a deed was recorded from Wil-

---

[11] *Union Presbytery Minutes;* The old and new school division took place in 1838.
[12] *McTeer,* 68. Called Columbian Hall because it ceased to be a church the year of the Columbian Exposition (New Providence Session Records).
[13] An unsigned manuscript giving history of Union Presbytery 1863–1874. In Maryville College vault; also Union Presbytery *Minutes.*
[14] *General Assembly Minutes,* 1797. (Report of Presbytery of Abingdon.)

liam McClung to the church at Baker's Creek for 4½ acres described as joining Samuel Henry. Trustees named were: Robert Thompson, James Houston and Samuel Montgomery.[15]

May 17th, 1806, Mr. Joseph R. Lapsley was ordained at Baker's Creek and became their first regularly installed pastor. The Rev. Lapsley served until 1810.[16] It is not stated what became of the Gallaher's Creek part of this congregation. However, since the Big Spring is the headwaters of Gallaher's Creek and a minister was settled for the Seceder Church, "Big Springs," in 1824, it is probable that at least a part of the congregation was absorbed by Big Springs.

When the division came in the Presbyterian churches of Union Presbytery in 1838, Baker's Creek was the only local church which went with the Old School group. Reunion took place in 1870. During the forties New Providence session records show that several members came from Baker's Creek congregation because they did not hold with the Old School beliefs.

There is a story told of the Rev. Daniel Baker who held a revival at Baker's Creek in 1842 and consequently made open criticism of the Rev. Isaac Anderson for the use of "raisin water" instead of wine for the Lord's Supper, which controversy was a common issue at that time.[17]

The organization of Clover Hill church began in 1841 and Cloyd's Creek in 1871. The above mentioned division and also the organization of Pine Grove Cumberland Presbyterian Church affected the membership of the Baker's Creek congregation, and it is not strange to learn that in 1906 the church was in a very weak condition. Investigation showed no charter, no trustees, and no deed to the property. The church at that time occupied their building on the same site. On account of a mortgage which they could not meet, the elders made a nominal sale of the property to the Methodist church and made a bond for the deed. When this was brought before the congregation, they immediately brought the matter before presbytery. Dr. S. T. Wilson and Major Will A. McTeer represented Union Presbytery, and moderated congregational meetings which eventually cleared up all matters satisfactorily. J. L. McCall, J. A. Hair, J. O. McCammon, D. M. Johnson and John F. Henry were elected a Board of Trustees and the charter was signed.[18]

Today Baker's Creek is an active rural congregation which has just built their fourth building, a lovely new, modern brick church on this historic spot.

Unitia Church was organized by Dr. Isaac Anderson, between October 1830 and April 1831. A deed was recorded in 1840 from John Griffitts and Henry Burem for 2½ acres on the south side of Cloyd's Creek,

[15] *Deeds*, Q, 183 (1821).
[16] *Union Presbytery Minutes*, 1806.
[17] J. J. Robinson, *Memoirs of Rev. Isaac Anderson, D.D.* (Knoxville, 1860), 127 ff.
[18] *Baker's Creek Trustee's Book* Maryville College vault.

to be used for a church and schoolhouse. They had 25 members in 1886. This group was no doubt a part of the Gallaher's Creek congregation listed in 1796. Unitia and Sinking Creek congregations were united in 1849 as Unitia, and continued as a church until the flooding of lands by Fort Loudoun dam made it advisable to dissolve Unitia Church in 1937, as it had been inactive since 1929. However, a Sunday school and occasional services are being held there at the present time.[19]

Dr. Anderson also organized, in 1833, a church on Nine Mile Creek called Mt. Vernon. A deed to the property by William Cooper to Trustees Henry Parker, the Rev. John G. Wilson, and Samuel Parks was registered in 1837. However, in 1838, we find that twenty-one members returned to New Providence—"the most of whom were members of this church and at their request were dismissed in order to form a church at Mount Vernon, which they did, but have now reunited with this church." The names listed are: Parker, Glass, Thompson, Kizer, Gardner, Ross, Snider, Morton, Strain, Martin, and Cook. In 1838, they had reported to presbytery, that "being feeble" they had made arrangements to join New Providence church.

This church was between Carpenter's Campground and Montvale, located near Chet McGhee's property. The deed had a reversionary clause which was repeated in two subsequent deeds, the last being from David Hamel to Moses Martin.[20]

The Louisville church was organized in 1837, by the Rev. Darius Hoyt. In 1838, twenty-eight members who had been dismissed to organize a Louisville church returned to New Providence because the congregation was not strong enough to stand alone. Thomas Rankin, John Hood and William Wallace were elders. The names, Hood, Dyer, Hartsill, Rankin, McClure, Wallace, Saffel, Corley, Gillespie, Patterson, and Spillman appear on this list.

Another group of members were dismissed by New Providence in October, 1851, and was organized by John S. Craig into the Louisville Presbyterian Church; William Wallace, Abraham Wallace, and Joseph Hart were elders. Names of charter members are: Corley, Wallace, Hartsill, Rankin, Spillman, Teffeteller, Price, Cummings, and Hart. Although the church had seventy-eight members in 1861, the Louisville church was not very active after the Civil War, although the Bartletts and other college professors held services, more or less, regularly. The building was sold to the M.E. Church in 1896, and used by them until it was struck by lightning in 1917, and burned.[21]

Sinking Creek citizens first petitioned presbytery to organize a church in 1835. A committee appointed for the purpose reported it as too near other churches. They continued to petition for organization

---
[19] *Deeds*, Q. 156; *Union Presbytery Minutes*, Passim.
[20] *Ibid.*, 316—Deeds containing reversionary clause M 336; also S 270; *New Providence Session Minutes* (1838); *Union Presbytery Minutes*.
[21] *New Providence Session Minutes* 1838, 1851; Adria B. Richmond (Cummings) *History of Louisville* in Maryville Enterprise. February 12, 1930, (Agricultural Educational Edition); A. H. Love, *History of Louisville* in 6 chapters (Unpublished) from a copy made in 1931.

at regular intervals and in April 1842, the Rev. Mr. Dyke reported that he had organized a church at Sinking Creek in Blount County. In April 1849, Sinking Creek was reported as having united with Unitia to form one church.[22]

The Clover Hill church was organized by John S. Craig as New Hope church, September 6, 1841. Elders ordained were: Henry Logan, John Gault, and William W. Dunn. Other names of membership were Boyd, Logan, Gault, Harris, Jackson, Bogle and Dunn. The deed from John S. Gault and Jesse Kerr is to trustees James Henry, Robert Culton and Wallace Edmondson. It was called Union in 1853. The name became Clover Hill in 1858, when the church moved to the present location. The membership in 1886 was seventy-eight.

The original building was replaced in 1924 by a brick structure which was enlarged in 1953.[23]

Bethel church was organized by Dr. Isaac Anderson in September 1853, and became officially known as Rockford in 1856. Clarks, Caldwells, Cowans, McCaullys and McCulleys were among the first members. Thomas Hart, son of the first clerk of New Providence, was the first clerk. The Rev. John M. Caldwell was the first regular pastor and the Rev. E. W. Hall was the last. The present building was built in 1890. The church disbanded in 1942 and the building was sold to the Wesley-Ann Methodist Church.[24]

The Forest Hill church was organized in October 1855, by the Rev. Fielding Pope. There were forty-three organizing members: Hoods, Broadys, McConnells, McGinleys, McCallins, McCullochs, Andersons, Boyds, Wallaces, Wrights, Scroggs, Blairs, Alfords, and Walkers. William Boyd, Jesse Wallace, and James McGinley were elected elders; William H. Anderson, and Andrew C. Broady were deacons. The Rev. John M. Caldwell, T. J. Lamar, R. E. Tedford, J. J. Robinson, J. T. Regan, and E. W. Hall were pastors. William Toole deeded 2½ acres of land to the church in 1859. The shed for camp meetings was still standing in 1869. Their church burned in 1889 and was almost immediately rebuilt. John M. Boyd, William Tulloch and Henry Lowry were the last elders and Joseph Miser and Henry A. Gardner last served as deacons. The last session recorded was September 1907. The Baptists bought the property in 1908, and have maintained a steadily growing active organization. A great many of the older Presbyterian families buried their dead in the old part of Forest Hill Cemetery.[25]

[22] *Union Presbytery Minutes*, Passim.
[23] *Clover Hill Session Records*, 1841–Present; the church was organized and first located at Rockdale School on James ("Specks") Henry Farm. List of Charter members found among papers of Mrs. John F. Henry, Sr. *Deeds*, X, 491 (Constitutional or "New School").
[24] Story in *Maryville Enterprise* February 12, 1930; *Union Presbytery Minutes*.
[25] *Forest Hill Session Minutes*. (In Maryville College vault); *Deeds*, Bk. Z, 303. Names of Trustees of Forest Hill church: A. C. Broady and Wm. H. Anderson, John DeArmond; An earlier deed for 3/4 acres in 1854 to "School House and Church" by Trustees; W. H. Anderson, John DeArmond, by John Hood is seemingly the same tract, before the organization of the church as two of the trustees are the same.

Little Tennessee near Morganton was organized by the Rev. John Dyke in 1853. Nothing is known of this church's activities and the church probably declined with the town which died with the advent of the railroad, and the subsequent decline of river traffic. The minutes of Cloyd's Creek church in 1879 speak of Morganton church as extinct. A Cumberland Presbyterian Church was organized at Morganton about the same time as Pine Grove and predated Little Tennessee.[26]

July 9, 1871, a portion of the members of Baker's Creek church was organized by the Rev. W. B. Brown and the Rev. A. Vance into the Cloyd's Creek church (Meadow). The lot for the church was given by James Alexander, Sr., of Blount County. Among the members were: Alexanders, Allens, Chapmans, Hudgeons, Hammontrees, Greers, McConnells, Stewarts, Robersons, Crys, Jones, Murrys, Sparks, Thompsons, Temples, and Turnbulls. Many others, not of the membership, had previously pledged to assist in building the church. The membership of this church was partly in Blount and partly in the newly organized County of Loudon. John A. Stewart and John J. Hudgeons, William Murry and William Alexander were ordained elders. Stewart had previously been ordained by Baker's Creek. In April, 1888, this church spread joint resolutions with Baker's Creek regarding the recent death of the Rev. Milton A. Mathes of Washington College who had previously served as their pastor. Cloyd's Creek is still an active church.[27]

Mt. Tabor church was organized at Kidd's Schoolhouse, June 3, 1871. Twenty-three members from Clover Hill and Louisville Presbyterian churches and William M. Lane from Maryville M. E. Church presented letters as Charter members. Among them were the Andersons, McCulleys, Talbotts, James, Browns, Badgers, Stallions, Taylors, Lanes, and Cashions.

John Brown and William M. Lane were elected elders. Brown had been an elder in Louisville church and Lane was ordained. It was decided to call the church Mt. Tabor. The present building stands on the site where the church was organized.[28]

Centennial was organized in the grove near the residence of J. H. Rowan, July 1st and 2nd, 1876, by the Rev. T. J. Lamar. The Charter members were: Gambles, Lowrys, Kinnamons, Caldwells, Rowans, Mortons, and Davises. Elders were A. K. Kinnamon, A. M. Gamble and William L. Caldwell.

J. H. Rowan offered a site for the church, as did John Gamble. Rowan's offer was accepted because it was more centrally located. The Gamble plot is still called the "Centennial Patch." It is the wooded knoll on the right of the curve near Little River on the Walland Highway. Gambles and Mortons have always been active in this church.

John Gamble suggested the name Lamar, but the Rev. Lamar sug-

---

[26] *Union Presbytery Minutes; Cloyd's Creek Session Book.* (In Maryville College vault).
[27] *Cloyd's Creek Session Book.* (In Maryville College vault).
[28] *Mt. Tabor Session* Book I. At home of clerk, J. E. McCall, Alnwick.

gested Centennial in commemoration of the hundredth anniversary of American Independence and of Col. Christian's campaign. Col. William Christian's campaign was the first organized expedition of white men into this country on record, and it was accompanied by the Revs. Charles Cummings and Joseph Rhea who were no doubt, the first Presbyterian ministers who preached on Blount County soil. This church is served by supply pastors from Maryville College and is a very active little congregation.[29]

We find in the New Providence Session records that a chapel was built near Mean's schoolhouse in 1886, and in 1897, we find that the building was sold to the congregation later called Oakview Cumberland Presbyterian Church. This site adjoined the present Fairview School. Nothing more is known about it as a church.[30]

In the New Providence Session minutes for 1886, we find the Session discussing the advisability of building a chapel at, or near Eagleton schoolhouse. (The traditional site of one of the first schools in Blount County, taught by Joseph Hart, 1790.) In 1889, they refer to the chapel recently built three miles north of Maryville in the Eagleton-Hart neighborhood. It was named Hart's Chapel. Elders Thomas N. Hart of Rockford church and John M. Lowry of New Providence church were appointed supervisors. Permission was given for the building to be used for day school providing no damages were incurred. It seems that all were not happy about the name Hart's Chapel and preferred the old name of Wear's Chapel, but no action was ever taken on the subject by New Providence Session. This church was in the neighborhood of Vose Station just off the Wright's Ferry Road. It was discontinued about the time the aluminum company came to Alcoa.[31]

In the New Providence Session records of 1886, we also find reference to the Pistol Creek Mission or Sunday school. The Big Springs Session November 3, 1888, asked the congregation to empower the trustees to dispose of the Pistol Creek church and grounds to the best advantage. This indicates that the church at Pistol Creek had been abandoned before this time and evidently the Presbyterian U.S.A. were trying to salvage the remains of the congregation and hold them together.

The Rev. John Eakin was at this time a student at Maryville College and was appointed to preach at Pistol Creek 1886–87 and to be Sunday school superintendent. Prof. W. R. Davison was his assistant.

---

[29] *Centennial Session Book*, at home of clerk of session, H. H. Henry. A letter from Mrs. Hetty Morton Lawson (widow of the Rev. J. D. ("Black Jim") Lawson) to Mrs. Lou Goddard Henry in February, 1926, relates how the Reverend Pope came to the house of her father James Morton for a great many years and conducted services for the local people who could not go to Maryville for services; 2 p.m. in winter and 4 p.m. in summer. James Morton died in 1859 and the Civil War came along and services were discontinued. Then in 1876 we find Centennial Church organized for this community. In her letter she deplores the fact that this church could not have been organized during her father's lifetime. Letter belongs to Mrs. Bessie Henry Olin, Maryville, Tenn.

[30] *New Providence Session Book*, 1886; *Oak View Session Book*, formerly in the hands of Mrs. Roy Pearson, Maryville.

[31] *New Providence Session Book*, 1886.

There is no record of how long this Sunday school continued. The property was taken over by the Yearout family and the building was later destroyed by a storm. The Seceder or "Cedar" graveyard was the only landmark left to mark the site of a historic church, until the establishment of West Maryville Presbyterian Church.[32]

In 1907 the Rev. Weaver reported to the Session that he had done some work preparatory to organizing a church at Walland. The membership of that church came to New Providence in 1914.

In 1917, Mrs. Martha Tedford Lamar, widow of the Rev. T. J. Lamar, at her own expense built a chapel near Sevierville Pike in East Maryville and named it "Malinda Gillespie Houston Tedford Memorial Chapel," in honor of her mother (a daughter of Major James Houston). It was to be an interdenominational community center. Locally it was generally called Lamar Chapel until 1947 when it became a full-fledged church known as Houston Memorial Chapel.

In 1936, the West Maryville Presbyterian Church was organized by the Rev. E. W. Hall at the site of the Pistol Creek Seceder Church. The Rev. W. T. Swain became the first pastor in June 1937, and their church was built during this year.[33]

The Second Presbyterian Church was set up as a separate organization soon after 1865. The building and lot which Maryville College had used as a boarding club on Church Street (next to the library) was given to the Negro brethren for their use as a church and school.

Later a white frame building was erected which they used until the forties when the congregation built a new church on Doll Street.

ASSOCIATE, OR SECEDER

The Associate Church is a descendant of the first secession from the established Church of Scotland, hence Seceder. Locally they have always been characterized by Psalmody or Psalm-singing.

According to tradition the Seceder congregation from Blount County petitioned the Associate Synod for a minister in the 1780's, but the organization date for Big Springs in the Associate records is given as 1821. United Presbyterian minutes give 1818 as the organization date of Pistol Creek. Both records list David Carson as the first pastor in 1824, which corresponds to local records and tradition. The Session minutes of the two congregations are combined which would indicate that they were organized at about the same time. Very little is known about David Carson, except that he was born in 1799, graduated at Cannonburg, Pennsylvania, and was licensed in 1823. He was ordained in 1824 as pastor of "Big Springs and connections" in East Tennessee. He married

---

[32] *Ibid., Big Springs Session Book,* (Formerly Big Springs and Pistol Creek combined).

[33] *McTeer,* 95; *Minutes of Union Presbytery.*

Mission stations, under the supervision of some minister, generally on the Maryville College faculty are maintained by college students at various points in the county. At present, Mountain View at Walland, Keeble's Chapel and Newcastle are churches under their care.

Jane Gillespy of Blount County in 1827. He was elected to a professorship in the Associate Seminary in 1833 and died in 1834, before taking the position.[34]

The first record of the United Congregation of Pistol Creek and Big Springs is described as Book II and begins in December 1830. This fact, together with the settlement pattern (most of the early settlers in Blount County had tarried for a while in the Upper East Tennessee counties before this section was open for settlement) would lead us to believe that Limestone was the mother church of these combined congregations. In the Big Springs records, various references are made to Limestone church. The Session record of Big Springs and Pistol Creek are one and the same. No deed is recorded directly to the church, but a transfer from James McWilliams in 1832, excepts the two or three acres given to the Seceder Church by William Gray.[35]

Slavery agitation became such a problem that many families: McKamey, Duncan, Delzell and Tedford emigrated en masse to Illinois. Henderson, McConnell, Hamil, Duncan, Edmondson, Rhea, and Walker families went to Iowa.

The Session records of these churches prove them to have been by far, the strictest church group among our local pioneers. We find them very concerned about "occasional hearing" (hearing other denominations) naming Covenanters, General Assembly, Hopkinsian, Baptists, and Methodists. If the guilty one could not see that he was wrong he was "dealt with." They were very strict about traveling on the Sabbath Day and censured many for such. Most of this travel was in hauling salt from Virginia. The records show that David Carson, T. S. Kendall and James Law served as pastors during the Associate period.[36]

In 1858, their minutes state: "previous to this, the Session excepted (accepted) of the Union, constituting the United Presbyerian Church of North America."

The church at Big Springs is listed as disorganized in 1860 as an Associate Church. David Strang was the first acting pastor after the change from Associate to United Presbyterian. The Session records do not show that any radical change was made in their procedure, except that the first mention of infant baptism is made in the Session record.

The Pistol Creek congregation is listed as disorganized in 1880, but it is not listed by the presbytery after 1871. The Big Springs Session record in November 1888, says: "The congregation was asked to empower the trustees to dispose of the Pistol Creek church and grounds to the best advantage." [37]

---

[34] W. M. Glasgow, *Cyclopedic Manual of the United Presbyterian Church*, (Pittsburgh, 1905); *The History of Big Spring Presbytery of the United Presbyterian Church*, 1750–1879, Harrisburg, 1879, 117.

[35] Book I is missing; Book II, III, and to date are in the house of church clerk, Roy Walker; Limestone was a Seceder church near Jonesboro, Tennessee, and was probably the mother church; *Deeds*, 4, p. 355.

[36] *Big Springs and Pistol Creek Combined Congregations Session Records*, Book 3.

[37] W. M. Glasgow, *Cyclopedic Manual of the United Presbyterian Church;* (Pittsburgh, 1903) 392; *Big Springs Session Records*, Bks. 2 and 3, Passim.

The West Maryville Presbyterian Church now stands on the site occupied by the Pistol Creek congregation of Seceders at the old "Cedar" graveyard on Morganton Road.

Several ministers served short or longer terms until 1887 when the Rev. A. S. Abbey came from Erie, Pennsylvania and became an integral part of the church community. He was postmaster of the post office Cliff until its discontinuance in 1903. The Rev. Abbey served as long as he was able. After that date ministers were only occasional.

In the United Presbyterian minutes, Big Spring is listed as disorganized after 1920. The Rev. E. W. Hall served until 1918, and because they could not secure United Presbyterian preachers, the church reorganized as a Presbyterian Church of the United States of America, so that they could get supply pastors locally. The Rev. Hall served as pastor until 1937. A new church was built in 1923 and the congregation has grown steadily.

In Nashville, there is an interesting petition concerning a tract of four acres of land donated to the "Trustees of the Sussession" congregation by one Henry Furgeson, and later by one Isaac Yearout. The land had reverted to the state and the trustees—Thomas Maxwell, Robert Sterling, and John McCulley in 1824 wanted to buy the four acres out of the tract. This evidently referred to the tract occupied by the Pistol Creek church and cemetery (now West Maryville Presbyterian Church.)[38]

CUMBERLAND PRESBYTERIAN CHURCHES

There is a scarcity of data in assembling the facts about the establishment of Cumberland Presbyterian churches in Blount County.

According to the best available information, Shady Grove is the oldest church in what is now Blount County. However, it is highly possible that Morganton and Pine Grove are of about the same date and all, prior to 1870, were included in what was then Blount County. The oldest Session record, which Shady Grove church has, begins in 1883 and the Pine Grove, now in Loudon County, begins in 1873. An older book predates each of these.

An agreement concerning the Shady Grove property made in December 1839 between Henry Pesterfield, Sr., and the Session of Shady Grove church, viz.: Lemuel Adams, Paten Lain, Joseph Dobson, John M. Bonham, and Robert C. Dobson, allowed them to use the property, including a small pond-spring, for a meeting house and campground for fifty years. So from this we can suppose the church had already organized in 1839 since the Session was named.[39]

The deed from Jesse Kerr, to the Pine Grove church by elders and trustees Andrew Cowan, Samuel Montgomery, Leonard L. McFarland, and Joseph A. Hutton, for a church and campground, was recorded in

[38] *Petitions*, Tennessee State Archives, Nashville, Tennessee.
[39] *Deeds*, Q, 89.

1840. This church is near Jena Station and Greenback and at that date was in Blount County. This land was first granted to Matthew Wallace, who was Justice of the Peace in Blount County in 1796. From these facts we would suppose that these two churches were organized about the same time. Pine Grove and Morganton joined with the Presbyterian U.S.A. at the time of the Union of 1902. Alleghany Station, later called Greenback, was formed from an arm of Pine Grove.[40]

The present Shady Grove church was built about 1881. In 1910, H. A. Miser and W. W. Key were already elders. G. L. Miser, and C. A. Hutton were elected elders and D. B. Johnson elected deacon and all were ordained. The church record from 1883 to September 1938 is in the hands of G. L. Miser. There is an active Sunday school here but the church has not been active since 1938.

The next church in point of the organization was Concord later called Holston College. This church was organized sometime between 1844 and 1848. The first log church stood within 100 feet of the cemetery. The first burial in the cemetery took place about 1841 according to tradition, however, there is reason to believe that it was used much earlier. Certainly, it is the oldest cemetery in the vicinity. The Rev. Thomas Small was the first preacher. This church was used as a school also. Tradition substantiated by Mr. E. J. Gillespy, says that Mr. William Warren solicited funds for a school and that as a result Ewing and Jefferson College was founded in 1851 and opened session in the old log church under the leadership of B. V. Irvine. The new brick building which we know today as Holston College was ready for the 1852 session. Gillespy said the first elders were probably Alexander Ish, Darby Ragan, and Thompson Barnet.[41]

The old log church was used for a time as the public school after being moved and rebuilt at the fork of the Friendsville Road. A Baptist church was later organized there.

The Rev. Thomas Small severed his relations with the church in 1853 when he left Tennessee to go to Oregon. The Gillespys sold their property at that time to go with him, but the ninety-year-old grandmother was not able to make the trip and they did not go. The Reverend Small was succeeded by David Amos who served two years. Amos was succeeded by S. A. Taylor, who was also president of the college until 1857, when he left.

Gillespy left the neighborhood to attend school at Lebanon where he was graduated in 1859 and never returned to the community, therefore, no further information was obtained through him.

Nothing definite is known of the church until 1893 when the Rev. J. C. Ritter became pastor of the church and revived the school which

---

[40] *Ibid.*, Q, 371; *Pine Grove Session Minutes* 1895.
[41] Session Record lost. Information from Mrs. Beulah O'Conner, Louisville, Tennessee. Information gleaned from correspondence with a cousin, Evander J. Gillespie at Palo Alto, California from June to November, 1926. He, at that time, was 91 years old. He had attended the first sessions of Ewing and Jefferson College. His family gave the land for the church and school.

had been inactive for a time. Ritter was followed by the Rev. A. M. Hunt. The school was permanently closed in 1900 and the building was used exclusively by the Holston College church until it was dissolved, in 1952.

The Clark's Grove church is next in organization. Their records begin with 1902, the date of their second church building. Fortunately a faithful clerk of the Oakview church, now extinct, had recorded the organization of the mother church in the beginning of their record. Accordingly, September 15, 1878, the following persons met at P. H. (Harve) Clark's, Blount County, Tennessee and associated themselves— to be known as Springfield Congregation of Cumberland Presbyterians: Martin C., Phebe, and Ann Eliza Brown; Alexander and Leona Eagleton; James N. and Sarah Lawson; Misses R. C. and Eletha S. Trundle; Mrs. S. E. George; Mary A., and Margaret J. Clark; Elias A. Lemons, James McKinnamon, Miss Charles E. McClure, Martin C. Brown and Alexander Eagleton (who were the elders), and the Rev. Solon McCroskey, organizer. The record further mentioned the church as being under the Hiwassee Presbytery. The members met for a few years at Eagleton schoolhouse and then in a shed at Clark's Grove. The frame building finished in 1902 was recently replaced with a modern brick structure. The elders named in their record beginning in 1910 are: W. E. McClure, Charles Thomas, M. Matlock, and W. C. Wrinkle; the Rev. D. C. Hoyle, pastor.

August 24, 1880, the Session of Springfield congregation being requested to form a branch at Sandy Springs schoolhouse received: W. M., Mrs. Elizabeth, Era L., and F. M. Watkins, Jr.; W. A. G., Sarah A., Nancy M., Rebecca J., and R. C. Snoddy; A. B. and Mrs. Montgomery; J. A., and Sophronia Porter; Dora L. Anderson, Albert Piper, Mary J. and Nancy Jones.

In 1896, William S. Smith took charge of the congregation known as the Arm of Springfield at Sandy Springs in Blount County, Tennessee. Organization was effected by election and ordination of ruling elders and deacons: James R. Feezell and J. N. Lawson, elders; T. J. McCampbell and N. R. West, deacons.[42]

In November 1897, the church appointed J. R. Feezell, Thomas McCampbell and J. N. Lawson to offer the Presbyterian Board $125.00 for Mean's Chapel (a mission chapel under the care of New Providence Presbyterian Church). The deal was effected, and in February 1898, the name was changed to Oakview instead of Arm of Springfield. This church stood on the east side of Niles Ferry, or Fairview School grounds. The last meeting of the Oakview Session was January 12, 1913.

The Maryville Cumberland Presbyterian Church was organized about 1914. The exact date is not known. The reversionary deed from Mr. Sam Everett and his mother, Mrs. R. E. Everett was recorded June

---

[42] *Oak Grove Session Record* 1880–1913. In hands of Mrs. Roy Pearson, Maryville, Tenn. *Clark's Grove Session Record*, 1910–Church clerk, Mr. Hall.

4, 1914, and named O. P. Sterling and T. W. Keller, of Knoxville, W. C. Wrinkle, J. C. McCampbell and D. C. Hoyle as trustees.

W. C. (Cowan) Wrinkle was an elder in the Clark's Grove church so it is to be supposed that he served as elder in this new organization which according to tradition he effected. The Rev. Hoyle was at that time pastor of Clark's Grove and since he was one of the trustees named, we would judge he was the first pastor. It will be noted that the organization of this church closely followed the close of the Oakview church. The McCampbells and others who had been members of the Oakview church were in the formation of this new church. It is unfortunate that the Session record of this church has been lost.[43]

PRESBYTERIAN, U.S.

On the first Friday in May 1871, a group of persons interested in organizing a Presbyterian Church, U. S., met at the Southern Methodist Church in Maryville to make plans. While in this meeting an invitation was given to meet the next day at New Providence Presbyterian Church, U. S. A. Accordingly, on Saturday, May 6th, 1871, the group met at New Providence church for a sermon at 11 o'clock, by a Mr. Morrison. At 2 P.M. the following persons presented themselves and were organized into a church: R. A. and Mrs. R. M. Ramsey from Sweetwater; William H. and Mrs. M. E. Henry, and Mrs. Mary S. Norwood from Clover Hill; Miss Ellen Gillespie, Mrs. Penelope Greenway, Misses Kate P. and Margaret V. Greenway, Mrs. Elizabeth M. and Lucinda P. Wear, Mrs. Elizabeth McTeer, James P. Wear, Mesdames Mary E. Cates, Ann E. Pope and Elizabeth McGhee from New Providence; Mrs. Margaret H. Cox from Pleasant Forest; Miss Nancy Strain from Western Presbyterian Church, Washington, D. C., Robert T. Corry, Mrs. Ann E. Thompson, Misses Phebe E. Malcom and Nancy C. Scribner and Charles E. McLin—by profession. The congregation elected R. A. Ramsey and William H. Henry to the office of ruling elders and ordained and installed them. James Parks was moderator. At a later date George Alexander McLin and D. D. Hurley were elders.[44]

Among the later members were: Hannum, McGhee, Russell, Wear, Everett, Hart, Wright, Porter, Thompson, Stone, Rhea, Hood, McTeer, Blackburn, McGinley, Hartsill, Boyd, Morrison, Gibbs, Hurley, Cox, Davis, and McKenzie.

According to their Session records, which were beautifully kept, the congregation met over Tedford's Drugstore ("Presbyterian Hall"). In 1876, the Maryville Baptist Church, organized the same year as this church, had just built their meeting house and had no furniture, as yet. The Maryville Presbyterian Church had furniture, but no church, so, it seems that they got together and signed an agreement, wherein the

---

[43] *Deeds*, 76, p. 72.
[44] Maryville Presbyterian Church Session Book, (in vault of New Providence Church), Passim.

Presbyterians would place their furniture in the Baptist house and both would meet in the same house for two years. The agreement was signed October 14, 1876, and the furniture moved the following day.

The last record of a congregational meeting of the Maryville Presbyterian Church was January 5, 1879.

At a meeting of the Session October 19, 1883, William H. Henry resigned as clerk of the Session and asked for letters of dismission for himself and wife to the New Providence church. This is the last Session meeting recorded in the book. However, it is known that the church continued to meet at least irregularly for some years after this date.[45]

The members gradually drifted away into other churches, some into New Providence, but the majority to the M. E. Church, South (now Broadway Methodist Church).

Trinity Presbyterian Church was organized by the Home Mission Committee of Knoxville Presbytery under the direction of Dr. B. M. Larsen in 1945. The Rev. W. J. Boyd was installed as first pastor.

THE METHODIST CHURCHES IN BLOUNT COUNTY

The first Methodist minister to visit any part of Tennessee, at least officially, was in 1783, when Holston Circuit was established. Locally, the first man that we have on record as a visiting minister was in 1792. A new circuit had been cut off Holston in 1788 called French Broad. This territory included all settlements west and south of Main Holston to the frontiers bordering on the Cherokee nation. At this time circuits required five and six weeks for the minister to make the rounds.

William Burke was the first man assigned to this circuit whom we actually know came into what is now Blount County; and he has the distinction of having been the first married man to travel a circuit west of the mountains. We know that Burke was in Blount County during his appointment in 1792 because of this story from his journal:

> On my next round the Cherokee war was just breaking out. After I crossed the French Broad and Little River and arrived at the extreme part of the settlement, I found the inhabitants in a state of alarm on account of the war ... in the morning I started for my next appointment on the south bank of Little River ... I arrived a little before noon but found it impossible to collect a congregation. The people were moving in ... and by night we were the frontier house. About 9 o'clock one of the men started out ... but returned and said the Indians were plenty in the neighborhood. I immediately determined to make my journey to the next preaching place which was about ten miles. I was obliged to travel under the cover of night. I put my trust in God and set off ... about 2 o'clock I arrived at the house where my appointment was for that day ... but found no inmates. I knew there were cabins on the other side of the marsh and commenced hallooing as loud as I could ... they then came over and conducted me to the place. The next day I recrossed over the French Broad which placed me beyond reach of danger. I passed up through the circuit leaving the frontier appointments on the south side of the river.

---

[45] Mrs. James M. Cates says that the last meeting was at her mother's house, but she cannot say when.

In 1794, Lewis Garrett says that there were few settlers south of French Broad and Holston and what were there either lived in forts cooped up in dread, or lived in strongly built houses with thick puncheon doors which were barred up strongly when night approached. The circuit riders visited these forts and scattering settlers in quest of "perishing souls."[46]

From several authorities we have the statements that nothing much was done south of the French Broad until 1810. We know, however, that there were active groups in Blount County before that time. From available data we know that it is strongly indicated that Middlesettlements was the oldest congregation. The date 1796, which is attributed to it can neither be proven nor disproven. It would appear that Burke in 1792 met with that congregation on the first day and that he may have gone to what was later known as the Logan's Chapel congregation, then south of the river, and left by night and went to the Forks of the River in Knox County. Another tradition says that Methodism entered Blount County about 1804; at this time Lorenzo Dow visited Maryville and spoke to a large crowd. He came primarily because he was interested in the "jerks," which were prevalent among the Presbyterians, locally. The first deed to a Methodist church in Blount County was from John Walker in 1814 and describes a tract "where two churches now stand." This tract was either across the river from the tract later deeded by his son, Samuel Walker, for Walker's Chapel, or where Miller's Cove Baptist Church now stands. The description is not too clear. The first congregation was no doubt composed of those members who later broke off to form various churches in the coves.[47]

On October 16, 1818, Bishop Asbury in his Journal records—"We crossed the Holston and rode ten miles to meet the people at John Saffles." This is the first actual record of a meeting of the Middlesettlements group as a congregation and their campground was by that time well known throughout the circuits.[48]

In 1811, at a camp meeting in Blount County there was a most extraordinary season of revival influence and scores were "gathered into the fold of Christ." This was the year that George Eakin was sent again to the circuit. Eakin was one of the most remarkable men in his time. He penetrated the hills and hollows, byways and hedges even into the Smoky and Chilhowee mountains. Dr. Job, in his Memoirs, speaks of hearing Eakin preach about 1824 in Cades Cove.[49]

It is also recorded that about this time a large encampment was erected in Blount County, south of the French Broad and Holston, and east of Little Tennessee called Middlesettlements, which was noted for the strength of its membership; its campground was a gathering place

---

[46] *McFerrin* V. 1, 1783–1804, 91.
[47] *Ibid.*, V. 2, p. 164; *Deeds*, 1, p. 282.
[48] Francis Asbury, *Journal* Vol. 3, p. 291.
[49] *McFerrin*, Vol. 1, p. 164; Dr. Abram Job, *Memoirs* (Unpublished) from the collection of Mrs. L. W. McCown, Johnson City, Tennessee.

for local preachers. Its patriarch, Father Saffold (Saffell) was outstanding. Much of the credit for local organization was due to the work of William Garrett, a local preacher of Cocke County, who began his labors with George Eakin on the local circuits in 1822.[50]

The earliest circuit records, that we have, are of Little River Circuit, beginning in 1830. Those early churches of Blount County which were not in this circuit are mentioned briefly here.

Middlesettlements has already been mentioned as the first congregation in the county. The Maryville church, in its beginnings, was called Mt. Gilead and stood where the armory now stands on Methodist Hill. The exact date of organization is not known. Lorenzo Dow preached here in 1804 to large crowds, and a general revival was held in Blount County in 1811, which should have brought about its organization at least by 1811. The lot was bought in 1824 and sold in 1862, when a new church was built on lot No. 1 immediately behind the present Methodist Church.[51]

In 1865, when Holston Conference reorganized, the M. E. group met wherever they could: in the old church, in New Providence church, and in the courthouse. In April, 1870, at a meeting held in the courthouse, they decided to build a church of their own. A lot was bought near the L. & N. depot site and a small frame building was erected there in 1871. In August, 1891, the present church lot was purchased and a building raised. At that time it was considered one of the best church buildings in the county.

The coming of the aluminum industry and the rapid attendant growth of the town soon made the building inadequate for the congretion's needs. Under the pastorate of the Rev. G. T. Francisco, the cornerstone of the present building was laid October 7, 1922, and dedicated August 1923. While building was in progress, the congregation again used the courthouse.

When the reorganization of Holston Conference came, at the end of the War Between the States, the Mount Gilead property was held by the Southern group and they continued to worship in the little church on Church Street until 1894, when they moved to the present building on Broadway. Dr. John W. Cates, A. K. Harper, W. Y. C. Hannum and John M. Clark, served as a building committee. In 1928, the Sunday school annex was built which included a fine gymnasium. This church has always had an active, progressive congregation.[52]

The second oldest deed for a Methodist church in Blount County is

---

[50] *McFerrin* Vol. 2. p. 243.

[51] *Deeds*, S, 351 (Trustees: Reuben L. Cates, John Ambrister, Michael Smith, John Biddle, Samuel Saffle, James Henderson); *Deeds*, Z, 361, (Trustees: Jos. Ambrister, Wm. H. Rogers, Henry Miller, Spencer Henry, John E. Hudson, W. W. Lawrence).

[52] A news item from the *East Tennessean (Kingston)* for October 6, 1870, says that the Methodist Church at Maryville is to remain in the hands of its rightful owners, the M. E. South, and that the Louisville Church has already been returned to the former owners.

for Logan's Chapel, 1816. "Two acres on which a meeting house is erected for a campground site." The first deed for a Methodist church at Louisville is in 1836 and again in 1844. Axley's Chapel and one on Gallaher's Creek from Alexander Ish in 1834 are all mentioned before 1840, but no official records other than deeds are in existence.[53]

Centenary Methodist Church was probably organized about 1839. At that date John Hays gave 1½ acres on Macklin's Branch, which adjoins William Pugh, "where they shall erect a house of worship." The cemetery was started here early, Baker's Creek, is the only cemetery in this part of the county which predates it. The earliest inscription is 1847. There is a story that an unknown man killed on the Great War Path was the first burial, also a man named George Best and his brother-in-law Simeon Crye were "bushwhacked" at Tomotley Ford during the Civil War and were buried here. Centenary Methodist Church ceased to function as a church between 1900 and 1908. At this time, the building was sold by the Methodists and the proceeds given to the Williamson church. A lot adjoining was later given by Willie Wilson for a Union church, and since that time a Baptist church has met regularly at this place.[54]

In 1842 Alexander Cook gave a tract of land at what is now Mint, between the railroad bed and the creek. In 1848, for a convenience of the population, a church was built in sight of the present church at Carpenter's Campground. Within a few years the church was moved to its present location at Carpenter's Campground where the church now occupies its fifth building on the same lot. The camps were used until about 1916. The land was given by Philip Costner and Thomas Carpenter. These named, together with Sloan, Gardner, Martin, Taylor, and Henry, often appear in their records. It was here, at a quarterly meeting, that the resolutions approving the action of the convention which transferred their relations from the Southern to the Northern Methodist Church were passed.[55]

Little River Circuit, in 1830, listed the following Blount churches: Logan's Chapel, Bethlehem, Samuel Walker's Chapel, Cades Cove and Millers Cove. Russam's seems to have been in Blount County, near Ellejoy and Eusebia, but must have been only an appointment, John Russam was later taken care of by the church as a retired local preacher. Regan's Chapel, now Bethel, probably grew out of this appointment.[56]

---

[53] *Deeds*, 2, p. 288 (Trustees: David Logan, Abraham Phillips, Archibald Murphy, James Edmondson, Robert McCally, Michael Swisher).

[54] *Deeds*, S, 48; X, 191 says: "Land that J. Hays gave to Centenary Meeting House"; *Recording Steward's Book*, Oakland Circuit, 1908. (Courtesy of Mrs. Ova Belt Lindsay).

[55] *Deeds*, S, p. 102 (Trustees; John Hays, Wm. Hale, Newton K. Williams, Alexander Cook, Wm. B. Bingham); History of Carpenter's Church written by W. E. Parham for dedication in 1938 (July 24) copy in author's collection; *Recording Steward's Book*, Little River Circuit, 1830-40, in Holston Conference Archives, Knoxville, Tennessee. Carpenter's Campground church was called Wesley Chapel for a time but that name did not take hold.

[56] John Russam is on the 13th district tax list for 1837, (Tennessee State Archives), copy in author's collection.

In 1831, trustees were appointed for Mt. Pleasant meeting house—Peter, Moses, and George Snider, Frederick Emmett, Isaac Hart and George Caylor. Locally this church was called Tuckaleechee Campground, and the campground was patronized by people from Wear's Cove, Miller's Cove and Cades Cove, until about 1880–90 as none of the other named communities had campgrounds.[57]

Trustees for Bethlehem were appointed in 1831: Adam and Isaac Kountz, James Julian, Samuel Palmer, and Alexander Logan. Bethlehem and Walker's Chapel were discontinued as churches in 1950.

Early local preachers in Blount County were Frederick Emert of Tuckaleechee, Spencer Henry, of Miller's Cove, James Rhea and George Julian of Logan's Chapel. James Cummings and Ashley Wynn of Sevier County were active in Blount County churches during the 30's as local preachers and later as traveling preachers. John Russam of Russam's, and Brittain Garrard, who was buried at Logan's Chapel, were later ministers.

Blount churches were first divided into two circuits in 1835 following Eakin's second term on the circuit. Thomas J. Brown, Elbert F. Sevier, Creed Fulton and James Cummings were the first presiding elders of the Maryville and Louisville circuits.[58]

In his "notebook" George Eakin listed the following appointments for 1845: Logan's Chapel, Peck's Chapel, Maryville, Carpenter's, Centenary, Howard's, Morganton, Mount Moriah, Axley's Chapel, Bowman's, Bussel's, Unitia, Middlesettlements, Louisville, Mount Pleasant, Zion, Gamble's, Colledge (sic), Cades Bluff, Rahobah.[59]

In 1850, we find the same churches in Little River circuit as in 1830. Russam's was dropped in 1853, (John Russam had been voted a pension in 1851). Jesse F. Bunker was a local preacher from Mt. Moriah, and Frederic Emert and J. D. Lawson, from Tuckaleechee. All churches except Cades Cove reported Sunday schools.

In 1852, C. Lemons, Josiah Regan, Walter Gregory, Nathan H. Sparks, Charles Fisher, Nathan Burchfield, and Bennett Bradford were appointed Trustees for Cades Cove Methodist Church. Trustees for Logan's Chapel in 1855 were: James and William McCamy, James Porter, Alfred Seaton, and A. McClain. W. H. Finley of Logan's Chapel was licensed to preach in 1858.

In 1858, we find the first listing of the churches in the Louisville circuit: Mt. Moriah, Louisville, Middlesettlements, Unitia, Jones, Bussel, and Salem. In 1862, Axley's Chapel, Morganton, Howard's, Centenary, Carpenter's and Peck's Chapel are listed in addition to the above.

---

[57] Interview with Mrs. Martha Crowson of Wear's Cove, 1952, age 92; *Recording Steward's Book*, Little River Circuit, 1830–40. In Holston Conference Archives, Knoxville, Tennessee.

[58] Minutes of Annual Conference, 1835–Passim.

[59] *Memorandum Book* of George Eakin. In Holston Conference Archives, Knoxville, Tenn.

Thompson's schoolhouse, and Kagley's appear next in 1871 while Kizer's and Best's schoolhouses appear in 1873, and Woods' schoolhouse, (later Mountcastle) in 1879.[60]

Best's schoolhouse became an appointment on the circuit in 1873. Ten or fifteen years later the Best's schoolhouse was replaced by Christy Hill school (named for Christy Best) and the church was built a mile or two nearer Six Mile on Kagley land, but was locally called "Red Stripe" because Henry Blevins had painted the corner strips and trim of the building red. Later this church was moved to Mint and called Mt. Olive and was dissolved as a church in the late thirties.

Exhorters were: B. F. Badgett, Peter Rule, Frances Kirby, John McCallie, Absolom Farr, James A. Goddard, John H. Jennings, Christopher Best, W. T. Dowell, and William H. Rogers. Trustees for Middlesettlements in 1866 were: G. G. O'Connor, M. Mizer, E. Moore, E. Wayman, T. Peterson, Robert Belt, J. M. Heiskell, and John Cummings; For Mt. Moriah: Richard Kirby, Peter Rule, David Chandler, Isaac Lebow, and John Chandler.

Maryville trustees were: W. T. Dowell, Spencer Henry, W. W. Lawrence, John E. Hudson, Joseph Armbrister and Andrew Hannah; later changed to: Ambrister and Henry, Michael Davis, W. T. Parham, Elisha Carpenter, J. A. Goddard, and Nimrod Byers. For New Salem in Blount County: Andrew Carpenter, Ezekias Kizer, William W. Ferguson, Henry Yates and M. M. Thompson.

In 1868, the following churches sent delegates to a lay meeting: Maryville, Peck's Chapel, Centenary, Carpenter's, Morganton, Axley's Chapel, Unitia, Middlesettlements, Louisville, Mt. Moriah, and Union Grove. In 1870, trustees for Centenary were: E. Carpenter, W. B. Bingham, John Ross, C. Best, and Spencer Henry. Trustees for a new church near Wright's Ferry were: Peter Rule, Perry H. Kidd, Preston Roddy, L. B. James, James Ackridge, William Ballard, and J. A. Bond. For Haven's Chapel: Peter Rule, James Ackridge, and Marcus Ballard. In 1879, the house built at Thompson's is mentioned. Williamson's and McMurry's Chapel appeared between 1880 and 1892. The Williamson congregation had been in existence for some time, meeting at Williamson schoolhouse, where according to the deed made by Lydia Williamson, the Missionary Baptists had the first claim. According to tradition an agreement was made whereby the congregation getting materials on the ground first could use the site. The Methodists placed their materials on the ground before daylight the next morning and thus won the building site.

McMurry's Chapel near Chilhowee was first listed as Ghormley's Chapel and later as McMurry's. Trustees for this church were listed in

---

[60] Hon. Charles T. Cates, Sr., said Peck's Chapel was named for Judge Peck, an honored friend of his grandfather, John W. Wilkinson; *Recording Steward's Book*, Little River Circuit, 1850-58; *Recording Steward's Book*, Louisville Circuit, 1851-61; Mountcastle was named for Rev. W. D. Mountcastle, then stationed in Maryville. (Maryville *Index*, 1879, Passim). The building was bought in the 1940's and rebuilt as Newcastle, a Presbyterian mission church.

1893 as: Boyd McMurry, Samuel McMurry, Joseph Nelson, George William Hamilton, and Pleas Henry.

In 1909, the recording steward for Oakland Circuit stated that Williamson's Chapel had collected the balance due for the sale of Centenary churchhouse. The property now known as Centenary was deeded to a Union group. The Baptists have a strong organized church there now but the title is still vested in a Union group.[61]

The A. M. E. Zion Church and Sunday school was organized in Maryville directly after Freedom, under the leadership of Thomas Lillard and Oscar Wilson. They were allowed the use of the Negro public school building until they were able to take over the property which they now occupy on Broadway. C. H. Gamble, G. W. Valentine, J. H. Hammond, David C. Henry, J. A. Davis and H. T. Gay are mentioned as active in the organization before 1900.[62]

In 1867, J. B. Cummings sold a house in Louisville, also a lot, to the A. M. E. Zion Union of America. Other Negro churches were organized later.

Methodism was already established in Blount when Burke came in 1792, and when Asbury preached in 1818. The revival of 1810 had set it on its feet. (It is said that George Eakin received ten thousand members into the church during his ministry, eight thousand of whom were converted under his ministry.) He also organized a Sunday school as early as 1813. Eakin did a mighty work of penetration into the coves and valleys, so that by 1830 and the first written Circuit Records, there were at least seven organized churches in Blount County, with others in the process of formation. Holston Conference since its organization in 1824, had been composed of young men, and they had injected the strength and enthusiasm of youth into their work.[63]

The work went on harmoniously within the conference. Locally the question of slavery posed no question, but at the highest level, the time came when the only solution was the Plan of Separation. Each annual conference was to vote whether they would be under the pastoral care of the Southern or Northern Church. Holston Conference voted to support the M. E. Church, South. This action made no apparent difference or interruption in the work of the church until 1862 and no break occurred until 1865.

In September 1864, at a quarterly meeting of the Maryville Circuit of the Holston Conference at Carpenter's Campground, they approved the action of the Knoxville Convention held in July, of the ministers and members of the M. E. Church, transferring their relations from the M. E. Church, South, to the M. E. Church, U. S. A., and that in the future their relations would be Holston Conference of said church.

---

[61] *Recording Steward's Book*, Oakland Circuit, 1892-1909; Interview with Joe A. Garner, oldest member of the Williamson church.
[62] *Maryville Times*, July 26, 1893.
[63] *McFerrin*, V. 2, p. 342.

This motion was made by Spencer Henry and seconded by Christopher Best. William H. Rogers was presiding elder.[64]

In 1865, The Methodist Episcopal Church reorganized in Holston Conference at Athens, Tennessee. Thirty-one preachers enrolled at that conference in the same church where, twenty years before, they had voted to adhere to the M. E. Church, South.

The confusion arising from the claims of the M. E. Church for church property practically paralyzed the M. E., South. Only one preacher was assigned to Blount County in 1865. The door of the Maryville church was barred and nailed. Some charges had appointees from both conferences, some had none. Neither sent anyone to the Little River Circuit. Only the Southern Conference sent an appointee to the Louisville Circuit, who did not remain the entire year.[65]

In 1867, the M. E., South sent Jacob Smith to the Little River Circuit, and the Rev. Henry C. Neal to the Louisville Circuit. The most open and brutal attack on a preacher which took place in East Tennessee during this period of unrest took place near Morganton in Blount County on February 2, 1868. The Rev. L. K. Haynes had been forced to leave the circuit the year before, and when Henry C. Neal came into the territory, he was threatened with violence if he tried to organize his churches. He went about his work in spite of threats. He was waylaid and taken from his horse one day and beaten cruelly and left unconscious in the woods. The physician who attended him, reported that a handful of splinters from withes were taken from the lacerations on Neal's back. In later years he said that the shock of the attack affected his mind and that he was ever conscious of it.

The following year, a little less brutal attack was made on Jacob Smith who was serving the Little River and Sevierville Circuit. He was the first preacher on the charge since the war, and no one had succeeded Neal on the Louisville charge. The element of mob violence was boldly present. Newspaper reports that a mob drove Smith away from Logan's Chapel on March 14, and that on April 25 the whipping took place. This was the end of violence and church affairs became more nearly normal with each succeeding year. It is unfortunate that two of the most flagrant acts of violence against ministers should have taken place in Blount County.[66]

Progress was very slow in working toward unification which was finally achieved, in 1936, after almost a hundred years of separation.

---

[64] Isaac Patton Martin, *History of Methodism in Holston Conference*, (Knoxville, 1945), 63, Hereinafter cited *Martin; Recording Steward's Book*, Louisville Circuit, 1864.

[65] *Martin*, 66; *Minutes of the Union League of Maryville* for April 8, and 25, 1867 show that they ordered Parson Haynes to leave the county and appointed a committee to "thrash" him if he did not.

[66] R. N. Price, *Holston Methodism* (Nashville, 1913), V. 4, p. 100, 492, 472, 507; Col. Fleming in the *Press and Messenger*, (Knoxville, Tenn.), 1869—March and April, Passim.

There are today, in Blount County, twenty-four Methodist churches working toward common goals and a closer union.[67]

THE BAPTIST CHURCH

The leavening agent of the Baptist church must have been introduced very shortly after the initial settlement of the coves of Blount County, if it were not brought in with the first wave of settlers. Elder Richard Wood was already established in his work in Sevier County when the coves were settled and it has been said by more than one authority that Richard Woods did more to establish churches along the streams and in the coves of Blount and Sevier counties than any other person.[68]

Certainly, he lost very little time from John Walker's arrival in Tuckaleechee Cove in 1793 or 1794 until 1803 when Tuckaleechee, a new constitution with a membership of 65 asked for admission to the newly formed Tennessee Association. Since Association records are all that we can rely on, we cannot know who was present at its constitution. The delegates who represented her at the Association are names of later note—James Taylor, a Revolutionary soldier from Virginia and North Carolina; William Davis to serve later in the War of 1812 and a grandson of William Johnson, the first Moderator of the Tennessee Association, . . . both were later ordained ministers of the Baptist church. William Davis' father, Richard Davis, was a licensed minister, active in Tuckaleechee and later Miller's Cove and Cades Cove churches. Tuckaleechee was represented in the Tennessee Association from 1803 to 1809 inclusive, with a membership ranging from sixty-five in 1803 to ninety-one in 1806; then it gradually decreased to fifty-nine in 1809. Among the delegates other than the two named were: Moses Crosen (Crowson), Thomas Suggs, Isham Guinn, John Friar, Henry Haggard, Thomas Morrison, Richard Davis, and Kinsey Veach.[69]

In 1810, Tuckaleechee did not appear, but a new church, Wear's Cove (Sevier County) was admitted with a membership of fifty-seven (Tuckaleechee had fifty-nine the year before). Their delegates were Isham Guinn, and Richard Davis who had represented Tuckaleechee the year before. The following year Miller's Cove appeared as a new constitution and the same Richard Davis represented Miller's Cove. Not many men have represented as an official delegate, three churches in three successive years!

The location of Tuckaleechee is halfway between Wear's Cove and Miller's Cove and evidently the Tuckaleechee Congregation was dissolved to form two new congregations better located to serve the twenty-mile radius of the three coves.

Miller's Cove appeared in 1811 as a newly constituted church repre-

---

[67] *Martin*, 281.

[68] *Minutes of the Tennessee Association of Baptists, 1802–1862*, Baptist Board vault, Nashville, Tennessee. Hereinafter cited *Tennessee Association Minutes*. (Copy in author's collection).

[69] *Miller's Cove Baptist Church Minutes*, 1812.

sented by Richard Davis, Billy Holloway and George Snider. Billy Holloway was later ordained as a minister and was active in Six Mile church as long as he was able to attend. He was a Revolutionary soldier from Virginia. George Snider was ordained as minister in 1814 and served one of the most useful ministries in the Baptist churches in Blount, McMinn, and Monroe counties. For a good many years he was the only ordained minister residing in Blount County. He was the father of many new churches in the above-named counties and was also instrumental in the organization of the Hiwassee and Sweetwater associations.[70]

The first pages of the Miller's Cove record are missing so it is not known who the contituting body was, nor the exact date of formation, but the term "New Constitution" would suggest the organization date was not prior to 1810. Due to the dissolution of Tuckaleechee to form two congregations—Wear's Cove and Miller's Cove—Miller's Cove thus became the mother of the Baptist churches in Blount County.

The Six Mile church began in 1813 as an arm of Miller's Cove and in May, 1814, the arm chose to build their first church in the flatland below the old cemetery. In August, they petitioned the body to be made a church. In November 1814, Six Mile was duly constituted by Elijah Rogers and George Snider. Thomas Morrison, James Taylor, Elihu Hicks, William Blair, Aaron Walker, Richard Davis, Zachariah Hicks, and John Snider were delegated by Miller's Cove to attend. Six Mile was admitted to the Association in 1815 with thirty-eight members. Their delegates were Billy and John Holloway. Billy Holloway and his five sons were very active in the church for some ten or twenty years. None were there after the Civil War.[71]

The first church at Six Mile was near the cemetery according to Mrs. Elijah Hatcher who learned of it from her father, William Grindstaff. The church record stated "where the logs is halled on Brother Boyd's Plantation." The deed for two acres was from John Boyd in 1818 and included a "never failing spring."

The second church was built on the one-acre lot deeded by Daniel D. Foute which was between the road and creek near Lambert's. A cloudburst occurred about 1870 while the church was in session and Six Mile Creek became a raging torrent. The water began to come up into the church and the congregation began to climb into the rafters and those who could pray, waxed eloquent, before the flood abated, and they were rescued. This incident is referred to by old-timers as the "Stout Flood" because the Henry Stout family had their house carried away. The present churchhouse was built on higher ground away from the creek on Ben Holder's land.[72]

[70] Six Mile Baptist Church Minutes, 1813—; J. J. Burnett, Sketches of Tennessee's Pioneer Baptist Preachers, (Nashville, 1919), 486. Hereinafter cited Burnett, Sketches.
[71] Minutes of the Six Mile Baptist Church, 1813–26, Copy in author's collection.
[72] Deeds, 1, 557; M, 166 (The deed was reversionary); Mrs. Elijah Hatcher and Bert Garner—Reminiscing, 1952.

In 1823, Ellejoy was admitted as a new church with twelve members. The presbytery constituting the church were: Elijah Rogers, Thomas Hill and James Taylor. It had been an arm of Miller's Cove since 1818 and was represented by Jesse Brown, deacon, and Augustine Bowers. Bowers became a licensed minister and was especially active in the border-line churches of Sevier and Blount counties.[73]

Crooked Creek, also an arm of Miller's Cove, first appeared in 1825, represented by William Billue, Robert Billue, and John Pigg. This church was represented until 1832 and then is seen no more. William Billue, who was a cripple as a result of "white swelling," had spent several years among the Cherokees. He joined the Miller's Cove church in 1822, was ordained to the ministry in 1823 and was a very successful minister. He served a large territory and exercised a strong influence in the Baptist cause. He was Moderator of the Tennessee Association for several years. Pleasant Grove and Piney Level originated from the Crooked Creek church.[74]

Cades Cove was admitted in 1829 with J. Johnson as delegate. Miller's Cove mentioned this group as an arm at one time, but the Cades Cove records say it was an arm of Wear's Cove church.

In 1832, Six Mile asked to be dropped from the Association and implied that there were difficulties with Miller's Cove, which very likely affected the Crooked Creek church also.

Nine Mile Creek appeared in 1830 represented by William Davis and Theophilus Lomax. This is the group mentioned in the Six Mile minutes as meeting at William Davis' on Nine Mile for a number of years. This church was built near the home of William Pugh on Centenary Creek very near the present Centenary Baptist Church. For some reason this church did not flourish and dropped out of the Association records in 1838. This is about the date that Centenary Methodist Church was organized and 1838 being the date that the separation took place in the Baptist Church on the question of missions, we can only guess what may have taken place. Delegates who represented Nine Mile are: William Davis, Theophilus Lomax, William Pugh, J. Anderson, J. Birdwell, J. Hampton, J. Henderson, J. Hendrixson, and C. N. George.[75]

Pleasant Grove replaced Crooked Creek in 1833, represented by Thomas Harper. It is thought by local people that Piney Level was probably organized about the same time due to factions in the Old Crooked Creek church, but Piney Level did not seek admittance to the Association for a period of years.

August 1833, Ellejoy church met at John Vineyard's on Nail's Creek

---

[73] *Tennessee Association Minutes;* Burnett, *Sketches,* Passim.; *Minutes* of Ellejoy Church. Photostats in McClung Room, Lawson McGhee Library, Knoxville, Tennessee.

[74] *Tennessee Association Minutes.* Community tradition from various older people.

[75] *Tennessee Association Minutes;* Six Mile Baptist Church Minutes.

and received twenty members. They continued holding regular monthly meetings until September 1834, when they agreed to call the name of their meeting house Cedar Grove. In March 1835, Cedar Grove petitioned to be made a church. The mother church, Ellejoy, agreed for the church to be constituted in May and also agreed to divide their church funds. Cedar Grove was admitted to the Association, represented by John Vineyard and J. Tipton.[76]

Tuckaleechee Baptist Church was constituted the second time, February 22, 1834, by Elders Johnson Adams and Eli Roberts. The church was admitted to the Association with William Brickey and Joshua Taylor as delegates from the new church. In 1839, following the division of the Baptists on the question of missions, thirty members withdrew from the Tuckaleechee church and formed the Tuckaleechee Missionary Baptist Church. This church met at the Tuckaleechee Methodist Campground until they were debarred in 1845. They then met for a while in George Freshour's new barn. In the 80's they built a house on the lower corner of the present cemetery lot and took the name Bethel. The plot was given by George Freshour.[77]

Pistol Creek church appeared in 1841. The land was deeded by James Houston for a new church to be used by all denominations and for a school. It was represented in the Tennessee Association until 1851. The building was used as a school for fifty years or more and was called the "White Church." It is now used as a tenant house on the Proffitt farm near the golf course on the Louisville Pike.[78]

Mount Lebanon church was begun as a Sunday school in the Rocky Ridge schoolhouse, which was an old log building. Columbus Cowan and Aunt Jennie Hitch (wife of Elias) were the leaders of the Sunday school. A church was built in 1858 and named Mt. Lebanon. It was admitted to the Association in 1859, just before the outbreak of the Civil War. Early delegates other than pastors were Sharp, Hitch and DeArmond.

In 1894, a news item stated that Mt. Lebanon had the finest church building in the county with the exception of the Presbyterian and Methodist churches in Maryville.

A new church was built on the present site in 1915 which burned in 1950 and the present building was finished late in 1951.[79]

The Civil War, of course, kept some churches from activity more than others. Representation at the Association was not very large during the war years. There is no record of any Association being held in

---

[76] Wm. Billue in a deed made in 1848 for the White's Mill Tract includes the Baptist Meeting House; *Deeds*, U, 26; *Ellejoy Church Minutes*. Photostats in McClung Room.

[77] *Tennessee Minutes*; *Deeds*, N, 71 (1837); *Tuckaleechee Minutes* (Copy in author's collection); *Bethel Baptist Church Minutes*, Jake Farmer, church clerk, Townsend, Tennessee (examined 1952).

[78] Interview with Mrs. Emma Worley whose sister Molly Caldwell taught there in the 90's.

[79] Maryville *Times*, January 24, 1894; August 28, 1895; *Tennessee Association Minutes*.

1863. This report from the Cades Cove Primitive Baptist Church minutes is an index to the local situation in many communities:

> We, the Primitive Baptist Church in Blount County, in Cades Cove, do show to the public why we have not kept up our church meeting. It was on account of the Rebellion and we was Union people and the Rebels was too strong here in Cades Cove. Our preacher was obliged to leave sometimes, but thank God we once more can meet, though it was from August, 1862, until June, 1865, that we did not meet.[80]

In 1868, districts were designated by the Tennessee Association and the Maryville Union was set up which included two or three Knox County churches (those south of the river). This was approximately the same group later organized into the Chilhowee Association.[81]

In 1871 after a powerful revival meeting, an interested group met in the kitchen of Dr. Benjamin A. Morton's house and effected the organization of the First Baptist Church of Maryville. Among the charter members were: Henry S. Catlett, stock trader, and his wife Martha; Elijah James and wife Dorcas of Blockhouse; W. D. McGinley, attorney; Eli McKinney and wife Susan; George Pearson, restauranteur (had first bicycle in Maryville); Margaret Sexton, (mother of the Rev. Tom Sexton); Stephen Wells, tanner and harness-maker and his wife Nancy; Mrs. M. E. Hutsell; Letitia and Sarah Youngblood; James Clemens; Nelson Stinnett; and Dr. Ben A. Morton (who was the backbone of the church as long as he lived). This group built their church in 1876. It was remodeled in 1902. The present church was built in 1914, but has been enlarged several times.[82]

In 1871, Four Mile Baptist Church was admitted to the Association. This church is a direct descendant of Miller's Cove through Six Mile. The Nine Mile church was admitted in 1830 and disappeared in 1838. After the Civil War we find some of the same people in the Four Mile organization.[83]

The Laurel Bank church had a deed in 1866 from Elkanah Johnson; the church was admitted to the union in 1872.

In 1872, Happy Valley, and Union Grove were admitted. Other Baptist churches which claim an organization date prior to 1900 are: First Chilhowee, Old Chilhowee, Galilee, Liberty, Piney Grove, Prospect and Salem.

In 1842, James Henry made a deed to New Hope (later Clover Hill Presbyterian Church) and the Commissioners of the Common Schools, for a school, later known as Rockdale, reserving to the Baptist church the second Saturday of every month. This was evidently the Baker's Creek Congregation referred to very early in the Six Mile Minutes. This congregation would also be the forerunner of the Salem, Hopewell

---

[80] Note in front of *Tennessee Association Minutes; Cades Cove Baptist Church* Minutes in hands of John Oliver, Townsend, Tennessee.
[81] *Tennessee Association Minutes* for 1868 (loose).
[82] *Minutes of First Baptist Church of Maryville;* Dr. Morton's brother, Rev. John H. Morton was active in Six Mile, Crooked Creek, and Pleasant Grove churches.
[83] *Tennessee Association Minutes,* 1871, 1872 (separate).

and Laurel Bank churches. In 1842, there was no organized Baptist church in the southwest quarter of Blount County.[84]

Although there had not been a Negro Baptist Church in Maryville within the remembrance of the present generation, a Congregation was listed in 1879 with John Clemens, as pastor. Other Congregations have been organized in the county in later years, but none in Maryville until recently.

To summarize briefly: Tuckaleechee was the first Baptist church organized in Blount County. Miller's Cove, by the dissolution of Tuckaleechee, became the mother church which supplied the leavening agent for: Six Mile, Ellejoy, Crooked Creek, Chilhowee and others. From the above named churches came all the later ones by a rapidly branching process.

George Snider was the first Baptist minister ordained in Blount County and he did a great work of organization here and later in Monroe and McMinn counties. James Taylor, William Holloway, William Davis, James Langford, William Billue, Isaac Elledge, Jeptha Ginn, Isaac Hinds, John H. Morton, and Augustine Bowers were some of the local ministers who are not well enough known to the public. There were a good many others who lived in Sevier County who did a tremendous work in our early churches; Richard Woods, Elijah Rogers, Eli Roberts, and Dr. Thomas Hill, especially. Others who were active later on: P. B. McCarroll, W. M. Burnett, William and Robert Atchley, Daniel Buckner, Michael Cate, J. W. H. Coker, Andrew Connatser, Richard Evans, and many others. Our records are few and sparse as to details, but to these poorly paid men and others the Baptist churches in Blount County owe a great debt.[85]

When the Baptist church divided on the mission question, in 1838, Tuckaleechee and Cades Cove were the only churches that had strong enough groups of the Old School faction to remain active without faltering. They took the name Old School or Primitive Baptist, while the other group were dubbed Missionary or New School. They are also referred to locally, as "Hard-Shell" and "Soft-Shell" respectively.

Miller's Cove, Law's Chapel, Old Piney, Antioch and Chilhowee along with Tuckaleechee and Cades Cove have been active Primitive Baptist churches. All of these except Old Piney, Antioch, and Cades Cove are still active churches. Cades Cove is inactive, but not altogether extinct. Among the outstanding local leaders in the Primitive Baptist Church since the Civil War were Elders William and J. B. J. Brickey, William H. Oliver, W. A. Gregory, John and James Abbott, Giles P. Dunn, John H. Brickey and G. P. Adams.[86]

---

[84] *Deeds*, B B, 294; S, 356; *Minutes of Chilhowee Baptist Association*, 1950, Table A. The Old Piney church first met in an old still house, and continued to meet there for a considerable time. The Rev. Mr. Gray preached the first sermon in the new house (interview with Mrs. Elijah Hatcher, Six Mile).

[85] Burnett, *Sketches*, Passim.

[86] Minutes of the individual churches and of the *Tennessee Primitive Baptist Association Minutes*: also *Tennessee and Nolachucky Consolidated Association of Primitive Baptists*.

No attemept has been made to touch the history of Baptist churches organized after 1900, even briefly, because it would require a separate work. The before mentioned facts serve only to bring to light and help preserve the early history which has too long been lost sight of.

THE LUTHERAN CHURCH

The only knowledge the present generation has of the existence of an early Lutheran church is the old Lutheran Cemetery on the Blockhouse road about three miles from Maryville.

The first trace of an official record of Lutheran connections in Blount County was in 1823, when Henry Long was a lay delegate from St. Paul's Church, Knox County to the 4th convention of the Tennessee Synod at Sinking Springs Church in Greene County. This is the first time that a Knox County church was represented at Synod.[87]

Among the Blount County deeds recorded in 1838 is one from Henry Long to the Lutheran Synod of Tennessee for one acre for St. John's Church. The odds are strong that this is the same Henry Long who in 1823 represented St. Paul's in Knox County.

No records have been found so far, between the registering of the deed for St. John's in 1838 and 1873 when William Wetzell was a delegate to the Evangelical Lutheran Holston Synod held at Blue Spring (Mosheim) in Greene County, Tennessee.

Patton Stone was a delegate in 1877. Nothing more is known until 1886. The Missionary superintendent in his report that year stated that "St. John's in Blount County is in a feeble condition but the way to assist it, just now, is not quite clear." [88]

An interview with an 87-year-old man who grew up in the community netted some information. The Longs—Jacob and Christian— Green Cupp, Patton Stone, Monroe and Mary Houser; the Wetzells— Jesse and his sons—William, Frank, and Isaac were members that he remembered. He could remember a Houser who preached there and a Cox as well as a one-armed man named Barb.[89]

The St. Paul's Lutheran Church was organized in Maryville during the year 1953 and has now a prosperous congregation meeting at the former location of the First Christian Church.

THE EARLY EPISCOPAL STORY

In the year 1852, the Rev. John Lenoir Gay came to the Diocese of Tennessee to undertake mission work in Blount, Loudon, McMinn, Bradley, Monroe, and Polk counties.

---

[87] Socrates Henkel, *History of the Evangelical Lutheran Synod of Tennessee* (New Market, Va., 1890), 54.
[88] *Deeds*, S, 23; *Evangelical Lutheran Holston Synod Minutes*, 1873; 1886, p. 10.
[89] Interview with E. L. Wilkinson, Maryville, Tennessee, March, 1953; J. C. Barb was a professor in various Lutheran church schools and is often mentioned in the minutes of Holston Synod.

As a result of his labors, church buildings were erected in Athens, Cleveland, Chilhowee, Riverside and Louisville.[90]

Before the Rev. Gay resigned in October 1854, he reported that he assisted in laying the cornerstone at Chilhowee in Blount County. He also reported the church buildings at Loudon and Ducktown as being well advanced.

In September 1854, Bishop Otey stated that on August 8, 1854, he appointed Mr. Robert Shepherd as Lay Reader at Chilhowee. He examined Mr. Shepherd for Deacon's orders and appointed his ordination. Mr. Shepherd was officiating at Chilhowee and hoping to collect a congregation and build a church.

In 1856, Mr. Shepherd was examined and ordained as priest in Knoxville. Shortly afterwards Bishop Otey went to Louisville where Mr. Shepherd was successful in raising money for a church. From Louisville, Bishop Otey went to Maryville where he preached in the Presbyterian College (Maryville) and on to Montvale, a "delightful summer resort," where he preached at the hotel. Leaving Montvale, he went to Chilhowee where he stayed with Mr. Robert James, the father-in-law of Mr. Shepherd and preached in Mr. James' factory. (Abram's Creek-Chilhowee Spinning and Weaving Manufactory.) From Chilhowee Bishop Otey traveled on to "Riverside" at the mouth of Tellico.[91] No further report can be found locally to indicate that an Episcopal church got further than the paper plans at this time.

In 1859, Otey reported that the Rev. Mr. Downing attempted to establish a school at Riverside but that he and the proprietor could not agree. He also reported that the Rev. Robert Shepherd had collected over a thousand dollars to construct a church at Louisville. He (Shepherd) loaned this money to a relative and left for England where he was understood to be acting as a curate to the Bishop of Durham. (Another report said that he went to Newcastle-on-Tyne.)

The James and Shepherd families left Chilhowee just before the Civil War and the church organization never revived after the war. No further reference is found of any attempts to establish an Episcopal church in Blount County until 1923.

May 21, 1923, Bishop Maxon of Tennessee, Dr. Walter Whittaker and the Rev. Leroy John of Knoxville met with a few interested people in Alcoa to talk over prospects of opening an Episcopal Mission. It was decided to operate as an unorganized mission under the direction of Dr. Whittaker, Dean of the East Tennessee Convocation. Services were held at a temporary mission on Nobel Street, in Alcoa. Pews were given by St. John's Episcopal Church in Knoxville.[92]

---

[90] Arthur Howard Noll, *History of the Church of the Diocese of Tennessee* (New York, 1900), 114.

[91] Bishop James H. Otey's *Journal* for 1854, 44; 1856, Passim. Riverside was St. Andrew's Church, on the McGhee farm at Nile's Ferry.

[92] Seymour, Charles M., *St. John's Knoxville*, 1947, p. 32; *Knoxville Sentinel* October 20, 1923.

The first service was September 2, 1923. Officers who served were: Warden, John A. Hunter; Treasurer, T. I. Stephenson; Secretary, D. W. Poage. A. G. Holland, Wm. H. Abbott and Robert G. Poage were to serve with the church officers as an executive board.

In 1947, the Episcopal group purchased the old Friends church property on Brodway in Maryville and St. Andrew's Episcopal Church was officially organized.

THE FRIENDS CHURCH

The exact date that Friends came into Blount County is not known but tradition in certain families has said that the date was about 1794. Officially the first church was organized in 1808.

The First Quaker meetings in Tennessee were Nolachucky in 1784 and Lost Creek in 1787. They appear to have been from New Garden, North Carolina, since that monthly meeting declined in 1787 to transfer their rights of membership, because they had settled on land to which the Indians still laid claim. Finally in 1795, New Hope (Greene County) became a monthly meeting and in 1797, Lost Creek (Jefferson County) was recognized.[93]

Lost Creek Monthly Meeting, 24th of 1st month, 1801 granted Friends of the Lower Settlement the privilege of holding meetings every first day except the one following monthly meeting. In 1802, this privilege was extended to include the holding of week-day meetings. At the session held 11th of 8th month, 1804, the Quarterly Meeting directed that a Preparative Meeting be established at the Lower Settlement, to be called by the name of Newberry. Lost Creek minutes mention the following persons as members of Newberry Preparative Meeting: James Allen, Mahlon Steveson, William Murdock, an elder; Walter Canaday, Ann Jones, an elder; Thomas Jones, an elder; William Durham, Mary Bonine and Margaret Jones. Other members mentioned in the first few pages of Newberry Monthly Meeting minutes include: Francis Jones, William Williams, a minister; Daniel Bonine, Ephraim Lee, Azariah Williams, an elder; Rachel Williams, an elder; Daniel Durham, Hugh Hackney, Benjamin Bailey, and Johnston Jones.[94]

The minutes of Lost Creek Meeting records the setting-off of Newberry Preparative Meeting as follows: on the 29th of 8th month, 1807, Newberry Preparative Meeting requested the privilege of holding Monthly Meetings among themselves. A committee was appointed to visit them and make a report. At the next meeting, held the 26th of the 9th month, 1807, the committee made a favorable report with which the Meeting concurred and ordered that a certificate be forwarded to the Quarterly Meeting. There is no further mention of the matter until

---

[93] Dorothy Lloyd Gilbert. *Quaker Migration to the Western Waters* in the E. T. H. S. Publications #18, p. 47–58, Passim.

[94] William Wade Hinshaw, *Encyclopedia of American Quaker Genealogy*, V. 1, p. 1137.

the 28th of the 5th month, 1808, when minutes were recorded stating that the request of Newberry to hold monthly meetings among themselves had been granted.[95]

The New Hope and Lost Creek Quarterly Meeting dated 14th of 5th month, 1808, stated that the committee had reported and on the basis of this report directed that Newberry Monthly Meeting be held on the first seventh day of the week on each month and their Preparative Meeting on the fourth day of the same week. A committee of nine was appointed to attend the first two meetings.

The minutes of the first meeting, evidently held in the 6th month, have been lost. The minutes of the second meeting, held 2nd of 7th month, 1808, have been preserved and their church records begin therewith. A deed to the church lot was made by Aaron Hackney and James Moore in 1822.[96]

In 1833 a complaint was lodged against certain persons, not Friends, having erected "artificial gravestones" to their dead in the Friends' burial ground, contrary to the custom of Friends. After much labor and reference to Quarterly Meeting the matter was compromised by sinking the slabs as low as would leave them legible.

It is interesting to note that they disapproved of their members accepting public office and also of their attending muster. They became concerned in the 1830's because so few local teachers were members of their society. Of five schools within the limits of their Meeting, only one was taught by a Friend. Fifty-three families are reported as not having a copy of Scriptures in the house. A survey to see if family records were kept, said all but one family kept records. Of 89 members interviewed to find if any used liquor for other than medicinal purposes, the report said only four.

In 1846, Friends on the west side of Cloyd's Creek requested a Meeting to be set up. The committee appointed found them capable and on December 12, 1846, Hezekiah Jones was appointed overseer of Hickory Valley Meeting.[97]

Newberry was the only Meeting of record in 1865, but there was before and after this date a number of "indulged Meetings." Among others, Hickory Valley and Bethel (near Montvale, chartered as Bethel Academy). Bethel was a church from its charter (1880) as Bethel Academy until 1900 on land given by John Farr. It was a subscription school only. Maryville, Tallassee (in Monroe County) and perhaps other points were meeting places for a while. Maryville and Hickory Valley became Meetings later.[98]

About 1820–30 the tide of emigration was strong toward Indiana,

---

[95] Samuel Dunlap, *History of the Society of Friends in Tennessee* (1899). An unpublished manuscript in the USD 1812 collection, hereinafter cited *Dunlap*.
[96] *Minutes of Newberry Monthly Meeting*, Friendsville, Tennessee, 1808–1848, copy at University of Tennessee Library, Knoxville, Tennessee. Hereinafter cited *Newberry Minutes;* Also in Church Library, Friendsville, Tennessee; *Deeds,* N, 200.
[97] *Newberry Minutes,* 109, 112, 171.
[98] *Dunlap.*

Illinois and Iowa as issues of slavery and States' rights grew stronger. By 1825, there were twenty-five Abolition Societies in the state. William Williams is credited with organizing several of the early ones in East Tennessee before he emigrated to Indiana. There are several petitions on this subject in the State Archives, bearing signatures of Friends and Methodists in the vicinity of Friendsville and Middlesettlement. At this time a proposition was laid before Newberry Monthly to close the Meeting entirely and emigrate to Kansas and form a colony. David Morgan, a minister, and James Allen, an elder, having been sent to seek out the land. The Meeting did not concur, and the subject was closed.[99]

Friendsville Institute and Newberry Female School was founded in 1854 and opened in 1857. Original plans called for two buildings but for economy's sake one building was constructed with a brick partition upstairs and down, and a high stout fence outside, separating boys and girls.[100]

Hickory Valley Meeting was set up 5th month, 20th day, 1871. Newberry and Hickory Valley composed Friendsville Quarterly Meeting. Newberry became Friendsville Monthly Meeting in 1875. Friendsville is still a strong church.

In June 1869, J. A. Grinnell bought forty-six acres at the north side of the intersection of Morganton Road and Main Street and lot No. 34 on Main Street. At this time we find that a group of Friends was meeting in the homes of Friends, at the A. M. E. Church, and at the courthouse. In 1871, we find that a deed was recorded from Grinnell to the Friends.

The following are identified as ministers in the minutes: the Revs. Jeremiah and Martha Grinnell, Rachel Binford, David Bowles, Joseph Haskins and wife. Trustees named in the deed were: John Morris, William Russell, and the Rev. David Bowles. In December, 1871, the overseers reported $2,286.95 spent on the house to date. From all indications the house was nearly complete. The treasurer named by the congregation was Dr. Franklin Elliott. Dr. Jeptha D. Garner, the Leverings, the Newbys, Professor Wilson Spray, Dr. W. C. Stanley and Orlando Winters are a few of the early members who made news locally during the 70's and 80's.[101]

The church was strong during the thirty years that the Quakers were operating local schools. The most prominent members were those who were active in the schools. By 1915 the schools had closed and the church was beginning to decline and continued to do so, for the next twenty years.

The Maryville church was attached to the Lost Creek Quarterly Meeting at first, and spent her energies working new territory in Blount, Loudon and Monroe counties.

---

[99] Tennessee State Archives, *Petitions*.
[100] *Dunlap*.
[101] An unsigned manuscript in the Minutes Book of the Maryville Church; *Deeds*, DD 64; *Minutes of the Maryville Monthly Meeting of Friends*, 1871–1910 at the parsonage at Friendsville, Tennessee.

After 1900, Friendsville was the only Quarterly Meeting in the state. It was composed of Friendsville, Maryville, and Hickory Valley.[102]

In June, 1935, it was suggested that the Maryville church be closed for an indefinite period. Later in the year it was reorganized, according to the records. The following April we find that they petitioned the Yearly Meeting to place the people and property under their care. During the last years of the congregation's existence, the members voted to use their "cemetery fund" to put a new roof on the building.[103]

In 1947, the property was sold to St. Andrew's Episcopal Church and so this quaint old building entered into another era of being. All that remains of the Friends property in Maryville is an overgrown, neglected, old cemetery lot on the Morganton Road.

CATHOLIC

There have been periods in the history of Blount County when there has been enough concentrated population of Catholics to warrant occasional official visits from churchmen. Especially was this true during the early days of the lumber mill at Townsend.[104] However, it was not until 1947 that Our Lady of Fatima Catholic Church was organized in Maryville. The temporary home of this church was on Ellis Avenue, until the completion of the new building at the corner of Hunt Road and Wright's Ferry Road in Alcoa, which was dedicated in 1953.

THE CHRISTIAN CHURCH

The Church of Christ at Liberty, Blount County, Tennessee was constituted by the Rev. Mattison (Madison) Love, December 25, 1850, and was afterwards more fully organized by the appointment of elders and deacons. Elders were John A. Hannah and John McClewer. Thirty-four original male members included: Anderson, Bicknell, Bise, Brown, Blow, Davis, Dunlap, Gorley, Grindstaff, Hannah, Harper, Hutsell, Hamel, Keller, Love, Learn, Land, McClure, Raulston, Rudd, Owen, Scott, Thompson, Waller.

In 1930, Mrs. A. C. Anderson (Mary E. Hannah) was 87 years old. At that time she was the only living charter member. She said that she pieced and sold quilts to buy the bell on the present building which is the second one since its organization. She also said that her great-uncle—John Davis Jr., was a minister of the church and preached here before he moved to Clay County, Illinois.[105]

---

[102] *Dunlap;* Stanley Pumphrey. *Missionary Work in connection with the Society of Friends,* (Phila., 1880), 35. A report to the Society of Friends given in 1879 says the membership of the Maryville Monthly Meeting is nearly 300, that about half are connected with the two newly established Meetings of Bethel and Tallassee, where meetings are held regularly twice a week. At another point meetings are held once a week and at three others once a month. A great many places are visited more occasionally. Eight meeting and schoolhouses have been built.

[103] *Maryville Friends Minutes,* 1910–1935.

[104] *Maryville Times,* July 22, 1905 stated that Father Cassedy had been visiting his parishioners. "The school has been built on the hill southwest of town, which will also serve as a church."

[105] Madison Love was prominent in Upper East Tennessee churches, and traveled widely; *Minutes of Liberty Church of Christ,* 1850. Mrs. C. R. Miller, clerk.

Mountain View Christian Church was organized October 6th, 1907, by George Martin and dedicated by E. C. Wilson, ministers, (from Johnson County, Tennessee) "with the Bible as our only rule of faith and practice" and the following officership: Elders I. W. Taylor, Nick Blevins, George T. Raulston, and later, James A. Kagley and William Crowder. Deacons: John Holder, John Rasor, Roy Howard and later Wade Raulston, and Cowan Willocks. Names found: Martin, Blevins, Taylor, Holder, Rasor, Chapman, Best, Willocks, Miller, Law, Raulston, Moore, Crisp, Farley, Boring, Hannah, Kagley, Howard, and Summey. The church was built on land given by Isaac W. Taylor. According to tradition the cemetery was started in 1910, but the first burial according to marked graves was in 1914. This is a very active rural church.[106]

The Maryville Christian Church was organized on the 26th day of January 1912 with twenty-five charter members and Brother Clark of Chattanooga as the pastor. Officers were elected the same day. Deacons were A. J. Coleman and W. A. Ball. Elders were C. S. Grove, W. H. Caldwell, J. F. Chappell, and E. C. Coleman.

The charter members included: Grove, Chappel, Caldwell, Ball, Walker, Miller, Anderson, Lonas, Smith, Steele, Keller. The church was located at the corner of College and Depot (Ellis Avenue) streets.[107]

This congregation moved in October, 1952, to a beautiful new church located at Court and Goddard streets and the old building is now occupied by St. Paul's Lutheran Church.

Sometime around 1890, a group of people met at Nelson School and was organized into a church body known as Nelson Chapel Church of Christ. They met there until 1894 when Ben Vaughn and his wife Martha gave a tract of land for a church and cemetery. The present churchhouse, which is the second, was built during the 1920's.

Among the first members were the families of William Heaton, Columbus Swaney, Ben Vaughn, and Robert Johnson. The first ministers were Alec Bruner who came from North Carolina, Dr. K. B. Lawson, an herb doctor, also from North Carolina, and S. T. Willocks.[108]

The first burial in the cemetery from the tombstone inscriptions seems to have been Moses Willocks in 1894, age 77.

The more recent church at Five Points is also of this faith.

CHURCH OF THE BRETHREN

The only Church of the Brethren, Dunker or Dunkard Church of record in Blount County is Oakland which was organized in 1870. In

---

[106] *Minutes of Mountain View Church of Christ*, 1907, James Clark, clerk; Information from Taylor's daughter, Mrs. Viola Taylor Raulston.

[107] *Minutes of the Maryville Christian Church*, 1912; this record was lost for about twenty years and was found when the church was moved to the new location in 1953.

[108] Interviews with various church members. They keep no records; They are also referred to as the "Antis" as opposed to the Christian Church. *Deeds*, 48, p. 199 (to D. C. Swaney, commissioner).

1874, Shem Zook of Mifflin County, Pennsylvania, transferred through his attorney, S. Z. Sharp, one hundred acres to John M. Bowman and his wife, Mary E. Bowman with the exception of one acre.

The Bowmans on the strength of this title bond then made a deed to George Kizer, Benjamin Sanborn and Joseph Fry, Trustees of Oakland Meeting House for one dollar, one acre, "on which is erected a house of worship known as the Oakland Meeting House of the Brethren (German Baptists)."

Matt Cochran and Hugh Young who were both past eighty years of age in 1952 remembered attending a school held in the old church building by John Bowman and Miss Lizzie McCracken under a Peabody grant some eighty years ago. Cochran was four years old at the time. He said the house was built by Joseph Fry, and that he clearly remembered how hard the backless split log benches (the bark still on them) were to one whose feet did not touch the floor.[109]

At a district meeting held at Mountain Valley, Greene County, Tennessee, in 1870, Oakland Church presented a letter stating their organization. Elder S. Z. Sharp represented the church in '71, '73, and '76. The church was represented by delegation only 14 out of 44 years of record. The Kleppers and Frys are the most often mentioned.

Elders G. C. Bowman and Samuel Molsbee, German Baptist evangelists from upper East Tennessee were conducting meetings in Blount County communities in 1880. Cloyd's Creek was particularly mentioned. The church was silent for fourteen years until 1914.[110]

February 28, 1921, the Mission Board of the Tennessee District, Church of the Brethren, signed an agreement with the following trustees: Floyd Bingham, G. W. Young, W. R. Cunningham, J. R. Lane, and O. M. Lane, that transferred the use of the property on condition that they either repair the old building or replace it with a new one such as would meet the needs of the community. The only condition of the agreement was that the Brethren should have the first Sunday in each month, provided they should want to hold services. The agreement was signed by: P. D. Reed; S. H. Garst, treasurer; J. B. Hilbert, president; A. E. Nead, member of the board. Garst is said to have lived at the Walter Pate place and taught school and preached at Oakland.[111]

Bowman, Kiser, Sanborn, Hutsell, McClanahan, Klepper, Crosswhite and Fry are among the early active members and the first five names may be found engraved on stones in the cemetery near the intersection of the Old Niles Ferry and Calderwood roads.

[109] *Deeds* PP, 86, 391; Interviews, July 1952. Later interview with Mr. A. B. Fry (son of Joseph).

[110] *District Meeting Minutes of Church of the Brethren,* 1870 . . . made available by Elder Reuel B. Pritchett of White Pine, Tennessee; Solomon Zook Sharp was principal of Maryville Normal School (Maryville College) during the seventies. He went to Ashland, Ohio, in 1878 (Maryville *Index*, December 11, 1878; March 5, 1880).

[111] Moses Cunningham, Interview March, 1953. Agreement registered April 15, 1922. (Agreement in Cunningham's possession).

Baldwin Hall   Anderson Hall   Memorial Hall

Maryville College 1879

CHAPTER VII

Education

From the earliest settlement, Tennessee was the pioneer in the dissemination and promotion of learning in the Southwest. This is all the more remarkable because Tennessee was an appendage of North Carolina which was the most backward of all the colonies in education. This is partly explained by the fact that the greater half of the population of Tennessee at this time was Scotch Presbyterian.[1]

Wherever there was a Scotch community there was a church, and in that church was a school or in a nearby building according as they had prospered. The teachers were generally the ministers who, on the whole, were well-educated. The first college west of the Alleghanies was chartered in 1783. Samuel Doak had started the school in 1780 which was chartered by North Carolina in 1783 as Martin Academy. It was recognized by the State of Franklin in 1785 and rechartered as Washington College in 1795 by the Territorial Assembly (Territory South of the River Ohio).

That the need for education was one of the foremost considerations of our forefathers is evidenced by the following excerpt from the Constitution of the State of Franklin, Sec. 41:

That a school or schools shall be established by the Legislature for the convenient instruction of youth, with such salaries to the masters paid by the public, as may enable them to instruct at low prices; and all useful learning shall be duly encouraged and promoted in one or more universities.

Section 32 of the rejected constitution of Franklin also provided for schools by naming a tax to support a grammar school for each county, etc.[2]

The early history of education in Tennessee is the story of the early colleges, and academies. The same is true of the early history of education in Blount County. Academies in general were private schools taught by ministers to supplement the meager support they got from their congregations and that fact is not exactly a misstatement when applied locally as will be shown.[3]

During the ten years prior to the erection of Blount County, the settlers were forced to enfort most of the time. Tradition says that schools were taught in these forts before 1790. Forts McTeer and Craig both carry such traditions. Unfortunately, our forebears did not record

---

[1] Goodspeed Publishing Co., *Tennessee History*, (Nashville, 1887) 413; hereinafter cited *Goodspeed*.

[2] Ramsey, *Annals*, 332; Samuel C. Williams, *State of Franklin*, (Johnson City, 1924), p. 56, (footnote); Appendix, 337.

[3] Robert H. White, *Development of the Tennessee State Educational Organization 1796-1929* (Nashville, 1929), 10, Hereinafter cited *White*.

their early acts regarding religion or education. An exception is the schoolhouse supposedly built in 1794 by Andrew Kennedy and Henry McCullock for the use of their own and neighboring children in which Sam Houston taught a school about 1811. A historical marker on State Highway 33 points out the fact. However, we are indebted to a couple of early travelers for this observation made November 9, 1799, as they passed through Maryville, "the County town of Blount County," on their way to the Cherokee Nation: "At the end of the place (Maryville) there is quite a large church built of hewn logs; further on we saw another (probably Baker's Creek) and several schoolhouses along the way." [4]

Mr. Parham said that the first school in Maryville was taught on lot No. 120 at the corner of Jail and Cates Street (near the spring) by the Rev. Mark Moore or Josiah P. Smith about 1797. (The Rev. Mark Moore was a Methodist Circuit Rider on Holston Circuit in 1786 who dropped out of the conference records until 1820.) It is not known where he lived except that Bishop Asbury mentioned stopping at his home near Maryville.[5]

From those references we have evidence of some sort of organized schools before 1800. The History of Eusebia Church says that a school was conducted in the church building at first and that later a schoolhouse was built nearby.

In 1806, Congress passed an act of great importance to the educational interests of Tennessee: "An act to authorize the State of Tennessee to issue grants and perfect titles to certain lands therein described and to settle the claims to the vacant and unappropriated lands within the same." This land act is important to Blount County for other than educational reasons because this act made it possible for the inhabitants of the county to obtain title to the lands on which they had lived for twenty years. The university phases of this act are not pertinent to this story.[6]

Following this action, the Tennessee Legislature passed an act chartering academies in twenty-seven counties of the state. Among those academies chartered was Porter Academy, in Blount County, with the following trustees: Gideon Blackburn, John Montgomery, John Lowry (merchant), Joseph B. Lapsley and Andrew Kennedy. The act provided that the trustees should purchase, receive and hold, or sell lands, etc., for the use and advantage of the academy. They were empowered to appoint a president, secretary, tutors, treasurer, and other persons necessary for conducting the business of the institution. Two-thirds of the trustees must concur on any matter of importance and any vacancy was to be filled by the Assembly. The trustees were to elect a treasurer, who should collect money (under bond) and might receive whatever salary was fixed by the trustees. The trustees were to purchase a site,

---

[4] Williams, *Early Travels*, 462. Report of Steiner and Schweinitz.
[5] *Parham Papers*; Francis Asbury's *Journal*, V. 3, 291; *Price*, V. 1, p. 95, 102.
[6] *White*, 11.

take subscriptions to pay for the site and erection of buildings and they had full power to recover, in case of a failure to pay, such subscriptions. The number of trustees could be increased up to thirteen. The first trustee named was to call a meeting at the courthouse and until the election of a president of the academy one of the trustees should be chosen to preside. (The trustees were required to visit the schools at least once each week, and later once each month.) Most of the academies were erected and financed by private subscriptions and donations. Some were financed by lotteries.[7]

Whatever the source of funds, the school opened in 1808 with the Rev. Mark Moore as teacher. He was to procure a teacher of Latin and Greek. It seems that at first the school was sharing a lot with the English school and that the arrangement was not satisfactory and they then moved to lot No. 110, formerly the site of Sterling Coal Company. The identity of this English school is not known but was probably the New Providence Church School.[8]

When the Board of Trustees for Porter Academy met in January 1807, the Rev. Joseph B. Lapsley was made chairman; the Rev. Gideon Blackburn, secretary, and John Lowry, (merchant) treasurer. In 1809, other trustees were appointed: James Houston Sr., John Lowry, attorney; Alexander McGhee and James Gillespy, Jr., of Little River. The board made eighteen rules to govern teachers and students. Among them: "School shall be opened with prayer; no student shall use profane and obscene language; they shall not attend horse races, balls, or frolicking assemblies and must attend divine services on the Sabbath." In 1809 John Caldwell and William Moore were teachers and in 1811 Josiah P. Smith was discontinued. In September 1811, a letter came from the Rev. Isaac Anderson recommending one Matthew L. Dixon. Additional trustees appointed in 1819 were: David Caldwell, Robert Houston, and John McGhee. (Gideon Blackburn had probably resigned when he left Maryville in 1810.) In 1813, the Rev. Isaac Anderson was elected principal and served an average of 15 students until 1817, when he became connected with the Female Academy. Some of the outstanding students mentioned in the early records were: Jacob Foute, who became clerk of the court; John Finley Gillespy, a prominent lawyer and politician; and William Eagleton, who was principal of Rittenhouse Academy at Kingston, instructor at Maryville College, and later pastor of the Presbyterian Church in Murfreesboro.[9]

In October 1813, an act was passed to establish a female academy in Maryville, Blount County. Andrew Thompson, David Caldwell, James Berry, John Montgomery, John Gardner, James Houston, William

---

[7] Porter Academy was probably named in honor of James P. H. Porter who was representative at this time; *Acts, 1806*, ch. 8, Sec. 1.
[8] *Parham Papers; Abstracts of Minutes of Board of Trustees of Porter Academy*, Property of James M. Cates. (Original minutes lost after abstracts were made. Copy in author's collection, Porter High School files and County Superintendent of Schools' office. Hereinafter cited *Academy Abstracts*.
[9] *Acts, 1809*, ch. 3, Sec. 3.

Aylett, and Isaac Anderson were elected trustees. The charter provided that any two members could hold a meeting and that five members would compose a board which could make all laws consistent with the State Laws.

In 1815, an act was passed authorizing the drawing of a lottery for the benefit of the Maryville Female Academy and Porter Academy. The amount was not to exceed $8,000. (The lottery was a common source of raising funds, in those days, which was outlawed in 1832.) In February 1819, the Trustees reported that the lottery would not work and ordered all money refunded. A week later they ordered the Female Academy building sold because they could not afford to repair it. It was sold to Isaac Anderson in 1820.[10]

In 1819 the Porter Academy building had fallen into such a state of disrepair that the property was advertised and sold to Jacob Foute in 1820 for $173.00. It is quite possible that the opening of the Southern and Western Theological Seminary at this time had an influence on the board's action. In 1822 some state funds to the amount of $300 were available and John Montgomery gave a lot across the street from the present courthouse for a new location.[11]

A committee was ordered to build a house of two ends, twenty feet square, connected in the middle with a partition of logs of one foot through at the butt. There were to be thirteen rounds of logs exclusive of the sills and plates; a chimney in the middle, with fireplaces above and below. There was to be a door and four windows in each end below and above (two windows at each end). This building cost $300.

In 1830, the title of all property belonging to the Academy was vested in the State of Tennessee in accordance with an act of Legislature, December 31, 1829, by James H. Gillespy, president of the board of trustees and James Berry, secretary.[12]

In 1831, $1,139.76 of Academy monies was allotted to each county which should have helped to get the academy back on its feet. Nothing seems to have been done about qualifying for these funds until 1835. To all appearances the school may not have been in operation. The appointment of trustees had been delegated to the county courts and up to this time none had been appointed and the fact that a full slate of trustees was appointed seems to support this idea. Major Jesse Thompson, Dr. Sam Pride, William Toole, Esq., William A. Spencer, Reuben L. Cates, Dr. James H. Gillespy, Thomas White, Esq., Col. William Wallace and Dr. Robert H. Hodsden were appointed trustees at the March term of court, 1835. They, together with Wilson L. Trundle and Samuel Wallace, made bond to receive the academy funds according to act of January 5, 1830.[13]

[10] *Acts, 1813*, ch. 30; *Academy Abstracts*, 1819; *Acts, 1815*, ch. 67.
[11] *Deeds*, 2, p. 271. Trustees were: John McGhee, James Berry, Andrew Thompson, John Montgomery, David Caldwell, James Gillespy, James Houston.
[12] *Academy Abstracts*, 1830; *Deeds*, 4, p. 124.
[13] *Senate Journal*, December 13, 1831; *Minutes*, March, 1835.

In May 1835, Mr. and Mrs. Sketchley advertised a "Female Academy" in Maryville, Tennessee, showing a cut of the old seminary building. They offered: needlework, lace work, embroidery, painting and music. Nothing more is known about this school. The Sketchleys owned property in Louisville. It seems that the Theological Seminary was not using all its building at this time so the Female Academy may have used part of that building.

In January 1836, mention is made of using a room in the seminary building for Porter Academy, "since it is gratuitously offered."

In 1843, the Rev. Fielding Pope was elected president of the academy. In 1848, Prof. T. J. Lamar was named head of the school, which was being operated as the preparatory department of Maryville College with twenty-seven pupils.[14]

Funds for the operation of the county academies were sketchy and variable. Most of the funds, of necessity, came from tuition fees and no one would suppose that a town the size of Maryville could support two or three such schools to a very satisfying degree.

Treasurer of Academy Funds Stephen J. McReynolds, reported $4,801.56 of academy monies loaned on security in July 1851. The income from this investment could not have been much.[15]

An act of 1840 provided that none of the county academy fund was to be used by a college unless there was no county academy. In that case a college might get the funds but the money must be applied to the academical department. The amount of money due each county in East Tennessee varied from $109 in 1840 to $304.44 in 1848. It can be seen from this that the state funds could not go very far toward operating the school for a year.

A petition of January 17, 1849 by Trustees of Porter Academy, Samuel Pride, Wm. McTeer, B. D. Brabson, Will Wallace, and John E. Toole, Sr., stated that for some years no regular teacher had been employed and it was believed that owing to the location of Maryville College at the same place, no regular teacher could be profitably employed. It was believed that if the trustees were authorized to use the academy funds in the academic department much good would be derived from it. There were seventy-three signers to the petition which reported "favorable." Maryville College had been chartered in 1842 and was steadily growing in strength.

The next school in point of organization was the Maryville Female Academy (act passed, 1813) which was organized in 1816 and it was probably the intention to split the academy fund between Porter Academy and the Female Academy as was done in many counties of the state. On this date (1816) a transfer from John Montgomery and James Berry to the Maryville Female Academy was registered for the

---

[14] *Academy Abstracts*, 1843–48; Photostat of Hand Bill printed by F. A. Parham (Parham Papers).

[15] *School Report*, Tennessee State Archives; *Acts, 1873*, Ch. 25.

back half of lot No. 42 (the former site of New Providence Presbyterian Church). No records are found for this school other than appeared in the records of Porter Academy's board of trustees which state that Isaac Anderson was the teacher in 1817 and that a brick building was completed in 1820. Several joint meetings of the Trustees of the Female Academy and Porter Academy are recorded. Four of the trustees are the same as those named for Porter Academy in the 1820 transfer. Dr. Isaac Anderson purchased the other half of lot No. 42, in 1819 and in 1820 the small unfinished brick building which had been intended for the Female Academy was purchased from the trustees for $600 by Dr. Anderson who moved his Southern and Western Theological Seminary into the building.[16]

When the Reverend Isaac Anderson accepted the call as pastor of New Providence Church in 1812 he brought his one-man academy with him. (He had operated Union Academy in Grassy Valley, Knox County, for ten years.) He continued to teach, first in Porter Academy and later in the Female Academy. All the while he was teaching one or more theology students on the side. He became worried because the number of ministers on the frontier was so few and began to cast about in his mind for a solution to the problem. He wrote appeals to ministerial students which were published in Northern newspapers and netted him one, Eli Sawtell, who after graduation became financial agent for the college.

In 1819, Dr. Anderson attended General Assembly in Philadelphia, and there appealed for ministerial help for the frontier to no avail. On his way home he talked at length of the problem to his companion, the Rev. James Gallaher, of Rogersville, a native-born Blount Countian, and they came to the conclusion that the solution was a seminary for the education of ministers sponsored by the Tennessee Synod.[17]

A few weeks later he went before Union Presbytery and persuaded them as a group to submit a plan to the Tennessee Synod for a Southern and Western Theological Seminary. The plan was accepted and the school was set up with thirty-six directors. In the fall of 1819, Dr. Anderson began his work with a class of five pupils. The plans called for one month's vacation in April and six weeks in September and October. The course of study was to cover three years, and was open to students of all denominations. Since the primary motive in establishing the school was to train ministers, students had to be recruited.[18]

The first class contained a shoemaker, a tailor, a blacksmith and a farmer, and the following ministers of the group that finished the course in 1825 are: Elijah Eagleton, Hilary Patrick, William Patrick, William Minnis, Wm. A. McCampbell, and Eli N. Sawtell. The semi-

---

[16] *Deeds*, 2, p. 14, 89; *Acts, 1840*, ch. 102, sec. 11; Tennessee State Archives, *Petitions*, Box #113.

[17] Samuel Tyndale Wilson, *A Century of Maryville College and Second Century Beginnings* (Maryville, 1935), 26-37, hereinafter cited, *A Century*, Passim.

[18] *Ibid.*, 40-46.

nary classes met for the first few years in a weathered old house on the lot next to the present bus terminal.

In 1820, a small unfinished, twenty-five by forty, brick building which had been intended for a female academy, was purchased for $600 from the trustees of the academy, one of whom was Anderson himself. This building was on the back half of the lot which Anderson had already bought in 1817. The building was described in the Boston Recorder as "brick, two stories high with six fire places." The building had one large room and two small rooms downstairs and similar rooms upstairs. The small rooms were used for dormitory space. The large room upstairs was used for a library and the large one downstairs for recitation. In 1827, Dr. Anderson says that of the forty-four students forty-three had free tuition and twenty-seven had free board. Union Presbytery records show that from time to time the Presbytery paid expenses of certain pupils. The efforts of Eli N. Sawtell in the field after he had finished the course was an influential force in getting financial help for the school and also in recruiting students for the "poor man's college."[19]

The story of Eli Sawtell who was the ministerial student who came from the North as a result of Dr. Anderson's first appeal for help is a fascinating one. He walked from New England to East Tennessee. Presbytery records show that he attended Greeneville College for a while and that Union Presbytery assisted him financially at various times. His reminiscences are preserved among the Presbytery records. He was a very earnest and successful financial agent for the college after his graduation.[20]

In 1826, the two-hundred-acre college farm south of the courthouse was purchased through Sawtell's efforts. Reuben L. Cates and John McCully were among those who had charge of the farm. In 1836 the manual labor idea was abandoned and a modified boarding house was established for the students.[21]

During the first few years Dr. Anderson had done all the teaching as well as pastoring New Providence Church, which by 1827 ranked thirteenth in size in the United States.

The Rev. William Eagleton was appointed instructor of Languages and Sciences in 1825. From 1831 onward there were usually three professors on the faculty. In 1829, the Rev. Darius Hoyt was elected Professor of Languages and served until his death in 1837. He was the son of the Rev. Ard Hoyt, a missionary to the Cherokees. Hoyt was educated at Maryville and served as tutor until he was elected professor.

---

[19] *Ibid.*, 95; *Knoxville Register*, November 15, 1827, (7th annual report of Southern and Western Theological Seminary says 31 students are studying theology. He gives a long detailed list of donations: food and clothing; 222 volumes to the library, and $1870.00 cash gotten by Sawtell).

[20] *Reminiscences* of Eli N. Sawtell in the Abingdon Presbytery Minutes Book in the Maryville College vault.

[21] *Deeds*, Z, 472 (Trustees; John Montgomery, James Houston, Alex McGhee, Andrew Early, Jacob F. Foute, James Berry).

The first literary professor was the Rev. Samuel McCracken and he was soon followed by the Rev. Fielding Pope, also a Maryville alumnus, who served for seventeen years. He resigned in 1850 when a shortage of financial aid caused retrenchment. The Rev. John S. Craig succeeded the Rev. Hoyt. He also was a Maryville alumnus who had served previously as tutor.[22]

The name was changed from the Southern and Western Theological Seminary to Maryville College in 1842. From the graduation of the first class in 1825 to that of 1852, Dr. Anderson assisted in the licensure of seventy-seven young men and the ordination of sixty-four in Union Presbytery alone. Among them, Thomas J. Lamar who appeared at Maryville as an eighteen-year old student in 1824. The Rev. John J. Robinson was elected professor of Sacred Literature in 1850. He stayed until 1855 and his "Memoir of Dr. Isaac Anderson" is a priceless contribution to Maryville history. Prof. Lamar succeeded the Rev. Robinson in this position very shortly before the death of Dr. Anderson.

Dr. Robinson became the second president of Maryville College on April 7, 1857. Two treasurers also had served during this same period. James Berry served until 1833 and General William Wallace served from this date to his death in 1864 and only eighty dollars was lost due to bad investment up to the time of the Civil War.

In 1833 a second building was completed—the same size as the first which faced Main Street and was flush with the street. The large room on the first floor was used as a chapel. It had a seating capacity of two hundred. The large upstairs room was used for a Literary Society Hall. The lot was covered with locust trees and besides the two buildings named had a small building used by Beth Hacima Ve Berith Literary Society.[23]

In 1853 a new building was started in the middle of the lot. By 1856, ten rooms were ready for use, and the frame building was removed. It is described as: "a three-story brick with a one hundred and ten foot front, containing a chapel, four recitation rooms, lodging enough for sixty to seventy students, and two halls for the use of literary societies. The building, when finished, will be worth $10,000." [24]

That building was never finished and the debt contracted came very near "finishing" the school at Maryville. It was actually voted by the Synod in 1855 to remove the school to Rogersville, but the action was rescinded at the next meeting.

In 1856, the New School Presbyterians of the South withdrew from the Constitutional General Assembly and formed the United Synod and Maryville College was transferred to this body by the Synod of Tennessee with a reversionary clause, which was evoked at the end of

---

[22] *A Century*, 73–78; *Knoxville Register*, May 2, 1827, (lists Isaac Anderson, William Eagleton, Robert Hardin as professors and Darius Hoyt as tutor. Tuition was $9 and Board $20 per session. Terms were May to September, November to March.)

[23] *Ibid.*, 82–98.

[24] *Ibid.*, 38.

the war, when it was found by the Synod that the college had been sold for debt by court order. The endowment had shrunk to $6,000, when obligations were cleared and only a shell of the building was left. During the Civil War the building had been torn away brick by brick to make ovens for the mess shanties of the soldiers who had occupied the town during the war. All the doors and window frames had gone for fuel. The library had been destroyed.[25]

In October 1865, Thomas J. Lamar went to New Market to attend the first Synod meeting since 1862. Under the leadership of the Hon. Horace Maynard the Synod was led to appoint new directors who should organize and redeem the college property. Professor Lamar was appointed as agent to try to secure funds to rebuild the college. His first efforts were fruitless, but like Dr. Anderson he decided to invest himself.

July 4, 1866, Ralph E. Tedford, recorder of the directors, and Professor Lamar issued a one-page circular stating that Maryville College would re-open in September 1866. On September 5th, Professor Lamar enrolled Frank W. Allen, George E. Bicknell, Gideon S. W. Crawford, Calvin A. Duncan, James A. Goddard, Benjamin H. Lea, Isaac A. Martin, Wm. H. Porter, Edward W. Sanderson, Hugh W. Sawyer, Joseph P. Tedford, Charles E. Tedford, and Edward W. Tedford. Four of these had been soldiers.

Professor Lamar was well educated. He was a graduate of Maryville College and Union Theological Seminary. He was licensed by the Presbytery of Brooklyn and ordained by the Presbytery of Lexington in Missouri. He was joined in 1867 by Prof. Alexander Bartlett from Connecticut and in 1869 by the Rev. Peter Mason Bartlett. Recitations were held in the old brick barracks for four years in spite of warnings against its use. In the spring of 1870 one wall collapsed and the building was abandoned. Part of the work was already being carried on in the old boarding-house which stood on the lot next to the city library, and the work continued here and in the house on the west corner of College and Broadway.[26]

Donations from three different sources made it possible to purchase a 65-acre tract from Julius Caesar Fagg and to erect the first four buildings. The first building was a residence for President Bartlett at the edge of the woods. Anderson Hall was begun in 1869, and Baldwin and Memorial halls the following year. Baldwin Hall is named for John Center Baldwin, who was one of the first donors and who helped to rebuild the endowment fund. William Thaw was a substantial donor and General O. O. Howard gave, in all, $16,000 from the Freedman's Bureau in behalf of Negro education which substantially helped to put the college on its feet. Memorial Hall commemorated the union of New and Old School Presbyterians. These buildings represented an outlay

---
[25] *Ibid.*, 117.
[26] *Ibid.*, 121–27. (The trustees of Porter Academy had voted that their funds for 1866 should go to Maryville College, since they had no building in which to operate a school).

of $90,000, only $3,000 of which was contributed locally and provided besides class rooms, a dining hall and dormitory rooms for one hundred thirty students.[27]

At the end of 1867, there were two college students and forty-three preparatory students. A class of five was graduated in 1871. The college department enrollment was seventeen, and there were eighty-three preparatory students including young women. (Maryville had been co-educational both as regards sex and color, since 1867.) In 1873 in addition to the president, there were two professors, three lady teachers; one graduate tutor, Thomas Theron Alexander; and two student teachers, Edgar Elmore, and Monroe Goddard. This same year one hundred and thirty students were enrolled. The Rev. Gideon S. W. Crawford joined the faculty in 1874. The enrollment increased steadily in spite of the panic of 1873 and by 1880 the enrollment was two hundred students mostly from Blount and nearby counties.

Professor Lamar made a supreme effort to establish an endowment fund of one hundred thousand dollars. He succeeded in this but died March 20, 1887, after thirty years' service to Maryville College.[28]

Mr. Thaw and the Northern friends that Professor Lamar had made for Maryville, led the movement for the Lamar Memorial Library Building, which he had planned to work for as his next project. It was erected soon after his death. This library has long since been outgrown and now serves as post office and book store. Professor Lamar's real monument is Maryville College. He kept it alive almost single-handedly for many years and gave his time, money, and eventually his life for the school.

The Rev. Dr. Bartlett resigned as president in 1887, and Prof. Edgar A. Elmore was acting president for two years.

The Rev. Samuel Ward Boardman, then of New Jersey, was elected president and took over the work in the fall. He was a close neighbor and friend of the Willard family who had helped in establishing the endowment fund. When President Boardman came to Maryville, Mrs. Willard gave eleven thousand dollars to build a home for the president as a memorial to Dr. Sylvester Willard who had recently died. The home was ready for occupancy by the Boardmans in December, 1890. This building was used as the presidents' home until the spring of 1952 when "Morningside" became the official residence of the president.[29]

While Professor Lamar was traveling in behalf of the endowment fund he met the Rev. Roswell D. Hitchcock, who influenced Mr.

---

[27] *Maryville Times*, March 5, 1880. General Howard had been in Maryville with Sherman's army during the war and his sympathies were strong for this section of the South. (He was one of the founders of Lincoln Memorial University). In 1868, the Synod of Tennessee passed a resolution making no difference in race and color, thus Maryville became the only old college in the South having co-education of the races. Without it the assistance of the Freedman's Bureau would have never been extended. (Lucius G. Merriam, *Higher Education in Tennessee*, U. S. Gov't. Printing Office, 1933, 231.)

[28] *A Century*, 128–147; Mary T. Wilson, who was graduated in 1875, was the first woman to receive a diploma from Maryville College.

[29] *Ibid.*, 149–154

Daniel B. Fayerweather, a wealthy leather merchant of New York, to include Maryville College in a list of twenty colleges to which he bequeathed most of his estate. By the end of the sixteen years litigation, the bequest had grown to over two hundred thousand dollars.

In 1892, an annex had been built to Anderson Hall, using part of this fund. Dr. Jasper Barnes became principal of the preparatory school in this same year. In 1893, a central heating plant and electric lights were installed. In 1895, an annex was built to Baldwin Hall for a dining hall and twenty-four dormitory rooms and in 1904 the annex was extended to make it a third larger.

In 1895, Bartlett Gymansium and YMCA Hall was built under the leadership of Kin Takahashi, a Japanese student. The Fayerweather Fund, Mrs. Nettie F. McCormick and Mrs. Elizabeth Voorhees all contributed to finish the work so heroically begun.

In October 1901, Samuel T. Wilson became President of Maryville College. His parents were Syrian missionaries and he had planned to be a foreign missionary. His health would not permit such strenuous work and he returned to Maryville College and served as professor from 1884 and dean of the college from 1891.

The same year the State of Tennessee had passed a law making it illegal for whites and Negroes to attend the same school. The board of directors voted to comply with the law, and $26,000 was set aside as a trust fund to be paid to Swift Memorial Institute at Rogersville, Tennessee. This fund represented the $16,000 originally given by the Freedman's Bureau and the $10,000 given by Mr. Thaw of Pittsburgh when the college was reestablished after the Civil War.[30]

Miss Margaret Henry started the Self-Help Scholarship Fund in 1903 which is still continued in connection with Maryville College.

The Elizabeth Voorhees Chapel was built in 1906. The chapel in Anderson Hall could no longer accommodate the six hundred students so the chapel filled a very real need. Seventeen music and expression studios were also provided on the basement level.

From 1905–1908, the Forward Fund was an absorbing project of Maryville friends and officials. As a result of this drive several new buildings appeared on College Hill. The first to appear was the Ralph Max Lamar Memorial Hospital, which was a memorial to the son of Professor Lamar who had died during the endowment campaign which indirectly took Professor Lamar's life. The building was given by Mrs. Lamar and dedicated May 4, 1910.

Pearson's Hall was erected in 1910 by Dr. Daniel K. Pearson. The Cooperative Boarding Club was moved to the first floor of this building. The second floor had halls for young women's literary societies and a parlor as well as thirty-four dormitory rooms.

Carnegie Hall, the largest and costliest building up to that date was dedicated in January 1911. It contained suites for two professors and

---

[30] *Knoxville Sentinel*, May 28, 1901, ff (W. H. Franklin, Principal of Swift was a Maryville Alumnus.)

their families and rooms for one hundred and twenty-five men. April 12, 1916, Carnegie Hall was totally destroyed by the first serious fire suffered by the institution. By January 1917, the rebuilt hall was occupied. The new Carnegie had five stories instead of three and had rooms for two hundred and thirty-eight instead of one hundred and twenty-five students. This building was made possible mainly by Blount County friends who raised $25,000 for this purpose.[31]

After 1867, the college had welcomed women as students and after World War I the enrollment of all types of students increased to the point that it seemed necessary to change the policy of the institution to meet the current demands. The best plan seemed to be to discontinue the Preparatory Department and build up the College Department, which plan was finally adopted and by a gradual process the Preparatory Department was eliminated and finally closed in 1925.

The high cost of living in the post-war period made additional endowments necessary which were providentially supplied by a gift from the General Education Board, and several new plans for self-help were evolved. The most notable of these was the College Maid Shop started by Mrs. Kathryn Romig McMurray in the fall of 1920. The story of its development is an almost unbelievable one and the shop is still continued on a large scale for such a project. The shop has averaged 100–150 girls earning as much as $8,000 a year. The student-help program started by Miss Margaret Henry had been seriously threatened by her untimely death in 1916 but Providence pointed to her cousin, Miss Clemmie J. Henry, who succeeded her in 1918.

A substantial gift from Mrs. Mary C. Thaw as a part of the Centennial Campaign (1919) made possible a much-needed new building. She was persuaded to allow the name Thaw Hall to be used. The building was dedicated in the fall of 1922 during a meeting of the Tennessee Synod. The library had become quite inadequate, so when Thaw Hall was completed, it was removed to the first floor of Thaw Hall. A special gift from Mrs. Thaw provided the necessary furnishings for the new quarters and the collection has grown into a very satisfactory organization. Rare books and manuscripts are housed in the college vault in Anderson Hall, where Union Presbytery also keeps its records.

The increase in enrollment and an enlarged program of athletics, and recreation made Bartlett Hall quite inadequate. The Alumni Association under the leadership of Professors Horace E. Orr, Edwin R. Hunter, and G. A. Knapp made possible an athletic field and the Alumni Gynasium. Various improvements have been made from time to time and substantial gifts have been made. One of the most invaluable was the donation of services as college pastor by Dr. William Patton Stevenson for twenty-three years. A friend of Mrs. Stevenson's erected "The House in the Woods" as a memorial to the parents of Mrs. Stevenson.[32]

---

[31] *A Century*, 154–76.
[32] *Ibid.*, 276–302.

Dr. Wilson resigned his office as president June 5, 1930 after fifty-seven years service to Maryville College. His resignation was accepted and he was made president emeritus and Dr. Ralph W. Lloyd was elected to the office of president. Dr. Wilson died in 1944 after 86 years of useful service. His writings are a worthy contribution to Blount County History. Dr. Lloyd is a Blount Countian by birth and a Maryville alumnus.[33]

In 1932, Mrs. John Walker of Pittsburgh came to Maryville and built a beautiful home "Morningside" in the college woods near the "House in the Woods," the home of her sister, Mrs. Stevenson. She did an extensive work in landscaping the campus, paving walks and drives, and improving the comforts and decorations of the parlors and dining hall for college students. Another of her major improvements was the developing of the natural amphitheatre in the college woods and the botany garden.

Perhaps one of the most worthy of her permanent contributions was joining the Stevensons in providing the College Cemetery endowment. She placed a new stone at the Isaac Anderson grave, and beautified the small cemetery where she has since joined Dr. and Mrs. Stevenson in the "last long sleep." [34]

"Morningside," since March 1, 1951, is the residence of President and Mrs. Lloyd. The azalea garden adjoining the house is one of the "show places" of Maryville. The nearby guest house which Mrs. Walker also built is a useful addition when official visitors are on campus. The work of Mrs. Walker in improving and beautifying the campus will be a continuing memorial.

A 1948 addition to the campus is the Student Center Building which combines the Recreation Hall and the Y-Store facilities.

The Fine Arts Building has excited nation wide interest and publicity because of its unique, ultra-modern functional design. It is the gift of Mr. and Mrs. Glenn A. Lloyd of Chicago. The building was finished in the fall of 1950 and was dedicated during commencement, 1951.[35]

On the evening of March 26, 1947, occurred the second major catastrophe in the college's history. The college chapel and all that it housed in the art and music departments burned. After seven years, a new chapel of modern design stands a little further down the hill than the old chapel and opposite the Fine Arts Building. The chapel has always been the heart of Maryville, and since 1954 she once again occupies a conventional chapel. The building includes one of the best equipped theaters in the country.[36]

---

[33] *Ibid.*, 304-306.
[34] Mrs. Stevenson died December 4, 1939; Dr. Stevenson, November 4, 1944; and Mrs. Walker died December 12, 1950 at the age of 98. (Alumni News, Passim.)
[35] Glen A. Lloyd is a brother of President Lloyd.
[36] *The Architectural Record*, June 1950; December 1951 (had a twelve-page feature including eight color-pages of features and pictures of the Fine Arts Building).

LOUISVILLE ACADEMY AND HOLSTON SEMINARY

There are two unchartered schools about which no tradition or trace of information has been preserved. The only evidence thus far gleaned is merely a newspaper notice of the initial opening of the schools.

In October 1841, Louisville Academy was advertised as lately organized by citizens at Louisville, Blount County. Trustees announced that they had procured the Rev. Thomas S. Kendall to superintend the management of the school. They recommended the village of Louisville as healthy, and stated that the society was good, and board moderate. The term was to begin in November 1841. Trustees were: H. C. Saffell, Hiram Hartsill, L. B. Saffell, Robert S. Cummings, Abram Hartsill, John Hood, and John F. Henry.

Most of these trustees were of strong Methodist leanings and the Rev. Kendall was a minister of the Seceder Church.[37]

In October 1844, the first session of the Holston Seminary was announced as beginning at Louisville, on the last Friday in the month. The trustees proudly announced that they had secured the services of Mr. Henry Saffell, former president of Holston College at New Market, who had consented to be principal. Hiram Hartsill signed the announcement as secretary.

Later a summer session was announced by the Board of Trustees: Alexander Ish, Daniel Taylor, Horace Foster, George S. Gilbert, William Prater, H. T. Cox, President; William Y. Warren, Vice President; and Hiram Hartsill, Secretary.[38]

Since the principal was lately from a Methodist College, this school seems to indicate a church school and the name of this school may explain why Ewing and Jefferson College which was established a few years later in the neighborhood was always locally referred to as "Holston College."

In 1856 an ad stated that Louisville High School would open on the first floor of the Masonic Building with Dr. J. M. Parker as teacher. No other reference is found to this school.[39]

EAST TENNESSEE MASONIC FEMALE INSTITUTE

July 9, 1849, a paper was laid before New Providence Lodge containing signatures of eighty subscribers stating that they, as subscribers to the Female Academy, in view of the fact that there was a deficit of five hundred dollars of the necessary funds to complete the building, agreed that the amounts should be used under the entire control and management of the New Providence Lodge No. 128 at Maryville, Tennessee.[40]

---

[37] *Argus*, (Knoxville), October 13, 1841; *Post*, (Knoxville), October 13, 1841.
[38] *Argus*, October 18, 1843; January 10, 1844; April 17, 1844; August 2, 1844.
[39] *East Tennessean*, (Maryville), April 4, 1856. (Miss Sophia Duncan).
[40] *Deeds*, X, 666. (The Masons had contracted with John E. Toole, for three lots in 1849. The deed was not prepared until 1854). All information, not otherwise accounted for, is from the first four books of Minutes of New Providence Lodge, No. 128, F. & A. M. (through 1869).

The Lodge agreed to complete the building and pay the deficit with the provision that the building should forever continue to be used as a Female Academy in the town of Maryville under the name of East Tennessee Masonic Female Institute with privilege of all attending said school whether they were daughters of Masons or not, provided they paid tuition fees.

The Articles of Agreement were adopted and J. E. Toole, J. G. Wallace and W. S. Porter were appointed a committee to devise a suitable plan for carrying out the part of the agreement devolving on the lodge, and report.

On July 19, 1849, in accordance with the report and recommendation of the above named committee, J. C. Fagg and J. A. McKamy were appointed agents to raise funds for the school on a 20 per cent commission basis. The agents were ex-officio members of an executive committee composed of J. G. Wallace, W. S. Porter, F. Pope, J. E. Toole, and Sam Pride. The agents were to visit other lodges in East Tennessee in person and solicit their cooperation and financial help. In August, a circular was prepared and distributed to the Masonic Fraternity at-large in the surrounding territory stating that the subject of education of the orphans of indigent Masons had long been a matter of concern; that while provision had been made for the sons of Masons, the daughters had been thus far overlooked. The fact was stated that two thousand dollars had been subscribed in Blount County for building a Female Institute at Maryville under the control and management of New Providence Lodge No. 128. The contract had already been entered into for erecting a brick building twenty-four by forty feet, three stories high, to be completed by May 1st, 1850. The advantages of the Maryville location were presented and an appeal was made for financial aid in enlarging the building by adding two wings twenty by twenty feet, two stories in height.

August 16, 1849, it was decided that any lodge in East Tennessee contributing one hundred dollars should have the right to appoint one trustee, and one trustee (up to three) for each additional one hundred dollars to represent the lodge on the Board of the Institute. New Providence Lodge, however, reserved the right to maintain a quorum on the board.

In September a committee was appointed to make plans for the laying of the cornerstone: J. G. Wallace, J. A. McKamy, and T. A. Pope. They were to issue invitations to all Masons in East Tennessee to attend the ceremonies.

On October 18, 1849, a procession formed at 1:30 P.M. composed of: members of New Providence Lodge; Maryville Division of the Sons of Temperance; Cadets of Temperance; and citizens. Led by Hardeman's Brass Band, they marched to the site of the contemplated building where the ceremony of the cornerstone-laying was conducted by Dr. Samuel Pride who officiated as Grand Master pro tem, assisted by the Rev. Fielding Pope and the Rev. Spencer Henry. These items were deposited in the cornerstone: a Bible, a copy of the chapter bylaws and charter members of New Providence Lodge; a list of present members and the constitution of the Maryville Division of the Sons of Temperance and their officers; an almanac for 1849; an address to the lodges of East Tennessee and adjoining states; a gold dollar; a Mexican quarter; and various other coins for 1849. The oration was then given by Jesse G. Wallace. Later, agents were appointed in Baltimore, Philadelphia, Nashville, and Memphis and other places from time to time under the commission agreement. The lodge secured remittance of their dues for 1849 from Grand Lodge to be applied on the building fund. Grand Lodge also subscribed $250.00.

March 21, 1850, a board of directors was elected: Sam Pride, John Davis, Fielding Pope, J. A. McKamy, Sam T. Bicknell, Spencer Henry, and James M. Toole. The five principal officers of the Lodge were to be ex-officio members of the board. Tellico Lodge No. 80 having made a donation of $100, George Brown was elected to the Board of Directors, to represent Tellico Lodge.

July 8, 1850, J. A. McKamy, secretary of the board, reported that the Rev. Fielding Pope was to be president of the institute; Miss Mary S. Towne, principal of the academic department; and Miss Mary J. Love, principal of the preparatory department—all of which had accepted. Assistants were to be employed if needed.[41]

The building committee was authorized to enclose the academy and to build "necessary" outbuildings. J. G. Wallace and J. M. Kennedy were to solicit books, funds, and apparatus for the school. The Grand Lodge was asked to donate a Charity Fund to East Tennessee Masons Female Institute for the education of the daughters of indigent Masons.

Trustees elected in December 1850 were: R. L. Cates, S. Pride, S. T. Bicknell, J. E. Toole, James Porter, and J. R. Love. In February it was decided that there should be twelve trustees and five more were elected: B. D. Brabson, J. A. McKamy, A. C. Montgomery, J. G. Wallace, and Wm. McTeer.

May 12, 1851, the wings were finished and the report of the building committee showed an unpaid balance of $2,808.47. In December the Rev. Fielding Pope assumed the debt, with the property as security, and was given the right to employ teachers and conduct the Literary Department according to the adopted regulations. Ads were ordered to be run in *The Presbyterian Witness*, and the *Christian Advocate*.[42]

In February 1855, it was voted that the lodge should act as a Board of Trustees, and in May, John E. Toole was elected to collect debts due the institute.

From the reports filed in 1855, it appears that the school was about "breaking even" financially. Teachers listed in 1855 were: The Rev. F. Pope; Misses Mary S. Towne, Mary J. Love, Minerva J. Cates; Prof.

---

[41] The salaries named varied from $750–$250 per year.
[42] A copy of the Rules and Regulations for 1850 is in the possession of John C. Crawford, Jr.

MRS. HARRIET C. J. M. HENRY
Lt. "Kim" McTeer of the Blount County Home Guards.

MISS MARGARET E. HENRY
Teacher and Scholarship Secretary at Maryville College for twenty-six years.

WOMEN OF NOTE

MISS A. BELLE SMITH
Teacher of Art and lover of books; Served as librarian for twenty years. Photograph of a self painting.

MRS. ELIZABETH K. BURGER
Effected the affiliation of local clubs with Federated Women's Clubs. Helped to found Blount County Industrial Home.

MRS. NANCY LEE BROADY MISER
Blount County's first Home Demonstration Agent and only woman to serve as County Superintendent of Schools to date.

MRS. MARY A. BIRD DUNN
Maryville's only Post Mistress to date; Active in church politics and civic clubs.

East Tennesseee Female Masonic Institute, later Maryville's first Public School.
(Photo courtesy Frank P. Clark.)

Friend's Normal Institute, formerly the Pride Mansion,
Maryville Public School after 1900.

G. R. Knabe (Music). Diplomas were awarded to Misses Sabina and Mary Alexander, and Mary Hurst. Major L. R. Hurst and Dr. Joseph Alexander were honored at a dinner with the graduates so we suppose them to be the "fond fathers" of the graduates.[43]

The lodge met as a Board of Trustees and decided that they should be relieved of liabilities and that if the school could not sustain itself, to let it "go down." They advised that it be leased for a term of years to private individuals and appointed S. Pride, Wm. McTeer, J. G. Wallace, J. M. Toole and S. T. Bicknell as a committee to make a contract excepting the Masonic lodgeroom (third floor) and Temperance Hall (on second floor).

The Rev. Fielding Pope, who had been principal for the five years it was operated by the lodge, signed the contract for one year with the privilege of making it three years.

The records from this point (1856) are missing but it is thought that the Rev. Pope continued to operate the school until the Civil War. However, since he became the pastor of New Providence church in 1857, he may not have.

Maryville was occupied by first one army and then the other for most of the war period and the schoolbuilding like the rest of the town suffered heavily. From the Minutes, it seems that the floors of the first story were gone except for one wing, and that shutters and windows were missing. (Everything that could be pried loose had been used for fuel.)

No mention of the Sons of Temperance is made after 1865. They had made a substantial contribution in the initial drive for funds and had had the use of "Temperance Hall" from the erection of the building.

In July 1867, minutes show that the Masonic Female Institute had been sold for debts of the lodge due Lucius Ardus, Wm. Wallace, and James M. Toole, and that Toole became the final purchaser and that W. D. McGinley and Thomas Pickens had taken steps to redeem the property. In August, a committee of three was appointed to have the Masonic buildings repaired and the lot fenced as soon as practicable. The committee: W. D. McGinley, C. T. Cates, and S. A. Rhea were to rent it for one year to the best advantage. However, in January 1868, the minutes flatly stated that the committee had no power to rent the property and that they refused to rent any part of the building for Common School purposes or any other school purposes unless it was under the control of the lodge. The Board of Trustees of Porter Academy had signed a lease for one year previous to this.[44]

In May 1868, the lodge passed resolutions to the effect that three trustees should be elected for 12 months to arrange for the establish-

---

[43] *American Statesman*, (Knoxville), February 2, 1953, carried an ad which listed the same faculty except Miss Towne.
[44] In 1864, Toole offered the property as security in a trust deed. *Deeds*, A A, 484.

ment of a school for both male and female children. The school was not sectarian nor political nor should any teacher be employed who was not a Mason or in some way connected with Masons. The Lodge would in nowise be responsible for any debts incurred. It was further voted that common decency required a neat fence and that G. W. Hutsell, R. L. McNutt, P. H. Clark, T. D. Edington and J. W. Cates should see that the house and grounds were put into good condition for school use as soon as possible.

In July, the trustees were empowered to hire Mr. S. Z. Sharp to open a school in this building September 1, 1868. Subscriptions were taken among lodge members for repairs which exceeded the amount subscribed and although other repairs were needed they were postponed.[45]

In March 1869, the committee appointed to attend the examination of Mr. S. Z. Sharp's school reported that they were well pleased with the manner in which the school was being conducted, and in July they asked him to continue for another year. They further proposed to rent him the two lower rooms on his own terms. (They, to have control of the school.) Action was also taken to raise one hundred dollars to put a floor in the main building for the use of groups for religious worship, but in no case was the use of the building by any group to interfere with school sessions.

Mr. Sharp operated the school until 1878, when he became the head of the Normal Department of Maryville College. The Masonic Female Institute, "in its 28th year," was headed by D. P. Hurley ("Both males and females are accepted.").[46]

In the summer of 1878, the Ninth Civil District of Blount County and the 21st school district completed negotiations with the New Providence Lodge for the school building and the deed was executed in September by R. N. Hood, W. O. Raulston and J. D. French for the Lodge to Will A. McTeer, H. L. McNutt, and Allen Garner, Jr., directors of the Common Schools for use as a school and no other purpose. The Masons reserved the third floor of the building for their use and the right to come and go at any time. Due to lack of funds, no public school was operated in 1878-79 and the building was leased to Blount County for a courthouse while a new one was being built.

The local newspaper carried advertisements from time to time of the opening of the school and continued to list it as the Masonic Female Institute but ordinarily it was referred to as the "Public School." Private sessions by subscriptions were taught after the public funds were exhausted each year.[47]

The public school used only four rooms in the old dilapidated building. From 1890 to 1896 the enrollment was from 250 to 300 students and there were four teachers.

---

[45] S. Z. Sharp was a minister of the Brethren Church (the Rev. Solomon Zook Sharp). See Oakland Church of Brethren.
[46] *Maryville Index*, July 10, 1878 (Hurley was editor of the *American Statesman* (Knoxville) above mentioned in 1853).
[47] *Deeds*, GG 396; *Maryville Index*, January 1, 1879.

In December 1897 the people of Maryville petitioned County Court to increase the tax rate so that better schools could be had. After this was refused, the school directors asked that a special school district be set up. While this project was in process, a mass meeting was held to raise money for a schoolbuilding. T. E. Cooper, Joseph Burger, S. L. Clark, David Jones and J. N. Badgett subscribed $100 each.

The school directors purchased the Friends school property where City Hall now stands in September 1900, and made whatever changes were necessary and the following year it became the "Public School." The following summer, after the close of the school session in 1901, the school directors: W. E. Parham, Fielding N. Lamon, and S. L. George transferred the "Public School" property back to the Masons through its officials: R. S. Walker, Luther Irwin, and Frank Mitchell for $450.00.[48]

In January 1905, the Masons transferred the property to Jo Burger. Shortly afterwards it was torn down and the following news item appeared. "The old Masonic Institute is a thing of the past. The old cornerstone was taken out on Wednesday, April 26th. At the time it was placed October 18, 1849, it contained a gold dollar, a quarter, and papers of various kinds. Only the silver coins and a sodden mass of materials were found. The cornerstone being placed low and not properly sealed." [49]

EWING AND JEFFERSON COLLEGE

The Concord Cumberland Presbyterian Church was organized some time between 1843 and 1848. The burial ground on the Gillespy plantation was at that time the only public institution of any sort in the community. So, it is not surprising that this location was chosen for the first church in that locality. Soon after the hewn log church was built, a school of sorts was started in the church. The leaders of the community and church wanted something bigger and better for their children, and even went so far as to visualize a school of higher education.[50]

According to tradition Mr. William Warren solicited funds for a school, and the brick building which we have known as Holston College was ready for use in 1852.

In 1850, Mrs. Jane Gillespy, widow of John Gillespy, deeded three acres to the Trustees of the Literary and Scientific Institute of the Hiwassee Presbytery of the Cumberland Presbyterian Church. The

---

[48] *Deeds*, 59, p. 199. (He sold to Keny who built the present building used by McCammon-Ammons Funeral Home.)

[49] *Maryville Times*, April 15, 1905.

[50] Much of the early information in this account is taken from letters written by the Rev. Evander J. Gillespy, of Palo Alto, California, to Miss Beulah Russell (now Mrs. Ross O'Connor) in 1926 when he was 91 years old. He attended the first session of Ewing and Jefferson College and was there until 1857. Hereinafter cited *Gillespy*.

trustees named were: Thomas H. Small, Alexander Ish, Thomas Boyd, William Rodgers, William Prater, Samuel B. West, Jesse Kerr, Jr., John Russell, and William Henderson. The cemetery, church and school lots were given by the Gillespys, nine acres in all, on the bank of the Holston River and included a spring near the creek.[51]

The school was evidently organized and set in operation under the Hiwassee Presbytery. It was named for Finis Ewing, one of the founders of the Cumberland Presbyterian Church and Thomas Jefferson, the great American statesman.

The school was begun in 1851 with Prof. B. V. Irvine as president. "He was a ripe scholar, but a poor disciplinarian." In the spring of 1852, he left. The school took a vacation for two years. In 1855, school opened again with the Rev. S. A. Taylor, president, assisted by Professor Wilson and Miss Garrett. The Rev. Taylor preached at the church also. At the end of five months Professor Wilson left and about the middle of the second year, Mr. Taylor was summarily dismissed and John Boyd was placed at the head of the school. The Rev. Gillespy says that although Taylor stayed at his house and that he was Taylor's most advanced student that he never knew why Taylor was dismissed but always thought it was for lack of scholarship.[52]

Ewing and Jefferson College was incorporated February 14, 1854. In 1855, the committee appointed by the General Assembly of the Cumberland Presbyterian Church to examine the minutes of the East Tennessee Synod discharged that duty and presented the following in their report: "This Synod has certainly taken high and laudable ground on the subject of education; they have in successful operation two academies, and have taken the necessary steps for the permanent establishment of a school of higher order under the name and style of 'Ewing and Jefferson College.'"[53]

The committee on education reported in 1855: "Ewing and Jefferson College, East Tennessee: three instructors, 80 pupils; property, $8,000." The charter of incorporation listed the trustees who were: A. Ish, William Rogers, A. Matlock, William Henderson, S. D. W. Law, Thomas Boyd, William H. Bell, William H. Russell, Joseph B. Dobson, James Blair, James Johnson, D. W. Amos, and A. I. McGhee. The committee on education in 1859 reported: "Ewing and Jefferson College, Blount County, East Tennessee has two professors, and about 60 students; estimated worth of college property and amount of endowment, we are not informed."[54]

The Rev. Gillespy says he left Blount County in 1857 and knew nothing more about the school. No account which named the head of

---

[51] *Deeds*, Y, 544.

[52] *Gillespy*. He says that at first there were no young ladies in attendance but that little girls attended.

[53] *Acts, 1853-54*, ch. 217, Sec. 28-35.

[54] *Minutes of the General Assembly of Cumberland Presbyterian Church*, 1855, p. 34, Bethel College, McKenzie, Tennessee (Archives of C. P. Church).

EDUCATION 153

the school has been found between the date which Gillespy says Boyd took charge and the advertisement in Brownlow's "Whig" which announced opening of the school with Professor Boyd in charge.

In the General Assembly minutes of 1862, Ewing and Jefferson was listed as one of the schools not reporting. This is the last time the school is mentioned in the reports to the General Assembly of the Cumberland Presbyterian Church.

Although the school is not identified with the Synod after 1860, it continued as a private church school under the sponsorship of the Concord Church or the Hiwassee Presbytery. A biographical account of the Rev. Solon McCrosky says that in 1860 he determined to get a better education and moved his wife and five children to Blount County and attended school at Ewing and Jefferson College for two years. From this it would appear that the school was in operation in 1860 and 1861.

In April 1865, an advertisement said: "Owing to influences introduced by the present war, operations of Ewing and Jefferson College have been suspended for some time and is now being opened at Concord, Prof. John N. Boyd in charge." A biography of T. W. Kellar says he was graduated from Ewing and Jefferson College in 1869.[55]

The Blount County Superintendent of Public Instruction, Thomas J. Lamar, in his report to State Superintendent, John Eaton, April 15, 1868, listed the school as Holston Academy, O. G. Park, teacher, 48 pupils. This is the only early use of this name but indicates a local tendency to use the name Holston. Officially, it was always called Ewing and Jefferson.[56]

There is no information about the school from this point to the year 1889. It is certain that there was no school session in 1888 and probably for some years previous. In 1889, the State Superintendent's report listed Ewing and Jefferson College as having four teachers and 210 pupils, and giving an A.B. degree. The 1890 report named G. W. Farmer as head of the school with three teachers and 79 pupils. The 1892 report listed three teachers.[57]

When the Rev. J. C. Ritter first came to Concord church as pastor from Greene County and saw the beautiful setting and the nice building already there, he resolved to realize his life-long ambition to operate a private school. (No plans had been made since the dismissal of Farmer.) After consulting with leading citizens and receiving favorable support he set the school in operation in the fall of 1893 and continued at its head until 1898. From various news items throughout those years he seems to have been the chief promoter of the Christian Endeavor movement in Blount County during that time.[58]

In 1894, the school patrons were reported as cleaning and painting in

---

[55] *Goodspeed*, 1005.
[56] Tennessee, *School Report*, 1868.
[57] *Ibid.*, 1889, 1890, 1892.
[58] Mrs. Beulah Russell O'Connor.

preparation for commencement. Shortly after the close of school, Mr. Ritter was busy collecting funds for the erection of another boarding-house for girls on the college grounds. A month later, $1,000 was reported and in July work was begun on the building.

In November 1895, the Board of Trustees bought the large brick house of S. A. Lackey for a boarding-house, and Mr. Ritter had a four-room annex built onto the college building for boys, making twenty-four dormitory rooms in all.

In 1897, according to a news item, the Rev. A. M. Hunt replaced Mr. Ritter as president because he was attending school at Lebanon. However, some of the local people say that Mr. Ritter was still at the school that year.[59]

In 1898 Prof. O. L. White was announced at commencement as the new president. Graduates for 1898 were: Mae Hertzler, Cora Davidson. Mabel Miser, and Charles Everett. Miss Miser taught part of the following year.

The school committee chose Mr. Croft for their president in 1899 and Frank Davidson, assistant, with Miss Margaret Prater, Primary teacher. Mr. Bechtel is named later in the year as teaching. February 22, 1900, some sort of disciplinary problem seems to have caused the principal to resign. Mr. Ritter came back and tried to straighten out the affair but the school never operated after this time.[60]

A county public school was operated at Holston College from 1900 until about 1920 when a frame building called Holston was built in the neighborhood. Holston, Cox, and Gravelly Hill schools were consolidated to form Mt. Vernon School in 1925.

It is highly possible that some public school funds were being used in the operation of the school all along because a great many private schools did qualify for such funds where other schools were not in operation.

The old college building was used by the Holston College Church until 1952 when it was dissolved, on the building's hundredth anniversary. The annex and the cottages on the grounds have long since been torn down and only the dilapidated shell of the old two-story brick building remains besides the old cemetery on the shore of Loudoun Lake.[61]

FRIENDSVILLE ACADEMY

In 1796, the nucleus of a colony of Quakers was formed near where the village of Friendsville now stands, by John Hackney, James Matthews, James Allen and John Walker.

---

[59] *Maryville Times;* 1894–97, Passim.
[60] *Ibid.,* September 11; December 4, 1897; May 21, 1898; February 25, 1899; *Ibid.,* January 27; March 10; April 21, 1900.
[61] Mr. Gillespy said that there were six "shanties" or cabins on the grounds at the beginning of the College. Four boys "batched" in each cabin. He told of "Moot" courts being held and of a "hanging" which was almost fatal. Cottages were still in use in 1888 when Miss Molly Caldwell taught school there. Mr. Ritter repaired or rebuilt these during his regime.

In due course after the establishing of a church in 1808, the church fathers turned their attention to proper cultural advantages for their children. Home schools and community schools were maintained according to the financial means of the populace.

In 1838, the observation was made that few teachers were Quakers. A survey showed that forty-six children of school age within the bounds of the church were not attending school. The report further stated that of five schools within the bounds of the church only one was taught by a Friend.[62]

Friends as a sect have always recognized the value of education and in the South where the public school system had been very deficient, they maintained a schoolhouse near every meeting house.[63]

In November 1854, the subject of education was brought before the Meeting and after due deliberation they came to the conclusion that it was their duty to make provisions for a "good scientific and religiously guided education" for their children. They resolved to collect funds for a school at Friendsville and further provided for the final disposition of the funds should the school be discontinued at Friendsville.

David Morgan, John Hackney, Jr., James C. Allen, and Ephriam Lee were named to solicit funds among the membership for establishing a system of education under the care of Friends. After their report in December a board of trustees: David Morgan, John Hackney, Jr., and Thomas M. Jones were elected for Friendsville Institute and Newberry Female School. They were to select and purchase two sites and apply for charters as above.

Francis Hackney and David Morgan donated lots. Plans were to set aside $2,000 for a permanent fund and build the boys' school first and put it into operation.

In September, 1855, the committees reported that after spending $500 on the building, a crack had appeared in the wall due to a fissure in the rock below and that they had decided to build a larger building on another lot and salvage whatever they could. They also reported that five trustees were necessary to obtain the charter and James C. Allen and Francis Hackney were accordingly appointed.[64]

In May 1856, the trustees were authorized to operate both schools in one house if they thought best and to employ such teachers as they thought proper; to fix a tuition rate and rules for the administration of the school to the best interest of the school and the society. Samuel Dunlap said that for economy's sake one building was constructed with brick partitions upstairs and down and a stout plank fence outside to separate the boys from the girls. Zimri S. Ellis explained this further as

---

[62] *Goodspeed*, 329; *Minutes of Newberry Monthly Meetings*, (Friendsville, Tennessee) 1808-1848. Hereinafter cited *Newberry Minutes*.

[63] Fernando G. Cartland. *Southern Heroes, the Friends in war times*. (Riverside Press) 1895, 214. Hereinafter cited Cartland, *Southern Heroes*.

[64] *Newberry Minutes*, 1824. 12th month; 1855, 3rd month; 5th month; 9th month.

a tight board fence seven feet tall and said that some of the boys cut holes in the fence to peek at the girls.

The second annual report made in July 1857, reported that funds from English and Philadelphia Friends as well as books from Philadelphia had been received. The school went into operation the first Monday in January 1857, with forty-four scholars and the number soon increased to seventy-three, a few of whom were not Friends. The session ran for twenty weeks in a very satisfactory manner.[65]

The total enrollment for 1858 was 120 with an average attendance of 69. Four teachers were proposed for the following year. Tuition was to be in five classes ranging from $3.75 to $12.50, one-fourth of which was to be paid in advance. No student could be admitted without a character certificate. All students were to attend worship on fourth days unless exempted. Teachers were: David Morgan, principal; Jeptha W. Morgan, first assistant; David Jones and Palmyra Jones, second assistants. Funds were raised and lightning rods installed and a fence was built. David Morgan was the head of the school and taught the girls. Jeptha W. Morgan taught the more advanced students on the second floor; David Jones (Ellis's uncle) taught the smaller boys.[66]

The 1860 report showed a decrease in attendance to 94, most of which were not members of the Society. David Morgan made a strong recommendation that the best interests of the Society would be served by the removal of the school from the South to one of the Western states or territories. This was due to the fact that four-fifths of the church families were planning to move to the Western states. It was decided that although such were the plans that it was not probable that all of them would move. Therefore the school would be continued "as long as it was sustained as a distinctive Friends School." In the event that in the judgment of the trustees it should be to the best interest of the Society to remove the school, it should be located in Kansas. A great many families did migrate West on the eve of the War Between the States, Morgan among them.[67]

The church at Friendsville lost heavily during the war because they were Union sympathizers. They lost $165,000 gold value; seventy-six out of ninety-six horses; 2,853 bushels of corn; 1,586 bushels of oats and other things.[68]

There are no records to show that the school was in operation from 1860–64, although a local tradition says that there was at least one student all during the war. Neither the church nor the school have any records for the war period, and the fact that the church speaks of "reviving" the school indicates inactivity.

---

[65] Samuel Dunlap. *History of the Society of Friends in Tennessee*, (1899) (Unpublished MSS. Copy in the U.S.D. 1812 collection); A letter to Friendsville Academy from Newburgh, Oregon, written in November, 1926 by Zimri S. Ellis. Published in the *Quaker Quill*, June, 1945; *Newberry Minutes*, 1857, 7th month.

[66] *Ibid.*, 1858; 6th month; 7th month; see note 6.

[67] *Ibid.*, 1860, 7th month; 9th month.

[68] Cartland, *Southern Heroes*, 315.

David Morgan, Thomas M. Jones, and John Hackney who were trutees of Friendsville Institute and Newberry Female School were among those who had gone West before the war, and T. R. Lee, William Lewis and Jonathan Lee were elected in their stead in 1864. Three months later L. L. Greer was elected to the room of James C. Allen, deceased. The church at that time directed the trustees to open the school following the same plans used when the school first opened.[69]

Friends in Indiana and Philadelphia contributed funds and books to help get the school back in full operation. In August 1868, 124 scholars were enrolled, only thirteen of which were Friends. Three teachers were employed. The school at this time was operating under the Baltimore Association of Friends.

In 1869, Wm. Lewis having moved from the bounds of the meeting, Hugh Hackney was elected trustee. In 1870 by direction of the yearly meeting a joint committee on education was appointed: Wm. Russell, John I. Morris, Wm. C. Endsley, John S. Mahoney, J. F. Beals, Lucinda Jones, S. S. Greer, H. S. W. Hackney, and E. C. Greer.[70]

The County Superintendent's report for 1868 named Franklin Elliott, Ester Newlin and Sarah Underhill as teachers and 112 students. (Elliott was a dentist who ten years later served as Blount County Superintendent of Public Instruction.)

About 1870 Rebecca Allinson accompanied by Marmaduke Cope and Sarah Cope, his wife, visited East Tennessee and saw the need of boarding facilities for students attending the Friendsville School. Assisted by Robert B. Haines, Sr., and his wife Margaret Haines, Edward Scull and Yardley Warner, who had also visited the territory, they built two boarding houses. The girls' home was named in honor of the distinguished English Friend, William Forster. The boys' home is generally referred to as Allen Hall but the records are silent as to where and for whom the name came into use.[71]

A news item in 1878 related that Prof. William Russell, principal of the Friendsville Institute had retired after six years hard labor. The

---

[69] David Morgan and others went to Iowa and took the school's permanent fund ($2,000) with them and according to report it was used in the founding of Penn College. He was later one of the promoters of the Iowa Central Railroad and died at New Sharon, Iowa. Jeptha Morgan also went to Oskaloosa and became a doctor and druggist. David Jones taught for awhile in the Richlands School (Ia.) and became a doctor and minister. (This information was taken from the letter referred to in Note 11.) Also from an article from *A Friend*, (Phila.) 6th month, 3, 1926, by William C. Price.

[70] *Newberry Minutes*, 1868, 8th month; 1869, 9th month; 1870, 6th month.

[71] *Maryville Times*, April 4, 1921: The first three named were of Philadelphia and were Trustees of the Maryville Normal School. (Friends Normal); Warner was a Massachusetts Friend who came to Maryville and supervised the building and establishing of the Freedman's Normal Institute; Forster, an English philanthropist, was traveling in the South in the interest of Manumission societies. He had visited Friendsville and left to continue his work. He became ill and died near Lowe's Ferry, January 27, 1854. (Ten miles distant). He was buried in the graveyard at Friendsville (Newberry Minutes 1854, 2nd month). His son, the Hon. William Edward Forster, M. P. visited his father's grave in later years and had an iron fence placed around the grave. For this reason the Forster family and English Friends have given generously to the Friendsville School. (Cartland, 308).

school advertisement stated that young ladies were boarded at Forster Home and "trained practically for the duties of life."

The following year it was noted that Prof. (Wilson) Spray and wife were at the Friendsville School.[72]

From its first beginnings in 1854 until February 12, 1881, Friendsville Institute belonged to the Newberry Monthly Meeting. At that date the Hickory Valley Monthly Meeting was asked to join with the Friendsville Meeting in asking for a new charter for Friendsville Academy to belong to the Friendsville Quarterly Meeting.[73]

At this time the plan of operation was to hire a principal to run the school for what he could make out of the project. Repairs had to be made how ever they could. The boarding homes seemed to operate in the same way. The principals' wives generally managed the Forster Home if they did not teach in the school.

William V. Marshburn was the first principal to try the lease plan. After two years he resigned on account of poor health.

Stephen M. Hadley was elected the following year but went into other work after one year. He was followed by Jesse W. Marshall and wife Annie from Penn College.

After two years Zeno H. Dixon succeeded Marshall in 1887. The school advertisement in 1889 listed tuition at $1.00 and $2.00 per month "for male and female." Later in the year Dixon resigned and went to Snow Camp, North Carolina.[74]

In 1889 the board decided that it was best to separate from the public schools. Evidently up to this date, they, like other private schools, had qualified for public schools funds to supplement their operation costs and to lengthen the school term.

Prof. A. H. Lloyd was chosen to head the school from 1889–93. In 1892, Philadelphia Friends who had paid the matron's salary for the Forster Home reduced or withdrew their aid. This in turn affected the cost of operation.

After one year, Charles W. Marshall was followed by Jesse H. Moore from Haverford College, who served until 1901.

In April 1897, Elizabeth Farnum of Philadelphia said that she could put the board in possession of at least $5,000 for a new building if she were assured that it would be finished within one year. Work was begun as soon as possible but school finally opened the first of October in the church building. This building was dedicated December 28, 1897.

In December 1901, the trustees of the Friends School in Maryville sold their property and offered the $3,000 derived therefrom to the Board of Friendsville Academy. This generous gift was accepted by the group.

---

[72] *The Maryville Index*, May 8, 1878; February 12, 1879.
[73] *Minutes of the Board of Managers of Friendsville Academy*. February 1881–December 1915. (at Friendsville Academy).
[74] *Maryville Times*, January 2, 1889; July 7, 1889. Report of the State Superintendent of Public Instruction for 1889 listed Friendsville Academy as having two teachers and 80 students.

The next two or three years were unsettled and principals kept resigning. Prof. Sam Miser filled the gap several times but finally refused to take the position again in 1904.

After another year of "short term" principals and a term by Frank Peters, Prof. Zeno H. Dixon was called back from North Carolina and offered a five-year contract. He was to have the total income from the school including the interest on the endowment after paying for insurance and incidental repairs. He resigned in 1907 and was followed by Ruthana Hadley for two years.

Daniel W. Lawrence of North Branch, Kansas was principal from 1909–12. He was followed by Dixon, who was again offered a long term contract. Sometime in 1914, Farnum Hall burned and Dixon went elsewhere. The insurance had been collected by December 15, 1914 and a committee was appointed to employ an architect to plan a new building.

About this time the high school proposition was taken up by the Blount County Court. The Quarterly Meeting was asked to give the academic site to the County High School Board to build a local public high school. The request was granted provided that the community would subscribe a like amount of money. The amount was subscribed but afterwards this contract was broken by the high school proposition being reconsidered by the County Court and voted down.

In February 1915, the managing Board named a building committee to rebuild Farnum Hall, the cost not to exceed $4,500.

The 1914–15 session of school was taught by Miss Ora Wright in the boys' home.

Friendsville Academy is the only survivor of the ten or more private schools and academies which were chartered in Blount County during the past hundred years. Its history is unique in many ways and it has continued for the last quarter of a century to carry on the same traditions as are shown in its early history.

THE FREEDMAN'S INSTITUTE

About the year 1867 a log house was built on the lot now occupied by the A. M. E. Zion church by the Negro people of Maryville. The money was raised mainly by the Negro Methodists. Fifty dollars was given by the Freedman's Bureau. Two years later, William B. Scott, Sr., headed a drive and raised $100 to purchase the lot on which the building stood from Alford McConnell who donated $20 of the amount himself.

The log building was then sold for fifty dollars and a joint drive among whites and Negroes, Presbyterians and Methodists, resulted in the erection of a new building costing $800. One-half of the amount was given at different times by the Freedman's Bureau. The building was primarily for school purposes, but with the Trustee's consent might also be used for church purposes. The trustees were: W. B. Scott, Sr., Jacob Henry, H. L. Cansler, and W. S. McTeer.[75]

---

[75] *Maryville Weekly Index*. March 5, 1880.

The first school session in this building was taught by Yardley Warner, under the auspices of the Friends Society, assisted by Miss Hannah Collins. Friends had always been sympathetic with the problems of the Negro race, so it was natural that they should turn to them with their educational problems.

W. B. Scott Sr., and a few others of the more enlightened local members of the race saw education as the major stepping-stone to the place they wanted in the world. They talked the matter over with the local Friends and as a result the New England Yearly Meeting was appealed to for help in solving their problem. About six months after their request was sent to New England, Yardley Warner, looking like a story-book character, arrived in Maryville. He walked the nine-hundred miles from New England, not because he couldn't afford to ride, but because he didn't see the point in paying for transportation as long as he was able to walk.[76]

He met with Scott and other interested parties and told them that the New England Friends were ready to assist in buying the land and erecting the necessary buildings, but that they would be expected to do their part; that bricks must be made and many strong arms and hands would be needed.

Preparatory to this meeting, a notice had appeared in a Knoxville newspaper calling for Negroes and their friends from Blount and surrounding counties to meet at the courthouse in Maryville, to see what could be done toward establishing a Normal Institute for training teachers for the Negro population.[77]

The call was signed by: W. B. Scott Sr., Hugh L. Cansler, Jacob Henry, W. S. McTeer, J. G. Ish, Thomas Lillard, and Henry DeBose. Appended to this call was a statement that the project was approved by: S. Z. Sharp, Yardley Warner, S. H. Gault, W. D. McGinley, Will A. McTeer, W. A. Walker, J. W. Greer, and S. P. Rowan.

At this meeting December 15, 1871, Scott and his associates outlined their plan and Yardley Warner presented the offer of the New England Yearly Meeting. The offer was unanimously accepted. Before he would undertake to raise the money, Mr. Warner desired that $2,000 should be subscribed locally, which was over-subscribed. In all, about $20,000 was raised. Of this amount, Friends in Great Britain and Ireland contributed about $12,000. Only six or seven hundred dollars of the local subscriptions were collected and the remainder of the amount was contributed in Pennsylvania and other states. In April 1872, the building was begun.[78]

---

[76] Charles W. Cansler, *Three Generations*. (Knoxville, 1939), 37 ff. Hereinafter cited *Cansler*.

[77] *Knoxville Chronicle*, November 29, 1871.

[78] *Maryville Weekly Index*. March 5, 1880. Deeds, EE, 117 (Trustees—Charles F. Coffin, Richard Padrick, Levi Jessup, Isaac C. Evans.) See also GG, 292; Stanley Pumphrey, *Missionary Work in Connection with the Society of Friends*. (Philadelphia, 1880), p. 74. Hereinafter cited *Pumphrey*.

Yardley Warner was principal of the school during its first year. William P. Hastings of Iowa took over January 1874, in its second year and acted for about twenty years. His daughter Letitia and her husband William O. Garner directed the school until its close in 1901.[79]

A typical advertisement in the local newspaper offered three courses: Elementary, Advanced, and Classical, "at terms within the reach of all." A total cost of $5.25 yearly; board for as little as .75 per week. "The school is especially recommended to those who wish to qualify themselves as teachers," and to "fill any calling creditable to themselves and their race." (A dormitory, 40 x 50 was, soon after the beginning, fitted up for the accommodation of self-boarders on the top floor. This made it possible for students to attend who otherwise could not have managed.)[80]

An 1879 report listed 175 scholars in the day school, and 54 in the training department. Eighty teachers had been sent out, 48 to teach in Tennessee, Alabama, and Georgia, with 2,500 pupils under their instruction. The Maryville students were in great demand and were able to hold their own in competition with graduates from Fisk University.

Booker T. Washington is quoted as saying, "When I first went to Tuskeegee—I felt that perhaps no other school in the South during that period was doing better work," (than Freedman's Normal).[81]

In 1878, a news item in the local newspaper stated that tuition was free to all from 6–18 years of age; and that the public school money enabled them to have 10 months of school instead of five. The work in this school continued but the interest in the higher phases of education tapered off and the enrollment was heavier in the lower grades. This may have been due partly to the fact that Negro students had been accepted by Maryville College since 1867. There were also in the town the schools for the younger children before-mentioned which were sponsored by the churches and since 1867 a public school. The Second Presbyterian Church had maintained a school since the close of the war, under the supervision of the Stated Supply. Mr. Parham mentions besides the Revs. Whittey and Trusty, Mrs. Stearns, Ella Brown Coulter, Maggie Bell Brown, the Rev. Daniel S. Baker, Ida Baker Parham, Mary Beeabout, Catherine Lillard and Ed Leeper as teachers who assisted in the church school.[82]

An index to the size of the Freedman's Institute may be had from

[79] *Cansler*, p. 39: (Garner was the son of Dr. J. D. Garner of Friends Normal).
[80] *Maryville Index*, random numbers; August 21, 1871.
[81] *Pumphrey*, 35; *Cansler*, 40.
[82] *Maryville Index*, August 21, 1878; Dr. Anderson had two theological students who were ordained by Union Presbytery before 1810. Jack, a man of color, bought his freedom and was allowed to take the name of Jack Gloucester and was ordained to do missionary work among his brethren after reference to General Assembly in 1807. George Erskine (Negro) was ordained and went as a missionary to Liberia in 1820. *(Union Presbytery Minutes*, Passim). The enrollment of Negro students in Maryville College averaged about 20 per cent at the most. They were debarred by state law in 1901; *Maryville Record*, July 8, 1904.

the 1889 report of the State Superintendent which listed 211 students and eleven teachers, but there is no indication as to the grades represented. The school finally closed in 1901 and lay idle for three years during which the property was transferred by the Friends to Letitia Hastings Garner and her husband, in payment of their last few years' work for which they had received no pay.

It has been said that Oscar Wilson was probably the first Negro teacher.

Among the early teachers listed by Mr. Parham were: Miss Mattie Strain, Miss Higgins, Hannah Rorex, Ellen Toole, Rosa McTeer, Catherine Lillard, Miss Morris, Mrs. Ida Woods, Blanche DeBose, Mr. Buck, Octavia Warren Hord, Pauline Hord Chandler, Ruth Fagg, Anna Richardson, Ed Leeper, Alice Gamble, Hannah Kennedy Argile, Olive Wallace, Savannah George Gore, and Lawrence Buford.

Paris Wallace was principal of the Negro public school in 1896, and was assisted by Minnie Valentine. The school continued at this location until the T. B. Lillard School was replaced by the Hale School in 1930, which is a twelve-grade school.[83]

MARYVILLE NORMAL AND PREPARATORY SCHOOL

In 1871, Dr. J. D. Garner came to the mountains of East Tennessee and devoted his energies for the next thirty years to the elevation of the religious, physical, and educational conditions of the rural and mountain people. More especially did he labor in the educational field. He was assisted in this work by members of his family. Jeremiah Grinnell, Rachel Binford, John Parker and Benjamin Coppock were also associated with him in this work. Goodspeed gives the organization date of the school as 1873.[84]

While the New England Friends were operating the Freedman's Institute for the purpose of training teachers for the Negro population, Dr. Garner, sponsored by Philadelphia and Indiana Friends, was operating the Maryville Normal and Preparatory School primarily for the purpose of training teachers for isolated mountain schools.

Prof. B. S. Coppock came to Maryville from Ohio about 1876 and took charge of the school, which was then being operated in the Friends Church. The school opened the first session with fifteen scholars. This number soon increased to sixty and the second year the en-

---

[83] Paris Wallace was one of the most brilliant students during his scholastic career at Maryville College, where he graduated with honors. He was later a Bishop in the A. M. E. Church. Thomas B. Lillard, confectioner, was one of the most progressive of his race and popular as a business man. The Lillard School was at the rear of the A. M. E. Church (now Gertrude Apartments). William T. Hale who was a graduate of Freedman's Institute was later one of the founders of the Tennessee Agricultural and Industrial College of Nashville.

[84] Stanley Pumphrey, *Missionary Work* . . . an address. (Philadelphia, 1880) 35, Passim.

rollment reached eighty. Professor Coppock was assisted by Misses Julia Garner and Sarah Moore.[85]

The need for a good Preparatory and Normal school was more and more apparent, so it was thought advisable to increase the facilities of the school. In 1878 the Pride mansion and grounds were acquired and the following year two dormitories, each containing eight apartments, were built on the grounds to accommodate young men and women who wished to board themselves. Normal students assisted in teaching the younger pupils.[86]

Newman reported to the Friends that thirty teachers had been sent out by 1878 and that thirty-five were in training. He also reported that eight school-meeting houses had been built through Dr. Garner's efforts and influence. He further stated that the schools with which Dr. Garner was connected were partly supported by public funds and partly by the Indiana Yearly Meeting of Friends and the voluntary contributions of other interested Friends.[87]

In 1878, the Dr. Samuel Pride residence was purchased with funds furnished by a few wealthy Friends of Philadelphia and Baltimore, who became members of the Board of Trustees and the school was conducted under Dr. Garner's supervision until 1884 when a new Board got control under a three-year lease. The original design was abandoned and it became a Normal and Preparatory or Intermediate School.[88]

An agreement was signed between E. L. Scull and J. D. Garner, May 14, 1878, which stated that Garner was to repair for school purposes and build such buildings as were necessary for the accommodation of a good Normal School and run the school without further trouble or expense to others. When Garner moved his Normal School into said property, when purchased, he was to "run and control it" . . . one object being to help him educate the worthy poor in the mountain districts of East Tennessee and Western North Carolina.[89]

Garner was to have entire power to hire principals and also to rent and lease property for school purposes and assume entire executive control, the Board being only as helpers and advisors.

---

[85] *Maryville Index*, August 14, 1878. An advertisement stated: "The aim of this school is to furnish first class opportunities for teachers and those preparing to teach to thoroughly qualify themselves. Tuition: Advanced—$7.00; Intermediate—$6.00; Incidentals, .75. B. S. Coppock, principal; Miss Sarah Morrison, James B. Bruff, Mrs. Julia (Garner) Coppock, teachers.

[86] *Maryville Index*, March 5, 1880.

[87] Henry Staley Newman (of England), *Memories of Stanley Pumphrey* (New York, 1883), ch. 11.

[88] *Deeds*, H H 356. Rufus B. Robinson and wife Elizabeth S., transferred four acres known as the Samuel Pride homestead to Edward L. Scull and Elizabeth Farnham of Philadelphia, Robert B. Haines of Montgomery County, Pennsylvania, Jeptha D. Garner and Benjamin S. Coppock of Blount County, Tenn., Trustees. (April 5, 1879); *Goodspeed*, 1005.

[89] Photostat. Original belongs to Bert Garner, Maryville, Tenn.; *Maryville Index*, May 15, 1878, "Stanley Pumphrey and wife of England, Robert Haines' wife, Edward Scull and Elizabeth Farnham of Philadelphia attended Quarterly Meeting at the Friends Church." (This was when the deed was signed by the Trustees named above.)

The Maryville Normal and Preparatory School opened in 1878 with Benjamin S. Coppock, principal, and four assistants. According to the terms of the deed, the school was to be devoted to the education of both sexes without distinction as to religious denominations. A charter was issued to Maryville Normal and Preparatory School in 1880.[90]

From 1886 to 1895 Timothy Wilson, Lindley D. Clark, Edgar Stinson and wife, of Jamestown, Ohio, and Prof. Wilson Hole who was followed by D. Riley Haworth in 1895 served as heads of the school. Matthew Terrill and Dr. W. C. Stanley were chairman and secretary of the Board during this period.

A local advertisement read: "Cheapest school in Tennessee." (Tuition was $10.00 a year. Room rent was fifty cents a month.) Professor Jonathan Wright was head of the school in the fall of 1899, assisted by R. C. Newlin and Carrie Moore. Professor Hadley was principal the following year which was the last session of the school, during which the enrollment was 179.[91]

The school property was sold to the City of Maryville in September 1900, and used for a public school building instead of the old Masonic building which was no longer safe. In 1910 the old Pride mansion was removed and the West Side School building was erected.[92]

It would not be fitting to neglect to mention the other work which Dr. Garner was doing while he was overseer of the "Quaker School." He was working under a contract with the Department of the Interior at $300 per year by which he had charge of the Indian schools in Tennessee, North Carolina and Georgia. He was also working as a missionary to the destitute and neglected mountain people of East Tennessee and Western North Carolina. His report filed for the years 1871–77 listed funds received from New England, Philadelphia, and Indiana Friends as $3,160.00. In 1877, he listed fourteen schools under his care. Twenty-three pupils in school at his expense were training as teachers. Forty-seven other pupils were being kept in school at his expense. He had furnished to various persons, 560 slates, 250 school books, fourteen sets of charts, over 860 second-hand garments and 3,000 yards of new materials. He had also organized ten new Sunday schools and distributed 125 Bibles and 230 Testaments. In fact, the report represented a prodigious amount of work and an almost unbelievable territory covered. Besides this work, he was a practicing physician, simultaneously.[93]

Dr. Garner and his family rendered a worthy educational service to

[90] *Deeds*, HH, 465. Trustees: Elizabeth Farnum, Robert B. Haines, Benj. S. Coppock, H. W. Spray, and J. D. Garner.

[91] *Maryville Times*, 1886, 1900, Passim.

[92] *Ibid.*, August 6, 1898; August 19, 1899; August 11, 1900; *Deeds*, 54, p. 200: J. D. Garner of Blount County, Edward M. Wistar, and John C. Whiston, of Philadelphia, Benjamin S. Coppock of Tallequah, Indian Territory, Trustees; to Fielding, H. Lamon, Samuel L. George, W. E. Parham.

[93] Photostat of Report. (Original of report belongs to Bert Garner, Route 6, Maryville, Tennessee); Cades Cove, Happy Valley and Bethel (near Christy Hill) were Blount County schools in which he was interested. Besides the Maryville Normal he also sponsored one at Hopewell Springs in Monroe County, Tennessee.

S. T. WILSON

WM. WALLACE

EDUCATIONAL LEADERS

SAMUEL TYNDALE WILSON, D.D.
Teacher and Dean of Maryville College, 1884–1901; President of Maryville College, 1901–1930; Author of *A Century of Maryville College*.

GENERAL WILLIAM WALLACE
Active in the early Railroad movements; Treasurer of Maryville College, 1833–1864.

CHARLES W. ("BILL JOE") HENRY
Founder of Maryville Polytechnic School; Early advocate of Free Public High Schools.

MAJOR BEN CUNNINGHAM
Holder of many Blount County offices; Treasurer of Maryville College, 1901–1914.

MAJOR WILL A. McTEER
Author of *A History of New Providence Presbyterian Church*; Attorney, and Treasurer of Maryville College, 1884–1901.

C. W. HENRY

BEN CUNNINGHAM

W. A. McTEER

Porter Academy

New Providence Presbyterian Church, 1852–1893; Columbian Hall, 1893–1911.

Blount County at the period when public education was in its infancy. Maryville College began to offer teacher-training courses soon after the establishment of the Normal. This and other general reasons caused the decline of the private school not only in Maryville and Blount County but all over the country.

MARYVILLE POLYTECHNIC SCHOOL

At the turn of the century there were as yet no public high schools in Blount County and no local opportunity for business training. The private schools were at that time slanted toward preparing for college and not toward earning a livelihood in the business world. Small businesses were springing up everywhere and "outsiders" were holding the key positions.

After graduating from Maryville College, C. W. Henry took a post-graduate course at the Commercial College of Kentucky University. He well knew that the youth of his native East Tennessee were well-qualified to become directors and managers of new enterprises if they were offered the opportunity to prepare themselves for this type of work.

On the 13th of November, 1901, Prof. Charles William Henry ("Bill Joe") opened a business school called "Maryville Business College" in a small upstairs room in the Gamble and Waller building on Main Street with one day, and four night pupils. These pupils were immediately employed after finishing their courses, and the reputation of the school spread. In 1902, Professor Sawers and John C. Crawford assisted, and in 1903 Miss Anna Newby taught shorthand.[94]

In due time larger quarters for shorthand was necessary and since the Freedman's Institute had closed its doors in 1901, that school plant seemed to be the answer to Professor Henry's problem. In the summer of 1904, the red tape was finally unwound and the three-story red brick building on West Main Street became the property of Professor Henry.[95]

The need for high school courses in connection with the business courses had been evident for some time, so with the addition of more room came an expansion to include a high school and grammar grades program, enriched by the cultural arts. So, on September 7, 1904— Blount County High School commenced its first year's work. Prof. H. B. McCall was Professor Henry's assistant in this venture and continued to be for several years, since his duties as county superintendent of schools constituted only a part-time job. The tuition fee was $16.00 for nine months.[96]

The school prospered and grew and in 1905 the enrollment reached

---

[94] *Maryville Times*, January 25, 1902; March 15, 1902.
[95] *Deeds*, 59, p. 140; see also 55, pp. 484, and 527.
[96] *Maryville Record*, July 8, 1904; *Maryville Times*, July 2, 1904.

151 and the staff increased to nine. A dormitory was built for boarding students in 1906.[97]

Even though his school was doing a wonderful job, Professor Henry knew that for every student who came to his school and other private preparatory schools there were possibly a hundred or more who could not. He wrote letters to the public in the local papers, showing that a system of public high schools could be operated at less cost than private schools and that all youth deserved an "even chance," but these appeals fell on deaf ears. A tentative move was made by County Court in 1914 and promptly reconsidered, thus it was not until 1918 that a definite move was made toward establishing public high schools.[98]

In 1908, Professor Henry made a statement that due to the fact that the title Blount County High School was misleading and that a majority of the people thought it was a school operating on state funds, and teaching those subjects offered in the common high schools, he felt compelled to change the title to: Polytechnic High School and Commercial College. In 1909 the name was changed to Maryville Polytechnic School.[99]

About this time, too, for the benefit of his rural patrons, he decided to offer some more practical courses, such as agriculture which would prepare rural students for a richer and more profitable way of life.

The music department and band were an integral part of the school from the beginning and Professor Henry himself was well qualified as a leader and was an accomplished clarinetist.

The athletic program was of the highest caliber and was the equal of any school in its class.

By 1908 the enrollment had grown to 385 in all its departments, which by then included beginners, high school, and commercial courses.

The fame of the school spread and students not only came from neighboring counties but neighboring states and finally far-away states. The reputation of Maryville Polytechnic School for a cultural Christian atmosphere was second to none.

By 1911, $15,000 had been spent on repairs and furnishings. The young men's home was improved and Martha Henry Hall was built to accommodate fifty young ladies.

The establishment of Maryville High School in 1917 and the county high schools from 1918–1922 marked the end of an era. Maryville College abolished their Preparatory Department in 1925 and the last session of Maryville Polytechnic School was in 1926. Professor Henry sold the school plant to the city of Maryville, and Maryville High School now stands on the campus first occupied by Freedman's Institute for 39 years, and by Maryville Polytechnic twenty-two years. The total enrollment of students for this period was 8,000 or an average of 300 per year.

[97] *Maryville Times*, August 18, 1905; August 3, 1906.
[98] *Ibid.*, January 2, 1906; Sept. 22, 1905.
[99] *Ibid.*, Sept. 8, 1908; (A historical sketch).

Whenever possible, Professor Henry got grants of state funds from the county which enabled students who otherwise could not have attended high school to do so. Too much value cannot be placed on the contribution made by Professor Henry and Maryville Polytechnic School to the educational program of Blount County and the practical cultural quality of the training given.

The most remarkable fact about the school is that it was always self-supporting and through the years maintained a program of expansion and improvement. This is all the more remarkable when one remembers that this school was started when other private schools were closing because of financial difficulties. The faculty of this school was always of the highest caliber as teachers and as individuals.[100]

After the close of Maryville Polytechnic School, Professor Henry served as teacher in the Lee School for boys; headmaster at the McCallie school for boys; associate-president of Sullins College; and president of King College. He resigned from the last-named position because of ill health and died in 1935.[101]

FROM ACADEMY TO HIGH SCHOOL

In 1866 there is recorded in the minutes of New Providence Lodge and also in the minutes of the Porter Academy Board of Trustees an agreement whereby the Academy was to have the use of two floors of the Masonic building and pay three-fourths of the upkeep. They were to rent the second floor to the Rev. Mr. Cherry and the first floor to Miss Sawyers for a school.

Evidently the academy did not get into operation and in 1867 the trustees for Porter Academy voted to give the interest on the academy funds to Maryville College for "the benefit of such young men of Blount County as may be entitled to it."

In 1868, a movement was inaugurated to rebuild the Porter Academy on the old lot but evidently the movement did not receive too much encouragement and since Maryville College was already in operation, the trustees, it seems, decided that another location might be better.

The trustees, after conferring with the general public, let it be known that the community subscribing the most money for a building and site would be favored for the location of the academy. Tradition has it that the eleventh district (Rockford) was outbid by a very small margin by the twelfth district (Wildwood) but it also said that other districts, especially the eighteenth, were close bidders also.[102]

A site of five acres was given by Thomas J. Pritchett which adjoined

---

[100] John E. Middlebrooks, *History of the rise and fall of Academies in Tenn.* 1923. (Peabody Thesis) says that in 1895 alone, 21 corporations were given legal permission to dissolve for: mortgages, indebtedness, repairs, or to invest in local public high schools.

[101] Information from Mrs. C. W. Henry.

[102] *Academy Abstracts*, 1866–67; *New Providence Lodge Minutes*, 1866–67; Mr. C. M. Kennedy, Interview July, 1953.

the Logan's Chapel Church property and an agreement was signed in October 1871, between S. C. Hinton, Elisha Carpenter, C. C. Cowan, John Edmondson, and James F. Beals, as trustees of Porter Academy, and C. B. Lord, William Goddard, Sr., Ben Cunningham, D. G. Wright, and Jacob Nimon who were acting as trustees and representatives of a voluntary association of persons who had signed subscriptions to erect suitable buildings near the Sulphur Springs and Logan's Chapel. $1,400 was subscribed to erect buildings and $900 to be used to carry on the school.

"It has been proposed to erect the building at divers other places but no other place has agreed to do so much. We consider the location beautiful and eligible. It is to remain a free academy and open to all denominations according to the original act. The buildings are to be erected within a reasonable length of time."

James Davis and David Jones built a two-story brick building thirty-two by eighty feet, with two rooms downstairs and one upstairs.[103]

The bricks were made nearby; the mud was ground by horsepower and the bricks hand-molded by Jim Scott (Negro) and sun-dried before being baked.

Prof. W. M. Rogers had the stairway changed in 1880 to the position remembered by later students. When the building was razed in 1921 the bricks from the old building were used in the new building.

In 1867, County Court elected William Goddard, R. J. Allen, H. H. C. Caruthers, S. F. Cowan and S. C. Hinton, trustees for Porter Academy. Thereafter, trustees were elected regularly every two years. James Waters was first elected to the board in 1872 and was chosen treasurer. He continued to serve as treasurer until about 1890. D. W. Trotter, John H. Pickens, and E. A. Walker were named as treasurers by various boards. (Pickens served from 1892 to 1910.)

R. N. Hood, C. T. Cates, James L. McCamey, R. L. Houston, Ben Cunningham, Robert Porter, Sam P. Rowan, J. B. French, W. D. McGinley, Monroe Goddard and M. H. Gamble were among those who served more than one term as trustees over a forty-year period.

At the January term of court in 1918, M. H. Gamble, one of the trustees of Porter Academy proposed the following resolution: "We believe that the public consolidated schools and the public high schools hold more nearly to the general cause of education formerly held by the academy . . ."

"The trustees of Porter Academy are authorized to transfer land, houses, and permanent fund to the County Board of Education according to the act of 1907."

---

[103] *Deeds*, E E, 217; p. 336; C. M. Kennedy. *History of Porter Academy*, (Kennedy Papers). Copy in author's collection. *The Comet*, (Johnson City) August 2, 1884 stated that Miss Rhoda Gifford had gone to Louisville, Tenn. to take charge of the Music Department of Prof. Gibb's School. No information has been found about this school.

The resolution was approved and the court ordered the transfer made.[104]

The Legislature had, in 1891, passed an act establishing two classes of school, primary and secondary, the first being "required" and the second "permitted." At this time it was also made a requirement that a school director be able to read intelligently and write legibly. In 1899 a law was passed permitting counties to levy a tax to establish and maintain one or more high schools in each county. In the same session that a uniform textbook law was passed in 1903, a law was passed requiring that school districts and civil districts be co-extensive.[105]

All these acts were building up toward the 1907 act creating a County Board of Education and the General Education Bill of 1909 which unified the public school system and for the first time made official reports mandatory before school funds could be received. Eight per cent of the general education fund was to be used for public high schools, to be graded by the State Board of Education. The Blount County Court in session "approved" of the act to establish high schools in 1907 and appointed W. E. Parham, Prof. M. H. Gamble, and H. B. McCall to recommend how the county should be divided into five school districts in accord with the recent act of Legislature. In July 1909, it was voted by County Court that the county superintendent of schools should devote his entire time to the job. Heretofore, it had been only a part-time job paying about $300 per year. In 1913 the General Education Law of 1909 was amended whereby thirty-three and one-third per cent of gross revenue of the state was appropriated to the maintenance of the public schools. Several other acts were passed by this legislature such as a compulsory attendance law and acts for consolidation and standardization of schools in general.

In 1914, we find that the Blount County Court appointed a high school board. The court authorized a $40,000 bond issue to be used to establish one or more high schools. When Farnum Hall burned at Friendsville Academy in 1914, the County School Board approached the trustees relative to acquiring the site for a county high school. They agreed and subscriptions were taken in the neighborhood. The rescinding of the act by the Blount County Court in 1915 canceled the contract. Farnum Hall was then rebuilt.[106]

In 1916, the County Court reconsidered the matter and voted a bond issue to establish high schools in Blount County. The board of trustees of Porter Academy, in 1918, transferred the academy property and funds to the high school board. In 1918 there was established three high schools in Blount County: Wildwood, Louisville, and Carpenter. The

---

[104] *Minutes*, Passim. 1918.

[105] Blount County *School Report* 1906–1907. H. B. McCall, Supt.; 1st School Dist. (1-2-7-17), 2nd (4-5-6-10), 4th (11-12-13), 5th (3-15-16-18), 3rd (8-9-14-19) —numbers refer to Civil districts; *Minutes*, 1907, 1909.

[106] *Minutes*, 1914; *Minutes of Managing Board of Friendsville Academy*, 1914. (In 1915 County Court rescinded its action of 1914.)

high school board at this time was: W. B. Townsend, Prof. H. L. Ellis, the Hon. Sam Johnson, J. A. Garner, Dr. W. B. Lovingood, and Will T. Harris. During that year, a new brick building was built at Wildwood, the first brick school building in Blount County and ten new frame buildings including Louisville and Carpenter. About the same time a committee was appointed to investigate the possibility of making Maryville Polytechnic School a county high school. No formal report was recorded. In 1919, a high school was established at Friendsville which was the first high school in Blount County to reach four-year status (in 1922).[107]

In 1922, high schools were started at Lanier, Prospect, Binfield, Townsend, Walland, and Everett. In 1923 Everett and Porter high schools graduated their first class. At this time it was decided to make Lanier a two-year high school and do away with the high school at Carpenter's. Transportation was furnished from Carpenter's to Lanier. This was one of the first transportation contracts in Blount County.

In 1926 Walland became a four-year high school, Townsend in 1927 and Lanier in 1928.

Louisville, Binfield and Prospect were junior high schools until 1932 when transportation, and consolidation made them unnecessary.

Porter High School at Wildwood Springs took its name from Porter Academy from which it was converted into a county high school in 1918. Porter serves the section roughly bounded by Little River on the west and Ellejoy on the south.

Friendsville High School, established in 1919 in the Quaker Village of Friendsville, serves the territory north of the Niles Ferry Road to the Tennessee River and east to Louisville.

Townsend High School serves Tuckaleechee and Cades Cove and has at times served Wear's Cove in Sevier County. During the days of Little River Lumber Company, Townsend was quite a flourishing village but the school is now semi-rural.

Walland High School is located in Walland which, from 1900 to 1930, was a prosperous village supported by Schlosser Leather Company. Walland had one of the first nine-month schools in Blount County (when other schools were having six months). The Tannery paid the extra month's salaries. Walland High School serves Millers Cove and the territory south of Ellejoy as far as Hubbard.

Everett High School is the only high school in Blount County which took only one year to reach senior high grade. The other five schools went through a transition period covering from two to six years. This school was made necessary by the rapid growth of the population east

---

[107] *Blount County School Report.* Nancy Lee Broady, Supt. 1917–18, ($7,000 and 5 acres of land were transferred by the Academy trustees.) Previous to her term as Superintendent of Blount County Schools Miss Broady served as the first Home Demonstration Agent for the county. She is the only woman to date who has held this office. During her term of office the first bond issue for schools was passed and the first high school established, also the first consolidated schools and school buses. It is noted further that the Blount County Teachers' Association and the Parent-Teachers' organizations were started during her regime.

EDUCATION

and north of Maryville. This growth was occasioned by the expansion of the Aluminum Company of America. Everett School gets its name from Mrs. Rosalie E. Everett, one of the donors of the building site. Everett High School draws its students from the territory covering a radius of from three to five miles in, and around Maryville.

Lanier is the only truly rural high school in Blount County. When established in 1922, it was a new creation, a consolidation of Woods and Williamson schools. The name Lanier was suggested by the late Hon. Sam Johnson, then chairman of the County School Board. The name was in honor of Sidney Lanier whose grandfather once operated Montvale Springs Hotel. Lanier High School draws patronage from that territory south of the Niles Ferry Highway from Carpenter's Campground to Monroe County, including Happy Valley and Calderwood. The elementary portion of Lanier is a consolidation or a combination of at least parts of eight or ten smaller schools.[108]

The beginnings of secondary school education in the City of Maryville dates a little further back than that in the county. Maryville High School was established in 1913 with Eva Alexander as principal. C. D. Curtis became principal of Maryville High School in 1914. The school became a four-year high school and graduated its first class in 1919.

In 1926, Charles W. Henry sold the Polytechnic School plant to the City of Maryville and in 1927, Maryville High School moved from the old East Side (later Fort Craig School) to this new location. In 1939, a modern building was erected on the five-acre campus.

Prior to the establishment of the public high school in Blount County, secondary education was an individual problem. A private boarding school was the only recourse. There was available in Blount County until 1900: Ewing and Jefferson or Holston College; near Louisville, Friendsville Academy at Friendsville, Porter Academy at Wildwood, Friends Normal and Maryville Preparatory School at Maryville College for white students, and Maryville Preparatory school and Freedman's Institute for Negro students.

After 1900 there was Friendsville Academy, Porter Academy, Maryville Preparatory School and Blount County High School (later Maryville Polytechnic School) in the private school category.

In 1918, Porter Academy became Porter High School; in 1925, Maryville Preparatory School was discontinued, and in 1926 Maryville Polytechnic was closed. Friendsville Academy since 1926 is the only private secondary institution in the county.

THE PUBLIC SCHOOL

The "Compact of 1806" would have set the common school system on its feet had not the lands been so involved. The advantages of such a system were appreciated from the beginning of the state and even before. The messages of all the Governors are filled with statements and suggestions which indicate interest in public education.

---

[108] Woods, Williamson, Four Mile, Union Grove, Brick Mill, West View, McCulloch, (which was formed from Nelson, Bryant, and Stony Grave schools.)

The first feeble attempt at anything like a public school was the Act of 1815 to provide education for the "orphans of the late war." This strengthened the prevalent idea that public education was for paupers, which idea prevailed to a great extent in parts of Blount County as late as 1920.[109]

Before public high schools were established in the county, snobbishness and a feeling of superiority to those who attended public schools was inbred and very evident. Even though a public school had operated in Maryville since the Civil War, as late as 1900, there was a strong prejudice, in the upper class, against attending the "Public Schools."

A number of laws were passed from time to time establishing on paper a common school law. Such was the law of 1823. "Five discreet persons" were to use the money for the education of the poor. This could be done either by establishing schools for this purpose or by paying their tuition in schools already existing. The only difference in this act and that of 1815 was the difference between the "poor orphans" and "poor children."

The "roving" teacher who went from county to county teaching certain subjects was common at this period. In 1827, Josiah Patty advertised that he would teach a surveying school in Blount County and also tailoring, to ten or fifteen ladies and gentlemen at $1.00 per scholar for five days and that he expected to be boarded. His advertisement further stated that he would go to any adjoining county for fifteen to twenty scholars. He would also teach other subjects for enough inducement.

The same season George McKay announced that he would teach a ten-day writing school at the house of Abijah Conger at Clover Hill. He would teach Copperplate and Business Hand at $1.00 per pupil, and Mr. Conger could furnish accommodations. These are typical examples of the sort of schools that were available to the general public before the general establishment of the common or public school.[110]

The first definite plan for common schools that evolved was the act of 1829. County Court was to appoint Commissioners to meet at Regimental Muster on the 3rd Saturday in April, 1830 to divide regiments into school districts and make registers of names of heads of families. The justices of the peace were then to give notice and hold an election of five trustees, who were to organize themselves into a board; the chairmen of which were to meet at the courthouse the first Saturday in June to choose Commissioners for the county. This bill gave existence to the Common School System of Tennessee which is the germ from which the present system developed.[111]

---

[109] *White*, 25-31.

[110] *Knoxville Register*, June 6, 1827; July 4, 1827.

[111] *White*, 34; A statement by Robert P. Duncan said that he attended Southern and Western Theological Seminary from 1825 to 1830; that in 1831 he taught a term of three months on the D. D. Foute plantation; in 1832 and 1833 he taught at the "meetinghouse" (Six Mile). (Miss Sophia Duncan's Papers).

There is no doubt that there were schools in operation in Blount County prior to 1834 of the "old field" category, and home-schools as well as the private school. There are no accurate records of the earlier schools, but a reference here and there established the fact that they did exist.

Early travelers mention schools before 1800 in their journeys through Maryville to Tellico Blockhouse. Dr. Job in his "Memoirs" mentions schools in Tuckaleechee and Cades Cove before 1830. We know that many schools were operated in church buildings and on private property without any written record being made of the fact.

The Friends mention that there were five schools within the bounds of the Friendsville Church about 1838. There were also recorded some half dozen deeds to schoolhouse lots before 1850 as well as the church lots which were also to be used for school purposes.[112]

In 1837, a report to General Assembly says: "The subject of education had never yet received in Tennessee that attention which it so vitally merits. Appropriations have been made to support of common schools, but the system adopted under that name has proved inefficient." This report was against entirely free schools, advocating partial self-taxation.

The school superintendent at this time was only an agent and there was no supervision nor unity in the system. The fund itself was prey to the unprincipled in that it passed through the hands of some ten people. In many cases the sheriff failed or refused to pay over funds collected.

On the 19th of February, 1836, an act was passed making it the duty of the Superintendent of Public Instruction to prepare plans for the improvement and organization of common schools, and the first scholastic year began in July, 1838. We have no reason to believe that a system was not begun in Blount County on or before this date.[113]

According to the best information available, the first commissioners of the Common Schools for Blount County were: David McKamy, Samuel Hamel, William McTeer, James Rhea, Joseph Johnson, and James McConnell.

In 1835, David McKamy, as chairman of the corporation of Common School Commissioners instituted a series of suits to recover school monies, loaned at interest to various individuals. In April 1839, certain citizens asked to be changed from one civil district to another because they would be more benefited by the common school system. So it would appear that some districts were more progressive than others.[114]

It seems that a judgment was rendered on the 31st of May, 1838 in the Circuit Court of Blount County for $4,257.34 against Daniel D. Foute, Michael Smith, Jesse Thompson, and Nelson Wright in a suit

---

[112] Deeds from: Hickey, James, Henry, Wolf, Kennedy, Houston, Griffitts and Burem, Eagleton, and Chambers are all for school lots before 1850.
[113] *House Journal, 1873-8*, 789; *Acts, 1835-6*, Ch. 27.
[114] *Minutes*, March 1835; April, 1839.

brought by: William Colburn, John Keys, Major Reeder, Robert A. Tedford and James H. Gillespy, successors to the above-named commissioners.

In 1847 William McTeer, trustee of Blount County, was authorized to sell any school land in the county bought by the former chairman of the Common School Commissioners if he saw fit. He was to manage and dispose of it to the best interest of the schools. At the same time a committee was appointed to settle the claim which the common schools had against Daniel D. Foute, former clerk and treasurer of the Board of Common School Commissioners. County Trustee McTeer made the bond as required for the disbursement of school monies.

In 1848, the committee recommended that since Foute had paid $2,645.42 and since the judgment was in their opinion oppressive and more than the amount actually due, that the remainder should be compromised. Foute proposed to pay $1,000 in eighteen months and they recommended that after he had made proper security the remainder of the amount should be released. This proposal was accepted by the court. The scholastic population in Blount County for 1849 was 4,044 and the appropriation was 40¾ cents per pupil.[115]

In 1845, a measure was passed which for the first time showed a correct understanding of the true principle of common education. This was the introduction of the feature of self-taxation for the support of common schools. The state was divided into districts which were to levy or not levy taxes according to the vote of the people. The Secretary of State was to match the amount raised by the district. In 1847, Governor Neill S. Brown in his message recommended that the county courts levy a tax in the county. Although not much was accomplished before the Civil War, the appreciation and estimate of the advantages of the public school system had been strengthened and spread.[116]

The main trouble in the educational idea as a whole in Tennessee was that the state had started at the top in evolving her educational system. There were three colleges already established within her borders when Tennessee became a state. Therefore the early history of education in Tennessee and Blount County lies entirely in the academies and private schools. Colleges were first provided, then the county academies and lastly the common schools.

In 1855, the question of levying a tax for schools was bypassed by County Court and voted down when submitted to the people. This was the result every time a proposition for taxation was submitted to the people of Blount County for the support of schools for several decades.[117]

Records in Nashville show that Blount County received from $1,600

---

[115] *Ibid.*, August, 1844; January, 1847; April, 1847; January, 1848; August, 1848.
[116] *White*, 60.
[117] *Minutes*, 1855.

to $3,400 per year from the Common School Fund from 1854–59. The Academy Fund netted from $206 to $225 per year.[118]

In 1857, the Rev. John S. Craig was named commissioner to examine teachers for the Common Schools. This is the last item of local school action until after the Civil War.

In 1865, the state teachers organized and worked for an organized system of education. The new school law was passed in 1867. Enumeration of children between six and twenty, white and Negroes and the election of school directors was ordered. No reports had been required under the Common School system and it was hard to get results immediately. Money was available for schools as soon as the district was organized and a house was available.[119]

Professor T. J. Lamar was appointed the first superintendent of Blount County Schools. January 1, 1869, he reported that all civil districts were able to draw 1866 money except two which could not get teachers. In August he reported general satisfaction, except for the uncertainty of state funds.[120]

In 1870, the law of 1867 was repealed and threw the support of the schools back on the county. Since Blount County had levied no local tax for a source of revenue this meant no schools except of a private nature. The record of a subscription school operated by J. H. Morton at Six Mile in 1868 is an example of the sort of educational program operated in Blount County from its organization to the inauguration of the Public School System on a county-wide basis. The account lists thirty patrons and 75 students. The rate is not given but one entry lists three children, 38 days, and $12.00. Other items seem to indicate that rates were $2.00 per month. John H. Morton as school Superintendent of Blount County in 1870 gave $2,557.80 as the amount of the school fund.[121]

Interested people were deeply concerned over the backward step in education, and a general reaction set in. Memorials and petitions were so rampant, that Governor John C. Brown in 1872 recommended that the Office of State Superintendent of schools be created.

In order to create public sentiment for the establishment and maintenance of a public school system, James K. Killebrew, who was selected by the State Teachers Association and paid by the Peabody Board, was named Assistant State Superintendent. He investigated the problem so promptly and reported his findings so forcefully and so accurately that the way was paved for the enactment of the Progressive

---

[118] Tennessee State Archives, Nashville, Tennessee; Porter Academy Trustees, for 1855 were: Dr. J. H. Gillespy, R. L. Cates, R. I. Wilson, Edward George, B. F. Duncan.

[119] *Minutes*, 1857; *Acts, 1866–67*, Ch. 27.

[120] John Eaton, Jr., *First report of Supt. of Public Instruction for the State of Tenn.* 1869.

[121] Tennessee Archives, *Petitions*, Box #109; private school record of John H. Morton, Mrs. John Hitch, Maryville, Tennessee.

Educational Act of 1873 which was the "Parent Act" of the present system of Public Education in Tennessee.

This act was very similar to the law of 1867 except that it was "an act to establish and maintain a uniform system of public schools." The funds were to be the interest from the permanent school fund and a one dollar poll tax on all male inhabitants plus one-mill tax on each dollar of taxable property. County courts were empowered to levy additional taxes.[122]

The county tax was voted down in Blount County. The county superintendent reported in 1874 that opposition had subsided and that schoolhouses were being built. Schools were late in starting because directors were not elected until August and 85 teachers were hired to teach in 78 schools. Nine of the schools were for Negroes. Peabody funds were available to schools which qualified for aid. Ten-month schools were possible under this plan. At least one school is known to have operated under a Peabody grant and we are sure that there were others. Under this plan a minimum enrollment of 100 pupils and two teachers netted $300 from the Peabody fund plus $600 furnished from the county. Negro and white schools alike could qualify. In 1874, Maryville schools drew $800 of Peabody funds.[123]

While the public schools were getting organized and in motion, several private schools were either being revived or organized. Most of these schools, if not all of them, utilized the public school funds to supplement their school term. Mr. Matt Cochran (age 86) said Oakland School under the direction of Prof. John W. Bowman was operating in 1880 under a Peabody grant. At least five private schools were chartered in Blount County in 1881, but due to the fact that the public schools took hold these schools never materialized. These schools were: Ellejoy Institute, Pleasant Grove, Louisville Academy, Grindstaff School, and Bethel Academy. Another reason for the chartering of so many private schools was to curb liquor sales through the four-mile law.[124]

The Bethel School and church house was built on the Farr land by the Friends, and a subscription school was conducted there for some years and this school eventually was absorbed by Christy Hill School, and the church later was abandoned.

The Friends through their missionary, Dr. Garner, also were instrumental in the inauguration of longer schools in Happy Valley and Cades Cove.

Another outside help in instituting schools in isolated communities

---

[122] *Senate Journal*, 1872; Appendix, 16; *Acts, 1873*, ch. 25; *Minutes*, 1874.
[123] *Minutes*, 1874; *School Report*, 1874.
[124] *Ellejoy Institute. Deeds*, H H, 470, Sept. 6, 1880, M. W. Rogers, Hugh H. Gamble, William Drake, Ben Cunningham and W. C. Davis, Trustees. *Louisville Academy, Deeds*, H H, 390, March 18, 1880. Madison Cox, H. G. Mead, S. H. Gault, James H. Henry, W. S. Keller, C. R. Love, S. T. Cox, Trustees. *Bethel Academy, Deeds*, H H, 441, July 14, 1880, John M. Tulloch, John H. Farr, J. D. Garner, William Conning, H. Wilson Spray, trustees. *Grindstaff School Deeds*, I I, 111, April 5, 1881, J. P. Raulston, S. H. Clemens, Abraham Simerly, Isaac T. Russell, Isaac Russell, trustees; Will A. McTeer, *Autobiography* (typewritten).

of Blount County was the work of the Mountain Settlement Department of the Tennessee Federation of Women's Clubs. In Walker's Valley, (later Tremont) "Black" Will Walker had lived for some twenty years. His family was later joined by two or three other families. They were seven miles from a school. Mr. Walker, after some years of agitation, got a two-month school for his community in 1901 which was taught by S. H. Dunn. In 1902 the term was extended to four months. In the summer of 1902 the settlement school was opened under the sponsorship of Ossoli and Newman circles of Knoxville and the Tuesday and Chilhowee clubs of Maryville. They were later joined by the Athena Club of Knoxville and the Kosmos Club of Chattanooga. The plan was formulated by the Chilhowee Club and Ossoli made the first donation of $50. The work was partly financed by the Massachusetts Federation from 1905–14. Mr. Walker made the Federation a reversionary deed for a tract adjoining the schoolhouse. Mrs. Emily Webb and her son Frederick undertook the work and Mr. Webb with Mr. Walker's assistance built the log cottage which became a model for local living. School opened with sixteen pupils which later increased to thirty with ages ranging from three to thirty.[125]

In 1913, it was voted to discontinue work in Walker's Valley since Little River Lumber Company had moved into the community. At this time it was decided to undertake a new school at Rocky Branch, at the foot of Chilhowee Mountain near Walland. A cottage was rented, and the county superintendent chose Miss Florence French for the teacher. She and Mrs. Sarah Henry Hood, settlement worker, began their work in 1914. A cottage was built for Mrs. Hood, in 1916, near the schoolhouse. Mrs. Julia Calloway, of Knoxville, and Mt. Nebo, donated $55.00 and local men contributed the labor. Mrs. Helsey, Mrs. Williamson, Miss Mollie Gamble and Miss Sallie Gamble each served as settlement workers. This work was continued until 1928 or 1929 and the cottage was later sold. Occasional work was also done at a place called Rocky Mountain, which was a boundary-line school between Sevier and Blount counties between Carr's Creek in Blount and Happy Hollow in Sevier County. A settlement school was also sponsored for one year in 1913 at the "Coal Pits." [126]

The Blount County schools developed as best they could on scanty funds. A. M. Gamble in his 1886 report stated that "some fossils were still teaching." The 1889 report listed fifteen log schools still in use. The first county school board elected after school directors were abolished was: W. J. Lewis, D. L. Edmondson, Alexander Gamble, C. C. Self, and N. B. Adams. In 1910, the largest number of schools in the county's history was reported (95).

---

[125] Tennessee Federation of Women's Clubs. *Woman's Work in Tennessee* (1916). 51 ff; Frederic Lee Webb, Margaret Henry, and S. T. Wilson were named trustees of the cottage site.
[126] When the settlement school was discontinued at Elkmont in Sevier County, the work was transferred to Park Settlement School in Happy Hollow. The "Coal Pits" was a small school, also called "Slab College," near Chilhowee View School.

In 1907 County Court approved of the state law to assist in establishing high schools but made no move toward establishing any local high school.

After the purchase of the Quaker School property by the ninth district in 1900, a special school district was set up for the 9th and 19th districts one mile east and west from the courthouse and one mile parallel with Main Street on both sides of town. County funds were to be allotted to the district based on the average daily attendance.

The old Public School building was sold back to the Masons, and in 1909 a bond issue was voted to finance two new buildings.

In 1910 the old "Quaker School" was removed and the West Side School building erected on the same lot. The same year the East Side School building was erected on a lot bought from David Jones. This school housed Maryville High School from its beginning in 1913 until 1927 when it moved to its present location. The name of East Side was changed to Fort Craig in 1928. A new building was completed in 1954. West Side was replaced in 1953, by the new Sam Houston School which is located more west and south of town than the old school. The Negro school was set up about 1867, on the lot now occupied by the A. M. E. Zion Church. Later they bought the lot and built a better building, the Freedman's Bureau contributing more than $400. The building could be used as a church at the discretion of the trustees: W. B. Scott, Sr., Jacob Henry, H. L. Cansler, and W. S. McTeer. About 1910, the T. B. Lillard school was built behind the first building (now Gertrude Apartments), which was replaced in 1930 by the William T. Hale, a twelve-grade school.

In North Maryville (now Alcoa) in 1917-18, the old Babcock School was replaced by the four-room Vose School and a four-room school with an auditorium was built on Lincoln Road (the "mule barn") for white children. A six-room building for Negro students was in the process of being built. This was the beginning of the Alcoa school system. The Springbrook Elementary School was built in 1920. This building also housed Alcoa High School from 1920 to 1939 when the present building was completed. The Bassel School building was completed in 1922 and replaced the "mule barn" which had been built by the county in 1918. The Charles Hall School for Negroes was completed in 1926. Before this time the Negro students had attended school in temporary quarters. Vose School was not used after Springbrook was built until 1947 when it was remodeled and modernized and is now used for the first four grades. Prof. V. F. Goddard has been superintendent of Alcoa schools since 1924. The Alcoa schools have never had to struggle to get equipment nor operate on a close budget like the county school system but have had the best of modern equipment and working materials.[127]

---

[127] *Blount County School Report*, H. B. McCall, Supt., 1908; Nancy Lee Broady, Supt. 1917-18; *Blount County School Board Minutes*, 1922—; Date from 1928—is from County Superintendent's office.

In 1923, the county agreed to pay one teacher and one-half the running expenses of Calderwood School. In 1928 the Calderwood School property was transferred to the county board, and became a county school.[128]

In 1908 there were eighty frame schoolhouses in Blount County and two log houses; all except four were one-room. In 1918 there were eighty-five schools, sixty of which were one-room; eleven two-room; twelve with more than two rooms. There was one newly erected brick building, Wildwood.

By 1928, there were six four-year high schools in operation and three junior high schools. Consolidation of small schools was taking a strong hold and transportation systems were being inaugurated in some sections of the county.

By 1938, all junior high schools had been discontinued. All four-year high schools had become transportation centers and all parts of the county including Happy Valley and Calderwood were being given high school service. The one-room school had been eliminated where it was at all possible.

Enforcement of standards which tend to improve have been consistently carried out insofar as funds have been available. No radical changes have taken place in the last two decades, other than to continue along the lines set and to strive for improvement.

The Negro population of the county has always been rather scattered. In 1870 there were ten Negro schools. The same number was reported in 1907. All were one-room schools except Rockford and Maryville. Six schools were listed in 1918. This did not include Maryville, but had added what is now Alcoa. In 1953, there were only three Negro schools listed in Blount County, other than Maryville and Alcoa: Wildwood, Chandler's Station and Rockford.

In June 1923, a delegation of Negro citizens asked for a consolidation of county and city funds to maintain a county high school for the Negroes. Nothing was done to remedy their lack of opportunity for higher education in Blount County until Charles Hall School in Alcoa first offered high school work in 1926. The city school board of Maryville inaugurated high school work at Hale School in 1932. The Hall High School is the only accredited high school in Blount County for Negro students. The city of Alcoa and Blount County have an agreement whereby the county furnishes transportation to Hall High School and pays tuition for county students who wish to attend high school, since the county does not have enough students to maintain an accredited school.

At present Blount County has forty schools, 366 teachers and more than 10,000 pupils with two full-time supervisors. There are six schools

---

[128] Calderwood had its beginnings as headquarters for the Aluminum Company's construction operations and was about to become a permanent community at this time.

offering grades one through twelve which employ 172 teachers and have an enrollment of almost 5,000 pupils.

Of the forty schools there are three one-room schools; one white and two Negro. There is one Negro two-room school and eleven white two and three-room schools. There are nineteen schools having more than four teachers. Forty-four buses transport about 7,500 pupils to and from these schools daily.

At first examination it would appear that our forefathers were slow in establishing a public school system but on further examination there seems to be some explanation for their failure to finance a school system.

Between 1830 and 1840 when the "common schools" were being established, it became necessary to build a new courthouse in 1839 and a courthouse tax was levied for several years to pay for it. In the meantime the school fund had been lost or misplaced and a judgment was awarded to recover it. This did not tend to excite the confidence of taxpayers in the school commissioners.

In 1848, a new jail was necessary and a jail tax was levied. By the time this was paid off, the Civil War came along and the Railroad tax had grown so oppressive during the last several years that consideration of any additional tax was out of the question.

When the school system was finally established in 1873 the county was in the midst of a depression and before the school system was organized and going, the courthouse burned in 1879 and it was necessary to build another courthouse.

In 1889 new school legislation for establishing a county system instead of district units was passed and also a public high school "enabling act." In 1901 the present jail was built. Again, when it looked like something would be done by the county, the courthouse burned and had to be rebuilt in 1906, and a county-wide road and bridge building program had been launched which lasted many years.

This is not an attempt to justify the failure to provide for adequate schools but is a logical explanation of why a conservative citizenry was slow to take advantage of various school legislations.

CHAPTER VIII

Medical Men and Institutions

IT IS impossible to say with certainty who the first practicing physician in Blount County may have been. Dr. Isaac Wright left a more definite record than any other of the early men but he is not necessarily the first nor the most important. Dr. Wright's name has been perpetuated in the Wright's Ferry Road. He operated a ferry at Louisville prior to 1816 when he was granted the right to build a warehouse on his land at Holston River. This point was later a regular shipping point or steam-boat landing on the river.[1]

According to tradition a Welsh youth named Isaac Wright was shipwrecked on the coast of Georgia in 1737. Soon after this date he married an Indian girl and their son was named Isaac II. Twenty-one years later a grandson was born who bore the name of Isaac III. He was married in North Carolina in 1792 at the age of 34 to Mary Rush. In 1800, they came to Blount County, Tennessee, and settled one mile below the mouth of Little River.

The Wrights were all herb doctors.[2] Dr. Wright III seems to have been master of herb lore and a past master at judiciously dispensing the prepared herbs from his deer-hide saddlebags, and ere long the public had beaten a path to his door. In his "Family Medicine" he relates the story of a patient who came to him from Oak Ridge in Knox County with a stomach complaint. The man said it felt like a "critter" was moving around in his stomach. Dr. Wright had his assistant to get him a small salamander or "water dog." He prepared a strong emetic and after the patient had discharged the contents of his stomach, he showed him the water dog and told him that it was probably responsible for all the gastric disturbance and that he had probably swallowed it from some mountain spring! This is an early example of scientific suggestion.

Dr. Wright related that in 1810, Reuben Charles of Blount County, who was "more famed for gallantry than domestic virtues" showed him his scrofulous thigh. Charles was subsequently treated by another doctor for twelve months and pronounced incurable, then Dr. Wright cured him. Some time later, Dr. Wright was summoned to appear in court and defend himself against charges that he had cured and turned loose on society "a most consummate scoundrel" among whose alleged crimes were lewdness, intemperance, profanity and counterfeiting. The doctor pleaded justification on two grounds: that the disease had been pronounced incurable and the discovery of a cure was of more benefit to society than all the evil Reuben Charles could perpetrate; and that

---
[1] *Minutes*, 1816; *Knoxville Republican*, December 19, 1832.
[2] *Knoxville Journal*, October 15, 1933; *Knoxville News-Sentinel*, April 22, 1934.

the cure was the result of an experiment and that better subject could not be found than Reuben Charles, and so the doctor was exonerated.[3]

Dr. Wright published a book in Madisonville (Henderson, Johnson, and Company) in 1833, which was the third medical book published in Tennessee. It was entitled *Wright's Family Medicine or System of Domestic Practices*, and was dedicated "To the Ladies—the fairest, dearest portion of creation." He set forth in his preface that he was merely trying, in publishing the book to "draw waters of wisdom from the wells of experience." He was, at this time operating a sanitarium at his home, and had patients who came from afar by stage, carriage, and river boat to "Mount Pisgah," near Louisville. He advertised as able to accommodate a number of "boarders."

His son, Willie Blount Wright was a physician as early as 1840. His advertisement stated that he had recovered his health and was at Wright's Ferry "ready to help all who called for a physician." Dr. W. B. Wright moved to Arkansas in 1859. He was killed there during the Civil War, in 1862, in a local skirmish.[4]

Dr. Isaac Wright's daughter, Matilda, married Dr. Azariah Shelton of French and Irish extraction, who was born in Patrick County, Virginia, in 1795. His family first moved to Grainger County, Tennessee and later to Rhea County. He came to Blount County, studied under Dr. Isaac Anderson, served as Clerk of the Circuit Court from 1820 to 1822, and read law. He then turned to medicine like two of his brothers, and studied with Dr. Caldwell in Maryville. He became associated with "the eccentric and self-made Dr. Wright" and practiced with him for a couple of years. During this time he noted and learned all Dr. Wright's peculiar preparations and practices.

Dr. Shelton had served a tour of eight months in the Creek War. He traveled extensively and later visited hospitals and institutions to learn more about diseases and drugs. He became acquainted with "the art of making, inserting and dressing teeth" from the most eminent dentists in the United States. He had also made a study of the Thompsonian Steam System.[5]

In 1834, the year following the publication of Dr. Wright's book, Dr. Shelton also published a book at Madisonville. The title was: *Shelton's American Medicine*. "The Valuable practice and preparation of Dr. Isaac Wright of Tennessee are fully developed in this work."

Dr. Shelton was living at Jacksonville, Alabama, when his book was published. It is remarkably concise and practical work for its time.

A Dr. Caldwell was practicing in Blount County prior to 1828. Dr. Shelton said that he studied medicine with Dr. Caldwell, practiced a few years with Dr. Wright, and did extensive travel prior to 1834 when his book was published. A contemporary advertisement stated that Dr.

---

[3] *Minutes*, 1800–1810–1813, Passim. Reuben Charles was mentioned in various connections. His lands were sold for taxes in 1813.
[4] *Knoxville Argus*, March 10, 1841, ff.
[5] T. J. Campbell, *Records of Rhea County*, (Dayton, 1940), 161. Information from the preface of his book (Copy in author's collection).

Samuel Pride opened his office in Maryville in 1828, "where Dr. Caldwell had been."[6]

A third Blount County man who published an early medical work, was Dr. William Spillman (son-in-law of John Ambrister). His "Simplified Anatomy for the Use of Families and Those Who Have Not Had the Advantage of a Teacher," was published at Madisonville in 1835. From 1833–37, Dr. Spillman was the publisher of the "Thompsonian Defender" in Maryville, which magazine defended the system of medicine advocated by one Samuel Thompson. In 1835, Dr. Spillman seems to have had financial difficulties, since he mortgaged a set of cabinet tools and a "lot of medicine." His Maryville property was sold in 1842, and he is mentioned no more.

Mr. Parham says that Dr. William Thomas lived and practiced in Maryville and died in 1829, while on a visit to Jackson County, Alabama. His house and doctor shop was on lot No. 34 and was sold by court order to R. L. Cates in 1833. Dr. Alexander McGhee had levied on Dr. Thomas's farm in 1829, according to court records.

By legislative act of 1829, a number of learned and intelligent practicing physicians was appointed to meet and constitute the Medical Society of Tennessee. At the organization meeting held on the first Monday in May, 1830 in Nashville, Blount County was represented by Drs. Samuel Pride and John Temple. At this meeting Drs. Alexander McGhee and James H. Gillespy were elected to membership from Blount County.

At this meeting, a Board of Censors for each of the grand divisions of the state was elected. Not more than two doctors on this board were to be from any one county. Dr. Temple was elected to this board. Dr. Pride was also elected, but declined to serve because he felt that the offices should be more generally distributed throughout East Tennessee.[7]

Very little is known about Dr. Temple. He was listed in the 1830 Census as a man between thirty and forty, with four children in his household. He seems to have left Maryville before 1834, since only three practicing physicians are listed in Maryville in 1834, one at Morganton and one at Unitia. However, Dr. Benjamin Cates in a biography of Dr. Robert Hodsden says that Dr. Hodsden came to Maryville in 1833 from Jefferson Medical School and formed a partnership with Dr. Gillespy.[8]

Dr. Alexander McGhee was a contemporary of Dr. Wright and Dr. Caldwell. He had petitioned the Legislature for vacant lands for a salt

---

[6] *Knoxville Register*, May 9, 1828.

[7] Tennessee State Medical Society, *Transactions*, (Nashville, 1830), 10–21.

[8] Eastin Morris, *Tennessee Gazeteer* (Nashville, 1834), 96. In 1834, Dr. Temple mortgaged his surgical and medical appliances, naming Dr. McGhee as the person to whom he is indebted. He obtained a letter of dismission from New Providence Presbyterian Church in 1834 also.

works in 1817. He is recorded as an atheist, who was converted and became a Presbyterian minister. He became the pastor of Eusebia church in 1824. He was also associated with Matthew and John McGhee in the firm of McGhee Brothers, merchants in Maryville (generally referred to as the "white store"). Dr. McGhee died in 1841.[9]

Of the early known physicians, Dr. James H. Gillespy enjoyed one of the longest spans of recorded activities. He became a trustee of Porter Academy very early in his career and was periodically identified with that institution as trustee for more than fifty years.

He was active in politics during the forties, fifties and sixties. He served as state representative to the Legislature for several terms, as did also his brilliant lawyer brother, John Finley Gillespy, who was burned to death while attending Legislature in Nashville. Dr. Gillespy was the Blount County delegate to the State Constitutional Convention in 1834. Dr. James Gillespy died in 1881. His son Samuel, began the study of medicine shortly before the Civil War at Jefferson Medical School in Philadelphia, but did not continue his studies after the war. However, he practiced medicine until his death.

Dr. James Gillespy kept a tavern during the thirties which was used by the County Court in 1839 and 1840 when a new courthouse was being built. He was postmaster in 1858 and from 1860 to 1864 he was register of deeds. His daughter, Ann Eliza Blackburn, was deputy register.[10]

Dr. Gillespy wrote that in 1844, there was an epidemic of fever caused by stagnant waters behind a large mill-dam west of town. The dam was ordered torn down and the fever disappeared.[11]

The land-holdings of Dr. Gillespy were vast. They were acquired with an eye to mineral wealth and he retained mineral rights to all lands which he sold. His "Memories" describe them in detail. He said he owned 10,000 acres stretching three miles on each side of Little River between Walland and Townsend. He operated a saw and grist mill in the flat below Sunshine and had a twelve-foot dam across Little River. He told of floating two loaded flat boats tied together with eighty-foot gunwales on a four-foot tide down Little River from that point.

The medical career of Dr. Sam Pride in Maryville began in 1828 when he took over the office of Dr. Caldwell and wed Miss Martha Sharp at Eusebia church in 1829. Dr. Pride was the first Clerk and Master of Blount County, the first Worthy Master of New Providence Lodge and the first Mayor of Maryville. He was also a member of the County Court for a good many years. In 1862, he appeared before the court and reported that he had been to Virginia and had contracted for 5,000 bushels of salt. This, in view of the blockade of ports of entry

---

[9] *Minutes of the Presbytery of Union*, 1824; various contemporary newspaper advertisements.
[10] *Minutes*, Passim. Family papers and data from Mrs. George Gillespy Dickerson.
[11] *Maryville Times*, May 15, 1889.

to the south, was important and impressed the court to the extent that they agreed to finance the deal so that he stood to lose nothing. Dr. Pride's son John M. was also a doctor. He served as a surgeon during the Civil War in the Confederate army and did not return to Maryville after the war. Dr. Pride is said to have contracted fever while assisting with the wounded at Chickamauga and died at Macon, Georgia in 1863.

Dr. Pride first lived on lot No. 40, then he built the three-story brick mansion on Main Street which was used by General Sherman as headquarters when he came to the relief of Burnside at Knoxville. Dr. Pride died about this time. In 1878, this property was sold to Friends of Philadelphia and became Maryville Normal and Preparatory School or the "Quaker School." When this school closed in 1900, the City of Maryville bought the property and in 1910 replaced the old building with the West Side School building. The West Side building was replaced in 1955 by the Municipal Building.[12]

Dr. Henry Hannum, a native of Pennsylvania and Kentucky, located in Maryville in 1834 and practiced here until his death. His residence was where the post office is, until he moved to the well-known Hannum estate, "Cedar Circle," where he died in 1845. His son James practiced medicine later.

In 1844 Drs. Gillespy, Pride and Hodsden were appointed trustees of Porter Academy. Dr. Robert H. Hodsden had learned the tailor's trade before studying medicine with Dr. John Hoyl of Rhea County. He came to Maryville in 1833 and entered into a partnership with Dr. Gillespy. In 1838 he served as a government physician in the Cherokee Removal (he made two trips). In 1844 he moved to Sevier County. In 1858 when a charter was issued to the East Tennessee Medical Society, Dr. Hodsden was named from Sevier County and Dr. Pride from Blount County. Dr. Hodsden died June 18, 1864 of heart disease.[13]

Another doctor with an interesting background came to Blount County in 1848. Dr. Jefferson Stone was born in Litchfield, Connecticut, December 15, 1806. He graduated from Yale in 1827 and practiced in Washington, Connecticut for ten years. He came to Knoxville in 1839 and practiced for five years. In 1845 he bought the farm in Blount County which was later the site of the Wildwood Springs Hotel. In 1847 he built an addition to the old log house on this farm and sealed a short sketch of himself in a bottle which was found sealed in the bricks of the chimney when the house was torn down in 1949. Dr. Stone operated a woolen mill in Maryville which was not very successful after the War Between the States. He practiced medicine until about 1870 when he reportedly went West.[14]

---

[12] *Minutes*, Passim.; *Minutes of New Providence Lodge #128 F. & A. M.*; various other local data referred to elsewhere; William B. Heseltine, ed., Dr. J. G. M. Ramsey, *Autobiography and Letters*, (Nashville, 1954) 142 ff.

[13] *Acts 1858* ch. 116; *East Tennessee History and Biography* (Chattanooga 1893). Dr. Cates also said that Dr. J. C. Cawood, Dean of the Tennessee Medical School, considered that Dr. Hodsden was one of the best surgeons of his day.

[14] Original document belongs to Joe D. Waters. Copied July, 1953.

Dr. George Hunt Chaffin came from North Carolina to Louisville in the late thirties and began the practice of medicine. He married the widow Cox in 1842 and they continued the operation of the local tavern until after the War. From 1825 to 1875 Louisville was in her heyday and bade fair for a time to outgrow Maryville. Other doctors who practiced in Louisville during this period were: Drs. John Singleton, Madison Cox, L. D. Carter, L. A. Gamble, Josiah T. Love, J. C. Gillespie (who later went to Inskip), and Dr. E. Goetz, a German, whose son later operated a clinic in Knoxville.

Several doctors are referred to as being located at Morganton in the early days but nothing definite is known about them. Doctors Anderson, Hugh Blair, W. W. Bayless, Francis Beals, James J. Bales, ... Carmichael, and W. G. McKenzie.

At least one local doctor, John Wilkinson, followed the gleam of gold to California with the "49ers." He was a cousin of Dr. John W. Cates. He was among the men who went across Panama on foot and reached California by boat up the West Coast. He did not strike gold, but he, no doubt, was a busy man in that new country.[15]

Dr. Sam T. Cox advertised as being located in Maryville opposite Barclay McGhee. He was also postmaster in 1846. Barclay McGhee was appointed Assistant Surgeon of the 5th Regiment in the Mexican War, and lived until about 1856.

Dr. A. J. Taylor had read medicine with his brother Dr. A. L. Taylor in Washington County before locating opposite the Eusebia Presbyterian Church in 1853. He served as contract surgeon in the United States Army during the War Between the States, and due to impaired health engaged in a very limited practice until 1870.[16]

Dr. Isaac Taylor had served in the Mexican War and practiced medicine in Madisonville and Maryville until the outbreak of the War Between the States. He died during the war.[17]

Dr. James B. Lackey, a native of Virginia, lived and practiced in the Holston College vicinity from about 1852 to 1867. He is buried on the old McReynolds' farm beside John Ish whose tombstone reads: "Killed by a Cherokee in 1794."

Dr. William S. Porter was active from Louisville to Rockford along the Little River and died on the eve of the War Between the States. Sam Sherrill, J. L. Russell and James H. Cowan also practiced along Little River beginning about 1850 and extending into the period after the Civil War. Cowan was a bachelor and said to be quite eccentric. He practiced until 1897.

The three Lane brothers came to Blount County from Washington

---

[15] *The Knoxville Argus*, January 10, 1844; October 16, 1844.
[16] Dr. A. J. Taylor made a trust deed to Sam Pickens at the outbreak of the war to keep his property from being taken by the Rebels as the Taylors were strong Unionists.
[17] Two articles written by Dr. Isaac Taylor have been found: "Dysentery" and "Epidemics of Blount County During 1856" published in the *Nashville Journal of Medicine and Surgery*, Vol. V (1853), 205; Vol. XII (1857), 502.

County in the early 1850's. James M., the father of Dr. Charles M. Lane, set up a practice at Brick Mill and was assisted by his brother Samuel D. Lane; the other brother, E. Ross Lane practiced at Unitia. The Lanes practiced until about 1885.

Dr. Samuel Ghormley of Chilhowee was one of the ten children of Hugh Ghormley and Nancy Charles. He married Anna James of the English James', who operated the woolen mill at Chilhowee. He began the practice of medicine about 1845. At the outbreak of the Civil War he was appointed Provost-Marshal of Tennessee by the Confederate States, but soon resigned and served as Lieutenant in the army, was taken prisoner and died in Federal Prison on Johnson Island, Sandusky, Ohio, January 9, 1865. His brother, Capt. DeWitt Ghormley was the Confederate recruiting officer stationed at Knoxville.

Dr. Calvin Post of Elmira, New York, came to Cades Cove in 1846 representing New York mineral interests and remained there until his death in 1873, practicing medicine and testing minerals for his employers. He owned large tracts of mountain land.

Dr. John W. Cates graduated from Maryville College in 1851 and later from Nashville Medical School. While in Medical School he was awarded a prize for proficiency in anatomy. He began his practice in Maryville in 1857 and soon earned an enviable reputation as a skilled physician and surgeon.

When the war broke out he enlisted in the Confederate Army as lieutenant, but resigned his commission and served as surgeon for the duration of the war. He served in the field and in the hospitals of Kentucky, Virginia and Tennessee. Among other battles he was present at the battle of Shiloh.

After the war, he returned to Maryville, married Miss Mary Elizabeth Brabson and resumed his practice. By 1867 he had built his home, "Sunny Hill," where he resided until 1906 when he sold the property to Blount County as a building site for the present courthouse. Dr. Cates died in 1916, at the age of eighty-three. Dr. Benjamin B. Cates of Knoxville was his son.

In 1866, occurred the first smallpox epidemic of sufficient seriousness to merit the attention of the County Court. All jail guards who had not had smallpox were dismissed and others hired who were immune. A delegation of citizens from Cook's Mill (Mint) asked the court to take measures to prevent the spread of the disease then raging in the neighborhood. R. J. Bishop, Jesse Kerr, Jr., and William B. Bingham were to enforce the quarantine and two guards were assigned to act under their orders.[18]

Dr. John P. Blankenship, who had begun practicing in 1858 and who had served as an army surgeon, was appointed as county physician and health officer at this time. Sanitary measures were ordered from time to time in regard to the courthouse, jail, and the streets and alleys

[18] *Minutes*, 1866.

of the town. He continued to act in this capacity until 1900. At times, Dr. B. A. Morton, James H. Martin, James Hannum, F. J. Arbeely and others assisted in attending the inmates of the jail and poor asylum.

In 1874, the State Board of Health was set up but it was not until after the yellow fever epidemic of 1878 that a state law was passed giving power to declare and enforce quarantines in handling epidemic diseases.[19]

Samuel H. Gault of Clover Hill was a third-generation Blount Countian. After attending Porter Academy, he joined the Union Army and served as an aide to General J. A. Cooper until the war ended. After three years in the mercantile firm of Walker and Gault, he sold out and read medicine with Dr. Blankenship for two years. Then he attended lectures at the University of Nashville as well as serving in the Legislature. He had quite a bit to say in letters to the newspapers about a smallpox epidemic in 1884, from Jones' Bend. He later moved to Rogersville.[20]

Dr. James H. Martin, a son-in-law of Dr. James M. Lane, occasionally assisted the county physician through the years. He enjoyed a wide practice in and around Maryville from about 1875 until well past the turn of the century.

Dr. T. F. Donaldson practiced from 1880 to 1912 around Rockford and Louisville, and lived at the Kirby or Donaldson Mill place, now Wheeler farm, on Little River.

Dr. Ben A. Morton was a popular physician and an ardent Baptist. The First Baptist Church of Maryville was reputedly organized in his kitchen. His son John D. Morton, later of Knoxville, and his nephew Wade Morton, who had a very successful career in California as a surgeon and head of his own hospital, both read medicine for a few years with Dr. B. A. Morton. Later the two attended Medical School in Nashville where they took the Paul Eve Faculty Award in successive years, graduating from medical school in 1888 and 1889. Another student who read medicine with Dr. Morton was Dr. J. H. Sherrill, who later attended lectures in Nashville. He practiced four years in Tuckaleechee and Cades Cove, then settled on Little River to practice until he retired. Dr. Ben Morton died in 1898.

Dr. John D. Nuchols also read medicine with Dr. Morton and after graduation spent a few years at Concord, Tennessee. He returned to Blount County and practiced five or six years near Union School. Shortly after 1900, he located in Polk County where he remained until his death.

Dr. J. D. Garner was a graduate of a medical school in Cincinnati. He practiced medicine along with his missionary and school work from the time he arrived here in 1871 until about 1900, when he retired from medicine and devoted his entire energies to school activities

---

[19] *Goodspeed*, 305.
[20] *Goodspeed; Whig and Chronicle* (Knoxville), July 26, 1882.

in Monroe County. Although he was a Quaker and opposed to fighting, he had worked in the Military Hospital in Cincinnati all during the War Between the States. Most of his Blount County practice was along the Chilhowee Mountain, Happy Valley and Cades Cove.

The Blount County Medical Society was organized about 1878 in the office of Dr. Ben A. Morton. The first officers were: Dr. Fordyce Grinnell, secretary-treasurer, Dr. John P. Blankenship, president, Dr. Ben A. Morton, vice president. Other members were: Drs. John W. Cates, J. D. Singleton, Samuel Gault, A. L. Jones, J. W. Hannum, C. P. McNabb, Finley Robbins, T. F. Donaldson, Alexander and Robert Goddard, A. B. McTeer, N. T. Krause, F. J. Arbeely, and J. H. Sherrill.[21]

A news item of this period names the following doctors as having attended an operation in Long Hollow performed by Dr. Arbeely (the "Syrian Doctor"): Drs. John Blankenship, B. A. Morton, John W. Cates, James Cowan, J. W. Hannum, Matt Cox, and S. H. McNeely.[22]

Among the charter members of this first Medical Society are some who have not been previously discussed. The secretary, Fordyce Grinnell was of one of the Quaker families, who came to Maryville in the 1870's. He had first read law and later studied medicine. He did not remain in Maryville very long and he became surgeon and physician to an Indian agency in South Dakota. He was in Pasadena, California, in 1924. Dr. F. J. Arbeely was a Syrian, who made capital of his nationality in his advertisement, and from all accounts seems to have been an able physician. His son was also a doctor. They went to Texas in 1875 soon after they came here. The son, Abraham, located there and the father remained in Maryville until 1886. Robert and Alexander Goddard were brothers from Friendsville. Both were dentists. Alexander went to Morristown soon after his father's death and Robert went to Hot Springs, Arkansas. Their brother, Samuel, began practice as an M.D. in 1886. After a few years, he moved to Middle Tennessee.[23]

Finley Robbins, one of a family having three generations of doctors, practiced along the Little Tennessee River and in the Alleghany section. S. L. Jones practiced at Unitia, Friendsville and Morganton. The two remaining charter members of the Medical Society for 1878, A. B. McTeer and J. D. Singleton may be found on the roster of the Blount County Medical Society for 1927, which is a span of fifty years.

The society met once each month, holding daylight sessions, presumably in the office where they organized. These sessions were devoted to the discussion of current cases and means of preventing diseases. After about twenty years or more of regular meetings, the organ-

---

[21] *Maryville Enterprise*, February 12, 1930.

[22] *Maryville Index*, November 20, 1878; September 24, 1880. Drs. J. W. Cates, T. J. Saunders, J. Blakenship, J. W. Hannum and F. Grinnell presented resolutions on the death of Dr. Chas. A. Fulton, druggist.

[23] *Parham Papers;* A son of Fordyce Grinnell, Joseph Grinnell is one of the outstanding ornithologists in the United States and an authority on West Coast birds.

ization disbanded, probably due to the relocation of most of the active members.

An interesting item which is not directly connected to Blount County medicine seems to merit mention at this point. In the summer of 1885, Dr. Felix T. Oswald of Ohio came to Montvale Springs for a stay. He persuaded the proprietor to build him a cabin in the "flats" of the Chilhowee Mountains. It was an exceptionally well-built double cabin with an extra fine chimney. Dr. Oswald lived here for two summers while writing *Household Remedies*. He was called the "Monkey Man" because his only companion was a monkey. In later years the abandoned cabin was referred to as the "Monkey House." Old-timers can still point out the location. Other books written by Dr. Oswald were: *Zoological Studies; the Poison Problem, a Temperance Plea; Physical Education; The Bible of Nature;* and *The Secret of the East* (a deep religious study of a heretical nature).[24]

Among those who moved away from Blount County were: Dr. James H. Alexander, who moved to Carter County about 1875 and James A. Brown, brother of the Hon. Thomas N. Brown, who returned to Pennsylvania after a few years' practice in the seventies and became a railroad company physician.

Dr. E. H. Mullendore practiced in the Wildwood Community after the Civil War. Dr. C. B. Lord did some practice also, after he bought Wildwood Springs. Dr. John N. McConnell practiced at Wildwood and Maryville from 1888 to 1919. During the decade preceding 1893, Dr. Henry Russell was practicing in Tuckaleechee Cove. Drs. W. H. Douthitt, Marcellus Gourley, J. H. Gothard, J. T. Sparks, Jesse Kerr, and Dr. Matlock practiced in the Louisville, Friendsville and Morganton sectors. Jesse Kerr, John Williamson, and W. M. Barr practiced mostly in Loudon County. Dr. Gothard moved to Knox County.

Prior to 1900, several new names appeared on the list of doctors: James M. Waters, T. S. Donaldson, J. W. Norton, W. O. Brickell, L. D. Webb, J. S. Tipton, S. S. Kittrell, Henry L. Harrison, A. B. Reagan, L. D. Lawson, W. R. Fronebarger, A. L. Jones, N. C. Ellis, S. L. Weagley, and W. E. Hathaway (homeopathist).

Beginning practice about 1900 or soon after were: A. M. Gamble, L. J. Jenkins, N. B. Adams, Charles M. Lane, S. L. Susong, J. D. Morton, George Robbins, John A. McCulloch, Wardell, E. L. Ellis, W. B. Lovingood, C. P. McNabb, G. F. Hannah, B. E. DeLozier, E. J. Foute, and J. A. McCall. Dr C. B. Lawrence advertised in 1908 as a specialist in women's diseases.

There are two women of Maryville families who studied medicine and entered the Foreign Mission field. Dr. Elizabeth S. Winters was the stepdaughter of Jesse Richardson, the photographer. After two

---

[24] Bert Garner's *Journal for 1931*, when he interviewed an old book-dealer in Cincinnati, who had known Dr. Oswald. The late Ludwig Pflanze had a collection of Dr. Oswald's works which were destroyed in the Montvale Hotel fire in 1932. Dr. Oswald was killed in a streetcar accident in 1922.

years in the foreign field (India) her health failed and she returned to Media, Pennsylvania where she operated the Innwood Sanitarium for Women.

Dr. Emma Garner, the daughter of Dr. J. D. Garner of Maryville, was educated at the "Quaker" School in Maryville and the Westwood School in Philadelphia. She received her surgical training at the Woman's Medical College of Philadelphia. She went to Shanghai, China, in 1895 where she was head of the Margaret Williamson Hospital for about 20 years.

Later names which could be elaborated on are: F. A. Zoller, C. C. Vinsant, E. H. Lowe, R. L. Hyder, C. F. Crowder, J. E. Carson, J. Walter McMahan, E. W. Griffin, A. J. Isham and J. E. Hall.

In 1900 Dr. A. M. Gamble succeeded Dr. Blankenship, who had served as county doctor and health officer for thirty-five years. After a year or two he was succeeded by Dr. John A. McCulloch.[25]

In 1901 a very serious smallpox epidemic broke out. The Board of Health was ordered to build "pest houses" and detention camps for the control of the disease. Detention camps were set up at Freedman's Institute for Negro victims and in the Home Avenue section for white people. Other camps were set at Louisville and in Cades Cove.

The health officer for 1901 reported a general epidemic of scarlet fever, and 107 cases of smallpox during the year. The first epidemic, carried from Knoxville, was fifty-two cases, thirty-one white and twenty-one Negro cases in the ninth, nineteenth, tenth, thirteenth and sixth districts. The second epidemic of fifty-five cases was in the lower end of the county and was brought in by a young man who came from Illinois to spend the Christmas holidays.

Over two thousand dollars was expended by the county for guards, supplies, and pest-houses, aside from medical care. The pest-houses were cleared and destroyed in July, 1902, and the wagon, utensils, bedding, etc., were sold or stored at the jail.

Small pox continued to be costly for several years, but was never equal to 1901.[26]

In 1906, an attempt was made to establish Blount Hospital. The charter was issued to: Dr. A. B. McTeer, Dr. John A. Goddard, William K. Weaver (pastor of the New Providence Church), Major Will A. McTeer, Elias ("Dick") Goddard and J. N. Badgett. A site was chosen and an option taken, on the lot at the intersection of Everett Street and Woodlawn Drive on Everett Hill. According to report it was not possible to raise enough capital for the building and equipment because of lack of professional cooperation and so the project was abandoned.[27]

In 1919, when the machinery of the City of Alcoa was set in motion, Dr. J. Walter McMahan was health officer. He had charge of a small

---

[25] In 1906 Dr. Blankenship was elected vice president of the American Anti-Tuberculosis Association.
[26] *Minutes*, 1898, 1900, 1901, Passim.
[27] *Corporations*, I, p. 275, *Notebook* C, p. 329. W. A. McTeer has original charter.

well-equipped hospital of ten beds, which was at that time the only hospital of any sort in Blount County. This was an important addition to the scheme of living, because at that time an emergency necessitated a "special train" to Knoxville. A great amount of difficult surgery was handled by Dr. McMahan and others, while this hospital was in operation.

In 1910, the Blount County Medical Society was re-organized at the courthouse with Doctors J. A. McCulloch, president; L. J. Jenkins, vice president; E. L. Ellis, secretary and treasurer. Other members were: Doctors A. B. McTeer, B. E. Delozier, N. C. Ellis, J. P. Blankenship, J. N. Norton, J. W. Cates, W. B. Lovingood, J. D. Singleton and A. M. Gamble.

Since that time the organization has enjoyed a rapid growth and has done much toward making Blount County a healthier place to live. Interest in problem discussions increased to the point in 1918 that the society started holding weekly sessions and has continued to meet every Thursday night since that time. Every active doctor in the county is a member of the society.[28] In 1925, there were twenty-five members of the Medical Society and in 1927 there were thirty-two.[29]

In 1930, Blount County was one of four county societies in the State of Tennessee, which was holding regular weekly meetings. Others met monthly or semi-monthly.

The Blount County Medical Society is largely responsible for the establishment of the Blount County Health Unit. The first tangible results which they produced were when the County Court appropriated $150.00 to be used with state funds for "Hookworm Dispensaries" in 1914. Dr. John M. Lee came from Nashville and did a Herculean work on this project under the State Board of Health.

The local Medical Society kept working to make the lay citizenry conscious of preventive measures in health. In July 1919, an appropriation of $600.00 was made by the Blount County Court for the beginning of a health program, teaching sanitation, and disease prevention in the homes and schools of Blount County.

In the fall of 1919, Dr. K. A. Bryant came to Blount County as director of Rural Sanitation. Most of the work done in this initial program was in Louisville, Rockford and Walland. The county failed to make an appropriation in January 1920, and Dr. Bryant went to Carroll County in February to set up a similar program there. In April the court reconsidered and made an appropriation for the rest of the year and Dr. Bryant was persuaded to return. In addition to sanitary work, he was also named County Health Officer.

The work continued on a larger scale in 1921, but in January 1922, the court again failed to make an appropriation. In February 1922, Dr. Bryant went to Roswell, New Mexico to engage in public health work,

---

[28] *Maryville Enterprise*, February 12, 1930.
[29] *Minutes of the Blount County Medical Society*, 1924.

and there was no program in force until October 1923, when Dr. Sullivan came to take charge.

In March 1924, Dr. Bryant returned to Tennessee and Dr. Bishop persuaded him to return to Blount County temporarily, and he remained with the work until 1932 when he resigned to enter private practice.[30]

At this time the County Court failed to make the requested appropriation until later in the year. This was during the "depression" years and there were intermittent outbreaks of typhoid fever throughout the county. For several years the Kiwanis and other civic clubs paid for the serum and the local doctors voluntarily took turns in administering the serum. The role that the local doctors played in keeping the struggling Health Unit alive cannot be over-emphasized. Nor can too much credit be given to them for their part in keeping the local civic organizations stirred up to the point of action. The doctors gave freely of their time, services, and money to keep the Health Program going and growing.

According to official records of the State Department of Health, Blount County was the first county in Tennessee to establish a full-time health service. The Board of Health, according to state law, was the county judge, the County Court clerk, and the county health officer. There was no nurse attached to the unit in the beginning. Under the general law of 1921, the unit was expanded to include one or more visiting nurses, and clinical assistants and a sanitary inspector. Locally, the personnel had to conform with the current budget. An appropriation was made for an extra nurse in 1929.[31]

Under a general law of 1935, the Board of Health consists of the county judge, the county superintendent of schools, two doctors, and a dentist. The last three named are elected by the County Court for a four-year term. This set-up is still in force.[32]

Our local Health Unit is now housed in its own $80,000 building on Court Circle, which was completed in 1953. This building was financed by 52 per cent Federal funds and the remainder shared equally by state and county.

The office of county physician, as such, was not created until 1885. He is elected for a four-year term. It is his duty to attend inmates of the jail and poorhouse. He makes yearly reports to the County Court, but is not required to keep any permanent record.

In March 1921, Dr. C. C. Vinsant, Dr. R. L. Hyder, Dr. J. E. Carson, Dr. G. D. LeQuire and J. G. Sims (attorney) pooled their assets and

---

[30] Interview with Dr. K. A. Bryant, July 23, 1954.

[31] Two men from Johns Hopkins worked with Dr. Bryant in 1920 under a Ford Foundation grant and did a prodigious amount of work running hookworm tests, etc. From time to time, men and women training for Public Health work were sent here for training in the field as this was one of the few units in operation.

[32] State of Tennessee, Department of Public Health, *The Monthly News Letter*, November 1, 1936.

opened Circle Drive Hospital as a hospital and Nurse's Training School, which was forced to close after two years.[33]

Soon after the close of Circle Drive Hospital (January 1, 1925), Dr. J. E. Carson began to operate a small private hospital on East Broadway, which he continued until 1928. Dr. C. C. Vinsant also operated a private hospital from 1926 until 1928.

In 1928, Dr. George W. Burchfield opened an eye, ear, nose and throat clinic and infirmary across from the courthouse, which he operated until his retirement in 1954. (Dr. Parke P. Swann, optometrist, who opened his office in 1909, was the first person to advertise locally in this field.)

After the close of the Circle Drive Hospital, the need for a local hospital was keenly felt, both by the public and the medical profession. In December 1928, the County Court appointed a Hospital Committee and asked that the Medical Society appoint a committee to work with them. Drs. A. M. Gamble, C. C. Vinsant and G. D. LeQuire were appointed to work with the committee. In January 1929, they asked the county judge to ask the Legislature to pass an enabling act allowing the County Court to issue bonds to build and maintain a hospital in Blount County. However, the "depression" evidently stopped this movement.

In the late twenties the Medical Society became actively interested in preventing tuberculosis among children. In March 1928, a plan for the organization and establishment of a tubercular prevention camp for the indigent to take care of twelve to fifteen children was presented to the Medical Society. A committee was appointed to act in conjunction with Blount County Welfare League and to assist in the plan and the organization. The charter was granted to: J. H. Webb, Ernest Koella, K. A. Bryant, J. L. Vineyard and Oliver Pickens.[34]

The plans were to treat patients free for one year. The doctors agreed to donate services and financial aid. Dr. G. D. LeQuire was recommended as chief-of-staff to organize a staff from among local men.[35]

The Aluminum Company of America gave the use of the hospital building near Bassel School and the idea became a reality. The first patients were admitted June 4, 1928. Fifteen children could be accommodated. No bed cases were admitted. Mrs. H. C. Bristol taught the day school for these children. Mrs. B. B. Johnson, assisted by Mrs. Ruth Hale, was in charge of the sanitarium. The Medical Society visited the sanitarium in a body in 1929 and soon after gave a benefit supper which netted over a hundred dollars for the project. In 1930, the doctors agreed not to send Christmas cards and to donate the amount saved to the support of the Mountain View Sanitarium. The sanitarium closed in 1931 or 1932 because of a lack of support from the general public.

---

[33] *Charters of Incorporations*, 2, p. 79.
[34] *Charters of Incorporation*, 2, p. 227.
[35] *Blount County Medical Society Minutes; Maryville Enterprise*, February 12, 1930.

In 1928, Dr. J. E. Carson assisted by Dr. C. C. Vinsant opened Fort Craig Hospital to the public which he later operated as an open-staff hospital. The hospital was gradually expanded and X-ray and the best of laboratory facilities were the equal of any large city hospital. After Dr. Carson's death the special services were gradually discontinued and the hospital was closed in 1944.[36]

February 7, 1943, the Doctors' Hospital was officially opened in the building at the corner of Ellis Avenue and College Street, and operated until 1947.

July 24, 1947, Blount Memorial Hospital, a fifty-bed institution was opened. This unit cost more than $500,000 and the Doctors' Hospital equipment was donated to the hospital. This was the most adequate hospital facilities that had so far been available to Blount County people, but it was not nearly enough to meet the demands for service.[37]

In 1948, work was started on a second unit, which when finished raised the capacity to 125 beds at about the same cost. The first and second unit were financed one-third by Federal funds. Plans are now under way for constructing a third unit which will raise the capacity to two hundred beds. The cost of the third unit is estimated as the same as the first two. The aluminum company has agreed to donate another $100,000 which will raise their investment to $350,000. This third unit will enable the hospital and the local medical profession to render a more efficient and satisfactory service to the citizens of Blount County.[38]

Finally, it is in order to say that it appears that the Blount County medical profession has pioneered throughout its history and that they are still continuing the tradition. Outside opinion has stated that the medical profession in Blount County has outstanding men in every field and bows to no group in the state or country as their peers.

DRUGGISTS

The early doctors prepared their own medical preparations, as Doctor Gunn so ably describes in his *Household Remedies*. They gathered their own herbs, compounded, concocted and brewed their own medicines. These herbs together with certain standard drugs which they purchased in quantity on annual (or oftener) trips to a distant apothecary.

There is no mention of any druggist doing business in Maryville prior to 1858. In 1857, Fagg and Miller began to do business as a firm. The name was changed in 1859 to Miller and Pope. The business operated under this name until the Confederates evacuated Knoxville. Dr. Sam Pride seems to have had an interest in the business according to references in the settlement of the Pride estate.[39]

---

[36] *Charters*, 2, p. 393, February, 1938.
[37] Charter issued January 12, 1946. This hospital was erected in memory of those who gave their lives in World War I and World War II.
[38] *Maryville Times*, April 9, 1954 (Editorial).
[39] *Deeds*, 1855–1876, Passim.; *Business Directory of Nashville, 1857*.

The Rev. W. T. Dowell seems to have taken over the business which passed through the hands of John M. Currier, G. A. Toole, and others until E. W. Tedford took over the business in 1878. He formed a partnership with James L. Lowe, and they operated a branch store in Morganton (later McClung and Lowe).

In 1879, Dr. Thomas O. Goetz opened a drugstore. His partner, Leo Ferrary became involved in some crooked whisky transactions and after grand jury action Dr. Goetz sold out to Dr. Charles A. Fulton, an experienced druggist. Dr. Fulton was assisted by Dr. George A. Warren. Both men were graduates of the Massachusetts College of Pharmacy. Dr. Fulton died in 1880.[40]

The present Byrne Drugstore in Maryville is a direct descendant of the first drugstore. Edward Tedford had various partnerships, previous to one with Samuel George. Mr. George had various partnerships until his death.

DENTISTS

Not more than one dentist advertised as such before the Civil War. As Dr. Shelton stated in his book, many local doctors "had learned the art of extracting, and inserting teeth" along with general medical knowledge. The medical doctor carried his forceps and extracted teeth whenever necessary.

The earliest local advertisement of a dentist is that of Dr. J. A. McFaul, Surgeon-Dentist, located at Louisville, Tennessee in 1844.[41]

After the War Between the States, at least four dentists came into Blount County with the "Quaker Migration": Drs. W. C. Stanley, and his son-in-law, H. P. Huddleston, a Dr. Ramsey, and Franklin P. Elliott, who later went to Shawneetown, Indian Territory, to work among the Indians.[42]

Dr. J. B. Williams did extensive local advertising during the seventies and eighties, especially appealing to timid ladies who might not want to go to his office, offering to go to their homes.[43]

Drs. Robert W. and Alex Goddard, and S. H. McNeely did not practice in Blount County very long before they moved on to other locations.

Dr. Thomas P. Cowan did not practice dentistry much. He was too busy with business projects such as the early Power and Light developments. Dr. Royal Jennings spent ten or fifteen years in the local field. Dr. J. H. Hughes was located here in 1894 for a while.

This brings us up to the time of Dr. John A. Goddard and Dr. W. H. Caldwell, which is within the memory of many today. The present roster of dentists follows closely after those already mentioned.

---

[40] *Maryville Index*, March 5, 1880; September 24, 1880.
[41] *Knoxville Argus*, October 16, 1844.
[42] Dr. Elliott resigned as County Superintendent of Schools when he left here.
[43] *Maryville Index*, January 22, 1879. "Toothache cured 10 cents, teeth extracted 25 cents, teeth filled 50 cents, (gold $1.00); can fix a tooth without "killing the patient."

JAMES HOUSTON GILLESPY, M.D.
Physician, State Representative and Senator; Inn-keeper, Post Master and Speculator.

JAMES MADISON COX, M.D.
Physician with the Cherokee Removal, 1838.

MEN OF MEDICINE

JOHN WILKINSON CATES, M.D.
Surgeon in Confederate States Army, 1861–1865.

SAMUEL PRIDE, M.D.
In organization of Tennessee Medical Association; First Clerk and Master of Blount County; First Worthy Master of New Providence Lodge F. & A. M.; First Mayor of Maryville.

BARCLAY McGHEE, M.D.
Assistant Surgeon 5th Regiment Mexican War, 1846–1848.

JOHN P. BLANKENSHIP, M.D.
Surgeon United States Army, 1861–1865; First County Physician; First President of Blount County Medical Association.

CAPT. W. Y. C. HANNUM, C. S. A.
Local chapter of United Daughters of the
Confederacy named in his honor.

CAPT. EMERSON J. LONES
First local American Legion Post named
in his honor.

MEN TO REMEMBER

JUDGE JESSE GEORGE WALLACE
Eloquent ante-bellum Attorney, prominent in Masonic circles; A post-war gift
to Middle Tennessee

ATTORNEY GEN. CHARLES T. CATES
Blount County's most outstanding legal
light.

CAPT. LEONARD S. GODDARD
One-time editor of *The Maryville Times*;
Enthusiastic recruiter for the Spanish-
American War; Advocate General of the
Philippines.

HON. EDWIN S. CUNNINGHAM
Consul General to China; Spent over
forty years in various Diplomatic capacities.

CHAPTER IX

Courts, Public Offices and Men of Law

WHEN Blount County was established in 1795 the Court of Pleas and Quarter Sessions was also set up, which functioned until 1836. As a Court of Pleas the body was a judicial group similar to our present day Circuit Court. This body was usually composed of three members and could empanel a jury. It heard civil and criminal cases, bound apprentices, probated wills and partitioned lands. As a Court of Quarter Sessions, it met four times a year. It was the legislative and chief executive body of the county.

Prior to statehood, the justices of the peace who composed the County Court were appointed by the Territorial Governor. After statehood they were appointed by the Legislature and served during good behavior and it was not until 1836 that justices were elected by the people. Under the first constitution the county political division or unit was the militia company. Each company was allowed two justices and one constable with an additional justice for the "town company." Eleven justices were appointed by Territorial Governor Blount in 1795. In 1812 there were 27 justices. When the 1835 constitution went into effect the county was laid off into seventeen civil districts and each district was allowed to elect two justices and a constable with an additional justice for the county town (later there was one justice allowed for each incorporated town in the county). Since 1836 justices are elected by popular vote for a term of six years.[1]

The Quarterly County Court is the county's governing body. It appoints many of the county officials; approves the bonds of nearly all the officials; levies property, privilege and poll taxes; borrows money to finance county activities; receives reports from county officials; zones the county for the benefit of public safety, health and morals; divides the county into civil districts and employs auditors for the examination of the county records.[2]

The business of the early court included the granting of mill rights, ferry rights, and the setting of toll rates; the opening of roads, the appointing of hands to work the roads; allotting of money for bridges, and the granting of the right to operate "ordinaries" as saloons or inns were then called. Courts also allotted bounties of $2 or $3 for killing wolves (this was discontinued in Blount County in 1889), and made

---

[1] *Constitution, 1834*, art. 6, sec. 15; *Constable's Bond Record* has been kept since 1888 in the County Court Clerk's office; *Private Acts*, 1835, ch. 1, sec. 3; *Constitution, 1870*, art. 6, sec. 15. Constitution hereinafter cited *Const.* and Private Acts hereinafter cited PA.

[2] *Acts, 1804*, ch. 1; *P A, 1836; Const., 1870*, art. 7, sec. 1; *P A, 1933* ch. 138, sec. 1; *P A, 1937*, ch. 307, sec. 8; *P A, 1939*, ch. 16, secs. 2–16; ch. 45, secs. 3–4; ch. 58, sec. 1.

plans for the temporary and permanent location of the seat of justice for the county.

According to the constitution, the Quarterly Court had the power to elect the Coroner and Ranger; to fill vacancies in the offices of the Sheriff and Trustee, as well as to elect some statutory officers. The County Court cannot be abolished but its powers may be removed and vested in another body such as a commission.[3]

Individually, the Justices of the Peace were minor judges and committing magistrates. Justices of the Peace tried minor cases where the penalty did not exceed a fifty dollar fine or thirty days in jail. A justice could issue warrants for arrest, appoint special temporary officers for making arrests and convene their courts whenever the occasion arose or as they saw fit. Whenever cases came before them which were out of their jurisdiction, they had power to bind the parties over to the proper higher court sitting in the county. After the justice had given this verdict and sentence if the verdict were unsatisfactory the case might be appealed to the District Court for another trial. These minor courts existed from 1795 until September 1, 1948 (Act, 1947). Severally, the justices of the Peace make up the Quarterly County Court, but there is no relation in this duality of function. The justices of the peace share with the Coroner the power to conduct inquests over the bodies of persons meeting death by "unlawful violence at the hands of some other person."

September 1, 1948, the justice courts were abolished and Will A. McTeer, by appointment, became the first judge of the Court of General Sessions of Blount County. It soon became evident that one judge could not handle the volume of cases which was presented and a second General Sessions judge was authorized in 1949. The General Sessions judge is elected by popular vote for a term of eight years.

The first presiding officer of the Quarterly Court was a Presiding Justice elected by the court for one year. After 1855, the court was presided over by a chairman of the County Court who was elected from the court for one year. Since 1875 the office of chairman has been practically synonymous with County Judge with the added advantage that he could act in an independent capacity of justice.[4]

The office of County Judge was created by a special act in 1919 (effective September 1, 1920). He is elected by popular vote for a term of eight years. The salary was fixed at $1200 in 1919 and increased by a special act in 1933 and again since, under the general law. The salary of the judge as general administrative, financial and executive officer of the county is fixed by the Quarterly County Court with an additional $5 per day during the sitting of the Quarterly and Probate Court.[5]

---

[3] *Const. 1870*, art. 7, sec. 1–2; art. 11, sec. 17.
[4] *Acts, 1796*, ch. 15, sec. 5; *1797*, ch. 39, sec. 2; *1811* ch. 67, sec. 2; ch. 86, sec. 2; *1817*, ch. 105, sec. s. 4, 12; P A, *1831*; ch. 89, sec. 2; *1836*, ch. 6, sec. 4; Under a general law of 1856 there was a county judge (Stephen J. McReynolds); *Acts, 1856*, ch. 253; The act was repealed in 1858—P A, *1858*, ch. 5.
[5] P A, *1919*, ch. 240; P A, *1925*, ch. 11, sec. 2.

COURTS, PUBLIC OFFICES AND MEN OF LAW 199

The County Court Clerk is clerk of the Quarterly, Probate and Juvenile courts and is the licensing and revenue-collecting agent of the state. The office is as old as the county. Prior to 1836 the clerk was elected by the court, and served during good behavior. Since 1836 he is elected by popular vote for a term of four years.[6]

The sheriff is the county's chief peace officer and the executive officer of its courts. The office dates from the establishment of the county. Until the War Between the States the sheriff acted as collector of property and poll taxes. The first sheriff was appointed by Governor Blount to perform that duty. Until 1897 he was the chief election officer. Under the first constitution the sheriff was appointed by the Court of Pleas and Quarter Sessions. Since 1836 he has been elected by popular vote for a term of two years.[7]

The Coroner has the power to conduct inquests over the bodies of persons meeting death "by unlawful violence at the hands of some other person." He acts as sheriff when the office is vacant or when the sheriff becomes incompetent. Since the organization of the state the coroner has been appointed for a term of two years by the Quarterly County Court. He is not required to keep records.[8]

One Constable is elected as a minor peace officer from each civil district with an extra one from the county seat. Constables serve as executive officers for justice of the peace courts, and as servers of certain processes for other courts.[9]

The office of Ranger is one of the oldest offices in the county, but was discontinued when there was no longer a need for an officer to receive and take up stray livestock. In the days when it was a criminal offense to steal a horse or to harbor stray livestock, it was highly important to have a person who was legally responsible for strays. Later when the laws were modified and people became more or less law-abiding the Ranger became less and less necessary. The Ranger was appointed by the Quarterly County Court for a term of two years. The Ranger was required to advertise any strays taken up and if the owner failed to claim the animal and pay for its keep within the year, the animal was sold for one-half its appraised value.[10]

From 1795 until 1836 one or two justices were designated to make tax returns for each militia company. These returns merely stated the number of acres of land owned, the number of white polls, the number of black polls, etc., with no valuation stated. The taxes were collected by the sheriff. The method of tax assessment varied after 1836. Some-

---

[6] *Acts, 1794*, ch. 1, sec. 50; *Const., 1796*, art. 5, sec. 10; *Acts, 1856*, ch. 253 sec. 7; *Const., 1834*, art. 6, sec. 13; *Const., 1870*, art. 6, sec. 13; *Acts, 1870*, 2d ses., ch. 23 secs. 1, 6; *P A 1911*, ch. 58, secs. 3, 7.
[7] *Const., 1796*, art. 6, sec. 1; *Const., 1834*, art. 7, sec. 1; *Const., 1870*, art. 7. sec. 1, *Acts, 1796*, 1st ses. ch. 9, secs. 2, 4; ch. 12, secs. 1, 3; *Acts, 1797*, ch. 2, sec. 13.
[8] *Const., 1796*, art. 6, sec. 1; *Const., 1834*, art. 7, sec. 1; *Const., 1870*, art. 5, sec. 1.
[9] *Const., 1796*, art. 6, sec. 1; *Const., 1834*, art. 6, sec. 15; *Const., 1870*, art. 6, sec. 15; A Constable's Bond Record has been kept in the County Clerk's office since 1888.
[10] *Const., 1796*, art. 6, sec. 1; *Const., 1834*, art. 7, sec. 1; *Const., 1870*, art. 7, sec. 1.

times a tax assessor was elected by popular vote for one year periods but more often one was appointed for each district by the County Court. In the 1880's the term was fixed at four years. Since 1909 there has been a County Tax Assessor elected by popular vote for a term of four years. The tax assessor since the creation of the office has been charged with evaluating property and listing polls for state and county taxation. However, since 1875 public utilities have been assessed by state officials. Since 1873 it has been the assessor's duty to enumerate persons engaged in trades, and professions taxable as privileges.[11]

The Register is elected for the purpose of registering deeds, liens, leases, charters, etc. The office dates from the formation of the county. Like the clerk the Register was elected by the court and served during good behavior until 1836. Since that time the Register is elected by popular vote for four years. Since 1927, the Register also acts as entry-taker.[12]

From 1799 to 1806 according to legislative act Blount County should have had an entry-taker. In 1806 the office was abolished, and the duties assigned to the District Surveyor, whose office combined the functions of entry-taker and surveyor. In 1823 the office of County Surveyor was re-created along with the office of Entry-taker. The office was abolished in 1875. In 1879 the County Court was authorized to impose the duties on the Surveyor or the Register. The Surveyor probably performed the duties which entailed very little work, since practically all lands open for entry were taken up by 1879. The books were closed in 1897.[13]

The office of Surveyor paralleled that of the office of Entry-taker from 1799 to 1806. The Surveyor was charged with surveying and making plats of lands entered with the Entry-taker. In 1806 the office was abolished and the duties assigned to the district surveyor. In 1823 the office of County Surveyor was recreated along with the office of Entry-taker. Prior to 1836 he had been elected by the Quarterly County Court for a term of four years. The Surveyor is not now concerned with the disposal of public lands, but he is required to make such surveys as any court of record may demand and to survey land at the request of an interested person.[14]

Blount County should have had a Board of Equalization of some sort since 1856. Its duties are to examine, compare and equalize the assess-

---

[11] *Acts, 1801*, ch. 13; *Acts, 1803*, ch. 3; *1804*, ex. ses., ch. 12; P A, *1836*, ch. 14; *Acts, 1873*, ch. 118; *1875*, ch. 81; *1877*, ch. 73; Other Acts were passed in 1883, 1885, 1895, 1897, 1903; *Acts, 1907*, ch. 602, sec. 9, subsec. 1.

[12] *Const., 1796*, art. 6, sec. 1; *Const., 1834*, art. 7, sec. 1; *Const., 1870*, art. 7, sec. 1; P A, *1927*, ch. 61.

[13] *Acts, 1899*, ch. 24; *Acts, 1806* (ex. ses.), ch. 1; P A, *1823*, ch. 49, sec. 1; There are three volumes of Entry-taker's books in the Register's office 1824–97. The Blount County entry-taker did not have authority to receive entries to lands in the Hiwasee District (Cades Cove and Happy Valley) until 1833 (P A, 1833, ch. 298); *Acts, 1870*, 2d ses., ch. 68; *Acts, 1875*, ch. 55; *Acts, 1879*, ch. 46; P A, *1927*, ch. 61.

[14] *Acts, 1799*, ch. 24, sec. 1; *Acts, 1806*, ex. ses. ch. 2; P A, *1823*, ch. 49, sec. 8; P A, *1836*, ch. 2, sec. 4; *Code, 1858*, 438; 1932, 789.

ments placed on properties in the county. Four members of the present board of equalization are appointed by the Quarterly County Court and one is appointed by the governing body of the City of Alcoa, for a term of two years.[15]

The office of Trustee is constitutional and as old as the county. Prior to 1836 the Trustee, who serves for a term of two years was appointed by the quarterly court, but since 1836 he is elected by popular vote. He is the treasurer of the county and since 1876 has been the collector of property and poll taxes. A general law of 1921 set $5,000 as the maximum fee which could be retained as compensation for this office. This act was replaced by a private act in 1923 reducing the amount to $3,000. This act was repealed in 1925 in favor of the general law. In 1927 the amount was again limited to $3,000.[16]

Between 1860 and 1876 Blount County had a revenue collector who was elected by popular vote for a term of two years. He served as collector of state and county property and poll taxes until the trustee was charged with this duty in 1876.[17]

A special act of 1923 created the office of Delinquent Poll Tax collector. He was appointed annually by the Quarterly County Court. He was under a $1,000 bond and served under oath. He was authorized to assess each delinquent tax payer 50 cents and retain that and the fee usually received by the County Trustee. The collector turned over his collection on or before the first court-day of each session of the Quarterly Court. Poll taxes became delinquent if not paid by the first Monday in July. The poll tax was not assessed in Blount County after 1952.[18]

The Revenue Commission consists of three members appointed for two years by the County Court and probably dates from the county organization with a lapse from 1858 to 1875. The members of the County Court and the Clerk of the Court are ineligible to serve on the commission. Under the general law the commission is required to examine and compare the quarterly records of the county collection and disbursement officers and report their findings to the court. If it is so directed, the commission is required to direct the sale of bonds and invest the sinking funds.[19]

Prior to 1900 the school system of Blount County operated almost exclusively under the general law. A special act of 1854 directed that $3,000 of the unappropriated money in the State Treasury be set aside

---

[15] *Acts, 1856*, ch. 74, sec. 26; *P A, 1858*, ch. 12, sec. 5, *Acts, 1873*, ch. 118, Sec. 35; *Acts 1877*, ch. 73, sec. 4; *Acts, 1907*, ch. 602, sec. 32 (some sort of legislation was introduced every two or four years from 1870 to 1907) *Acts, 1909*, ch. 495, sec. 1.

[16] *Const., 1796*, art. 6, sec. 1; *Const., 1834*, art. 6, sec. 1; *P A, 1835*, ch. 2, sec. 4; *Code 1858*, 822; *Const., 1870*, art. 7, sec. 1; *Acts, 1875*, ch. 91, sec. 1; *P A, 1925*, ch. 481; *P A, 1927*, ch. 305; *P A, 1925*, ch. 136; *P A, 1921*, ch. 101; *P A, 1923*, ch. 677.

[17] *P A, 1860*, ch. 9; *Acts, 1875*, ch. 91, sec. 1.

[18] *P A, 1923*, ch. 676, sec. 1–7.

[19] *Acts, 1787*, ch. 14, sec. 2; *P A, 1819*, ch. 38, sec. 1; *P A, 1840*, ch. 160, sec. 7; *Acts, 1875*, ch. 91, sec. 15, 16; *Acts, 1907*, ch. 602, sec. 76; *P A, 1913*, 1st ex. ses. ch. 26, sec. 4, 6; *P A, 1919*, ch. 175, sec. 4, 5. There are many, many others not cited especially between 1875–1907.

as a school fund for the benefit of the township composed of the 17th districts of Blount and Monroe counties. This was in lieu of the failure to set aside school lands for this township.

The office of County Superintendent of Schools was created in 1867 with the election of T. J. Lamar and has existed since that time. Under a special act of 1929, amended in 1933, the superintendent is elected by popular vote for a term of four years. Prior to this he was elected by the County Court for a term of two years.[20]

Under the Common School System set up in 1836 each separate school was governed by five school directors and the school funds were administered by a Common School Commission. After 1867 a county superintendent coordinated the individual schools into one system. In 1873 when the present general school plans had their beginning, each civil district was under a board of directors. The general education bill of 1907 abolished the district directors and divided the county into five school districts and provided for popular election of board members to constitute the County Board of Education. This board had general supervision over the elementary system.

There should have been a high school board soon after the law was passed in 1899 allowing a high school tax to be levied. Blount County did not elect such a board until 1914 and it did not succeed in getting a high school system set up until 1918 when Porter Academy was transferred to the county. A special act in 1919 directed the Count Trustee to pay any incorporated town its pro rata share of the high school tax.

A general law of 1921 created a board of seven members appointed by the County Court for terms of seven years (the first board was appointed with terms arranged so that one new member should be appointed each year). This board replaced the high school and elementary boards which had formerly functioned as two separate bodies. The bulk of the power from 1921 to 1929 was vested in the superintendent.

Under the act of 1929 the board was called the Board of Supervisors. The seven members were elected by popular vote for a term of two years, but the powers were the same as under the act of 1925.[21]

Two special high school districts have been created from sections of Blount County. In 1911 the Trigonia High School district was created from parts of Blount, Loudon and Monroe counties. The district operated under the supervision of three directors elected by popular vote within the district. In 1918 when Blount County set up a County High School System, the Blount portion was withdrawn from the district. The Meadow High School district was set up in 1913 from Blount and

---

[20] *Acts, 1854*, ch. 95; *Acts, 1856*, ch. 267, sec. 9; *P A, 1867*, 2d, ses., ch. 27, sec. 22-45; *Acts, 1873*, ch. 26; *Acts, 1875*, ch. 138; *P A, 1929*, ch. 45; *P A, 1933*, ch. 266.

G. S. W. Crawford, Capt. F. M. Smith, and Sam W. Sherrill of Blount County have held the office of State Superintendent of Public Instruction.

[21] *Acts, 1907*, ch. 236; *Acts, 1899*, ch. 279, sec. 3; *P A, 1919*, ch. 522; *1921*, ch. 120, sec. 1, 2; *1925*, ch. 115; *1929*, ch. 436.

Loudon counties under the same plan as the Trigonia District. It was dissolved in the same way.[22]

In 1933 when the superintendent's term was changed to four years and became subject to popular vote, the election of the County School Board became subject to popular vote in their respective districts.

The Poor Commission consists of three members appointed by the County Court for a three-year term since 1827. The superintendent is chosen by and is subject to the will of the commission. The commission and the superintendent are responsible for the operation and supervision of the poor home. Before the War Between the States the farm was near Middlesettlements and since the war, near Alnwick. A contract was let in 1889 for a new building. The Poor Farm was abolished in July 1955.[23]

The County Industrial Home is managed by a board consisting of the County Judge and four trustees appointed for a four-year term by the judges of the Circuit and Chancery courts. The superintendent is appointed by and serves at the will of a board of trustees. The home was privately sponsored when first established in 1895. A few county charges were kept at first and later it was taken over by the county. The Daniel Griffin house on Cunningham Street was rented in 1895 and Mrs. Ann Eliza Blackburn was the first matron. Mrs. Blackburn, Dr. A. B. McTeer and Mrs. S. T. Stanley acted as an admission committee. The property was bought in 1897, by supporters of the project. Judge R. P. McReynolds suggested the present location on the Louisville Pike which was secured in 1926, after his death. The capacity of the house is fifty children. Mrs. Ica McCampbell has been matron since 1922.

The County Health Department is discussed fully in the chapter on Medicine.

Prior to 1901 the roads were laid out and maintained under general laws except for acts which allowed private individuals to build and operate toll roads. The County Trustee was ordered to buy and take charge of a set of tools for blowing rocks in 1852. This was the first county expenditure for equipment for road building. The general law of 1883 authorized the County Court to build improved roads. No improvements of account were made on Blount County roads prior to 1900, although an attempt was made in 1892 to improve all the main roads in the county by the Blount County Turnpike Company. The first rock crusher was bought in 1894. In 1909 the County Court elected a road commissioner in each district who had had experience in road building. Each district was divided into sections and an overseer was appointed for each section. Failure to serve when appointed was a misdemeanor. Every able-bodied male between the ages of 21 and 45 was

---

[22] *P A, 1911*, ch. 248; *1915*, ch. 665; *1917*, chs. 74, 508; *1919*, ch. 779; *1913*, 1st ex. ses., ch. 75.

[23] *P A, 1827*, ch. 112, sec. 3-6, 7, 8, 9; *Acts, 1879*, ch. 102; *Acts, 1889*, ch. 150; *Minutes*, 1889.

[24] *Acts, 1895*, ch. 60, sec. 2, 8, 12; *Minutes*, 1852; *Acts, 1909*, ch. 268, sec. 1; *P A, 1911*, ch. 282, sec. 1; *P A, 1911*, ch. 473, sec. 1; *Minutes*, 1892.

required to work from five to eight days or pay the commissioner of his district $1 for each day he did not work. The overseer could be paid $1 per 8-hour-day and up to $6 for extra days. The proceeds of the road tax were to be spent by the commissioner for labor, tools, and materials. Such expenditures had to be endorsed by the County Judge before being honored by the Trustee. Annual reports were required by the county court.[25]

A county road supervisor was authorized by an act of 1919 to be elected by the County Court biennially. His salary was fixed at $3 per day.

The district road commissioners continued as before with a salary of $2 per day. The overseer received $1.50 per day for his excessive days and the maximum age was advanced to 50 years. District commissioners were required to remove roads from streams and excessive grades. The road supervisor was to settle all right-of-way disputes and assess any damages arising from such changes.

Overseers were required to report to the commissioners the names of all road hands who failed to report for work. The commissioners and county supervisor were required to make an annual report to the County Judge of road tools and machinery on hand.[26]

The act of 1919 seems to have been modified by an act of 1921 which raised the rate of compensation of the commissioner to a yearly maximum of $1.00 to $3.50 per day and an overseer's rate of $3.00 per day. Under this act section overseers were appointed by the district commissioner and not the County Court. The days of labor required was set at 4 to 6 days at $1 to $2 per day.[27]

In 1925 the present County Highway Commission was created. The commission was appointed by the court from 1925–31; elected by popular vote from 1931 to 1937; elected by the County Court from 1937 to 1939; and since then by popular vote. From 1931 to 1937 the term was six years, otherwise the term has been two years. The commission can transact business if two members are present.[28]

The commission has general supervision over all roads, highways, bridges, culverts and public ferries. This commission also has charge of the workhouse and can use workhouse inmates for road maintenance. Compulsory road duty was discontinued in 1931. Construction and maintenance since that time is done by private contractors, workhouse prisoners, or labor hired by the commission. The commission has always had the power to purchase such tools, machinery, equipment, and materials as it has needed and the power to exercise the right of "eminent domain."

[25] *Minutes,* 1852; *Acts, 1909,* ch. 268, sec. 1; *P A, 1911,* ch. 282, sec. 1; *P A, 1911,* ch. 473, sec. 1; *Minutes,* 1892.
[26] *P A, 1919,* ch. 777, secs. 1–9.
[27] *P A, 1919,* ch. 20, secs. 1–5.
[28] *P A, 1925,* ch. 55, sec. 2; *P A, 1931,* ch. 357; sec. 5; *P A, 1937,* ch. 550, sec. 1; *P A, 1939,* ch. 302, sec. 1.

Applications for changing old roads or opening new roads have always been addressed to the road commission. Damages are assessed by the commission which reports to the County Judge. The decisions of the commission can be appealed to the Circuit Court. The commission is the county's agency for dealing with State and Federal agencies in highway matters. Highway funds are disbursed by the County Trustee through combined endorsement of the commission's secretary and chairman and the County Judge. The commission is required to submit an annual budget to the County Court and to keep a full set of minutes, a perpetual inventory and a warrant register.[29]

Since 1900 several acts authorizing bond issues for road-building have been passed. The act of 1909 authorized the issuing of $400,000 in bond and required the court to levy a tax to establish a sinking fund. In 1911 an act authorized the issuing of an additional $25,000 to supplement the 1909 issue. These bonds were to mature in forty years. The sale of these bonds and a 30 cent bridge tax made possible the building of the first concrete bridges in Blount County.

In 1919 a $500,000 road improvement bond issue was authorized which was to mature in thirty years. A "good roads commission" was created to act as a purchasing agent and to employ a civil engineer to supervise the work done by private contractors. A bond issue was also authorized by another special act of 1919 for the purpose of connecting Blount County and Loudon County roads. An act of 1921 authorized an additional $250,000 of road improvement bonds. This was when the Knoxville Highway by way of Rockford was built. Later acts have carried on the work begun under the early bond issues. Later highway programs have been subsidized by Federal funds.[30]

CIRCUIT COURT

Prior to 1810 all cases in law and equity originating in the county which were not tried before the Court of Pleas and Quarter Sessions, or Justices of the Peace, were tried before the Superior Court of Law and Equity held in Knoxville. Under the general law it had exclusive jurisdiction in civil and criminal cases triable before a jury. It also had certain probate jurisdiction and the power to hear and determine any equity matter wherein the parties did not object to its jurisdiction.

The Circuit Court tried those cases arising from the breaking of state statutes that called for a penalty higher than justices of the peace could

---

[29] *P A, 1919*, ch. 256, sec. 7–14.

[30] *P A, 1919*, ch. 619, sec. 1—Lon Bible operated the first bus between Maryville and Knoxville in 1919. In 1921 he was succeeded by Bale and Learn. The Mary-Knox Coach Company was chartered in March, 1924 by A. D., S. H., and C. W. Dunn; Joe Broyles and J. L. Kizer. The White Star Lines was chartered in January, 1926 by J. B. and T. R. Cochran; H. L. Hoffmeister, R. D. Russell, and Fred Ballard (*Charters* 1, pp. 133, 171; *Knoxville Journal*, March 20, 1955.) White Star Lines secured the Townsend Bus Lines in 1928, the Alcoa Bus Lines in 1938, and the Friendsville Bus Line in 1947.

impose and also for trying cases which had been appealed from the lower courts. Appeals from the District Courts were taken directly to the State Supreme Court at Nashville, which reviewed the evidence as presented in the District Court and then sustained or over-ruled the decision of the court.[31]

Up to 1836 the Circuit Judge was appointed by the General Assembly and held office during good behavior. He, in turn, appointed the clerk under the same terms. From 1836 until 1854 he was appointed for a term of 8 years. The clerk was elected by popular vote for a term of 4 years. Since 1854 the Circuit Judge has been elected by popular vote.[32]

A special act of 1917 increased the salary of the Circuit Court Clerk from $750 to $1800. In 1929 the clerk was allowed to retain up to $600 of the fees collected by him as clerk of the Criminal Court. Robert Houston, son of Major James Houston was one of the first clerks of the Circuit Court. (Dr.) Azariah Shelton was a later clerk.[33]

In 1925 a special act was passed which has relieved the Circuit Court of all criminal jurisdiction since that time.[34]

There are no preserved early papers of this court. When the courthouse burned the second time in 1906, few of the Circuit Court records were saved. The criminal Rule Docket from 1852–1924 is about the only surviving court record.

Dr. John A. Goddard and Major McTeer have left us the story of Blount County's three hangings which are related hereinafter. The first hanging was that of a man named Brice who was convicted of stealing slaves on the strength of a North Carolina law passed in 1779. The case was appealed to the Supreme Court but was affirmed and Brice was hung July 20, 1814.

The second hanging was Henry Lunsford on the 26th of September 1828, for killing one Thompson. The story goes that Lunsford had struck Thompson on the head at a log-rolling with a hand spike. Thompson went about his work for a month before he died suddenly from the effects of the blow.

The third hanging was Charles Cox, a Negro slave, October 25, 1839. David Humes owned Cox's wife and had her whipped for some misdemeanor. Cox was angered by this and sought revenge by firing a shot at Humes through the window while he was engaged in a checker game with Billy Hackney. The gun which Cox had used had been borrowed from a free Negro, Andy Tedford, who was acquitted of being an accessory. All three of these hangings took place on top of the hill at the head of McGhee Street.

About 1868 John Murphy shot and killed one Lunsford. He was tried

---

[31] *Acts, 1809*, (Sept. ses.), ch. 49; *Const., 1834*, Art. 5, secs. 1, 3, 13; *P A, 1836*, ch. 5, sec. 3; *Const., 1870*, art. 6, secs., 1, 3, 13.
[32] *Acts, 1809*, Sept. ses., ch. 49; *Const., 1834*, art. 6, sec. 3.
[33] *Acts, 1903*, ch. 255; *P A, 1917*, ch. 628; *P A, 1929*, ch. 62.
[34] *P A, 1925*, ch. 15; chs. 58, 105.

at the May term of court in 1868 and sentenced to hang. Murphy was such a handsome rascal that he aroused quite a bit of sympathy. He appealed his case but before the hearing he escaped to Kentucky. He was apprehended and returned to Knoxville. He was given a second trial and the judge ruled that since the crime had taken place in that part of Blount County that was cut off as part of Loudon County in 1870 that the case must be tried in Loudon County. Murphy was taken to Loudon County for trial and the same judge again ruled that since the murder was committed in Blount County that it could not be tried in Loudon and threw the case out of court. Murphy later met his match in Campbell County and was killed in a brawl.

Accounts of two duels have been preserved through A. B. Gamble who was an eye-witness to at least one of these duels. In 1845 a barbecue was held in Maryville in honor of Sam Houston who was on his way to Washington, D. C. to serve as State Senator from Texas. The barbecue was held at the old campground at the intersection of Harper and Aluminum Avenue, and was largely attended. In the course of the afternoon a bloodless duel with pistols was fought between Jim Wolfe and Frank Reeder near Broadway Viaduct. About two years later two Maryville College students from Alabama met with their seconds near the same spot and fought with pistols without serious injury.[35]

CHANCERY COURT

There was no Chancery Court held in Blount County until 1852. Equity cases arising in Blount County were tried in the Blount County Circuit Court in 1810 and 1811; and before the Supreme Court of Errors and Appeals sitting at Knoxville from 1813 to 1822. Between 1822 and 1824 equity suits not brought in the Circuit Court of Blount County were tried by a Court of Equity held at Knoxville by one of the judges of the Supreme Court of Errors and Appeals. From 1824 to 1831 such cases were tried in a Chancery Court held at Kingston in Roane County. From 1831 to 1833 equity cases in Blount County were tried at Madisonville, in Monroe County. From 1833 to 1852 the Chancery Court at Madisonville and the Chancery Court at Knoxville had concurrent jurisdiction in Blount County equity cases. In 1836 the Circuit Court was divested of jurisdiction in equity cases involving more than $50, but since 1852, has had the power to decide all equity cases in which parties did not object to its jurisdiction. In 1852 Blount County was created as a separate Chancery district and provision was made for the court to be held in Maryville.[36]

The Chancery Court is chiefly a court of equity but also has considerable concurrent jurisdiction with the Probate and Circuit courts over the appointment and supervision of personal representations and the partition and distribution of estates as well as concurrent jurisdic-

---

[35] Dr. John A. Goddard, *History of Maryville*, in *Maryville Times*, April 9, 1902.
[36] *Acts, 1808*, ch. 49, secs. 1, 5; *Acts, 1811*, ch. 72, sec. 4; *Acts, 1813*, ch. 77, sec. 3; *Acts, 1838*, ch. 116, sec. 12; *Acts, 1852*, ch. 345, ch. 152, sec. 9.

tion with the Circuit Court in all civil cases at law except in liquidated damages.³⁷

Prior to 1854 the Chancellor, the judge of the Chancery Court, was appointed by the General Assembly. Since then he has been elected by popular vote. Before 1836 the Chancellor held office during good behavior; since then he has served for a term of 8 years. The Clerk and Master, appointed by the Chancellor, served during good behavior prior to 1836. Since 1836 his term has been limited to 6 years.³⁸

PROBATE COURT

The Probate Court is the judicial branch of the County Court which meets to expedite the probate of wills, the appointment and supervision of personal representatives, the partition and distribution of estates and to establish and supervise special road improvement, levees and drainage districts. The Probate Court has existed in one form or another since the organization of the county. The old Court of Pleas and Quarter Sessions, the Quorum Court, the County Chairman's Court and the present County Judge's Court.³⁹

JUVENILE COURT

The Juvenile Court with jurisdiction over juvenile delinquencies is regulated by the general law and dates from 1911. The court is held by the county judge. The Juvenile Court tries those cases classed as Juvenile (minors under the age of sixteen). Juveniles cannot be confined with adult prisoners in the jails. Offenders between sixteen and eighteen years of age may be tried in the regular courts but the sentence to labor must be to the State Agricultural and Training School at Nashville. The court convenes when need arises.⁴⁰

CRIMINAL COURT

An act of 1925 created the Criminal Court of the Fourth Judicial Circuit of which Blount County is a part. There is a separate criminal judge for this circuit who is elected by popular vote for a term of eight years. The clerk of the Circuit Court is the clerk of this court. The Criminal Court has exclusive common law and statutory jurisdiction, original and appellate, over criminal cases arising in Blount County.⁴¹

City Recorder, or Police Courts exist in Maryville and Alcoa which

---

³⁷ *Code 1858*, 3441; *P A, 1831*, ch. 107; *Acts, 1852*, ch. 57, sec. 1; ch. 92, sec. 1; *Acts, 1873*, ch. 64; *P A, 1915*, ch. 47; *P A, 1919*, ch. 42, sec. 3; ch. 150, sec. 4; *P A, 1927*, ch. 75, sec. 6; *Acts, 1836*, ch. 20, sec. 1; *Acts, 1846*, ch. 194, sec. 1.

³⁸ *Const., 1796*, art. 6, sec. 3; art. 5, sec. 2, 10; *P A, 1827*, ch. 79, sec. 2; *Const., 1834*, art. 6, sec. 3; *Acts, 1852*, Resolution 3; *Acts, 1854*, Res. 16; *Const., 1870*, art. 6, sec. 4, 13; *Acts 1870*, 2d ses., ch. 23, sec. 3, 6, 7.

³⁹ *P A, 1919*, ch. 240; *Acts, 1856*, ch. 253, sec. 7.

⁴⁰ *P A, 1911*, ch. 58.

⁴¹ *P A, 1925*, ch. 15; sec. 6, 9; ch. 58, sec. 6, 9; ch. 105; *P A, 1929*, ch. 142; ch. 159; *P A, 1931*, 2nd ex. ses., ch. 58.

try those persons brought before them by the city police for the violation of city ordinances of various natures, disorderly conduct, etc.

A Jury Commission has existed in Blount County since 1925. This commission is charged with the selection of jurors for the courts of the county, a task which ordinarily belongs to the Quarterly County Court. The board consists of three "discreet residents of the county appointed for terms of four years by the Circuit and Criminal judges who designate which commissioner is to be chairman." Not more than two can be of the same political party. Practicing attorneys and county and district officials elected by popular vote are not eligibile for membership on the commission. The Circuit Court Clerk is the clerk of the board. All members of the board are required to take an oath to be impartial in selecting jurors and to keep selections secret. A jury commissioner receives $4 per day of service and the clerk receives 5 cents for each name entered on the jury list. It is the duty of the board to draw up a list of four to eight hundred names biennially from election sheets, tax lists, and other sources and record them in a well-bound book. The clerk must write the names upon slips of paper and put them in the jury box, which is to be kept locked and opened only by the Circuit Judge, the Criminal Judge, the Jury Commission or the Circuit Court Clerk. Before each regular or special term of the Criminal Court the commission meets and opens the jury box from which the names for the panel of Grand and Petit jurors are withdrawn by a child under ten years of age. Jurors for the Criminal, and Circuit Court are chosen at the same time. The panels and also a list of people whose names are drawn who are unable to serve are reported to the court concerned. If some of the jurors selected are not qualified the judge can have the box brought into court and take other names from the box or he can direct the sheriff to summon whomever he wishes to be summoned. The slips of paper drawn from the jury box containing names of persons selected as jurors who fail to serve are returned to the box.[42]

The lawyers who are mentioned as practicing in Blount County courts prior to 1800 were: Ephriam Dunlap, Thomas Gray, John Lowry, Drury W. Breazeale, Benjamin Lowry, James Porter, Townsend Stuart Dade, John F. Jack, Arch Leake, Stephen Heard, Pleasant M. Miller, and Samuel L. Crawford. Luke Boyer was named in 1796 as the first county solicitor. Luke Bowyer was State's Attorney for the Watauga Association in 1776. He is said to have been of turbulent disposition and was once confined in the stocks for contempt of court. His name disappeared from records soon after this.[43]

After 1800 another group is mentioned: Andrew M. Lusk, James Rodgers, Andrew White, Samuel Lane, Simeon B. Grigsby, William E. Brown, George Moore, Thomas Dardis, William Thompson, William B. McNutt, Charles Keith, and Enoch Parsons.

Enoch Parsons seems to have lived in Maryville since he was a prop-

---

[42] *P A, 1925,* ch. 521, secs. 1, 2; *P A, 1931,* ch. 556, secs. 1, 2.
[43] Joshua W. Caldwell, *The Bench and Bar of Tennessee,* (Knoxville, 1898), p. 2.

erty owner. Parsons began to practice here about 1804 and continued until about 1819. He was appointed county solicitor in 1806 with Thomas Dardis as his alternate. (The salary of solicitor at that time was $10 for each term of court that he served.) In August 1806, Enoch Parsons and Gavin Black were fined $5 each for affray in open court. This is interesting because it is the only such incident on record in the Blount County Records. Enoch Parsons was a candidate for governor against Joseph McMinn in 1819. After his defeat, Parsons moved to Alabama.

John Lowry was licensed by Governor Blount in 1793 to practice in the Court of Pleas and Quarter Sessions of the Territory South of the River Ohio and later he served as Attorney-General. He is often mentioned in various town and county records. The term "John Lowry, attorney" is used to distinguish him from John Lowry, merchant. Lowry was County Representative to the State Legislature in 1809, 1817, and 1827.

John Gardner was active in various county businesses for forty or fifty years. (His name has been confused with that of John Garner.) Gardner seems to have made a practice of buying real estate which was sold in the settlement estates. He, at one time, owned "Methodist Hill," (the present Armory site), and other interesting properties. Samuel Glass practiced law locally, and served as State Senator in 1799. He was one of the commissioners appointed to lay out the town of Maryville.

Four lawyers are listed in the *Gazeteer* for 1833, but only John Wilkinson and Jacob F. Foute are named. Foute was active in the organization of the Masonic Lodge and served from 1817–1836 as County Court Clerk. (His brother, Daniel D. Foute was his deputy, and the first proprietor of Montvale Springs.) John Wilkinson served as an early solicitor and was deputy surveyor under Robert Wear for the Territory South of the Ohio River. He was State Senator in 1801, 1805, and 1807. He was the father of Dr. John Wilkinson who was a "49'er" and the grandfather of Dr. John W. Cates and Attorney Charles T. Cates, Sr.[44]

G. W. Churchwell maintained an office in both Maryville and Knoxville in 1840, and operated the ferry at the Holston River on the Maryville-Knoxville road. Quite a bit of advertising can be found for his ferry in the then current newspapers.

Among the mid-century attorneys were: John S. McNutt, John Finley Gillespy, who was Senator in 1829 (his brother Dr. James H. Gillespy was Representative at the same time), Joseph W. Lemons, J. H. Parsons, James A. Houston, S. T. Bicknell, and Alexander M. Wallace. Bicknell served several terms in the Legislature. He was also one

---

[44] All names were taken from the Blount County Court Minutes, 1795–1818. Although Sam Houston never practiced law here, he was a native of Blount County and the only native son who had thus far occupied the Governor's chair; Eastin Morris, *Gazeteer of Tennessee*, (Nashville, 1834) Appendix.

COURTS, PUBLIC OFFICES AND MEN OF LAW   211

of the leading merchants in the 1840's and 1850's. He moved to Monroe County about the time of the Civil War. He served as Assistant Quartermaster under General Caswell in the Confederate Army.[45]

John E. Toole was very active in social and political activities in the forties and fifties. He began his law practice in 1845 and took a very active part in pre-war politics. He served as Provost-Marshal with the Confederate Army. After the Federal occupation of East Tennessee, Toole did not return to Maryville, but moved to Alabama. Jesse G. Wallace was a brilliant young man with journalistic and oratorical tendencies who was quite active in Masonic circles. He was acting Attorney-General in 1857. Like Mr. Toole, he began his law practice in 1845 and espoused the Southern Cause. He moved to Franklin, Tennessee after the war and led a very active, useful life. He wrote many newspaper articles reminiscent of East Tennessee.

Stephen J. McReynolds was a practicing attorney and a member of the County Court twenty or thirty years. He served as County Judge from 1856 to 1858 which was the only time the county had a judge until 1919. He was also Presiding Justice for several years.

There were three Negro men who read law and practiced in Maryville for a while. Allen Garner was a very intelligent free Negro. After the Civil War, Garner was elected justice of the peace and did most of the justice business in Maryville for several years. His office was in the courthouse and in 1879 the courthouse fire started in his office. He later served as courthouse janitor for a good many years. Charles P. Whitlock made a brilliant record as a student at Maryville College, but did not have enough business here. He moved to Loudon about 1880 where he served as justice of the peace. Alex George also read law but only practiced here for a short while before moving elsewhere.

The lawyers who practiced in Maryville during the fifty years after the Civil War were: W. D. McGinley, R. N. Hood, C. T. Cates, Sr., Sam P. Rowan, M. L. McConnell, Will A. McTeer, Thomas N. Brown, D. L. Bryan, Charles T. Cates, Jr., A. G. Howe, W. B. Stevens, J. W. Culton, F. H. Lamon, Sam Nuchols, Andy Gamble, G. S. W. McCampbell, John M. Rorex, James M. Cates, M. H. Gamble, John C. Crawford, Sr., Homer A. Goddard, W. C. Chumlea, John L. Goddard, Edwin S. Cunningham, George C. Jackson, J. Merritt DeArmond, R. R. Kramer, J. G. Sims, J. L. Tweed, Sam Johnson, Sam H. Dunn, T. C. Drinnen, Wood Wright, Charles C. Jackson, Pat Quinn, George D. Roberts, Will A. McTeer, Jr., and D. S. Kramer.[46]

There were twenty Democrats and twenty Republicans in this group and one of unknown political leanings. Twenty-eight of those were natives of Blount County.

---

[45] Names given by W. E. Parham in article *Maryville*. J. H. Parsons died in Rusk County, Texas about 1880 and his estate was settled here.
[46] Names and information given in a paper given by the Hon. Thomas N. Brown before the Maryville Bar Association March 1, 1929. (From files of the Maryville Bar Association.)

There were two other lawyers who were here for a while that Mr. Brown did not mention. Brinton Gregory was a brilliant young man, who practiced in Maryville during the seventies and eighties. He lectured on law at the old Quaker School one year. Gregory became frightened that he would be prosecuted for selling insurance without a license and left Maryville. He was a very successful prosecuting attorney in Denver, Colorado.

Fordyce Grinnell gave promise of becoming a legal light when he was admitted to the bar in the seventies. He suddenly decided that he wanted to study medicine and he became a leading physician before he went West to an Indian Reservation in the Dakotas, where he practiced until his retirement to California in 1924.[47]

After the Civil War, the oldest and most picturesque lawyer in speech and dress was W. D. McGinley. He was described by Major McTeer and various contemporaries as being an excellent lawyer before a jury but not very successful in Chancery practice. The Hon. Thomas N. Brown described him as a good all-round lawyer, with a pleasing personality. McGinley Street is named for him.

Robert N. Hood, Charles T. Cates, Sr., Will A. McTeer, M. L. McConnell and Sam P. Rowan had all served in the War Between the States as officers and shortly became the leading lights in the legal field.

General R. N. Hood was the partner of W. D. McGinley for several years. He was an excellent lawyer and could turn out a prodigious amount of work. In fact, it has been said that he "burned himself out." He was an excellent scribe and could write almost as fast as a stenographer can take dictation. General Hood represented the Knoxville and Augusta Railroad from Knoxville to Maryville and later became president of the road. At a railroad convention after listening to others boasting of their many miles of railroad, Hood is reputed to have stated in his report that his line was only fifteen miles long but that it was the same width as the best of them. General Hood was president of the Farmers Bank established in Maryville in 1882 and later, established the Third National Bank in Knoxville and served as its president until his death. General Hood died at the height of his career from the effects of over-work.[48]

Charles T. Cates, Sr., was considered by his contemporaries as the best all-round lawyer in the Maryville Bar and was without peer in the State of Tennessee.

In his latter days, he is described as a very courtly figure who always wore a cape, and carried a cane. He was very logical and convincing in all his arguments. He was the father of General Charles T. Cates, Jr., of Knoxville and James M. Cates of Maryville. Gen. Chas. T. Cates, Jr., served as Attorney-General for 16 years.

---

[47] Will A. McTeer, *Autobiography* (Unpublished).

[48] R. N. Hood served as Brig. Gen. on the staff of Gov. James D. Porter and as captain and adjutant in the 2d Tennessee Cavalry.

Captain Sam P. (Pres) Rowan was a well-read lawyer who made a specialty of Supreme Court decisions. He had a very pleasing personality and as a rule he was very pleasant in court, but when aroused, he became a cyclone of eloquence. His contemporaries described him as a safe counselor, who would not bring suit unless he was convinced that he had a good case. Captain Rowan as before indicated was popular and represented Blount County several times in the Legislature. He evidently made his impression abroad because a story is told of Chancellor Staley at one time addressing him in court as the "tall statesman from Pistol Creek." Captain Rowan is given credit for clearing up some very difficult cases especially those involving the railroad bonds which the county issued and later repudiated.

Lamar McConnell served in the army, and a term as sheriff before he decided to read law with Charles T. Cates, Sr. He is conceded by all who ever heard him to be the most eloquent member of the Blount County Bar of this period. He edited the *Blount County Democrat* also, but sold the paper when he became Attorney-General of this district. He served in that capacity for eight years. He was generally slow in getting "wound up" to speak, but once started, he became very eloquent. Lamar McConnell's son Lincoln inherited this capacity for eloquence and earned a nation-wide reputation as a minister and lecturer.

Major Will A. McTeer was clerk of the Circuit Court for several years before he was admitted to the bar. He was a fluent writer and well versed in law, but a poor speaker. He was among the best technical and chancery lawyers. Major McTeer had a wide variety of civic interests and did a great deal of writing for local newspapers which have preserved valuable information for future generations. His histories of New Providence and Eusebia churches as well as his autobiography are good examples. Major McTeer represented our county in the Legislature for several terms during 1880–90. He was later commissioner of Internal Revenue, City Recorder of Maryville, Trustee of Maryville College, as well as holding other posts of responsibility.

A. G. Howe came to Maryville from Indiana with his father-in-law, Dr. Royal Jennings. Dr. Jennings built the Orr House on Indiana Avenue, Howe built the Dr. Wilson house (now Morton). Howe never seemed to get along with the local people although he was a good lawyer. He spent most of his time dealing in real estate and developed the Howe addition and probably is responsible for the name of Indiana Avenue since he came from that state. He moved to Knoxville in a few years and that is the last knowledge we have of him.

W. B. Stevens was admitted to the bar in the 1870's. He was an excellent speaker and sometimes depended on his ability to speak rather than on factual evidence. He drifted away from Maryville after a while.

Sam Nuchols was a very promising young lawyer with a great deal of ability. After practicing here for a short time he moved to North Dakota where he was very successful and became judge of one of the courts. He was a brother of Dr. John Nuchols, who moved to Polk County, Tennessee.

Andrew Gamble was a partner of Major McTeer. He was a fine jury lawyer. He could present a fine argument and was excellent on examination of witnesses. He gave most of his attention to real estate and related business and was very successful financially.

John M. Rorex was a native of Cocke County who settled in Maryville to practice. He had an unusually fine law library and was a promising young man. He had an ample allowance from a well-to-do father, which robbed him of the incentive to apply himself seriously to his profession. He soon sold his library and went to Texas where he became a newspaper publisher.

Edwin S. Cunningham, the eldest son of Major Cunningham, was a well-read young lawyer who was in the office of Charles T. Cates, Sr. He was appointed in 1897 to foreign service and served in various capacities in the foreign service for about fifty years, mostly in China, where he was twice decorated for services to the Chinese government. He retired in 1935 and after his wife's death came to Maryville, where he died in 1953.

J. Merritt DeArmond was a well-educated young lawyer who became impatient with the slowness of building up a clientele. He followed Greeley's advice "go West, young man" and moved to Texas, where he became judge of one of the courts. He died in 1955.

John L. Goddard became interested in politics soon after he was admitted to the bar. Through Congressman Gibson he was appointed postmaster in Maryville. He served for eight years and died in 1910.

G. S. W. McCampbell was a very good collection lawyer but never seemed to make much impression at the bar. After a few years he went back to his native Knox County. He did well in the collection business, and the insurance field.

J. Wright Culton was a very energetic and successful lawyer with a fine gift of oratory. He was the partner of Thomas N. Brown for six years. He moved to Knoxville about 1890 and became a partner in the firm of Taylor and Culton.

W. C. Chumlea was a licensed lawyer but held the office of Clerk and Master from 1890–1903, after which date he moved to Knoxville.

Fielding H. Lamon was a fine office lawyer and a good businessman whose career was cut short by an early death.

Mason Bartlett, one of Maryville's most colorful and interesting men, was admitted to the bar in his youth. After he came to Maryville from a protracted Western tour, he never got around to law practice.

George C. Jackson was a legislator, educator and innkeeper. He served as County Superintendent of Schools, teacher and justice of the peace. He was licensed to practice law in 1878. However, he is more remembered as the builder and operator of the Jackson House, which he built in 1885. Jackson died about 1914 and since 1919 the building is known as Blount Hotel.

Jancer L. Tweed was a promising lawyer who was elected City Recorder for Maryville soon after his arrival here. He later moved to Ohio and entered law practice.

J. G. Sims came to Maryville after World War I and set up a practice. He was very active in the state organization of the American Legion and has held all important offices. When Gen. L. D. Tyson was elected Senator from Tennessee he asked Mr. Sims, with whom he had been associated in the late war, to serve him as secretary. Since 1935, Mr. Sims has been connected with the Tennessee Veterans' Administration.

D. L. Bryan was a native of Sevier County, who had read law in North Carolina before he came to Blount County to teach. He carried on a law practice for about thirty years before his death in 1927.

James M. Cates read law with his father, Charles T. Cates, Sr. He began practice in 1897 in the old Cates law office at the corner of Love and Broadway. He was postmaster for nine years. The post office building, city delivery and the Maryville College Station were all instituted during his term as postmaster.

R. R. Kramer was born in Pennsylvania, studied law at the University of Michigan and came to Maryville in 1913. He formed a partnership with Will A. McTeer. His brother D. Sylvan Kramer came to Maryville in 1926 after five years' practice in Lenoir City and the firm of Kramer and Kramer was formed. After the death of D. S. Kramer in 1934, R. R. Kramer joined the law firm of Poore and Testerman in Knoxville. He is now associated with the firm of Kramer, Dye, McNabb and Greenwood where he was recently joined by two sons, Arnold and Jack. (Mr. Kramer still maintains his residence in Maryville.)

Sam Johnson was born in Loudon County, and studied law at Valparaiso, Indiana, and the University of Tennessee. He began practice in Maryville in 1913 and was active in Democratic politics. In 1919 he was appointed Chancellor of the 13th Chancery Division. He served as corporation lawyer for a long list of firms until his death in 1935.

C. C. Jackson was born in Morgan County, and attended the American Temperance University at Harriman, Tennessee. He was appointed Assistant Attorney-General in 1921. He came to Maryville soon after this date and formed a partnership with Sam H. Dunn. He served as a member of the Legislature from both Morgan and Blount counties. He died some years ago.

Thomas N. Brown served about sixty years as a lawyer in Blount County and during that time took an active part in every progressive civic movement that transpired. He was active in the organization of the First National Bank and served as financial adviser to a dozen or so corporations. He died in 1936.

John C. Crawford, Sr., read law with Major McTeer and took his degree from the University of Tennessee in 1900. After his admission to the bar he formed a partnership with Moses H. Gamble. He served as Clerk and Master from 1903–1909; as State Senator in 1912 and County Judge from 1924–34. Judge Crawford served on the local school board, election commission, city council, as bank director and on the Executive Committee of Maryville College as well as being active in church affairs. The law firm of Gamble, Crawford, and Goddard was dissolved about 1932 to form the firm of Crawford and Crawford with John Crawford, Sr. and John Crawford Jr. as partners. Judge Crawford passed away in 1934 and the firm at present is composed of John Crawford, Jr., and Roy Crawford, another son. (John Crawford, Jr., is at present District Attorney of the Supreme Court at Knoxville.)

Moses H. Gamble served as principal of Porter Academy and later as Superintendent of Public Instruction before he was admitted to the bar in 1900. He served several terms as Representative from Blount County, and a term as Chancellor. He was a very able lawyer, and was well known for his oratory. Judge Gamble died in 1934 and is succeeded by two sons in the legal field: Joe C. Gamble and Moses H. Gamble, Jr.[49]

Judge Pat Quinn was a native of Morgan County, who had attended Maryville College and entered the law firm of McTeer, Kramer, and Quinn. In 1926, he was named Circuit Judge for the Fourth Judicial Circuit composed of Blount, Loudon, Monroe, Bradley, McMinn, Polk and Roane counties. Judge Quinn was active in church, American Legion, and Kiwanis circles. His death occurred February 13, 1949.

George D. Roberts, a native of Cades Cove, was a teacher for about ten years. He was justice of the peace 1912–18. From 1918–30, he served as County Court Clerk. He had been admitted to the bar in 1925 and practiced law from 1930–34, when he was elected County Judge. Judge Roberts served in this position until his death in 1954. He was very active in church and was a charter Kiwanian.

T. C. Drinnen was born in the Dumplin Community of Sevier County, read law with James R. Penland at Sevierville and got his degree from the University of Tennessee in 1900. He served as City Recorder of Sevierville, and County Superintendent of Sevier County. He began the practice of law in 1911, and came to Maryville and formed a partnership with J. G. Sims in 1919. In 1932 his son Frank joined the firm and this partnership lasted until his death in 1953.

Only one older lawyer who was practicing in Maryville twenty-five years ago is still active—Sam H. Dunn. Homer A. Goddard has retired from active practice and left the practice to his two sons: Houston and Arthur B. Goddard. John W. Morton, who was in the firm of Kramer and Kramer, is now practicing in Oak Ridge.

The practicing lawyers not previously mentioned are: R. L. Meares, D. K. Thomas, William B. Felknor, Frank Bird, D. H. Rosier, Jr., Hugh DeLozier, Ben W. Kizer, Marinell Ross Waggoner, William H. Shields, Hubert Patty and Thomas D. Kelly.

W. A. McTeer, Jr., who began the practice of law in 1927, and Frank Drinnen, who was admitted to the bar in 1932, are now judges of the General Sessions Court of Blount County.

---

[49] Moses H. Gamble, Jr. was Blount County Representative to the Constitutiona Convention, 1952.

CHAPTER X

Industries and Occupations

THOSE who are unfamiliar with the topography of Blount County wonder why there are no large plantations or wealthy landowners. The explanation is simple: the land did not lend itself to that pattern of life and the grants were all small due to a limitation on the number of acres allowed to an individual. A letter from Benjamin Hawkins to Daniel Smith in 1790 strikes the keynote of the average way of life in Blount County—"impress as early as possible on your citizens the necessity of attending to their home manufactures—This is indispensible to your prosperity. You can raise fruit trees of all sorts, grapes of all sorts for wine . . . salt, iron, and clothing of cotton, wool, and silk. You can never have much money but you will have facility in acquiring the necessaries and comforts of life from the richness of your soil and the mildness of your climate." [1]

A few months after the first settlers arrived and planted their first crop, small mills began to appear along the streams of the territory. Several mills were already in operation before the establishing of Blount County. Tub mills and mortar and pestle had to suffice until mills were available.

The first mill in what is now Blount County was mentioned in 1788. John Kirk went to John Sloan's mill on Nine Mile Creek the morning that his family was massacred. This mill was later operated by Cook and then by Griffitts at Mint. In 1792, Thomas McCullock was granted leave by the Knox County Court to build a mill on Pistol Creek (probably near its mouth at Rockford). This mill was later operated by Sam George, Jim Thomas, and then Williams. It burned in the 1940's. The same year John Craig was given leave to build on Pistol Creek but evidently did not do so as he got another permit from the Blount County Court in 1795. Knox County permits were issued to Robert McTeer on Ellejoy Creek and Nicholas Bartlett on Stock Creek. It is not known when Martin's Mill on Nail's Creek nor Ish's Mill on Gallahar's Creek were built but Ish's was built before 1794 because John Sevier's Report to Governor Blount is headed "Ish's Mill." Kelly's Mill on Lackey's Creek was already in operation when the county was erected, as the Knox County Court voted to lay out a road to that point in 1792.[2]

In 1795 when Blount County Court first met, permits were granted for mills to John Walker in Tuckaleechee Cove; Samuel Thompson and Joseph Colville on Crooked Creek; Thomas and Elizabeth Ish on Gallahar's Creek; Samuel Henry, Matthew Wallace and David Ed-

---
[1] *Carter*, 26.
[2] The Griffits Mill was dismantled in 1952 and the wheel was taken to the Dover's Mill on the Alleghany Road.

mondson on Baker's Creek; Joseph Wittenberg on Cloyd's Creek; John Hess on Murphy's Creek (now Hess) in Miller's Cove, and to James Willis on Hannah's Branch. Permits for a saw and grist mill were granted to James McNutt on Pistol Creek (near Veach-May-Wilson), and to Andrew Kennedy on Little River (now Cave Roller Mill.)[3]

Later permits were issued to William Burk to build a mill on Nine Mile Creek, Thomas Cochran on Lackey's Creek, Richard Hudson (later to Reuben Charles) and Hugh Kelso on Baker's Creek. The Kelso Mill was at what later became Morganton. On Cloyd's Creek Charles Baker and Samuel Shaw got permits to build. Shaw's Mill was near the mouth of Cloyd's Creek and Unitia. His permit was for a saw and grist mill (the third sawmill in the county).

In 1797 Josiah Danforth was granted permission to build a mill on Pistol Creek. In 1802 he sold a 10-acre tract of land to John Lowry which included a powder, grist and saw mill. This mill was in Maryville at the foot of Cusick Street.

In 1800 John Lackey got permission to build a mill on Sinking Creek and James Scott on Baker's Creek. Reuben Charles protested Hugh Kelso's permit in 1799 but Kelso was issued a second permit to build at the mouth of Baker's Creek. William Hughes got a permit to build a mill in Tuckaleechee Cove (Walker evidently had not built his mill as permitted in 1795).

In 1803 James Houston, James Campbell and James Gillespy were to build a mill and "other works" on Pistol Creek. Cornelius Alexander was to build a mill on Pistol Creek and Christopher Hussey to build on Gallahar's Creek. The following year it appears from the records that John Craig's mill was transferred to Thomas Berry. By 1806 Berry seems to have transferred his mill claims on Pistol Creek to John Woods. Thomas Berry was at that date operating a mill and distillery on Gallahar's Creek (where David Oats had lived).

In 1809 Daniel Best was authorized to build a mill on Nine Mile Creek. This was on the site of the Wellsville Mill which was dismantled after the death of John B. Wells in 1954. In the partitioning of the George Best estate in 1869 the mill tract was sold to Robert M. Anderson and Stephen Wells. Wells bought Anderson's interest in the mill in 1876 and it was operated by Stephen M. Wells and later by his son John until 1954.[4]

By 1813 Bowerman was operating a still on Bowerman's Creek also known as Ish's. It is possible that Bowerman took over Elizabeth Ish's Mill. This mill, or its successor was later known as the Johnson or Mahoney Mill which is still standing on the road to Friendsville.

---

[3] The Legislature passed the act in 1803, which declared Little River open to navigation from its mouth to Bradley's Mill in Tuckaleechee. Nothing else is known about this mill. (John Bradley was major in the Blount County Militia and lived in Tuckaleechee). An interesting feature about Kennedy's Mill is that he discovered and used a natural tunnel through the rocks for a millrace, which is still in use.

[4] *Deeds*, F F, 196.

In 1815 Samuel Henry installed French burrs in a new brick building on Baker's Creek. Afterwards this mill was called the Brick Mill and was later operated by J. M. Rorex, John R. Henry and George Montgomery. The mill ceased operation in the late 1940's. The Henry descendants also operated a small mill on the main stream of Baker's Creek. In 1817 Josiah Johnston built a mill on Cloyd's Creek. The same year Jehu Stephens was authorized to build a mill on Little River (now Rockford) provided that he leave a lock or passage for boats on the river. (Later a petition represented that he had not complied with the specifications.) The Friendsville Mill was begun by John Hackney in 1819.[5]

In 1828 James Kirby and William McNabb were authorized to build a mill dam on Little River. This mill was later called Donaldson's Mill and McNabb's Mill, and was located a little below Rockford.[6]

The 1834 *Gazeteer* listed three grist mills in Maryville, two mills at Louisville and one at Morganton. We are reasonably sure that Kennedy's Mill and Stephen's mills on Little River; Martin's Mill on Nail's Creek; Best's Mill at Wellsville, the Brick Mill, Bowerman's Mill, Hess's Mill in Miller's Cove, Hughes' Mill in Tuckaleechee and many others were in operation at this time. Birdwell's Mill at the Big Springs on Highway 411 at Spring View grocery was in operation in 1831.[7]

In 1842 Samuel Henry of Little River was allowed by the Legislature to build a dam across Little River. This place was near the present site or Peery's Mill.[8]

In 1842 Isaac White built a mill on Crooked Creek on land bought from George Snider, which is on the road from Maryville to Law's Chapel and Rocky Branch. The mill is still in operation and the road, since the building of the mill has been called the White's Mill Road.

Sometime in the 1840's Michael Best built a mill on the waters of Nine Mile Creek on the lower road to Montvale. The road leading from Maryville to the mill is still called the Best Mill Road. This mill was later operated by Elijah Brown, James Murphy, and Zephaniah Cotant. The Best Mill Road passes by the Anderson Mill, which is between the McCammon dairy farm and the Marley Francis farm. William H. Anderson built the mill and it was operated after him by his son Isaac and a grandson, Thurston Anderson.

In 1849 David McKamey who lived at the spring which is now at the intersection of highways 411 and 129, built a mill. He built it a quarter of a mile from the house where he also had a distillery. This was near the Clover Hill Post Office which had been established in 1823. McKamey was in the Legislature during the next few years and he sold

---

[5] *Acts, 1817*, ch. 147.
[6] *P A, 1828*, ch. 209.
[7] Eastin Morris, *Tennessee Gazeteer*, (Nashville, 1834), Passim.
[8] *Acts, 1842*, ch. 87 (This Samuel Henry was the son of James Henry, Sr., and a nephew of the Samuel Henry, Sr., who had a permit to build a mill on Baker's Creek in 1796 and again in 1815).

the mill to J. L. Hackney. The mill seems to have been held in partnership by J. N. Badgett and John Gardner during the Civil War and later Alexander Kennedy bought it. The mill has been in continuous operation from 1849 to the present. Gilbert Blankenship, the Russells and Perkinses have been operators since 1875.

In 1838 a River Commission was appointed composed of Alexander Kennedy, John Henry, Alexander McNutt and Jehu Stephens. They were allowed $2,000 to improve navigation on Little River. The plans, according to a contract let to B. L. Badgett, James Porter, and Thomas McCullock, called for wing dams to be erected on all gravel bars or bottoms. Burrel Badgett, Samuel Pickens, John S. McNutt, James L. Porter and Thomas McCullock all rendered various bills for building wing dams and removing obstructions.

This project was very important to Alexander Kennedy who operated the mill at "Horseshoe Bend" on Little River (Cave Roller Mill). He manufactured gunpowder and sent it to Jackson at New Orleans in 1814. He not only operated a flour mill and sawmill, but built flatboats 60 to 80 feet long on the sand bar above the mill and loaded them with his own and other people's produce (especially lumber from his own and Martin's Mill on Nail's Creek) and floated them downstream to the market. The Kennedy correspondence contains information about the market from Brown's Ferry, Ditto's Landing, Gunter's Landing and other points. Arthur Kennedy and Isaac Thompson handled the downstream business in the 1840's.

In one letter in 1846 Arthur Kennedy asked for more lumber and reported poplar weatherboarding at a premium. Corn was 40 cents per bushel and meal 50 cents, flour $4.50 to $5.00 per barrel; "cornmeal, bacon, flour, plank and thread will sell best." Whisky was not so popular that season. Flatboats sold for $2 per foot. "Lighters" or small boats sold for $1 per foot. After the Civil War Arthur Kennedy located on a plantation near Montgomery, Alabama and wrote about the market for mules which they drove down from Tennessee and sold to plantation owners.[9]

Cades Cove probably had several small "tub mills" during the early years. Dr. Job said that a flour mill was built soon after 1824, but in 1850 the references all mentioned Foute's Mill and Emert's Mill, and 1883 references named Fred Shields' Mill. The 1887 *Gazeteer* listed William Shields' grist mill and John P. Cable's flour mill. The Cable Mill has been preserved by the Smoky Mountains Park authorities.

In Tuckaleechee, Bradley's Mill was mentioned in 1801. Hughes should have built a mill about that time. In 1850 John Chambers operated a saw and grist mill in the Dry Valley area. Dr. Gillespy owned a saw and grist mill above the "Narrows" below Sunshine. William Myers had a saw and grist mill on Little River above the Cedar Bluff.

[9] *Acts, 1838*, ch. 191, sec. 4; *Acts, 1842*, ch. 4, sec. 12; "River Papers" and correspondence in C. M. Kennedy Papers. (Kennedy headed his letters "Horseshoe Bend." He also did business at Morganton in 1833 according to his account books).

In later years Yearout and still later Willis Lequire had a flour mill and cotton gin on Short Creek. Fayette Wear had a grist and sawmill at the site of the present power dam above Townsend and Lawson Brothers had a roller mill at Townsend. Giles Dunn built a small grist mill about 1870 near Wear's Cove and John Burns built a more elaborate grist mill at the same site in 1910 which operated about thirty years.

In Miller's Cove the Hess Mill which was built in 1796 in the west end was succeeded by Martin's Mill which continued operations until recent years. An early deed referred to the Blair Mill tract in Miller's Cove. John Waters operated a saw and grist mill on Reed's Creek from about 1815 and was succeeded by his sons, Adam and Enoch. Steve Huskey was the last operator at this site.

At the mouth of Abram's Creek Joshua Parsons operated a grist mill in the 1840's and later (near the turn of the century) Dave Smith was operating the mill.

The Samuel Henry Mill on Little River was succeeded by Scales Amerine, who sold to Bud Hitch about 1906. It was later Hitch and Peery, Peery Brothers, and Little River Mills.

The Trigonia Mill was built about 1850 by George, Ike and Jim Swaney. After 65 years of operation, the mill was sold to John Cook in 1915. Brown operated the mill from 1930 to 1951. White owned the mill when it burned in 1954.

Silas Pearson's saw and grist mill was also operated between Howard's and Trigonia Mills before 1900. It was operated mostly for sawing lumber for Pearson's own use in his contracting business. It was later known as Shadden's Mill.

The 1860 census is the first census which has information about mills. Fourteen mills which employed 19 hands, were in operation at that date. The total value of goods produced by mills was $223,000, and the total value of all industries in the county was $300,000. Hence, mills represented two-thirds of the total cash income to the county.[10]

In 1870 the census reported 10 flour mills employing 19 hands, and Killebrew listed 16 grist mills in Blount County in 1874. The 1880 census listed 12 flour and grist mills employing 17 men. Three of these mills were in Maryville. Others were: Mahoney's Mill at Miser's Station, Heiskell's Mill at Morganton, Clover Hill Mills, Trigonia Mills, Kennedy's, McNabb's and Sanderson's. Boyd and Coulter were operating along Little River and Nail's Creek. Two grist and sawmills were operating on Ellejoy.[11]

An 1887 *Gazeteer* listed: J. M. Rorex at the Brick Mill; Miser and Mahoney at Miser's; Donaldson's Mill and Sam George's Mill at Rock-

---

[10] *Manufactures of the U.S. in 1860*, (Washington, 1865), 560.

[11] *Statistics of Wealth and Industry of the U.S., 9th Census*, (Washington, 1872) Vol. 3, p. 732; *Report of the Manufactures of the U.S. at 10th Census* (1880), Vol. 2, p. 355; *Gazeteer*, 1881 (K & C Railroad); *Tennessee State Directory*, (Nashville, 1887), Passim.

ford; J. Hines on Nails Creek; Sam Griffitts at Mint; three flour mills in Maryville—Rhea's, Pedigo's, and Hackney's; John P. Cable's flour mill and William Shields' grist mill in Cades Cove; Martin and West at Clover Hill; C. A. Hafley on Ellejoy; Jones-Beals and Co. at Friendsville; Zephaniah Cotant at Huffstetler's Store; Weaver-Mitchell and Co. at Louisville and the Trigonia Mills operated by Swaney Brothers.

The mill at Springfield was built and operated by A. C. Montgomery before the Civil War. In the 1880's it was renovated and operated by Hackney. The foundation is still standing.

In 1893 Dr. A. B. Reagan built a grist and sawmill on Nine Mile Creek between Mint and Wellsville which was operated by his son P. C. Reagan. From 1924 to 1934 the mill was operated by William Willocks. From 1934 until it was discontinued in 1941 the mill was operated by Charles Chambers.

In 1900 the Harris Mill, formerly Kennedy or Cave Roller Mill, machinery and all, along with 500 bushels of wheat was washed away in a flood. This was the second time that this mill had been washed away, Kennedy's Mill having been washed away in 1875. The mill was operated by Jack Rorex after it was rebuilt. James R. Harris owned the property from 1912 to 1935 when he sold it to E. A. Walker. The present owner is Floyd West.[12]

Many small mills were operated about which information is lacking such as: J. Gray Smith's near Montvale, later operated by Heaton. Daniel Rasor's and Isaac Taylor's were also in the Montvale to Alleghany vicinity as well as Blair's and Dover's at a later period.

This is by no means a complete story on mills but is a record of the better known locations.

WOOL CARDING

The census report for 1820 listed one wool-carding machine in operation which employed one man and handled 4,000 pounds of wool per year.

The first definite reference to a wool-carding machine was in a deed by Josiah Danforth to Berry and Foute in 1829. This was at the saw and grist mill in Maryville at the foot of Cusick Street.

The *Gazeteer* of 1834 listed two carding machines in Blount County, one at Maryville and one at Unitia. A trust deed from Samuel Steele to James Houston in 1834 named a wool-carding machine, but did not locate the property. A. C. Montgomery was operating a wool-carding factory at Springfield in 1851. A trust deed from John Gardiner to Thomas Sanderson in 1860 named a wool-carding machine located at the Clover Hill Mill. No information is given about the operation of the machinery. It was moved to Sanderson's Mill (Martin's) on Nail's

---

[12] *Maryville Times*, October 6, 1900; *Deeds*, 67, p. 22; 69, 255; 76, p. 420; 111, p. 238.

Creek, in 1866. Only one machine is listed as operating in 1860. Two men and one woman were employed.[13]

Three carding machines were listed in operation in 1870 and again in 1874, which employed five hands, according to a survey made by Killebrew.

A wool-carding factory located on Pistol Creek near Hannum's on the Louisville Road and one operated by Henry Blevins and H. I. Hodge at Christy Hill (later Isaac Taylor) were in operation in 1880. Hodge was still operating as late as 1894, and the factory as late as 1906.[14]

COTTON GINS

After the law was passed requiring that an inspector be assigned for each cotton gin, most of the owners of cotton gins were appointed to act in that capacity. These cotton gins were usually located in connection with a saw or grist mill since gins were seasonal in operation. The tax on cotton gins was in accordance with an agreement with Eli Whitney and his agent Phineas Miller.

In 1802 Thomas Berry, James Scott, Samuel Houston, William Stanfield, William Lowry, and Patrick Collins were named as inspectors at their own gins.

In 1803 John Regan, Thomas McCullock, John Black, and William L. Taylor were named in addition to the above-named inspectors.

In 1806 John Lowry, James Cunningham, William Griffitts, David Campbell, Robert Gillespie and John Frazier were named as owners of cotton gins.

It seems that the tax was not collected after 1803 as prescribed. In 1807 an act was passed requiring tax collectors to report saw gins from 1804 to 1808 by June 1808.

The following gins were reported in 1808: John Regan and John Lowry reported 40 saws; James T. Steele reported 36 saws; William Griffitts reported 32 saws; and John Carroth reported 25 saws.[15]

The importance of cotton gins declined after this time. The census report of 1820 did not list the number of gins but listed five men employed in the work and 157,000 pounds of cotton handled during the year worth $14,040. In 1820 John Thornbury sold a grist mill and cotton gin on Pistol Creek to Jacob Foute.

In 1834 Samuel Steele mortgaged a 45-saw cotton gin, grist mill and wool-carding machine to James Houston.

---

[13] *Digest of Accounts of Manufacturing* . . . (Washington, D. C., 1825), 25; Eastin Morris, *Gazeteer of Tennessee* (Nashville, 1834), 96, 166; *Deeds,* Passim.; Tennessee State Business Directory, 1857.

[14] J. B. Killebrew, *Resources of Tennessee* (Nashville, 1874), 460; Maryville *Index*, May 5, 1880; *Manufactures of the United States in 1860,* (Washington, D.C., 1865), 560; *The Statistics of Wealth and Industry of the U. S.,* Ninth Census (Washington, D.C., 1872), Vol. 3, p. 732.

[15] *Minutes,* 1802–1808; Passim.; *Acts, 1807,* ch. 15.

In 1834 there were three cotton gins in Blount County located at Louisville, Maryville, and Unitia.[16]

William Myers operated a cotton gin on Little River in Tuckaleechee Cove in 1852 and one Yearout in the lower end of Tuckaleechee Cove until well past the turn of the century. There were several others who operated throughout the county. There was a cotton gin operated at Wellsville probably from its beginning in 1809, until 1953.

There was probably a gin operated at the mill in Friendsville since an early date. The only charter for a gin, on file in Blount County was to the Friendsville Ginning Company in 1925.[17]

In 1857 A. C. Montgomery operated a cotton-picking machine at his mill in Springfield, and no doubt for many years later. John Jackson operated a gin on Reed's Creek in 1887 and which would indicate a span before and after this time.

Six bales of cotton were marketed in Blount County in 1850 and 21 pounds of silk cocoons. Nothing appears in county records to indicate who was employed in silk culture.

A hemp factory for manufacturing rope and bagging was operating at Morganton in 1834. We do not know anything about the culture of hemp, but evidently it was tried as an experiment.

We know of course, that every self-sufficing housewife had her own cotton and flax patch and flock of sheep from which she spun her own thread and wove her own cloth until the advent of machine-made thread and cloth, but no data concerning flax has been found.

COTTON AND WOOLEN MILLS

In 1837 the mill dams of William Oldham's cotton spinning factory in Knox County were destroyed by floods. In 1838 he moved his machinery to the mill site of Jehu and Holston Stephens on Little River (Rockford).[18]

In 1845 the Stephens Brothers and Mr. Oldham sold their mill to Alexander Kennedy. In 1850 a news story told about an excellent cotton factory on Little River owned by Mr. Alex Kennedy which was to manufacture good quality yarn, domestics, and tickings.[19]

In 1852 the Rockford Manufacturing Company was organized and bought a tract of land from David Caldwell on the east bank of Little River. A charter was issued to: John M. Coffin, Alexander Kennedy, James R. Love and Richard I. Wilson to manufacture wool, cotton, silk, and hemp, as well as to build mills for grinding grain. Kennedy transferred the saw and grist mill to the Rockford Manufacturing Company in 1855. An 1857 bill-head featured shirtings and cotton yarn and listed domestic, yarn and calico.[20]

---

[16] Eastin Morris, *Tennessee Gazeteer* (Nashville, 1834), 92-166.
[17] *Charters*, 2, 152.
[18] William, Rule, *History of Knoxville* (Chicago, Ill.), 195; *Deeds*, p. 137.
[19] *Knoxville Register*, June 8, 1850.
[20] *Deeds*, X, 261; Y, 175; *Acts, 1855*, ch. 178; Kennedy Papers (correspondence and bills).

In 1860 only one cotton mill was in operation in Blount County which employed 12 men and 13 women. The value of the manufactured goods was $24,834.[21]

The company was re-chartered after the Civil War to Richard I. Wilson, A. A. Kennedy, and James Rogers and continued business. In 1870 there were 42 employes turning out goods worth $66,985. In 1874 the factory had 1600 spindles and employed 60 persons and was the leading manufactory in the county.[22]

In 1880, eight men and 30 women, and one child were turning out goods worth $31,461. In June, 1885, F. P. Toof came from New York State and bought one-half interest with H. M. Wilson (son of R. I. Wilson) and in 1887 he became the full owner of the business. By 1889 Rockford Mills Co. with 5,000 spindles had become one of the largest cotton factories in the state.[23]

In 1895 McElwee, Magill, Greenlee, Magill and Matthews were issued a charter under the same name. Gettys and McKeldin were the men in charge of operations. In 1899 the name was changed to McElwee Company, with F. Bond, H. M. McElwee, James A. Goddard, Charles Chandler and J. L. Clarke as a corporation. The name was changed in 1901 to Rockford Cotton Mills when John and Fritz Staub, Joe Burger, Max Lobenstein and Ernest Koella took over the company. The mill burned in 1909.

In 1910 the Rockford Manufacturing Company was chartered to Major Ben Cunningham, J. L. Clarke, Joe Burger, Ernest Koella and J. A. Cox. The business has been operated by Koella and sons since the early 1930's and is the most important and oldest locally owned and operated business in the county.[24]

The same news item that spoke of the fine new factory on Little River spoke of another extensive factory which was in process of erection on Abram's Creek under the direction of a company of Englishmen. A charter had been issued in 1848 to the Chilhowee Spinning and Manufacturing Company at Chilhowee Old Town. The proprietors were William and Robert James.[25]

The mill was evidently in operation by 1853. An advertisement stated that Robert James had the greatest part of the machinery in successful operation of the Abram's Creek, Chilhowee Cotton and Woolen Spinning and Weaving Manufactory. James proposed to supply any quantity of thread or goods of an equal if not better quality than any other establishment. The business closed before the Civil War and was never re-opened.[26]

[21] *Manufactures of the U.S. in 1860* (Washington, D.C., 1865), 560.
[22] *Statistics of Wealth and Industry of the U.S.* (Washington, D.C., 1872), 732; *Acts, 1866*, ch. 68, sec. 71; J. B. Killebrew, *Resources of Tennessee* (Nashville, 1874), 460.
[23] *Reports of Manufactures* ... 10th census (1880) vol. 2, 355.
[24] *Deeds*, 48, p. 358; The mill and properties were purchased from the Bank of Maryville in 1895 by the corporation; *Charters* I, 126, 159, 188, 355, 381, 11, 33, 223.
[25] *Acts, 1848*, ch. 68, *Knoxville Register*, June 8, 1850.
[26] *Knoxville Register*, June 22, 1853.

WOOLEN MILLS

In 1873 Dr. A. J. Stone, formerly of Massachusetts who lived at what was later Wildwood Springs built a woolen factory in Maryville. The machinery may have been the same that John Gardner mortgaged to Thomas Sanderson in 1860 because of a debt to Joseph Hodgson (Hodgson was an Englishman as were also Sanderson, J. Gray Smith and the James family at Chilhowee).[27]

In 1874 J. T. Hanna took over the property in partnership with W. M. Watkins. In 1876 and 1877, W. T. Parham bought out all interests and became sole proprietor of the Maryville Woolen Mills. About 15,000 yards of cloth were manufactured and twelve persons were employed about 8 months of the year. There were 3 looms, one set of 40" cards and 260 spindles.[28]

J. T. Hanna and I. J. Thorne established the Anchor Woolen Mills in 1880 which were later operated by J. T. and R. H. Hanna. This mill was famous for the excellent quality of its woolens.

In 1888 the total of the two woolen mills was 44 looms, 908 spindles and 60 employes. They used 150,000 pounds of wool yearly.[29]

The Maryville Woolen Mills continued operations until 1901 when the machinery was moved to Knoxville and became the Jefferson Woolen Mills. The Anchor Woolen Mills continued until soon after 1906 when operations were discontinued.

Soon after the Maryville Woolen Mills closed, Robert B. Oliver, who had just finished building the L. & N. Railroad across Blount County formed a partnership with C. S. Groves, N. B. Morrel and Joe Burger and the Maryville Hosiery Mill was chartered, in 1910 and set up operations in the old woolen mill building. This plant was described as one of the best in the South, and employed 75 to 100 men. The building was destroyed by fire and was rebuilt.

In 1912 the Madison Hosiery Mill was bought and removed to Maryville. The new unit made it possible to employ 150 more men.[30]

In 1922 the company was organized again and a new charter was issued to the Ideal Hosiery Mills and was further amended in 1929. In 1934 the business was closed due to labor troubles and the machinery was moved to Knoxville.

THE PRESS

The *Maryville Religious and Literary Intelligencer* was edited by Darius Hoyt. In 1834 the name was changed to the *Millennial Trumpeter* with Mr. Hoyt still acting as editor.

This publication was identified in the *Millennial Harbinger* as a pub-

---

[27] J. B. Killebrew, *Resources of Tennessee* (Nashville, 1874), 460; *Goodspeed*, 1095.
[28] *Maryville Index*, March 5, 1880.
[29] *Goodspeed*, 1095.
[30] *Charters*, I, 359; *Charters*, II, 105, 244; *Maryville Times*, April 9, 1912.

lication with 400 to 500 subscribers which was "a constant loss to the publisher."[31]

From 1833 to 1837 Dr. William Spillman published the *Thomsonian Defender*, which defended the system of medicine advocated by one Samuel Thomson.

F. A. Parham was operating a printing press in 1836 and printed a music book for William Caldwell (Sr.). It would appear from various mortgages that F. A. Parham was operating the press and that Hoyt was editing the newspaper. On May 10, 1837, the Rev. Hoyt began the publication of the *Temperance Banner*, a monthly magazine devoted to the Prohibition cause. (Subscription rates were fifty cents per year.) Parham moved his press to Chattanooga late in 1837.[32]

The *American Journal of Productive Industry*, a bi-monthly, was published by Montgomery McTeer in 1838. It was devoted to domestic economy and agricultural arts.[33]

In 1840 Eliza C. Bunker sold to Hyram Barry a Super-Royal printing press with all its fixtures which had belonged to Montgomery McTeer.[34]

Nothing seems to have been published locally during the 1840's. The *Blount County Advocate* was founded in 1853 by W. P. Collins. He mortgaged this press late in 1853.

The *East Tennessean* was edited by James Z. Swann and printed by Collins from January 18 until November 18, 1856. This newspaper was published upstairs over Crawford and Caldwell Hardware. James Z. Swann later signed an agreement with B. C. Edwards which involved the press and the subscription list of *The East Tennessean*.[35]

There were no more press activities until after the Civil War. W. B. Scott & Son, had printed the *Colored Tennessean* in Nashville, August 12, 1865. This was the first newspaper published in Tennessee by a Negro. The Scotts were free Negroes who had settled in Blount County in 1847. William B. Scott, Jr., had worked in a printing office in Knoxville for two years prior to the launching of the *Colored Tennessean* in Nashville. After a year, the Scotts moved their press to Maryville, where they had formerly resided.[36]

The *Maryville Republican* was published in 1867 with R. C. Tucker as editor, and Scott as publisher. When Tucker died in 1869, M. L. McConnell became editor and continued until his appointment as Attorney-General in 1878. McConnell had started the publication of the

---

[31] The Dr. Thomas property was sold to R. L. Cates after being advertised in the *Intelligencer* in 1832. William C. Brownlow, *Helps to the Study of Presbyterianism*, 145; *Millennial Harbinger*, vol. 6, p. 133.

[32] *Knoxville Register*, May 31, 1837; Parham Papers; (Hoyt died August 8, 1837.)

[33] Dr. John A. Goddard, *History of Maryville*, in the Maryville *Times*, April 9, 1902.

[34] *Deeds*, Q, 95.

[35] *Goodspeed*, 830; *Deeds*, Z, 178; Miss Sophia Duncan has several copies of The East Tennessean.

[36] Charles W. Cansler, *Three Generations* (1939), 34.

Soldier's Gazette in 1869, and discontinued it after a few months to take over the *Republican*.

Soon after Yardly Warner came to Maryville, to superintend the building of Freedman's Institute, there appeared a new publication, *The Maryville Monitor*. Warner was editor and W. B. Scott, Sr., the publisher. Three issues (1872–73) have been brought to light through the efforts of S. Allen Warner, of Didcot, England, (Warner's son). The avowed purpose of the publication was: "In the interest of the freed man's education and religion." One of the numbers brings out the fact that Scott's office and fixtures had recently been burned.[37]

The *Blount County Standard* was established in December, 1877, by an attorney, George Woodward. Only a few issues were published.

The *Independent* was edited and published by the Rev. George Coleman who had purchased in 1876 the *Daily News* from Charles F. Brause of Kingston and moved the press to Maryville. His print shop was upstairs in the old hotel, which was later known as Sam Houston Inn.[38]

The *Indicator* was also published by W. Y. C. Hannum for a few months about this time.

The *Maryville Index*, edited by J. A. Silsby, succeeded *The Republican* and *The Standard*. The first number of the *Index* was published March 2, 1878, and continued until 1882. Silsby also edited, in collaboration with William A. Cate, the *Tennessee Normal Teacher*, a monthly.

The *Blount County Democrat*, a small 5¼ x 7½ newspaper, was first published May 10, 1878. It was printed on Wednesdays and Saturdays by Preston B. Love, and had several editors. It was eventually owned by Gen. R. N. Hood. W. B. Scott, Sr., was said to have written many of the editorials of these various newspapers as well as being the publisher.

The *Maryville Watchman* was edited by Will A. McTeer in 1882 and published by J. W. Culton Company. The *East Tennessee News* was published about the same time by John T. Anderson. In 1885 *Today's News* was published by the News Publishing Company.[39]

In 1884 *The Maryville Times* was established by A. J. Neff and son George. It was taken over by Leonard Goddard about 1890 and continued by his father Andrew Goddard and brother Clyde when Leonard enlisted to serve in the Spanish-American War. Clyde B. Emert became the owner and editor of *The Times* in 1915. At that time the circulation was 1,000. In 1921 *The Times* became a semi-weekly and had a circulation of 4,500. In 1944 the name was changed to *The Maryville and Alcoa Daily Times* and was changed to a daily newspaper. By

---

[37] Photostats of the originals are in the A. K. Harper Memorial Library at Maryville, Tennessee. One number has a map showing the location of Negro schools in East Tennessee, etc. Another gives a detailed account of progress in building of Freedman's Institute; (William P. Hastings was Assistant Editor).

[38] *Goodspeed*, 831; Emma Middleton Wells, *History of Roane County* (Chattanooga, 1927).

[39] *Tennessee State Gazeteer and Business Directory* (Nashville, 1887).

1955 the circulation had grown to 8,500.⁴⁰ In November 1955, Tutt S. Bradford of Bristol became owner and publisher of the *Times*.

The *Alliance Advocate*, a weekly, was published at Louisville from 1890 to 1892, by the Advocate Publishing Company.⁴¹

The *Maryville Record* was begun February 18, 1904 with William Koehler, of Indiana, as editor and publisher. The *Record* was described by a Memphis paper as a "dyed-in-the-wool Republican" paper. The *Record* continued until 1906.

Mr. Parham said that *The Maryville Enterprise* was established by George C. Jackson in 1905, but the only file of early papers begins October 11, 1906 with C. B. Lawrence as editor through May 1908. John A. Everett was editor from August 13, 1908 until September 1, 1911. W. D. Williams was owner for a few months and sold the paper to James B. Hedge, Jr. in 1912. Mr. Hedge was owner and proprietor until his death in the early 1940's. His son James R. Hedge continued the business until his death in 1953, and is now continued by his widow, Kathryn Rees Hedge.

LUMBER

One of the major sources of income to the county has been the lumber industry. It would be impossible to enumerate all the small businesses which have existed, so only those of economic importance and of early record will be mentioned.

Alexander Kennedy received the first permit to operate a sawmill in Blount County in 1796. His mill at the Horseshoe Bend of Little River is still an institution as a flour and grist mill. He sawed and shipped large quantities of lumber downstream to the market from this place. James McNutt received the second county permit to operate on Pistol Creek at a location identified as approximately the same as that occupied later by Babcock Lumber Company, Bond-Woolf, and Veach-May-Wilson. The third permit was to Samuel Shaw to operate at the mouth of Cloyd's Creek, or Unitia.

These mills became more important as the demand for lumber and cabinet work grew with the communities. Warner Martin's Mill on Nail's Creek, later operated by Brown, Sanderson, Beeson, Wells and others, became one of the industrial centers of the county, along with the three named. Reference is found before 1800 to Ambrose Legg's sawmill but its location is not known. Practically every well-located grist mill in the county became a sawmill, a cotton gin and a distillery. In 1834 there were three sawmills at Louisville and one at Morganton.

The first definite information about the lumber industry is compiled from the 1860 census report. There were six establishments in Blount

---

⁴⁰ Information from Clyde B. Emert, Publisher. L. S. Goddard remained in the Philippines at the end of the Spanish-American War, and was appointed Associate Justice of the Supreme Court of the Philippines January 23, 1934.

⁴¹ *East Tennessee History and Biography* (Chattanooga, 1893).

County at that time. They employed eight men and turned out about $18,000 worth of products. In 1880 the number of establishments was unchanged, but the number of men employed had increased to 19 and the income to $24,000.[42]

One of the establishments in 1880 was Mount and Hooper who had the courthouse contract and set up a planing mill in the old carding mill on the Louisville Pike. McCoy and Chapman had a sawmill at their flour mill in Springfield.

The steam sawmill of Curtis and Snyder at Miser's Station was sold to Andrew Purdy and Samuel Cozart in 1880. Mr. Snyder went to work at Gaddis's Mill at Rockford. The Hackney Mill at Friendsville was probably in operation as well as the Kennedy Mill on Little River.[43]

David Jones, contractor, began operating a steam sawmill about 1885 along with his brickyard.

The McDonalds from Pennsylvania came into Blount County in the late eighties and operated about twenty years. They practically denuded the accessible forests of Blount County of choice poplar timber, which was shipped to a Northern market.

In the 1890's the Englishes and their associates operated a mill below Rockford to which logs were "splashed" down Little River from the virgin forests on the headwaters of the river. "Lumber-jacks" from Pennsylvania and North Carolina carried on this operation. Firms such as Tuckaleechee Timber and Boom Company, Chilhowee Lumber Company, and Tennessee Manufacturing Company, also Tennessee Lumber Canal Company, among others were chartered to operate in Blount County.[44]

Of the companies mentioned above, the Tennessee Lumber Canal Company merged into Little River Railroad and Lumber companies. These were chartered in 1901 to operate. Little River Lumber Company was the result of an investigation of lumber resources in 1900 of W. B. Townsend, William McCormick, William Wrigley, Joe Dickey, and Asbury Lee. This company acquired approximately 100,000 acres of land on the waters of Little River which enabled the company to operate on a large scale for forty years.

The first Little River Lumber Company mill went into operation in 1901 and burned in 1905 and was immediately rebuilt. Fifty-seven varieties of hardwood were marketed by Little River in the early years of operation. Little River Railroad built extensions onto Eldorado Creek and Laurel Creek into the Cades Cove Section as well as up the

---

[42] *Manufactures of the U. S. in 1860* (Washington, D. C., 1865), 560; *Report of Manufactures* . . . Tenth Census, Vol. 2 (Washington, 1880), 355; Killebrew listed 20 sawmills in operation in 1874, operated by water power and three by steam.

[43] *Maryville Index*, March 5, 1880.

[44] Maryville *Times*, July 9, 1886; April 18, 1897. The sawmill at Rockford had handled 2,000 logs that spring. This was a contract between Yellow Poplar Lumber Company and Alex Watts. Forty million feet were cut in Blount and Sevier County. Twenty men were employed at the Rockford Mill and 60 men at logging. The flood of 1900 broke through the boom at Rockford and hundreds of logs were lost.

middle prong into Walker's Valley (Tremont) and the east prong above Elkmont. The railroad was finished into Elkmont in 1908.

The mill town had been named Townsend in 1902 in honor of W. B. Townsend, the managing-president of the corporation. The mill burned a second time in 1916 and was again rebuilt.

By the late 1920's the resources had been heavily depleted and with the initiation of the Smoky Mountains National Park movement, 77,000 acres were offered to the government by the Little River Lumber Company. The park became a reality in the early 1930's. A Civilian Conservation Corps camp was set up at Walker's Valley on the middle prong of Little River which operated about 8 years. Camp Margaret Townsend for Girl Scouts is still maintained on the middle prong of Little River.

The mill at Townsend officially closed in 1938 and all signs of the plant have been removed.

Vestal Lumber Company has held extensive acreages and leases since 1901 when they were issued a charter to operate in Blount County but have never set up operations in the county. McCoy and Vandevoort have also held some acreage of timber. F. McDonald of Loudon leased the Hamilton Slate tract for lumbering purposes and utilized the Little Tennessee River for transportation after 1900.

Among miscellaneous lumbering projects was Hanlon and Company's Spoke and Stave Company which operated at Carpenter's Campground in 1903. After a few years the supply of good white oak was exhausted as well as the company's funds. Hardwood Lumber Company operated between the Little Mountain and the Big Mountain near Alleghany about 1910, for about ten years.

The only other large scale lumber operations in Blount County was by Babcock Lumber Company. In 1916 they purchased 35 acres near Vose Station in North Maryville and built a modern sawmill, planing mill, dry kilns, etc., and 200 modern dwelling houses.

The logs to support this operation came from the Jeffrey's Hell and Citico Creek sections of Monroe County by way of the Tennessee Carolina Southern Railroad. This operation was completed in 1934 and the plant was sold to Bond-Woolf Company. Later the plant was taken over by Veach-May-Wilson who continue to process lumber.

CABINET-MAKING

There were numerous early cabinet-makers in the county, but the only clue to their identity is contained in mortgages which mention their tools. In 1833 there were four cabinet-makers listed in Maryville and one in Morganton. Abram Hartsell was a cabinet-maker at Louisville, in 1854. Henry J. Tilson mortgaged a lot of mahogany and cabinet-tools in 1841. Montgomery McTeer, and Dr. William Spillman also had tools in their possession.[45]

---

[45] Eastin Morris, *Tennessee Gazeteer* (Nashville, 1834).

Two or three generations of the Dupes men engaged in cabinet work on Nail's Creek and the Wildwood section. Henry Dupes and his son George are especially remembered.

C. E. Aaron and son operated a sawmill and cabinet shop on the Montvale Road at the intersection of Mountain View Avenue. They manufactured furniture, some fine specimens of which are much prized by local owners. Simeon Mook worked with them and was famous as a coffin-maker. He later worked for Mr. Pflanze. The Aaron mill was taken over by William Goddard and operated by B. F. Willard and was one of the finest circular saw and planing sawmills in the county in 1880.

Charles Pflanze started a cabinet-working shop in 1870 and kept a good stock of furniture of all sorts in his shop. He was classed as an undertaker at this date and is the first man in Blount County to advertise himself as such. George Allen Brown entered the furniture and undertaking business soon after this. The Pflanze furniture shop gradually evolved into the manufacture of dining tables which were shipped to market in the North, South and Middle-west.[46]

In 1916, on the death of Charles Pflanze, Sr., the firm was consolidated with Bogle & Frye. Pflanze had already begun to sell lumber under the name of Cherokee Lumber Company in 1912. Bungalow Town was developed from the Pflanze estate.[47]

Southern Coffin and Casket Company was established in 1898 in Knoxville, Tennessee. In 1904 the plant was moved to Maryville. At that time the shop employed 40–50 men and was turning out 300 to 400 coffins per week, and were shipping to a large area. I. B. Zeigler was president, J. H. Staley, general-manager, and Clay Cunningham was secretary-treasurer. The business still continues to operate.

The Dixie Mantle and Manufacturing Company was another woodworking establishment chartered in 1907. This business was located on Short Street and was operated by Richey and Benedict four or five years.[48]

There have been many other small businesses in lumber and woodworking lines and many such firms are now in operation.

THE ALUMINUM COMPANY

In 1910, the first of a series of seven power dams on the Little Tennessee and its tributaries was begun at Tapoco on the Cheoah River. This project extended, over a period of thirty-some years and includes Calderwood (Cheoah, Santeetlah, Nantahala, and Glenville. All of these are in North Carolina except Calderwood. The Fontana Dam, built by TVA, was originally part of the Aluminum Company Development plan.[49]

---

[46] *Maryville Index*, March 5, 1880. (The swastika was the Pflanze trademark).
[47] *Maryville Record*, August 19, 1904.
[48] *Charters*, I, 303.
[49] Maryville City Directory, 1923, p. 63.

The Pittsburgh Reduction Company was organized in 1888 and the name was changed to Aluminum Company of America in 1907. The Tennessee Legislature in 1905 (ch. 394) had granted Knoxville Power Company the right to build a dam across the Little Tennessee River above Tallassee Ford. In July 1910, ALCOA bought the stock of Knoxville Power Company. Cheoah Dam was finished in 1919, Santeetlah in 1928, and Calderwood in 1930.

The purchase of the farmlands north of Maryville for the location of plants and housing was begun in 1913. The first reduction units, or the South Plant, were started in 1914 and the construction of the first 150 houses was begun in 1916. This area was known as North Maryville until 1919 when it was incorporated as Alcoa.

In 1917, the Carbon Plant was built and in 1919 the first power was received from the company's own power development at Tapoco. In the same year the construction of the "Sheet Mill" or West Fabricating Plant was begun and the first sheet was rolled August, 1920. In this same year the brick plant was built with a Dresler gas-fired kiln.

In 1929 the Aluminum Powder Plant was built for the manufacture of aluminum bronze for paint.[50]

The construction of the North Fabricating Plant was begun in 1939 and began operations in 1942. The North Plant is said to be the largest factory under one roof in the world, and covers 54 acres.

The social and economic influence of the Aluminum Company and its power holdings on Blount County and the surrounding counties is far-reaching and cannot be over-estimated.

The building of another power dam on the Little Tennessee at Chilhowee, which was initiated in 1955, is a progressive step in the development of the original plan. The average number of employes is in excess of 7,000.

FERRIES

Fords or ferries were the only means of crossing streams in the early days and since Blount County was bounded on the north, west and south by streams, ferries were important. The first permit issued in 1796 by the Blount County Court was to John Trimble. Trimble's Ferry was just above the forks of Holston and Little Tennessee and was No. 11 on the Holston River and in later years was known as Bussel's Ferry. This ferry was on the main road to Southwest Point or Kingston, and Nashville.

The second permit was issued in 1796 to William Stockton and its location is not fixed but was along the upper section of the river. The third permit was issued in 1797 to Major George Farragut to keep a ferry at Stony Point. This ferry is known as (Abraham) Lowe's Ferry and is No. 5 on the river.

[50] *Maryville Enterprise*, February, 1930.

Samuel Shaw's ferry was established about 1800 at the mouth of Cloyd's Creek and Unitia. Some years later the ferry was operated by Leeper. This ferry was No. 10 on the river.

No. 6 was Townsend's Ferry which was established about 1800. By 1840 it was Prater's Ferry. This ferry was located near Holston College.

Wright's Ferry was operated by Dr. Isaac Wright near the mouth of Little River as early as 1810. This ferry was No. 1 on the river.

No. 2 was John Rankin's Ferry and was established by 1824. This ferry was three miles above Louisville. Later it was known as Henry's Ferry and operated as such for many years. No. 4 was operated just above Lowe's Ferry by Captain Bird for a few years. No. 3, Louisville, was in operation by 1838 by Samuel Saffell. The Saffells sold the ferry to Wisecarver, and Wisecarver sold his ferry rights to TVA.[51]

Russell's Ferry was a private ferry and was No. 7 on the river just below Prater's Ferry. Park's Ferry was No. 9 and was just above Leeper's Ferry. It was in use by 1840.

Trimble's Ferry was the only one of these ferries which was on a main or important road, being located on the road from Maryville to Nashville.

On the Little Tennessee River, Calloway's Turnpike crossed at Tallassee Ford, now Calderwood. Dave Smith operated a ferry just above the mouth of Abram's Creek in the 1880's and nineties. Pleas Henry operated a ferry above the mouth of Citico Creek about the same time.

John B. McGhee was issued a permit in 1876 to operate the ferry later known as "Sunline" below Citico Creek which operated until a few years ago.

Henley's or Bacon's Ferry is near the village of Chota just below the mouth of Four Mile Creek and is still in operation. Russell's Ferry was just below this ferry on the Bacon Farm and was on the road connecting Maryville by way of Thompson Bridge with the Unicoi Turnpike. This ferry was first operated about 1817.

Just below the mouth of Nine Mile Creek was (Barclay) McGhee's Ferry which was operated by William Blair, and later William Lowry, McGhee's son-in-law, from 1819–1840. Later it became known as Nile's Ferry, named after J. W. J. Niles who had married one of John McGhee's daughters.

Kelso's Ferry was at the mouth of Baker's Creek and was established by 1800. In 1813 Morganton was established and the ferry was generally referred to as Morganton but the ferry was operated by Tipton after Kelso.[52]

Below Morganton was the Hughes, the Davis and Wyley, or Coyatee, ferries. Only the Morganton and Davis Ford ferries have been operated of late years. None are operated now below Bacon's Ferry.

---

[51] It is interesting to note that in 1821, some forty citizens petitioned the Legislature to prohibit the establishment of too many ferries and roads. (*Petitions*, Tennessee State Archives, Nashville, Tenn.).

[52] Permits are found in Blount County Court Minutes; *Parham Papers*.

RAILROADS

Although Blount County was not directly concerned in the outset of the railroad movement, there was intense interest.

The Hiwassee Railroad was the first local attempt to establish direct connection with the Atlantic Seaboard. Muscle Shoals prevented the Tennessee River from being an easy outlet and the Hiwassee Canal plan to connect the Hiwassee and Coosa rivers to form a short-cut to Mobile had failed. The next step was to plan to build a railroad to connect the Hiwassee and Coosa rivers.

By 1831 East Tennessee had gone beyond this idea to the direct line idea. The Knoxville and Southern Railroad was chartered in 1831 to operate from some point of navigation on the Tennessee River to the southern boundary of the state where connections could be made with one of the Georgia or Carolina railroads. Various plans were in progress for railroads over the mountains by the French Broad route, south from Cincinnati, and down the valley from Virginia. However the Hiwassee Railroad was the first to which Blount County subscribed.[53]

Dr. J. H. Gillespy, Wm. A. Spencer, Wm. Wallace and John Sample served as commissioners for the Hiwassee Railroad from Blount County. Although the Hiwassee Railroad actually was the first to break ground in Tennessee, the work was entirely suspended in 1839 and was not reorganized until 1848. The failure of this company was caused by the panic of 1837; too liberal state aid; inefficiency of methods; purchase of materials at high prices; and poor management.

The Hiwassee Company was reorganized under the name of the East Tennessee and Georgia Railroad and by August 1852, the road was in operation from Dalton, Georgia, to Blair's Ferry (now Loudon). The project hung here for a while which was what the Loudon people wanted. They thought that they could draw Knoxville into its suburbs by withholding the railroad.

The Junction Railroad was incorporated in 1852 to build a road from Loudon to Knoxville if the directors of the East Tennessee and Georgia refused to extend their line. Jabez Coulson, H. T. Cox, James Donaldson, John E. Toole and William Wallace were commissioners for this railroad. This company did not have to function because the East Tennessee and Georgia Railroad pushed on to Knoxville. Under the presidency of Campbell Wallace the first train steamed into Knoxville on the East Tennessee and Georgia Railroad July 4, 1855.[54]

This gave direct rail connections by way of Atlanta to Charleston, South Carolina; Savannah, Georgia; and Montgomery, Alabama. Chattanooga and Nashville were connected by rail, but in order to reach Chattanooga from Knoxville, one must go to Dalton, Georgia, and return on the Western and Atlantic Railroad to Chattanooga.

---

[53] E. T. H. S. Publications No. 5, p. 81 ff; Blount County Court subscribed 7 shares to the Hiwassee Railroad.

[54] January 1852, the County Court through its chairman, Dr. Sam Pride bought stock in the E. T. and Ga. R. R.

On the same day that the first train came to Knoxville, track-laying was begun on the East Tennessee and Virginia line. John Allison, B. D. Brabson, Dr. J. H. Gillespie, Robert Porter, Dr. Sam Pride, John E. Toole, and William Wallace were Blount County men who were interested in this project. The last spike on the East Tennessee and Virginia was driven by May 14, 1858, which indirectly connected Memphis and New York by rail.

The next movement was the Knoxville and Charleston Railroad, which was organized locally in 1856. This project was very staunchly supported by citizens of Blount County.

The K. & C. stockholders met in Maryville July 18, 1856, and elected directors: William G. Swann, Sam Pride, William Wallace, John E. Toole, Edward George, R. I. Wilson, John J. Craig, and William McTeer. Porter Swann was elected president and John Toole, secretary-treasurer. In 1857, General William Wallace was president and John E. Toole, secretary-treasurer.

The Blount County Court in 1854 had bought 120,000 shares in the K. and C. Railroad, but in 1856 they applied to Chancellor Van Dyke for an injunction to restrain collection of railroad tax for the benefit of the K. and C. This opposition slowed down enthusiasm and a contract was let for only 16 miles instead of the advertised thirty miles.

This project failed due in part to the Panic of 1857 and in part to the failure of other roads with which it was designed to connect.

After the war the project was revived and the K. and C. Railroad was completed into Maryville in 1868 and the name was changed to the Knoxville and Augusta Railroad in 1879.[55]

In 1900 the K. and A. Railroad was extended to Walland where it met the Little River Railroad which was operated from this point to Townsend and from there, up the east prong of Little River to the North Carolina line (Elkmont), and to the North Carolina line up the middle prong and up Laurel Creek to Laurel Gap.[56]

The Knoxville, Montvale and Chilhowee Railroad Company was chartered in 1891, to construct a railroad from K. and A. Railroad in Maryville to near Montvale, then to, or across, the Little Tennessee River near Chilhowee or Abram's Creek and thence to the North Carolina line with the privilege of connecting with the East Tennessee, Virginia and Georgia Railroad.

In 1907 the Tennessee and Carolina Southern Railroad which had been chartered in 1892 and again in 1902 was built south of Maryville to the Little Tennessee River and up the river as far as Chilhowee. When the Aluminum Company of America began their contruction operations at Tapoco and Santeetlah they extended the railroad from Chilhowee to those points for transporting machinery and supplies.[57]

---

[55] *Knoxville Register*, February 2, 1856; March 3, 1856; July 17 and 24, 1856; *Deeds*, H H, 255.

[56] *Charters*, I, 193 (An earlier charter had been issued to Tennessee Lumber Canal Company). The railroad to Walland and Townsend was discontinued in 1937.

[57] *Charters*, I, 15; *Deeds*, SS, 93.

By 1901 the Louisville and Nashville Railroad had finished their road across the southwestern section of the county through Louisville and Friendsville to cross the Little Tennessee River at Niles Ferry.

The Louisville and Nashville Railroad did not touch Maryville but when they re-routed the railroad in 1906 they built a branch line into Maryville.

Several minor railroads were chartered for construction within the bounds of Blount County which did not materialize. One of these was the Maryville and Little Tennessee Railroad in 1887. The Lenoir City, Montvale and Carolina Railroad Company was chartered in 1891 to build a railroad from Lenoir City by way of McGhee Station to Montvale Springs, to Sevierville and to Paint Rock.[58]

In 1901, W. D. Hamilton was granted a right of way by the County Court to build a railroad from the Howard farm (Calderwood) in the 17th district to Maryville or some point in Loudon County.

There was also another interesting project in 1906, which did not materialize; the Knoxville and Maryville Electric Railroad Company from Maryville to Stock Creek (to extend 1½ miles below Maryville on the old Federal Road). This project was revived by charter in 1913 under the title Maryville-Knoxville Interurban Railway Company. The idea died with the advent of World War I and was never revived.[59]

MARBLE

The Marble belt in Blount County is about three miles wide and from the Little Tennessee River near Morganton, extends sixteen miles northeast to Louisville. At least twenty-four quarries have been opened in this area, most of which have been discontinued. The L. & N. Railroad which crosses the belt near Meadow gives good transportation facilities.[60]

The first marble quarry was opened soon after the Civil War by E. H. Copley, who came from New York State. After his death T. Copley continued the operations.

The Juniata Marble Company began operations in 1883. It employed thirty-five men and had machinery for sawing marble into blocks.

In 1886-7, the Evans Marble Company of Baltimore acquired quite a number of twenty-five year leases and was chartered in 1892 and operated for a while thereafter. In 1889, they were operating the Cliff Quarry at Louisville, which was said to contain 20 or 30 varieties of marble.[61]

In 1888, the Great Southern Marble Company of Knoxville acquired a lease in Blount County and in 1895, the Royal Tennessee Marble

---

[58] *Deeds*, M M, 412; *Charters*, I, 5.
[59] *Minutes*, 1901, 1906, Passim.
[60] *Tennessee, Division of Geology*, (Bulletin #28), 63.
[61] A. H. Love, *History of Louisville*, Ch. 5; Maryville *Times*, May 29, 1889.

Company of Baltimore was transacting business. The Tennessee Variegated Marble Company was operating in 1902. The Quaker Marble Company in 1906, and the Tennessee Producer's Marble Company in 1907.[62]

The Gray-Knox Marble Company was founded by J. B. Jones, Sr., in 1917. They have operated two quarries near Friendsville.[63]

The Friendsville Marble Company was chartered in 1949 by Endsley and others.

The John J. Craig Company has been operating since its incorporation in 1896. They are now operating six quarries at four locations. In 1902 they built a tram road connecting the main quarry with the railroad. The original quarry is at Marmor (near Friendsville), where a sawmill was built with eight gang-saws. They sell blocks to Candora Marble Company and rough sawed blocks to trade. The crushing machinery is located at Marmor. The Hamil Quarry at Rega and the Light Pink at Louisville are also well-known quarries.[64]

BUTTONS

A news item in 1880 reported that Mr. A. P. Thompson and others had bought the machinery for a button factory which would begin work in a week or two. This factory was located where the railroad to Walland crossed the creek (on the Sevierville Pike).[65]

In 1882 Representative Will A. McTeer presented his colleagues in Nashville some Tennessee pearl buttons made at the Eagle Button Factory in Maryville. The buttons were made of mussel shells gathered from various rivers. A. P. Thompson was manager of the works which employed eight men. A later account said that about one hundred people were engaged in gathering of the shells and manufacturing the buttons.[66]

J. T. Hanna and others also operated a button factory about the same time near his woolen mill on Pistol Creek. It was called the American Button Factory, and in some deeds is referred to as Bartlett's Button Factory. Hanna's Button factory is listed for taxes as late as 1908.[67]

---

[62] *Leases, Options, and Contracts*, Book 1, Passim.; also *Charters*, Passim.; W. M. Crawford was Vice-President and General Manager of the Quaker Marble Company and prior to this had held the same office in the Olentangy Mining Company of Knoxville and Friendsville (1903). His correspondence over a period of ten years deals with chances of development of manganese deposits in the Friendsville vicinity (Roll Hanna papers).

[63] Hai Chuan Teng, *Marble Deposits and the Marble Industry of Knoxville Area* (Thesis, 1948, University of Tennessee), 89, 101-3.

[64] Letter from John J. Craig Co., February 19, 1954.

[65] *Maryville Index*, March 5, 1880.

[66] *Nashville American*, May 10, 1882; A. J. McWhirter, *Revised Handbook of Tennessee* (Nashville, 1885), 92; A. P. Thompson, locally referred to as "Apple Pie" Thompson, was born in Wisconsin. He tried his hand at a great many businesses in Blount County. After the above-named venture he manufactured insulator pins for telephone lines in Cades Cove.

[67] Information from Mrs. A. J. McKenzie; Hanna Papers.

THE SLATE INDUSTRY

The Abram's Creek Roofing Slate Company was incorporated under the laws of Tennessee, September 29, 1886, by W. A. Haskins, W. B. Lenoir, Robert Pritchard, C. C. Hann, and F. Gibson. The land involved was part of a tract of 5,000 acres granted by the State of Tennessee to James C. Wright and Joseph S. Milligan which had been sold at Madisonville in 1856 by court order to W. D. McGinley and conveyed by him to Pleasant Henry in 1876. Henry sold the property to Ida F. Haskins and W. Morris for conveyance to the Abram's Creek Roofing and Slate Company in 1886.[68]

The stated purpose of the company was to "erect warehouses, storehouses, etc., for mining, quarrying and manufacturing slate." They were to use water power on Panther Creek, and have harbor privileges on the Little Tennessee River. According to the deed, the corporation was unable to carry out its contract and the property was conveyed back to Haskins and Morris in November, 1888.

In 1890, Col. W. D. Hamilton bought a tract from James B. Seaton and James A. Moore of Jefferson County, deducting twenty acres of the Williams, or Deal tract and two acres to David L. Smith (near the mouth of Abram's Creek where he operated a store).[69]

The Tennessee Slate Company was incorporated October 28, 1890, by D. G. Crudup, B. M. Hord, J. H. Warner, John G. Rawlings, and T. H. Snow. (Crudup and Warner seem to have gotten title to the two tracts formerly owned by Haskins and Morris in September 1890 and later transferred the property to the Tennessee Slate Company.)[70]

According to the best information, three slate quarries were opened at various times; purple, green and black. A tram road was built from the quarries down Panther Creek, and Abram's Creek to the Little Tennessee. The slate was stacked like cordwood on the river bank and shipped down the river on barges. It is said that heavily loaded barges occasionally went "wild" and collided with the bluff above Niles Ferry and sunk with their cargo.[71]

In the case of Wilburn Morris vs. The Tennessee Slate Company, Morris purchased all the personal property of the company also known as Abram's Creek slate, marble, iron, and timber property. The Warner interest in the property, transferred to J. H. Warner and Frank Spurlock, was later vested in Porter Warner in a settlement of the Warner estate in Chattanooga.[72]

Southern Slate Company was incorporated December 7, 1893 by: Thomas H. Welch, W. S. Hamilton, Richard J. Edwards, Charles T.

---

[68] Charter information from the office of the Secretary of State, Nashville, Tennessee; *Deeds*, MM, 43; NN, 56; FF, 204.
[69] *Deeds*, 42, p. 512; p. 171, p. 271.
[70] *Ibid.*, 44, p. 118; p. 135.
[71] *Maryville Times*, February 13, 1896.
[72] *Deeds*, 106, p. 278.

Cates, Sr., and Foster Clarke. They installed very expensive and elaborate cutting equipment, but were not successful in business.

In 1932, the Southern Slate Company transferred 2,300 acres and the quarry tools to William E. Hamilton of Franklin County, Ohio.

In 1934, The Knoxville Power Company bought railroad, telephone and power-line right-of-ways over these lands.[73]

In 1931, Stuart Fonde and J. T. Roberts leased the slate quarries, warehouse sites, and the use of the road into the purple slab quarry for a period of fifteen years on a percentage basis. They removed slate for structural and flagstone purposes.[74]

This contract was terminated by the Smoky Mountains National Park taking over all of the tract except 87.5 acres in 1942.[75]

TANYARDS

The earliest reference to tanyards is the location of Daniel Taylor's on lot No. 112 in Maryville in 1797 and the transfer of a tanyard on Holston in 1818 from Wallace to Campbell. George Howard settled on Nine Mile Creek in 1818 and soon had a saw-grist-mill and tanyard. The 1820 census listed 7 tanners in operation in Blount County, employing 15 men. An average of 3,000 hides and skins were processed annually. Humphrey Montgomery located at the head of Cloyd's Creek in 1802 is listed as "breeches and skin dresser." [76]

In 1834 three tanners resided in Maryville and one tanyard was in operation in Unitia. Lots 14 and 15 in Maryville was Wallace's Tanyard in 1834. In 1836 Sam Saffle was getting water for his tanyard at Louisville from John and James Gillespie's mill dam and further reference was made to Robert Gillespie's mill tract and tanyard lot. The Saffle Tanyard and Brickyard was operated until 1854 when it was sold to W. W. Lawrence who continued operations until the Civil War. From 1862 to 1870 Lawrence owned and operated the old Ambrister tanyard at Springfield.[77]

Willis was a later tanner at Springfield. His daughter married William Burton, who learned the tanner's trade and later the shoemaker's trade. He had an unusual mechanical aptitude and began working at Maryville Woolen Mills where he became foreman. He invented and patented several gadgets and when the woolen mill was moved to Knoxville, Burton went with it and became chief machinist.

---

[73] *Ibid.*, 108, p. 82; 106, p. 340; 121, p. 60.
[74] *Leases,* Book 5, p. 417; 438; In 1896, the steamer "E. F. Dawson" was running within two miles of the quarries. At that time five quarries were being operated, employing 30 or 40 men. R. W. Owens was operating one quarry on his 700 acre tract and W. B. Hall was also operating a quarry. Hamilton, Warner and Haskins had 20,000 acres.
[75] *Deeds,* 130, p. 488.
[76] *Deeds,* Passim.
[77] Eastin Morris, *Tennessee Gazeteer* (Nashville, 1834), Passim; Five tanners were operating at Louisville in 1854; William T. Johnson, Wm. W. Lawrence, G.

In 1837, William Gamble sold his half-interest in the land where Andrew Peery had his tanyard on Ellejoy Creek.

In 1839 George S. Gilbert of Louisville mortgaged: six vats of leather (40 sides in each vat), 20 cords of tanbark and all his tanning tools.

In 1843, Sam T. Glass mortgaged: 18 sides of skirt leather, 25 sides of upper leather, and 16 kip skins of upper leather.

John Davis entered into a partnership with William Toole for a tanyard business in Maryville and Louisville in 1849 which was dissolved in 1851. In 1856 Johnson and Swan bought a lot for a tanyard in Louisville. The Toole tanyard in Maryville was near Anderson Lumber Company on McGhee Street.

In 1856, William Ambrister mortgaged a set of tanning tools which he had some years previously gotten from Abraham Davis in payment for a debt. In 1862 John Ambrister willed his tanyard to his son Asa.

In 1860 there were four tanning establishments operating in Blount County employing nine men.[78]

In 1870 five establishments employed nine men and manufactured both tanned and curried leathers.

The tanyard in Maryville, about which most information is available, was operated by Andrew McClain at the corner of Cusick and Church Street extending to the creek. It was operated from 1840 to 1865 by McClain who sold three lots, forty vats with 1,088 pieces of leather, tanbark and tanner's tools to W. T. Parham. Stephen Wells bought the tanyard. About 1872, Loney Wells took over the business. Mr. Sprinkle was the last operator of this business which closed near the turn of the century.

Stephen Wells bought the Best Mill at what was later known as Wellsville in 1876. Soon after this date he was operating a tanyard. His son Anderson Wells lived on Walker Ridge and had a small tanyard near the old school site at Brownlow Tindell's. When he moved a few miles west on Nine Mile Creek, tanning operations were moved to that point.

Barton Warren had charge of a large tanyard on his farm near Louisville from an early date and according to his family always had a large number of apprentices for the tanner's trade working with him. William Warren was operating a saddle shop in Louisville in 1839. The Lawrences learned the trade here and later owned and operated tanyards in Louisville and Maryville.

After the Civil War James Millsaps operated a considerable tanyard at Melrose Springs which was patronized by the "Cove trade."

Robert Bogle at an early date operated a tanyard and mill near the large spring at Spring View. In 1887 Hale and Hollifield were proprietors of the business and Hollifield was a harnessmaker. Leonard Wood had a tanyard on Baker's Creek about mid-century.

W., W. N., and W. T. Price.
[78] *Manufactures of the U. S. in 1860* (Washington, D. C., 1865), 560.

In 1848 Blackburn was in business on Sinking Creek. J. L. Hackney was at Friendsville, Sam McMurray at Chilhowee, Brickell at Miser's Station, and Samuel Koonts on Ellejoy.

Taylor Long built a tanyard at Six Mile which was later sold to Mr. Sprinkle. He had previously been in business at Chilhowee.[79]

In connection with the leather industry, Barclay McGhee, James Turk, Eli Nunn, D. N. Broyles, G. W. Lawson, H. Berry and R. L. Cates were named as saddlers. These saddlers were working in Maryville in 1834. (The fact that Daniel D. Foute sold a town lot for two saddles in 1830 gives some idea of the approximate value.) J. W. Tilton was at Morganton in 1887, having previously worked at Springfield.

W. B. Scott, Sr., Rufus Taylor, A. L. Wells, J. T. Long of Chilhowee, James W. Holt of Ellejoy, J. D. Hollifield of Brick Mill, R. S. and Paul Kitchart are listed as working with harness and leather at various times.

In 1854, W. R. Wilkinson, B. F. Doughty, T. J. Robinson and John Sparger, were saddletree workers in Louisville and John C. Ferguson was a harnessmaker.

In 1843, James Blount mentioned among his assets 70 shoemaker's lasts. After the Civil War the following are referred to as shoemakers: John Goodwin, David Henry (Negro), Kaleel Arbeely, "Cad" Hayes, Matt Barger (Negro), Joseph Aken, Calvin Davis, S. J. Farr, L. C. Kay, A. T. and B. T. Moody, W. H. Dodd, W. A. Steele, L. Clark, John Potter, Sam Malcom, J. L. and W. M. Vineyard and William Morton. Needless to say every small community had its own shoemaker and every man was his own cobbler to a certain degree until midway between the Civil War and the turn of the century, when factory products began to take the place of hand-manufactured goods except for highly specialized work.[80]

In May 1901, Schlosser Leather Company was chartered "to tan hides and manufacture leather . . . to act as general dealers in hides and leather . . . to manufacture all kinds of leather goods and products." The construction of a tannery was immediately begun under the supervision of J. W. Fisher. The site was at the mouth of Reed's Creek on a tract of land bought from Josias ("Stutt") Gamble.[81]

This tannery began operation in 1902 and then it was that Walland was born. The tannery handled an average of 3 to 4 hundred hides per day and each hide was in process five months. A. J. Fisher was superintendent for twenty years. The business grew and prospered until January 1931, when the tannery burned. Due to injunctions and litigations the tannery was not rebuilt and Chilhowee Inn and a few company houses are all that remain of a once-prosperous industrial village.

---

[79] *Deeds, Directories of Tennessee;* Parham Papers, Miscellaneous sources.
[80] *Maryville Index,* March 5, 1880.
[81] *Corporations,* 1, p. 169, 179.

DISTILLERS

One of the most important of the early industries was the manufacturing of whisky which found a ready market down the Tennessee River. In 1820 there were 47 distilleries in operation in the county which employed 52 men. There were 67 stills in use at the 47 distilleries. The yearly cash income to the county from distillers was $26,000. The same number of men were engaged in smith work, but the income was only $20,000. Iron, cotton and leather were the only other industries which at that time netted an income over $1,000.

Very little information is available on the proprietors of these businesses except from mortgages, and deeds. Thomas Berry was mentioned as owning stills in Maryville in 1799. In 1806 he was operating on Gallahar's Creek. Trimble's at Morganton was mentioned in 1817. Practically all of these were mentioned in connection with mills. In 1822 James Clark sold a distillery and mill to McMurray. Edward Buchanan had a distillery at Six Mile very early.

Between 1830 and 1840, Arch McCallie sold three stills and apparatus to Andrew Kirkpatrick in the Eusebia neighborhood. Peter Kee sold a still and 12 tubs to Phillip Myers near Middlesettlements and was to receive his pay in whisky, at $33\frac{1}{3}$ cents per gallon.

Robert Thompson was located in 1839 on the Tellico Road next to Norwood's. He had bought the distillery in 1830 from Abraham Utter. George Snider was operating two stills on Crooked Creek in 1834 which were later taken over by Isaac White and was referred to as White's Mill place and stillhouse. Two stills and apparatus were sold to Cox at Louisville in 1838. Tuck was operating a still on Gray Ridge at about the same time, and in 1848 William Fann sold to J. A. McTeer.

Between 1848 and 1860 several others are mentioned: among them are James Henry's stillhouse on Nine Mile Creek; Daniel Yearout's 90-gallon and 40-gallon stills on Pistol Creek near Alnwick; Michael Gardner in the 7th district; William S. King near Louisville; Blackburn on Sinking Creek; John Roddy on Roddy's Branch; and David McKamey at Clover Hill were all engaged in distilling spirits. Alexander Kennedy operated a large distillery at his mill in Rockford.

In Miller's Cove John Blair's distillery was sold to Samuel Cochran at Blair's death in 1847. Peter Brickey operated a distillery in Tuckaleechee from 1810 to 1856. John Chambers was in business in the Dry Valley section about the same time. George Powell's distillery in Cades Cove carried over into the illicit period after the Civil War. This distillery probably grew out of William Davis' setup which consisted of a 115-gallon still, a 65-gallon still, 40 tubs, three 15-gallon barrels and 18 one-gallon kegs. George Ramsey was named by Love as an early distiller at Louisville.

In 1860 there were only five distilleries in operation which employed 8 men. In 1870 only one distillery was listed which required five men to operate.

In 1878 legal distilling operations were outlawed and according to newspapers, Hutsell Amerine and George Powell were keeping revenue officers busy. John Cooper was killed during one of these raids and Amerine became a fugitive from justice. He was captured after six months and later escaped from the Knoxville jail and went West. He was not considered guilty by those who knew him best and was aided in his "scouting." George Powell, Jr., was eventually killed from ambush in 1898.[82]

IRON

The Iron industry was developed very early in a small way. Many early settlers located iron deposits from which they supplied their own and probably their neighbors' wants. One example of this type was Cook's forge on Nine Mile Creek near Cook's (later Griffitts) Mill at Mint and Matthew Houston's forge. Mention is made in a great many early deeds of ore banks and forges and of land condemned for iron works.

The Gillespie Ironworks was the first reported in operation in Blount County. It was owned by James and Robert Gillespie and located near the mouth of Lackey's Creek. The iron was shipped down the Tennessee River from Gillespie's Landing. Operations were not too profitable and the business was discontinued after a few years. This forge was not in operation when Lesley made his survey and so was not mentioned by him.

The only definite information on the early iron industry is from the 1820 census which stated that there were two establishments, but that the returns were imperfect. The annual income was $17,000. The same report recorded that two men were engaged in manufacturing axes and hoes, using 1,000 pounds of iron which cost $100 and the products sold for $500. In 1820 Benjamin Duncan bought a farm at Wildwood from Abijah Conger and paid for it with 1,500 axes and mattocks. Therefore, it seems that Benjamin Duncan was the manufacturer of tools referred to in the report.[83]

The first forge to officially begin operations in the county was the Cades Cove Bloomary Forge. It was built about 1827 by Daniel D. Foute on land acquired from William Tipton and referred to by him as the "Forge Tract" which implies that a primitive operation probably preceded Foute's Bloomary. This forge was located near where the millrace now leaves Forge Creek and the ore was removed about a mile northeast of this site. The Bloomary operated for about twenty years. Coaling signs are still to be found in the vicinity.

Carson's Iron Works was first built and operated by James Carson in 1827. This forge was located on Abram's Creek about a mile above

---

[82] Maryville Newspapers, Passim.
[83] *Digest of Manufacturing Establishments* . . . (Washington, D. C., 1823), 25; The Tiptons were engaged in iron manufacture in Carter County and probably began operations here as soon as they settled.

the present campground in Happy Valley. It was taken over by Daniel D. Foute and operated as the Abram's Creek Forge until 1847 when it was abandoned. The big wheel which operated the hammer is still beside the creek. The ore banks were four miles north and at one time 50 per cent ore was taken. Coaling signs are plentiful nearby.

The Shields Bloomary Forge was located on Little River at Sunshine near where the branch crosses the highway. It was built by Robert Shields and used ore from the "Flats" or White Oak Cove near Schoolhouse Gap. The ore was of poor grade, consequently when the forge was washed away in the 1850's, it was not rebuilt.

The largest and most productive of the local iron works was the Amerine Bloomary Forge which was located on Hess's Creek in Miller's Cove at the lower end of the "Mountain Homes" meadowland. It was built by George Amerine about 1845. It had two bloomary fires and one waterdriven hammer. In 1856, the output was fifteen tons of bar iron. The ore came from the Chilhowee "flats" about four miles west. This forge operated until the Civil War and possibly after. Huge piles of slag mark the furnace site on Hess's Creek.[84]

In 1890 an attempt was made to begin a factory for manufacturing iron hand car couplings. N. L. and W. P. Hastings; Burger; Cowan; McTeer and Goddard were named in the charter, but the project did not progress very far.[85]

During the early 1900's a great deal of iron ore was taken from at least three locations near Carpenter's Campground and shipped to Rockwood. This was a period of "mineral hunter's" and many options were taken by outside interests with a view to future developments but no "rich strikes" were located and options expired without any further activities.

In 1904 a Board of Trade was organized in Maryville to promote new industries in Blount County and the Golden Rule Stove Company was chartered by George and Merrill R. Holliday and A. A. Coventry. Sam Everett gave a tract of land for the factory near Cherokee Street. Twenty men were employed. They manufactured stoves and ranges and made all sorts of castings.

By 1910, the stove business had gradually evolved into a foundry. The Furnace Equipment Company was organized by McNaughton and others known as McNaughton Grate Bar Company, who proposed to do foundry business of all sorts. In 1916 the firm was known as McNaughton Manufacturing Company. During World War I, they did a large business in castings. They continued in business until the late 1930's when they moved to Knoxville. (Mr. Hart McNaughton had worked for McCormick in Chicago and is a highly skilled craftsman.

---

[84] Information gleaned from *Deeds*, Passim; A. H. Love, *History of Louisville*; J. P. Lesley. *Iron Manufactures Guide* (Phila., 1859), 202, 594.

[85] *Notebook* 42, p. 561.

He was closely associated with the cultural group at Maryville College over a long period—Mme. Denne, Miss Bell Smith, Dr. G. A. Knapp, Miss Susan Green and others.)

BANKS

In 1817 a branch bank was incorporated for Blount County. In 1833, there was a State of Tennessee Bank with an agent in Maryville; in 1837 the Planter's Bank in Athens had an agent here. In 1848, the Union Bank at Knoxville served this area.

In 1880, the Farmer's Bank was chartered locally. Joe Burger was cashier and R. N. Hood, president. The Farmer's Bank was discontinued in 1884.[86]

The Bank of Maryville was chartered in 1885 and opened across the alley from the present post office. P. M. Bartlett was president and Joe Burger, cashier. It was moved to the present location in 1932 when it was consolidated with the Bank of Blount County. The Bank of Maryville is now the 6th largest bank in the state.[87]

The Bank of Blount County was chartered in 1893, and S. T. Post was the first president. It was located four doors west of Cusick Street, and later built the building now occupied by the combined banks.[88]

The First National Bank with Thomas N. Brown as president and E. F. Ames, cashier, opened in 1914. In 1921, they built the five-story First National Bank Building on Broadway. It closed its doors in 1932. The Blount National Bank was organized in 1934 and continues operation in the same building.[89]

From 1908 until 1912 a bank was operated in Friendsville under the presidency of Dick Morris and later Hugh Griffitts. The People's Bank of Friendsville was chartered in 1914 and opened for business May 5, 1915. O. L. Defoe was president until the bank was closed June 30, 1936.

The Profit-Sharing Investment Company began in 1932. The Maryville Savings and Loan Corporation began operation in 1933. (A Building and Loan Association had operated as a branch of the Knoxville office from 1890 to 1908.) The First Federal Savings and Loan Association was established in 1921, as Mutual Building and Loan Association. July 1, 1935, it began operation under a Federal Charter.

TAILORS

A great many early housewives did tailoring for their own families except for very special occasions. The first mention of tailoring in Blount County was Josiah Patty's offer to teach a tailoring class in 1827 if enough people were interested.[90]

Berry and Hoffar advertised as tailors in Maryville in 1828. The next year, Thomas White stated that he had taken over Hoffar's business.[91]

---

[86] *Notebook* D, p. 133.
[87] *Notebook* K, 223.
[88] *Charters*, 1, p. 174.
[89] *Charters*, 412.
[90] *Knoxville Register*, June 6, 1829.
[91] *Ibid.*, October 29, 1828; September 2, 1829.

The 1834 *Gazeteer* listed three tailors in Maryville. William McTeer had a partnership with N. R. Maroney in Louisville and with James Nance in Maryville, which he dissolved in 1842 and announced that he would continue in business. McTeer closed his business and left Maryville and went North in 1860.

James Temple had a shop in Louisville in 1850. W. C. Warnack, Philander P. Houston, James M. Toole, Thomas A. Pope, Will Toole, Jr., and I. N. Hair were in business before the Civil War period, severally and in combination.

F. M. Hood was in tailoring business in 1880 and Sophronia Small was dressmaker and milliner.

Button and Swan; Button and Chumlea and Button alone advertised after 1900.

CROCKS AND TILE

In 1859, John E. Glass mortgaged the proceeds of his Crock Factory to Jacob Best. Glass was then living on Six Mile Creek near the Albert Conning place. Nothing more is known about Glass as a potter.

At the close of the War Between the States a considerable migration from Carter County to Blount County took place. These people settled in Happy Valley and along the west side of the Chilhowee Mountains. Among others were Boones, Whiteheads, Herrons, Gourleys, Blevins, Borings, and Grindstaffs. William Grindstaff settled in Happy Valley and operated a pottery on the hill opposite the Baptist church near the house of the late Jerry Hearon.

About 1870 William Grindstaff moved his operations across the mountains and set up a crock factory at the intersection of the "Lower Road" to Montvale and the Christy Hill-Six Mile Road. He advertised as making "all kinds of crockeryware such as crocks, jars, jugs, flower pots and tiling." He gave the location as "Murphy's Mill" and his post office as Huffstetler's Store.

Numerous pieces of Grindstaff Pottery are still in use. Some of it is stamped with "W. Grindstaff," and the date. Pieces bearing the dates 1871 and 1885 have been found.[92]

Some time in the eighties, Grindstaff moved to a location which was in the yard of the present Carpenter's School and operated at this location for four or five years.

About 1888, Dr. J. D. Garner set up a tile business with elaborate machinery about one mile north of Carpenter's. He imported two potters from Ohio, Gunion and Nooncesser, who operated the kilns. They did a larger business in tile than in crockery, shipping most of it. About 1896, William Rasor bought this pottery and continued operations until 1898.

Doubtless other potteries operated in Blount County. A few pieces have been found stamped "Maryville Pottery." It is not known where

---

[92] *Maryville Times*, May 28, 1885 (The G and part of the date is backwards!)

these pieces were made or by whom, but it is said that a pottery operated in Maryville for a while. Neither Grindstaff, nor Rasor stamped all their pottery, and Dr. Garner didn't use a stamp.

BLACKSMITHS AND WAGON SHOPS

Sam Houston is one of the first blacksmiths mentioned in Maryville. He was a cousin of the Rev. Sam Houston and Gen. Sam Houston. He was also a surveyor.

According to the 1820 census there were 52 wagonsmiths and two wheelwrights in 27 different establishments. The goods produced were worth $20,500.[93]

Most men could do ordinary smith work such as shoeing horses, but later, work became more specialized. Strain's Smith Shop is mentioned in 1832 in Maryville. Morris' *Gazeteer* listed three blacksmiths in Maryville in 1834, and three wagonmakers, who were probably identical. Morganton, Louisville and Unitia each had a smith shop.

At Morganton, James McTeer's smith shop and Edward Wayman's wagon and carriage shop are referred to many times in the records. Later the firm was Wayman and Cummings. Wm. P. L. Cummings had a wagon and blacksmith shop on lots 40, 7 and 8 in Maryville. John Cummings also had a shop earlier on lot 72. John M. Bonham and Jesse Carter mortgaged wagonmaker's tools about 1840. James Henry (of William) had a wagon and blacksmith shop on Ellejoy Creek in 1840 and at that time had a set of wheels and a stage bed. The Rev. Brittain Gerrard had a set of wagonmaker's tool in his possession along with "a Yankee wooden clock." There were many others engaged in the trade, but no mention is made of names.[94]

In 1835 only two 4-wheel carriages were owned in Blount County and one 2-wheel carriage, so we can see that the demand was greater for wagons.

John Sparger came to Louisville about 1840 and opened a wagon shop and after M. Dunlap learned the trade he opened his own shop. J. M. George and James K. Orr also ran wagon shops in Louisville. Joe Brown and a Negro man, Joe Cox, operated large blacksmith businesses in Louisville. Three wagonmakers and five blacksmiths were listed in 1854 at Louisville.[95]

In Maryville about the same time Cummings and Carnes were operating a carriage and wagon works.

The 1860 census listed one carriage shop which employed six men.[96]

Hugh Lawson Cansler's wagon shop seems to have been the most prominent shop in operation after the war. It was located next to Jacob Henry's blacksmith shop. Henry was assisted by Alex Fagg in black-

---

[93] *Digest of Accounts of Manufacturing Establishments* . . . (Washington, D. C., 1822), 25.
[94] *Deeds*, Passim.
[95] Love, *History of Louisville;* 1854 Tax list for Louisville Corporation.
[96] *Manufactures of the U. S. in 1860* (Washington, 1865), 560.

smithing. Both were excellent workmen and outstanding Negroes. F. T. Sexton was mentioned in 1887 as a wagonmaker.

In the 1870's Stephen Post, one of the many Quakers who came to Maryville, opened an extensive wagon works in Maryville in the basement of the McKenzie Hotel, the present site of the Broadway Methodist Church. He manufactured farm wagons and "post hacks" which were popular as public conveyances to the various "Springs." Hacks were operated regularly from the depot in Maryville to Mt. Nebo, Montvale and Alleghany Springs. This wagon works moved to Knoxville about 1890. (The Post Sign Company in Knoxville is operated by the same family.)

In 1889 Linnaeus Hastings announced that he had bought the stock, tools and machinery of Frank Post and had rented the shops of Stephen Post and would continue the manufacture of road wagons, and would continue to sell the Post hack, or spring wagon. Also that he would give special attention to blacksmithing and repairs. Hastings was an unusually clever workman with an inventive mind, who had been forced by loss of hearing to give up teaching.

H. O. Wilson was an outstanding blacksmith and wagonmaker in the 1880's and until his death in 1893. David Morrison also did smith work in Maryville during the same period.[97]

During the nineties while progressive citizens were agitating for more industries in Blount County, several companies were chartered which never reached successful operation.

The Maryville Butter and Cheese Manufacturing Company was chartered in 1894 by William H. Henry, James A. Goddard, Thomas P. Cowan, and John P. Duncan. A building was erected near the Cedar Spring and equipment installed representing an investment of $5,000. The business was operated for a while, but lack of experience and "know how" led to its failure. The building was used for mission work and a community school for under-privileged children for a while. When the building burned in 1904, a news story described the creamery as a "monument to the gullibility of people when a smooth operator gets hold." [98]

After the creamery was closed another promoter came along and the equipment was changed to a steam laundry, but this business did not flourish either. After this the building was used to house the engine which pumped water to the jail and courthouse, until it was destroyed by the above-mentioned fire.

CANNERIES

The Friendsville Canning and Manufacturing Company was chartered in 1893 soon after the opening of the railroad and named fourteen prominent Friendsville men in the Charter. They had ambitions to

---
[97] *Maryville Times*, May 29, 1889.
[98] Charters I, p. 111; *Maryville Record*, March 18, 1904.

reach out into Monroe and Loudon counties but apparently did not catch hold.[99]

The L. B. Sutton Canning Company began as a family enterprise at Armona in 1912. The business was carried on in an 8 by 10 shed by Mr. and Mrs. Sutton and turned out 150 cans per day. Beans and tomatoes were handled mostly under the "Sunshine Valley" brand. They were marketed locally. The output in 1913 was enlarged to 500 cans daily.

In 1915 a modern canning plant was installed at Mentor which turned out 1,000 cans per day and employed 8 to 19 persons. The brand was changed to "Sycamore Spring." By 1917 the plant was turning out 10,000 cans daily and used 20 employes.

By 1923 the business had grown to the extent that the cannery was moved to Maryville to the site now occupied by Texas Oil Company and the daily output was 30,000 cans. At this time the brand was changed to "Pride of Blount." By 1927 there were 170 employes on the payroll at the peak of the season and the bean crop was so heavy that the cannery could not handle it even by running day and night; hundreds of bushels spoiled before they could be processed.

In 1930 the Blount Cannery Company was sold to J. W. Gillespie and managed by Mike Ballard. Mr. Sutton managed the business in 1932. Srawberry-growing in Blount County was at its peak at this time and strawberry preserves was one of their specialties. A carload of preserves was shipped to the Northern market just at the time that the market fell and the company lost heavily on this shipment. This lead to the close of the cannery business.

Mr. Sutton later became Area Supervisor for the Works Progress Administration Canning Project and helped to set up 23 canneries in the 27 counties under his supervision.[100]

Frank C. Gibbons came to Maryville from Ohio in 1911 and organized the Tennessee Canning Company which was backed by Knoxville capital. The cannery was operated in the building formerly occupied by the Dixie Mantle Company. The company canned vegetables, fruits, apple butter and preserves. During World War I they had numerous government contracts. When the war ended and contracts were canceled the business was forced to close.

The business was reorganized as Frank C. Gibbons and Sons and operated under this name until the beginning of World War II. This company made only jams, jellies and preserves under the "Knox-Pure" label. In the late thirties Mr. Gibbons died and the business was carried on by Averell S. Gibbons until restrictions imposed by the government after the beginning of the war made it unprofitable to operate.

---

[99] *Charters*, 1, p. 64.
[100] *Maryville Enterprise*, February 12, 1930; Personal interview with Mr. Sutton. This canning project was another government sponsored agency to relieve unemployment along with the C. C. C. mentioned earlier in this chapter.

CONTRACTORS

The earliest local contractors mentioned were Pride and Barnes who got the jail contract in 1849. They dissolved their partnership in 1855. Barnes is spoken of as a brick mason. (Six bricklayers were listed in Maryville in 1834 and one painter.)

L. B. Saffle's brickyard is mentioned at an early date in Louisville, and later Foster's brickyard.

Elliott Carnes was mentioned about 1850 as a plasterer, and Joe Miller who built the Melrose Springs Hotel was also a plasterer.

Alford McConnell was an extensive contractor in the period after the Civil War. Among other buildings, he built Anderson Hall on the Maryville College Campus in 1869.

Mount and Hooper had the carpentry contract for the 1880 courthouse and David Jones had the masonry contract. By 1885 Jones was operating a steam sawmill and a brick plant. By 1900 he was able to turn out 30-40,000 bricks daily. Bricks from Jones' brickyard were specified in many local contracts as being of superior quality, and he was not always able to meet the demand. David Jones built, among other things, the 1879 courthouse and the New Providence Presbyterian Church which was recently razed. His residence, now owned by Highland Presbyterian Church, is a good example of Jones' work. He supervised the burning of the bricks for the Freedman's Institute and the Friends Church building which is now St. Andrew's Episcopal Church, and many other local buildings for which the bricks were burned on the spot.

OTHER INDUSTRIES AND OCCUPATIONS

The Scott Brickyard near the Knox County line at Stock Creek was established in the 1870's by James F. Scott of Knoxville. The K. and A. Railroad built a switch-yard at this point (between Tipton Station and Little River Station) for loading purposes. This brickyard operated for forty or fifty years. The elder Scott was succeeded by his son Alex, a widely traveled man, who had accompanied wagon trains West and had spent some years as a prospector and miner.

Alex A. Scott, Sr. was of an inventive turn and before 1930 the Scott Manufacturing Company was manufacturing bakelite products. This was perhaps one of the first plastic molding companies in the South. Their products were radio knobs, electric switch plates, electrical components, razor handles, iced tea coasters and other "custom molded products."

In May 1931 the Molded Cap Corporation was established under the leadership of Alex Scott, Jr. under the same roof with the above enterprise. (A 1934 news item mentioned that they were turning out 300,000 bottle caps per week.)

In 1933 the Molded Cap Corporation became connected with the Patent Button Company of Connecticut and was re-chartered as the

Patent Button Company of Tennessee. In April 1934 the Patent Button Company began operations at Townsend (near Derris House) and manufactured buttons exclusively. After three years at this location, The Patent Button Company in January 1937 moved to Knoxville. At that time all of the equipment of the Scott Manufacturing Company was purchased and the business was enlarged to include a wide variety of custom molded products.[101]

W. H. Kirk opened a watch repair shop in 1868 and soon after this added a stock of "jewelry, eyeglasses, fishing tackle, cutlery, guns, ammunition, etc." Kirk was also acting as postmaster for Maryville at the same time. He was assisted in 1880 by Martin Simpson.

In 1879 S. A. Patton came to Maryville from Rockwood and opened a similar business on the corner of Main and Court streets. His business was one of the substantial fixtures on Main Street until well into the new century.

A. E. McCulloch opened a jeweler's shop on Main Street in 1906 which was a fixture for about forty years.

A man by the name of Baker opened a bake-shop at the corner of Broadway and Cusick Street in the 1870's. He was followed by Herman Reuter's father in a few years, who operated the business for a while and then left town. The City Bakery was operated in the nineties by Callahan and Best. They were succeeded by H. Rueter who carried on the business for twenty or thirty years. He was succeeded by Reagan and Presley (next to Candy Kitchen) who operated about ten years.

The first reference to photography is an early reference to H. J. Yearout, a daguerreotypist. Jesse Richardson came to Maryville in 1876 and opened a shop in the Austin Hotel (formerly McKenzie House). He did business in Maryville for thirty or forty years.

The 1887 Directory listed W. A. Reese at Brick Mill and S. W. Colburn at Miser's Station as photographers.

In the early nineties Miss Annie Lord, who had operated a small studio at Wildwood Springs, moved into Maryville and operated a studio in a small building at the back of the lot where the Tarvin building now stands. In the late nineties she sold her business to E. L. Webb who operated here under the name "Aristo" until 1907. Then he moved to the College Street location where he continued the business until the late 1940's.

J. W. Stewart opened a studio in 1904 for a few years. Mr. A. L. Butcher did photography and repair work for ten or twenty years. The caption over his doorway read "mends everything but broken hearts."

Other than those mentioned the photography field belonged to the roving photographer who made his yearly rounds.

In 1880 the Maryville Broom Factory on Church Street operated by

---

[101] Patent Button Company of Tennessee, *Employe's Manual*; Letter from E. C. Snoddy, General Manager of Patent Button Company, September 6, 1955.

James M. Greer and Elijah Walker was turning out 8,000 dozen brooms per year. F. Clute was operating a small business near Maryville at the same time. In the nineties Pink Haggard operated a large broom factory on East High Street. He did a great deal of work on the "shares" system (taking a percentage of the product for his work). Robert Martin also operated a broom factory in the late nineties. Many other small shops have been operated now and then through the years.

The first barber to open a full-time shop in Maryville was Charles Wallace, a Negro, who had done a flourishing Saturday business before the war. Hyram Gay, another Negro, soon followed Wallace in this work. Joe Patterson and David Hannum exercised their skill a little later, and R. D. Hunnicutt was the leading barber after 1900. These names are reminiscent of 5 cent shaves and 15 cent haircuts!

No mention has been found of tinshops and tinners until after the Civil War. Reference is made to a copper and tin shop on lot 108 about that time. Ben Yearout, Joseph and Frank R. Hood, Dan and Jim Broyles, and Wells and Irwin were all in the tinner's business. Charles Rafter had a tinshop on Harper Street and Sam Lee on the corner of Depot and College streets about the turn of the century.

The Maryville Bottling Works had its origin in the company operated by Dr. John M. McConnell, Sam Feezell and others at Wildwood for the purpose of selling mineral waters. This business was taken over about 1906 by Clay Cunningham, Lowry McCulley, Dr. Lloyd Prater and Will Lawrence. They manufactured "pop" and after six or seven years they sold the business to Mr. Webster who was the local agent for the K. and A. Railroad. In the late twenties the business was taken over by Mr. C. E. Weems. The business was continued until World War II when the sugar shortage made it necessary to close the business.

Prior to 1919, Coca Cola was shipped into Maryville. At that time the company opened their own business on Church Street where they operated until the present building was opened.

The Maryville Steam Laundry was established in 1906 by F. M. Medlin and J. D. Ammons in a building especially planned for it, belonging to T. A. Hill. In 1928 the business was taken over by Blount Sanitary Laundry with W. B. Riley as manager. With an occasional change of management the business has continued to the present.

The Maryville Ice and Coal Company was established in 1914 by Charles, Walter and E. E. Hunter. The first capacity of the plant was 25 tons per day. In 1917 the firm was reorganized with E. E. Hunter, J. L. Edmondson, and D. F. Young. By 1919 the capacity of the plant was increased to 50 tons daily, and house to house deliveries were being made.

In 1930 the company owned four trucks, and seven wagons which were used to make deliveries, and employed 30 men in the summer (ten in the winter). Two cold-storage rooms had been built which at that time were rented to the Fuller Packing Company. The ice business has shifted somewhat with the advent of automatic refrigerators, but there still is a demand for ice. Several ice and coal companies have come and gone since the establishment of this firm but none has occupied the field so long.

Harrison Construction Company opened an office in Alcoa and began operation in the Blount area in 1940 when they began grading operations for the Aluminum Company's north fabricating plant. They set a construction record by removing a million feet of timber, pulling stumps and moving 320,000 cubic yards of earth in a few months on the 58 acres now covered by the north plant.

In 1946 they purchased a permanent location in Alcoa for their Southern division which operates throughout the South. The firm at present has about 450 local employes and spends more than $4,000,000 within the state. At the same time they offer quick service on small local paving jobs as well as handling large contracts.

Blount County's newest industry is the Tennessee Textile Corporation on McArthur Road which began operation in 1954. The company manufactures work clothes. The location of this industry here was made possible by the subscription of local citizens to a twenty-five year bond issue to be amortized by the industry.

CHAPTER XI

Communities

BLOUNT County, the tenth county created in Tennessee, lies in the extreme eastern portion of the state. The county is bounded on the north by Knox County, on the east by Sevier County, on the southeast by North Carolina, on the southwest by Monroe County, and on the west by Loudon County.

Blount County's present area of 571 square miles gives it a rank of twenty-fourth among the state's 95 counties in size. The county's altitude ranges from 700 feet above sea level to more than 5,400 feet in the high peaks of the Smoky range. Maryville, the county seat is 980 feet above sea level. The northwestern portion of the county is composed of valley lands which are immediately south and east of the Tennessee River. The southeastern portion of the county is a rugged mountainous section which contains three beautiful coves (Cades Cove is now in the Smoky Mountains National Park). The average annual rainfall is approximately 50 inches and the mean annual temperature is about 50° Fahrenheit. The county is drained by three major streams and their tributaries. Little River flows through the northeastern portion of the county and empties into the Tennessee River a few miles northeast of Maryville and its twin city, Alcoa. The Tennessee River forms part of the county's northern boundary. The Little Tennessee drains the southern areas of the county.

Indian title to this region was extinguished by three treaties between the Cherokees and the Federal Government. The Treaty of Holston, or Blount's Treaty of July 2, 1791 gained the cession of that portion northeast of the Hawkins line which ran just south of Maryville. The first Treaty of Tellico, October 2, 1798, ceded the land south of the Hawkins line and east to the Chilhowee Mountains. By Calhoun's Treaty of February 27, 1819, the Indians finally gave up claim to all lands included within the bounds of present Blount County.

MARYVILLE

In July 1795, the General Assembly of the Territory South of the River Ohio appointed commissioners to lay out a county seat to be called Maryville in honor of Mary Grainger Blount. The commission chose to locate the town on fifty acres adjoining Captain John Craig's Fort on Pistol Creek which was 16 miles south of Knoxville. The tract was laid out in 120 lots with streets and alleys. This tract was a part of 343 acres which John Craig had bought from the 100,000 acres granted by the State of North Carolina to Stockley Donelson.[1]

The first courthouse was erected on the lot west of the present jail, which was followed in 1805 by a second courthouse on the Bank of Maryville lot (which had been reserved for the city square). Three courthouses occupied this site. The courthouse was removed to the present site in 1906 after two courthouses had burned on the old site.

The first jail was on the present site, the second and third were on McCammon Street (the third is still standing there). The present jail is the fourth building. The stocks and pillory were on the city square as long as they were used.

In 1799 a traveler described the town as three years old, consisting of 20, mostly frame, houses. At the end of the place was quite a large church of hewn logs. (By 1811, this church (New Providence) had 217 members).[2]

In 1803 the following merchants paid the $25 state license fee: King & Montgomery; John Lowry; Josiah & John Nicols; Lowry & Waugh; Love & Co.; and Henderson & Company.

The Rev. Mark Moore and Josiah P. Smith taught first in the New Providence Church School and later in Porter Academy and the Female Academy. The Rev. Isaac Anderson joined them in this work by 1812. Early Maryvillians had hats from Samuel Love; coats tailored by Caldwell; saddles made by James Turk or Barclay McGhee; smithy work done by Samuel Houston; grain ground by John Craig and did their drinking and entertaining at Cunningham's or Taylor's taverns.

Diversion was occasioned by courts meeting, or by the stages from Knoxville and from Hot Springs, North Carolina, passing through as they did two or three times weekly. In 1810, the Circuit Court began meeting, and the first hanging occurred in 1814.[3]

By 1834, Maryville had 600 inhabitants, three churches, five stores, two taverns, four clergymen and four lawyers. Three hatters, three tailors, three saddlers, and two silver smiths were then in business, and Maryville College had 22 students. Wallace and Jacobs, Wilson & Saffell (who also had a store at Louisville), Spencer & Wallace, and C. & J. H. Gillespy, were among the places doing business. Later John Brabson and his associates, B. D. Brabson, and Reps J. Davis were the leading merchants. Joseph Cusick and his brother-in-law Rice, and Price

---

[1] *Acts of the General Assembly, 1795,* ch. 6, sec. 2; *Acts of Tennessee, 1796, 1st ses.,* ch. 26; A post office was established in 1800 with John Montgomery as postmaster.

[2] Williams, *Early Travels,* 462.

[3] Tennessee State Archives, Nashville, Tenn., *Tax Lists;* John A. Goddard, in Maryville *Times,* April, 1902.

were in business as well as Wm. Toole, Coffin & Wilson, Cox & Devers and others.[4]

By 1842 Henry Sesler was operating a stage route from Knoxville to Athens and listed a 4-horse carry-all among his assets. Twenty years later he offered stage and buggy harnesses as security for a debt. L. D. Bencini and William Cummings were engaged in driving hacks and stages to Montvale during the same period. After the Civil War, Roderick McKenzie operated a stage and hack line from Maryville to Montvale.

One of the biggest events in local history happened when the citizens of Blount County entertained with a barbecue for General Sam Houston in August, 1845. Gen. William Wallace, Dr. Sam Pride, and Col. Hiram Heartsill were very active in the movement. About fifty men were appointed to the committee on arrangements and all the surrounding counties were invited. Part of the entertainment was a duel which was probably of little note at that time. Also, according to Hyram Gay, an old Negro man, a man named Childers imbibed too much spirits and emulated Samson by wielding the thigh bone of the beef.[5]

At this period there is evidence of some sort of social or intellectual gathering of leading citizens. In 1848, the Polymathic Society of Maryville was chartered. All the leading business and professional men are listed. The nature of the Society was not stated.[6]

In 1852, a circus came to town and created some welcome diversion. Welch, Delevan and Nathan's National Circus arrived on May 13th. Admission was 50 cents for adults; children and Negroes were half-price. The imperial chariot was drawn by 30 elegant horses.[7]

Another movement of an intellectual nature was the local plan to establish the East Tennessee Female Masonic Institute. The Masons throughout East Tennessee and beyond the state were solicited for help and the cornerstone was laid in 1849 with great ceremony and the help of Hardeman's Brass Band. The school was not too successful and the building was eventually sold to the city of Maryville.[8]

In 1853, the leading merchants were Toole, Pope & Co.; Wm. McTeer & Co.; A. M. & J. G. Wallace; Bicknell & Wallace.

By 1857, S. J. McReynolds, J. A. Houston & Co.; Geo. W. Lawson & Co., Grocers; and Fagg and Miller's Drugstore were the chief businesses. The Wilson Flour Mill and Teffeteller's Blacksmith shop were in operation.[9]

[4] Parham Papers, *Maryville;* Eastin Morris, *Tennessee Gazeteer,* Passim.
[5] *Knoxville Register,* August 13, 1845; Dr. John A. Goddard in the Maryville *Times,* April 9, 1902.
[6] *Acts, 1848,* ch. 139. John Singleton, John B. Cox, John E. Toole, Jesse G. Wallace, Wm. S. Porter, James R. Love, S. T. Bicknell, Thos. A. Pope, Sam T. Cox, R. I. Wilson, Sam Pride, D. D. Foute, B. D. Brabson, John S. McNutt, J. C. Fagg, D. C. Bicknell, James M. Toole, Montgomery McTeer, W. W. Wallace, James A. McCamey, J. M. Kennedy, Wm. McTeer, S. J. McReynolds, W. D. McGinley, R. L. Cates, James F. Dever, D. W. Tedford, John D. Tedford.
[7] *Knoxville Register,* May 1, 1852.
[8] *Minutes of New Providence Chapter, F. & A. M.;* Passim.
[9] *Campbell's Business Directory* (1851); p. 258.

Many business changes were influenced by the shadows cast by war clouds and the railroad controversy. When the war actually came, the sentiments of the citizenry were pretty well divided and each followed the dictates of his own conscience. Many valuable men of Southern inclinations left Blount County and never returned after the war.

Maryville suffered heavily during the war and the fire which accompanied the siege of the courthouse destroyed almost all the business section on the main street. After the war the influx of monied Quakers from Indiana practically took over the business section of town and rebuilt it. They also acquired a great deal of property in Maryville west of Cates Street and completely changed the character of the town. These people became some of Maryville's most valued citizens and did much toward building a bigger and better Maryville. They also built Freedman's Institute and the Maryville Normal School and helped establish the public schools in the county. One of the Quakers, who came to Maryville, was John Collins, a painter. Among other things, he painted the only existing reproduction of the ante-bellum courthouse in 1872. The courthouse burned in 1879, and he painted the new one in 1883. The originals are now owned by Will A. McTeer.

Reference had been found to a fire of importance in Maryville in January, 1868. Mention was made in the *Maryville Monitor* in 1873 that William B. Scott's printing shop and equipment had been recently damaged by fire. The courthouse and some of the surrounding buildings burned in 1879.

The Union League was active in the period directly after the Civil War and elected four Negro men out of seven to the city commission and this group was also active in persecuting the Southern Methodist ministers who were sent to Blount County circuits. The activities of the group played out about the time that the Rev. W. T. Dowell, one of the active organizers, died in 1869.[10]

In 1837, the town of Maryville was permitted by law to incorporate and elect seven aldermen, but no record exists to indicate that it was done. In April, 1850, Dr. Sam Pride was elected Mayor. Aldermen were: John E. Toole (lawyer), Samuel T. Bicknell (planter, lawyer, and politician); Andrew McClain (tanner), and Reuben L. Cates (saddler). In 1851 East Maryville (to Washington Street) was taken into the corporate limits.

In 1879 the citizens finally voted to dissolve the corporation because they could not control the sale of liquor under the "four mile law" which was passed in 1877.[11]

A taxing district was set up, with R. N. Hood as mayor, which operated until 1883 when the town came under the jurisdiction of the

---

[10] *Minutes of Union League*, McClung Collection, Lawson McGhee Library, Knoxville, Tenn.

[11] Saloon Keepers whose names are known were Johnson and Cassidy, Joseph Anderson and Leo Ferrary.

County Court by special act. This plan continued until the town was again incorporated in 1907.[12]

A city water system was a perennial subject. An act had been passed in 1807 which provided that the Cedar Spring should never be sold, but kept for the benefit of the town. (The same year $100 was appropriated by the County Court to bring water into the town.) Many references to attempts to install waterworks are found, but the first charter was issued in 1889. Evidently this attempt did not go very far because the County Court voted $1,000 in 1901 to install water works at the jail and courthouse.[13]

Another attempt was made to install waterworks in 1902. In 1908, 14 water customers were reported to the County Court as paying from $5 to $30 yearly. In 1911, the Maryville Water Commission was founded with J. C. Bittle as chairman and the water pipes were re-laid in iron. By 1913 water lines and sewer connections were being laid along the Friendsville and Montvale roads by Messrs. Cooper, Willard, Broyles and Gamble. Many improvements and changes have taken place since that date and additional water supplies have become necessary with the growth of the town. Mr. Bittle and Jasper Henry served on the Water Board for more than twenty years and personally supervised the installations.

A new two and one-half million dollar sewer and water system has been installed which brings water into Maryville from Little River. The source of water supply up to the present has been from two wells and two springs.[14]

The Gay Fire Company (Hiram Gay, a Negro barber) was given permission to erect a building at the rear of the courthouse to keep fire apparatus in 1894. Later fire-fighting equipment was located near Columbian Hall. These and other privately owned vehicles were the forerunners of the organized fire department of the town.[15]

The Maryville Fire Department was organized about 1915 with John H. Mitchell as chief. The personnel was entirely volunteer. Glenn Huffstetler was appointed chief in 1918 and at that time a light truck was purchased to carry the hose which was kept in a public garage and operated by employes of the street department.

By 1930 the personnel was composed of a chief, assistant chief, two captains, two drivers, an electrician, a hoseman and 25 trained firemen. The equipment at that time was an American LaFrance 750-gallon

---

[12] *Acts, 1837*, ch. 246; *Acts, 1850*, ch. 225, sec. 7; The minutes of the Corporation were stored in the courthouse basement and were lost in the fire of 1906 (Mr. Parham had abstracted them); *Acts, 1879*, ch. 175, sec. 1, 3; *Acts, 1907*, ch. 116.

[13] *Acts, 1807*, ch. 84, Sec. 4; *Charters*, T, 343; *Minutes*, Passim. Water was piped from Cates Springs.

[14] Wm. O. Garner in 1898 piped water from the Tucker Spring to a storage tank between Mt. View and Lawrence St. for the use of Freedman's Institute and others in that part of town.

[15] Mr. Thomas F. Broady says that Linnaeus Hasting took the old Gay fire engine with its brass fittings and converted it into a heavy farm wagon and sold it to his father.

pumper fire truck and between 5,000 and 8,000 feet of hose. This equipment was housed in the new fire station on Church Street which has since been enlarged to house the larger engines and equipment necessary to keep up with the growth of the town.

The Blount County Fire Department was organized in 1949 by W. L. (Jack) Huffstetler (son of Glenn Huffstetler mentioned above). This company is operated on a yearly subscription basis. Four trucks and 6 men are employed in this business which affords fire protection to property-owners in outlying districts.

The first electric plant in Maryville was used exclusively by the Maryville Woolen Mills in 1890. In 1892 Thomas F. Cooper, Joe Burger, Thomas P. Cowan, James A. Summers, and Will A. McTeer recorded a charter as Maryville Electric Light and Power Company. Their power was both hydro and steam-generated at the City Flour Mill.

By 1894 Charles M. French and Thomas P. Cowan were operating their own plant at McGhee and Cates Street and Sam A. Walker and Jesse Groner had joined the firm. Between 1899 and 1904 the plant was owned successively by Rockford Mills, McElwee Company, and the Bank of Maryville before it was purchased by a company chartered as the Rockford Electric Company.

In 1910 the Bays Mountain Electric Company was chartered with Joe Burger, J. L. Clark, Ernest Koella, Clay Cunningham and Thomas M. Brown named. They had 80 customers in Maryville when they sold their power rights in 1916 to the Maryville Lighting Company. In 1924 the plant was sold to the Tennessee Electric Power Company and in 1939 to the City of Maryville.[16]

Schlosser Leather Company had a power plant at Walland in 1909, and Little River Light and Power Company had a power plant at Townsend by 1904. The dam at Walland was washed away before the tannery closed and the Townsend community outgrew the capacity of the local power plant, and arranged for supplemental power in the 1930's. The Rural Electrification Administration has furnished power to Tuckaleechee Cove since 1952.

TELEPHONES

The East Tennessee Telephone Company was chartered in 1894 to maintain and operate telephones and exchanges. Evidently this group which was chartered from Bowling Green, Kentucky did not get into operation.[17]

---

[16] In 1911, Maryville Light, Heating and Power Company obtained a charter to build a dam and manufacture power at Abram's Falls. The idea was abandoned in 1916 and the Maryville Lighting Company bought the power rights in Maryville of the Bays Mountain Electric Company. *Deeds,* UU, 10; *Charters* 1, p. 205, 259, 447; *Maryville Electric System* (a pamphlet) 1939.

[17] *Charters,* 1, p. 97.

Little is known about the early telephone systems. There were People's Telephone switchboards operated at Wildwood, Clover Hill, Townsend, Walland, Brick Mill and other rural points before 1900.

A right of way was granted to the People's Telephone Company composed of Will A. McTeer, J. C. Bittle, T. F. Cooper, W. E. and C. L. Parham, in 1896 to bring lines from Knoxville into Maryville and to various points in the county.

According to report, Joe Burger, cashier of the Bank of Maryville, had the first telephone in Maryville—a private line from his house to the bank. The first switchboard was located in the Central House, while Z. H. Lasseter was proprietor.

The first Bell Telephone was installed in Maryville at Harper's Furniture Store. The local people who were subscribers to the People's Telephone Company and the Maryville Exchange were violently opposed to the introduction of the Bell System. The first line was free of tolls to Knoxville. An exchange was set up at J. M. Goddard's house on the Montvale Road about 1905. There were about twenty-five subscribers. After two or three years the exchange was moved into town.

In 1915 G. C. Jackson put up a telephone line to Brick Mill. This was evidently a private line.

In January 1922, it was voted to put the $10,000 in the Maryville Telephone Exchange into the People's Telephone Company, which was rebuilding its lines and installing new equipment.[18]

In 1928 the People's Telephone Company was merged with Southern Bell Telephone Company, and the building on Church Street was occupied. In 1955 work was begun on a new and up-to-date exchange and in June 1956 the change-over to the dial system was effected. At this time all points in the county were made available without tolls.

Along the line of diversions and amusements, fairs were the earliest form. Blount County was the first county authorized to hold a fair. In connection with the fair, horse-racing and other amusements were participated in by those in attendance. (Horse-racing was forbidden in town.) The racetrack at the fairgrounds was in the field where the T. C. & S. Railroad crossed the Sandy Springs Road. A field on the Calvin and Rufus Davis farm on Ellejoy Creek was also referred to as the "Race Track."

Fairs continued in popularity, but the character changed after the Civil War. After country stores became pretty well distributed and goods were more easily available, the fair was more like it is today. There seems to have been periods when there were no fairs held for a few years. The fairs were moved nearer to the town about the turn of the century and of late years were held near the courthouse.

In 1932 P. A. Waters, Cam Sterling and Shan Wilcox bought the present Fairgrounds near Five Points and the County fair has been held there since that time. In 1956 the Fairgrounds were taken over by the

---

[18] *Minutes*, Passim; *Maryville Enterprise*, February 1930.

American Legion Post of Maryville and they plan to establish buildings and recreational facilities of a more permanent nature.

Sam Everett in his "Reminiscences" recorded by John Everett when he was editor of the *Maryville Enterprise* said that John Robinson's Circus was the first circus to come to Maryville by train. They had a big parade up Main Street and the wagons got stuck in the mud. The circus elephants were barely able to get out of the mud in time for the afternoon performance where Fort Craig School now stands.

Chatauqua programs were regularly brought to Maryville during the summer season. Oratorical contests and debates were popular as well as stock performances of such plays as the "The Drunkard's Warning." Columbian Hall was much in demand for these gatherings. Maryville College Literary Societies also put on various types of public programs. "Lawn Socials" at the churches were also popular pastimes.

The first motion picture theater opened in Maryville in 1909. The program was a 3-reel feature with a reel of illustrated music as an added attraction. The Dreamland Amusement Company was chartered by H. Rueter and others in 1915 and a more elaborate program was furnished thereafter as new developments in movies were introduced. The Crescent Amusement Company now operates the movie houses in Maryville.[19]

One of the major problems from the earliest times was the problem of furnishing free public schools. Not until 1879 did the city own a public school building. At this time they bought the Masonic schoolbuilding but were not able to pay a teacher that year. Fortunately, for the city, the courthouse burned in 1879 and the city leased the building to the county for a courthouse for a year while a new one was being built. The problem of financing the public school was hard to solve because the county would not vote for an adequate school tax and it was not settled until a special school-taxing district was set up in 1898 with the courthouse as the center to extend one mile in every direction. The Friends Normal School property was bought for a public school in 1900 and the Masonic building was sold back to the Masons. In 1910 the East Side and West Side buildings were built. The free Negro school had been financed by Freedman's Bureau and had been in operation since 1867 and the Negro population fared better than the white prior to 1898.

In 1889 a group of local businessmen organized themselves into the Maryville Improvement Company and sent out advertisements to induce business firms to locate here. Among the "wants" was a hotel to accommodate 100 boarders. A site was offered gratis for this purpose. A spoke factory, canning factory, furniture factory, hosiery mill, wagon factory, pork-packing house, soap factory, foundry and machine shop, and cotton factory were all listed. Two factory sites were offered free. A new factory already built was offered for $1,200. The bankers

---

[19] *Maryville Times,* September 6, 1909; *Charters,* 1, p. 4, 69.

and lawyers were the chief promoters. Within the next ten years some of these businessses tried to get established and failed.

The "Novelty Store" started operation about 1880. The "Racket Store" was a later novelty store. Walker's Stationery Store was another shop in that category. These were the forerunners of the modern "5 and 10."

A great many organizations had their beginnings in the 1880's and nineties.[20]

The local chapter of the W. C. T. U. was organized in 1885 by Mrs. Saxon, a national W. C. T. U. lecturer. (Mrs. Frances Willard was an occasional visitor in the house of Captain William H. Henry, who was several times Prohibition candidate for governor.) They maintained "Bands of Hope," organizations for both white and Negro children, and a Loyal Temperance League. The W. C. T. U. was very active in welfare work and it is said that the Blount County Industrial Home was founded as a result of a discussion at a W. C. T. U. meeting at the home of Mrs. Mary Wilson McTeer in 1894. As an attempt to curb drinking in town, the W. C. T. U. got permission to install the first public drinking fountains in Maryville.[21]

Chilhowee Club was organized in 1891 by six faculty wives of Maryville College for "mental improvement and the improvement of humanity." The Tuesday Club was organized in 1894 under the leadership of Mrs. Keith Follett. Their avowed object was "to stimulate intellectual and moral growth." Their library was the nucleus of the city library when it was organized. These clubs continued to support the library through the lean years of the "depression."

Although numerous editorials had been written on the need for incorporating, and civic improvement for more than fifteen years, it was not until April 1907 that the town was again incorporated. A. K. Harper was elected mayor, and Will A. McTeer, recorder. There were five aldermen. Will A. McTeer was recorder every term but one until 1915 when J. L. Tweed was elected. Harper, Roll Hanna, Harper again and Sam Everett for three successive terms served as mayors until 1919 when the form of government was changed to the mayor-commission type.

Sewers were promoted during 1915–16. A police department was first named in 1919. A macadamizing program was initiated and Cates Street was named in honor of Charles T. Cates Sr., an honored citizen, who had recently died. The name of Austin Street was changed to Harper Street in honor of Lt. Milton L. Harper, the son of Maryville's first mayor, who was killed in France.

The first Red Cross work was initiated in Blount County in 1914 through the Tuesday Club chairman, Mrs. Keith Follett, as an auxil-

---

[20] *Maryville Enterprise* (Historical edition), February 12, 1930.
[21] It is said that once when the Owl's Club (in the old jail building) was raided that the W.C.T.U. "bid off" the confiscated liquor so that they could burn it on the street. It was almost a failure because some one had "watered" the whisky!

liary of the Knox County Chapter. The Blount County Chapter was organized in 1917 and has been active since that time.

The movement for the organization of a public library in Maryville was the result of the efforts of Mrs. Jane Alexander, who had been operating a private loan collection of 500 volumes for some years. The Tuesday Club had also accumulated a small library at their clubrooms.

The first meeting relative to establishing the library was late in 1918. A Board of Directors was elected in April 1919, with James B. Hedge, Jr., as chairman. There were two ladies each from the Tuesday Club, Chilhowee Club, and W. C. T. U., and six businessmen on the first Board.

The library was opened over the Service Barber shop with a book shower, October 24, 1919. Miss A. Belle Smith was librarian from 1919 until her death in May 1939. Miss Lida Hooke was the first assistant. Some of the opening gifts were the Tuesday Club collection and 500 volumes from Miss Anne Cheney (of the Cheney Silk family) of Massachusetts, a special friend of Mrs. Alexander, and her sister Miss Smith.

In 1924 the city was contributing $400 yearly toward the upkeep and Prof. J. W. Hughes got a grant of $200 from the county to supplement the subscriptions.

The Board began to cast about for a building which could be used for a library. Among the locations considered was the old jail building. In 1926, the board was incorporated and it was agreed to buy the Toole property at the rear of the post office.

A gift of $1,000 some years previous to this date from Miss Cheney was used as part of a down payment and a later gift of $1,000 from Miss Cheney was used to remodel the building for library purposes. The library moved into its new quarters in January 1927.

In July 1927 Miss Smith presented 5 books as a memorial to Miss Lida Hooke, assistant librarian who had died in 1926, and suggested the Memorial Shelf as a means to build up the book collection.

In May 1930 the Maryville Public Library Board met to consider how Mrs. A. K. Harper's proposal to erect a memorial to her husband could be combined with the library. The details were worked out and a deed of trust to the library building was made to the city commissioners in August 1930. A contract was let for the A. K. Harper Memorial Library in October and the building was dedicated in February 1931.

In January 1931 the city commissioners elected the first Board of Directors for A. K. Harper Memorial Library. Mr. Hedge, Miss Edith Goddard, and Mrs. Hugh Norton had been on the library board since its beginning. (Mr. Hedge served until his death and Miss Goddard and Mrs. Norton are still on the Board.) Mrs. A. K. Harper, A. D. Huddleston, Miss Della Goddard, and J. L. Vineyard were also named to the new Board. Miss A. Belle Smith and Miss Jonnie B. Coulter were librarian and assistant, respectively. (Miss Coulter had been elected in 1926 to succeed Miss Hooke.)

Miss A. Belle Smith died in May 1939 and was succeeded by Miss Jonnie B. Coulter as librarian. Mrs. Frank Nance began work as assistant in February 1939. The Children's Room was opened early in 1940 as a memorial to Miss Smith, who besides her library work did much to promote the appreciation of literature and art in schools and clubs.

Mrs. Nance succeeded Miss Coulter who resigned as librarian in June 1944. The library now has a well-rounded collection of some 14,000 volumes.

Maryville at present has a population of about 8,000, covers two square miles and has 11 miles of hard-surfaced streets. An excellent recreation program is being developed as part of a county-wide movement.

The new municipal building ornamented with Tennessee marble from Friendsville and utilizing a great deal of aluminum began construction early in 1956 on the old West Side School site on Broadway. Dedication services were held on May 26, 1956. It houses the public utilities offices, the police and fire departments, and other city offices.

The grounds are spacious enough to provide for a front lawn, parking space and storage yards for utilities vehicles.

MORGANTON

Morganton was established in 1813, by act of legislature, on the Little Tennessee River eleven miles above its junction with Holston. The town was laid off as Portsville with 19 lots in the original plot, on the land of Hugh and Charles Kelso, but was chartered as Morganton. The commissioners were: William Lowry, James J. Greene, John Eakin, Richard DeArmond, Matt Wallace, James Wyley, John Lambert, Sr., and Joseph Duncan. The post office was established in 1816 with Samuel McCroskey, postmaster.[22]

Kelso's Mill had been built here in 1799 previous to the establishment of the town. (It burned in 1936.) A ferry has always been operated here, for a time as Wear's, and later Tipton's. The stationing of an official shipping inspector here brought about the founding of the town. In 1823, Morganton was one of the three voting places in the county. (Maryville and Tuckaleechee were the others.)

Taverns and general stores, and shops of all sorts sprang up immediately. By 1832, there were eighteen houses, seventy inhabitants, one physician, a hatter's shop, a cabinet shop, smith shops, a silver smith, a gun smith, a grist mill, a sawmill and a hemp factory for manufacturing rope and bagging. Nathaniel Reagan, and Utter and Stephens were storekeepers. Later Blair, McGhee & Bros., Jabez Coulson & Co., J. P. Lawrence & Bros. were in business.[23]

Edmund Wayman operated a wagon shop and manufactured wagons and buggies.

---
[22] *Acts, 1813,* ch. 49. Morganton was probably named for Gideon Morgan.
[23] Eastin Morris, *Tennessee Gazeteer* (Nashville, 1835), 104.

James McTeer operated an early blacksmith shop. Jonathan Tipton (son of Colonel John), state representative, and Robert Wear (son of Colonel Samuel), district and county surveyor, were early citizens.

Since an inspection port was established here in 1801 a great deal of shipping was handled. The Dawsons of Unitia operated barges and steamboats, and the Loves of Louisville also operated steamboats which plied up and down the river from Knoxville to Alabama. Morganton was an exchange point for Maryville and Kingston merchants. For this reason the Morganton Road became an important thoroughfare early in the county annals.[24]

In 1853, there were three dry goods, grocery and general merchandise stores operated by Messrs. Coulson, Tipton, and Jones. In 1857, the proprietors had changed to Jones and Cowan, J. B. Gaston & Co., Stevens and Tipton. Hugh Blair and W. G. McKenzie were practicing medicine.

In 1859, the Legislature was petitioned by one group to repeal the act incorporating Morganton, but a larger group asked that the charter not be repealed. They were, however, excused from paying corporation taxes on vacant lots.[25]

When Loudon County was erected in 1870, Morganton ceased to be a part of Blount County.

The advent of the railroad about 1900 drew attention and business away from Morganton and the river to Alleghany Station, now Greenback. Morganton is now a forgotten town with most of the old landmarks gone.

LOUISVILLE

It seems that Alexander Kelly, the first Lt. Col. Commandant of Blount County, probably first settled on the site of Louisville. He sold his holdings to William Rooker and Samuel Saffle. Robert and John Gillespie acquired a large tract of land in the same vicinity. The first road was cut by the Gillespies across the Saffle land to the river in order to haul their iron to the river for shipping. This boat-landing at the mouth of Lackey's Creek was called Gillespie's Landing. The Gillespies' Iron Works was located on Lackey Creek where Cox's milldam later stood. The iron ore was hauled by ox-wagons from the Ambrose Cox farm about three miles west of the works and from a mine up Little River near Russell's Ford (Rockford). The charcoal was burned in the valley just back of the hill and the extracted tar was used by settlers to lubricate their wagons (in early days each wagon carried a tar bucket for lubrication). This valley was called "Tar Kiln Valley." Later the

---

[24] *Acts, 1801*, ch. 5, sec. 24.
[25] *Petitions*, Tennessee State Archives, Nashville, Tennessee. *Acts, 1824*, ch. 36, sec. 3.

Gillespies could not compete with the price of iron manufactured in upper East Tennessee and discontinued operations.[26]

In 1838, Samuel Saffell established a ferry, at the mouth of Rooker Branch below Louisville and a new road was built from Middlesettlements by the "Dug Gap" to connect with his ferry. At the same time the Henry brothers were allowed to establish a ferry at the mouth of Lackey's Creek at the site of Gillespie's Landing.[27]

The first roads were to Maryville and to Lowe's Ferry. The Coxes: John, Nathaniel, and Ambrose, and two sisters, Nancy Cox and Elizabeth Cox Saffell settled here about 1800. Nathaniel went into the mercantile business soon afterwards and operated an inn. All merchandise at this time was hauled by wagon from Baltimore. Mrs. Cox said that when she first came to Louisville that there were two houses, a blacksmith shop and a hut occupied by Indians. The Louisville Post Office was established in 1828 with Nathaniel Cox as postmaster. He was succeeded by his son, H. Talbott Cox in 1839. On the death of Nathaniel Cox, his widow married Dr. George Hunt Chaffin who had come from North Carolina. They continued to operate the inn, and the sons, Henry T. and J. L. Cox, continued the mercantile business.

In 1833, Louisville was described as one-fourth mile from Holston River with four dwelling houses, one store, one blacksmith shop, one cotton gin, two grist mills, three sawmills, and an iron works, a quarter mile from town.[28]

Ambrose Cox was injured by a falling timber at a barn-raising on the farm of Dr. Isaac Wright and died in 1836. One of John Cox Sr.'s sons, James K., was the local schoolmaster. The other son, Madison, was a doctor.

Soon after the coming of the Coxes, John F. and James Henry built a two-story building and operated as commission merchants under the style "Samuel Henry and Sons." The Brick Mill Henrys also shipped flour and other goods from Louisville. The Henrys did extensive river trade between Louisville and New Orleans. Later they sold this property to H. T. Cox and built a store or warehouse closer to the river. In the late 1840's they sold their business to Horace Foster and moved to Knox County where John F. Henry was elected to the State Senate. Then he returned to Blount County and built a fine home and served as Representative to the Legislature from Blount County.[29]

Barton L. Warren operated a large tannery and leather business on his plantation east of town. Many young men served their apprenticeship in the tannery business with Mr. Warren.

---

[26] Information from A. H. Love, *History of Louisville* (an unpublished manuscript in six chapters). John and Robert Gillespie were sons of William Gillespie. James built the stone house still standing west of Louisville.

[27] *Minutes*, Vol. 5, pp. 174, 75, 79.

[28] Eastin Morris, *Tennessee Gazetteer* (Nashville, 1834), 92.

[29] John F. Henry was Speaker of the Senate during one term. His only child was the mother of the Rev. A. N. Jackson.

Steamboat service was initiated on the river in 1828 when the "Atlas" made her first run. From 1835 to 1845 Louisville enjoyed a boom and the "Jim Williams" was locally owned and operated but was finally sunk on the Little River Shoals. The inland country, even to western Carolina, shipped goods down the river from this point and Louisville was a busy exchange center. H. T. Cox and Bros., Gilbert Bros., Henry Bros., Byerly and Owens, Finley Bros., Steele and Bros., all did wholesale business here.

J. B. and W. F. Cummins opened the first store after the Civil War, followed soon after by H. G. and J. L. Cox, and Sam Snapp. Snapp soon moved away to Texas and was succeeded by F. W. Keller and Co.

Pelts, hides, tallow, beeswax, dried fruits, feathers, whisky, grain, flour, and bacon were all standard goods. The smithy business was a lucrative occupation. B. F. Wilkinson operated four forges. Joseph Brown (a Canadian) and Miss Nancy Cox's handy man Joe (a Negro), all did smith work.

About 1840, John Sparger came from Virginia and operated a large wagon shop and saddletree shop. An 1850 news story said that the saddletree shop was turning out 100 trees weekly. J. M. George worked with Sparger and later opened shop for himself. James K. Orr was also a later wagonmaker. Abram Hartsell had a cabinet shop.

Horace Foster and L. D. Skinner ran cooper shops and manufactured barrels, tubs, water buckets, churns, etc. They supplied barrels for George Ramsey and other local distillers as well as for shipping bacon and flour down the river. There were two saloons in the town.

The local shoemakers were Obediah McKenzie, Riley and Bart Milligan.

There were two large warehouses on the riverfront. One was owned by Henry C. Saffle, who owned a sawmill on Lackey's Creek west of town, and the other by Arthur Kennedy, who owned the flour mills at the east end of town. There was a wharf extending about one hundred feet along the waterfront.

According to information gleaned from the Kennedy Papers, the shipping downstream was done by flatboat. The common price for flatboats was $2 to $2.25 per foot. The boats were generally sold for the lumber when the produce was disposed of.

A news item in *Brownlow's Whig* in December 1850 stated that A. Kennedy that season had already slaughtered 250 head of cattle and lots of hogs for shipping. Gilbert and son had slaughtered near a hundred. If barrels were available there would likely be 1,000 hogs and 500 cattle processed for shipping. This account gives an idea of the volume of business carried on.

In March 1851, a petition signed by forty citizens was recorded asking the County Court for permission to incorporate the town of Louisville by right of a charter issued in January 1850. Hiram Hartsell was the first mayor, M. L. Teffeteller, Horace Foster, R. S. Cummings, A. Heartsill, W. T. Johnson and G. S. Gilbert were aldermen; W. W. Eagleton, recorder; and Joseph Hart, town constable. A patrol of five citizens was appointed by the mayor, whose duties were mostly concerned with runaway Negroes. Those found in town after 9 P.M. without a pass were publicly whipped by the town constable. A. H. Love described one such whipping and says 39 lashes were laid on with a leather strap. He also related the incidents leading up to the hanging of one of Jack Cox's Negroes in Maryville for the murder of a Mr. Humes. Charles had borrowed the shotgun used to kill Mr. Humes from Andy Tedford, a free Negro, who lived in Louisville and was proven innocent of the murder. Love mentioned a dozen or two "Free Negroes," among them, Cox, Henry and Warren.[30]

The Masonic building was erected in 1847 and is still in use. The town was divided into six sections. B. F. Owens operated the hotel during this era. The aldermen voted to spend $160.00 on the wharf to facilitate river trade. In June 1855 Mayor Hiram Hartsell appointed a committee to erect a "calaboose" or "lockup" of heavy hewn logs.

Thomas Barnett raised tobacco and had a tobacco press and manufactured "plug" tobacco. Prior to 1850 Dr. G. H. Chaffin, John Singleton, J. T. Love, and Dr. Madison Cox practiced medicine in Louisville. L. D. Carter and L. A. Gamble were dentists. Drs. Sam Gault, E. Goetz, N. T. Kraus, W. M. Douthit, J. C. Gillespy and A. B. McTeer are listed as later practitioners.

The flood of 1867 is described as the worst ever known in the Tennessee Valley. The river at Louisville rose to 42½ feet. The water was 8 inches deep in the aisles of the Methodist church. Kennedy's warehouse was washed away, and Saffles' warehouse was saved by the weight of the grain which was ruined.

Transportation on the river was at low tide, due partly to the establishment of the railroad to Maryville, in the 1870's. H. C. Saffell continued to operate a warehouse. In the spring of 1875 another flood swept down the Tennessee Valley. It lacked two feet of reaching the height of the 1867 tide. Saffell's warehouse was saved this time by being weighted down with rocks. From 1875–80 river traffic picked up, stimulated by the building of the Cincinnati Southern Railroad and heavy traffic was carried on between Louisville and Cooper's Landing on the Emory River.[31]

When this boom died down, J. E. Hartsill and A. H. Love built a large freight boat which operated by manpower and plied between Louisville and Concord mostly. Love took over the business and later went into partnership with F. W. Keller and bought the steamer "Tellico" which operated between Knoxville and Rockwood Landing. Later A. H. Love bought the Saffle warehouse where he operated a

---

[30] *Minutes*, Vol. 7, March 1851 and December 1853; A. H. Love, *History of Louisville*, ch. 3; R. C. Saffell signed the petition, provided that the town did not attempt to control the wharfs. The charter of incorporation was repealed in 1860. (*Acts, 1860*, ch. 103).

[31] *Maryville Times*, March 8, 1902 related a story of a third flood "highest in 33 years."

store and continued steamboat operations with the "Clinton B. Fisk"; "Water Lily"; and later the "Walter A. Love." S. H. Wilkinson (Sim) was pilot and Ed Coker, mate, during the 80's and 90's when the marble business was in full swing at the Bond and Great Bend quarries on the Knox County side of the river and the Sheep Pen quarries on the Louisville side. The "Water Lily" made daily trips to Concord where the marble was shipped by rail to various points.

After the completion of the L. & N. Railroad line from Knoxville to Marietta, Georgia, about 1900, the town lost its importance as a river town, and became more or less static.

In 1943 the formation of Ft. Loudoun Lake flooded part of the original townsite and necessitated the relocation of roads and old landmarks. The cemeteries in the vicinity were moved to a new location on the hill adjoining the Interdenominational Holiness Association Campground (now Nazarene) about one mile east of Louisville on the Maryville Pike.

UNITIA

The first settlements in the vicinity of Unitia were made about 1791 by a group of Friends: Matthews, Griffitts, Hackney, Allen and Jones. In 1799, Samuel Shaw built a grist and sawmill about a mile from the mouth of Cloyd's Creek. He later operated a ferry and a warehouse for storing grain and merchandise on the river.

The first post office was established in 1824 with John E. Haire, postmaster. He was followed in 1825 by James Jones who served for twenty years. Unitia was one and one-half miles from the mouth of Cloyd's Creek, which was Shaw's Ferry as early as 1800, later called Leeper's Ferry.

In 1833, there were seventy inhabitants, one store, a blacksmith shop, a hatter, one doctor, a tanyard, a wool-carding and a cotton-picking machine.[32]

In 1853, J. H. Donaldson, S. M. Leeper and S. Matthews were the merchants.[33]

Unitia Presbyterian Church was organized in 1820 (the Shaws and several other local families belonged to the Seceder Church at Big Springs). The church was moved to the hill at the cemetery when the waters of Loudoun Lake covered the old site in 1943. The Methodist church was organized in 1875 and a good per cent of the local people belonged to the Friends Church in Hickory Valley. Unitia is in that section of Blount which became part of Loudoun County when it was erected in 1870.

The Masons had an active organization as early as 1861. The Odd Fellows were meeting by 1890 and the Junior Order in 1901. When the

---

[32] Eastin Morris, *Tennessee Gazeteer*, 166.
[33] Campbell's Directory, 1853–54, p. 259.

railroad was finished about 1900, a station was set up at Kizer nearby which became a post office in 1893. The post office at Unitia was discontinued in 1903.

TUCKALEECHEE COVE AND TOWNSEND

The first definite reference to Tuckaleechee is made by the trader Vaughn in 1740. He spoke of following an Indian trading path through the cove.[34]

The next reference is a North Carolina grant in 1791 for 1,000 acres to Charles McClung and James Woods Lackey, adjoining their two thousand acre survey which included the Tuckaleechee Towns.

All evidence seems to point toward John Walker, Sr., as the first settler. The first registered transfer of lands was from John Walker, Sr., to John Walker, Jr., April 22, 1793. John Walker was also granted permission to build a mill on his property when the first session of Blount County Court met in 1795.[35]

A file of depositions relative to certain land claims prove that Hughes, Snider, Cameron, Quiett, McClanahan and other later settlers got their land from Walker and that grants were later issued to these people.[36]

When the Indian depredations became so prevalent in 1794, it was decided by the Territorial Assembly that a post or fort should be erected in Tuckaleechee on Little River. However, there is no indication that this was ever done.[37]

In 1797, a check of the Hawkins line found two "intruders" in Tuckaleechee Cove. By the first Treaty of Tellico, October 2, 1798, Tuckaleechee was open for legal settlement. Rapid settlement is indicated by the extensive tax list for 1800. Fifteen of this list received land grants in Tuckaleechee by 1810.[38]

John Walker had been granted leave in 1795 to build a mill. William Hughes was granted leave to build at the same place in 1801. However, the Legislature declared Little River navigable to Bradley's Mill in Tuckaleechee Cove. We suppose Bradley was the Major John Bradley of the Blount County Militia, but no reference has been found as to how he got a permit for the mill.[39]

The first Baptist church in Blount County was organized in Tuckaleechee Cove in 1802, and was dissolved in 1810 to form the Wear's Cove and Miller's Cove congregations. Presbyterians had held services in 1799 and 1800. The Methodists organized in 1830 at the "Campground." The division of the Baptists in 1838 and the Methodists in 1865 completed the church picture up to 1900.[40]

---

[34] *Haywood*, 40.
[35] State of North Carolina, Grant #969; *Knox County Deeds*, A, 4; *Blount County Deeds*, 1, p. 175; *Minutes*, 1795, September session.
[36] *Petitions*, Tennessee State Archives. Nashville, Tennessee.
[37] *Knoxville Gazette*, March 14, 1794; May 22, 1794.
[38] *Tax Lists*, Blount County, 1800. Tennessee State Archives, Nashville, Tenn.
[39] *Acts, 1801.*
[40] *Tennessee Baptist Association Minutes*, 1802—*Minutes of Union Presbytery*, 1799, 1800; *Recording Steward's Book*, Little River Circuit, 1830—Passim.

There are nine cemeteries in Tuckaleechee Cove: Myers, Campground, Bethel Baptist, Tuckaleechee Chapel, Tuckaleechee Primitive Baptist (Coker Hill), Caylor's Chapel, Brickey, Burns and the Davis-Lane.

Schools were established early, but no definite information is available. Roads were established as soon as the county was erected; first to Maryville, and then to Sevierville. Regular twice-weekly mail routes were established by 1832.

Grist mills were established with the first settlement and other industries added as demanded. A distillery and cooper shop was operated by Peter Brickey until the Civil War. An ironworks was operated by Robert Shields in 1843 at Sunshine but it was not rebuilt when destroyed by high waters.[41]

William Myers operated a grist, sawmill, and cotton gin above Cedar Bluff on Little River prior to the Civil War. Richard Burns operated a sawmill later, and was followed by Fayette Wear. George Snider and the Emerts operated the first general stores in the cove. George Snider was the first postmaster in 1833 and no doubt the post office was in the store.[42]

It was in 1855 and 1856 that John Mitchell, the exiled Irish patriot, "rusticated" in Tuckaleechee Cove.

The lumber industry is strongly interwoven in the history of Tuckaleechee Cove. The first chapter involves the work of Captain Duncan McDonald and his son Harry who cut most of the virgin poplar in the cove from three sets: the "Sleepy" John Myers place, the Dry Valley, and Laurel Creek.

The second chapter was the "lumberjack" period between 1896 and 1900. Those "splash" operations were in charge of J. L. English, who operated a mill near Rockford.

In April 1900, a party of five men: W. B. Townsend, William McCormick, William Wrigley, Joe Dickey, and Asbury Lee visited Tuckaleechee Cove and in February 1901, the Little River Lumber Company was chartered. The Little River Railroad was chartered in November the same year to operate between Townsend and Walland which was the terminus of the K. and A. Railroad.[43]

The town which sprang up about the sawmill became Townsend officially with the establishing of a post office in 1902. Tuckaleechee Cove in the lower part of the cove was a post office from 1833 to 1906. Tang operated at the house of "Sleepy John" Myers from 1886 to 1906. Sweet in the Dry Valley was operated from 1898 to 1904 by Joe L. Walker.[44]

---

[41] J. P. Lesley, *Iron Manufacturer's Guide* (Philadelphia, 1859), 202.

[42] *Deeds,* AA, 274.

[43] *Corporations,* 1, p. 169, 193.

[44] Photostats of post office data from National Archives, Washington, D. C. The name Tang came from "Mustang" Liniment.

The mill burned in 1906, and again in 1916, and was rebuilt each time. The railroad was finished to Elkmont in 1908. The middle prong (Tremont) was the last site of lumbering operations. A post office was established there in 1926. All operations ceased in 1938 and practically all signs of lumber operations have disappeared from Tuckaleechee Cove.

When the Smoky Mountains National Park movement was initiated, Little River Lumber Company offered 77,000 acres to the Park Commission. The main highways through the Little River Gorge now follow the roadbeds of the Little River Railroad lines.

The Patent Button Company of Tennessee operated in Tuckaleechee from 1934 to 1937 when they moved their operations to Knoxville.

The chief interest aside from agriculture is tourist developments. Tuckaleechee Caverns are being developed as a side attraction. Along the highways are found ultra-modern accommodations while almost within view in the fastnesses of the hollows and side coves can be found Elizabethan customs and speech.

From Tuckaleechee Cove one can climb three hundred feet into Wear's Cove in Sevier County; or seven hundred feet into Cades Cove; up Little River Gorge and over the mountain; or down the gorge to Miller's Cove which stretches along the back side of the Chilhowee Mountains.

MILLER'S COVE AND WALLAND

Miller's Cove stretches along the Chilhowee Mountains for about ten miles. Little River flows across the cove and through the gap of the Chilhowee range at Walland.

The earliest grant on record is a North Carolina grant to John Rhea in 1794 for 940 acres in Greene County on both sides of Little River in Murphy's Cove.[45]

The east end is drained by Reed's Creek (named for Alexander Reed who died before 1810). Walden's Creek can be reached from the east end by a three-mile stretch of unimproved road.

The west end of Miller's Cove which is drained by Hess' Creek (named for John Hess, a Swiss immigrant who came from Carter County, and died before 1808), is about seven miles long.

Early references to this cove call it Murphy's Cove, but very soon after settlement it was consistently called Miller's Cove probably from Andrew and Alexander Miller who were listed with the 1800 taxpayers. A report on the Hawkins Line listed four "intruders" in Murphy's Cove in 1797. John Hess, most certainly must have been one of these.[46]

Amerine's Forge which was operated by George Amerine from 1845 to the beginning of the Civil War was the largest ironworks operated in Blount County. It was a two-bloomary forge located on Hess' Creek

---

[45] *Deeds*, 1, p. 142 (Grant #1502).
[46] *Minutes*, September 13, 1796. "John Hess is to have leave to build a mill in a place called Murphy's Cove near the mouth of Murphy's Creek.

just below the open fields on the present Mountain Homes tract in the west end of Miller's Cove. Huge piles of slag are at the site and excavation signs are plain in the Chilhowee "Flats" where the ore was removed.

Above the open fields previously mentioned is the junction of Hess and Cane creeks. A road formerly led from Miller's Cove over the Cane Creek Divide, down Abram's Creek to Happy Valley. Most of this road is still open and used by park rangers (at least from the site of the Cane schoolhouse and the Buchanan Cemetery).

At one time, houses were scattered along Cane Creek and along this road to Happy Valley. The Great Smoky Mountains National Park owns all the land on the south side of Cane Creek and about a mile from its junction with Hess' Creek takes in both sides.

John Waters built the first grist and sawmill in the east end and the descendants of Waters and James Walker have populated that section up to the present. A post office (Waters) was operated here from 1884 to 1912.

Dr. James H. Gillespy, was quite a land speculator and in his later days settled in Miller's Cove to oversee and dispose of his thousands of acres of mountain land.

Miller's Cove became the 18th district in May, 1880. (It had previously been a part of the 15th with Tuckaleechee Cove.)

In October, 1900, the Tennessee Lumber Canal Company was chartered to operate a railroad from Maryville to the Fork of Little River in Tuckaleechee Cove. When the right of way was obtained, this company quietly disappeared and the K. and A. or Southern Railroad took over the railroad to Walland, which was finished late in 1901.

In May 1901, Schlosser Leather Company was chartered to "tan hides and manufacture leathers." They were also empowered to operate flour mills, and build railroads.[47]

Five days later, Josias ("Stutt") Gamble sold a tract of 223 acres on the northeast side of Little River to Schlosser Leather Company and the company under the supervision of J. W. Fisher began the construction of a tannery in Miller's Cove.

The tannery began operations in 1902. Walland was officially born with the establishment of a post office in March 1902. The name Walland was a combination of Walton and England, two of the chief men in the Schlosser Leather Company combination. A. J. Fisher was the superintendent of the tannery from its beginning until 1922. This plant handled an average of 300–400 hides per day and each hide was five months in process. About 250 carloads of tanbark per year were used (some of it, hemlock especially, was bought locally). This company had their own power plant in 1909.

---

[47] *Corporations*, 1, p. 169, 179. The taxes paid by the tannery to the county were remitted to them until they had recovered the amount expended by them for right-of-way under the style Tennessee Lumber Canal Company.

COMMUNITIES 275

This plant was destroyed by fire in January 1931. On account of an injunction, it was decided not to rebuild at Walland, and whatever materials that had been salvaged were removed to the Unaka Tannery at Newport or to the Junaluska Tannery at Hazelwood, North Carolina.

There has been a Methodist church since 1830. The Miller's Cove Baptist Church, established in 1810, was the first permanent Baptist church in Blount County. Both denominations used the same building until 1890, when Dr. Samuel Gillespy and Aaron Burns headed a movement to build a Methodist church in the east end, which was also to be used by the Presbyterians. About 1910, the Presbyterians were barred from the use of the church.

The main cemetery is at the Missionary Baptist Church in the west end. There are three small family cemeteries in the west end of the cove as well as the one on Cane Creek and a small one on another stream to the right of Cane Creek.

CADES COVE

The first official reference to Cades Cove is contained in a North Carolina grant issued to Hugh Dunlap in 1794 for 5,000 acres in a place called Cades Cove. This grant was mislaid and when re-issued in 1809 by the State of Tennessee was subject to previous occupant-entries and school reservations.[48]

A petition from Aaron Crowson to the Tennessee Legislature, June 10, 1820, stated that his father, William Crowson, and a Mr. James Ross, both possessed the right of occupancy and pre-emption to a tract of land in Cades Cove on the 6th of February, 1796. References are also found to a Linville improvement in Cades Cove. Earlier, in 1809, John Smith and William Crowson had petitioned for entry rights for land in Cades Cove for which they held North Carolina grants. These were confirmed in 1820 and a grant based on these was issued to William Tipton March 23, 1821, which is the first Tennessee grant issued for land in Cades Cove which was not legally open for entry until after 1819.[49]

From 1821 to 1836 William Tipton ("Fighting Billy") sold about 2,000 acres to his Carter County relatives, some of whom moved on to Walker County, Georgia, about 1830, when the Indian lands further south were opened. His son Jacob stayed in Cades Cove until the 1840's when he went to Missouri along with the Hyatts and others but left two sons Isaac and John ("Jack") in the Cove.

The Cables, Burchfields and Olivers came to Cades Cove before 1825, and the Sparks family in 1833. After the 1830 emigration to Georgia,

---

[48] North Carolina grant #172, registered April 18, 1794, Eastern District, Book 7, p. 263; Book 9, p. 155. Tennessee State Archives, Nashville, Tenn.
[49] Register of East Tennessee, Book O, p. 538. *Deeds,* 3, p. 3; *Petitions,* Box 24, Tennessee State Archives; Letter from Charles A. Richey, Chief of Land Planning, Department of Interior, Washington, D. C., October 2, 1950. An unregistered deed from James Smith's heirs to John Smith in the writer's possession.

several new families came to Cades Cove. A great many families left Cades Cove, among them Foute, Bradford, Lemons, Cobb, Campbell, and Pearce, after the Civil War on account of war happenings.

The Cades Cove Bloomary Forge was built on Forge Creek about 1827 and was operated by Daniel D. Foute. The Tiptons had previously carried on some sort of forge operations. Coaling signs are still visible.[50]

A post office was established in 1833 which continued until 1947. Cable Post Office operated in 1896 and 1897.

Dr. Abraham Job in his diary says that the soil was rich and that stock-raising was good, but that it was two or three years before they had a flour mill in the cove. Only tub mills were first built, and orchards had to be planted.[51]

Some of the first settlers left because they were too "shut-off" from the rest of the world. Daniel D. Foute did much to try to make it easier to get in and out. He built a road from Maryville to Cades Cove and a road out through Chestnut Flats to Parson's Turnpike to North Carolina. These roads were at first bridle paths or pack trails, and were later widened into wagon roads. The Cooper road was probably the improved version of Foute's first road.[52]

George Powell operated one of the most elaborate distilleries in Blount County, at first as a licensed distiller. He had an orchard of several hundred fruit trees and manufactured fine brandies. A "revenuer" raid at his place once destroyed eleven tubs of beer and mash, four tubs of pomace, 130 gallons of "singlings," five bushels of meal, two bushels of rye, and two bushels of malt.[53] About forty shots were exchanged with no injuries. The "engineer of the mash mill" escaped. Powell's wagon was the most popular "apple wagon" which came to market during the court week, and he always had choice quarters at the livery stable where he slept close to his wagon.

The Baptist church was established in 1827 and the Methodist church in 1830. This sufficed until the Baptist split in 1838 and the Methodist division at the end of the Civil War.

There are cemeteries at each one of the four churches in the cove. The Cable graveyard is in the lower end where the Cable School stood. Two groups of graves are at the Post place (later Willie Myers) and one at the Burchfield farm as well as a cemetery in the Chestnut Flats.[54]

Since all of Cades Cove was taken into the Smoky Mountains National Park, it seems proper to review the Park movement at this place.

---

[50] J. P. Lesley, *Iron Manufacturer's Guide* (Phila., 1859), 202; *Deeds*, Passim.

[51] Dr. Abraham Job, *Memoirs or Diary* (unpublished manuscript). Mrs. L. W. McCown collection, Johnson City, Tenn. (He said that they attended school in Tuckaleechee Cove at first. They also got their fruit there from Mr. Scott.).

[52] *Acts* and *Deeds*, 1820–1855, Passim; When Blount County was divided into districts, Cades Cove was made the 16th district and Capt. Jacob Tipton's house was the voting place.

[53] Maryville *Index*, September 18, 1878.

[54] The M. E. Church stood on top of the rise in the woods just past Caughron's beehives on the south side of the cove. The church was removed, but the cemetery is still there.

The Park and National Forest movement toward a Southern park started in 1899, which was merely a sectional movement in forest conservation.

Through the efforts of Mr. and Mrs. W. P. Davis, the Great Smoky Mountains Conservation Association was formed in 1923, and in 1925 it was incorporated to raise money to purchase land. The Tennessee Great Smoky Mountains Park Commission was created in 1927.[55]

The actual achievement of the park may fairly be attributed to Col. D. C. Chapman as chairman of the association and of the Tennessee State Commission.

The Great Smoky Mountains National Park became a national park in 1930 with the help of five million dollars given by John D. Rockefeller, Jr. The park stretches 71 miles along the summit between Tennessee and North Carolina from Davenport Gap to Deal's Gap or from Big Pigeon River to Little Tennessee River. It extends an average width of fourteen miles. It contains 687.5 square miles of which nearly half is primitive, which makes it the sixth largest national park.[56]

77,000 acres were taken from Little River Lumber Company, which had already depleted its forests. The Blount County sector of the park stretches from seven miles east of Thunderhead to Deal's Gap, and includes Meig's Falls and Abram's Falls. All of Cades Cove and its environs, the mountains enclosing the headwaters of Hess's Creek in Miller's Cove and the Richwood section of Happy Valley is included and keeps the waters of Abram's Creek under control practically to its mouth. Titles had been cleared and the State of Tennessee had transferred 72,000 acres lying in Blount County, to the Federal government by 1933.

One of the most fascinating and thus far unexplained things in the Smokies is the "balds." Three of these are in Blount County; Thunderhead, Gregory's and Parson's Bald and also the Spence Field. These open grass ranges gave livelihood to a great number of Cades Cove men prior to 1930. There have been many theories advanced as to how these balds happened to be, and whether they will eventually become forest. It is evident that Gregory and Parson's balds are gradually becoming shrub balds. Since the removal of grazing and forest fires, blueberries and azaleas are spreading in all directions. Every season the azaleas on Gregory's and Parson's balds are becoming more of an attraction for those who are hardy enough to climb the six miles to the top.[57]

---

[55] The term "smoky" was first used by Governor Campbell of Virginia in 1781.

[56] *Living Wilderness*, March 1942, p. 3–19. Tennessee *Wildlife*, December, 1939 (Great Smoky Mountains National Park ed.); Dept. of Interior, *Great Smoky Mountains National Park*, 1941.

[57] The Diary of Samuel McCammon, 1846–54 (McClung Collection) tells every April about "belling" and driving his cattle from Knox County to Spence Field and to Gregory's Bald and leaving his cattle with various herders, according to whether he thought their ranges good. In April, 1847, it snowed when they got to the top and some of the cattle died. In 1848, there was trouble about a new North Carolina law and he took his cattle up the Little Tennessee River and in 1849 to the Cumberland Mountains. Sometimes they had trouble rounding up their cattle.

The most enthusiastic early press agent that Cades Cove had was Dr. William Clark of Franklin, Tennessee, who was with General Wilder's expedition in the late 60's. He wrote a series of descriptions under such titles as "A Tennessee Paradise" and "The Switzerland of America." [58]

A few families are still living in Cades Cove and some restoration has been done, notably the Cable Mill and some of the houses. The campgrounds are being enlarged, and roads improved as the budget allows. The new road up Laurel Creek was finished in 1951 and has made this garden-spot available to everyone and its popularity continues to grow.

HAPPY VALLEY

Running parallel along the south side of the Chilhowee range is a narrow cove known as Happy Valley. This valley connects with the Chilhowee Cove along the Little Tennessee River.

Robert Rhea, who had fought in the Revolution and the Indian Wars, in 1823, asked the Tennessee Legislature to give him a quarter section in the Hiwassee district "whereon to spend his declining years in peace." In early records, this cove is spoken of as Rhea's Valley. Robert Rhea was the first coroner of Blount County and lived until 1850, and is buried in the Chilhowee Primitive Baptist Cemetery ("Red Top").

After the Civil War, County Court minutes refer to the place as Happy Valley. This name is perhaps explained by the fact that the Whiteheads, Rasars, Herrons, Gourley's, Boones, Borings, and numbers of other families who are still living in Happy Valley came from Carter County at the end of the Civil War and that the name is reminiscent of Happy Valley in Carter County.

Carson's Iron Works on Abram's Creek at the head of Happy Valley, was a post office in 1833 and was listed as a point on the 1832 mail route from Sevierville to Chilhowee.

Happy Valley became the third district in 1880, replacing the district lost to Blount County in 1870 when Loudoun County was erected. There were fifty voters at that time and the schoolhouse at Aaron Crumley's was the voting place. James H. Rasar and David L. Smith were prominent citizens. (Smith was mill operator and storekeeper.) The Rasar Post Office with James H. Rasar as its postmaster was established in 1882 and still serves the population.

There is a Missionary and a Primitive Baptist Church in Happy Valley. There is a cemetery at each of these churches and the Boone Cemetery between the two. The Richwood section at the head of the valley, which supported several families, was taken into the Great Smoky Mountains National Park.

---

[58] Dr. Clark was editor of the newspaper which is now the Nashville *Banner*. Dr. Sam Clark of Vanderbilt Medical School has a scrapbook of these materials.

ROCKFORD

From the earliest days of the county's history the Federal road from Knoxville to Maryville and Tellico Blockhouse crossed Little River at McCullock's. When regular stage lines were established, this was a stopping-place.

The first industry to be established here was a mill built by Jehu and Holston Stephens in 1817. This act provided that provisions must be made for boats to bypass the dam. Another Act relating to this project, provided for a commission to examine the dam when finished.[59]

In 1837, William Oldham, who had been operating a cotton mill in Knox County which was destroyed by flood. Evidently he removed the machinery to the Stephens mill site and rebuilt it, since a deed from Jehu and Holston Stephens to Oldham in 1840 refers to the mill site and factory erected by Oldham.

In 1845 the Stephens brothers sold their saw and grist mill on the south side of Little River to Alexander Kennedy. A news items stated that a most excellent cotton factory on Little River was owned and operated by Mr. Kennedy, that a good quality of yarn, domestic and tickings were made.[60]

In 1852, David Caldwell sold a tract of land opposite the Kennedy factory to the Rockford Manufacturing Company. The company was represented by: William Wallace, James M. Toole, Alexander Kennedy, Arthur A. Kennedy, R. I. Wilson, William C. Gillespy, Edward George, James Porter, John M. Coffin, James R. Love, and John E. Toole. This is the first appearance of the name Rockford, probably taken from "Rocky Ford."

An 1854 directory listed B. F. Reeder as engaged in a dry goods and grocery business at Rockford. In 1855 Alexander Kennedy sold his saw and grist mill to the Rockford Manufacturing Company, which under various ownerships has continued operation to the present and is still an outstanding business.[61]

The Rockford Post Office was established in 1854, with William McCampbell as postmaster. The Little River Post Office had been established in 1849 with Thomas McCulloch as postmaster, and was discontinued in 1852.

---

[59] *Acts, 1817*, ch. 147; *1823*, ch. 250. Jehu Stephens was a son-in-law of William Tipton and had served as Captain in the War of 1812.

[60] *Deeds*, 1840–50, Passim. Knoxville *Register*, June 8, 1850; a bill head for 1857 said: "Manufacturers of 4-4 shirtings and cotton yarns" and listed domestic yarn and calico. (Kennedy Papers).

[61] *Deeds*, X, 261; Y, 175.

Business continued throughout the Civil War under permission. A few incidents were recorded in the war record. Ten cotton bales from Rockford were requisitioned by General Burnside and were used in the building of Fort Sanders. In 1889 a special bill allowed Alexander Kennedy $3,375 for this cotton.[62]

The company was re-chartered after the Civil War. In 1874 the factory was described as the most important industry in the county.[63]

From 1886 to 1909 there was also a South Rockford Post Office operated by E. E. and A. A. Wrinkle.

A Presbyterian church was organized here in the 1850's and disbanded in 1943 and the property was taken over by the Wesley Ann Methodist Church, which prior to this, had been located at the mouth of Roddy Branch. The Baptist church was established in 1885.

A fine modern school of city dimensions was built in 1952. An active Masonic lodge is also located here.

CHILHOWEE

The Indian village, Chilhowee, near the mouth of Abram's Creek, was in existence before white settlement, so it is safe to assume that it would have been seized by some white person as soon as possible after the Indian evacuation. At any rate Hugh Ghormley became postmaster at Chilhowee in 1828 and regular twice-weekly mail service was established in 1832.[64]

In 1830, Daniel D. Foute, who owned Montvale Springs, built a road across Chilhowee Mountain down Rhea Valley to Chilhowee. This road to Maryville was used until the railroad was built in 1907.

In 1844–46, two attempts were made to establish Jones County with Joseph Ashley's (Chilhowee) as county seat. These attempts failed because they could not get the minimum territory required without encroaching on Blount and Monroe counties.

In 1850–53, William and Robert James, Englishmen, built the Chilhowee Spinning and Manufacturing Company which operated until the Civil War when the factory was closed and the James family returned to England. During this period an Episcopal church was established at Chilhowee.[65]

Riverboats operated irregularly as far up the Little Tennessee River as Chilhowee. A road from Cades Cove to Chilhowee was also opened in the 1850's. The opening of Parson's Turnpike into North Carolina 1830–50 also helped Ashley and Ghormley to do a thriving drygoods business with North Carolina clients. William Ashley sold the business to Caswell Davis in 1859.[66]

---

[62] Bill S. 151, 51st Congress, 1st Session, December 4, 1889 (Kennedy Papers).
[63] *Acts, 1866–67*, ch. 68, sec. 71; J. B. Killebrew, *Resources of Tennessee*.
[64] Post Office data from National Archives, Washington, D. C.; *Knoxville Register*, August 15, 1852.
[65] *Acts, 1848*, ch. 68; *1843*, ch. 196; *P A, 1829*, ch. 178; *Knoxville Register*, June 22, 1853.
[66] *Deeds*, 3, 254; *Acts, 1825*, ch. 312; *1830*, ch. 178; *Knoxville Register*, June 8, 1850 tells about the "Cassandra" making a trip to Chilhowee.

The various slate interests which developed in the 1879–1900 era helped to boost Chilhowee and the building of the Tennessee Carolina Southern Railroad to this point in 1907 gave the surrounding country a permanent outlet. The post office has been in continuous operation since 1828.

There are two cemeteries at Chilhowee: one, a very old neglected one at the early church site on top of the hill at the mouth of Abram's Creek; the other at Chilhowee Baptist Church about one mile down the river from Chilhowee.

FRIENDSVILLE

By 1808, a Friends Church had been officially established among those families who had located in this community twelve miles west of Maryville in the early 1790's.

John Hackney, in 1819, built a sawmill and a grist mill on Gallahar's Creek which became a part of the town when it was built. This mill was later operated by William and Elias Jones and James F. Beals, and more recently by Moses Gamble.

By 1850, David Morgan sold town lots and opened a store and established a post office called Friendsville. The church was then considering the advisability of establishing their own school, which was done in 1857. Morgan had set aside a lot for the school when the town was laid out.

About 1883, the first marble workings began in the vicinity of Friendsville which has varied in volume, but it is now one of the more important county industries.

Friendsville is a station on the L. & N. Railroad since about 1900 and this has helped to boost the marble industry. The town was incorporated in 1952 to facilitate the administration of utilities.

The People's Bank of Friendsville was the only banking institution in Blount County outside of Maryville. It operated from May, 1915 to June, 1936.

CLOVER HILL

A post office was established by Abijah Conger in 1823 by the name of Clover Hill. Conger had planted the first clover in the county about this time and was proud of the fact. Conger evidently operated a sort of store and tavern on the road to Morganton.

David McKamey built his mill and distillery on a branch of Baker's Creek about a mile from the main road in 1849, and a small commnuity grew around these operations.

Dr. Samuel Gault began his medical practice here in 1869 and he also was postmaster. At one period a telephone exchange was operated here. The Presbyterian church location was moved to Clover Hill about 1850 and a school was located here after the Civil War.

The post office was discontinued to Binfield in 1915. The Clover Hill Mill is still in operation.

BRICK MILL

The name of the community of Brick Mill was taken from Samuel Henry's second mill which he built in 1815 to house his French burr millstones.

The first mill and Baker's Creek Church were both established simultaneously with the county and the state at Henry's Station or Fort.

A large commission trade was carried on by Samuel Henry's sons from the Brick Mill. They even "wagoned" as far as Atlanta with their flour, grain, domestic produce, and livestock.

A post office was established here in 1858 by James A. McKamey. The post office was continued until 1907 when rural routes were established in Blount County.

Robert Bogle operated a large tanyard at his "Hide Park" farm nearby at an early date. Later Hale and Hollifield carried on tanning and leather operations.

CARPENTER'S CAMPGROUND

The name Carpenter's Campground has been attached to the community from the Methodist church and campground. The community has been known by various other names. The term applied from 1870–1891 was Huffstetler's Store which was the local post office. From 1891 to 1903, the post office was McKinley. Another name applied locally was Montvale Station which was the railroad station from 1907 to 1932.

The church name predates and has outlasted the other terms. The church was located at two other sites nearby before settling on the present site about 1850 on land given by Thomas Carpenter and Phillip Costner. The cemetery at this place is predated by the Hamil Graveyard which has been abandoned and most of the graves lost.

WELLSVILLE

The little community of Wellsville sprang up around the mill and tanyard of Stephen Wells. Daniel Best had built the mill in 1809 and Wells bought it from the Best heirs in 1876.

A post office (Houk) was established here with Wells as postmaster in 1879. Various postmasters served until 1892 when R. L. Belt was appointed postmaster. The name was changed to Wellsville in 1894. The post office remained at Belt's store until it was discontinued in 1937. Mr. Belt's daughter, Mrs. Ova B. Lindsey succeeded him as postmistress.

Wells' Mill was an institution in constant use until the death of John B. Wells in 1954. A cotton gin, grist and sawmill and other works were operated at this site for over one hundred and fifty years.

SUNSHINE

In 1894, Mr. E. J. Kinzel came to the west entrance of Tuckaleechee Cove and settled on the south side of Little River. The Kinzel Springs Hotel was built in 1914 and a railroad station was established called Kinzel Springs. Mr. Kinzel named the four peaks surrounding the hotel for the Apostles: Matthew, Mark, Luke and John.

Mr. Kinzel gave a site on the north side of the river to the International Sunshine Society to build a rest cottage for working girls. It is from this that the name Sunshine sprung.

The Kinzel Springs Post Office operated from 1925 until 1945. An average of seventy-five to one hundred summer cottages has existed for the past forty years. Part of the time two hotels operated. The old Sunshine Hotel burned in the forties and Kinzel Springs Hotel is now abandoned.

TALLASSEE

Tallassee was a station on the Tennessee Carolina Southern Railroad which went as far as Chilhowee in 1907. It is unfortunate that this name was applied here, because the Cherokee Indian village, Tallassee, was on both sides of the river at Tallassee Ford near where Calderwood now stands.

The post office, Tallassee, was established in 1928. At this time, a summer resort development was launched. A lodge was built across the river, and lots were sold for summer cabins along the mountain streams and several cabins were built. Interest waned in a few years and most of these cabins have been abandoned.

A sizable permanent community has grown up around the general store and post office.

ARMONA

Armona is an L. & N. Railroad station about four miles northwest of Maryville. In the early thirties, when strawberry-raising reached its peak, Armona was the main shipping point.

L. B. Sutton carried on his first canning operations at Armona.

The depression caused strawberry growers to become discouraged and shipping has never again reached the peak that it did in 1933 and 1934.

MENTOR

Mentor is located five miles northeast of Maryville at the junction of the through-line and the L. & N. Railroad loop. It sprang up as a construction camp and was later a section headquarters. Stores and churches were built as the community grew.

Charles H. Logan was postmaster when the post office was established in 1891 soon after the L. & N. main line went into operation. This is one of the few small post offices still in operation in the county.

BINFIELD

The community of Binfield was formed about the L. & N. Railroad station by that name. The L. & N. Railroad finished this line in 1906. William M. Carpenter who had been operating a store at Clover Hill moved his store near this station and in July 1907, he was appointed postmaster for Binfield Post Office and served in that capacity most of the time the post office existed.

In 1918, a high school was established at Binfield and a new consolidated school built there. This school never developed beyond the junior high stage and was abolished in 1932 and the high school students were transported to Friendsville.

The post office was discontinued in 1934 and a rural route now serves the community. There are three churches in the community: Clover Hill Presbyterian Church, Salem Baptist Church and Binfield Methodist Church.

The spring at the boyhood home site of Sam Houston is located within a stone's-throw of Salem Baptist Church.

CALDERWOOD

By 1910 the Aluminum Company of America had purchased the site of Calderwood from John Howard. A post office was established as Alcoa in September, 1912. In 1916, Calderwood, about 31 miles south of Maryville on the Little Tennessee River, became the construction camp for the Cheoah and Santeetlah dams which were being built just over the line in North Carolina.

The name Calderwood was officially given to the community in March 1920, when the post office name was changed from Alcoa to Calderwood. The name was given in honor of Mr. I. G. Calderwood who was superintendent of construction and was later in charge of building the Calderwood Dam.

In 1928 it was decided to build a dam about one and one-half miles above the town near a place called the "Narrows." This dam is built of concrete in the shape of a vertical arch. It is approximately 200 feet high and 708 feet long. The water is carried through a 2,700-foot tunnel, bored through solid rock 27 feet in diameter to the turbines in the powerhouse.

The Calderwood Dam was finished in 1930 and the railroad which had been built and operated from the terminus of the Tennessee Carolina and Southern Railroad at Chilhowee to Cheoah and Santeetlah, North Carolina was removed. By 1932, the rails had been removed to the switchyard at the Montvale Road in Maryville.

Calderwood, loosely speaking, occupies the site of the Indian village, Tallassee. Tallassee Ford was the terminus of the Calloway Turnpike or its junction with the Parson's Turnpike which led over the mountain into North Carolina. This road was in use from 1830 to 1910.

Movies and other community recreational features were established with the first permanent housing facilities and a progressive school was maintained by the company at first and later taken over by the county.

ALCOA

In 1910, the Aluminum Company of America started a long-range power development on the Little Tennessee River which included the erection of seven power dams, over a period of thirty years. This development required the continued services of engineers and buyers for five to ten years and necessitated the acquisition of more than five thousand separate parcels of land.

The site was chosen for the future city and its wide-spreading plants and in June 1913, the purchase of farm lands was begun. The first two reduction plant units (pot-rooms) were started in 1914 and the construction of about 150 houses was begun in 1916. This development was known as North Maryville. The erection of three or four service buildings and the installation of the necessary water, sewer and lighting systems was instituted and by 1919 the town was ready to be set into operation.[67]

The city was planned by E. S. Fickes, then chief engineer, and Robert F. Ewald, one of the company's hydraulic engineers. The plan provided zoning for industry, business, and residential areas with provisions for schools, churches, parks, playgrounds and recreational facilities. Streets, water and sewer lines, and park areas were laid out and initial plans provided for a city from five to six thousand people.[68]

In April 1919, the City of Alcoa was chartered for the commission-manager form of government and was incorporated July 1, 1919 with C. L. Babcock, S. A. Copp, and W. V. Arnold as commissioners. Victor J. Hulquist was appointed as City Manager, who was also president of the Knoxville Power Company and manager of the Alcoa Brick and Tile Works. A. B. Smith was City Recorder and Treasurer, and succeeded Hultquist as City Manager. The first engineer was Blair Wilcox, the health officer was Dr. J. Walter McMahan and chief of police was Henry Grizzard. Alcoa has had six mayors: C. L. Babcock, R. F. McLaughlin, L. S. Munch, George U. Thompson, J. H. Studley and O. W. Brumfiel.[69]

In 1917, the Carbon Plant was built and in 1919, the first power was received from the company's power development at Tapoco. The same year, the construction of the "Sheet Mill" or West Fabricating Plant was begun as a separate unit and the first sheet was rolled in

---

[67] The data used here is a combination of materials from miscellaneous clippings from the *Broady* collection and the files of the Maryville *Enterprise* and the Maryville *Times*, from 1910 to the present.

[68] Alcoa has an acre park for every 100 inhabitants and maintains a municipal swimming pool (for whites) and a fishing pool. A swimming pool for the Negro population was opened in 1956.

[69] *Acts, 1919*, The composite Alcoa had been first used for the construction headquarters now known as Calderwood, but was given to this town when it was incorporated.

August 1920. In this same year, the Brick Plant was built. In 1929 the Aluminum Powder Plant was built for the manufacture of aluminum bronze for paint. Increased demands for aluminum made the expansion necessary. Construction of the North Fabricating Plant was begun in 1939 and began operations in 1942.

In 1920 the population was 3,358. In 1944 the total population was about 6,500. Various sub-divisions have arisen: Rock Gardens, Springbrook, Meadowbrook, Lincoln Park, Eagleton Village, Blount Hills gradually merging into Alcoa and Maryville. Alcoa proper has 5½ square miles, 22 miles of paved streets, and 35 miles of water mains. The municipal swimming pool in Alcoa is one of the finest in the South. In 1955 a small lake was stocked with fish for the benefit of Alcoans under 15 and over 60 years of age.

The first and closest sub-division of Alcoa was Vose. At the time the aluminum company decided on the development of the city, the Babcock Lumber Company had acquired 350 acres on the eastern side (third ward), and in 1916, began the construction of a modern sawmill, planing mill, dry kiln, machine shop, necessary auxiliary buildings, commissary and recreational facilities. Two hundred modern dwelling houses were erected.

The timber for this operation was brought from the Jeffrey's Hell section on the waters of Citico Creek in Monroe County by way of Babcock Siding to the T. C. and S. Railroad. C. L. Babcock was manager of this operation and became the first mayor of Alcoa. This operation was completed in 1934 and the plant was sold to Bond-Woolf, and later Veach-May-Wilson, which continues to manufacture and process timber products.

BIG SPRINGS

The large springs which form the beginnings of Gallahar's Creek gave the name Big Springs to the community. Early in the 1800's a group of "Seceders" migrated from the vicinity of Limestone in upper East Tennessee and settled in this vicinity.

By 1820 they had grouped themselves into two congregations known as Pistol Creek and Big Springs. (The name Big Springs may have been taken from a Seceder church group in Pennsylvania by that name.) The Pistol Creek congregation dwindled away and only the Big Springs congregation remained. Soon after 1900 this church ceased to be Seceder or Associate (later United Presbyterian) and became Presbyterian, U. S. A., but the name Big Springs has prevailed.

Cliff was the post office from 1888 until 1903.

ELLEJOY

Ellejoy Valley stretches along the back side of Chilhowee Mountain from the Sevier County line to Little River. McTeer's Fort was built on one of the tributaries of Ellejoy and later the mill and blacksmith shop began to be quite a gathering place. This is said to have been the site of the first school in the county and the first election. The name Ellejoy is a loose term, however, since it covers so much territory.

The muster ground was probably on the Davis farm where the "Race Track" was located. This was the scene of many political and social gatherings as related by Major McTeer.

The Gambles, McTeers and Perrys operated wagon shops, blacksmith shops, distilleries and tanyards as well as mills for the public. Due to the fact that the community was near the "War Path," later the main road to Sevierville, the citizenry was above the average in knowledge of what was happening in the world.

WILDWOOD

Soon after 1800 a Methodist Campground was established on the north side of Little River at a place later called Logan's Chapel. Nearby there were mineral springs which attracted many.

In 1870, the Rev. Claudius Lord (also an M.D.) came South seeking a more healthful climate for his family. He bought the estate of a fellow-Yankee, Dr. Stone. Eventually he enlarged his dwelling and built cottages to house paying guests. His talented family helped to attract guests. The son Claudius was a painter and the daughter Annie was a photographer. One of the daughters reportedly named the resort "Wildwood Springs."

Porter Academy was built on a lot adjoining the hotel property about the same time and students and teachers at the academy found the hotel most convenient for lodging.

The Bank Post Office was established in 1880, which continued until 1912.

Cave Roller Mill was only a short distance away from Wildwood, which made this a rather independent community.

MINT

Mint, eight miles south of Maryville, is the official name of the community which grew up around Cook's Mill. The first post office in 1850 was called Plum Grove. In 1881, the Mint Post Office was established.

When the T. C. & S. Railroad was built, Mint was a station on the railroad. The railroad was abandoned in 1932, the post office was discontinued in 1934, and the mill was dismantled in 1955. Today Mint is merely the intersection of the War Path and the Alleghany Road.

EAGLETON VILLAGE

In 1941 a Federal Housing project was begun to take care of the increased population of the Maryville-Alcoa area occasioned by the expansion of war industries. The original plans were to build 500 units but only half of that number were judged sufficient. This project was finished in 1942 and was named Eagleton Village. This community soon had their own school and recreation center. Government ownership continued until 1950 when the project passed to private ownership.[70]

---

[70] There were 88 five-room houses, 150 four-room houses and 12 three-room houses according to Mr. Herschell Burger who had charge of the project during its entire existence.

HISTORY OF BLOUNT COUNTY

BLOUNT COUNTY REVOLUTIONARY SOLDIERS
Data gathered from Pension Rolls, Court Minutes and other sources.

Agnew, Martin			Eusebia
Allison, John			
Aylett, William			
Berry, George			
Bingham, Benjamin	Pvt. Va. Mil.		
Bogle, Andrew	Penn. Mil.	(widow Elizabeth)	Eusebia
Bogle, Joseph		(widow Margaret)	Eusebia
Boyd, John	Pvt. Penn. Cont. Line	(widow Catherine)	
Brakebill, Peter	Va. Line	(widow Catherine)	
Brewer, William	Pvt. N.C. Line		
Bryant, Robert			
Byerly, Jasper			Byerly Cemetery, Louisville
Capshaw, John		(widow Catherine)	
Caruthers, James	Va. Line		
Clampet, Govey		(widow Sarah)	
Clark, James	Pvt. Va. Line		Clark's Grove
Clayton, John		(widow Hannah)	
Caldwell, George	Va. Line		
Costner, Jacob		(widow Lucy)	
Cummings, Andrew	Pvt. Penn. Line	(widow Jane)	
Davis, John	N.C. Line		New Providence
Divine, Thomas		(widow Jemimah)	
Downie, Alexander	Pvt. Va. Cont. Line		
Duncan, George			
Duncan, John		(widow Margaret)	New Providence
Etheridge, John	Pvt. N.C. Line		
Everett, Robert	Pvt. Va. Line		Law Farm on Crooked Creek
Ewing, George	Pvt. Va. Line	(widow Margaret)	
Fergus, John		(widow Milly)	
Forrester, Robert			
Garner, John Foushee	Pvt. N.C. Mil.		Headrick Cemetery
Haddon, George	Pvt. Va. Line		
Hall, Joel		(widow Margaret)	
Harris, Benjamin		(widow Elinor)	
Harrison, Joseph	N.C. Line		
Harrison, Nathaniel	Pvt. N.C. Line		
Hamby, William	Pvt. Va. Line		
Hanley, Samuel			
Hart, Joseph	Removed to Indiana		
Henry, James	Va. Line		Headrick Cemetery
Henry, Samuel	Va. Mil. (Q.M. Sgt.)		Baker's Creek
Hill, James	Pvt. N.C. Line		
Holloway, Billy	Pvt. Va. Line		
Houston, James	Ens. Va. Mil.		New Providence
Hook, Willoughby	Pvt. N.C. Line		
Houston, John	Pvt. Va. Mil.		
Hunter, Thomas	Pvt. N.C. Line		
Ish, John	Penn. Mil.		Private Cemetery
Jackson, William	Pvt. Va. Line		
Johnston, Joseph			Big Springs
Jordan, John	Pvt. Md. Line		
Keeble, Thomas			
Keeble, William	Pvt. Va. Line	(widow Mary)	Keeble's Chapel
Kennedy, Andrew	N.C. Mil.	(widow Rachel)	
Kilbourn, Benjamin	Sgt. Va. Line	(widow Diana)	

APPENDIX 289

Leay or Lee, William	Pvt. Va. Line		
Mathews, James	Pvt. N.C. Line		Friendsville Cemetery

Mathews, Susannah Laughlin (used her home as a hospital and buried the dead). She was buried in the Friendsville Cemetery (wife of James)

Mackey, William	S.C. Line	(widow Nancy)	
Menably, Michael	Pvt. Va. Line		
Miller, — —		(widow Martha)	
Minnis, John	Sgt. Va. Line		
Minton, Ebenezer	Pvt. Va. Line		
McCallie, John			
McCallon, James	Pvt. S.C. Mil.		New Providence
McCoy, Robert	Sgt. N.C. Mil.		Big Springs
McClung, William			
McDonald, John	Penn. Line		
McGinley, James			New Providence
McGinley, William			New Providence
McKamey, James	Va. Line		
McNabb, William			Clark's Grove
McTeer, Robert	Penn. Mil.		Eusebia
Neel, John	Pvt. N.C. Mil.		
Nelson, Elijah			Piney Level
Newman, Jacob			
Northern, Solomon	Pvt. N.C. Mil.		
Norton, Alexander	Pvt. Va. Mil.		
Norwood, John	N.C. Line		Middlesettlements
Parks, James		(widow Nancy)	
Paul, James			
Pride, Burton			
Pritchett, Edward			
Phillips, Abraham			
Ray, James			Middlesettlements
Rhea, Robert	Va. Line	(widow Mary)	Happy Valley
Robertson, Joseph	Pvt. N.C. Line		
Robinson, James	Penn. Line		
Rudd, Burlingham	N.C. Line		
Scott, Robert			New Providence
Sharp, John			
Simerly, John		(widow Wilmuth)	
Simms, James	Pvt. Va. Mil.		Eusebia
Sims, John	Pvt. N.C. Line		
Sterling, Robert	Pvt. N.C. Line		
Taylor, James	Ens. N.C. Line		Centenary Cemetery
Tedford, George			Probably Hamil Cemetery
Tedford, James			Probably Hamil Cemetery
Tedford, John	Ens. Va. Line		Probably Hamil Cemetery
Tedford, Joseph		(widow Mary)	Probably Hamil Cemetery
Tedford, Robert	Sgt. Va. Line		Probably Hamil Cemetery
Thompson, Isaac			
Thompson, Samuel	Sgt. Va. Line		
Thurman, John		(widow Nancy)	
Tipton, Benjamin	Va. Line	(widow Rebecca)	Probably Eusebia

HISTORY OF BLOUNT COUNTY

Tipton, William — Va. Line — Private-Badgett Farm
Utter, Abraham
Walker, John — Pvt. Penn. Line
Wallace, Jesse — New Providence
Wallace, Matthew — New Providence
Wallace, William — New Providence
Weir, James — (widow Margaret)
Weir, Joseph — (widow Margaret)
White, Gordon — Pvt. Va. Line — Logan's Chapel
White, William — Pvt. N.C. Line
Wood, John — Pvt. N.C. Line
Wourley, James — Sgt. N.C. Line
Wyley, James — Pvt. Va. Line

PASSPORTS TO ENTER THE CHEROKEE COUNTRY IN 1798

Filed in Box No. 1, Tennessee State Archives
(Names are spelled as they appear in the records)

John Cowan
Robert Cowan
William Adams
James Montgomery Jr.
Alexander Montgomery
Hugh Montgomery
William Hutton
Josiah Hutton
Arch. Slone
James Martin
James Gealy
David Edmondson
William Condren
Samuel Handley
Thomas Vance
David Oats
Thomas Gallaher
Capt. Alex. Lackey
Thomas Gibson
James Hogg
John Gibson
Samuel Read
John Allison
Baldwin Howard
Ephriam Howard
Alexander Craig
John Ore
Hugh Gilbreath

Samuel Norwood
John Wallace
William Wallace
Samuel Cowan
Martin Cook
John Williams
Moses Justice
Prettyman Jones
Zachariah Jones
John Hackney
David Satyrwhite
Edward Casteel
Joshua Parsons
Christopher Huzy
Alexander Ford
Joseph Gomery
  (Montgomery)
Charles Logan
John Craig
Nathaniel Bigham
Robert Howel
Solomon McCampbell
James Gallahar
Humphrey Montgomery
Robert Ailens
Robert McCulley
Samuel Orr
John McCulley

Andrew Gibson
Sarah Logan
Zachariah Gillespie
Zachariah Saterwhite
Alex. Craig, Senr.
James Houston
John Houston
John Edwards
John Simmons
Thomas Simmons
Thomas Tedford
Matthew Houston,
  wife & Negro girl
James Gillespie
William Small
Ebenezer Jones
James Gillespie, wife
  & girl
Isaac Hannah
James Boid
Nancy Simpson
John Simpson
Thomas Richey
Jonathan Matthews
Arch. Cowan
James Simpson
Isham Hale
Elija Hussy

Several of these people had more than one permit issued to go into the Cherokee lands to take care of their crops and to remove their cattle after they were removed from their lands by order of the Federal Government in 1798. After the Treaty with the Cherokees was effected, the people returned to their homes.

NORTH CAROLINA LAND GRANTS WHICH ARE REGISTERED IN BLOUNT COUNTY

Bonine, Daniel, 1794, south of Holston on Ish's Creek.
Chamberlain, Hannah, 1795, south of Holston on Chamberlain Branch.
Colville, Joseph, 1790, Greene County, Crooked Creek (jns. Berry, Lowry, and Wear).
Conner, Terrence, 1791, Greene County, south side of Holston
Donelson, Stockley, Alex. Kelly and Arch. Lackey, 1794, north side of Tennessee River (Col. James White's Camp).
Donelson, Stockley, 1795, 100,000 acres south of Holston opposite Turkey Creek.
Dunlap, Ephraim, 1789, west bank of Little River at Christian's War Ford.
Dunlap, Ephraim, 1793, Hawkins County, south of Holston at junction of Tennessee.
Dunlap, Hugh, 1794, 5,000 acres in Cades Cove on the waters of the Tennessee.
Gillespie, James, Sr., 640 acres in Greene County on south side of Little River.
Greer, Andrew, 1791, Greene County, west side of Four Mile Creek where Indian path crosses the creek.
Greer, Andrew, 1791, Greene County, on Four Mile Creek, joins self.
Hannah, John, 1791, Greene County, on Nine Mile Creek, south side.
Ish, John, Greene County, head of Black Creek.
Ish, John, Greene County, 1791, south side of Holston, jns. Peter Bowerman.
King, William, 1789, Greene County, west bank of Little River.
Lackey, Arch., 1791, Greene County, at foot of Bays Mountain.
Lackey, J. W. and Arch., 1794, 1,000 acres opposite Coyatee Island, north side of Tennessee River.
Lackey, J. W. and William Tyrell, 1795, on west side of Six Mile Creek to Chilhowee Mountain (1,200 acres).
Lackey, J. W., 1795, 1,500 acres in Tuckaleechee Cove, joins Lackey and McClung.
Lackey, J. W., 1799, Greene County, north side of Tennessee (surveyed 1783).
Lackey, J. W., 1795, 5,000 acres at head of Lackey Creek.
Lowry, John, 1797, Greene County, Crooked Creek.
Miller, Alexander, Assignee of Edward Green, 1791, Greene County, south side of Nine Mile Creek.
Miller, Andrew, Greene County, 1791, Nine Mile Creek.
McMurry, William and Samuel, 1793, Crooked Creek.
Moor, Elizabeth, Washington County, includes an island opposite Holston River.
McTeer, Robert, 1791, Greene County, 800 acres on Ellejoy Creek.
Pritchett, Edward, 1795, northeast side of Little River, joins former entry of 1,000 acres.
Rhea, John and William Tyrell, 1,000 acres on north side of the Tennessee, 1796.
Rhea, John, 1794, Greene County, both sides of Little River in Murphy's Cove.
Rowan, Henry, 1794, Greene County, Nine Mile Creek on the waters of the Tennessee, includes two improvements—Carroway and James Walker, dec'd, on which *David Craig now lives*.
Sloan, Arch., Washington County, North fork of Nine Mile Creek, includes the big spring on the war path, (1778).

Wear, Hugh, 1791, Greene County, head of Pistol Creek.
Wear, Samuel, 1790, Greene County, North fork of Crooked Creek.
Wear, Samuel, 1791, Greene County, Crooked Creek.
Worley, James, (Assigned to Thomas Supret), 1795, southeast side of Little River.

MILITIA CAPTAINS WHO SERVED IN BLOUNT COUNTY

Data taken mostly from reports filed in the State Archives, Nashville, Tennessee

(Names are spelled as they appear in the records)

1792
Ewing, Tedford, Singleton, Henry, Black (?).
1793
Ewing, Tedford, Singleton, Henry, Flenniken (?), Black (?).
1794
Singleton, Flenniken, Henry, Tedford, Ewing, Black.
1795 & 1796
Boyd, Ewing, Scott, Tedford, Singleton.
1797—Samuel Bogle, Joseph Colville, Clendennen, James Moor, Robert Rhea, James Scott, Arch. Lackey.
1800
Samuel Bogle, Joseph Colville, John Alexander, James Scott, John Cowan, David Caldwell, James Gillespie, Richard Dearmond, Alexander Montgomery.
1801
Samuel Bogle, Joseph Colville, John Alexander, James Scott, John Cowan, James Gillespie, Richard Dearmond, Alexander Montgomery, John Kelley, John Allison, James McGinley.
1802
Samuel Bogle, John Alexander, John Cowan, James Gillespie, Richard Dearmond, Alexander Montgomery, John Kelley, John Allison, James McGinley, — Walker, — Hanna.
1803
Samuel Bogle, John Alexander, John Cowan, James Gillespie, Richard Dearmond, John Kelley, John Allison, James McGinley, — Hanna, McClanahan, Reagan, Parkhill.
1804
Wilkinson, Walker, Watson, Moor, Ewing, Kirby, McRenels, Norwood, Taylor, Craig, McGinley, Tuckaleechee Company (no Captain named).
1805
Wilkinson, Walker, Watson, McRenals, Taylor, Davidson, Murrin, Wheeler, Reagon, McCamble, Kelso, Harriss.
1807
Cusick, McCammon, Harriss, Kelso, Beard, Watson, Roops, Walker, Wheeler, Davidson, Logan, Caldwell.
1808
Cusick, Kelso, Beard, Wheeler, Davidson, Caldwell, Dixon, Thompson, Houston, Garner, Forester, Allen, Buchanan.
1809
John B. Cusick, — Caldwell, John P. Houston, William Garner, — Wheeler, Edwin Allen, Edward Buchannon, — Henderson, Eli Dixon, Samuel Davidson, Samuel Thompson.
1810

APPENDIX

Cusick, Beatty, Dixon, Thompson, Houston, Garner, Wheeler, Allen, Buchanan, Henderson, Davis.
1814
Alex. Biggs, David McCamey, —— McKee, Isaac Campbell, —— Davidson, Bonham, Joseph Duncan, Regan, Harriss, William Wallace, Thomas Wallace, Love, Jehu Stephens, Garner.
1815
Alexander Biggs, Kendrick, Jones, David McCamey, Whittenbarger, Davidson, Bonham, Joseph Duncan, Regan, Harriss, Thomas Wallace, Boyd, William S. Taylor.
1814
McKamey, Campbell, Davidson, Bonham, Duncan, Regan, Harriss, Love, Stephens, Thompson, Wallace, McGhee, Thornbury, Buchanan.
1812
Houston, Garner, Allen Gay, McCamey, Buchanan, Beatty, Campbell, Thompson, Duncan, Wheeler, Biggs, Tuckaleechee (no Captain named).
1813
Biggs, Duncan, McCamey, Orr, McKee, Thompson, Gay, Campbell, Reagon, Tuckyleachy (sic), Buchanan, Thornbury, Wheeler, Harriss.
1817
Toole, James, Wallace, McCartney, Boyd, Greenway, Hogan, Bonham, Lowe, Whittenbarger, Kendricks, Harriss, Rhea, Panter.
1818
Toole, Harriss, Kendricks, Duncan, James, McCartney, Whittenbarger, Morrison.
1819
Warren, McMahan, Lambert, Rush, Rhea, Wallace.
(There were 22 acting justices.)
1820
Barnett, Duncan, Gay, Lambert, McMahan, Morrison, Reeves, Sloane, Tedford, Tuckaleechee, Tipton, Tharp, Warren, Wilson, Martin.
1821
Coleburn, Duncan, Gay, Lambert, Morrison, McMahan, Maddon, Ruch, Sloane, Turk, Tharp, Tipton, Tedford, Wilson, Martin.
1825
There were 32 acting justices and 16 militia companies.
1827
Jacob Tipton, Josiah Gamble, William Flinn, Kirkpatrick, Harriss, Warren, Houston, Duggan (town company), Morton, Frew, Kerr, Hale, Howard, Hammontree, Blankenship, Douthitt, Ferguson.

A LIST OF TAXABLE PROPERTY AND TAX FOR BLOUNT COUNTY 1801

There are two early tax lists for Blount County on file in the State Archives in Nashville: 1800 and 1801. The statement has been made that two companies are missing from the 1800 list. A careful check of names shows that actually there are about thirty more names on the 1800 list and a breakdown of personnel shows that Captain John Alexander's Company (the town company) was divided in 1801 and part of it was given to Captain John McGinley. Capt. David Caldwell was replaced by Captains John Allison and John Kelly and that company was divided in 1801. There was some shift of personnel but the other companies remained substantially the same. The list used is the 1801 tax list. Those names checked are not on the 1800 tax list.

There were six columns on the original sheets in the following order: Land, White Poles (polls), black Poles (polls), town lots, billiard tables, and studs. (No billiard tables were listed.)

Captain Alexander's Company

Name	Land	White poles	Black poles	Town lots	Studs
Alexander, Oliver	300		1		
Alexander, Benjamin		1			
Alexander, John	150	1	2		
Alexander, John	100	1			
Burk, William	233½	1	1	1	
Berry, Thomas	200	1		1	
Boles, James	100	1			
Brown, Isaiah		1			
Blackburn, Gidion	505	1			
Cunningham, David		1	½		
Cunningham, Miles		1	½		
Culton, Robert	190	1			
Drew, John	640	1		1	
Danforth, Josiah	7,640	1	3		
Donahoe (Donohoo), Charles		1			
Denning, Matthew		1			
Donaldson, Robert	200	1			
Fitzgerald, Patrick		1			
Garrison, John		1			
Glass, William	300	2			
Gardner, John		1		1	
Hart, Joseph		1			
Hargas (Hargis), William		1			
Hart, Alexander	200	1			
Hooks (Hooke), Robert	150	1			
Lowry, John, Atty.	500	1	1	2	1
Lowry, John, Mcht.		1	1	2	
Logan, Alexander	400	1			
Montgomery, John		1		2	
Montgomery, James S.		1			
McClanahan, James		1			
Minnis, John	640				
McBath, William	200	1			
McFaddian (McFadden), Joseph	80	1			
McNeely, Samuel		1			
McNutt, Alexander	130				
Ogleby, David	100	1			
Paxton, Samuel	200	1			
Panther, Alexander		1			
Pedigrew (Pettigrew), Matthew		1			
Russell, John		1			
Russam, John	33½	1			
Rhea, John, Atto.	900				
Stone, Edward		1			
Sharp, John	400	1	3	1	1
Thairman (Thurman), Joseph		1			
Taylor, John		2		1	
Woods, John	123	1	5	5	
Wilkinson, John		1		3	
Wilson, James		1			
Wallace, William	400	1	1		
Whiteaker (Whittaker), John	200	1			
Wier, Joseph, Jr.		1			
Wier, Joseph, Sr.	300	1			

APPENDIX

Captain Alexander's Company

Name	Land	White poles	Black poles	Town lots	Studs
Wier, James, Sr.	300	1			
Wier, James, Jr.	100	1			
Wier, John	300	1			

Captain John Allison's Company

Name	Land	White Poles	Name	Land	White Poles
Allan (Allen), James	50	1	Jones, Thomas	100	2
Akin, Samuel		1	Jones, Samuel		1
Alensan, Robert		1	James, Samuel		1
Alkenson (Allison), John	200	1	Jones, Francis	100	1
Brown, David	100	1	Johnston, John, Jr.		1
Bowerman, Michael	300	1	Jones, Al	200	
Boen (Bowen), Wm.	100		Jones, Priteman		1
Baker, Wm.	50	1	Knox, Joseph		1
Brown, Eliah		1	Lackey, Andrew		1
Boyd, Alexander		1	McCalister, John	600	1
Cowan, Arch.		1	Montgomery, Humphrey	300	1
Canedy (Kennedy), Walter	60	1	Matthes, James	640	
Clemens, John		1	Matthes, Jonathan		1
Cochain (Cochran), James.		1	Mardick (Murdock), Wm.	90	1
Ford, Alex	200	1	McCulley, Solloman	300	1
Gillespie, Alex		1	McCulley, Robert		1
Gillespie, Zacharia		1	Oatts, David		1
Ghormley, Joseph	100	1	Osburn, Alexander	100	1
Gamble, Andrew	350	1	Rogers, James	100	1
Gray, Wm.	300	1	Russel, James		1
Gibson, John	300	1	Rhodes, George	200	1
Gailey, James		1	Reid, Samuel	600	1
Gibson, Andrew		1	Small, William		1
Gibson, Thomas		1	Shaw, Samuel		1
Hussey, Christopher	250	1	Smart, Francis	200	1
Hall		1	Wilson, David		1
Hackney, Hugh		1	Watson, James	300	1
Husse (Hussey), Elijah	200	1	Woody, John	100	1
Ish, Elizabeth	640	1	Walker, John	150	1
Jones, Johnston	100	1			

Slaveowners: John Allison 1, James Gailey 1, David Oatts 1, Samuel Shaw 1, Francis Smart 1.

Captain Bogle's Company

Name	Land	White Poles	Name	Land	White Poles
Bogle, Samuel	150	1	Cup (Cupp), David*		1
Bell, John	150	1	Coats, John*		1
Bogle, Joseph	150	1	Cup, Jacob	80	1
Boyd, Robert	100	1	Caldwell, Carson		1
Boyd, Wm.	200	1	Durham, William	200	1
Bowerman, John	30	1	Davis, Samuel	150	1
Bogle, Hugh*		1	Dunlap, James	100	1
Bogle, Andrew	200	2	Dunlap, John	100	1
Carson, David	200	1	Davidson, James*		1
Cusack (Cusick), John B.*.		1	Davis, James	100	1
Cunningham, John	100	1	Dunlap, Adam	100	1

Captain Bogle's Company

Name	Land	White Poles	Name	Land	White Poles
Davis, Elijah	500	1	McMurry, James*	100	
Finley, Robert	300		McCauly (McCallie), John	200	1
Graves, Stephen	50	1	Martin, Luke*	100	1
Garnor, James		1	Nyman (Neiman), Margaret*	100	
Garnor (Garner), John F.	400		Nyman, Michael	80	1
Houston, William	100	1	Pickens, John	200	1
Halfley, Conrad	300		Palmer, Samuel*		1
Kunse (Koontz), Adam	400	1	Richardson, John	200	1
Kirkpatrick, Charles	300	1	Rhea (Ray), John	100	1
Kirkpatrick, Thomas		1	Reed, Lambert Senr	50	
Kennedy, John	100	1	Reed, Lambert, Jr.	50	1
Kunse, John*	100		Simms (Sims), James	100	1
Kunse, Henery	100	1	Skean (Skeen), James	100	1
King, Jonston	50	1	Trimble, John		1
Kirkpatrick, James*		1	Thomas, Adam	100	2
Legg, Jonathan		1	Thompson, John	50	1
(Leg)7, Matthew*			Tipton, Benjamin	250	1
(Ki)ng, Robert	100	1	Tipton, Joseph	122	1
(Ma)rtin, Warner	500	1	Upton, James	100	1
McMurray, Samuel	150		Upton, Isaac*		1
Malcom, Alexander*	100		Vickers, James	300	1
McTeer, Robert Senr	600	1	Vance, David*	100	1
McTeer, Robert Junr	50	1	Williams, John Junr	50	1
McKain, Nancy	100		Wallace, George		1
Murrin, Robert	100	1	Williams, Richard	50	1
McCammon, Samuel	150	1	Williams, John, Stiller	100	1
McCammon, Thomas		1			

Slaveowners: Joseph Bogle 1, William Durham 3, John F. Garnor 2, John McCauly 1, Warner (Ma)rtin 2, David Vance 1, Richard Williams 1.
Town lots: Richard Williams 1.
Studs: William Boyd 1, Michael Nyman 1.

Captain Colville's Company

Name	Land	White Poles	Name	Land	White Poles
Beard, Arch	100	1	Gamble, John*		1
Barnet, Joseph		1	Gamble, John		1
Breeze, Thomas		1	Gamble, Josiah	1,380	1
Beard, James		1	Greer, Arthur		1
Beaty, John*		1	Henery, Wm.		1
Campble (Campbell), Robt.	100	1	Henery, Samuel		1
Colville, George		1	Holton, John		1
Campble, James	100	1	Kennedy, Andrew	200	1
Caldwell, George		1	Keeble, Wm.*		1
Coulter, Richd Junr		1	McMurry, Wm.	290	1
Coulter, Charles		1	McCulloch, John		1
Caldwell, John	400	1	Moor, Thomas		1
Colville, Joseph	430	1	McCanles, John		1
Caldwell, David		1	McCulloch, Samuel		1..
Davidson, Andrew*		1	Nicolson, John		1
Ewing, John	120	1	Partin, Samuel*		1
Ewing, George	300	1	Phillips, Abraham	180	1
Ewing, James		1	Walker, Samuel		1
Ewing, Wm.		1	Regan, Ahimas		1
Gillaspie, James		1	Regan, John		1

APPENDIX

CAPTAIN COLVILLE'S COMPANY

Name	Land	White Poles	Name	Land	White Poles
Regan, Charles			Smith, Andrew*		1
Rider, John		1	Taylor, James		1
Rhea, Hugh		1	White, David		1
Rhea, James		1	Wier, Samuel	532	1
Rogers, Benj.		1	Wier, John	300	1
Snider, John		1	Walker, John		1
Snider, George*		1	Wilson, Isaac*		1

Slaveowners: George Caldwell 1, David Caldwell 1, George Ewing 1, James Gillaspie 1, Josiah Gamble 2, Andrew Kennedy 3, Samuel McCulloch 1, Charles Regan 2, John Rider 1, Hugh Rhea 1, James Rhea 1, Andrew Smith 1, David White 1, Isaac Wilson 1.

Town lots: Andrew Kennedy 1.

CAPTAIN COWAN'S COMPANY

Name	Land	White Poles	Name	Land	White Poles
Arehart (Earhart), Henery	300	1	Martin, James	250	1
Alexander, Wm.*		1	Montgomery, Hugh	300	1
Alexander, Thomas		1	Millar, David*		
Armstrong, Wm.*		1	McCord, David*	75	1
Alexander, Jeremiah		1	Montgomery, George*		1
Besley (Beasley), Wm.*	200		Montgomery, David		1
Bigham (Bingham), Wm*	225	2	Montgomery, James		1
Bigham, Samuel		1	Null, John Junr*		1
Boyd, James	300	1	Nicles (Nichols), George*.	50	1
Boyd, George		1	Norwood, Samuel		1
Bigham, Natth	100	1	Null, John Senr		1
Cowan, Robert		1	Orr, Joseph		1
Carr, Samuel	300	1	Rogers, Joseph		1
Cowan, John Senr	150	1	Richey, James*	75	1
Carr, David*	200	1	Robenson, Daniel*		1
Coope, Baracias		1	Russel, Hance		1
Dickson, Thomas		1	Sheets, Jacob		1
Dickson, John		1	Skiles, Wm.		1
Edmondson, John	100	1	Skiles, George*		1
Gilbreath, Hugh	100	1	Stuart, Wm.		1
Gilbreath, Thomas	100	1	Townsley, George		1
Hanna (Hannah), Joseph*		1	Thompson, John	150	1
Hanley, Samuel	400	1	Utter, Abraham	150	1
Hanley, Samuel for*		1	Wallace, John		1
J. Cowan	100	1	Wallace, Wm.	200	1
Kelsoe, Hugh*	400	1	Wiley, Alex*	200	1
Logan, Wm.	125	1	Wallace, David	100	1
Licans, John	100	1	Woolf, Jacob	100	1
Lassiter, Burrel	300	1	Wallace, Matthew		1
Montgomery, John	100	1			

Slaveowners: Henry Arehart 3, Wm. Besley 2, Hugh Kelsoe 1, Burrel Lassiter 1, James Martin 1, David Millar 4, Alex Wiley 1, Matthew Wallace 2.

Captain DeArmand's Company

Name	Land	White Poles	Name	Land	White Poles
Baugher (Boyer), Jacob	150	1	Irvin, Robert		1
Brumley, Barnet*	100		Irvin, James*		1
Barclet, Joseph*		1	Kirbey, Richard	100	
Brim, Edmond*		1	Kirbey, Joseph		1
Boghard, Cornelius		1	Loveless, David		1
Carter, Mcaja (Micajah)*		1	Liddy, John*		1
Chanler (Chandler), Richd	80	1	Lackey, Jas. W. for		
Caldwell, Thomas	50	1	Maj. Lackey	800	2
Charles, Isaac*		1	McClure, Charles	150	1
Cawood, Moses*		1	Moor, Mary*		
Cochain, John		1	McCullock, Thomas		
Doherty, John*	100	1	McCulloch, James		1
DeArmand, David	100	1	Maxwell, Mary*		
DeArmand, Richard	150	1	Pearce, Robert	200	1
DeArmand, Samuel		1	Pearce, James	200	1
Edington, John*	100	1	Pearce, John		1
Frew, Arch.		1	Rogers, John	100	1
Glass, Samuel	350	1	Rogers, Isaac*		1
Gillaspie, Alex		1	Rogers, Reuben		1
George, Samuel		1	Rankin, John	300	1
Gillaspie, Wm.		1	Stockton, Marshall*		1
Houston, James	300	1	Singleton, John	500	1
Hudson, Richd.	100	1	Thornhill, Armsted*	100	1
Hanna, Andrew*	150		Wheeler, Wm.	200	1
Hanna, Robert Junr		1	Woods, Patrick		1
Hanna, Robert Senr		1	Woods, Joseph Junr		1
Harris, Samuel		1	Woods, John		1
Jones, Lewis	228	1	Willis, James	100	1

Slaveowners: Thomas Caldwell 1, Moses Cawood 1, John Cochain 1, Samuel Glass 1, Samuel George 1, James Houston 1, Richard Kirbey 3, Joseph Kirbey 2, Lackey, Jas. W. for Maj. Lackey 2, Mary Moor 1, Thomas McCullock 3, Mary Maxwell 1, John Singleton 2.
Town lots: Thomas McCullock 1.

Captain Gillaspie's Company

Name	Land	White Poles	Name	Land	White Poles
Able, Cain		1	Gillaspie, Wm.		
Bowerman, Peter		1	Gillaspie, James		1
Broils (Broyles), George		1	Henderson, Joseph	175	1
Adams, Thomas	100	1	Henderson, John	50	1
Bice, Wm.	100	1	Hichland, John	640	1
Barnes, Wm.	100	1	Henderson, Wm.		1
Boterite, Daniel*		1	Hampton, Joshua		
Bourden, Adon*		1	Hail, Wm.		1
Conner, Terrance	300	1	Hucheson, Samuel*		1
Castalor, Martin	100	1	Laurence, Martin		
Casteel, Joseph*		1	Lackey, Arch	640	1
Craig, Alexander	100	1	Miser, George		1
Chamberlan, Hanna	500	1	Maxwell, Robert		1
Fouster, Robert		1	McCulley, John	100	1
Gaut, Wm.*		1	Meriot, John	100	1
Gaut, John		1	Maxwell, John*		
Gillespie, John		1	O'Conner, Thomas*		1
Gillaspie, Robert		1	Rule, Wm.*		1

APPENDIX

Captain Gillaspie's Company

Name	Land	White Poles	Name	Land	White Poles
Rogers, Thomas		1	Teel, John*		1
Sullavan, John		1	Vaught, Andrew*		1
Stewart, Alexander	100	1	Walker, James	100	1
Sherrel, John	323	1	Whitenbarger, Henery	250	1
Taylor, David		1	Young, Wm.	200	1
Taylor, James	175	1			

Slaveowners: Wm. Gaut 1, Wm. Gillaspie 2, James Gillaspie 2, John Hichland 1, Wm. Henderson 2, John Sherrel 1.

Captain Kelley's Company

Name	Land	White Poles	Name	Land	White Poles
Anderson, James*	470	1	McKinley, James*		1
Bond, Henry*	460	1	Mayo, Valentine	250	1
Bonham, Daniel*	150	1	Michel, Mordecai*		1
Bibles, John*	200	1	Millar, Andrew	400	1
Bailey, Robert*		1	Millar, John*	100	1
Casteel, Edward	50	1	Maxwell, James		1
Cook, George*	50	1	McComes, John	200	1
Casteel, John*	150	1	McKinzey, Daniel	150	1
Caldwell, David	400	1	Nave, George		1
Cartrite, Thomas		1	Parkhill, David	100	1
Cart, Richard	300	1	Pride, Burtin	250	1
Essery, Thomas	150	1	Robenet, Moses*		1
Franks, John	150	1	Richey, Andrew*		1
Folkner, Joseph	150	1	Richey, Thomas	275	1
Ferguson, Henery*	300	1	Stephenson, Nicolas	480	1
Greenaway, James	950	1	Saterwhite, David	100	1
Griffitt, Wm.*	100	1	Simpson, Thomas*		1
Hughs, Robert	200	1	Taylor, Thomas*		1
Hughs, Moses	229	1	Trimble, Arch	100	1
Hail, Isom*	50	1	Trimble, John	250	1
James, Bennet*	150	1	Washam, Jeremiah*	100	
Jones, Ebenezer	200	1	Whitenbarger, Abraham	100	1
Kelley, Alexander	600	1	Washam, Alexsan	200	1
Kelley, John	300	1	Winters, Samuel	1060	1
King, John		1	Washburn, Sherord*		1
King, Samuel	200	1	Washam, Jeremiah*	100	

Slaveowners: David Caldwell 3, James Greenaway 3, Moses Hughes 1, Bennet James 1, Alexander Kelley 2, Valentine Mayo 1, Andrew Millar 4, John McComes 2, Thomas Richey 1, Thomas Taylor 1, John Trimble 1.

Captain McGinley's Company

Name	Land	White Poles	Name	Land	White Poles
Alexander, Ebenezer		1	Ferguson, John		1
Alexander, Joseph		1	Fergusson, Hugh		1
Bowers, Daniel		1	Finley, Joseph		1
Buchanan, Edward		1	Gilbreath, William		1
Culton, James		1	Gilmore, John		1
Crawford, James		1	Gold, John		1
Duncan, John		1	Houston, Samuel		1
Ferguson, Robert		1	Harriss, John		1

Captain McGinley's Company

Name	Land	White Poles	Name	Land	White Poles
Harriss, William		1	Timberman, Jonathan		1
Harriss, Jonathan		1	Timberman, Matthew		1
Houston, John		1	Timberman, Jacob		1
James, John		1	Timberman, George		1
Ingland, Thomas		1	Trippett, Jonathan		1
Long, Henery		1	Thomas, George		1
McGinley, James		1	Thomas, Henry		1
McCanles, Robert		1	Tedford, Joseph		1
McRanels, John		1	Wallace, Joel		1
Posey, Daniel		1	Wallace, Abram		1
Rorax, Martin		1	Wallace, Benjamin		1
Rowan, Samuel		1	Wallace, William		1
Sloss, Joseph		1	Wallace, David		1
Simons, William		1	Weir, Abraham		1
Thomas, Jacob		1	Weir, Hugh*		1
Timberman (Stephen?)		1	Weir, Jonathan	640	1
Thompson, James		1	Wallace, John		1
Thomas, John		1	Wallace, Andrew		1

Slaveowners: John Duncan 1, Samuel Houston 1, Jonathan Harriss 1, Henery Long 1, James McGinley 1, John McRanels 1, Wm. Simons 1, Joel Wallace 1.

Captain Montgomery's Company

Name	Land	White Poles	Name	Land	White Poles
Bromley, James		1	McClanahan, James		1
Beard, George		1	Millar, Alexander	200	1
Blair, John		1	McClanahan, Matthew		1
Blair, William		1	Montgomery, Robert		1
Brown, John		1	More, James		1
Blizard, Thomas		1	More, Alexander		1
Black, Gavin	200	1	Miller, Andrew	300	1
Bradley, John			McClanahan, David		1
Beard, Henry		1	Manuel, Cudbert		1
Beaty, Samuel		1	Manuel, Valentine		1
Conway, Thomas		1	McMurry, Robert		1
Conway, Joseph		1	McClung, Charles	500	
Conway, Jessey		1	Nelson, John		1
Camron, Samuel		1	Rhea, Jesse		1
Campbell, John		1	Rhea, John		1
Davis, James		1	Richardson, Obediah		1
Davis, Thomas	50	1	Ramsey, Richard		1
Davidson, William			Smith, John		1
Finley, John		1	Stafford, Stephen		1
Finn, Jesse		1	Snider, Peter		1
Frier, John		1	Smith, Samuel		1
Goodman, Stephen		1	Tate, Isaac		1
Goforth, Zachariah		1	Tipton, Meshech		1
Hesse, John		1	Tarwater, Jacob		1
Little, Thomas		1	Tarwater, Lewis		1
Lowry, Wm. for Jas. W. Lacky	1,500	1	Walker, Joseph		1
Morrison, Thomas		1	Walker, Isaiah		1
Montgomery, Alexander		1	Wise, John		1

Slaveowners: James More 1.
Studs: William Davidson and Meshech Tipton one each.

APPENDIX 301

Captain James Scott's Company

Name	Land	White Poles	Name	Land	White Poles
Airhart, Nicolus	150	1	McGhee, Barcley	2,300	1
Adams, William	200	1	McNabb, William		1
Boyd, John	100	1	Montgomery, Alex.	150	
Blackburn, Benjamin		1	McCartney, John	200	1
Cooper, John	500	1	Millar, Samuel		1
Cooper, George		1	Mowrey, John		1
Craig, John		1	McTeer, James Junr.		1
Craig, David	500	1	McKemy, James		1
Chaffin, Robert		1	McCampbell, Sollomon	400	1
Craig, James, Jr.		1	McGill, Robert	300	1
Cook, Michael	100	1	McConald, James		1
Craig, James, Sr.		1	McKee, John Junr.		1
Craig, William		1	McGhee, John	167	1
Copland, David		1	Means, William	400	
Dickson, Samuel	200	1	Maxwell, Thomas		1
Dunlap, George		1	McMeans, John		1
Delzell, John	100	1	McClurkin, Thomas	100	
Dothero, Michel		1	McTeer, James Senr.	100	1
Ewing, John	200		Mayben, by J. W. Lackey*	500	1
Edwards, Mark	100	1	Posey, Joseph	200	1
Edwards, John		1	Parks, John		1
Evans, Edward	200		Ross, John	50	1
Edmondson, James		1	Ritchey, David		1
Fisher, John		1	Sloan, Robert		1
Gould, Samuel	50	1	Sloan, William		1
Hanna, John, Jr.	200		Simons, John		1
Henery, Charles		1	Sloan, James	200	1
Hanna, Wm. Senr.			Sloan, John	200	1
Hamontree, James		1	Sloan, Alex.		1
Hack, Andrew			Scott, James	640	1
Hamontree, Jeremiah	100	1	Shields, Robert		1
Holoway, John	60	1	Tedford, George		1
Hanna, Wm., Jr.		1	Tedford, Robert		1
Henery, Samuel	300	1	Tedford, Thomas		1
Hogg, Samuel		1	Tedford, Alex.		1
Houston, James		1	Tedford, John		1
Hutton, Josiah	500	1	Wilson, Robert		2
Hammantree, John		1	White, James		1
Holten, Daniel*		1	Wilcox, Isaac	200	1
Jackson, John	100		Waren, Michael		1
Jackson, Andrew	200	1	Williams, Samuel		1
Kennedy, John		1	Yarien, Michael	146	1
Logan, James	600		Yarien, Frederick		1
Logan, Henery		1	Young, John		1

Slaveowners: John Craig 3, David Craig 2, James Craig Sr. 1, Edward Evans 1, Samuel Henery 1, James Houston 2, Barcley McGhee 9, John McGhee 2, Wm. Means 1, Robert Wilson 1.

Town lots: John Craig 1, Barcley McGhee 3.

BLOUNT COUNTY TAX LIST—1800

The following names do not appear on the 1801 tax list for Blount County.

Alexander, Abner
Alexander, John
Alkeson, Robert
Asbil, Solomon
Bacon, Wm.
Beard, David
Bell, Robert
Berry, George
Black, John
Blair, James
Boutwell, Stephen
Bowan, Esias
Braidey, Thomas
Brein, Abraham
Brown, Joseph
Carpenter, George
Caruthers, James
Clark, David
Clark, James
Cloud, Jason
Cobb, Samuel
Coils, George
Conally, Walter
Condran, Wm.
Coulter, Francis
Cowan, Andrew
Craig, Susanna
Davenport, Wm.
Davis, George
Duiry, Ruben
Edwards, Charles
Ewing, Nathaniel
Ewing, Wm.
Everett, Robert
Ferguson, Hugh
Ferguson, Robert
Ford, Alexander
Forester, Robert
Frow, Archibald
Furgue, John
Gamble, Moses
Gamble, Thomas
Gaut, Ison
Gaunt, Robert
Gay, Wm.
Gibson, Wm.
Glass, John
Gower, Matthies
Griffith, Viney
Hail, John
Hail, Luke
Harison, Gideon
Hay, James
Henderson, Alexander
Hill, Peter
Hogg, Samuel
Holway, Joseph
Houston, John
Houston, Samuel
Irvin, Benj.
Johnston, Francis
Justice, Moses
Legg, Ambrose
Loins, Thomas
Lively, John
Logan, Charles
Logan, William
Lowrey, John
McAmmon, Robert
McCarmack, Wm.
McClure, James
McCollom, Alexander
McCollom, John
McCoy, Michel
McCullock, Alex.
McCurdy, Robert
McDonald, David
McDowell, John
McKee, John
McClurg, Wm.
McNeely, John
McNutt, James
Mackey, John
Malcom, Wm.
Miser, George
Mizer, John
Montgomery, Thomas
Montgomery, Wm.
Netherton, John
Paine, Josiah
Palmer, Wm.
Parks, Samuel
Reeves, Moses
Regan, Ahimas
Rhea, James
Rhea, Robert
Roberts, John
Rogers, Thomas
Rowan, Samuel
Russel, Matthew
Simon, Wm.
Singleton, John
Sloss, Joseph
Spilman, Thomas
Stuart, Alex.
Taylor, Magnus
Tedford, James
Thomson, Robert
Tippett, Erastus
Timberman, Stephen
Vaught, David
Waller, Thos.
Weese, John
Weir, Samuel
Williams, Joseph
Wilson, David
Witt, James
Yarin, Matthies

CAPTAIN EDWARD BUCHANAN'S COMPANY
WAR OF 1812

(Photostats from National Archives)

Muster roll of a company of East Tennessee's drafted militia under the command of Capt. Edward Buchanan in the regiment command of Col. Samuel Wear in the service of the United States from the 10th day of January to the 20th day of May, 1814. (Those with a D after the name joined from Capt. Duncan's Company.)

Name	Rank	Name	Rank
Edward Buchanan	Captain	William Martin	Pvt.
Joel McCorkle	1st Lt.	James McClenahan	Pvt.
Ellet Holliday	2nd Lt.	George McFarland	Pvt.
Arthur Campbell	Ensign	Robert Murrian	Pvt.
Jacob Keeny	Sgt.	John Murrian	Pvt.
John Pearson	Sgt.	James McNeely	Pvt.
John McDaniel	Sgt.	John McCauley	Pvt.
William Davis	Sgt.	John Medlock	Pvt.
Athiel McCollister—D	Sgt.	Thomas Morrison	Pvt.
John Black	Cpl.	Absolem McNabb—D	Pvt.
John McGinley	Cpl.	Samuel Orr—D	Pvt.
Charles Taylor	Cpl.	John Patty	Pvt.
Silas Hart	Cpl.	Joel Prewet—discharged	
Samuel Ross—D	Cpl.	Samuel Ranken	Pvt.
James Anderson	Pvt.	Ewel Roper	Pvt.
Jacob Bordon—D	Pvt.	David Roper	Pvt.
James Boaz	Pvt.	Lot Rogers	Pvt.
Uriah Black	Pvt.	John Rogers	Pvt.
David Caldwell	Pvt.	Ahimas Ragan	Pvt.
John Casteel	Pvt.	John Read—D	Pvt.
Thomas Davis	Pvt.	James Smith	Pvt.
Arch. Davis	Pvt.	John A. Smith	Pvt.
James Erwin	Pvt.	William Spragan	Pvt.
George Erwin	Pvt.	Thomas Spragan	Pvt.
William Eakin	Pvt.	Elisha Skeen	Pvt.
John Finley	Pvt.	John Sterling	Pvt.
Robert Goodwin	Pvt.	John Soffle	Pvt.
Thomas Gaston	Pvt.	John Stone	Pvt.
Samuel Houston—apptd. wagon master—1-28-14	Pvt.	James Thompson	Pvt.
		Joseph Tipton	Pvt.
Bevin Hattocks	Pvt.	Joseph Teffeteller	Pvt.
Isaac Hicks	Pvt.	Jacob Thomas	Pvt.
William Huse	Pvt.	Benjamin Taylor	Pvt.
Edmond Halloway	Pvt.	Wallace Thompson	Pvt.
Allen Henderson—D	Pvt.	John L. Tulloch	Pvt.
Elisha James	Pvt.	Samuel Wear	Pvt.
Benjamin James	Pvt.	James Wise	Pvt.
Williams Kinnard	Pvt.	John White	Pvt.
John Kibble	Pvt.	John Wolf	Pvt.
Samuel Knave—D	Pvt.	James Williams	Pvt.
John Low	Pvt.	Jacob Yount—died 3-29-1814	Pvt.
Alex. Logan	Pvt.	Peter Yount	Pvt.
Nehemiah Lacy	Pvt.	John Yearout—D	Pvt.
Jonathan Lacetor—D	Pvt.		

CAPTAIN JOSEPH DUNCAN'S COMPANY
WAR OF 1812

(Photostats from National Archives)

Payroll of a Company of East Tennessee Militia commanded by Captain Joseph Duncan of a Regiment commanded by Col. Samuel Bunch—attached to Col. Ewen Allison in the service of the United States from the 10th of January 1814 to the 21st day of July 1814.

The personnel of this company seems to have shifted quite a bit. Men who transferred to the company will be indicated thusly: Captain Allen—A, Buchanan—B, Duncan—D, Gibbs—G, Howell—H, McNair—M, Yarnell—Y; those who transferred out to other companies are indicated thusly: Captain Berry—tr Be, Buchanan—tr Bu, English—tr E, and Houk—tr H.

Name	Rank	Name	Rank
Joseph Duncan	Captain	William Dynes—tr E	Pvt.
William Colbert—A	1st Lt.	James H. Doyle—tr E	Pvt.
John Johnson	1st Lt.	Thomas Davis—B	Pvt.
Eli Barton	Ensign	Arch. Davis—B	Pvt.
Aaron Lambert—died 3-25-1814	1st Lt.	Benjamin Durham	Pvt.
Joseph B. Woods—tr E	Ensign	Adam Dinsmore	Pvt.
James Hamilton—H	Sgt.	William Eaken	Pvt.
John McDaniel—B	Sgt.	William Eakins	Pvt.
Marvel Duncan (promoted 3-11-14)	Sgt.	Jonathan Eakins	Pvt.
Geo. W. Reed (promoted 3-11-14)	Sgt.	Soloman Eakins	Pvt.
James Morrow	Sgt.	James Ervine—B	Pvt.
Isaac Adams	Sgt.	Robert Evans—H	Pvt.
John Aiken	Sgt.	Right Edwards—Y	Pvt.
Joseph McManis—died 4-13-1814	Sgt.	Thomas Farmer	Pvt.
James Riddle—A	Cpl.	Samuel Farr	Pvt.
Henry Newman—M	Cpl.	Martin Foster	Pvt.
Bartlett Quinn	Cpl.	William Farmer	Pvt.
Azariah Orr	Cpl.	John Finley	Pvt.
Samuel Ross—B	Cpl.	Andrew Fergusson	Pvt.
Athiel McAllister	Cpl.	Joel Fargusson—Y	Pvt.
Josiah Brown	Cpl.	Robert Fargusson—Y	Pvt.
Thomas Adams	Pvt.	Thomas Gaston—B	Pvt.
Michael Anderson	Pvt.	Joseph Hamilton—H	Pvt.
John Adams—A	Pvt.	Thomas Harper	Pvt.
William Brickey—A	Pvt.	Solomon Humphreys	Pvt.
Robert Bandy	Pvt.	Joseph Havens—G	Pvt.
James Baxter	Pvt.	Edward Hall	Pvt.
Francis Brown—M	Pvt.	Zachariah Hall	Pvt.
John Brown	Pvt.	Jesse Henderson—Y	Pvt.
John Blakely	Pvt.	Henry Hide	Pvt.
Ezra Buckner—G	Pvt.	Allen Henderson—tr Bu	Pvt.
Thomas Brook	Pvt.	James Hamontree—tr Be	Pvt.
James Campbell—A	Pvt.	William Hamontree	Pvt.
Meshac Casteel	Pvt.	Martin Hicks—tr H	Pvt.
Joseph Casteel—tr Bu	Pvt.	Jesse Hoffman—disch. 5-1-14	Pvt.
Caleb Casteel—tr Be	Pvt.	Tarlton Herl	Pvt.
John Casteel—tr Bu	Pvt.	Elisha James—tr. Bu	Pvt.
Barachias Coop	Pvt.	Benjamin James—tr Bu	Pvt.
William Cunningham—A	Pvt.	John Jamison	Pvt.
William Coose—H	Pvt.	Alex. Jenkins—A, died 5-9-14	Pvt.
John Crawson—Y	Pvt.	Beverage Lawrence	Pvt.
Benjamin D. Clift	Pvt.	George LaRue—Y	Pvt.
Isaac Corban	Pvt.	Daniel Lambert—tr E	Pvt.
Jacob Dyre	Pvt.	John Low—B	Pvt.
Quintian Dynes	Pvt.	Jonathan Lacetor	Pvt.

Name	Rank	Name	Rank
Solomon Lowdermilk—M	Pvt.	Robert Rhea	Pvt.
James Ledgerwood—G	Pvt.	John Rhea—tr Bu	Pvt.
Robert Murrian—B	Pvt.	Henry Stephenson—E	Pvt.
John Murrian	Pvt.	James Stephenson	Pvt.
William Maxwell—A	Pvt.	George Stone	Pvt.
Price McNare—M	Pvt.	John Simmons	Pvt.
Peter Moses—H	Pvt.	John Sterling	Pvt.
Jesse Marten	Pvt.	John A. Smith	Pvt.
Pleasant Miller—G	Pvt.	Elijah Skeen	Pvt.
Luke Mitchell	Pvt.	Thomas Spraggins	Pvt.
Simeon McCarroll—Y	Pvt.	William Spraggins	Pvt.
Joseph Mayberry	Pvt.	John Saffle	Pvt.
Josiah McGuire	Pvt.	Martin Stegall—A	Pvt.
Blackman Mayo—tr E	Pvt.	Jesse Smith—M	Pvt.
David Martin	Pvt.	James Smith—Y	Pvt.
Absolem McNabb	Pvt.	Jonathan Simmons—H	Pvt.
William Moore	Pvt.	John H. Sappington—G	Pvt.
Carolinus Miller (sub. for Jesse Huffman)	Pvt.	Samuel Tummins	Pvt.
		John L. Tulloch—tr Bu	Pvt.
Samuel Nave—tr Bu	Pvt.	Jesse Vaughn—tr Bu	Pvt.
Samuel Orr	Pvt.	Daniel Vance—M	Pvt.
Joel Prewett	Pvt.	William Williams—A	Pvt.
John Putty	Pvt.	Nicholas Woody	Pvt.
Thomas Palmer—A	Pvt.	Silas Woody	Pvt.
William Patton—H	Pvt.	John A. Wright	Pvt.
Daniel Pew—G	Pvt.	Thomas Wright	Pvt.
William Rutherford	Pvt.	Robert Wilson	Pvt.
Joseph Rutherford	Pvt.	Daniel Whittenbarger	Pvt.
George Rigney—Y	Pvt.	James Young	Pvt.
John Redman—H	Pvt.	John Yearout—tr Bu	Pvt.
Joseph Rogers	Pvt.	Peter Yount—B	Pvt.
John Roach (promoted 4-27-1814)	Sgt.		

CAPTAIN JAMES GILLESPIE'S COMPANY
WAR OF 1812

(Photostats from National Archives)

The payroll of a company of Militia Infantry commanded by Captain James Gillespie of the Reg't of East Tennessee Militia under the command of Col. Sam'l Wear in the service of the United States from the 23rd day of September 1813 to the 31st day of December 1813.

Name	Rank	Name	Rank
James Gillespie	Capt.	John McNabb	Cpl.
William Henry	1st Lt.	Benjamin Irwin	Cpl.
James Gardner	2nd Lt.	Phillip Able	Pvt.
Robert Boyd	3rd Lt.	Gasper Bright	Pvt.
Samuel Montgomery	Ensign	John Bastic	Pvt.
John Thornberry	Sgt.	John Bundy	Pvt.
Samuel Henry	Sgt.	Jesse Bean	Pvt.
Matthew Whittenbarger	Sgt.	John S. Burnette	Pvt.
Robert Thompson	Sgt.	John Culph	Pvt.
John McKee	Sgt.	Walter Carruth	Pvt.
Alexr. Rider	Sgt.	Nelson Crowder	Pvt.
John Lambert	Cpl.	Cylas Casteal	Pvt.
Patrick McClung	Cpl.	Silas M. Caldwell	Pvt.
William Thompson	Cpl.	James Corley	Pvt.

Name	Rank	Name	Rank
William Edminston	Pvt.	William McGill	Pvt.
William Forrester	Pvt.	James McCabe	Pvt.
Robert Gaines	Pvt.	John Miller	Pvt.
Charles Goldsby	Pvt.	John Pennell	Pvt.
James Griggsby	Pvt.	James Page	Pvt.
Reynolds Gentry	Pvt.	Abner Parks	Pvt.
William Green	Pvt.	William Rudd	Pvt.
Adam Graves	Pvt.	John Rodgers	Pvt.
James Gamble	Pvt.	George Rolsten	Pvt.
James Hicklan	Pvt.	John Rider	Pvt.
Samuel Houston	Pvt.	Able Rice	Pvt.
Jacob Hammontree	Pvt.	William P. Reed	Pvt.
John B. Hail	Pvt.	William Rodgers	Pvt.
Donathan Hicklan	Pvt.	Jesse Rucker	Pvt.
Nelson Hudgeons	Pvt.	George W. Reed	Pvt.
Thomas Heart	Pvt.	Joseph Ray	Pvt.
James Henry	Pvt.	William Russell	Pvt.
John Hanby	Pvt.	Patterson Rodgers	Pvt.
Robert Hood	Pvt.	Peter Summerford	Pvt.
Alexander Ish	Pvt.	John Stewart	Pvt.
Jesse James	Pvt.	John Short	Pvt.
Andrew James	Pvt.	Thomas W. Smith	Pvt.
John Jackson	Pvt.	William Sathewhite	Pvt.
John Jameson	Pvt.	James Townsly	Pvt.
James Kendrick	Pvt.	William Tool	Pvt.
Peter Key	Pvt.	David Thompson	Pvt.
David Key	Pvt.	Jesse Teavault	Pvt.
John Knave	Pvt.	John Toole	Pvt.
John Reagon	Pvt.	Joseph Utter	Pvt.
William Long	Pvt.	William Utter	Pvt.
George Lowe	Pvt.	John Williams	Pvt.
David Leatherdale	Pvt.	Hugh Wear	Pvt.
John McCarroll	Pvt.	James Woody	Pvt.
James McAlester	Pvt.	Joseph B. Woods	Pvt.
John Montgomery	Pvt.	Thomas Wear	Pvt.
Samuel Montgomery	Pvt.	David Williams	Pvt.
Hugh McGil	Pvt.	Barney Casteal	Pvt.
John Moore	Pvt.		

CAPTAIN DAVID McKAMEY'S COMPANY
WAR OF 1812

(Photostats from National Archives)

A Muster Roll of Captain David McKamey's Company of East Tennessee Drafted Militia under the command of Col. William Johnson from the 29th of September 1814 to May 18th, 1815.

Name	Rank	Name	Rank
David McKamey	Captain	Arch. Sloan	2d Cpl.
George Black	1st Lt.	John Minis	3d Cpl.
Thomas D. DeArmond	2d Lt.	James McGaughey	4th Cpl.
James Tedford	Ensign	James McCallen	5th Cpl.
James McCartney	1st Sgt.	William McCarty	Fifer
John M. Clute	2d Sgt.	William Blithe	Pvt.
Peter Brakebill	3d Sgt.	Isaac Brooke	Pvt.
James McKamey	4th Sgt.	Edward Boman, Campbell Co.	Pvt.
John Means	Cpl.	Samuel Boman, Campbell Co.	Pvt.

APPENDIX

Name	Rank
John Brakebille	Pvt.
Joseph Brown	Pvt.
James Brown	Pvt.
Nicholas Boring	Pvt.
William Bowman, Campbell Co.	Pvt.
Alasander Black	Pvt.
Stephen Boling, Campbell Co.	Pvt.
Henry Boin, Campbell Co.	Pvt.
William Cross, Campbell Co.	Pvt.
John Canon	Pvt.
John Cruiz, sub. for A. Rogers	Pvt.
John Cannon, Sr.	Pvt.
George Crider	Pvt.
David Cup	Pvt.
Peter Davis	Pvt.
William Dunlap	Pvt.
James Dunlap	Pvt.
William Donaldson, sub. for James Strain	Pvt.
William Davis, sub. for Wm. Dever	Pvt.
Richmond Davis	Pvt.
Moses Dougherty, Campbell Co.	Pvt.
Emens Dosert, Campbell Co.	Pvt.
Walter Edwards, Campbell Co.	Pvt.
Elijah Farmer	Pvt.
John Fortner, Campbell Co.	Pvt.
Samuel Givens	Pvt.
James Glass	Pvt.
Peter Grenfield	Pvt.
John Gormley	Pvt.
Samuel Gibbs	Pvt.
Zephaniah Gideon, Campbell Co.	Pvt.
Richard Green	Pvt.
William Hickman, sub. for John Branson	Pvt.
William Hamilton	Pvt.
James Hannah	Pvt.
Fredrick Harges	Pvt.
John Holoway	Pvt.
Thomas Henderson	Pvt.
John Ingram	Pvt.
John Henry	Pvt.
John Long	Pvt.
John Lowe	Pvt.
Jonathan McMurry	Pvt.
Robert McTeer, sub. for John Hamell	Pvt.
William Murray, sub. for John Ewing	Pvt.
Asberry Mash	Pvt.
Montgomery McTier, sub. for Joseph Utter	Pvt.
William McCulloch	Pvt.
Robert McGill	Pvt.
Jacob McGhee	Pvt.
John McCullough, Campbell Co.	Pvt.
John Peck, sub. for Eli Dickson	Pvt.
Jacob Pope, Blount Co.	Pvt.
Lewis Paret, Campbell Co.	Pvt.
John Richey, Blount Co.	Pvt.
Andrew Rogers, Blount Co.	Pvt.
Robert Rhea, sub. for Wm. Kilburne	Pvt.
Joseph Reagan	Pvt.
William Richmond	Pvt.
Harmon Shook	Pvt.
Jacob Simons	Pvt.
David Smith	Pvt.
James Scott, sub. for James Cawhorn	Pvt.
James Scott	Pvt.
John Shrowe	Pvt.
John Stuart	Pvt.
Parks Shelton, Campbell Co.	Pvt.
Samuel Tipton, Blount Co.	Pvt.
Samuel Tual	Pvt.
Frederick Thomas	Pvt.
John O. Wilson, sub. for Arthur Hanley	Pvt.
Robert Wilcox, sub. for Lewis Jones	Pvt.
William Walker	Pvt.
James White	Pvt.
George Williams	Pvt.
William White	Pvt.
Robert Witt	Pvt.
John Weese	Pvt.
William H. Walker	Pvt.
Thomas Woodall	Pvt.
John Wier	Pvt.

CAPTAIN JEHU STEPHENS' COMPANY
WAR OF 1812

(From the original Muster Roll kept by Sgt. William McTeer)

Muster Roll of Captain Jehu Stephens' Company of Volunteer Mounted Gunmen from East Tennessee under the command of Col. Samuel Wear and Brig. Gen. John Coffee. In the service of the United States from the 6th of October 1814 when mustered into service until the 6th of April 1815, the expiration of their service.

This Muster Roll was preserved by William McTeer, who was 1st Sgt. of the company. Most of these men were from Blount County.

Name	Rank	Name	Rank
Jehu Stephens	Captain	Samuel M. Johnson	Pvt.
William Upton	1st Lt.	Thomas M. Jack	Pvt.
James Henry	2d Lt.	Milton Jack	Pvt.
Ransom Peery	3d Lt.	John Knight	Pvt.
William Bates	Ensign	George Kennard	Pvt.
William McTeer	1st Sgt.	Jesse Kerr	Pvt.
Nelson S. Wright	2d Sgt.	Samuel Legg	Pvt.
Hugh Henry	3d Sgt.	Henry Logan	Pvt.
Alexander Sharp	4th Sgt.	Samuel McClung	Pvt.
William Glass	5th Sgt.	James McCallen	Pvt.
James Bogle	1st. Cpl.	Samuel McCurry (died 2-14-1815)	Pvt.
William Taylor	2d Cpl.	George McFarlin	Pvt.
John Henry	3d Cpl.	Spencer McBrient	Pvt.
William Garner	4th Cpl.	Robert Martin	Pvt.
Samuel Read	5th Cpl.	Thomas McCallie	Pvt.
John Regan	6th Cpl.	Hugh Murphy	Pvt.
Robert Beaty	Pvt.	William Martin	Pvt.
John Cooper	Pvt.	John McCallon	Pvt.
James Conner	Pvt.	Alexander McKee	Pvt.
Alexander Coulter	Pvt.	Charles W. C. Norwood	Pvt.
Benjamin Carter	Pvt.	Thomas Oens	Pvt.
Gabriel Crawley	Pvt.	Semple Ore	Pvt.
James Caldwell	Pvt.	James Page	Pvt.
William Caldwell	Pvt.	George Pate	Pvt.
James Davis	Pvt.	Elijah Rudd	Pvt.
John Douglas	Pvt.	Ephraim Rossen	Pvt.
James Douglas	Pvt.	George Snider	Pvt.
Samuel C. Davidson	Pvt.	Thomas Snider	Pvt.
William Davidson	Pvt.	William Sims	Pvt.
Hiram A. DeFrees	Pvt.	Addison Sharp	Pvt.
James Delzell	Pvt.	William Stephens	Pvt.
John Duglas, Jr.	Pvt.	Jesse Thompson	Pvt.
James Eagleton	Pvt.	Jesse Tevault	Pvt.
Henry Ewing	Pvt.	William Trotter	Pvt.
William Farmer	Pvt.	James Taylor (died 1-22-1815)	Pvt.
William Graves	Pvt.	James Wolf	Pvt.
Thomas Gray	Pvt.	William R. White	Pvt.
Moses Gamble	Pvt.	William Wallace	Pvt.
John Houston	Pvt.	John Wear	Pvt.
Cornelius Hafley	Pvt.	William Weldon	Pvt.
John Harriss, Jr.	Pvt.	Jesse Hird	Pvt.
Samuel Henry	Pvt.	William Harriss	Pvt.
Edwin Harriss	Pvt.	James Lusk	Pvt.
William Henry	Pvt.	Abraham Barrett	Pvt.
John Harriss, Sr.	Pvt.	Jesse Harriss	Pvt.
Toliver Harriss	Pvt.	James Price	Pvt.
Nathaniel Jeffries	Pvt.	Lewis Black	Pvt.
Solomon Henson	Pvt.	William Price	Pvt.

CAPTAIN JAMES TEDFORD'S COMPANY
WAR OF 1812

Pay Roll of a company of Militia Infantry commanded by Captain James Tedford of the Regiment of East Tennessee Militia under the command of Col. Samuel Wear in the service of the United States from the 23rd day of September 1813 to the 31st day of December 1813. (Mustered out at Kingston.)

Name	Rank	Name	Rank
James Tedford	Captain	Benjamin Harrison—apptd. Major by Col. Wear 10-6-1813	
Thomas Maxwell	1st Lt.	John Jones	Pvt.
David McKamey	2d Lt.	Thomas Jack	Pvt.
James McCartney	Ensign	Joseph Johnson	Pvt.
Robert R. Young	Sgt.	John Lowe	Pvt.
John Tedford	2d Sgt.	Armond Means	Pvt.
Samuel Caldwell	3d Sgt.	David McRanalds	Pvt.
William Black	Cpl.	John McCartney	Pvt.
Alex. Ewing	2d Cpl.	John Morrison	Pvt.
Jonathan Whister	3d Cpl.	Samuel Menis	Pvt.
Job Allen	Pvt.	Thomas Menis	Pvt.
Alexander Cook	Pvt.	William McMakin	Pvt.
Thomas Cooper	Pvt.	William McCampbell	Pvt.
William Cooper	Pvt.	John Pierson	Pvt.
Thomas Cummings	Pvt.	Jacob Pursley	Pvt.
William Caldwell	Pvt.	Gideon Richey	Pvt.
John Caldwell	Pvt.	John N. Rankin	Pvt.
Alexander Cahorne	Pvt.	John Snider	Pvt.
Jacob Coiles	Pvt.	James Sloan	Pvt.
Thomas Caskright	Pvt.	Hugh Skott	Pvt.
James Dickson	Pvt.	John Simans	Pvt.
Andrew Davis	Pvt.	James Tedford, Jr.	Pvt.
Robert Delzell	Pvt.	Robert Wilson	Pvt.
Alexander Eagletin	Pvt.	John Wilson	Pvt.
Henry Frushour	Pvt.	James Wallice	Pvt.
Stafford Gibbs	Pvt.	Samuel Wear	Pvt.
John B. Harriss	Pvt.	Matthew M. Young	Pvt.
Hugh Hamille	Pvt.		
Daniel Hails	Pvt.		

CAPTAIN JOHN TRIMBLE'S COMPANY
WAR OF 1812

(From Photostats from National Archives)

Muster Roll of Mounted Infantry commanded by Captain John Trimble in the Battalion commanded by Major William Russell of Brig. Gen. Coffee's Brigade in the service of the United States commencing on the 5th day of October 1814 and ending on the 5th day of April 1815.

Name	Rank	Name	Rank
John Trimble	Captain	Michael Gormley	Cpl.
*John Wilson	1st Lt.	James McMahan	Cpl.
James Cunningham	2d Lt.	William Laney	Cpl.
Henry Freshour	Ensign	James McCabe	Cpl.
Matthew Young	Sgt.	Robert Robertson	Cpl.
Samuel McConnell	Sgt.	Wiley Adams	Pvt.
James Gamble	Sgt.	James Boyd	Pvt.
Alesar Hannah	Sgt.	John Boyd	Pvt.
Samuel Roark	Sgt.	John Blackwell	Pvt.

Name	Rank	Name	Rank
Thomas Blair	Pvt.	John McCartney	Pvt.
Welcome Bayard	Pvt.	John McConnell	Pvt.
David Caldwell	Pvt.	John Maxwell	Pvt.
Isam Cordill	Pvt.	John McMahan	Pvt.
James Caruth	Pvt.	Robert McGaughey	Pvt.
Joseph Cook	Pvt.	Thomas Minnis	Pvt.
Moses Cunningham	Pvt.	William McNabb	Pvt.
Samuel Carruthers	Pvt.	William McConnell	Pvt.
Thomas Carns	Pvt.	Thomas H. Neil	Pvt.
William Cook	Pvt.	Wilsey Pride	Pvt.
James Caldwell[1]	Pvt.	Lewis Russell[2]	Pvt.
Isaac Dial	Pvt.	Joseph Runnington	Pvt.
James Dickey	Pvt.	Thomas Roark	Pvt.
John Gould	Pvt.	William Raper	Pvt.
John Gormley	Pvt.	James Sloan	Pvt.
Carolinus Hannah	Pvt.	John Sloan	Pvt.
Daniel Hoyle	Pvt.	Abel Stafford	Pvt.
George Hutcheson[2]	Pvt.	John Varner	Pvt.
Jesse Harriss[1]	Pvt.	Charles Walker	Pvt.
Jesse Heard[1]	Pvt.	George Williams	Pvt.
John Hannah	Pvt.	Jeremiah Woodart	Pvt.
Moses Hannah	Pvt.	John Wright	Pvt.
Matthew Hannah	Pvt.	Joseph Wilson	Pvt.
Robert Harriss	Pvt.	Robert Williams	Pvt.
William Hambrey	Pvt.	John Young	Pvt.
William W. Harges	Pvt.	Joseph Morton	Pvt.
James Kelso	Pvt.	John Williams	Pvt.
John Kitchen	Pvt.	Markes Orr	Pvt.

*Arrested on the 12th of January 1815 and in preference of standing trial suffered his sword broke over his head—ordered to the ranks and done duty as a private the remainder of the term.
[1]Transferred from Captain Stephens' Company December 12, 1814.
[2]Transferred from Captain William Russell's Company December 18, 1814.

CAPTAIN REUBEN TIPTON'S COMPANY
WAR OF 1812

Muster Roll and description List of Captain Reuben Tipton's Volunteer Company of Mounted Gunmen raised in East Tennessee, mustered into the service of the United States on the 20th day of September 1814. (Served until May 1, 1815.) (Major John Chiles.)

Name	Rank	Age	Hgt	Complexion	Hair	Eyes	Regt.	County
Reuben Tipton	Capt.	33	5-8	fair	fair	blue	40th	Knox
Thomas McEldry	1st Lt.	24	5-9	dark	black	hazel	10th	Knox
James W. Flenniken	2d Lt.	37	6	dark	black	black	40th	Knox
Jacob Tipton	Ens.	22	5-9	fair	fair	blue	12th	Blount
Carey Thatcher	1st Lt.	17	6	dark	dark	blue	40th	Knox
Perey Wilkinson	2d Sgt.	26	5-11	dark	black	blue	6th	Jefferson
Ichabod Hansley	3d Sgt.	20	5-9	dark	black	black	40th	Knox
Andrew Gass	4th Sgt.	23	6	fair	dark	grey	6th	Jefferson
John Hood	1st Cpl.	22	6	fair	dark	blue	40th	Knox
Benjamin Johnson	2d Cpl.	22	5-10	fair	dark	black	40th	Knox
John Lowe	3d Cpl.	41	5-10	dark	black	grey	12th	Blount
Jonathan Shelley	4th Cpl.	20	5-8	fair	sandy	blue	6th	Jefferson
John Franklin	5th Cpl.	21	6-2	dark	black	blue	6th	Jefferson
Jacob Shelley	Tru'pet	19	5-7	fair	fair	blue	6th	Jefferson

APPENDIX

Name	Rank	Age	Hgt	Complexion	Hair	Eyes	Regt.	County
William Baker	Pvt.	17	5	dark	dark	black	40th	Knox
John Baker	Pvt.	18	5-8	fair	fair	blue	6th	Jefferson
George Bowman	Pvt.	21	5-10	dark	dark	black	6th	Jefferson
Henry Butrage	Pvt.	28	5-4	dark	dark	blue	6th	Jefferson
Adam Carter	Pvt.	27	5-10	dark	fair	blue	6th	Jefferson
Robert Childress	Pvt.	33	5-7	dark	dark	black	12th	Blount
William Childress	Pvt.	17	5-5	fair	fair	black	40th	Knox
Benjamin Carr	Pvt.	20	5-9	dark	dark	grey	40th	Knox
Walter Childress	Pvt.	23	5-8	dark	dark	black	40th	Knox
Gallion Crews	Pvt.	22	6	fair	dark	black	10th	Knox
John Crews	Pvt.	19	5-9	dark	dark	black	10th	Knox
Francis Collins	Pvt.	22	5-7	fair	fair	blue	6th	Jefferson
John Darr	Pvt.	37	5-6	fair	dark	dark	6th	Jefferson
Asa DeLozier	Pvt.	20	5-10	dark	dark	black	12th	Blount
William DeArmond	Pvt.	18	6	dark	dark	grey	40th	Knox
Richard Dodd	Pvt.	25	5-9	dark	dark	black	10th	Knox
Samuel Flenniken	Pvt.	32	5-8	dark	black	grey	40th	Knox
James Gass	Pvt.	18	6	dark	black	black	6th	Jefferson
Elijah Harriss	Pvt.	17	5	dark	black	black	10th	Knox
James Harriss	Pvt.	35	6	dark	black	black	12th	Blount
Matthew Houston	Pvt.	21	5-10	fair	fair	blue	10th	Knox
Charles Hodge	Pvt.	23	5-11	fair	brown	blue	6th	Jefferson
John Hill	Pvt.	18	6	dark	black	blue	40th	Knox
John R. Hanson	Pvt.	21	5-7	dark	black	grey	40th	Knox
George Hanson	Pvt.	19	5-11	fair	fair	blue	40th	Knox
John Hays	Pvt.	21	5-10	fair	fair	blue	6th	Jefferson
Bevin Haddox	Pvt.	25	5-10	fair	fair	grey	12th	Blount
James Hines	Pvt.	25	5-9	fair	fair	blue	10th	Knox
Isaac Hines	Pvt.	transferred from Captain Conway's company						
Robert Jack	Pvt.	21	5-10	fair	dark	blue	10th	Knox
Giles S. Bogas	Pvt.	22	5-6	dark	black	black	10th	Bledsoe
James Kemp	Pvt.	36	5-10	dark	dark	blue	6th	Jefferson
James Moore	Pvt.	44	5-11	dark	dark	blue	40th	Knox
James Murphy	Pvt.	31	5-10	fair	dark	blue		Bledsoe
Samuel McEldry	Pvt.	22	5-11	fair	dark	blue	10th	Knox
Uriah Murphy	Pvt.	36	5-2	fair	fair	black	40th	Knox
James McKeehan	Pvt.	40	5-11	fair	fair	blue	10th	Knox
Andrew McBath	Pvt.	19	5-7	fair	fair	blue	10th	Knox
Cullinas Miller	Pvt.	33	6	fair	fair	blue	12th	Blount
William McKinley	Pvt.	22	5-11	fair	black	grey	6th	Jefferson
John Roddy	Pvt.	19	6	dark	dark	black	12th	Blount
Andrew Roddy	Pvt.	26	5-5	dark	dark	black	12th	Blount
Nathan R. Sellars	Pvt.	19	5-6	dark	dark	black	6th	Jefferson
David Smith	Pvt.	26	6	fair	fair	blue	6th	Jefferson
William Sassean	Pvt.	42	5-7	fair	black	black	6th	Jefferson
Hugh Seahorne	Pvt.	21	5-10	fair	fair	blue	6th	Jefferson
Jonathan R. Tipton	Pvt.	17	5-5	fair	fair	blue	12th	Blount
Isaac Tipton	Pvt.	23	5-8	fair	fair	blue	12th	Blount
John Tipton	Pvt.	23	5-10	fair	fair	blue	12th	Blount
John Witt	Pvt.	27	5-9	dark	fair	grey	6th	Jefferson
Silas Witt	Pvt.	24	5-11	dark	dark	blue	6th	Jefferson
John Ward	Pvt.	30	5-8	dark	black	black	10th	Knox
George Wells	Pvt.	21	5-5	fair	fair	grey	40th	Knox
Thomas Wright	Pvt.	30	5-8	dark	black	blue	10th	Knox
Joel Woods	Pvt	27	5-7	fair	fair	blue	6th	Jefferson
William Wheeler	Pvt.	23	6	dark	dark	black	12th	Blount
Benjamin Wheeler	Pvt.	18	6	dark	black	black	12th	Blount
John Webb	Pvt.	28	5-6	dark	dark	black	40th	Knox
Elijah Bogas	Pvt.	19	5-6	dark	black	black		Bledsoe

Signed by John Russell, Brigade Major at Fort Montgomery January 19th 1815

CAPTAIN WILLIAM WALKER'S COMPANY
WAR OF 1812

(Photostats from National Archives)

Muster Roll of a company of Mounted Volunteers from East Tennessee under the command of Col. John Williams in the service of the United States. Commanded by Captain William Walker from the 1st of December 1812 to the 25th of March 1813 inclusive. (See Samuel Cole Williams, *A Forgotten Campaign*, in The Tennessee Historical Magazine, v. 8, No. 4, p. 266.)

Name	Rank
William Walker	Captain
Richard Meredith	1st Lt.
Joel Denton	2d Lt.
John Chiles	Ensign
Joseph Hart	1st Sgt.
John P. Houston	Sgt.
Thomas H. Miller	Sgt.
William H. Greenway	Sgt.
William Armstrong	Pvt.
Marshall Ayers	Pvt.
John W. Alston	Pvt.
Jesse Bartlett	Pvt.
James D. Burnett	Pvt.
Allen S. Bacon	Pvt.
Alexander Campbell	Pvt.
Andrew Cowan	Pvt.
English Crawford	Pvt.
Francis Collins	Pvt.
Thomas Davis	Pvt.
Benjamin Dean	Pvt.
Charles Douglas	Pvt.
Richard J. DeArmond	Pvt.
Phillip Edington	Pvt.
Jacob Fornwalt	Pvt.
Arch. W. Gordon	Pvt.
Bevin Grady	Pvt.
Daniel Graves	Pvt.
Joseph Gerring	Pvt.
Charles C. Hodge	Pvt.
Robert Handcock	Pvt.
James H. Hindman	Pvt.
William Hughs	Pvt.
Hezekiah Jackson	Pvt.
Luke Lea	Pvt.
Henry Mattock	Pvt.
James McConnell	Pvt.
William Malcom	Pvt.
Pleasant M. Miller	Pvt.
William C. Mynatt	Pvt.
Samuel McEldry	Pvt.
Hathan B. Markland	Pvt.
Gideon Morgan	Pvt.
Valentine Mayo	Pvt.
William Mayo	Pvt.
James Murphy	Pvt.
Thomas McConnell	Pvt.
John McNair	Pvt.
Thomas Nolan	Pvt.
Alexander S. Outlaw	Pvt.
Enoch Parsons	Pvt.
Peter Parsons	Pvt.
James Page	Pvt.
Isaac Pangle	Pvt.
Joseph Peterson	Pvt.
William Purvis	Pvt.
Henry Stephens	Pvt.
George Smith	Pvt.
Benjamin C. Stout	Pvt.
William Sawyers	Pvt.
Stephen Skaggs	Pvt.
Jesse Turner	Pvt.
James Turner	Pvt.
Jacob Tipton	Pvt.
Abraham Tipton	Pvt.
Thomas Williams	Pvt.
Richard G. Waterhouse	Pvt.
Moses White	Pvt.
Benjamin Wheeler	Pvt.
John Williams	Pvt.
Thomas F. Wells	Pvt.
James Tunel	Pvt.
Coleman Cox	Pvt.
James Dell	Pvt.
Maxey Dell	Pvt.
William Vince	Pvt.
Wade Hampton	Pvt.
Joseph Muse	Pvt.
Henry Newman	Pvt.
David Nelson	Pvt.

APPENDIX

CREEK REMOVAL

Information taken from the War Papers of Newton Cannon Tennessee State Archives, Nashville, Tennessee.

The Fifth Brigade of the First Division of Mounted Volunteers in 1836 was made up of five companies: Captain Morrow of Knox County; Captains Cunningham and Tedford of Blount County; Captains West and Ellis of Sevier County.

June 30, 1836 Captain Ben Cunningham reported a company of volunteers from the twentieth Regiment Tennessee Militia consisting of himself, 1st Lt. William Deever, 2nd Lt. William Hendrick, Ensign Jacob Tipton and 63 privates. These men rendezvoused at Athens, July 7, 1836 for 6 months against the Creeks.

Captain James Tedford reported a company of volunteers from the 21st Regiment Tennessee Militia on July 1, 1836. He was accompanied by 1st Lt. John Stratton, 2nd Lt. Barkly M. Russell, Ensign James Hendron and 53 men.

CHEROKEE REMOVAL

A Company enlisted under Captain Robert A. Tedford May 26, 1838 at Camp Cass (Charleston, Tennessee).

1st Lt.—James M. Johnson.
Ensign—Perry Clifton.
Sgts.—Thomas C. Dotson, Jesse B. Thompson, James A. Murry, and James Strain.
Corporals—Pleasant L. Futhy, Thomas P. White, Joel Sharp, Park B. Nicols.
Drummer—Joseph Runnions.
Fifer—David Tarwater.
Privates:

James Branham
William Branham
Thomas Bright
Jesse Bawner
John D. Bruster
Harvy Cameron
Samuel Carr
William E. Carter
William Claiborne
William Clifton
Robert Cochrane
Newton Cook
Jesse Cox
Lewis Cox
David Deal
Henderson P. Dobins
Thomas Dodson
William Dodson
Isaac T. Douthitt
James Early
Joseph Emery

John D. Eppes
Eli Fox
Richard Gentry
Jeptha Ginn
(Baptist minister)
William E. Graham
Stephen Hensley
Aaron Hickman
Humphrey Hickman
Benjamin Hitch
James Keen
William Key
James Martin
David Smith
Gabriel Turner
William Turpin
Burches Ward
Riley Waters
H. G. W. Whittenbarger
Thomas J. White
Benjamin Wilkinson

                Jesse Wells   James Woods
                John Wilson   William Woods
                James W. P. Wilson (1st Lt.)

   Another company enlisted at Madisonville, July 8, 1838 under Captain Thomas J. Caldwell which contained about 80 men, some of whom were Blount Countians.

CAPTAIN JULIUS CAESAR FAGG'S COMPANY
MEXICAN WAR
(Photostat from National Archives)

Muster Roll of Julius C. Fagg's Company (F) in the 5th Regiment of Tennessee Foot Volunteers, commanded by Col. George R. McClelland, called into the service of the United States by the President, under the Act of Congress approved May 13, 1846, at Knoxville, Tennessee (the place of general rendezvous) on the 12th day of November 1847, to serve for the duration of the War with Mexico, from the date of enrollment, unless sooner discharged; from the 30th of April 1848 (when last mustered) to the 20th day of July 1848, when mustered out of the service. The company was organized by Capt. J. C. Fagg at Maryville, Tennessee, in the month of September 1847 and marched thence to Knoxville, where it arrived the 11th of November, a distance of twenty miles.

Name	Rank	Age	Enlisted
Julius C. Fagg	Capt.	39	Knoxville
James A. McKamey	1st Lt.	22	
James M. Kennedy	2nd Lt.	21	
James W. Gault	2nd Lt.	21	
George H. Maxwell	1st Sgt.	25	
DeWitt C. Ghormley	Sgt.	22	
Adam P. Mooty	Sgt.	22	
Hugh Gamble	Sgt.	21	
Lewis R. Young	Cpl.	19	
William C. Norton	Cpl.	21	
Isaac Taylor	Cpl.	19	
Cornelius Y. Lambert	Cpl.	19	
Cliff, John B.	Music.	44	
Owens, John	Music.	20	
Allen, Reuben	Pvt.	33	
Barns, Jason	Pvt.	20	
Baty, William B.	Pvt.	23	
Boling, Mitchell	Pvt.	22	
Bicknell, William	Pvt.	24	
Brown, William	Pvt.	25	San Juan
Brown, Alexander	Pvt.	20	Louisville
Cunningham, Riley	Pvt.	18	Knoxville
Cain, Ruben	Pvt.	19	
Davis, Rufus M.	Pvt.	22	
Cummings, Joseph	Pvt.	18	Louisville
Dunaway, Leroy	Pvt.	22	Knoxville
Davis, William M.	Pvt.	19	
Dillow, Joseph	Pvt.	19	
Everett, Abraham	Pvt.	18	
Ellige, William	Pvt.	21	
Ellige, Joseph P.	Pvt.	19	
Esslinger, William	Pvt.	18	
Ellis, Alexander	Pvt.	22	Tazewell
Folkner, John	Pvt.	19	Knoxville

APPENDIX

Name	Rank	Age	Enlisted
Ferguson, John A.	Pvt.	20	
Grace, George C.	Pvt.	19	
Gamble, Moses	Pvt.	21	
Givens, Temple	Pvt.	24	Maryville
Hinds, Joseph H.	Pvt.	21	Maryville
Hicks, Henderson H.	Pvt.	21	Knoxville
Huffman, James	Pvt.	21	
Howard, John M.	Pvt.	22	
Hutsell, George W.	Pvt.	19	
Hubbard, James J.	Pvt.	21	
Hope, James B.	Pvt.	19	
Hand, James A.	Pvt.	19	Knoxville
Hicks, Thomas	Pvt.	22	
Holder, Thomas F.	Pvt.	22	
Leak, Peter	Pvt.	20	
Langford, John	Pvt.	20	
Lea, John L.	Pvt.	19	
McGhee, Barclay*	Pvt.	31	
Murrin, James M.	Pvt.	24	
Meroney, Matthew H.	Pvt.	18	
Nelson, William J.	Pvt.	20	San Juan
Palmer, James G.	Pvt.	25	Knoxville
Phelps, John	Pvt.	26	
Potter, John	Pvt.	18	
Roberts, Frederick	Pvt.	37	
Rose, Daniel M.	Pvt.	18	
Rollins, George	Pvt.	21	
Sparks, Robert A.	Pvt.	19	
Taylor, Benjamin	Pvt.	21	
Thomas, John S.	Pvt.	18	
Turner, Ward	Pvt.	20	

*Assistant Surgeon from 3-25-1848

Names	Rank	Age	Enlisted	Remarks
Transferred				
Durham, Ruben	Pvt.	22	Knoxville	Tr to Capt. Rose's Co.—11-12-1847
Ferguson, James	Pvt.	19		Tr to Capt. Rose's Co.
Fulkerson, Isaac	Pvt.	19		Tr to Capt. Powell's Company
Kinsley, William	Pvt.	20		Tr to Capt. Shaver's Company
Young, Jesse	Pvt.	44		Tr to Capt. Rose's Company

Discharged at Vera Cruz on Surgeon's Certificate

Name	Rank	Age	Enlisted	Date	Reason
Austin, Nathan	Pvt.	40	Knoxville	4- 6-1848	Disability
Dyer, William	Pvt.	22		2-14-1848	Disability
DeLosier, Jesse	Pvt.	22		4- 6-1848	Disability
Kerrick, John W.	Pvt.	19		4- 6-1848	Disability
McCulley, John	Pvt.	19		2-14-1849	Disability
Ogle, Thomas	Pvt.	25		March 1848	Disability
Phillips, William	Pvt.	21		2-14-1848	Disability

Died

Name	Rank	Age	Enlisted	Remarks
Gowers, Powers C.	Pvt.	20	Knoxville	Result of sickness at San Juan 1-5-1848
Roberts, George W.	Pvt.	19		Result of sickness at New Orleans 7-5-1848

Deserted

Name	Rank	Age	Remarks
Huckaby, Thomas	Pvt.	26	Deserted at Knoxville 12-8-1847
Warnick, William	Pvt.	22	Deserted at Knoxville 12-8-1847

DELEGATES TO THE UNION CONVENTION
at Knoxville and Greeneville
May 30th and June 17, 1861 from Blount County

Those marked with an asterisk were present at both conventions.

S. F. Bell
Henry Brakebill
The Rev. J. S. Craig
F. M. Cruze
W. H. Cunningham
The Rev. W. T. Dowell*
W. L. Dearing
Robert Eagleton
Solomon Farmer*
S. C. Flannagan
Horace Foster
David Goddard
William Goddard
John Godfrey
J. R. Frow
Henry Hammell
J. M. Heiskell
The Rev. H. J. Henry
James Henry
Isaac Hinds
W. A. Hunter
G. W. Hutsell
John Jackson
Alex. Kennedy
Edward Kidd
James Henry
A. Kirkpatrick*
Sanders Leeper
Stephen Matthews
Fleming Mays
Andrew McBath
M. McTeer
Robert Pickens
Thomas Pickens
James H. Rowan
John Trew
James H. Walker
Levater Wear*

From Thomas W. Humes, *Loyal Mountaineers* (Knoxville, 1888), Appendix.

1862 AND 1863 ACCOUNTS OF SALT SOLD IN THE 7TH DISTRICT FOR BLOUNT COUNTY
by James M. Henry, Esq.

1862

December 18th	Gould Wilson 25 lbs.	$15.00
	William Ross 15	9.00
	Mike Huffstetler 10 lbs.	6.00
December 19th	Sam P. Pugh 4¾	2.90
	J. C. Hutton 8½	5.00
	Hiram Walker 29	17.00
	P. Costner 16 2/3	10.00
	J. M. Best 8½	5.00
	A. Ross 10	6.00
	A. Hannah 8½	5.00
	Betsy Farr 4½	2.55
	Christopher Best 16½	10.00
	A. J. Wilson 25	15.00
	Wm. Robbins 72½	43.50
	Cooper Baumgardner 2½	1.50
	John A. Hannah 25	15.00
December 20th	Wm. Kiser 5	3.00
	Joseph Tuck 50	30.00
	Ellison Scott 8½	5.00
	Will Roddy 36	21.60
	Greenberry Hill (?) 2 2/16	1.25
	Betsy Ann Miller 16¾	10.00

APPENDIX

	Wm. McGhee 21⅔	13.00
	Moses Martin 8⅔	5.00
	Joseph Tuck 13⅓	8.00
	Wm. Ross 10	6.00
	John M. Best 16⅔	10.00
	Mrs. Riddle 13½	8.15
	Laban Rhyne 20	12.00
	Joseph Kagley 10	6.00
	Mrs. Kagley 1⅔	1.00
	Margaret Ross 16⅔	10.00
	George Thompson 25	15.00
	Alfred Cunningham 41⅔	25.00
	James Taylor 35	21.00
	Spencer Henry 13⅔	7.00
	1863	
January 1st	Joseph Kagley 11	6.60
	Mrs. Kagley 8⅓	5.00
	J. M. Henry 10	6.00
	William Gardner 18½	11.00
	George Taylor 7¼	4.25
	Wm. R. Henry 149	89.40
	Wilson Hays 41⅔	25.00
	Levi Johnston 6⅔	4.00
	G. B. Saffle 16⅔	10.00
	Mat Gardner 8⅓	5.00
	J. C. Hutton 16⅔	10.00
January 6th	Gould Wilson 10	6.00
	Jacob Best 50	30.00
	John T. Hargis 6¼	3.70
	Sanders Hinton 6⅔	4.00
	J. M. Henry 10	6.00
	A. Cook 159	89.40
	Jesse Kerr 61	36.60
July 22nd	Riley McGhee 25	6.25
	David Giffin 40	15.00
July 23rd	A. W. Emmitt 36	9.00
	Mrs. Kiser 20	5.00
	Spencer Henry 30	7.50
	Mrs. Means 50	12.50
	Johnathan Tharp 16	4.00
	Sanders Hinton 45	11.25
	Alfred Cunningham 39	9.75
	Margaret Ross 15	3.75
	Adrian Martin 40	10.00
	Amos Riddle 20	5.00
	Addison Hannah 42	10.50
	Presley Bennett 20	5.00
	J. M. Hill (?) 40	10.00
	Mariah Wilson 16	4.00
	John Houston 35	8.75
July 25th	G. B. Saffle 38	9.50
	Hiram Walker 27	6.75
	Mrs. McGhee 20	5.00
	Mrs. Keys 9	2.25
	Lissa Saffle 16	4.00

Betsy Ann Miller 15	3.75
Wilson Mays 30	7.50
Mrs. Tuck 20	5.00
Henry Hamil 33	8.25
July 30th Thos. E. Scott 26	6.50

Taken from the account book now belonging to Mrs. Bessie Henry Olin, grand-daughter of James M. Henry.

copied June 17, 1954

BLOUNT COUNTY HOME GUARD
7th CIVIL DISTRICT, 1861-65

As remembered by Christopher Hannah in 1929 and recorded by Mr. W. E. Parham.

Larkin Anderson, killed on Nine Mile Creek by Rebel "bushwhackers."

Jackson Best	S. C. Hinton
Martin C. Best	D. Addison Huffstetler
Caleb Carpenter	John Hoyle
Phillip Costner	Robert Ross
Samuel Costner	William Saffell
Simeon Crye, killed with Anderson	Greenberry Saffell
Elijah Cunningham	Tobe Tuck (said to have killed M.
Lawson Fields, killed with Anderson	Wilson who with others had gone to
John Farr	Morganton to rob a store.)

MUSTER ROLL OF THE HOME GUARD
15TH CIVIL DISTRICT, 1865

Muster Roll of the 1st Company of Volunteer Infantry, in the 15th Civil District of Blount County, East Tennessee, for three years, or during the War. Made up expressly for home duty and to scout the frontier of our district and county. This, the 18th day of February, A.D., 1865.

Volunteer's Name	*Number*	*Volunteer's Name*	*Number*
Jacob Bird	1	Jonas Jenkins	20
L. P. Dunn	2	Joseph Lukewire	21
Nathan Sparks	3	J. W. R. Harrison	22
William Oliver	4	David Wadkins	23
H. N. Tipton	5	A. G. Dunn	24
Nathaniel Burchfield	6	Henry Web	25
W. P. Dunn	7	C. S. Fancier (Fancher)	26
Philip Davis	8	W. L. Welch	27
E. M. McCampbell	9	J. H. Gregory	28
John Myres, Jun.	10	Thos. B. Chambers	29
John Wadkins	11	N. A. Miller	30
John McCampbell	12	J. E. Chambers	31
Drury Gregory	13	Thomas Henry	32
Harmon Roberts	14	E. R. W. Bird	33
J. W. Sparks	15	Daniel Headrick	34
T. J. Wear	16	Wm. Walker	35
E. A. Gregory	17	John Myres, Sen.	36
Jim M. Bird	18	D. H. Myres	37
J. P. Dunn	19	M. Cameron	38

APPENDIX 319

Volunteer's Name	Number	Volunteer's Name	Number
David Web	39	J. A. Shields	44
D. L. Bird	40	James Shields	45
J. A. Bowers	41	W. M. Dunn	46
I. W. Lukewire	42	J. W. Lane	47
Pete Burchfield	43	Joel Johnston	48

SULTANA SURVIVORS FROM BLOUNT COUNTY STILL LIVING IN 1892

A monument to the Sultana victims was erected in Mount Olive Cemetery in Knox County. No distinction is made between survivors and the dead.

COMPANY A 3RD TENNESSEE CAVALRY

Sgt. Samuel A. Cowan
James Curtis
Elias Farmer
Cpl. Alex. Kidd
L. M. Kidd

Thomas Linginfelter
Robert Rule
Calvin Russell
Nicholas Russell

COMPANY B 3RD TENNESSEE CAVALRY

Cpl. James Millsaps
Jesse W. Millsaps

William M. Millsaps
Bart McMurray

COMPANY H 3RD TENNESSEE CAVALRY
Pleasant M. Keeble

COMPANY I 3RD TENNESSEE CAVALRY

Sgt. H. Linginfelter   Mart Thompson

COMPANY L 3RD TENNESSEE CAVALRY
William S. Hill

COMPANY B 2ND TENNESSEE CAVALRY
George A. King (captured while carrying a dispatch from Athens to Gen. Morgan)

BLOUNT COUNTY SCHOOL DIRECTORS FROM THE 1869 REPORT

1st Dist.—John Garner, Brick Mill
    Daniel Brewer
    John Ross
    James Tallen
2nd Dist.—F. F. Fulkerson,
    Morganton
    Hugh Eaken
    H. Hammontree
3rd Dist.—W. V. Griffitts, Unitia
    Johnston Jones
    William Phillips
4th Dist.—R. F. Walker
    J. O. Jones
    Joseph Mathes

5th Dist.—T. J. Robinson,
    Friendsville
    John Jones
    T. Baldwin
    J. P. Chapman
6th Dist.—S. H. Gault, Maryville
    S. McCammon
    M. Cochran
7th Dist.—S. H. Hinton
    Joseph Kagley
    A. M. Emmett
    E. Carpenter

8th Dist.—S. F. Bell
O. Miller
James Raulston
J. M. Scott
P. Raulston
M. McConnell
N. McConnell
S. Clemens
G. C. Capp
9th Dist.—C. C. Cowan
Alex. Eagleton
A. D. Sanders
10th Dist.—J. Mead, Louisville
W. Anderson
A. Love
11th Dist.—H. T. Linginfelter, Rockford
Rich Lebow
Milus Hooper
J. P. Cochran
12th Dist.—J. P. Hook
W. A. Hunter
John Beal

13th Dist.—S. C. Flanagin, Ellejoy
Robert Pickens
J. H. Boyd
W. E. Davis
C. Dunlap
W. Hafley
14th Dist.—John Garrett, Gamble's Store
Thomas Broady
James Walker
James Henry
A. M. Smith
A. Waters
15th Dist.—H. Tipton, Tuckaleechee
Robert Emmett
William Myers
Elijah Emmett
F. M. Snyder
Jas. McCampbell
16th Dist.—John Oliver, Cades Cove
Will Lawson
Calvin Post
A. B. Burchfield
J. B. Gregory
17th Dist.—James Harrison, Chilhowee
Jesse Carr
John Ghormley

COPY OF A REPORT

filed in the County Court Minutes July 1872
(Made by County Superintendent of Schools, Thomas J. Lamar for 1869.)

From State Superintendent John Eaton, 1866 .... $2299.66
From State Superintendent John Eaton, 1867 .... 6089.25
Privilege tax collected by County Clerk 53.65
From Dr. B. B. Sears, agt. of Peabody fund 300.00
  (for 10th district)
Total $8742.56

1st District
  Daniel C. Brewer $123.10
  A. L. Dewberry 116.52
  M. E. Amerine 119.19
                          ———
                          $358.81
2nd District
  Miss T. A. Evans $100.00
  R. M. Evans 195.65
  E. H. Mathes 96.05
  M. L. Isbill 130.55
                          ———
                          $522.25

3rd District
  H. T. Quillen $130.00
  Rhoda Crumley 64.83
  F. M. Allen 148.84
  Simeon Griffitts 200.00
                          ———
                          $543.67
4th District
  S. L. Greer $108.10
  A. L. Maupin 146.75
  W. E. Sheddan 144.72
  Miss A. B. Snapp 48.00
  J. F. Beals 116.63
  Miss Rhoda Crumley 27.59
  Miss S. E. Jones 37.14
                          ———
                          $628.93

APPENDIX

5TH DISTRICT
Miss R. E. Baldwin $120.27
Miss M. J. Elliott 110.69
Miss Esther Newlin 81.41
T. J. Robinson 142.04
Hugh Jenkins 52.04

$506.45

6TH DISTRICT
S. L. Greer $107.81
J. H. McConnell 144.90
S. H. Gault 150.00

$402.71

7TH DISTRICT
J. T. Harges $120.67
S. H. Clemons 125.00

$245.67

8TH DISTRICT
Samuel H. Clemons $112.50
J. V. Iddins 94.11
J. V. Iddins 40.00
J. V. Iddins 120.00
Miss Mary Burchfield 100.00
E. L. Wilkerson 100.00
D. H. Tedford 62.00

$628.61

9TH DISTRICT
J. A. Greer $196.70
J. H. McNabb 116.20
Mrs. S. M. Alexander 124.25
Geo. E. Bicknell 150.00
J. H. Boyd 117.20

$704.35

10TH DISTRICT
W. F. Cummins $250.00
Miss M. L. McKelvy 200.00
H. M. Bonham 112.50
Henry H. Stephens 125.00
C. M. Parker 101.03
W. F. Cummins 82.39
Miss M. L. McKelvy 84.15
J. M. Singleton for use
 of Masonic Hall 25.00
J. M. Cummins & Sons for
 incidentals 24.00

$1004.37

11TH DISTRICT
W. R. Goddard ....$ 58.58
R. W. Goddard 112.58
W. B. Johnson 86.25
S. H. Badgett 150.00

$407.41

12TH DISTRICT
Mrs. E. M. Copley $109.54
Miss Euphrasia Goddard .. 100.00
S. B. Hart 149.83
Miss N. L. Dunaway 39.01

$398.38

13TH DISTRICT
W. M. Burnett ....$ 92.35
J. B. Sutton 111.83
E. S. Thompson 89.58
John Dunlap 121.10
A. P. Hodges 83.15
A. K. Kinnamon 99.25

$585.85

14TH DISTRICT
D. L. Beaver $100.00
William Farmer 111.83
J. H. Morton 89.58
A. M. Gamble 71.75
H. T. Clemons 60.00
William Henry 67.52
J. M. Walker 91.30
Miss H. E. Rowan 99.40

$691.38

15TH DISTRICT
W. F. Whitesides ....$ 60.00
J. B. J. Brickey 100.00
L. G. Camp 108.25
L. Wear 125.45

$393.70

16TH DISTRICT
W. F. Rodgers $141.30
D. L. Brewer 100.00

$241.30

17TH DISTRICT
F. M. Ramsey ....$ 82.50
A. L. Dewberry 75.00
L. M. Medlin 75.00

$232.50

Aggregate Total $8,496.36

SPANISH AMERICAN WAR—CUBA

Company B, 4th Tennessee United States Volunteers. Mustered in at Camp Bob Taylor, Knoxville, Tennessee, August 13, 1898. (Most of these men were from Blount and Loudon counties.)

John J. Blair, Capt.
Leonard S. Goddard, 1st Lt.
Samuel R. Rodgers, 2nd Lt.

SERGEANTS

Hugh L. Matthews (1st)
Henderson Phillip (2nd)
H. Nicholson (3rd)
W. Ellis Tatom (4th)
John W. Broyles (5th)
Richard A. Smith (Q.M. Sgt.)

CORPORALS

John Edgar Harvey
Daniel M. Posey
James L. Henderson
Guy M. Badgett
John G. Burns
Caleb J. Fancher
Joseph Furrow
Jesse E. Wallace
Walker Bacon
John R. Baldwin
James L. Jeffries
George Humphrey

MUSICIANS

George Riddle (died of measles and TB in Cuba)
Wm. Sexton
Huse Walker (Artificer)
Robert S. Watson (Wagoner)
Reason H. Cecil (Clerk)

PRIVATES

John A. Anderson
John W. Billingsley
Robert L. Blair
Wm. Boone
Dock Brewer
John R. Bryant
Thomas J. Bryson
Wm. H. Baldwin
George H. Bales
Wm. H. Bright
Matthews Bolin
Andrew Caylor
James A. Caylor
Charles A. Chapman
Crawford Cecil
Marion R. Davis
John W. Dean

Robert R. Dunn
John L. Erwin
Esaw Foster
James Frazier
Samuel Gillespy
David Gorly
James Greenway
Charles Harvey
Solon Haskins
John Dodson
Floyd E. Holloway
Major Hudgens
Thomas L. Hutsell
James Harvey
John S. Henson
Robert Johnson
David M. Jones
Isaac N. Jones
John S. Jenkins
Joel H. Keaton
Richard M. Kidd
Wm. Kidd
Joseph L. Kidd
David T. Love
Elihu M. Lee
John McCabe
John McCauly
Charles F. McPherson (Spring City)
Millard A. Morton
Gus Murr
Michael Murphy
John H. McNeal
John B. Owens
Elvin L. Phillips
Jeffries Phillips
John Phillips
David Ridge
Hays Ridge
Shade Roberts
Wm. H. Scott
Elisha Slovin
John C. Sloan
Edward Smiddy
John H. Smith
Robert Southerland
Ellis Stallions
James Stockwell
John R. P. Thomas
Johnathan Thomas

Charles Towle
James Wallace
Thomas Wadkins
Charles Ward
Wm. R. E. West
John H. Webb
Wm. W. Williams

Charles N. Wood
James J. Woodard
William P. Wilson
John Williams
Ruben West
A. Y. West

COMPANY H, 47TH VOLUNTEER INFANTRY, SPANISH AMERICAN WAR

The following men left Maryville, Tennessee September 23, 1899 for Camp Meade, Pennsylvania where they became a part of the 47th Infantry.

Blair, Sherman
Brickey, Daniel L.
Brickey, Wiley J.
Burns, Frank W.
Burns, Richard G.
Bond, James A.
Chapman, Charles A.
Childress, Charles L.
Cochran, Rosco G.
Delaney, James H.
Gardner, Homer
Hitsell, Thomas L.
Johnson, Robert
Keeble, John R.
Kidd, James W.
Love, James A.

Merritt, Samuel
Murr, William J.
Phifer, Robert
Roberts, William E.
Russell, Charles G.
Russell, Charles H.
Russell, Charles I.
Russell, William
Scott, Sherman
Seaton, Amos A.
Teffeteller, Edgar
Walker, Walter W.
Walker, James C.
Walker, John D.
Weagley, Perry J.
Weagley, William J.

The following Negroes went on the same date to Fort Thomas, Kentucky and joined the 48th Regiment:

Coffin, King
Hodsden, Alonzo

Tate, Dock

POST OFFICES OF BLOUNT COUNTY

Those starred are still in operation

Alcoa—est. September 11, 1912; name changed to Calderwood March 3, 1920
*Alcoa—est. November 25, 1921
Alleghany—est. September 21, 1886; to Mint September 30, 1907
Bank—est. August 26, 1880; to Maryville May 31, 1912
Big Gully—est. March 17, 1879; to Greenback September 30, 1903
Binfield—est. July 29, 1907; 1934
Blockhouse—est. October 5, 1889; to Maryville January 27, 1907
Bonum—est. December 6, 1892; to Maryville December 12, 1893
Brick Mill—est. January 29, 1858; to Maryville January 2, 1907
Cable—est. December 18, 1896; dis. January 28, 1897
Cades Cove—est. June 28, 1833; dis. October 31, 1947
Carson's Iron Works—est. June 28, 1833; dis. June 29, 1834
*Calderwood—est. as Alcoa September 11, 1912; changed to Calderwood March 3, 1920
Chandler—est. May 16, 1891; dis. December 31, 1912
*Chilhowee—est. July 7, 1828
Chota—est. April 29, 1818; Monroe County

Cliff—est. October 9, 1888; to Greenback September 30, 1903
Cloyd's Creek—est. February 25, 1837; to Greenback September 30, 1903
Clover Hill—est. March 27, 1823; to Binfield December 31, 1915
College—est. November 23, 1898; dis. July 8, 1902
Corn—est. June 22, 1883; to Blockhouse October 15, 1900
Coytee—from Monroe County September 3, 1868; Loudon County
Dell Grove—est. May 10, 1834; dis. December 14, 1839
Disco—est. September 29, 1884; to Friendsville January 15, 1903
Double—Late Dammit, Sevier County February 6, 1885; to Grapeton (Sevier County) June 7, 1887
Drake—est. August 30, 1880; to Uceba December 5, 1883
Ellejoy—est. April 12, 1830; to Bank April 28, 1904
Ellsworth—est. July 27, 1889; to Maryville December 12, 1903
Evans—est. May 31, 1832; to Trundle's Cross Road, Sevier County
Ewing—est. October 31, 1889; to Louisville July 8, 1902
Fisher's Landing—est. June 27, 1866; dis. January 26, 1871
*Friendsville—est. July 27, 1850
Gamble's Store—est. July 3, 1855; to Bank September 15, 1906
Gentry—est. August 29, 1881; to Ebenezer September 18, 1882
Glenlove—est. January 19, 1892; to Louisville December 21, 1893
Grayridge—est. November 5, 1897; to Louisville May 5, 1899
Hebronville—est. August 24, 1889; to Gamble's Store September 6, 1893
Houk—est. December 23, 1879; changed to Wellsville October 12, 1894
Huffstetler's Store—est. September 9, 1870, changed to McKinley April 11, 1891
Kinzel Springs—est. April 1, 1925; to Townsend May 30, 1945
Kizer—est. January 27, 1893
Lanier—est. April 11, 1899; to Louisville July 31, 1902
Little River—est. May 17, 1849; dis. May 26, 1852
*Louisville—est. May 24, 1828
*Maryville—est. October 6, 1800
Matlock—November 6, 1888; dis. May 31, 1895
McKelder—est. March 30, 1901; to Mint January 5, 1922
McKinley—est. April 11, 1891; to Maryville December 12, 1903
*Mentor—est. March 20, 1891
Militia Springs—est. June 23, 1834; to Mouth of Tellico October 17, 1836
Miller's Cove—est. June 28, 1833; to Walland November 20, 1902
Miser's Station—est. April 26, 1867; to Miser November 29, 1882
Miser—est. November 29, 1882; to Friendsville April 13, 1903
Montvale Springs—est. July 15, 1837; to Maryville March 31, 1907
Morganton—est. November 14, 1816; in Loudon County after 1870
Mouth of Little River—est. September 22, 1851; dis. May 11, 1853
Mouth of Tellico—est. November 15, 1837; Monroe County
Mount Pisgah—est. June 18, 1834; dis. January 4, 1836
Mint—est. February 7, 1881; 1934
Nichols—est. August 23, 1890; to Trundle's Cross Roads December 21, 1903
Nine Mile Creek—est. February 27, 1828; dis. January 8, 1835
Notime—est. May 23, 1883; to Gamble January 31, 1902
Plum Grove—est. July 19, 1850; dis. January 8, 1852
Rado—est. February 7, 1898; to Mint March 30, 1907
*Rasar—est. April 19, 1882; to Chilhowee 2-3-87 to 8-14-89; to present
*Rockford—est. April 25, 1854; to present
Slate—est. February 6, 1897; to Bank August 15, 1906
Sweet—est. April 26, 1898; to Townsend September 30, 1904
South Rockford—est. January 12, 1886; to Rockford May 31, 1909
Seaton—est. December 14, 1881; to Walland September 30, 1903

APPENDIX 325

Tang—est. August 31, 1880; to Townsend July 31, 1906
Tuckaleechee Cove—est. June 6, 1833; to Townsend August 23, 1906
Tut—est. June 15, 1883; to Friendsville October 7, 1903
*Tallassee—est. June 5, 1928; to present
Tremont—est. February 13, 1926; dis.
Truceangle—est. March 23, 1900; to Greenback September 30, 1903
*Townsend—est. July 26, 1902; to present
Unitia—est. May 6, 1824; Loudon County after 1870
Uceba—est. December 5, 1883; to Trundle's Cross Roads July 17, 1904
Waters—est. August 21, 1884; to Walland May 31, 1912
*Walland—est. March 20, 1902; to present
Wellsville—est. October 13, 1894; dis. 1937
Woodson—est. July 15, 1899; to Clover Hill December 22, 1902
Wildham—est. October 25, 1899; dis. February 1, 1921
Yellow-Sulphur—est. June 29, 1860; dis. 11-9-69 to 6-22-74; dis. 1-15-1909

COMPANY "B" 117TH INFANTRY, 30TH DIVISION
April 3, 1919
Captain George H. Post, Commanding Company

First Lieutenant Robert M. Lindsay
First Sergeant Edgar L. Boyd
Supply Sergeant Conda U. Hunley
First Lieutenant Carl F. Gehring

First Sergeant Arthur Waldroup (Attached)
Mess Sergeant Thomas B. Thompson

SERGEANTS
Looney L. Lones
Freland T. Godfrey
Edward S. Campbell
John C. Robbins
Burgin Dockery
Jackson Parks
William J. McDade
Julis Burchfield
Arthur B. Burgess
Virgil M. Latham
Frank C. Dockery
Fred Whitehead

CORPORALS
Carl M. Curtis
Samuel H. Hatcher
William M. Holt
Doctor W. Kimsey
James M. Raines
James H. Rowan
Charles M. Tabor
Alexander Woodby
Henry H. Smith
Raymond Perkins
James A. Rose
Brownlow Hensley
John M. Burchfield
Thomas O. Gilbert
William E. Gilbert
Walter A. Gregory
James E. Harmon
Hafford Jurney
Patrick A. Mogan
Roy Rushing

Daniel W. Walker
Nick Weaver
Paul S. Richards
Murray T. Boring
Charles H. Parker

COOKS
William A. Contz
Hugh Hicks
Charles W. Presley
Robert B. Wilson

MECHANICS
Joseph C. Melton
Thomas F. Dew
Jacob A. Miller

BUGLERS
Jeff Warricks
Bernard K. Carter

PRIVATES
(1st Class)
Arnold, John W.
Ball, Tossie R.
Bonine, Charles
Boone, Horace
Bright, Fred C.
Byrd, Elwood
Coffman, George J.
Cope, James H.
Cowell, Clarence C.
Davis, John I.
Dunkin, John R.
Ellis, Robert J.
Ferguson, Walter B.

Goodson, Mina
Greene, John L.
Gregory, Alexander
Hair, Hobert
Hamby, Percie
Harrison, Thomas
Hill, Adren L.
Hill, Pearlie D.
Holland, Juney J.
Johnson, Joe H.
Johnson, Wilson S.
Kidd, David S.
Larkins
Long, Eulis
Lowe, Homer
Mack, Charles M.
Massey, Cave O.
McNatt, Porter
Ogle, Forest
Russell, Arthur B.
Russell, William
Tipton, Mike H.
Turner, Hal
Walker, James L.
Wilkinson, George L.
Woodby, Joe

PRIVATES
Allen, Daniel G.
Bradburn, Hobert
Baker, Robert L.
Bailey, John A.
Ballew, William H.
Blakeley, Robert M.
Brewer, Benjamin F.
Burk, Milum

Byrd, William A.
Chandler, Felix H.
Clabough, Bascom H.
Coatney, William R.
Coulter, Guy
Curtis, Homer D.
Carrier, Earnie A.
Dockery, Ben
Durden, Marvin A.
Everett, Clyde
Fry, William A.
Grizzle, Judd P.

Gudger, Andrew J.
Hamby, Horace
Harris, Martin L.
Hicks, John
Holt, Ernest
Hughes, Huddy
Jackson, Edward
Lawson, Russell
Leach, Lonnie L.
Lusk, Noah O.
McCaulley, Archie H.
Morrison, Enoch

Oatsvall, Elmer W.
Parker, Wilbur E.
Pass, Eulis
Perkins, Minis
Ready, Lueker
Rice, Vanderbilt
Rogers, Jim
Sweeney, William T.
Teffer, James
Uphlett, Elton
Vaughan, Carl B.
Vinson, Thomas W.

Company "B," 117th Infantry, was organized by Captain Emerson J. Lones at Maryville, Tennessee, and was trained at Camp Sevier, Greenville, S.C. Left Camp Sevier May 2nd, 1918, for New York, arriving in New York City May 5th, 1918; was stationed at Camp Mills until May 10th, when the Company embarked on the transport North Umberland, and arrived at Liverpool, England, May 23rd, disembarking same day, and entrained for Dover, England, arriving at Dover after a journey of twelve hours. Embarked at Dover May 24th, arriving at Calais, France. Left Calais May 27th and took station at Menteque, about eight miles from Saint Omer, France, where the next few weeks were spent in hard training preparatory to going to the front. On July 2nd the Company left for the Ypres Sector, Belgium, arriving at Proven July 4th. On July 17th the Company brigaded with the First British Army, commanded by General Plumer; went into the front line trenches at Ypres, occupying same until July 24th, when the Company was relieved and went back to the reserve. Left Ypres Sector September 5th for the Somme front. On the Somme front from the 24th of September to October 20th, taking part in the following engagements: Hindenburg Line, near Bellicourt and Nauroy, September 29th-30th; Premont and Busigny October 7th-8th-9th; Molain and Ribeauville October 17th-18th-19th. During the Somme offensive, Captain Lones and 27 enlisted men were killed in action. Lieutenant Gaston E. Crosby and 103 enlisted men were wounded. On October 20th the Company left for Heilly, France, remaining there until the latter part of November, when the Company went to the LeMans Area, remaining there until March 10th, 1919, when they left for St. Nazaire, where they embarked on the transport U.S.S. Pocahontas March 16th, arriving at Charleston, S.C., March 28th, 1919.

FAMILY DATA

Families about whom data may be found in the Parham Papers in the McClung Collection in Lawson McGhee Library, Knoxville, Tennessee.
*Indicates a folder of materials.

Abernathy*
Adams
Alexander*
Allen*
Ambrister
Anderson*
Armstrong
Atchley
Aylett
Axley
Ayer
Badgett*
Bailey-Conner
Baker*
Ball*
Barclay*
Bartlett*
Beard-Stoner
Bearden*

Bennett*
Berry*
Best*
Bell*
Billew-Billue
Bingham
Birdwell
Bittle
Blackburn*
Blackwell
Blair
Blankenship*
Blount
Boaz*
Bond*
Bonham*
Boyd*
Bogle*
Brabson

Bradburn
Bradley
Brakebill-Brown*
Briant
Brickey
Brock
Brown
Broyles
Bryan-Henry
Brown*
Buchanan-McDaniel
Burum-Gallahar
Byerly-Scaggs
Caldwell*
Callaway*
Campbell*
Cameron*
Carmichael*
Carpenter*

APPENDIX

Carr
Carson*
Casey
Cates*
Cavin
Cawood*
Chamberlain
Chambers
Childress
Clack*
Clark*
Clemens*
Cobb-Abernathy*
Cochran*
Collett
Courtney-Waters-
　Cottrell
Copeland-Henderson-
　Parsons
Coughron
Corley
Cottrell
Coulton-Alexander*
Cowan*
Cox*
Craig*
Crawford
Creswell-Whittle*
Cummings*
Cunningham*
Cupp*
Currier*
Cusick
Curtis
Dalton-Odle
Daniels
Davidson*
Davis*
Dearmond
Deaver
Delzell-Dalzell*
Dildine
Debusk
Dobson*
Doherty*
Donaldson*
Donohoo
Douglas*
Douthitt
Downey
Dozier
Duncan-Tear-McTeer-
　Pierce-Green*
Dunlap-Lonas*
Dunn*
Dyer
Eagleton-Hook*
Eakin*
Early*
Edmonson-Edmiston*
Elliott
Ellis
Emert

Epps
Erwin-Irwin*
Evans-Creswell
Ewing
Fagg*
Fancher*
Farmer*
Farr*
Ferguson-Carson*
Feezell-Henniger*
Fields-Johnson*
Finley*
Flenniken-Cottrell*
Foute*
Freeman*
French-Rule*
Fryar*
Fulkerson*
Gallahar-Goliher-
　Houston*
Gamble*
Garner*
Gault-Taylor-Logan*
George-Paul-Kidd-
　Chandler*
Ghormley*
Glass*
Gourley-Gurley-
　Goorley*
Gillespie-Gillespy*
Graves
Gray
Gregg-Gragg-Grigg*
Green
Greenway*
Greer
Griffitts*
Grisham*
Hackett
Hackney*
Hadden
Hafley-Haffly-Hafly*
Hair*
Hale
Hamby
Hamill-Hamil
Hammontree*
Handley
Hanna*
Hanna-Hannah*
Hinshaw
Harden-Hardin
Hardwick-Knoblett
Hargis
Harper
Harris*
Harrison*
Hart*
Haskew*
Hatcher*
Hawkins*
Hays*
Hayden

Hayes
Headrick*
Heard
Hearn
Heartsill-Atchley*
Heath
Heiskell
Henderson*
Henley*
Henshaw
Hill-Shaver*
Hines-Hinds*
Hitch*
Hix*
Hodsden
Hoge-Hogg-Hogue*
Holliday*
Holt
Hood*
Hooke-Hook*
Hoover*
Hope*
Horner*
Howard*
Hoyle
Huffstetler*
Hughes*
Henry*
Houston*
Humphreys*
Hutsell*
Iles
Inman
Ish
Jackson*
James*
Jeffries*
Jerries
Jenkins-Jinkins
Jobe*
Johnson*
Johnston*
Kagley
Kee
Keeble-Kibble*
Keewood-Keywood-
　Caywood-Cawood
Keith
Keller*
Kelley*
Kelso*
Kendrick*
Kerr-Carr*
Key*
Kennedy*
Kidd*
King*
Kinney-Kidd*
Kinser-Perry*
Kirby
Kirk-Sloan-Cook
Kiser
Knox

Lackey
Lamon*
Lane*
Langston
Lapsley
Leatherwood*
Lebow*
Leeper*
Leming*
Lemons
Lewis
Lillard-Keith
Lockhart
Logan-Gault*
Long
Love*
Lowry
Lusk
Majors
Maroney
Martin*
Matthews*
Maxey
Maxwell*
McCaine*
McCall*
McCallie-McCauley*
McCampbell-Anderson
McCammon*
McChesney*
McClain
McClanahan*
McClellan (Wallace-Black-Valkenburgh-Bradley)
McClung-Houston
McClure
McCroskey
McCulley*
McCulloch*
McDowell
McDonald
McGaughey-McTeer-Boyd*
McGhee*
McGill
McGinley*
McConnell*
McCoy
McGauhey
McGhee-Russell*
McKaskill
McKaslin-McCaslin
McKee*
McKenzie
McLin
McMillan*
McMurry
McNabb*
McNutt*
McReynolds
McTeer*
McWhinney*

McCoy-McKay*
Means*
Meggison
Mercer*
Miller*
Minnis*
Minton*
Mitchell-Peak
Misemer
Moore*
Morrison*
Morrow
Morton
Murray
Myers
Montgomery*
Nance
Nelson*
Norton
Norwood*
Nunn
Orr*
Overton
Parker*
Parkins
Parks
Pass-King
Pate*
Patterson-Stevenson*
Patton
Paul-Kidd*
Parham*
Paxton*
Pearce
Phillips*
Pickens-Henry
Pomfret*
Pope
Plumlee
Porter
Post-Thompson-Wallace
Prater
Pride
Pritchett*
Pruett-Prewitt*
Pruner
Pugh-Steele
Rankin*
Rasor
Redman
Ray-Rhea*
Rector
Rider-Thompson
Reed-Reid*
Reeder*
Ritchie*
Roberts*
Robinson-Robertson*
Robinet
Rogers
Rooker*
Rorax-Rorex
Ruble

Rule
Russell
Saffle*
Saffell-Cox
Sater-Dyer-Calloway
Scott*
Scroggs-Scruggs
Seaton*
Shaver*
Shaw
Shook
Sharpe-Sharp*
Simmons
Sims-Simms*
Simerly*
Singleton*
Skiles*
Sloan*
Smith*
Snider*
Snoddy*
Sparks*
Spillman*
Sowers
Stafford
Steele*
Stanfield
Stephens
Sterling*
Stewart
Stitch*
Stout
Strickler
Swan
Sypert
Tallent
Talliferro-Tolliver
Tathero
Taylor*
Tedford*
Teffeteller*
Thompson*
Tipton*
Thomas
Timberman*
Tofflemire
Toole*
Townsend*
Trice*
Trimble*
Trotter
Tuck*
Waldrup
Walker*
Warren*
Waters*
Watkins*
Wallace*
Wallace-George*
Wells*
Webb*
Wear-Weir*
Wetsill-Whetsell

White
Whitehead-Hearn
  (Herron)*
Whittle*
Wilhite*
Wilkinson*

Williams-Keen*
Williamson
Willoughby
Wilson*
Winton*
Woody*

Wright*
Wynn-Parham
Wyley*
Woods*
Yearout*
Young*

BLOUNT COUNTY CEMETERIES

This is a fairly complete list of the Cemeteries of Blount County. The date indicates the oldest date appearing on a marker. There are hundreds of unmarked graves which are older than these dates especially in New Providence, Hamil, Friendsville and Eusebia cemeteries.

     Abram's Creek.
1869 Amerine
1916 Armona.
1834 Baker's Creek (Presbyterian).
1853 Ballard's Chapel (Baptist).
1904 Bethel Baptist (Townsend).
1868 Bethlehem (Methodist).
1812 Big Springs (Presbyterian).
     Birdwell (on Everett Road).
1882 Boone.
     Bogle—Baker's Creek.
1851 Brakebill.
1856 Brickey.
1892 Buchanan.
1902 Burchfield.
1848 Burns.
1871 Cable.
1861 Cades Cove Primitive Baptist.
1861 Cades Cove Methodist.
1919 Cades Cove Missionary Baptist.
1862 Carpenter's Campground.
1917 Caylor's Chapel.
1865 Cates or Cupp.
1930 Cedar Grove.
1831 Centenary.
     Chestnut Flats.
1870 Chilhowee (Lower)—Tallassee.
1850 Chilhowee Primitive Baptist (Red Top)
1934 Central Point (Baptist).
1812 Clark's Grove (Presbyterian).
1872 Clear Springs.
1832 Clover Hill (Presbyterian).
1870 Cloyd's Creek (Presbyterian).
1944 Cold Springs
1856 Davis-Lane.
1921 East Maryville (Baptist).
1857 Ellejoy (Baptist).
1790 Eusebia (Presbyterian).
1858 Forest Hill (Presbyterian & Baptist).
1870 Friends (Maryville).
1802 Friendsville (Quaker).
1850 Four Mile (Baptist).
1874 Garner.
1840 George.
1922 Grandview.
1807 Hamil or Tedford.
1843 Hardin (Calderwood).
1843 Hardin (Caldwell Farm).

1882 Happy Valley (Baptist).
1845 Harriss.
1810 Headrick or Henry.
1841 Holston College (Presbyterian).
1907 Hopewell (Baptist).
     Houston Homestead (Binfield).
1885 Howard's Mill (Hardscrabble).
1794 Ish or Henderson.
1891 Kagley (Methodist).
1886 Kagley's Chapel (Baptist).
1834 Keeble's Chapel (Baptist).
1835 Kirby.
1880 Lambert or Howard.
1883 Laurel Bank (Baptist).
1884 Law's Chapel (Baptist).
1892 Lawson (Cades Cove).
1870 Liberty (Baptist).
1865 Liberty (Christian).
1833 Logan's Chapel (Methodist).
1838 Louisville (moved and combined).
1873 Lutheran.
1879 Magnolia.
1841 Maryville College.
     Methodist Hill (Negro).
1815 Middlesettlements (Methodist).
     Mingle.
1808 Miller's Cove (Baptist).
1882 Mount Tabor (Presbyterian).
1851 Mount Moriah (Methodist).
1863 Mount Lebanon (old).
1924 Mount Lebanon (new).
1895 Mountain View (Christian)—
     Christy Hill.
1807 Myers.
1860 Montgomery-Trigonia.
1830 Montgomery—Baker's Creek.
1827 McGinley or McConnell.
1894 Nelson Chapel (Church of Christ).
1799 New Providence (Presbyterian).
1884 Nail's Creek (Old).
1919 New Providence Primitive Baptist.
1950 Oak View.
1876 Oakland Methodist—Trigonia.
1814 Oakland (Dunkard).
1876 Old Piney.
     Parkins.
1840 Parsons-Ghormley.
     Poor Farm.
1870 Pleasant Grove (Baptist).
1890 Pleasant Hill (Methodist).

1859 Peck's Chapel (Methodist).
1852 Piney Level (Baptist).
1925 Providence (Baptist).
1892 Prospect (Baptist). Reagan.
1886 Russell (on Blockhouse Road).
1865 Russell (on Cutshaw Farm).
1900 Russell (on Pearlie Anthony Farm).
1941 Russell (near Mt. Tabor).
1882 Salem (Baptist)—Binfield.
1840 Shady Grove (Miser's Station), (Presbyterian).
1827 Six Mile (Baptist).
1860 Seceder (now West Maryville Presbyterian).
1840 Tipton.

1855 Tuckaleechee Campground (Methodist).
1903 Tuckaleechee Chapel (Methodist).
1935 Tuckaleechee Primitive Baptist (Coker Hill).
1894 Union Grove (Methodist).
1880 Union Grove (Baptist).
Union Temple (Negro)—Pea Ridge.
1850 Walker's Chapel (Methodist).
1891 Walker's Valley.
1886 Wesley Ann (Methodist).
Wilder's Chapel (Negro).
1880 Williams-Younce (Miller's Cove).
1835 Williamson's Chapel (Methodist).
1843 Wright's (Wright's Ferry).
1887 Wear.
1874 Zion's Chapel (Baptist).

BLOUNT COUNTY OFFICEHOLDERS

January session 1907

"It being represented that part of the records burned when the Courthouse burned July 28, 1906, a committee reported: Trustee's records—all saved; County Court records—all saved (old tax schedules, etc. stored in the basement were lost; Register's records—all saved; Clerk and Master's records—all the records and most of the files were saved; Circuit Court records—*all records lost from 1810-1870* except one execution docket; the greater part of the Supreme Court records were saved.

(Those records lost were in locked cases in the Circuit Court Clerk's office and no one present could open them.)

COUNTY COURT CLERKS

John McKee 1795-1796
James Houston (Major) 1796-1818
Jacob F. Foute 1818-1833
Nathaniel Reagan 1833-1840
Jeremiah Kennon 1841-1844
William Lowry 1844-1848
Robert A. Tedford 1848-1853
Spencer Henry 1853-1854
J. C. McCoy 1854-1862
W. L. Dearing 1862-1866
R. C. Tucker 1866-1871
T. D. Edington 1871-1872
J. A. Greer 1872-1880
Ben Cunningham (Major) ..1880-1902
Clay Cunningham 1902-1910
C. B. Badgett 1910-1918
George D. Roberts 1918-1930
E. A. Walker 1930-1938
R. D. Hunnicutt 1938-1946
Joe L. Marshall 1946-

REGISTERS OF BLOUNT COUNTY

William Wallace 1795-1799
J. Wallace 1799-1820
Andrew Thompson 1820-1836
James M. Anderson.......1836-1840
Andrew McClain 1840-1864
Ralph E. Tedford 1864-1868
Fletcher Wallace 1868-1874
J. C. Hutton 1874-1878

J. N. Badgett 1878-1890
F. M. Webb 1890-1898
Charles E. Kidd 1898-1902
Carson Caldwell 1902-1914
N. H. Tipton 1914-1921
Ila Tipton Lawson 1921-1930
R. C. Parkins 1930-1946
Runa S. White 1946-1953
Mildred M. Watson 1954-

CHANCERY COURT CLERKS OF BLOUNT COUNTY

Samuel Pride 1853-1862
William A. Walker 1862-1864
William C. Pickens 1864-1867
Elias Goddard 1867-1883
James T. Gamble 1883-1885
J. A. Greer 1885-1890
W. C. Chumlea 1890-1903
John C. Crawford 1903-1909
R. S. Walker 1909-1918
Joe H. Gamble 1918-1932
R. Dot Wynn 1932-1947
Leonard McCulloch 1947-

CLERKS OF THE CIRCUIT COURT OF BLOUNT COUNTY

Robert Houston 1810-1814
Jesse Bean 1814-1820
Azariah Shelton 1820-1822
Daniel D. Foute 1822-1836

APPENDIX

Ake Henry 1836-1840
Daniel D. Foute 1840-1848
William A. Walker 1848-1862
James A. Houston 1862-1864
Montgomery McTeer 1864-1868
Will A. McTeer 1868-1878
William C. Chumlea 1878-1890
James C. Stanfield 1890-1898
W. P. Seaton 1898-1906
Charles E. Kidd 1906-1910
Joe H. Gamble 1910-1918
John L. Law 1918-1926
Peter Rule 1926-1938
Leonard McCulloch 1938-1946
Wade Everett 1946-1954
W. Chet Young 1954-

SUPERINTENDENTS OF PUBLIC INSTRUCTION OF BLOUNT COUNTY

Thomas J. Lamar 1867-1869
John H. Morton 1873-1875
Wm. H. Henry 1875-1879
Franklin Elliott 1879-
John V. Griffitts 1879-1881
G. C. Jackson 1881-1884
A. M. Gamble 1884-1887
J. W. Duggan 1887-1893
Robert Walker 1893-1896
M. H. Gamble 1896-1898
J. F. Iddins 1898-1902
H. B. McCall 1902-1914
Nancy Broady 1914-1918
Joe Miser 1918-1922
H. B. McCall 1922-1930
Eugene Williams 1930-1932
Claude D. Curtis 1932-1938
L. M. Ross 1938-1950
Hugh A. Coulter 1950-

TRUSTEES OF BLOUNT COUNTY

John McKee 1795-1796
David Eagleton 1796-1802
John Lowry, Merchant ...1802-1816
Samuel Love 1816-1820
Jesse Thompson 1820-1836
R. L. Cates 1836-1846
William McTeer 1846-1852
Ralph E. Tedford 1852-1858
D. N. Broyles 1858-1862
Francis M. Hood 1862-1866
Eli Nunn 1866-1872
Daniel Broyles 1872-1874
J. W. Eakin 1874-1878
James A. Goddard 1878-1886
A. M. Rule 1886-1896
W. A. Dunlap 1896-1900

William Wine 1900-1904
Lowry McCulley 1904-1908
John L. Law 1908-1912
William McCulloch 1912-1916
H. B. McCall 1916-1920
J. A. Costner 1920-1924
D. O. Waters 1924-1928
J. C. McConnell 1928-1932
J. E. Webb 1932-1936
J. O. McCammon 1936-1942
W. F. Walker 1942-1948
Clyde L. Curtis 1948-1952
Robert M. Rule 1952-1956

SHERIFFS OF BLOUNT COUNTY

Littlepage Sims 1795-1796
Joseph Colville 1796-1800
William Burk 1800-1804
William Lackey 1804-1806
Samuel Cowan 1806-1814
David Russell 1814-1816
Charles Donahoo 1816-1820
William Wallace 1820-1842
Calvin D. Anderson.......1842-1848
James M. Henry 1848-1854
Campbell Gillespie 1854-1858
W. L. Hutton 1858-1862
William H. Finley 1862-1864
Moses Gamble 1864-1866
M. L. McConnell 1866-1868
John D. Alexander 1868-1872
J. P. Edmondson 1872-1876
Robert P. McReynolds 1876-1878
A. M. Rule 1878-1882
M. H. Edmondson 1882-1888
John M. Armstrong 1888-1894
S. A. Walker 1894-1898
A. M. Rule 1898-1900
John H. Pickens 1900-1902
M. H. Edmondson 1902-1906
G. C. Whitehead 1906-1910
Jesse Hutton 1910-1914
H. B. Webb 1914-1918
M. H. Edmondson 1918-1922
J. C. McCampbell 1922-1924
Walter R. Pate 1924-1926
J. C. McCampbell........1926-1928
Walter R. Pate 1928-1932
R. E. McReynolds 1932-1936
Robert B. Young 1936-1940
W. B. Carringer 1940-1942
John C. McCampbell 1942-1944
William B. Carringer 1944-1946
Ben Mayes 1946-1950
W. B. Stinnett 1950-1954
Edward C. Guinn 1954-

INDEX

Aaron, C. E., 232
Abbey, Rev. A. S., 106
Abingdon Presbytery, 139n
Abingdon, Va., 10
Abbott, James, 123
Abbott, John, 123
Abram's Creek, 41, 51, 84, 221, 225, 234, 236, 244, 260, 274, 277, 278, 280, 281
Abram's Creek-Chilhowee Spinning and Weaving Manufactory, 125
Abram's Creek Roofing Slate Company, 239
Abolition and Colonization, 59, 128
Academies, 133–36
Ackridge, James, 115
Act to incorporate Maryville, 51
Adair, James, 3
Adams, G. P., 123
Adams, Johnson, 121
Adams, Lemuel, 106
Adams, Dr. N. B., 177, 190
Address to Cherokees, 24, 27
Agricultural Training School, 208
Air Defense Command, 69
Air National Guard Armory, 69
Airport, 52
Aken, Joseph, 242
A. K. Harper Memorial Library, 228
Alabama, 81, 210, 266
Alamo, 57
Alcoa, 51, 70, 178, 201, 255, 285
Alcoa Brick Plant, 285
Alcoa Bus Line, 205
Alcoa High School, 178
Alexander, Eva, 171
Alexander, Cornelius, 218
Alexander, James, Sr., 102
Alexander, Dr. James H., 190
Alexander, Mrs. Jane, 228
Alexander, Capt. John, 35, 294
Alexander, John, 30
Alexander, Rev. John, 96
Alexander, Joseph, 17
Alexander, Dr. Joseph, 149
Alexander, Mary, 149
Alexander, Oliver, 32, 34
Alexander, Sabina, 149
Alexander, Thomas Theron, 142

Alford's, 101
Alleghenies, 12–14
Alleghany, 189
Alleghany Springs Hotel, 84, 87, 249
Alleghany Road, 289
Alleghany Station, 89, 107, 266
Allen, 102, 270
Allen, Capt. Edwin, 55
Allen, James, 126, 128, 154
Allen, James C., 155–57
Allen, R. J., 65, 168
Allen, Frank W., 141
Alliance Advocate, 229
Allinson, Rebecca, 157
Allison, Capt. John, 44, 236, 295
Alnwick, 203
Aluminum Avenue, 207
Aluminum Company of America, 52, 103, 171, 179, 194, 233, 236, 254, 284, 285
Aluminum Powder Plant, 233
Ambrister, John, 77, 112n, 183, 241
Ambrister, Joseph, 115
Ambrister, William, 241
Ambrister and Henry, 115
Ambrister Tanyard, 240
A. M. E. Zion Church, 116, 128, 158, 178
Amelia County, Va., 3
American Airlines, 52
American Button Factory, 238
American Journal of Productive Industry, 227
American Legion, 68, 69, 216, 262
American Temperance University, 215
Amerine Bloomary, 283
Amerine, George, 245, 283
Amerine, Hutsell, 244
Amerine, Scales, 221
Ames, E. F., 246
Amos, David, 109, 152
Ammons, J. D., 253
Anchor Woolen Mills, 226
Anderson Hall, 141, 143, 251
Anderson Mill, 219
Anderson, 41, 101, 129
Anderson, Mrs. A. C., 129
Anderson, Andrew L., 41
Anderson, Dora, 108

334 INDEX

Anderson, Rev. Dr. Isaac, 17, 41, 98, 99, 101, 133, 136, 138, 140, 145, 182, 186, 256
Anderson, James, 58, 83, 120
Anderson, John, 41n
Anderson, John T., 228
Anderson, Joseph, 19, 29, 36, 258
Anderson, Larkin, 65n
Anderson, Lyle, 76
Anderson, Robert H., 80
Anderson, Robert M., 218
Anderson, Thurston, 219
Anderson, William H., 101
Annexation of Texas, 59
Antioch, 123
Anti-slavery Society, 28, 58
Appellate Court, 208
Arbeely, Dr. Abraham, 189
Arbeely, Dr. F. J., 189
Arbeely, Kaleel, 242
Arcadia, Fla., 68
Architectural Record, 145n
Ardus, Lucius, 149
Argile, Hannah Kennedy, 162
Argonne, 67
Arlington National Cemetery, 67
Armistice, 68
Arm of Springfield, 108
Armona, 283
Armory Building, 69
Armstrong, John, 12, 13
Armstrong Land Office, 12
Army Surgeon, 187
Arkansas, 182
"*Aristo*," 252
Arnold, W. V., 285
Asbury, Bishop, 11, 116, 134
Ashley, Joseph, 43, 280
Ashley, William, 280
Ashley & Ghormley, 280
Ashmon, David, 93
Assembly of North Carolina, 19
Associate Church, 104
Associate Presbyterian Church, 286
Associate Synod, 104
Atchley, Robert, 123
Atchley, Wm., 123
Atchley farm, 68fn
Atheist, 96
Athens, 57, 77, 117, 125, 257
Athena Club, 177
Atlanta, 235, 282
"Atlas", 268
Attorney-General, 227
Augusta County, Va., 95
Augusta, Ga., 41
Austin, H. C., 75

Austin Hotel, 252
Austin House, 75
Austin Street, 263
Australian troops, 68
Avery's Treaty, 11
Aviation Corps, 68
Axley's Chapel, 113, 114, 115
Aylett, Wm., 135
Azalea garden, 145

Babcock, C. L., 285, 286
Babcock Lumber Company, 94, 299, 231, 286
Babcock School, 178
Babcock Siding, 286
Bacon Farm, 234
Bacon's Ferry, 234
Badgers, 102
Badgett, B. F., 115
Badgett, Burrel, 220
Badgett, J. N., 151, 191
Bailey, Benjamin, 126
Bailey, M. T., 76
Bakelite, 251
Baker, Charles, 218
Baker, Rev. Daniel, 99
Baker, M. D., 75
Baker's Creek, 25, 36, 39, 98, 99, 102, 113, 122, 218, 219, 234, 241, 281, 282
Bakeshop, 252
Balds, 277
Baldwin, D. B., 84
Baldwin Hall, 141, 143
Baldwin, John Center, 141
Bales, James J., 186
Ball, Nicholas, 27
Ball, W. A., 130
Ballard, Fred, 205
Ballard, Marcus, 115
Ballard, Mike, 250
Ballard, Wm., 115
Baltimore, 267
Baltimore Association of Friends, 157
"Bands of Hope", 263
Bank of Blount County, 246
Bank of Maryville, 31, 37, 72, 89, 246, 256, 260
Bank Post Office, 289
Baptist Church, 271, 275
Barb, J. C., 124
Barber, 253
Barger, Matt, 242
Barges, 239
Barnes, Dr. Jasper, 143
Barnet, Thompson, 107
Barnett, Amos, 39, 77

INDEX

Barnett, Thomas, 269
Barnhill, Jennie, 93
Barnhill, W. P., 74, 93
Barrels, 268
Barry, Hyram, 227
Barry, William, 190
Bartlett, Prof. Alexander, 141
Bartlett, Mason, 214
Bartlett, Nicholas, 32n, 217
Bartlett, Rev. Dr. Peter Mason, 141, 142, 246
Bartlett's Mill, 33
Bartlett's Button Factory, 238
Bartlett, Gymnasium, 143
Bartlett Hall, 144
Bassell, G. M., 74
Bassell School, 178
Base-Community Welfare Council, 70
Battery A 114th AAA, 69
Battery C 191st AFA Battallion, 69
Battle of Alamance, 12
Battle of Hillobees, 55
Battle of Horseshoe, 39, 55, 56
Battle of Island Flats, 11
Battle of Mexico City, 58
Battle of Vera Cruz, 58
Battleship Maine, 66
Bauman, J. F., 48
Bauman Bros., Architects, 48, 51
Baumgardners, 92
Bayless, Dr. W. W., 186
Bays Mountain, 61n
Bays Mountain Electric Co., 260
Beals, James F., 157, 168, 281
Beals, Francis, 186
Bean, William, 1, 8
Beatty, Arthur, 97
Beatty, General, 62
"Beauty Spring", 73
Beavers, Major, 73
Beeabout, Mary, 161
Bechtel, Mr., 154
Beeson, 229
Belden, Col. Wm., 94
Belgium, 68
Bell, James, 80
Bell, Samuel W., 58
Bell, S. F., 48
Bell, William H., 152
Bell Telephone, 261
Belt, R. L., 89, 115, 282
Bencini, L. D., 257
Berry Field (Nashville), 69
Berry, H., 242
Berry, James, 79n, 135, 136, 137, 139n, 140
Berry, Thomas, 72, 218, 223, 243

Berry and Foute, 222
Berry and Hoffar, 246
Best, 130; Best's Mill, 219, 241; Best's Schoolhouse, 115
Best, Christopher, 115, 117
Best, Daniel, 65 fn, 218, 282
Best, George, 113, 218
Best, Jacob, 247
Best, Martin Christopher, 46
Best, Michael, 219
Bethel, 101
Bethel Academy, 76
Bethel Baptist Cemetery, 272
Bethesda Springs, 80n
Bethlehem, 113, 114
Bibles, 164
Bicknell, 129
Bicknell, D. C., 257
Bicknell, George E., 141
Bicknell, Lt. John Y., 58
Bicknell, Samuel T., 44, 148, 149, 210
Bicknell & Wallace, 257
Biddle, John, 112n
Big Bend Quarry, 270
Big Springs, 59, 103, 105, 106, 219
Biggs, Capt. Alexander, 56
Big Spring, 41, 59, 99, 286
Billue, Robert, 120
Billue, William, 120, 121n, 123
Binfield, 281, 284
Binfield Methodist Church, 284
Binfield Post Office, 284
Binford, Rachel, 162
Bingham, Floyd, 131
Bingham, William B., 113n, 115, 187
Bird, Frank, 216
Bird, Captain, 234
Birdseye, Ezekiel, 59
Birdwell, Dora Jackson, 63
Birdwell, J., 120
Birdwell's Mill, 219
Birks, James, 84
Bird's Station, 25
Bise, 129
Bishop, R. J., 187
Bishop, Dr., 193
Bishop of Durham, 125
Bittle, J. C., 76, 259, 261
Black, Gavin, 210
Black, John, 223
Black, J. E., 84
Black, Joseph, 31, 33n, 34
Black, 25, 28n
Black's Blockhouse, 20, 21
Black Sulphur Spring, 74, 79, 80
Blackburn, 37n, 109, 242, 243
Blackburn, Ann Eliza, 50n, 184, 203

Blackburn, Rev. Gideon, 96, 97, 134, 135
Blacksmiths, 248
Blair, Charles D., 93
Blair, Col., 26
Blair, Dr. Hugh, 266
Blair, James, 32, 34, 152
Blair, Capt. John J., 66, 243
Blair, William, 119, 234
Blair, McGhee & Bros., 265
Blair's Ferry, 235
Blair's Mill, 221
Blankenship, Dr. John P., 48, 50, 61, 65, 94, 187, 188, 189, 191, 192, 220
Blevins, 247
Blevins, Henry, 46, 115, 223
Blevins, Nick, 130
Blount, Gov. William, 19, 20, 24, 26, 28, 30n, 31, 32, 49, 53
Blount, Mary Grainger, 255
Blount Cannery, 250
Blount College, 31
Blount County, 14, 15, 19, 20, 26, 30, 31, 58, 61, 66, 119
Blount County Advocate, 227
Blount County Cemeteries, 329
Blount County Court, 32, 44, 159
Blount County Court Clerks, 330
Blount County Chancery Clerks, 330
Blount County Circuit Court Clerks, 330
Blount County Democrat, 213, 228
Blount County Fire Department, 260
Blount County Forts, 23
Blount County High School, 165, 166
Blount County Home Guard, 318
Blount County Industrial Home, 49, 263
Blount County Medical Society, 89, 189, 192, 194
Blount County Sheriffs, 331
Blount County Superintendents of Public Instruction, 331
Blount County Third District, 47
Blount County Trustees, 331
Blount County Standard, 228
Blount County Turnpike Company, 203
Blount Hotel, 191, 214
Blount Memorial Hospital, 52, 195
Blount Fraction of Loudon County, 45
Blount Hills, 296
Blount Hospital, 191
Blount Laundry, 40, 253
Blount's Treaty, 255
Blow, 129
Blue Spring, 124
Board of Aldermen, 65
Board of Censors, 183
Board of Equalization, 200

Board of Health, 50, 191, 193
Board of Supervisors, 202
Board of Trade, 245
Boardman, Rev. Samuel Ward, 142
Bogle, Andrew, 30, 33, 34, 35
Bogle, Joseph, 96
Bogle, Robert, 59, 241, 282
Bogle, Capt. Samuel, 30, 73, 295
Bogle and Frye, 232
Bond, F., 225
Bond, J. A., 115
Bond-Woolf, 229, 231, 286
Bond Quarry, 70
Bonham, John M., 248, 106
Bonine, Daniel, 126
Bonine, Mary, 126
Bonner, Frederick, 84
Boones, 247
Boone, Daniel, 6, 9, 278
Boone's Creek, 8, 9
Borings, 130, 247, 278
Boring, Hart, 64
Boston Recorder, 139
Boteright, Daniel, 35
Bounds, Capt. (of Hawkins County), 58
Bounds, Thomas, 29
Bowers, Augustine, 120, 123
Bowerman's, 64n, 218
Bowerman, Peter, 28
Bowerman's Creek, 218
Bowerman's Mill, 41, 219
Bowles, David, 128
Bowling Green, Ky., 260
Bowman, 114
Bowman, G. C., 131
Bowman, John M., 131
Bowman, Prof. John W., 176
Bowman, William, 76
Boyd, 96, 101, 109
Boyd, Alexander, 72
Boyd, John, 152
Boyd, Major Leslie, 69
Boyd, Robert, 30
Boyd, Captain, 34
Boyd, Thomas, 152
Boyd, Rev. W. J., 110
Boyd and Coulter, 221
Boyd's Creek, 10n, 12, 13
Boyd's Creek-Ellejoy, 95
Boyd's Plantation, 119
Boyer, Luke, 33, 34, 209
Brabson, B. D., 43, 44, 137, 148, 236, 256, 257
Brabson, John, 256
Brabson, Mary Elizabeth, 187
Brabson's Ford, 51, 77, 79, 97
Bradford, 276

Bradford, Bennett, 114
Bradford, Tutt S., 229
Bradley, Major John, 218, 271
Bradley's Mill, 220, 271, 278
Bradley County, 216
Branam, John, 17
Brandies, 276
Brause, Charles E., 74, 228
Breazeale, 18, 209
Brethren, 130, 150
"Breeches and skin Dresser", 240
Briar Knob, 41
Brice, 206
Brickell, 242
Brickell, W. O., 190
Brick Mill, 24, 41, 63, 77, 171, 187, 219, 221, 233, 252, 261, 282
Brick Mill Henrys, 267
Brick Mason, 251
Brickyard, 251
Brickey, D. L. (Fate), 66
Brickey, John H., 123
Brickey, J. B. J., 123
Brickey, Peter, 243
Brickey, Sgt. Wiley J., 67
Brickey, William, 121, 123
Bridge-burning, 60
Bristol, Mrs. H. C., 194
British Agents, 53
Broadway Methodist Church, 75
Broady, 101
Broady, Mrs. India Patton, 72n
Broady, Nancy Lee, 17n, 170
Broady, Thomas F., 259n
Brock, Dr., 84
Brooks, Joseph, 29
Brooks, Moses, 29
Broom Factory, 253
Brown, 129, 229
Brown, Ann Eliza, 108
Brown, Elijah, 219
Brown, George Allen, 232
Brown, George, 148
Brown, Governor, 57
Brown, Jacob, 9, 10
Brown, Jesse, 120
Brown, John, 102
Brown, John C., 175
Brown, John T., 63
Brown, Joseph, 268
Brown, Col. Leroy, 66
Brown, Maggie Bell, 66
Brown, Martin C., 108
Brown, Gov. Neill S., 174
Brown, Phebe, 108
Brown, Thomas J., 114

Brown, Thomas N., 17, 190, 211, 212, 214, 215, 246, 260
Brown, Rev. William B., 102
Brown, William E., 209
Brown's Ferry, 220
Brownlow, Parson, 60n, 65, 83, 97
Brownlow's Whig, 153, 268
Broyles, 259
Broyles, D. N., 242
Broyles, Dan and Jim, 253
Broyles, Joe, 205
Bruff, James B., 163
Brumfiel, O. W., 285
Bruner, Alec, 130
Bryan, D. L., 211, 215
Bryants, 171
Bryant, Dr. K. A., 192, 193, 194
Buchanan, 39
Buchanan, Capt. Edward, 55, 243, 303
Buchanan Cemetery, 274
Buck, Mr., 162
Buckner, Daniel, 123
Buffalo Trails, 1
Buford, Lawrence, 162
Bullock, 17
Buly (Bewley), George, 17
Bunker, Eliza C., 227
Bunker, Jesse F., 114
Burchfields, 275
Burchfield, Dr. George W., 194
Burchfield, Nathan, 114
Burem, Henry, 99
Burger, Joseph, 151, 225, 226, 245, 260, 261
Burger, Lizzie K., 49n
Burger, Herschell, 289
Burk, William, 34, 218
Burke, Edward, 10, 116
Burke, William, 95, 110
Burkhart, Thomas, 60
Burnett, W. M., 123
Burns, Aaron, 275
Burns, Sgt. Frank W., 66, 67
Burns, John, 221
Burns, Richard, 66, 272
Burns Cemetery, 272
Burnside, General, 62, 63, 64, 280
Burton, William, 240
Bussel's, 114
Bussell's Ferry, 233
Butcher, A. L., 252
Butler, Captain, 72
Butler, Lt. Col. Thomas, 36, 37
Buttons, 247, 238
Button and Chumlea, 247
Button and Swan, 247
Byerly, 77

INDEX

Byerly and Owens, 268
Byers, Nicholas, 71
Byers, Nimrod, 115
Byrne Drugstore, 196

Cables, 275
Cable, John P., 220, 222
Cable graveyard, 276
Cable Mill, 278
Cable School, 276
Cabinet Making, 231
Cades Bluff, 114
Cades Cove, 3, 42, 50, 65, 80, 91, 111–20, 164, 170, 173, 176, 191, 238, 243, 244, 255, 273, 275, 276, 277, 278, 280
Cades Cove Bloomary Forge, 276
Cades Cove Baptist Church, 122, 276
Cadets of Temperance, 147
"Calaboose", 269
Calamity Corner, 37
Calderwood, I. G., 284
Calderwood, 40, 42, 171, 232, 233, 237, 283, 284
Calderwood Dam, 284
Calderwood School, 177
Caldwells, 41, 101, 256
Caldwell, David, 135, 136n, 224, 279
Caldwell, John, 34, 135
Caldwell, Molly, 121n, 154
Caldwell, Robert, 73
Caldwell, Thomas J., 57
Caldwell, William Sr., 227
Caldwell, Dr. W. H., 130, 196
Caldwell, Doctor, 182
Calhoun's Treaty, 240, 255
Calico, 224
California, 186
Calloway, Mrs. Julia, 77
Calloway, Sue S., 86
Calloway Turnpike, 40, 234, 284
Callahan and Best, 252
Cameron, 271
Camp Bob Taylor, 66
Camp, Carroll, 58
Camp, Cass, 57
Camp Dewey, 66
Camp, Margaret Townsend, 231
Camp Meade (Penna.), 66
Camp Morgan, 60
Camp Oglethorpe, 68
Camp, Sevier, S.C., 68
Camp Meeting, 111
Camp Ground, 271
Campaign of 1793, 31
Campbell, 35, 276
Campbell, Governor of Va., 277
Campbell, David, 15, 19, 223

Campbell, James, 218
Campbell County, 207
Canaday, Walter, 126
Candora Marble Company, 238
Candy Kitchen, 252
Cane Creek, 6, 274
Cane Schoolhouse, 274
Canneries, 249
Canning Factory, 262
Cannon, Newton, 57n
Cannonburg, Penna., 104
Cansler, Charles W., 160
Cansler, Hugh Lawson, 159, 160, 178, 248
Carbon Plant, 233, 285
Capital Airlines, 52
Carey, James, 20
Carmichael, 87, 186
Carnegie Hall, 143
Carnes, Elliott, 251
Carpenter, Andrew, 115
Carpenter, Elisha, 115, 168
Carpenter, Thomas, 115, 282
Carpenter, William M., 282
Carpenter's Campground, 83, 113, 114, 115, 116, 169, 231, 245
Carpenter's School, 247
Carr's Creek, 177
Carriages, 248
Carrick, Rev. Samuel, 95
Carroth, John, 223
Carson, David, 102, 105
Carson, Fannie C., 86
Carson, James, 73, 244
Carson, Dr. J. E., 76, 191, 193, 194, 195
Carson's Ironworks, 244, 278
Carter, Jess, 248
Carter, John, 13
Carter, Landon, 14
Carter, Dr. L. D., 186
Carter County, 83, 247, 275, 278
Carter's Valley, 9
Cartright, 10
Carruthers, Harvey H. C., 168
Cashions, 102
Cassandra, 280
Cassedy, Father, 129n
Cast, Richard, 72
Caswell, Capt. William, 58
Caswell, General, 62
Cate, Michael, 123
Cate, William A., 228
Cates, Dr. Benjamin B., 183, 185, 187
Cates, Charles T., Jr., 211, 212
Cates, Charles T., Sr., 51, 115n, 210, 212, 213, 215, 239, 263
Cates, James M., 135 fn, 211, 212, 215

INDEX 339

Cates, Dr. John W., 61, 112, 150, 186, 187, 189, 210
Cates, Mary E., 109
Cates, Minerva J., 148
Cates, Mrs. Neppie Hannum, 110n
Cates, Reuben L., 44, 112n, 136, 139, 148, 175, 183, 227, 242
Cates Law Office, 215
Cates Street, 31, 263
Catlett, Henry S., 48, 75, 122
Caughron's, 276
Cavalry, 53, 57
Cave Roller Mill, 218, 220, 222, 289
Cavet's Station, 26
Cavin's Blockhouse, 28
Cawood, Dr. J. C., 185
Caylor, George, 114
Caylor's Chapel Cemetery, 272
Cedar Bluff, 220, 272
"Cedar Circle", 185
"Cedar Graveyard", 106
Cedar Grove, 121
Cedar Spring, 259
Cemeteries, 272, 281
Centenary, 65n, 114, 115, 116, 120
Centenary Methodist Church, 113, 120
Centennial, 102
Centennial Campaign, 144
"Centennial Patch", 102
Central House, 76, 261
Cerro Gordo, 58
Cession by North Carolina, 35
Chaffin, Dr. George Hunt, 77, 186, 267, 269
Chambers, Charles, 222
Chambers, John, 220, 243
Chancery Court, 207, 208
Chancery Court Clerks, 330
Chancellor, 208
Chancellor Staley, 213
Chancellor Van Dyke, 236
Chandler, Charles, 225
Chandler, David, 115
Chandler, John, 115
Chandler, Pauline Hord, 162
Chandler, R. F., 85
Chapman, 102, 130
Chapman, D. C., 277
Chappell, J. F., 130
Charles I, 1
Charles, Nancy, 187
Charles, Reuben, 181, 218
Charles Hall School, 178
Charleston, S.C., 2, 3, 44, 68, 235
Chatauqua, 262
Charcoal, 266

Cheoah Dam, 233, 234
Cheoah River, 232
Cherokees, 3, 6, 8, 10, 14, 15, 19, 20, 21, 24, 26, 28, 29, 31, 93, 120, 134, 139, 186, 255
Cherokee Removal, 57, 185
Cherokee warfare, 53
Cherokee Lumber Co., 232
Cherry, Rev. Mr., 167
Chestnut Flats, 276
Chief Atta-Culla-Culla, 6, 7
Chief Dragging Canoe, 10, 11
Chief Oconastota, 6
Chief Ostenaco, 7
Chief Standing Turkey, 7
Childers, 257
Childress, 66
Chilhowee, 16, 21, 25, 41, 43, 61n, 82, 123, 125, 225, 233, 236, 242, 280, 283, 284
Chilhowee Association, 122
Chilhowee Baptist Church, 281
Chilhowee Flats, 274
Chilhowee Inn, 94
Chilhowee Lumber Company, 230
Chilhowee Medical Spring, 87, 88
China, 214
Chota, 4, 7, 19, 234
Christian, Gilbert, 8
Christian, John, 20
Christian, Col. William, 11, 15, 26, 95, 103
Christy Hill School, 115, 176, 223, 247
Christian Advocate, 148
Christian Endeavor, 153
Chumlea, W. C., 211, 214
Churchwell, G. W., 210
Cincinnati, 188
Cincinnati Southern Railroad, 269
Circle Drive Hospital, 194
Circular Saw, 232
Circuit Court, 32, 39, 78, 173, 197, 208, 213, 256
Circuit Court Clerks, 44, 209, 330
Circuit Court Records, 330
Circus, 257
Citico, 18
Citico Massacre, 17
City of Alcoa, 191, 285
City Bakery, 252
City Flour Mill, 260
City Manager, 285
City of Maryville, 171, 213
City Offices, 265
Citizen's Hotel, 75
Civil Aeronautics Administration, 52
Civil Districts, 41

INDEX

Civil War, 78, 81, 182, 225, 242, 272, 278, 280
Civilian Conservation Corps, 231
Claiborne, W. C. C., 36
Clark, 101, 130
Clark, Foster, 75, 240
Clark, James, 243
Clark, John M., 112
Clark, J. L., 50, 225, 260
Clark, Lindley D., 164
Clark, L., 242
Clark, Margaret J., 108
Clark, Mary A., 108
Clark, P. H., 108, 150
Clark, S. L., 151
Clark, Dr. William, 91n, 278
Clark's Grove Church, 108, 109
Clay County, Illinois, 129
Clemens, James, 122
Clemens, J. L., 49
Clemens, S. H., 176
Clemens, John, 123
Clerk and Master, 184, 208, 214, 215
Cleveland, 125
Cliff, Post Office, 286
Cliff Quarry, 237
Clinkenbeard, John, 13
Clinton B. Fisk, 270
Clingman, Thomas Lanier, 83
Clingman's Dome, 83
Clover Hill, 41, 74, 85, 101, 102, 122, 172, 188, 219, 243, 261, 284, 286
Clover Hill Presbyterian Church, 99, 284
Clover Hill Mill, 221, 222, 281
Clover Hill Road, 63
"Cloudland Spring", 90
Cloyd's Creek, 99, 102, 127, 131, 218, 229, 234, 270
Clubs, 193
Clute, F., 253
"Coal Pits", 177
Cochran, John, 20, 30, 35, 37
Cochran, Matt, 131, 176
Cochran, Roscoe, 66
Cochran, Samuel, 243
Cochran, Thomas, 218
Cochran, T. R., 205
Cocke, Major John, 55
Cocke County, Tenn., 86, 112, 214
Coffee, Col. John, 56
Coffin, Charles, 64, 160
Coffin, John M., 224, 279
Coffin, King, 67
Coffin and Wilson, 257
Coker Hill Cemetery, 272
Coker, Ed, 270

Coker, J. W., 123
Colburn, S. W., 252
Colburn, William, 174
Cold Springs, 91
Cold-storage Rooms, 253
Cole Alexander, 29
Coleman, E. C., 130
Coleman, Rev. George, 74, 288
Coleman, A. J., 138
Coleman, Mrs. Virginia, 65
Collector of taxes, 201
College Cemetery, 145
"College Inn", 75
College Maid Shop, 144
College Vault, 144
Collins, John, 258
Collins, Patrick, 225
Collins, W. P., 227
Colonization, 59
Colored Tennessean, 227
Columbian Hall, 50, 98, 262
Colville, Capt. Joseph, 34, 35, 217, 296
Colville's Ford, 33
Common Schools, 171, 173
Common School Commissioners, 80, 149, 150, 173, 174
Common School Fund, 175
Common School Law, 172
Common School System, 202
Compact of 1806, 38, 171
Concord, 107, 151, 153, 188, 270
Confederate Army, 60, 61, 187
Confederate Cavalry, 60
Confiscation, 64
Conger, Abijah, 85, 172, 244, 281
Congress, 14
Congressman Gibson, 214
Connaster, Andrew, 123
Conning, Albert, 247
Conning, William, 176
Conner, 25
Conscript Agents, 66
Constable, duties of, 199
Constitution of the U. S., 32
Constitution convention, 216
Cook, Alexander, 113n
Cook, John, 221
Cook's Mill, 46, 187, 289
Cook's Forge, 244
Cook's 100
Cooperative Boarding Club, 143
Cooper, 259
Cooper, J. A., 188
Cooper, Thomas F., 84, 151, 260, 261
Cooper, William, 100
Cooper's Landing, 269

INDEX 341

Cooper Road, 80, 84, 276
Cooper Shop, 268, 272
Coosa River, 55
Cope, Marmaduke, 157
Coply, E. H., 237
Copp, S. A., 285
Copperplate and business hand, 172
Coppock, Benjamin, 162, 163, 164
Corley, 100
Corporation Minutes, 259
Coroner, 198, 199, 278
Corry, Robert T., 109
Costner, Phillip, 113, 282
Cotant, Zephaniah, 219, 222
Cotton Factory, 224, 262
Cotton-Picking machine, 270
Cotton Gin, 39, 272
Coulson, Jabez, 44, 235
Coulson, John, 58n
Coulson, Tipton and Jones, 266
Coulter, Jonnie B., 264
County Chairman, 208
County Clerk, 216, 330
County Court, 33, 45, 47
County Election, 39
County Fair, 261
County Judge, 211, 215
County Judge's Court, 208
County Physician, 187
County Solicitor, 34
County Superintendent of Schools, 202
County Tax Rate, 35
Court of Equity, 207
Court of Errors and Appeals, 207
Court of Pleas, 31, 197, 210
Court of Quarter Sessions, 31, 197
Courthouse, 41, 43, 36, 37, 38, 50, 51, 180, 187, 256
Courthouse Fire, 330
Courthouse Painting, 258
Courthouse Tax, 51
Covenanters, 58, 105
Coventry, A. A., 245
Cowan, 101, 245
Cowan, Andrew, 43, 58n, 106
Cowan, Archibald, 32, 33, 34, 72
Cowan, Bob, 92
Cowan, C. C., 121, 168
Cowan, James, 186, 189
Cowan, John, 36, 297
Cowan, S. F., 168
Cowan, Dr. Thomas, 47, 196, 249, 260
Cowan Spring's, 91
Cox, 109
Cox, Ambrose, 266, 267
Cox, Charles, 206

Cox, H. Talbott, 44, 146, 235, 267, 268
Cox, Henry T., 267
Cox, H. G., 268
Cox, Jack, 269
Cox, James K., 267
Cox, John B., 257
Cox, J. L., 267
Cox, Dr. Madison, 64, 176, 186, 269
Cox, Mrs. Margaret, 109
Cox, Matt, 189
Cox, Nathaniel, 77, 267
Cox, R. W., 86
Cox, Dr. Sam T., 176, 186, 257
Cox and Devers, 257
Cox school, 154
Cox's Milldam, 266
Coyatee Ford, 28n
Coyatee Ferry, 234
Cozart, Samuel, 230
Craig, Major David, 16, 20, 24, 27, 28, 29, 30, 31, 32, 33n, 34
Craig, Capt. John, 17, 24, 26, 28, 31, 32, 33, 100, 218, 256
Craig, Rev. John S., 59, 73, 101, 140, 175
Craig, John J., 45, 236, 238
Craig, William, 72
Craig's Fort, 20, 31, 95
Crawford, 216
Crawford, G. S. W., 141, 142, 202
Crawford, John C., 165, 211, 215, 216
Crawford, John C., Jr., 148, 216
Crawford, Roy, 216
Crawford, Samuel L., 209
Crawford and Crawford, 216
Crawford and Caldwell Hardware, 227
Creeks, 20, 21, 24, 26, 29, 56
Creek Removal, 313
Creek War, 182
Crescent Amusement Co., 262
Creswell, Andrew, 58n, 96
Criminal Court, 206, 208
Criminal Judge, 209
Criminal Rule Docket, 206
Crisp, 130
Crooked Creek, 20, 21, 28, 32, 64, 120, 123, 217, 219, 243
Crooked Creek Church, 120
Crock Factory, 247
Croft, 154
Crosswhite, 131
Crothers, William H., 98
Crowder, C. F., 191
Crowder, William, 130
Crowson, Aaron, 275
Crowson, Mose, 118
Crowson, William, 275

Crudup, D. G., 239
Crudup and Warner, 239
Crum, Major M. B., 69
Crumley, Aaron, 278
Crutchfield, Thomas, architect, 43
Crye, Shimmon (Simeon), 65n, 113
Crys, 102
"Cudjo's Cave", 64
Culton, J. W., 228
Cumberland Gap, 2, 8, 60, 61
Cumberland Mountains, 8, 277
Cumberland Presbyterian Church, 102, 106
Cumberland River, 10
Cummins, J. B., 268
Cummins, W. F., 268
Cummings and Carnes, 248
Cummings, Rev. Charles, 10, 95, 103
Cummings, Franklin, 66n
Cummings, James, 114
Cummings, John 115, 248
Cummings, J. B., 116
Cummings, Robert S., 146
Cummings, R. S., 268
Cummings, William, 257
Cummings, Wm. P. L., 248
Cunningham, Ben, 51, 57, 61, 168, 176, 225
Cunningham, Clay, 232, 253, 260
Cunningham, David, 72, 73
Cunningham, Edwin, 211, 214
Cunningham, George, 29
Cunningham, James, 28, 30, 223
Cunningham, Miles, 73
Cunningham, W. R., 131
Cunningham, 256
Cunningham Tavern House, 73
Cure-all Springs, 91, 92
Curried leathers, 241
Cullen, Cyrus, 94
Culton, J. Wright, 211, 214
Culton, Robert, 101
Cupp, Green, 124
Currier, John M., 73, 195
Curtis, C. D., 171
Curtis and Snyder, 230
Cusick, 218
Cusick, Capt. John B., 39
Cusick, Joseph, 256
Cypress, 81

Dade, Townsend Stuart, 209
Daguerrotypist, 252
Daily News, 74, 228
Dakotas, 212
Dalton, Ga., 235

Dam, 184
Danforth, Josiah, 34, 37, 72, 218, 222
Dardis, Thomas, 209, 210
Daughters of Masons, 148
Davenport Gap, 277
Davidson, Cora, 154
Davidson, Frank, 154
Davidson, Ensign Samuel, 27
Davidson, William, 21, 24, 25
Davis, 102, 109, 129
Davis, Abraham, 241
Davis, Calvin, 242, 261
Davis, Caswell, 280
Davis, E. F., 240
Davis, James, 92, 94, 168
Davis, J. A., 116
Davis, John, 129, 148, 241
Davis, John S., 61
Davis, Michael, 115
Davis, Reps J., 256
Davis, Richard, 118, 119
Davis, Rufus, 261
Davis, W. C., 176
Davis, William, 94, 118, 120, 123, 243
Davis-Lane Cemetery, 272
Davis and Wyley, 234
Davis Farm, 261, 289
Davis Ford, 234
Davidson, Prof. W. R., 103
Dawsons of Unitia, 266
Dayton, Ohio, 6, 8
Deal Tract, 239
Deal's Gap, 52, 84, 277
Dean, Jonathan, 17
DeArmond, David, 72, 121
DeArmond, John, 101n
DeArmond, J. Merritt, 211, 214
DeArmond, Richard, 21, 39, 265
DeBose, Blanche, 162
DeBose, Henry, 160
DeBrahm, J. W., 5
Declaration of Independence, 11
Defeat Ridge, 41
Defoe, O. L., 246
Delinquent Poll Tax Collector, 201
Delozier, Dr. B. E., 190, 192
Delozier, Hugh, 216
Delozier, Jesse, 73
Delta C. & S., 52
Delzell, 105
Delzell, David, 58n, 79
Demeré, Capt. Raymond, 5
Demeré, Capt. Paul, 5, 6
Denné, Mme., 246
Dentists, 182, 189, 196
Denver, Colorado, 212

INDEX

Derris House, 252
Dever, James F., 257
Dever, Wm., 57n
Dickerson, Mrs. George Gillespy, 184
Dickey, Joe, 230, 272
Didcot, England, 228
Dill, Capt. (McMinn County), 58
Distillers, 219, 243
Distinguished Flying Cross, 67, 69
Distinguished Service Cross, 67, 68, 69
Distinguished Service Medal, 67
Districts, 33
District Attorney, 216
District Courts, 206
District Surveyor, 200
District Voting Place, 41
Division, 30th, 325
Ditto's Landing, 220
Dixie Mantle and Manufacturing Company, 232, 250
Dixon, Matthew L., 135
Dixon, Zeno H., 158, 159
Doak, Rev. Samuel, 12
Doak, Samuel, 133
Dobson, Joseph, 106
Dobson, Joseph B., 152
Dobson, Robert C., 106
Doctor Gunn, 195
Doctor's Hospital, 195
Dodd, W. H., 242
Dog Tax, 47
Doherty, Cornelius, 3
Donaldson, James, 44, 235
Donaldson, J. H., 270
Donaldson Mill, 188, 221, 219
Donaldson, Dr. T. F., 188, 189
Donaldson, T. S., 190
Donnelson, Stockley, 31n, 256
Dorton, Capt. James M., 62
Doughty, B. F., 242
Douglas, Lt. Col. John R., 69
Douthitt, Dr. W. H., 190, 269
Dover's Mill, 217
Dow, Lorenzo, 111
Dowell, W. T., 59, 61, 65, 115, 196
Downing, Rev., 125
Drake, William, 176
Dreamland, Amusement Co., 262
Drinnen, Frank, 216
Drinnen, T. C., 211, 216
Druggists, 189, 195
"The Drunkards Warning", 262
Dug Gap, 267
Dry Valley, 243, 272
Ducktown, 125
Dumplin Community, 216
Dumplin Creek, 15

Duncan, 105
Duncan, Benjamin, 244
Duncan, B. T., 175
Duncan, Calvin A., 141
Duncan, John P., 74, 249
Duncan, Joseph, 55, 265, 304
Duncan, Robert, 172
Duncan, Sophia, 172
Dunkard Church, 130
Dunlap, 96, 129
Dunlap, Ephriam, 33, 209
Dunlap, Hugh, 275
Dunlap, James, 96
Dunlap, Samuel, 129, 155
Dunn, 101
Dunn, Capt. Cynthia, 63
Dunn, Giles, 221
Dunn, Green, 65
Dunn, Rhad, 61, 63
Dunn, Sam, 211, 215
Dunn, A. D., S. H., and C. W., 205
Dunn, S. H., 177, 216
Dunn, Wm. W., 101
Dunkin, Joseph, 39
Dunmore, Gov., 10
Dupes, Henry, 232
Dupes, John, 91
Durham, Daniel, 126
Durham, Wm., 126
Dye, 215
Dyer, 100
Dyer, Major Charles W., 67
Dyke, Rev. John, 102

"Eagle", 73
Eagle Button Factory, 238
Eagle Ford on Clinch River, 27
Eagleton, Alexander, 108
Eagleton, Elijah, 59, 138
Eagleton, Ethie, 65n, 85n
Eagleton, W. W., 268
Eagleton Schoolhouse, 108
Eagleton Village, 286, 289
Eakin, John, 286, 289
Eakin, Rev. John, 103
Eakin, William L., 87
East Maryville, 258
East Side School, 171, 178
East. Tenn. Convention, 59
East Tenn. Female Masonic Institute, 146, 147, 257
East. Tenn. Telephone Co., 260
East Tenn. & Georgia Railroad, 44
East Tenn. & Virginia Railroad, 44, 236
East Tennessean, 53, 227
Eaton, John, 153

Ecuador and Peru, 67
Edington, T. D., 150
Edmondson, 105
Edmondson, David, 217
Edmondson, D. L., 177
Edmondson, John, 168
Edmondson, J. L., 252
Edmondson, R. M., 61
Edmondson, Wallace, 101
Edwards, Col. R. M., 61
Edwards, Richard, 239
Education, County Board of, 168, 169
Education Bill, General, 169
Ekaneetlee Gap, 3, 80n
Elder, Lt. Col. John L., Jr., 69
Elizabeth Voorhees Chapel, 143
Elkmont, 177, 231, 236, 273
Elledge, Isaac, 123
Elledge, William, 60
Ellejoy, 32n, 51, 60, 66, 121, 123, 170, 221, 241, 242, 286
Ellejoy Church, 120
Ellejoy Creek, 7, 217, 248, 261
Ellejoy Institute, 176
Elliott, Dr. Franklin, 128, 157
Ellis, E. L., 190, 192
Elmira, New York, 187
Elmore, F. A., 86
Ellis, H. L. Prof., 170
Ellis, 57
Ellis, Zemri S., 155
Ellis, N. C., 190, 192
Emancipation, 3
Emert, 272
Emert, Clyde B., 228
Emert, Frederick, 60n, 114
Emert Mill, 220
Emory, Rev. Isaac, 86
Emory River, 269
Endsley, 238
Endsley, William C., 157
Engel, David, 83
Engel, J. C., 84
England and Bryan, 49
English, 156
English, J. L., 272
English, William, 17
Entry-taker, 200
Episcopal Church, 80, 83
Episcopal Diocese of Tenn., 124
Episcopal Mission, 125
Equity cases, 207
Erie, Penna., 106
Erskine, George, 39, 59, 161
Estabrook, Joseph, 41n
Estanaula, 20, 26

Etowah, 26
Eureka House, 74
Eusebia, 15, 95, 96, 97, 184, 186, 213, 243
Evans, Capt. Nathaniel, 17, 18, 27
Evans, Isaac C., 160
Evans, Richard, 123
Evans Marble Co., 237
Evangelical Lutheran Holston Synod, 124
Everett, 170
Everett, Charles, 154
Everett, John, 262
Everett, John A., 229
Everett, Mary, 76
Everett, Rosalee, 171
Everett, Sam, 50, 245, 262, 263
Everett, Will, 86
Everett, W. W., 76
Everett High School, 170
Everett Hill, 191
Ewald, Robert F., 285
Ewing, Capt. George, 30, 32, 33, 34, 35
Ewing, Finis, 152
Ewing and Jefferson College, 107, 146, 153, 171
"Eye Spring", 88

F-86A, 70
"Factory" on the Holston, 4, 8
Fagg, Alex, 248
Fagg, Capt. Julius Caesar, 44, 58, 141, 147, 257, 314
Fagg, Ruth, 162
Fagg Bushnell & Sesler, 77
Fagg and Miller's Drugstore, 195, 257
Fain, Capt., 16, 17
Fairs, 37, 261
Fair Grounds, 261
Fairview School, 103
Fall of Charleston, 12
Falling, William, 11
Family Data (Mr. Parham), 326
Family Medicine, 181
Fann, William, 243
Farmer, Adam, 60
Farmer, G. W., 153
Farmer, Jake, 121n
Farmer, William, 61
Farmer's Bank, 212, 246
Farnham, Elizabeth, 158, 163, 169
Farley, 130
Farr, Absolom, 115
Farr, John, 127, 176
Farr, S. J., 242
Farragut, Major George, 35, 233
Farragut, Adm. David Glasgow, 35n

INDEX

Fauquier, Governor, 7
Fayerweather, Daniel B., 143
Federal Cavalry, 66
Federal Funds, 52, 66, 193, 195
Federal Government, 14, 28, 277
Federal Housing Project, 289
Federal Prison, 189
Federal Road, 71, 78, 279
Feezell, James R., 108
Feezell, Sam, 253
Felknor, William B., 216
Female Academy, 135, 137, 138, 146, 256
Ferguson, James, 28
Ferguson, John C., 242
Ferguson, Lt. Vernon, 69
Ferguson, Wm. H., 115
Ferrary, Leo, 195, 258
Ferrary Saloon, 49
Ferries, 34, 39, 233
Fickes, E. S., 285
Fields, Lawson, 65n
Fifth, Regiment, 58
Fighting Creek Gap, 66
Fincastle County, Va., 9
Fine Arts Building, 145
Finly Bros., 268
Finley, W. H., 114
Fire, 258
Fire Dept., 265
First Baptist Church of Maryville, 122
First Federal Savings and Loan Corp., 246
469th Fighter-Squadron, 69
460th Fighter-Interceptor Squadron, 70
First National Bank, 215, 246
First Superintendent, 175
First Tennessee Regiment of Mounted Volunteers, 58
Fisher, A. J., 242
Fisher, Charles, 114
Fisher, J. W., 86, 242, 274
Fisk University, 161
Five Points, 261
516th Air Defense Group, 70
Flanders, John C., 83
Flats of Chilhowee, 245
Fleming, Col., 117n
Flint Gap, 84
Flood, 222
Flood of 1875, 269
Flood of 1867, 269
Flood of 1902, 269
Florida, 53
Floyd, William, 72
Follette, Mrs. Keith, 92, 263

Fonde, Stuart, 240
Fontana Dam, 232
Ford Foundation, 193
Forge Tract, 244
Foreign Mission Board of the Presbyterian Church, 26
Forest Hill Church, 101
Forgotten Campaign, 55n
Forster, Hon. William Edward, 157
Forster, William, 157
Forster, Home, 158
Foster, Horace, 63, 146, 267, 268
Fort Craig, 76, 96, 97, 133, 178
Fort Craig Hotel, 76
Fort Craig Hospital, 77, 195
Fort Craig School, 51, 171, 262
Fort Deposit, 55
Fort Henry, 2
Fort Loudoun, 5, 6, 7, 8
Fort Loudoun Dam, 100
Fort Loudoun Lake, 270
Fort McTeer, 133
Fort Mims Massacre, 55
Fort Montgomery, 55
Fort Necessity, 3
Fort Prince George, 4, 5
Fort Robinson, 6, 7
Fort Sanders, 280
Fort Stanwix, 8
Fort Thomas, Kentucky, 67
Fort on Watauga, 11
47th Volunteer Infantry, 66, 67, 323
48th Regiment at Fort Thomas, Kentucky, 66, 67
"49ers", 186
Forward Fund, 143
Four Mile, 171
Four Mile Creek, 13, 71, 234
Four Mile Baptist Church, 122
Four Mile Law, 176, 258
Foute, 267
Foute, Daniel D., 41, 65, 79, 80, 85, 119, 173, 174, 210, 244, 242, 276, 280
Foute, D. D., Plantation, 172, 242, 244
Foute, E. J., 190
Foute, Jacob F., 39, 135, 136, 139n, 210, 223
Foute's Bloomary, 244
Foute's Mill, 220
Foute's Road, 87
"Foute Trail", 80, 84
Foundry and machine Shop, 262
Francisco, Rev. G. T., 112
Franklin, 14
Franklin County, 240, 249

Franklin Movement, 15
Franklin, State of, 18, 19, 97, 133
Franklin, Tennessee, 211
Frank Post, 249
Frazier, John, 223
Free Negroes, 269
Free Negro School, 262
Free Public Schools, 262
Free Schools, 173
Freedman's Bureau, 141, 142, 143, 159, 262
Freedman's Institute, 49, 50, 159, 162, 165, 166, 171, 191, 228, 251, 258, 259
Freedman's Normal, 161
Freeman, John, 73
Freeman, Capt. John, 75
French, Charles M., 260
French, Miss Florence, 260
French, J. B., 168
French, J. D., 150
French Broad, 3, 15, 19, 29, 31, 95
French Broad River, 10, 13, 110, 111
French and Indian War, 3
French Propaganda, 3
Freshour, George, 121
Friar, John, 118
Friends, 155, 157, 270
Friends Society, 160
Friends Church, 126, 151, 156, 158, 162, 251, 281
Friends Normal, 171, 262
Friends in Great Britain and Ireland, 160
Friends of the Lower Settlement, 126
Friendsville, 27, 63, 64, 70, 128, 154, 155, 156, 171, 189, 190, 222, 230, 238, 242, 246, 265, 281
Friendsville Academy, 158, 159, 169, 171
Friendsville Bus Line, 205
Friendsville Canning and Manufacturing Co., 249
Friendsville Church, 173
Friendsville Ginning Co., 221
Friendsville Institute, 128, 155, 157
Friendsville Marble Co., 230
Friendsville Mill, 219
Friendsville Quarterly Meeting, 128, 129
Friendsville Road, 259
Fry, Joseph, 131
Frys, 131
Fuller Packing Co., 253
Fulton, Dr. Chas. A., 189, 196
Fulton, Creed, 114
Furgeson, Henry, 106
Furnace Equipment Co., 245
Furniture Factory, 262

Gaddis's Mill, 230
Gailbraith, 36
Gailey, James, 32
Gallaher, Rev. James, 24, 138
Gallaher, Thomas, 35
Gallaher Creek, 32, 98, 99, 100, 113, 122, 217, 218, 243, 281, 286
Gambles, 15, 102, 114, 181, 216, 259, 289, 275
Gamble's Station, 21, 25, 75
Gamble, A. B., 207
Gamble, Alexander, 77, 80
Gamble, Alice, 162
Gamble, Dr. A. M., 49, 50, 61, 75, 76, 92, 177, 190, 191, 192, 194
Gamble, Andrew, 84, 211, 214
Gamble, C. H., 116
Gamble, Hugh H., 176
Gamble, Joe, 92, 216
Gamble, John, 102
Gamble, Josias (Stutt), 242, 274
Gamble, Dr. L. A., 186, 269
Gamble, Mary, 76
Gamble, Miss Mollie, 177
Gamble, Mose, 92
Gamble, M. H., 168, 169, 211, 215, 216, 281
Gamble, Moses H., Jr., 216
Gamble, Miss Sallie, 177
Gamble, William, 241
Gardner, 100, 113
Gardner, Henry, 101, 135, 210, 220, 222, 226
Gardner, Michael, 243
Garner, Allen, 211
Garner, Allen, Jr., 150
Garner, Bert, 164
Garner, Dr. Emma, 191
Garner, Joe A., 116n, 170
Garner, Julia, 163
Garner, Dr. Jeptha D., 128, 162, 163, 164, 176, 188, 191, 247
Garner, William O., 161, 259
Garrard, Brittain, 114
Gerrard, Rev. Brittain, 248
Garrett, Lewis, 111
Garrett, 152
Garrett, Wm., 112
Garst, S. H., 131
Gass, Juliett, 75
Gaston, J. B., 266
Gatlinburg, 60n, 66
Gault, John, 101
Gault, S. H., 160, 176, 188, 189, 269, 281
Gault, William, 73, 87
Gault House, 73

INDEX 347

Gay Fire Co., 259
Gay, H. T., 116
Gay, Hiram, 253, 257, 259
Gay, Rev. John Lenoir, 124, 125
Gayley, James, 34, 36
General Assembly of the Territory, 31, 97, 138, 206, 208, 255
General Caswell, 211
General Education Board, 144
General Sessions Court, 216
General Sherman, 185
George, Alex, 211
George, C. N., 120
George, Edward, 43, 45, 175, 279
George, J. M., 248, 268
George, S. E., 108
George, Samuel L., 76, 151, 164, 196
George's Mill, 51
Georgia, 40, 53, 55, 57, 79, 81
Gertrude Apartments, 178
Gettys and McKeldin, 225
Ghormley, Capt. Dewitt, 65
Ghormley, Hugh, 187, 280
Ghormley, Dr. Samuel, 187
Ghormley's Chapel, 115
Gibbons, Averell S., 250
Gibbons, Frank, 250
Gibbs, Prof. School, 168
Gibbs, 109
Gibson, F., 239
Gifford, Miss Rhoda, 168
Gilbert Bros., 268
Gilbert, George S., 146, 241, 268
Giles County Virginia, 87
Gillespy, 20, 21, 39, 100, 107, 151
Gillespy, Campbell, 73, 256
Gillespie, Miss Ellen, 109
Gillespy, E. J., 107, 151, 152
Gillespy, James, 25, 55, 73
Gillespy, James Jr., 135, 136, 218
Gillespy, Capt. James, 44, 136, 298
Gillespy, Dr. James, 136, 174, 175, 183, 184, 210, 220, 235, 236, 274
Gillespy, Jane, 105
Gillespy, John, 151, 266
Gillespy, Dr. J. C., 186, 269
Gillespy, John Finley, 135, 184, 210, 250
Gillespy, Robert, 223
Gillespy, Dr. Samuel, 275
Gillespy, Wm., 33, 85, 209
Gillespie's Landing, 244, 266, 257
Gillespie's Ironworks, 244, 266
Gillespie's Mill dam, 240
Gillespie's Mineral Springs, 86
Gillespy's Station, 18

Gillespy, James H.'s Tavern House, 43, 73
Gingko Trees, 81
Ginn, Jeptha, 123
Girl Scouts, 231
Glass, 100
Glass, John E., 247
Glass, Samuel, 30, 31, 33n, 43, 210, 241
Gloucester, Jack, 161
Goddards, 216, 245
Goddard, Alexander, 189, 196
Goddard, Andrew, 228
Goddard, Arthur B., 216
Goddard, A. O., 93
Goddard, Edith, 264
Goddard, Della, 264
Goddard, Capt. Elias, 61, 191
Goddard, Gladys, 93n
Goddard, Homer A., 211, 216
Goddard, Houston, 216
Goddard, James A., 65, 115, 141, 225, 249
Goddard, Dr. John A., 191, 196, 206, 207
Goddard, John L., 211, 214
Goddard, Leonard, 66, 228
Goddard, Monroe, 142, 168, 261
Goddard, Robert, 189
Goddard, Samuel, 189
Goddard, Lt. Thomas W., 68
Goddard, Prof. V. F., 178
Goddard, William, 74, 160, 232
Goetz, Dr. E., 186, 269
Goetz, Dr. Thomas O., 195
Goforth, Zachariah, 34
Gold Creek Falls, 84
Gold Creek Mine, 84
Golden Rule Stove Co., 245
"Good roads commission", 205
Goodhue, Daniel F., 84
Goodpasture, 1
Goodwin, John, 242
Gore, Savannah George, 162
Gorley, 129
Gossett, Calvin, 58n
Gothard, Dr., 83, 190
Gourley, 247
Gourley, John, 64
Gourley, Dr. Marcellus, 190
Governor Blount, 210
Governor Dinwiddie, 4
Governor Glen, 3, 4
Governor Lyttleton, 5
Grace, George, 56n
Graham, Thomas E., 98
Graham, Wm. E., 98
Grainger, Mary, 31

Grainger County, Tenn., 58, 182
Grand Lodge, 148
Grand and Petit jurors, 209
Grant, 63
Granville, Lord, 9
Grassy Valley, Knox County, 138
Gravelly Hill School, 154
Gray, Rev., 123n
Gray, Thomas, 209
Gray, William, 105
Gray-Knox Marble Company, 238
Gray Ridge, 243
Great Smoky Mountains Conservation Association, 277
Great Smoky Mountains National Park, 277, 278
Great Southern Marble Co., 237
Great Tennessee, 15
Great War Trail, 7
Great War Path, 15
Green, Miss Susan, 246
Greene, James J., 39, 265
Greene County, 13, 14, 31, 64, 87, 124, 153
"Green Tree", 73
Greenback, 107, 266
Greenback Industries, 78
Greenlee, 225
Greeneville, 15
Greeneville College, 139
Greenaway, James, 32, 33n, 34
Greenway, Kate P., 109
Greenway, Margaret V., 109
Greenway, Mrs. Penelope, 109
Greenwood, 215
Greers, 102
Greer, Andrew, 10, 13
Greer, Arthur, 74
Greer, E. C., 157
Greer, J. M., 85, 253
Greer, Joseph C., 88
Greer, J. H. and Co., 74
Greer, J. W., 160
Greer, L. L., 157
Greer, S. S., 157
Greer, S. L., 48
Gregg, Herman, 17
Gregory, 277
Gregory, Brinton, 212
Gregory, Russell, 65
Gregory, Walter, 114
Gregory, W. A., 123
Gregory's Bald, 84
Griffin, Daniel, 203
Griffin, E. W., 191
Griffitts, 217, 270

Griffitts, John, 99
Griffitts, Sam, 222
Griffitts, William, 225
Grigsby, Simeon B., 209
Grindstaff, 129, 247
Grindstaff, William, 119, 247
Grindstaff Pottery, 247
Grindstaff School, 176
Grinnell, Dr. Fordyce, 189, 212
Grinnell, Jeremiah, 128, 162
Grinnell, J. A., 128
Grinnell, Joseph, 189
Grinnell, Rev. Martha, 128
Grizzard, Henry, 285
Groner, Jesse, 260
Grover, Sam, 64
Groves, C. S., 130, 226
Guilford, Martha, 86
Guinn, Isham, 118
Gunion and Nooncesser, 247
Gunn, Lt. (later Capt.), John T., 63
Gunnings Chapel, 10
Gunpowder, 56
Gunsmith, 265
Gunter's Landing, 220
Guyot, Arnold, 83

Hackney, 222, 270
Hackney, Aaron, 58, 127
Hackney, Billy, 206
Hackney, Francis, 155
Hackney, Frank, 64
Hackney, George, 64
Hackney, Hugh, 126, 157
Hackney, H. S. W., 157
Hackney, John, 41, 154, 157, 281
Hackney, John, Jr., 155
Hackney, J. L., 220, 242
Hackney, William J., 63
Hackney Mill, 230
Haddon, Elisha, 17
Hadley, Ruthana, 159
Hadley, Stephen M., 158
Hafley, C. A., 222
Haggard, Henry, 118
Haggard, Pink, 253
Haggard, Una, 73
Haggard Family, 93
Haines, Margaret, 157
Haines, Robert B., 157, 163
Hair, I. N., 247
Hair, J. A., 99
Haire, John E., 270
Hale, William, 113n
Hale, William T., 162, 178
Hale School (Negro), 162

INDEX

Hale & Hollifield, 241, 282
Halifax County, Va., 8
Hall, 101
Hall, Allen, 157
Hall, Charles, 179
Hall, Rev. E. W., 96, 101, 104, 106
Hall, Dr. Joe E., 89
Hall, J. E., 191
Hall, Nellie Leonard, 91n
Hall, W. B., 240
Hamil, 105, 129
Hamil, David, 100
Hamil, Henry, 43
Hamil, John W., 65
Hamil, Samuel, 173
Hamil Graveyard, 282
Hamil Quarry, 238
Hamilton, George William, 116
Hamilton, Mrs., 65
Hamilton, William, 32, 34
Hamilton, Col. W. D., 237, 239
Hamilton, W. S., 239
Hamilton, William E., 240
Hamilton County, 40
Hamilton District, 29n
Hamilton Slate, 231
Hammond, 116
Hammontree, 102
Hampton, J., 120
"Hanging Maw", 24, 27, 28, 29
Hanging, 269
Hanlin, John T., 89
Hanlin, Lydia E., 89
Hanlon Spoke and Stave Company, 231
Hann, C. C., 239
Hannah, 129
Hanna, Andrew, 29, 115
Hannah, Bob, 88n
Hannah, Chris, 65n
Hannah, G. F., 190
Hannah, Col. Harvey, 66
Hannah, John, 36, 97
Hannah, John A., 129
Hannah, Joseph, 72
Hannah, J. R., 89
Hanna, J. T., 226, 238
Hanna, Roll, 263, 226
Hannah, Sam, 36
Hannah, William, 97
Hannah's Branch, 218
Hannah's Button Factory, 238
Hannum, 109, 223
Hannum, David, 253
Hannum, Dr. Henry, 43, 185
Hannum, James, 188
Hannum, Dr. J. W., 189

Hannum, Capt. W. Y. C., 61, 62, 76, 112, 228
Hanover Presbytery, 97n
Happy Hollow, 177
Happy Valley, 79, 122, 164, 171, 176, 179, 189, 245, 247, 274
Hard Labor, Treaty of, 8
Hardeman's Brass Band, 147, 257
Hardin, John, 43
Hardin, Jordan C., 83
Hardin, Robert, 140n
Harding, Monroe, 86
"Hard Shell", 123
Hardwood Lumber Company, 231
Harnessmaker, 241
Harper, 129
Harper, A. K., 112, 263
Harper, Mrs. A. K., 264
Harper, Lt. Milton L., 68, 263
Harper, Thomas, 120
Harper Furniture Store, 261
Harper Memorial Library, 264
Harper Street, 263
Harrill, Dr. J. G., 93
Harris, 101
Harris, James R., 222
Harris, Will T., 170
Harris Mill, 222
Harriman, Tenn., 215
Harrison, Henry L., 190
Harrison, Capt., 26
Harrison, Rev. William, 98
Harrison Construction Company, 254
Hart, 101, 109
Hart, Isaac, 114
Hart, Joseph, 97, 100, 103, 268
Hart, Thomas N., 103
Hart's Chapel, 103
Hartsell, Heartsill, 109
Hartsell, Abram, 77, 146, 231, 268
Hartsell, Hiram, 77, 146, 268, 269
Hartsell, J. E., 269
Haskins, Ida F., 239
Haskins, Joseph, 128
Haskins, W. A., 239
Haskins and Morris, 239
Hastings, Letitia, 162
Hastings, Linnaeus, 50n, 259
Hastings, William P., 161, 228, 245
Hatcher, Elijah, 65n
Hatcher, Mrs. Elijah, 119
Hatcher, Pvt. Sam, 68
Hathaway, Dr. W. E., 190
Haven's Chapel, 115
Haverford College, 158
Hawkins, 35
Hawkins, Benjamin, 217

350 INDEX

Hawkins Line, 255, 273
Hawkins County, 15, 58
Haworth, D. Riley, 164
Hayes, "Cad", 242
Haynes, Rev. L. K., 66, 117
Hays, George, 29
Hays, John, 113
Haywood, 17
Hazlewood, N. C., 275
Hazen, James, 36
Headquarters and Headquarters Battery 191st AFA, 69
Headrick, Wm., 59n
Health Department, 48, 203
Health Officer, 48, 187, 191, 192
Health Unit, 192, 193
Heard, Stephen, 209
Herrons, 247
Hearons, 278
Hearon, Jerry, 247
Heaton, Wm., 130
Heaton's Station, 11
Hedge, James B., 264
Hedge, James R., 229
Hedge, Kathryn Rees, 229
Heiskell, J. M., 115
Heiskill's Mill, 221
Helsey, Mrs., 177
Hembree, Sgt. Wm. T., 69
Hemp Factory, 224, 265
Henderson, 26, 105
Henderson, James, 112n
Henderson, J., 120
Henderson, Richard, 10
Henderson, William, 152
Henderson and Company, 256
Henderson Johnson and Company, 182
Hendrixson, J., 120
Hendron, James, 57n
Henley's, 234
Henley, Arthur H., 71
Henley, Lena, 89
Henry, 113
Henry, Alexander, 76
Henry, Arthur, 43
Henry, Brothers, 267, 268
Henry, C. W., 165, 167, 171
Henry, Miss Clemmie, 144
Henry, David, 242
Henry, David C., 116
Henry, Ezekiel, 36
Henry, George, 77
Henry, F., 63
Henry's Ferry, 234
Henry, H. H., 103n

Henry, Jacob, 159, 160, 178, 248
Henry, James H., 176
Henry, James, 43, 101n, 101, 122, 243, 248
Henry, James W., 36
Henry, James M., 61
Henry, Capt. James M., 63
Henry, Jasper, 259
Henry, John, 220
Henry, Mrs. John, 101n
Henry, John F., 59, 99, 146, 267
Henry, Mrs. John F., 63
Henry, John R., 219
Henry, Lou Goddard, 103n
Henry, Margaret, 177
Henry, Miss Margaret, 143, 144, 177
Henry, Mrs. M. E., 109
Henry, Pleas, 116, 234
Henry, Samuel, 98, 99, 217, 219, 221, 282
Henry, Samuel of Little River, 219
Henry, Capt. Sam., 27
Henry, Sam, 31
Henry, Samuel and Sons, 267
Henry, Spencer, 41, 112n, 114, 115, 117, 148
Henry, Rev. Spencer, 148
Henry, Spenser, 45
Henry's Station, 15, 20, 21, 26, 28, 282
Henry Mill, 41
Henry, Samuel's Station, 24
Henry, W. H., 61
Henry, William H., 249
Henry, Wm. H., 109
Henry, Capt. W. H., 263
Herders, 277
Hertzler, Mac, 154
Hess, John, 218, 273
Hess's Creek, 245, 273, 277
Hess's Mill, 219, 221
Hickory Grounds, 55
Hickory Valley, 270
Hickory Valley Meeting, 128, 129
Hickory Valley Monthly Meeting, 158
Hicks, Elihu, 119
Hicks, Zachariah, 119
"Hide Park", 282
Higgins, Miss, 162
High School Board, 159, 169, 202
High School, 170
Highland Presbyterian Church, 251
Highway 411, 79, 219
Highway Commission, 204
Hilbert, J. B., 131
Hill, Albert, 94
Hill, Owen, 94
Hill, Thomas, 120
Hill, Dr. Thomas, 123

INDEX 351

Hillsboro, North Carolina, 12, 13
Hinds, Isaac, 123
Hines, J., 222
Hindenburg Line, 68
Hindman, Samuel, 29
Hinton, Jeff, 64
Hinton, S. C., 168
Historical Marker, State Highway, 134
Hitch, 121
Hitch, Aunt Jennie, 121
Hitch, Mrs. John, 175
Hitch and Peery, 221
Hitchcock, Rev. Roswell D., 142
Hiwassee, 12, 29, 99
Hiwassee Association, 119
Hiwassee Canal, 235
Hiwassee District, 200
Hiwassee Presbytery, 108, 151, 152, 153
Hiwassee Railroad, 44, 235
Hiwassee River, 16
Hodsden, Alonzo, 67
Hodsden, Dr. Robert H., 136, 183, 185
Hodge, H. T., 223
Hodgson, Joseph, 92, 93n, 226
Hodson, Robert, 57n
Hoffmeister, H. L., 205
Holder, Ben, 119
Holder, John, 130
Hole, Prof. Wilson, 164
Holiness Campground, 270
Holland, A. G., 126
Holland, Capt. William, 61
Holliday, George and Merrill, 245
Hollifield, J. D., 242
Holloway, Billy, 119
Holloway, John, 119
Holloway, William, 123
Holston, 6, 13, 19, 21, 24, 26, 154, 233
Holston Academy, 153
Holston Circuit, 110
Holston College, 107, 108, 112, 116, 146, 151, 234
Holston College Church, 154
Holston River, 7, 35, 181, 210, 265
Holston Seminary, 146
Holston Treaty, 35
Holston Valley, 8
Holt, James W., 242
Home Avenue, 50, 191
Home Guard, 59, 63, 65
Home Guard Muster Roll, 318
Homeopathist, 190
Honeycut, John, 9
Hood, 100, 101, 109
Hood, Frank Marion, 75
Hood, F. M., 247
Hood, John, 100, 101n, 146

Hood, Joseph and Frank R., 253
Hood, Robert N., 61, 84, 212
Hood, R. N., 85, 150, 168, 211, 246, 258
Hood, Gen. R. N., 228
Hood, Mrs. Sarah Henry, 177
Hooke, Lida, 264
"Hookworm Dispensaries", 192
Hopkins, Johns, 193
Hopkinsian, 105
Hopkinsian Sacrament, 94n
Hopewell, 122
Hopewell Springs, 164
Hord, B. M., 239
Hord, Octavia Warren, 162
Horse races, 135
Horse racing, 261
"Horseshoe Bend", 220, 229
Hosiery Mill, 262
Hospital Committee, 194
Hot Springs, Arkansas, 189
Hot Springs, North Carolina, 77, 256
Houk Post Office, 282
"The House in the Woods", 144
Housem, Robert, 17
Houser, Jonathan, 60, 61
Houser, Monroe, 124
Household Remedies, 190, 195
Houston, 15, 96
Houston, James, 30, 33n, 34, 58n, 99, 121, 136n, 139n, 218, 222, 223
Houston, James, Jr., 33
Houston, James, Sr., 135
Houston, Maj. James, 16, 39, 104, 206
Houston's Station, 15, 17, 19, 95
Houston, James A., 210
Houston, J. A. and Co., 257
Houston, John, 17n, 40
Houston, Matthew, 244
Houston, Robert, 39, 135, 206
Houston, R. L., 168
Houston, Sam, 30, 34, 39, 54, 56, 77, 207, 210, 284
Houston, Samuel, 33, 223, 256
Houston, Gen. Sam., 25n, 248, 257
Houston, Maj. Sam, 25n
Houston, Rev. Sam, 14, 97
Houston Memorial Chapel, 104
Howards, 114, 221
Howard, George, 240
Howard, Gen. O. O., 62, 141
Howard, Gen., 142n
Howard, Roy, 130
Howard, W. B., 51
Howard Farm, 237
Howe, A. G., 211, 213
Hoyl, Dr. John, 185

Hoyle, Rev. D. C., 108, 109
Hoyt, Rev. Ard., 139
Hoyt, Rev. Darius, 100, 139, 226
Hubbard, 68n, 170
Hubbard, Major, 16
Hudgeons, 102
Hudson, Jeremiah, 73
Hudson, John E., 112n, 115
Hudson, Richard, 218
Huddleston, A. D., 264
Huddleston, Elizabeth, 49n
Huddleston, Dr. H. P., 196
Hughes, 234, 271
Hughes, J. W., 264
Hughes, William, 218, 271
Hughes' Mill, 219
Huffacre, George, 21
Huffsteller, Glenn, 259
Huffsteller, W. L. (Jack), 260
Huffsteller's Store, 222, 247, 282
Hulquist, Victor J., 285
Humes, David, 206
Humes, Mr., 269
Hunt, Rev. A. M., 108, 154
Hunnicutt, R. D., 253
Hunter, Charles, 253
Hunter, E. E., 253
Hunter, Edwin R., 144
Hunter, John A., 126
Hunter, Walter, 253
Hunter's Station, 16
Huntsville, Alabama, 73n, 77
Hurley, 109
Hurley, D. D., 109
Hurley, D. P., 150
Hurst, Major L. R., 149
Hurst, Mary, 149
Huskey, Steve, 221
Hussey, Christopher, 218
Hutton, C. A., 107
Hutton, Joseph A., 106
Hutsell, 129, 131
Hutsell, George, 61
Hutsell, G. W., 150
Hutsell, Mrs. M. E., 122
Hyatts, 275
Hyder, R. L., 191
Hyder, Dr. R. L., 193

Ideal Hosiery Mills, 226
Incorporate, Act to, 42
Indian Depredations, 271
Indian Line, 35
Indian School, 164
Indian Territory, 21
Indian Trading Post, 271
Indiana, 128, 157, 229

Indiana Yearly Meeting, 163
The Independent, 74, 228
The Indicator, 228
Industrial Home, 48, 203
Industrial School, 50
Infantry, 57
Inglis, Thomas, 29
Ingleside Hotel, 76
Illinois, 85, 105, 128
Illinois Cavalry, 62
Innwood Sanatarium, 191
Inskip, 186
Inspection Port, 266
"Intruders", 35, 271, 273
Iowa, 105, 128, 157
Iredell, James, 49
Iron Industry, 244
Iron Spring, 84
Ironworks, 272
Irvine, Prof. B. V., 107, 152
Irwin, Luther, 151
Isbill, John, 41
Ish, Alexander, 29, 107, 113, 146, 152
Ish, Ben, 64
Ish, Elizabeth, 217, 218
Ish, John, 18, 28, 29, 32n, 186
Ish, J. G., 160
Ish, Thomas, 217
Ish's Mill, 27, 217, 218
Ish's Station, 20, 21, 26
Isham, A. J., 191

Jabez Coulson & Co., 265
Jack, John F., 209
Jackson, 26, 40, 101
Jackson, General, 55, 56, 73
Jackson, Andrew, 36, 53
Jackson, Rev. A. N., 267n
Jackson, Charles C., 211, 215
Jackson, Eva, 63
Jackson, George C., 76, 211, 214, 229, 261
Jackson, John, 224
Jackson, "Stonewall", 62
Jackson, House, 76, 214
Jackson County, Alabama, 183
Jacksonville, Alabama, 182
Jail, County, 35, 37, 40, 43, 46, 48, 49, 50, 187, 256, 264
James, 83, 102
James, Anna, 187
James, Elijah, 122
James, L. B., 115
James, Robert, 125, 225, 280
James, William, 225, 280
James Family, 226
Jay County, Indiana, 87, 89
Jefferson, Thomas, 152

Jefferson Medical School, 183
Jefferson Woolen Mills, 226
Jefferson County, 15, 24, 30, 58, 96, 239
Jeffrey, Jeremiah, 29
Jeffrey's Hell, 231, 286
Jeffries, William, 60, 61n
Jena Station, 107
Jenkins, Dr. L. J., 190, 192
Jenkins, Tom, 66
Jennings, John H., 115
Jennings, Dr. Royal, 196, 213
Jessup, Levi, 160
Job, Dr. Abraham, 111, 173, 220, 276
John, Earl of Loudoun, 5
John, Rev. Leroy, 125
John, Mrs., 63
Johnson, Mrs. B. B., 194
Johnson, D. B., 107
Johnson, D. M., 99
Johnson, Elkanah, 120
Johnson, J., 120
Johnson, James, 152
Johnson, Joseph, 173
Johnson, Luther, 17
Johnson, Robert, 130
Johnson, Hon. Sam, 170, 171, 211, 215
Johnson, William, 118
Johnson, Sir William, 8
Johnson, W. T., 268
Johnson and Cassidy, 258
Johnson and Law, 76
Johnson and Swan, 241
Johnson Mill, 218
Johnson County, 130
Johnson City, Tenn., 83
Johnson Island, Sandusky, Ohio, 187
Johnston, Josiah, 219
Jones, 114, 270
Jones, Ann, 126
Jones, Dr. A. L., 189, 190
Jones, David, 48, 85, 86, 151, 156, 230, 251
Jones, Capt. Caleb, 17
Jones, Charles, Sr., 88
Jones, Mrs. Charles, 87n
Jones, Elias, 281
Jones, Francis, 126
Jones, Hezekiah, 127
Jones, James, 59, 270
Jones, Gov. James C., 43
Jones, Johnston, 126
Jones, Josh R., 87n, 89
Jones, J. B., Sr., 238
Jones, Lucinda, 157
Jones, Margaret, 126
Jones, Mary J., 108

Jones, Moultrie, 88
Jones, Nancy, 108
Jones, Ole Bull, 88
Jones, Palmyra, 156
Jones, S. L., 189
Jones, Thomas, 126
Jones, Thomas M., 155, 157
Jones, William, 281
Jones, 102
Jones Beals and Co., 222
Jones' Bend, 188
Jones Brothers Orchestra, 88
Jones and Cowan, 266
Jones County, 280
Jonesboro, 13, 14, 105n
Julian, George, 114
Julian, James, 114
Junaluska Tannery, 275
Junction Railroad, 44, 235
Juniata Marble Company, 237
Junior High School, 170
Jury Commission, 209
Justices of the peace, 198
Juvenile Court, 199, 208

Kagleys, 92
Kagley, James A., 130
Kagley's Schoolhouse, 115
Kansas, 128, 156
Karr, Matthew, 21
Kay, L. C., 242
Kee, Peter, 243
Keeble's Chapel, 104
Keith, Charles, 209
Keller, 129, 130
Keller, F. W., 269
Keller, F. W. & Co., 268
Keller, T. W., 109, 153
Keller, W. S., 176
Kelly, Col. Alexander, 30, 32n, 266
Kelly, Captain Alexander's Company, 299
Kelly, Thomas D., 216
Kelly, Field, 69
Kelly's Mill, 33, 217
Kelly's Station, 25
Kelso, Charles, 39, 265
Kelso, Hugh, 39, 218, 265
Kelso's Ferry, 234
Kelso's Mill, 265
Kendall, Thomas S., 59, 105, 146
Kentucky, 10
Kennedy's, 221
Kennedy, Alexander, 73, 75, 85, 220, 224, 229, 243, 279, 280
Kennedy, Andrew, 56, 134, 218

Kennedy, Arthur, 220, 268
Kennedy, A. A., 225, 279
Kennedy, C. M., 92, 167, 168
Kennedy, Col. Daniel, 16
Kennedy, J. M., 148, 257
Kennedy's Mill, 51, 219, 222, 230
Kennedy Papers, 224, 268
Kennedy's Warehouse, 269
Kerr, 101
Kerr, G. C., 87
Kerr, Jesse, 106, 190
Kerr, Jesse, Jr., 87, 152, 187
Kerr, John, 29, 174
Kerr (Kyker) House, 62
Kerr, W. W., 107
Kidd, J. M., 61
Kidd, Perry H., 115
Kidd Farm, 51
Kidd's Schoolhouse, 102
Killebrew, James K., 175, 221
King, Charles S., 83
King, George, 5
King, Henry, 60n
King, James I, 1
King, Joseph L., 82, 83
King, Major, 19, 28
King, William S., 243
King College, 167
King & Montgomery, 256
King's Mountain, 12
Kingsport, 8
Kingston, 63, 77, 207, 233, 266
Kinzel, E. J., 90, 283
Kinzel, Sophie, 90n
Kinzel Springs Hotel, 283
Kinzel Springs, 90
Kinnamon, A. K., 102
Kip Skins, 241
Kirby, 188
Kirby, Frances, 115
Kirby, James, 219
Kirby, Richard, 115
Kirk, John, 16, 17, 217
Kirk, W. H., 252
Kirkpatrick, 96
Kirkpatrick, Andrew, 243
Kirkpatrick, Robert, 29
Kithcart, Paul & R. S., 242
Kithcart, R. S., 50n
Kittrell, S. S., 190
Kiwanis, 193, 216
Kizer, 271
Kizer, Ben W., 216
Kizer, Ezekias, 115
Kizer, George, 131
Kizer, J. L., 205

Kizer's Schoolhouse, 115
Kleppers, 131
Knabe, G. R., 148
Knapp, Dr. G. A., 144, 246
"Knights of the Grip," 74
Knox County, 13, 14, 24, 27, 29n, 30, 31, 42, 52, 55n, 57, 58, 217, 255
Knoxville, 13, 26, 31, 52, 58, 62, 257
Knoxville and Augusta Railroad, 212, 236, 251, 253, 272, 274
Knoxville and Charleston Railroad, 44, 45, 49, 83, 236
Knoxville Garden Clubs, 70
Knoxville and Maryville Electric Railroad Company, 237
Knoxville, Montvale, and Chilhowee Railroad, 236
Knoxville Municipal Airport, 52
Knoxville Power Company, 233, 240, 285
"Knox-Pure," 250
Knoxville and Southern Railroad, 235
Koehler, William, 229
Koella, Ernest, 194, 225, 260
Kountz, Adam, 114
Kountz, Isaac, 114
Koonts, Samuel, 242
Kosmos Club, 177
Kramer, 215
Kramer, D. S., 211, 215
Kramer, R. R., 211, 215
Kramer & Kramer, 215, 216
Krause, Dr. N. T., 189, 269

Lackey, Captain, 35
Lackey, Dr. James R., 156
Lackey, James W., 16
Lackey, James Woods, 30, 271
Lackey, John, 218
Lackey's Creek, 32n, 217, 218, 244
Lackey, S. A., 154
Lain, Paten, 106
Lake Sidney Lanier, 84, 85
Lamar, Mrs. Martha Tedford, 49n, 104
Lamar, Prof. T. J., 137, 140, 141, 153, 175, 320
Lamar, Rev. T. J., 98, 101, 102, 104
Lamar Chapel, 104
Lamar House, 81, 84n
Lamar Memorial Library, 142
Lamberts, 119
Lambert, James, 77
Lambert, John Sr., 39, 77, 265
Lamon, F. H., 49, 151, 164n, 211, 214

INDEX 355

Lamon, H., 164
Land, 129
Lane Brothers, 186
Lane, Charley, 85
Lane, Dr. Charles M., 187, 190
Lane, Dick, 85
Lane, E. Ross, 187
Lane, Elder Tidence, 12
Lane, Dr. James M., 188
Lane, J. R., 131
Lane, O. M., 131
Lane, Samuel D., 187, 209
Lane, William A., 74, 84
Lane, William M., 102
Langford, James, 123
Lanier, 170
Lanier, Sampson, 81
Lanier, Sidney, 82, 171
Lanier, Sterling, 81
Lanier, William B., 82
Lanier High School, 171
Lapsley, Joseph R., 99, 134, 135
Larsen, Dr. B. M., 110
Lashley, 20, 24, 21
Lasseter, Wiley, 76
Lasseter, Z. H., 261
Laurel Bank Church, 122, 123
Laurel Creek, 230, 236, 272, 278
Laurel Gap, 236
Laurel Lake, 91
Law, 130
Law, James, 105
Law, S. D. W., 152
Laws Chapel, 123, 219
Lawn Socials, 262
Lawrence, 240
Lawrence, C. B., 229
Lawrence, Daniel W., 159
Lawrence, Joseph P., 84, 89
Lawrence, Will W., 85, 112n, 115, 253
Lawson Brothers, 221
Lawson, Geo. W. & Co., Grocers, 242
Lawson, Hetty Morton, 103n
Lawson, Rev. J. D., 60, 66, 103n, 114
Lawson, J. N., 108
Lawson, Dr. K. B., 130
Lawson, L. D., 190
Lea, Benjamin H., 141
Lea Springs Hotel, 84n
Leake, Arch, 209
Learn, 129
Lebanon, 107
Lebanon in the Forks, 95
Lebow, Isaac, 115
Le Conte, Joseph, 83
Lee, Asbury, 230, 272
Lee, Ephriam, 58n, 126, 155

Lee, Jonathan, 157
Lee, Dr. John M., 192
Lee, Riley, 64n
Lee, Sam, 253
Lee, T. R., 157
Lee, Wayne, 64
Lee, William, 29, 58n
Lee School for Boys, 167
Leeper, 234
Leeper, Ed., 161, 162
Leeper, S. M., 270
Leeper's Ferry, 270
Le Mans, 68
Legg, Ambrose, 229
Lemons, 276
Lemons, C., 114
Lemons, Elias A., 108
Lemons, Joseph W., 210
Lenoir, W. B., 239
Lenoir City, 237
Lequire, Dr. G. D., 193, 194
Lequire, Willis, 221
Lewis, Major Andrew, 4, 6, 63
Lewis, W. G., 177
Lewis, William, 157
Levering, 128
Liberia, 59, 161
Liberty, 122
Liberty Christian Church, 129
Library, 263
Library Board, 264
Light Pink, 238
Lighters, 220
Lillard, Catherine, 161, 162
Lillard, Thomas, 116, 160
Lillard, T. B. School, 162, 178
Lillard, William C., 80
Limestone Church, 105
Limestone, 286
Lincoln Memorial University, 142n
Lincoln Park, 286
Lincoln Road, 178
Lindsay, Mrs. Ova Belt, 89n, 113n, 282
Linville Improvement, 275
Litchfield County, Conn., 94, 185
Liquor-selling, 51
Literary Society Hall, 140
Lithia Springs, 93
Little Mountain, 231
Little Pigeon, 3
Little River, 13, 15, 18, 19, 20, 21, 25 31, 61, 63, 77, 102, 113n, 114, 170, 218, 219, 220, 224, 229, 230, 255, 259, 279, 181, 283, 184, 186, 188, 117

356 INDEX

Little River Circuit, 113, 114, 117
Little River Gorge, 273
Little River Light & Power Co., 260
Little River Lumber Company, 170, 177, 230, 272, 277
Little River Post Office, 279
Little River Railroad, 230, 236, 272
Little River Railroad Line, 273
Little River Shoals, 268
Little River Station, 251
Little Tennessee, 3, 5, 25, 31, 102, 233, 239, 255
Little Tennessee River, 4, 13, 189, 265, 280, 284, 285
Lloyd, Prof. A. H., 158
Lloyd, Dr. Ralph W., 145
Lloyd, Glenn A., 145
Lobenstein, Max, 225
Lomax, Theophilus, 120
Lonas, 130
Lones, Captain, 68
Lottery, 136
Lawrence, J. P. & Brothers, 265
Love, 129, 243, 266
Love, A. H., 62n, 77, 269
Love, C. R., 176
Love, James R., 148, 224, 257, 279
Love, Dr. John T., 62, 63, 186, 269
Love, Mary, 63, 74n
Love, Rev. Mattison, 129
Love, Preston Blount, 228
Love, Samuel, 38, 74, 256
Love, William H., 76
"Love's Tavern," 74
Love & Company, 256
Lovingood, Dr. W. B., 190, 192
Louis Philippe of France, 72
Louisville, History of, 62
"Lower Road," 81, 247
Lower Towns, 4, 6, 21
Lowe's Ferry, 35n, 157, 267
Lowe, Abraham's Ferry, 233
Lowe, Lt. Claude O., 68
Lowe, E. H., 191
Lowry, 102
Lowry, Benjamin, 209
Lowry, Henry, 101
Lowry, John, Merchant, 38
Lowry, John, attorney, 38, 210
Lowry, John, 30, 33, 34, 35, 37, 71, 209, 210, 218, 223, 256
Lowry, John M., 103
Lowry, William, 39, 37, 34, 32, 30, 223, 234, 265
Lowry & Waugh, 72, 256
Loyal Temperance League, 263

Loyal League of America, 65
"Loyal Ladies Home Guard," 63
Lumber, 229
Lumber-Jacks, 230
Lunsford, Henry, 79, 206
Lusk, Andrew M., 209
Lutheran Church, 124

McAfee, John A., 98
McAlister, John, 25
McArthur Road, 254
McBath, A. R., 48
McCall, Prof. H. B., 165, 169, 178
McCall, J. A., 190
McCall, J. E., 102n
McCall, J. L., 99
McCallie, 96
McCallie, Arch, 243
McCallie, John, 115
McCally, Robert, 113n
McCallie School, 167
McCallins, 101
McCamie, Texas, 65, 80n
McCamy, James, 114
McCamy, James A., 257
McCamey, James L., 168
McCamey, Wm., 79, 114
McCamy's Ford, 79
McCammel, Andrew, 29
McCammon and Ammons, 76
McCammon, J. O., 99
McCammon, Oliver, 61
McCammon, Samuel's Diary, 277
McCammon Street, 40
McCampbells, 41
McCampbell G. S. W., 211, 214
McCampbell, Mrs. Ioa, 203
McCampbell, J. C., 109
McCampbell, T. J., 108
McCampbell, William, 79
McCampbell, Wm. A., 138
McCampbell, Wm. C., 61
McCarrol, A. B., 123
McCarty, John, 29
McCaully, 101
McClain, A., 114
McClain, Alexander, 46
McClain, Andrew, 44, 241, 258
McClanahan, 60, 131, 271
McClelland, Col. George R., 58
McClelland of Sullivan, 58
McClewer, John, 129
McClung, 35
McClung, Charles, 271
McClung Collection in Lawson McGhee Library, Knoxville, Tenn., 326

McClung, Wm., 99
McClung and Lowe, 195
McClure, 100, 129
McClure, Charles E., 108
McClure, W. E., 108
McCollock, Alexander, 33
McCollum, Alexander, 41
McConnells, 101, 102, 105
McConnell, Alfred, 159, 251
McConnell, James, 173
McConnell, Dr. John M., 253
McConnell, John N., 190
McConnell, Lamar, 213
McConnell, Lincoln, 213
McConnell, M. L., 61, 211, 212, 227
McCormick, Nettie, 143
McCormick, William, 230, 272
McCown, Mrs. L. W. Collection, 84, 111n, 276
McCoy, James F., 88
McCoy, Nathan, 87
McCoy and Chapman, 230
McCoy and Vandevoort, 231
McCracken, Miss Lizzie, 131
McCracken, Rev. Sam., 140
McCroskey, 96
McCroskey, Samuel, 265
McCroskey, Rev. Solon, 108, 153
McCulleys, 101, 102
McCulley, John, 106, 139
McCulley, Lowry, 253
McCullocks, 101, 171
McCullock, A. E., 252
McCullock, Dr. John A., 191
McCullock's Ford, 33
McCullock, Henry, 134
McCullock, J. A., 192
McCullock, John, 24
McCullock, John A., 190
McCullock place, 77
McCullock, Thomas, 30, 32, 217, 220, 223, 279
McDonalds, 230
McDonald, Captain Duncan, 272
McDonald, F., 231
McDowell, Ephraim, 18
McElwee Company, 225, 260
McElwee, H. M., 225
McFarland, Leonard L., 106
McFaul, J. A. Dr., 196
McGhee, Dr. Alexander, 133, 96, 183
McGhee, Alex, 139n
McGhee, A. I., 152
McGhee, Matthew and John, 184
McGhee, Dr. Barclay, 37, 57n, 58, 186, 242, 256

McGhee, Elizabeth, 109
McGhee, John, 135, 136n, 234
McGhee, John B., 234
McGhee, Mary K., 87, 88n
McGhee Brothers, 184
McGhee's Ferry, 234
McGhee House, 75
McGhee's property, 100
McGhee Street, 206
McGhee Tyson Airbase, 51, 52, 69, 70
McGhee Rest Camp, 70
McGinley, 101, 109
McGinley, W. D., 49, 122, 139, 149, 160, 168, 211, 212, 257
McGinley, Col. James, 24
McGinley, Street, 9, 212
McKamy, 105
McKamy, Capt. David, 39, 56, 175, 219, 243, 281, 306
McKamy, J. A., 147, 148
McKay, George, 172
McKee, 29, 35
McKee, John, 30, 32
McKennamon, James, 108
McKenzie, 109
McKenzie, Capt., 58
McKenzie's Hack, 84
McKenzie Hotel, 249
McKenzie House, 75, 252
McKenzie of Meigs, 58
McKenzie, Obediah, 268
McKenzie, Roderick, 73, 75, 257
McKenzie, W. G., 186
McKenzie, Dr. W. G., 266
McKinney, Eli, 122
McKinney, Irwin and Cowan, 48
McKinley Post Office, 282
McLaughlin, R. F., 285
McLin, Charles E., 109
McMahan, Dr. J. Walter, 191, 192, 285
McMinn County, 40, 61, 119, 123, 216, 58
McMinn, Joseph, 210
McMurray, 96
McMurray, Boyd, 116
McMurray, Mrs. Kathryn Romig, 144
McMurray, Samuel, 116, 242
McMurray, William, 28
McNabb, 215, 221
McNabb, Dr. C. P., 189, 190
McNabb's Mill, 219
McNabb, William, 219
McNaughton, Hart, 245
McNaughton Grate Bar Company, 245
McNaughton Manufacturing Company, 245

McNeely, Dr. S. H., 196, 189
McNutt, William B., 209
McNutt, R. L., 150
McNutt, Robert, 97
McNutt, John S., 210, 220, 257
McNutt, James, 218, 229
McNutt, H. L., 150, 47
McNutt, Alexander, 220
McReynolds Farm, 186
McReynolds, R. P., 51
McReynolds, Judge R. P., 203
McReynolds, Stephen J., 137, 43, 198, 211, 257
McTeer, 15, 63, 77, 109, 245, 289
McTeer, Dr. A. B., 50, 61, 189, 191, 192, 203, 269
McTeer, Mrs. Elizabeth, 109
McTeer, Lt. Harriet, 63
McTeer, J. A., 243
McTeer, James, 248, 266
McTeer, Mrs. Mary Wilson, 263
McTeer, Montgomery, 63, 75, 227, 231, 257
McTeer, Robert, 32n, 217
McTeer, Rosa, 162
McTeer, W. S., 159, 160, 178
McTeer, Major, 24
McTeer, Will A., 49, 51, 60, 61, 86, 99, 160, 198, 211, 212, 213, 215, 228, 258, 260, 263
McTeer, W. A., Jr., 216
McTeer, William, 41, 44, 45, 75, 81, 137, 148, 149, 150, 173, 174, 236, 238, 247
McTeer, William & Company, 257
McTeer, Kramer, Quinn, 216
McTeer's Fort, 95, 286
McTeer's Mill, 41
McWilliams, James, 105

Macadamizing Program, 263
Madison Hosiery Mill, 226
Macklin's Branch, 113
Madisonville, 57, 182, 183, 207
Magill, 225
Magill, J. H., 76
Mahoney, John S., 157
Mahoney Mill, 218
Main Street, 51
Malcom, 96
Malcom, Phebe, 109
Malcom, William, 93
Malcom, Sam, 242
Malinda Houston Tedford Gillespie Memorial Chapel, 104
Manumission, 58

Maple Springs, 82n
Marble, 237, 281
Marcum, Mrs. Josie, 74
Margaret Williamson Hospital, 191
Marietta, Ga., 270
Marmor, 238
Marquette and Joliet, 2
Marshall, Charles W., 158
Marshall, Jesse W., 158
Marshburn, William V., 158
Martha Henry Hall, 166
Martin, 113, 130
Martin Academy, 12, 133
Martin, Dr. James H., 89, 188
Martin, General, 16, 17, 18
Martin, George, 130
Martin, Governor, 10, 14
Martin, Isaac A., 141
Martin, Rev. Isaac Patton, 117n
Martin, John, 90
Martin, Moses, 100
Martin, Robert, 253
Martin, Samuel, 28
Martin's Mill, 217, 219, 220, 221
Martin and West, 222
Martindale, Franklin, 84
Mary-Knox Coach Company, 205
Maryville, 7, 24, 31, 40, 41, 42, 44, 62, 114, 115, 224, 260, 265, 272
Maryville Alcoa Daily Times, 228
Maryville Bar Association, 211, 212
Maryville Board of Commissioners, 38
Maryville Broom Factory, 252
Maryville Business College, 165
Maryville Butter and Cheese Manufacturing Co., 249
Maryville Christian Church, 130
Maryville Circuit, 116
Maryville College, 41, 59, 86, 96, 140, 166, 171, 187, 216, 256
Maryville College Literary Societies, 262
Maryville Cumberland Presbyterian Church, 108
Maryville Division of the Sons of Temperance, 147
Maryville Electric Light and Power Co., 48, 260
Maryville Enterprise, 229, 262
Maryville Exchange, 261
Maryville Female Academy, 136
Maryville Fire Department, 259
Maryville High School, 166, 171, 178
Maryville Hosiery Mill, 226
"*Maryville Hotel*," 73
Maryville Ice and Coal Co., 253
Maryville Improvement Co., 262

INDEX 359

Maryville Index, 228
Maryville Lighting Company, 260
Maryville and Little Tennessee Railroad, 237
Maryville, Map of, 38
Maryville Methodist Episcopal Church, 114
Maryville Monitor, 228
Maryville Normal and Prep. School, 162, 258
Maryville Polytechnic School, 165, 166, 170, 171
Maryville Pottery, 247
Maryville Preparatory School, 171
Maryville Presbyterian Church, 109
Maryville Religious and Literary Intelligencer, 226
Maryville Republican, 227
Maryville Savings and Loan Corporation, 246
Maryville Steam Laundry, 253
Maryville Telephone Exchange, 261
Maryville Times, 228
Maryville Union, 122
Maryville Watchman, 228
Maryville Water Commission, 259
Maryville Woolen Mills, 226, 240, 260
Maryville-Knoxville Road, 52, 66
Maryville-Knoxville Turnpike, 42
Massachusetts, 226
Massachusetts College of Pharmacy, 196
Masonic Building, 167
Masonic Female Institute, 149, 150
Masonic School Building, 262, 269
Masonic Lodge, 149, 210, 280
Mathes, Rev. Milton A., 102
Matthews, 225, 270
Matthews, General Calvin B., 67
Matthews, George, 17
Matthews, General Hugh, 66, 67
Matthews, James, 154
Matthews, S., 270
Matlock, Dr. A., 152, 190
Matlock, M., 108
Maxon, Bishop, 125
Maxwell, 77
Maxwell, Thomas, 106
Maynard, Horace, 59, 141
Mayor, 258, 263, 268
Mead, H. G., 176
Meadow, 237
Meadow High School District, 202
Meadowbrook, 286
Mean's Chapel, 108
Mean's schoolhouse, 103
Meares, R. L., 216

Media, Pennsylvania, 191
Medlin, F. M., 253
Medlock, John, 17
Meigs Co., 58
Meigs Falls, 277
Melrose Springs Hotel, 85, 251
Melrose Springs, 90, 241
Memoir of Dr. Anderson, 97
Memorial Hall, 141
Memorial Shelf, 264
Memphis, 58
Mero District, 19
M. E. Church, U.S.A., 116, 276
M. E. Church, South, 116, 117
Methodist Campground, 289
Methodist Circuit Rider, 134
Methodist Hill, 112, 210
Mexican War, 186
Mexican Muster Roll, 314
Mexican Border, 67
Mexico City, 58
Middle Cherokee Towns, 3, 6, 11, 12
Middle Tennessee, 8, 189
Middlesettlements, 95, 111, 114, 115, 128, 243
Mifflin County, Penna., 131
Mineola, New York, 68
Minnes, 97n
Minnis, John, 87
Minnis, William, 138
Minnis, Fort (Ala.), 55
Mint, 113, 115, 187, 217, 222
Mint Post Office, 289
Military Hospital, 189
Militia, 40, 53, 96
Militia Captains, 292
Militia Companies, 33, 199
Militia Spring, 36, 72
Mill Dam, 184, 224
Millennial Harbinger, 226
Miller, 130
Miller, Adalia and Samantha, 63
Miller, Andrew, 34, 273
Miller, Alexander, 273
Miller, David, 72
Miller, Henry, 112n
Miller, John, 85, 90
Miller, Joe, 251
Miller, Phineas, 223
Miller, Pleasant M., 55, 209
Miller's Cove, 42, 65n, 113, 114, 118, 122, 123, 218, 219, 221, 245, 271, 273, 275, 277
Miller's Cove Baptist Church, 111, 119, 120
Millican, Thomas, 29
Milligan, Bart, 268

Milligan, Joseph S., 43, 239
Milligan, Riley, 268
Milliken, James, 29
Millsaps, Hugh, 90
Millsaps, James, 241, 90n
Millsaps, Mrs. Nola, 90n
Millsaps, Spring, 90
Millsaps, Tanyard, 90n
Miser, G. L., 107
Miser, H. A., 107
Miser, Joseph, 101
Miser, Mabel, 154
Miser, Prof. Sam, 158
Miser and Mahoney, 221
Miser's Station, 221, 230, 242, 252
Mission Board of the Tennessee District, 131
Mississippi River, 14, 80
Missouri, 275
Mitchell, Frank, 151
Mitchell, John, 81, 272
Mitchell, John H., 259
Mobile, 235
Molded Cap Corporation, 251
Molsbee, Samuel, 131
Monkey House, 84, 190
Monkey Man, 190
Monroe County, 14, 40, 58, 119, 123, 164, 171, 189, 202, 207, 211, 216, 255, 286
Montgomery, A. B., 108
Montgomery, Andrew C., 43, 80, 148, 222, 224
Montgomery, David, 36
Montgomery, George, 219
Montgomery, Humphrey, 240
Montgomery, John, 38, 134, 135, 136, 137, 256
Montgomery, Major Lemuel P., 55
Montgomery, Capt. Robert, 300
Montgomery, Samuel, 99, 106
Montgomery, Ala., 82, 220, 235
Montvale, 41, 75, 79, 100, 125, 171, 190, 210, 219, 249, 257, 280
Montvale and Carolina Railroad, 237
Montvale Company, 82
Montvale Road, 232, 259, 261, 284
Montvale Station, 83
Montvale Turnpike Company, 75n, 84, 87
Moody, A. T. and B. T., 242
Mook, Simeon, 232
Moor, Captain (James), 35
Moore, 130
Moore, Carrie, 164
Moore, E., 115

Moore, George, 209
Moore, James, 127
Moore, James A., 239
Moore, Jesse H., 158
Moore, Rev. Mark, 134, 256
Moore, Sarah, 163
Moore, William, 135
Morgan, David, 128, 155, 157, 281
Morgan, Gideon, 39, 265
Morgan, Jepthah, 64n, 156
Morgan, Col. John H., 60
Morgan County, 215, 216
Morganton, 39, 77, 102, 106, 114, 115, 183, 186, 189, 190, 195, 218, 219, 221, 229, 234, 242, 243, 248, 265, 281
Morganton, N. C., 18
Morganton Road, 266
Morningside, 145
Moroney, Mrs. Diva Jones, 88n
Moroney, N. R., 247
Morrell, N. B., 226
Morris, John, 34, 128, 157
Morris, W., 239
Morrison, 109
Morrison, Sarah, 163
Morrison, Thomas, 118, 119
Morrow, Capt. (Knox County), 57
Morton, 102
Morton, Dr. Benjamin A., 122, 188, 189
Morton, Glenn, 69
Morton, James, 103n
Morton, Dr. John D., 188, 190
Morton, John H., 61, 90, 122, 123, 175
Morton, John W., 216
Morton, Dr. Wade, 188
Morton, William, 242
Morton Bluff, 92
Morse, George, 20
Motion Picture Theater, 262
Mt. Gilead, 112
Mt. John, 283
Mt. Lebanon, 121
Mt. LeConte, 83
Mt. Luke, 283
Mt. Mark, 283
Mt. Matthew, 283
Mt. Moriah, 114, 115
Mt. Nebo, 177, 249; Hotel, 76, 85, 86
Mt. Olive, 115
"Mount Pisgah," 182
Mt. Pleasant, 114
Mt. Tabor, 102
Mt. Vernon, 55, 100
Mt. Vernon Church, 98
Mt. Vernon School, 154
Mount and Hooper, 48, 230, 251

INDEX 361

"Mountain Homes," 245, 274
Mountain Settlement, 177
Mountain View Christian Church, 130
Mountain View Sanitarium, 194
Mountcastle, Rev. W. D., 115n
"Mule Barn," 178
Mullendore, Dr. E. H., 190
Mullendore, W. W., 93
Munch, L. S., 285
Municipal Building, 265
Munson, Spencer, 83
Murdock, William, 126
Murfreesboro Presbyterian Church, 135
Murphy, Archibald, 113n
Murphy, James, 219
Murphy, John, 206
Murphy, Nina Gamble, 91n
Murphy's Cove, 35, 273
Murphy's Mill, 247
Murray Gap, 79, 84
Murrys, 102
Muscle Shoals, 235
Music Book, 227
Muster Ground at James M. Kerr's, 41
Muster Roll, Descriptive, 53
Muster Rolls—1812, 303
Mutual Building and Loan Association, 246
Myers, "Sleepy John," 272
Myers, Phillips, 243
Myers, William, 220, 224, 272
Myers, Willis, 276
Myers Cemetery, 272
Nail's Creek, 120, 217, 220, 222, 229, 232
Nance, Mrs. Frank, 265
Nance, James, 247
"Narrows," 220, 284
Nashville Banner, 278
Nashville Medical School, 187
Natchez, 53
National Bridge (Mexico), 58
National Forest Movement, 277
National Guard, 67
Nazarene, 270
Nead, A. E., 131
Neal, C. B., 87
Neal, Rev. Henry C., 117
Neal, Nicholas, 29
Neal, William M., 87
Needham, James, 2
Neff, A. J., 228
Negro Race, 59, 211
Negro Schools, 179
Negro Baptist Church, 123
Negro Industrial Home, 49
"Neighborhood House," 50

Nelson, Joseph, 116
Nelson, 171
Nelson Chapel, 130
Newberry Female School, 128, 155
Newberry Monthly Meeting, 126, 127, 158
Newberry Preparative Meeting, 126
Newby, Anna, 165
Newcastle, 104, 115n
Newcastle-on-Tyne, 125
New England Architecture, 92
New England Friends, 160, 162
New Garden Meeting (N.C.), 126
New Hope, 122, 126, 127
New Orleans, 39, 53, 56, 57, 220, 267
Newport, 77, 275
New Providence, 15, 95, 96, 97, 100, 108, 109, 138, 139, 149, 183, 191, 213, 256.
New Providence Lodge No. 128, 146, 147
New Providence Church School, 135, 256
New Salem, 115
New School Presbyterians, 140
New Sharon, Iowa, 157
New York, 68, 225
Newman, Bluford, 91
Newman, Capt., 58
Newman, Fannie, 91n
Newman Circle, 177
Newlin, Ester, 157
Newlin, R. C., 164
Nicarauguan National Guard, 67
Nichols, Josiah and John, 256
Niles, J. W. J., 234
Niles Ferry, 108
Niles Ferry Highway, 52, 170
Nimon, Jacob, 168
Nine Mile Creek, 16, 19, 20, 28, 30, 32n, 71n, 72, 100, 120, 122, 212, 217, 218. 222, 234, 239, 240, 241, 243
Nolachucky, 9, 97n, 126
"Noonday," 24
Normal Department of Maryville College, 150
North Dakota, 213
North Branch, Kansas, 159
North Fabricating Plant, 233, 286
North Maryville, 178, 231, 285
Northwest Territory, 17
North Carolina, 6, 9, 14, 18, 19, 40, 126, 186, 271, 275, 280, 284
North Carolina Grant, 273, 291
North Carolina Legislature, 15
North Carolina Line, 13, 41

Norton, Mrs. Hugh, 264
Norton, J. N., 192
Norton, J. W., 190
Norwood, C. W., 87, 78
Norwood, John, 73, 78
Norwood, Mrs. Mary S., 109
Norwood Inn, 78, 243
Norwood Street, 31
Novelty Store, 263
Nuchols, Dr. John D., 188, 214
Nuchols, Sam, 211, 213
Nunn, Eli, 242
Nurse's Training School, 194

Oak Ridge, 70, 181, 216
Oakfuskee, 29
Oakland, 130
Oakland Circuit, 116n
Oakland Church of the Brethren, 150
Oakland Meetinghouse, 131
Oakland School, 176
Oak View, 108, 109
Oak View Cumberland Presbyterian Church, 103, 107
Oats, Roger, 27
Oats, David, 218
Obongphohego, 29
Occupancy and Pre-Emption, 275
O'Connor, Beulah Russell, 151, 107n
O'Connor, G. G., 115
Ogle, S. H., 86
Old Abraham of Chilhowee, 11, 16
Old Chilhowee, 122
"Old Field," 173
Old Hickory Division, 68
Old Piney, 123
Old School Presbyterians, 99, 122, 141
Oldham, William, 224, 279
Olentangy Mining Company, 238
Olin, Bessie Henry, 46n, 103n
Olivers, 275
Oliver, John, 122
Oliver, Robert B., 226
Oliver, William H., 123
105th Fighter-Interceptor Squadron, 69
119th Aircraft Control and Warning Flight, 69
117th Infantry Muster Roll, 325
178th Field Artillery (National Guard), 69
Optometrist, 194
Ordinary-Keepers, 34; rates, 71
Ore, Joseph, 36
Oregon, 107
Ornithologist, 189
"Orphans of the late War," 172

Orr, Horace E., 144
Orr, James K., 248, 268
Orr House, 213
Oskaloosa, 157
Ossoli, 177
Oswald, Dr. Felix, 190
Otey, Bishop, 83, 125
Our Lady of Fatima Catholic Church, 129
Outlaw, Alexander, 55

Packinghouse, 262
Padrick, Richard, 160
Palmer, Samuel, 114
Panama, 186
Panic of 1857, 236
Panther Creek, 239
Parent-Teacher Association, 170
Parham, C. L., 261
Parham, Ida Baker, 161
Parham, W. E., 49, 151, 164, 169, 183, 261
Parham, F. A., 137n, 227
Parham, W. F., 226
Parham, W. T., 65, 115, 241
Park, Jabel, 87
Park, James, 109
Park, O. G., 153
Park, Samuel, 100
Park's Ferry, 234
Park Settlement School, 177
Parker, Henry, 100
Parker, John, 162
Parker, Dr. J. M., 146
Parsons, Enoch, 55, 209, 210
Parsons, Joshua, 41, 210, 221
Parsons Bald, 84, 277
Parsons Turnpike, 41n, 276, 280, 284
Pasadena, California, 189
Passports to enter Cherokee lands—1798, 290
Pate, 77
Pate, John, 21
Pate, Walter, 131
Patent Button Company of Connecticut, 251; Tennessee, 252, 273
"Path" Deed, 10
Patrick, Hilary, 138
Patrick, William, 138
Patrick County, Va., 182
Patterson, 100
Patterson, John, 29
Patton, A., 252
Patty, Hubert, 216
Patty, Josiah, 172, 264
Patty, Joshua, 61n

INDEX 363

Pauley and Co., 49
Paul Eve Faculty Award, 188
Paul, James, 20
Payne, Charles, 17
Peabody Board, 175
Peabody Grant, 176
Pearce, 276
Pearson, Abel, 39
Pearson, Dr. Daniel K., 143
Pearson, George, 122
Pearson, Mrs. Roy, 103n
Pearson, Silas, 221
Pearson Hall, 143
Peck's Chapel, 115
Peck, Judge, 115n
Pedigo's, 222
Penland, James R., 216
Penn, W. C., 74
Penn College, 157, 158
Pennsylvania, 190, 215, 286
Penney, J. C., Store, 72
Pensacola, 56, 57
Pension Files, 53
People's Bank (Friendsville), 281
People's Telephone, 49, 261
Percefield, Van, 17
Peery Bros., 221, 281
Pershing, Gen., 68
Pesterfield, Henry Sr., 106
Pesthouse, 191
Peters, Frank, 159
Petersburg, Va., 2
Peterson, T., 115
Pfanze, Charles, 232
Pfanze, Ludwig, 84, 190
Philadelphia Friends, 155, 157, 158, 162
Philippines, 66, 229
Phillips, Abraham, 113n
Physical Education, 190
Piedmont, Airlines, 52
Pickens, 35
Pickens, John H., 168
Pickens, Oliver, 194
Pickens, Sam, 61, 186, 220
Pickens, Sam W., 61
Pickens, Thomas, 149
Pickens, William C., 61
Pigg, John, 120
Pine Grove, 102, 106, 107, 99
Piney Grove, 122
Piney Level, 120
Piper, Albert, 108
Pistol Creek, 18, 20, 25, 28, 32, 51, 104, 105, 106, 213, 217, 218, 223, 230, 256, 286
Pistol Creek Baptist Church, 121

Pistol Creek Mission, 103
Pistol Creek Seceder Church, 104
Pittsburgh Reduction Co., 233
Pittsylvania County, Va., 8
Plan of Separation, 116
Pleasant Forest, 109
Pleasant Grove, 120, 176
Poage, D. W. and Robert, 126
"Pole Bridge," 41
Police Courts, 208
Police Department, 263, 265
Polk County, 188, 214, 216
Polymathic Society of Maryville, 257
Polytechnic School, 171
Polytechnic High School and Commercial College 166
Poor Commission, 49, 203
Poor Farm, 203
Poor Tax, 38
Poore and Testerman, 215
Pope, Ann E., 109
Pope, Rev. Fielding, 137, 147
Pope, Marshall, 47
Pope, Thomas, 147, 247, 257
Porter Academy, 135, 136, 137, 138, 141, 149, 167, 171, 188, 202, 216, 256, 289
Porter High School, 170
Porter, J. A., 108
Porter, James, 45, 114, 148, 209, 220, 279
Porter, J. L., 74
Porter, James P. H., 73, 135
Porter, Robert, 44, 168, 236
Porter, Dr. William S., 86, 141, 147, 257
Portsville, 265, 39
Post, Dr. Calvin, 187
Post, Frank, 249
"Post Hacks," 249
Post place, 276
Post, Stephen, 249
Post, S. T., 76, 246
Post's Wagon Works, 75
Post Offices of Blount County, 323
Pot Rooms, 285
Potter, 247
Potter, John, 242
Powell, George, 243, 244, 276
Powell, Lt. Col. Wm. H., Jr., 69
Powell, River, 8
Powell's Station, 50
Powers, J. Pike, 86
Prater, Margaret, 154
Prater, William, 146, 152
Praters Ferry, 234
Pre-emption and Occupation, 38
Preparatory Department of Maryville College, 144, 166

Presbyterian Church, U.S., 109
"Presbyterian Hall," 149
Presbyterian Witness, 148
Presbytery of Lexington, 141
Presbytery of Brooklyn, 141
Presiding Justice, 198, 211
Price, 100, 256
Pride, John M., 185
Pride, Dr. Sam, 43, 45, 62, 136, 137, 148, 149, 163, 183, 184, 195, 236, 243, 246, 244, 257, 258
Pride Mansion, 163, 164
Pride and Barnes, 44
Priest, Martin, 29
Primitive Baptists, 123, 278
Printing Shop, 227, 258
Pritchett, Reuel B., 131n
Pritchett, Thomas J., 167
Pritchard, Robert, 239
Probate Court, 198, 208
Proffitt's, 72
Prohibition, 227
Prospect, 122, 170
Provost-Marshal, 211, 187
Psalmody or Psalm-singing, 104
Public Education, 176
Public High School, 169
Public Library, 264
Public school, 172, 151, 150, 115
Public Utilities, 265
Pugh, Wm., 113, 120
Punk Knot, 29
Purdy, Andrew, 230

Quakers, 58, 59, 63, 128, 154, 189, 258, 249
Quaker Marble Company, 238
Quaker Meetings, 126, 127
Quaker School, 62, 164, 178, 185, 191
Quarterly County Court, 209
Quiett, 271
Quinn, Pat, 211, 216
Quorum Court, 208

Racetrack, 261, 289
Racket Store, 263
Radar, 69
Rafter, Charles, 253
Ragan, Darby, 107
Ragan, Henry, 30
Ragan, John, 30
Ragan, William, 21, 30
Ragsdale, Emma, 91n
Rahobah, 114
Raiders, 64
"Raiders," 66

Railroads, 235
Railroad Fund, 45
Railroad Movement 44.
Railroad Tax, 46, 180
Ralph Max Lamar Memorial Hospital, 143
Ramsey, 18
Ramsey, George, 243
Ramsey, Dr. 196
Ramsey, R. M., 109
Randolph, William, 13
Rangers, 24, 198, 199
Rankin, 100
Rankin's John, Ferry, 234
Rankin, Rev. John, 58
Rankin, Thomas, 100
Rasars, 278
Rasar, James H., 278
Rasar Post Office, 278
Rasar, Daniel, 222
Rasar, John, 130
Rasor, William, 247
Rates, Tavern, 34
Raulston, 129
Raulston, J. P., 176
Raulston, George T., 130
Raulston, Mrs. Viola Taylor, 130n
Raulston, Wade, 130
Raulston, W. O., 150
Rawlings, John G., 239
Ray, Col. D. M., 61
Reagan, A. B., 190, 222
Reagan, Nathaniel, 265
Reagan, P. G., 222
Reagan and Presley, 252
Reconstruction Period, 98
Record the Wills, 46
Recreation and "Y" Store, 145
Red Cross, 263
"Red Stripe," 115
Reed, Alexander, 273
Reed's Creek, 221, 224, 273, 242
Reed, P. D., 131
Reeder, B. F., 279
Reeder, Frank, 207
Reeder, Major, 174
Reese, Capt., 58
Reese, W. A., 252
Reese of Jefferson, 58
Rega, 238
Regan's Chapel, 113
Regan, John, 223
Regan, Josiah, 114
Regan, Rev. J. T., 101
Regimental Muster, 172

Register, 199, 330
Register of East Tennessee, 38
Register's Record, 47
Representative, 210
Republic F, 69
Republican, 228
Revenue Commission, 201
Revolutionary Soldiers, 12, 118, 119, 288
Revolutionary War, 14, 53
Rhea, 105, 109
Rhea, Capt., 35
Rhea County, 58, 182, 185
Rhea, James, 173, 114
Rhea, John, 273
Rhea, Rev. Joseph, 10, 95, 103
Rhea, Robert, 30, 32, 56n, 278
Rhea, S. A., 149
Rhea Valley, 79, 280, 278
Rhea's, 222
Rice, 256
Richards, John, 2
Richardson, Anna, 162
Richardson, Jesse, 75, 190, 252
Richie and Benedict, 232
Richie, Thomas and Wm., 29
Richmond, Adria B., 100n
Richwood, 277, 278
Riddle, George, 66
Rife, Jacob, 18
Riley, W. B., 253
Rio Grande, 58
"Rising Sun Tavern," 71
Rittenhouse Academy at Kingston, 135
Ritter, Rev. J. C., 107, 153, 154
River Boats, 280
River Commission, 220
River Papers, 220
Riverside, 125
Road Commissioners, 204
Road Duty, 204
Road Improvement Bond Issue, 205
Road Supervisor, 204
Road Tools, 46
Roane County, 42, 55n, 207, 216
Robbins, Finley, 189
Robbins, George, 190
Roberson, 102
Roberson, James, 9
Roberson, Jesse, 41
Roberts, Eli, 121, 123
Roberts, George, 211, 216
Roberts, Robert B., 76
Roberts, J. T., 240
Robinson, 36
Robinson's, John (Circus), 262
Robinson, J. J., 99n, 101, 140

Robinson, Rev. J. T., 97
Robinson, Rufus B., 163
Robinson, Thomas, 29
Robinson, T. J., 242
Rock Crusher, 48
Rock Gardens, 286
Rockdale, 122
Rockdale School, 101n
Rockefeller, John D. Jr., 277
Rockford, 41, 62, 161, 186, 192, 217,
    219, 230, 243, 266, 272, 279
Rockford, Bridges at, 51
Rockford Cotton Mills, 64, 225
Rockford Electric Co., 260
Rockford Manufacturing, 224, 225, 279
Rockford Mills, 225, 230, 260
Rockwood Landing, 245, 269
Rocky Branch, 177, 219
Rocky Branch School, 86
"Rocky Ford," 279
Rocky Mountain, 177
Rocky Ridge Schoolhouse, 121
Roddy, John, 243
Roddy, Preston, 115
Roddy's Branch, 243
Rodgers, James, 209
Rodgers, William H., 112n, 117, 152
Rogers, Elijah, 119, 120, 123
Rogers, James, 225
Rogers, M. W., 176
Rogers, Prof. W. M., 168
Rogers, William H., 115
Rome, Ga., 27
Rooker Branch, 267
Rooker, William, 266
Rorex, Eliza, 90
Rorex, Hannah, 162
Rorex, John M., 211, 214, 219, 221
Rorex, Jack, 222
Rorex, Mary, 90
Rose, Eagle, 67
Rose, James, 275
Rosier, D. H. Jr., 216
Ross, 100
Ross, John, 115
Roswell, New Mexico, 172
"Royal Proclamation," 7
Royal Tennessee Marble Company, 237
Rowan, J. H., 102
Rowan, Sam P., 61, 160, 168, 212, 213
Roylston, Frank and T. A., 76
Rudd, 129
Rueter, Herman, 252, 262
Rule, Peter, 115
Rural Electrification Administration, 260

366   INDEX

Rural Sanitation, 192
Russell, 109
Russell, Barkley, 57n
Russell, Charles, 66
Russell, David, 38, 71, 72, 73
Russell, Hance, 36
Russell, Dr. Henry, 190
Russell, Isaac T., 176
Russell, Dr. J. L., 186
Russell, John, 152
Russell, R. D., 205
Russell, William, 128, 152, 157
Russell, W. L., 50
Russell's Ferry, 234
Russell's Ford, 266
Russam, John, 113
Rush, Mary, 181
Rusk County, Texas, 211
Rumbley, Mrs. Alice Taylor, 74n
Ryan, John, 9
Sabre Jet, 70
Saddle Shop, 241
Saddlers, 242
Saddletree, 242, 268
Saffle, 100
Saffle, Elizabeth Cox, 267
Saffell, Henry, 146, 268, 269
Saffles, John, 111
Saffell, L. B., 146
Saffle, Samuel, 112n, 240, 243, 266, 267
Saffle Tanyard, 240
Saffle's Warehouse, 269
St. Andrew's Episcopal Church, 126, 129, 251
St. John's Church, 124
St. John's Episcopal (Knoxville), 125
St. Nazaire, 68
St. Paul's, 124, 130
Sale Creek, 97
Salem Church, 12, 114, 122, 284
Saloons, 268
Saloon Keepers, 258
Salt, 184; sold in Blount County, 1862, 316
Salt Works, 46
Saltville, 9
Sams, J. T., 49
"Sam Houston" Inn, 74, 228
Sam Houston School, 178
Sample, John, 235
Samuel Shaw's Ferry, 234
Samuel Walker's Chapel, 113
Sanborn, Benjamin, 131
Sancti Spiritus, Cuba, 66
Sanderson's, 221, 229
Sanderson, Edward, 65, 141

Sanderson, Thomas, 92, 222, 226
Sandy Springs road, 261
Sandy Springs Schoolhouse, 108
Santeetlah, 232, 233, 236
Santeetlah Dam, 284
Sapling Grove, 9
"Saratoga of the South," 79
Savannah, Georgia, 235, 66
Saw gins, 223
Sawmill, 272
Professor Sawers, 165
Sawtell, Eli, 138, 139
Miss Sawyers, 167
Sawyer, Hugh W., 141
Saxon, Mrs., 263
Scaba Bay, 55
Scarlet Fever, 191
Schools, 173, 175
School Directors From the 1869 Report, 319
School Districts, 169, 172
School Funds, 48
School House Gap, 41, 245
School System, 201
School tax, 47
School taxing district, 262
Schoolmaster, 267
Scott, 129
Scott, Capt. James, 34, 35, 301
Scott, Col. James, 20
Scott, Gen., 58
Scott Brickyard, 257
Scott, Rev. Archibald, 95
Scott, Alex A. Sr., 251
Scott, James, 30, 32, 168, 218, 223, 251
Scott, W. B. Sr., 227, 228, 242, 258, 178, 159, 160
Scott, Winfield, 57
Scott Gap, 84
Scott Manufacturing Co., 251, 252
Schlosser Leather Company, 94, 170, 242, 260, 274
Scribner, Nancy C., 109
Scroggs, 101
Scull, E. L., 157, 163
Seaton, Alfred, 114
Seaton, James B., 239
Seceder Church, 59, 99, 146, 270
Seceder or "Cedar Graveyard," 104, 286
Secessionists, 59
Second Presbyterian Church, 104, 161
Second Tennessee Infantry, 62
The Secret of the East, 190
Secretary Smith, 26
Secretary of War, 20, 21, 24, 27n, 35, 36

Self-Help Scholarship Fund, 143
Self, C. C., 177
Seminole Indians, 53, 55, 56n
Service Barber Shop, 264
Sesler, Henry, 43, 44, 257
Sessler, Jake, 77
74th AirBase Squadron, 70, 69
Sevier, Elbert F., 114
Sevier, Gen., 26, 21
Sevier, Major John, 9, 11, 12, 14, 15, 18, 20, 27, 31, 34, 36
Sevier County, 13, 15, 55n, 57, 61, 114, 118, 170, 177, 185, 215, 216, 255, 273
Sevierville, 30, 77, 272, 289
Sevierville Circuit, 119
Sewers, 263
Sewer and Water System, 259
Sexton, F. T., 249
Sexton, Margaret, 122
Sexton, Rev. Tom, 122
Shadden, 96
Shadden's Mill, 221
Shady Grove, 106, 107
Shank's Spring, 41
Shanghai, China, 191
Sharp, 121
Sharp, S. Z., 160, 150, 131
Sharp, William, 29
Sharp, Robert, 20
Sharp, Miss Martha, 184
Shaw, Samuel, 270, 218, 229
Shaw's Mill, 218
Shaw's Grave, 65
Shaw's Ferry, 270
Shawneetown, Indian Territory, 196
Shelton, Dr. Azariah, 182, 196, 206
Shelton, *American Medicine*, 182
Sheriffs of Blount County, 331
Sheriff, 199
Sherril, "Bonny Kate," 11
Sherril, Dr. G. H., 188, 189
Sherril, Sam, 186, 202
Sherman Heights, 66
Sherman, General, 62
Shepherd, Robert, 125
Sheep Pen Quarries, 270
"Sheet Mill," 285, 233
Shelby, Isaac, 12
Shelby, Col., 15, 11, 9
Shields, Henry, 65
Shields, Robert, 245, 272
Shields, William, 220, 216
Shields Bloomary Forge, 245
Shields Grist Mill, 220, 222
Shoaff, A. A., 88

Shockland, John, 20
Shoemakers, 242
Shoemaker's Trade, 240
Shine, Daniel, 13
"Shin Plasters," 62
Shipping Inspector, 77
Short Creek, 221
Siege of Knoxville, 46
Silk Cocoons, 224
Silsby, J. A., 228
Silversmith, 265
Simerly, Abraham, 176
Simms, John, 96
Sims, 84, 96
Sims, Gray, 32
Sims, James, 33
Sims, Lt. Col. J. G., 69, 193, 211, 216, 215
Sims, Littlepage, 30, 32
"Simplified Anatomy," 183
Simpson, Martin, 252
Singleton, Captain, 28, 38, 30
Singleton, Dr. John, 186, 189, 192, 257, 269
"Singlings," 276
Sinking Creek, 100, 101, 218, 242, 243
Sinking Springs Church, 124
"Sinks," 60n
Six Mile, 80n, 115, 119, 122, 123, 175, 242, 243
Six Mile Church, 119
Six Mile Creek, 120
Sixth Tenn. Infantry, 60
Sketchley, 137
Skinner, L. D., 268
Slate Industry, 239
Slim Tom, 16
Sloan, 113
Sloan, Archibald, 13
Sloan, Mill, 217
Slone, 28n
Slone, John, 32n
Small, Rev. Thomas, 107
Small, Thomas H., 152
Small, Phrona, 49n
Small Pox, 50, 191
Small Pox Epidemic, 46
Smith, 138
Smith, A. Belle, 246, 264, 285
Smith, Daniel, 217
Smith, Bowman, 74
Smith, Charles C., 88
Smith, Dave, 221, 234, 239, 278
Smith, Captain F. M., 202
Smith, J. Gray, 222, 226, 80

Smith, Rev. Jacob, 117
Smith, John, 275
Smith, Joseph, 64
Smith, Josiah P., 134, 135, 256
Smith, Lewis, 42
Smith, Michael, 73, 112n
Smith, Stanfield, 72
Smith, Rev. W. A., 98
Smith, Wiley, 80
Smith, William S., 108
"Smoky," 277
Smoky Mountains, 41
Smoky Mountain Park Authorities, 220
Smoky Mountain Inn, 91
Smoky Mountain National Park, 52, 91, 231, 240, 255, 273, 276
Snapp, Sam, 268
Snider, 100, 271
Snider, George, 114, 119, 123, 219, 243, 272
Snider, Moses, 114
Snider, Peter, 114
Snider's Ford, 51
Snider, Peter's Store, 41
Snoddy, Nancy M., 108
Snoddy, R. C., 108
Snoddy, Rebecca, 108
Snoddy, Sarah A., 108
Snoddy, W. A. G., 108
Snow, T. H., 239
Snow Camp, North Carolina, 158
Snyder, Mr., 230
Soap Factory, 262
"Soft Shell" Baptists, 123
Soldiers Gazette, 228
"Soldiers in Hoopskirts," 63
Somme Offensive, 68
Sons of Temperance, 148, 149
Souers, Dr. J. A., 61
South Carolina, 3
South Dakota, 189
South Plant, 233
South Rockford Post Office, 280
Southern Coffin and Casket Company, 232
Southern Depot, 76
Southern Park Movement, 277
Southern Slate Company, 239
Southern Bell Telephone Co., 261
Southern and Western Theological Seminary, 136, 138, 140, 172
Southwest Point, 35, 77, 233
Spanish American War, 228, 232, 322
Sparks, 102
Sparks, J. T., 190, 248, 268
Special High School Districts, 202

Spence, Col. Cary F., 67
Spence Field, 277
Spencer, 15
Spencer, William A., 44, 136, 235
Spencer and Wallace, 256
Spillman, 100
Spillman, Dr. William, 183, 227, 231
Spindles, 225, 226
"Splash Operations," 272
Spoke Factory, 262
Spray, Prof. Wilson, 128, 158, 176
Springbrook, 176, 288
Springfield, 77, 108, 222, 230, 240, 242, 224
Spring View, 219, 241
Sprinkle, Mr., 241
Spurlock, Frank, 239
Stage Line, 279
Stage Route, 77, 73n
Staley, J. H., 232
Stallions, 102
Stanley, Sarah, 49n
Stanley, Dr. W. C., 128, 164, 196
Stanley, Mrs. S. T., 203
Standard-bearer, 34
Stanfield, William, 223
States Attorney, 209
State Board of Health, 188, 192
State Department of Health, 193
State Constitutional Convention, 33, 184
State of Franklin, 31
State Senator, 215
State Teacher's Association, 175
State of Tennessee, 32
State of Tennessee Bank, 246
Staub, John and Fritz, 225
Steam Sawmill, 230
Stearns, Mrs., 161
Steele, James T., 223
Steele, 130
Steele, John, 29
Steele, Samuel, 222
Steele, W. A., 242
Steele and Bros., 224
Steiner and Schweinitz, 134
Stephen, Col. Adam, 6, 8
Stephens, Holston, 224, 279
Stephens, Jehu, 56, 220, 224, 279, 308
Stephens Bros., 224
Stephens Mill, 41, 219, 279
Sterling, Cam, 261
Sterling, O. P., 109
Sterling, Robert, 106
Stevens, W. B., 211, 213
Stevens and Tipton, 144
Stephenson, "Jacky," 65

INDEX

Stephenson, James, 84
Stephenson, T. I., 126
Stevenson, Dr. William Patton, 144
Steveson, Mahlon, 126
Stewarts, 102
Stewart, John, 102
Stewart, J. W., 252
Stewart, Major Thomas, 17
Stinnett, Nelson, 122
Stinson, Edgar and wife, 164
Stock Creek, 32n, 77, 217, 237, 251
Stocks and Pillory, 34, 256
Stockton, William, 34
Stone, 109
Stone, Dr. Jefferson, 92, 94, 185, 226, 289
Stone, Patton, 124
Stone House, 267n
Stony Grave School, 171
Stony Point, 35, 253
"Stout Flood," 119
Stout, George, 29
Stout, Henry, 119
Strain, 100
Strain, Mattie, 162
Strain, Nancy, 109
Strang, David
Strutton, John, 57n
Stuart, Capt., 58
Stuart, John, 8
Stuarts Company of Rhea, 58
Stuart, William, 72
Student Center Building, 145
Studley, J. H., 285
Subscription School, 175
The "Suck," 6
Suez Canal, 66
Suggs, Thomas, 118
Sullins College, 167
Sullivan County, 12, 13, 58, 73
Sullivan Dr., 193
Sultana Survivors, 61n, 319
Summers, James A., 260
Summey, 130
Sumter, Sgt. Thomas, 7
Sunline, 234
Sunshine, 90, 245, 272, 283
Sunshine Rest Cottage, 91
Sunshine Society, International, 91
"Sunshine Valley," 250
"Sunny Hill," 187
Superior Court, 14, 205
Supreme Court, 206, 208, 216
Supreme Court Records, 330
Superintendent of Schools, 320; List of, 331

Surveying School, 172
Surveyor, 248
Susong, S. L., 190
Sutton Canning Company, 250
Sutton Transfer Co., 65n
Swain, Rev. W. T., 104
Swann, James Z., 227
Swann, Dr. Parke P., 194
Swann, William G., 45, 236
Swaney, Columbus, 130
Swaney Bros., 222
Swaney, George, Ike and Jim, 221
Sweet, 272
Sweetwater Association, 119
"Sweet William Spring," 84
Swift Memorial Institute, 143
Swisher, Michael, 113n
Switchboards, 261
"Switzerland of America," 91, 278
"Sycamore Spring," 250
Sycamore Shoals, 10, 11
Synod of Tennessee, 97n
Syrian, 189

"Tail," 20
Tailors, 246
Takahashi-Kin, 143
Talbotts, 102
Tallassee, 21
Tallassee, 283, 284
Tallassee Church, 127
Tallassee Ford, 40, 233, 234, 284
Tallassee Post Office, 283
Tallassee Town, 16
Tallassee Old Town, 30
Tallapoosa, 55
Tallequah, Indian Territory, 164
Tanbark, 241, 274
Tang, 272
Tannery, 274
Tanyards, 240
Tapoco, 233, 236, 285
Tar kiln Valley, 266
Tarvin Building, 252
"Tassell," 16
Tate, Doc, 67
Tavern rates, 35
Tax Assessor, 47, 200
Tax List-1800, 302
Tax List-1801, 293
Tax for schools, 174
Taxes, 33
Taxing District, 258
Taylors, 92, 113
Taylor, Dr. A. J., 186
Taylor, Rev. B. C., 74

Taylor, Daniel, 146, 240
Taylor, David, 35, 71, 72
Taylor, Gen., 56n
Taylor, Hugh O., 87
Taylor, Dr. Isaac, 186
Taylor, Isaac, 222
Taylor, I. W., 130
Taylor, James, 118, 119, 120, 123
Taylor, John, 36
Taylor, Joshua, 121
Taylor, Rufus, 242
Taylor, Rev. S. A., 109, 152
Taylor, William L., 223
Taylor's Tavern, 256
Tedford, 105
Tedford, Andy, 206, 269
Tedford, Chas., 141
Tedford, D. W., 257
Tedford, Edward W., 141, 196, 195
Tedford, E. Drugstore, 47, 109
Tedford, George, 30
Tedford, James P., 25, 55, 57n
Tedford, Capt. James, War of 1812, 309
Tedford, John D., 257
Tedford, Joseph, 25, 30
Tedford, Joseph P., 141
Tedford, Rev. Ralph E., 98, 101, 141
Tedford, Robert A., 57, 174
Tedford, Capt., 34, 39
Tedford, Lt., 24, 25, 26
Tedford's Rangers, 25
Teeguarden, W. R., 76
Teffeteller, 100
Teffeteller, M. L., 268
Teffeteller's Blacksmith Shop, 257
Telephone, 51, 260
Tellico Blockhouse, 20, 25, 27, 29, 30, 33, 35, 36, 71, 72, 77, 173, 279
Tellico Lodge No. 80, 148
Tellico Plains, 27
Tellico River, 5
Tellico Road, 243
Tellico Treaty, 37
The "Tellico," 269
Temperance, 190
Temperance Banner, 227
Temperance Hall, 149
Temple, 102
Temple, James, 247
Temple, John, 183
Tenn. Agricultural and Industrial College, 162
Tenn. Assoc. of Baptists, 118, 120, 122
Tennessee Canning Co., 250
Tenn. Carolina Southern Railroad, 231, 236, 261, 281, 283, 284, 286, 289
Tennessee Congregation, 98
Tennessee Country, 1, 8, 9, 10, 14, 20, 29, 95
Tenn. Electric Power Co., 260
Tenn. Federation of Women's Club, 177
Tenn. Legislature, 275
Tenn. Lumber and Canal Co., 49, 274
Tennessee Marble, 265
Tennessee Normal Teacher, 228
Tennessee Paradise, 91n, 278
Tenn. Producer's Marble Co., 238
Tenn. River, 8, 13, 36, 39, 170, 255
Tenn. Slate Co., 239
Tenn. Synod, 124, 138
Tenn. Textile Corp., 254
Tenn. Valley, 269
Terrill, Matthew, 164
Territorial Assembly, 30, 133, 271
Territorial Governor, 32, 197
Territory South of the River Ohio, 18, 210, 255
Texas Rangers, 64
Texas, 214
Texas Oil Company, 250
Textbook law, 169
Thaw, Mrs. Mary C., 144
Thaw, Wm., 141, 142, 143
Thaw Hall, 144
Theological Seminary, 137
Third Nat'l. Bank of Knoxville, 212
Third Regiment, 61
Thirtieth Division, 67
Thirty-ninth Reg. U. S. Infantry, 55
Thirty-ninth Regulars, 56
Thunderhead, 277
Thomas, Col. Abithia, 27
Thomas, Charles, 108
Thomas, D. K., 216
Thomas, Isaac, 11, 30
Thomas, Jacob, 72
Thomas, Jim, 217
Thomas, Dr. William, 183
Thomas Dr., 227
Thomason, Capt. (Grainger Co.), 58
Thompson, 79, 100, 102, 109, 129, 206
Thompson, Andrew, 34, 37, 38, 135, 136n
Thompson, Ann E., 109
Thompson, B. W., 61
Thompson, Elizabeth, 68n
Thompson, George U., 285
Thompson, Isaac, 220
Thompson, Jesse, 43, 79, 80, 173
Thompson, Maj. Jesse, 136

INDEX

Thompson, M. M., 115
Thompson, Robert, 99, 243
Thompson, Samuel, 32, 56, 71n, 183, 217, 227
Thompson, William, 209
Thompson's Bridge, 62, 71n, 234
Thompson's Schoolhouse, 115
Thomsonian Defender, 227
Thomsonian Steam System, 182
Thornburg, John, 223
Thorne, I. J., 226
"Tiger Lilies," 82
Tile Work, 285
Tilson, Henry I., 231
Tilton, J. W., 242
Timberlake, Ensign Henry, 6, 7
Tindell, Brownlow, 241
Tinshop, 253
Tippet, Erastus, 34
Tipton, 39, 234
Tipton, Capt. Jacob, 42, 276
Tipton, Jacob T., 57n
Tipton, Jonathan, 266
Tipton, Col. John, 266
Tipton, J., 121
Tipton, J. S., 190
Tipton, J. W. H., 58n, 90
Tipton, Lt. Ray, 69
Tipton, Capt. Ruben, 53n, 56
Tipton, William, 275, 279
Tipton's Ferry, 265
Tipton Station, 251
Tobacco, "plug," 269
Tomotley Ford, 65n, 113
Toof, F. P., 225
Toole, Ellen, 162
Toole, George, 62
Toole, G. A., 195
Toole, James M., 80, 148, 149, 247, 257, 279
Toole, John E., 44, 45, 61, 74, 137, 146, 147, 148, 211, 235, 236, 257, 258, 279
Toole, Sam, 61
Toole, Wm., 43, 73, 101, 136, 241, 247
Toole, Will Jr., 247
Toole, Wm. "Well Place," 41
Toole, Polly, 47
Toole, Pope and Co., 257
Toole Property, 264
Toole Tanyard, 241
Toqua, 24
Towne, Miss Mary S., 148
Townsend, W. B., 51, 170, 230, 231, 272
Townsend, 129, 170, 221, 231, 236, 252, 260, 261, 271, 272

Townsend Bus Line, 205
Townsend's Ferry, 234
"Trail of Tears," 57
Transportation, 170
Transylvania Co., 10
Treaty of Coyatee, 15
Treaty of Dumplin Creek, 13, 31
Treaty of Holston, 25, 27, 31, 255
Treaty of Hopewell, 19
Treaty of Long Island, 11
Treaty of Saluda, 4
Treaty of 1798, 35
Treaty of Tellico, 36, 255, 271
Tremont, 177, 231, 273
Trigonia High School, 202
Trigonia Mill, 221, 222
Trimble, 39, 243
Trimble, James, 39
Trimble, John, 30, 31, 33, 34, 56, 72, 233
Trimble, Capt. John, (War of 1812), 309
Trimble, Wm., 29
Trimble's Ferry, 233, 234
Trinity Presbyterian Church, 110
Trotter, D. W., 168
Troy Coaches, 81
Trundle, Eletha, 108
Trundle, James, 43
Trundle, Wilson L., 136
Trustee, 201
Trustees of Blount County, 331
Tub mills, 217, 220, 276
Tuberculosis Association, 191, 194
Tuckaleechee, 28n, 32, 42, 65, 68, 95, 114, 123, 170, 173, 218, 219, 220, 243, 265
Tuckaleechee Baptist Church, 121
Tuckaleechee Primitive Baptist Cemetery, 272
Tuckaleechee Caverns, 91, 273
Tuckaleechee Methodist Campground, 114, 121
Tuckaleechee Chapel Cemetery, 272
Tuckaleechee Cove, 35, 41, 42, 58, 60, 65, 81, 90, 118, 190, 217, 218, 224, 260, 271, 283
Tuckaleechee Road, 41
Tuckaleechee Towns, 3, 271
Tuckaleechee Villages, 68
Tuckaleechee Timber and Boom Company, 230
Tucker, R. C., 65, 227
Tucker Spring, 259
Tuckaseegee River, 41
Tuesday club, 177, 263, 264
Tullock, John M., 176

Tullock, Samuel, 41
Tullock, W. H., 74
Turk, James, 242, 256
Turnbulls, 102
Tuskeegee, 5, 161
T V A, 70, 232, 234
Tweed, J. L., 211
Tweed, Jancer L., 214, 263
Twentieth District, 42
Typewriter, 50
Tyson, Charles McGhee, 52n
Tyson, Gen. Lawrence D., 52, 67, 215

Unaka Tannery, 275
Underhill, Sarah, 157
Unicoi Turnpike, 40, 71, 80, 234
Union Academy, 138
Union Army, 64
Union Camps, 60
Union Convention Delegates, 316
Union Grove, 115, 122, 171
Unionists, 59
Union League, 65, 258
Union Presbytery, 59, 96, 98, 99, 138, 139
Union Rally, 59
Union Sympathizer, 156
Union Theological Seminary, 141
United Presbyterian, 104, 106, 286
United Presbyterian Church, 105
United Synod, 140
Unitia, 59, 84, 100, 101, 114, 115, 183, 187, 189, 218, 222, 224, 229, 234, 240, 270
Unitia Church, 99
Unitia Presbyterian Church, 270
University of Michigan, 215
University of Nashville, 188
University of Tennessee, 31, 215
Upper Cherokee Chiefs, 20
"Upper" Road, 81
Upton, James, 96
U. S. Government, 25
U. S. Navy, 52
U. S. Regular Army, 55
Utter, Abraham, 243
Utter and Stephens, 265

Valentine, G. W., 116
Valentine, Minnie, 162
Valley of Virginia, 9
Vance, Rev. A., 102
Vanderbilt Medical School, 278
Van Dyke, Chancellor, 45
Van Kirk, John, 89

Vaughn, Capt. (Monroe County), 58
Vaughn, 3, 271
Vaughn, Ben, 130
Vaults, 50
Veach, Kinsey, 118
Veach-May-Wilson, 218, 229, 231, 286
"Verandah Hotel," 75
Vestal Lumber Company, 231
Veteran's Administration, 215
Viaduct, Broadway, 207
Vineyard, J. L., 184, 264
Vineyard, John, 120, 121
Vineyard, J. L. and W. M., 242
Vinsant, C. C., 191, 193, 194, 195
Virginia, 186, 268
Virginia Fort, 4, 5
Virginia Military Institute, 61
Virtue, 84
Voorhees, Mrs. Elizabeth, 143
Vose School, 178
Vose Station, 103, 231

Waddell, Col. Hugh, 7
Wagon Shop, 248, 262
Walden's Creek, 273
Walden's Ridge, 8
Walker, 39, 101, 105, 130
Walker, Aaron, 119
Walker Chapel, 111, 114
Walker County, Georgia, 275
Walker, E. A., 168, 222
Walker, Elijah, 253
Walker, George, 29, 49
Walker, Hiram, 87
Walker, James, 29, 61, 274
Walker, Joe L., 272
Walker, John, 32, 41, 111, 118, 154, 217
Walker, John Sr., 271
Walker, John Jr., 271
Walker, Mrs. John, 145
Walker Ridge, 241
Walker, Roy, 105n
Walker, R. S., 151
Walker, Samuel, 111, 260
Walker Springs, 85
Walker's Stationary Store, 263
Walker, Dr. Thomas, 6
Walker's Valley, 177, 231
Walker, "Uncle Johnny," 92
Walker, W. A., 160
Walker, Capt. Wm., 55, 312
Walker, "Black" Will, 177
Wallace, 101
Wallace, Alexander M., 210
Wallace, A. M. & J. G., 257
Wallace, Campbell, 73, 235

INDEX

Wallace, Ensign Joel, 25, 21, 30
Wallace and Jacobs, 256
Wallace, Judge Jesse, 60, 73, 79
Wallace, J. G., 147, 148, 149, 211, 257
Wallace, John, 34, 37, 71
Wallace, John and James, 36
Wallace, Matthew, 33n, 34, 35, 39, 107, 217, 265
Wallace, Matthew's Mill, 35
Wallace, Oliver, 29, 72, 162
Wallace, Paris, 162
Wallace, Samuel, 36
Wallace Tanyard, 240
Wallace, T. F., 61
Wallace, Wm., 30, 31, 32, 33, 34, 35, 41, 44, 45, 55, 61, 76, 100, 136, 137, 140, 149, 235, 236, 279
Wallace, W. W., 257
Walland, 49, 59, 104, 170, 177, 192, 272, 261, 236, 260, 274
Walland Gap, 59
Walland High School, 170
Waller, 50, 129
Walton and England, 274
"Walter A. Love," 270
Walton, George, 37
Wardell, 190
Ward, Nancy, 11
Warehouse, 268
Warehouse on Holston River, 39
Warnack, W. C., 247
Warner, S. Allen, 228
War of 1812, 53
War Path, 95, 113, 289
Warner, J. H., 239
Warner Martin Mill, 229
Warner, Porter, 239
Warner, Yardley, 157, 160, 228
Warren, Barton, 241, 267
Warren County, La., 64n, 64
Warren, George A., Dr., 195
Warren, Wm., 107, 146, 151, 241
War with Mexico, 57
Washington, Booker T., 161
Washington College, 133
Washington, Connecticut, 185
Washington County, 11, 12, 13, 186
Washington District, 10, 11, 13, 19
Washington, Gen., 73
Washington, New Preston Society, 94
Washington, President, 19
Watauga, 8, 9, 12
Watauga Association, 9, 10, 209
Watauga Purchase, 10
Watauga River, 8

Waters, 274
Waters, Adam and Enoch, 221
Water Board, 259
Waters, Carl, 94
Waterhouse, Richard, 55
Waters, James, 48, 190
Waters, Joe, 92
Waters, J. D., 94, 185
Waters, John, 221, 274
"Water Lily," 270
Waters, Otis, 92
Waters, P. A., 94, 261
Water System, 50
Water works, 48, 259
Watch repair, 252
Watkins, Era L., 108
Watkins, Elizabeth, 108
Watkins, F. M., 108
Watkins, W. M., 108, 226
Watson, Asa, 80, 82
Watts, 26
Watt, Abram P., 81
Watt, Alex, 230
Watt, John, 18, 21, 24, 27, 30n
Wayland, F. G., 76
"Wayland House," 76
Waggoner, Marinell Ross, 216
Wayman and Cummings, 248
Wayman, E., 115, 248, 265
Wayne Co., North Carolina, 15
W C T U, 263, 264
Weagley, Perry and William, 66
Weagley, S. L., 190
Wear's, 39
Wear, Abraham, 32
Wear, Elizabeth M., 109
Wear, Samuel, 28, 266
Wear's Chapel, 103
Wears Cove, 3n, 60, 60n, 66, 114, 120, 170, 221, 271, 273
Wear's Ferry, 265
Wear, James P., 109
Wear, Lucinda P., 109
Wear, Robert, 266
Wear, Fayette, 221, 272
Weaver's, 10
Weaver-Mitchell and Co., 222
Weaver, Rev., 104
Weaver, William K., 191
Webb, E. L., 252
Webb, Frederic Lee, 177
Webb, J. H., 194
Webb, L. D., 190
Webb, Mrs. Emily, 177
Webster, 253

Weems, C. E., 253
Weir, Joseph, 37
Welch, Delevan and Nathan's National Circus, 257
Welch, Thomas H., 239
Welfare, League, 194
Wells, 229
Wells, Abraham, 25
Wells, A. L., 242
Wells, Anderson, 241
Wells and Irwin, 253
Wells, John B., 218, 282
Wells' Mill, 282
Wells' Station, 21, 25, 27, 28
Wells, Stephen, 122, 241, 282
Wellsville, 219, 222, 241
Wesley-Ann Methodist Church, 101
Wesley Chapel, 113n
West, 57
Western and Atlantic Railroad, 235
West Fabricating Plant, 233, 285
West, Floyd, 222
West Maryville Presbyterian Church, 104, 106
West, N. R., 108
West Point, 58
West, Samuel B., 152
West Side School, 51, 164, 178, 265
West View, 171
Westwood School, 191
Wetzell, Wm., 124
Wheeler's Cavalry, 62, 64
Wheeler Farm, 188
Wheeler, Peter, 41
Whetsell, 64
Whiston, John C., 164
White, Andrew, 209
White, Bill, 86
White, Capt., 60
White, Col., 21
White, Isaac, 219
White, John, 90
White, Lt., 60
"White Church," 121
White's Mill, 243
White's Mill Road, 219
White's Mill Tract, 121n
White Oak Cove, 245
White, Sophronia, 94
White, Thomas, 136, 246
Whiteheads, 247, 278
"White Store," 184
Whitlock, Charles P., 211
Whitney, Eli, 223
Whittaker, Dr. Walter, 125
Whittey and Trusty, Revs., 161

Wiggs, A. R., 61
Wilcox, Shan, 261
Wilcox, Blair, 285
Wilder, Gen., 91n
Wildwood, 167, 169, 171, 179, 190, 261, 289
Wildwood Mineral Springs, 93, 252
Wildwood Springs Hotel, 74, 92, 185
"Wildwood Sulphur Springs," 93
Wilkinson, John, 186, 210
Wilkinson, B. F., 268
Wilkinson, W. R., 242
Wilkinson, S. H., 270
Will I Omaugh, 29
Willard, 259
Willard, B. F., 232
Willard, Mrs. Frances, 263
Willard, Dr. Sylvester, 126
Williams, Azariah, 126
Williams, James, 85
Williams, John and Enoch, 36
Williams, Col. John, 55
Williams, John, 190
Williams, Dr. J. B., 196
Williams, Luther A., 89
Williams, Mary J., 91n
Williams, Mrs. William, 177
Williams, Newton K., 113n
Williams, Rachel, 126
Williams, Richard, 59
Williams, Sam, 86
Williams, Wm., 126, 128
Williamson, Col. John, 11
Williamson, John W., 38, 73, 115n
Williamson, Lydia, 115
Williamson's Chapel, 113, 116
Williamsons and McMurray Chapel, 115
Williamson School, 171
Willis, James, 218, 240
Willocks, Cowan, 130
Willocks, Moses, 130
Willocks, S. T., 130
Willocks, William, 222
Wills Town, 20
Wilson and Anderson, 84
Wilson, Abner, 86
Wilson, Clem, 86
Wilson, E. C., 130
Wilson Flour Mill, 257
Wilson, H. M., 225
Wilson, H. O., 249
Wilson, Rev. John G., 100
Wilson, Mrs. Mary A., 86
Wilson, Mary T., 142
Wilson, Oscar, 116, 162

Wilson, R. I., 44, 45, 64, 85, 152, 175, 177, 224, 225, 236, 257, 279
Wilson, Dr. S. T., 99, 145, 213
Wilson & Saffell, 256
Wilson, Timothy, 164
Wilson, Willie, 113
Winchester, 35
Winters, Dr. Elizabeth S., 190
Winters, Orlando, 128
Wisecarver, 234
Wistar, Edward M., 164
Wittenberg, Joseph, 218
Wolf Hills, 10
Wolfe, Jim, 207
Woodlawn Drive, 191
Wood, Leonard, 241
Woods, Abraham, 2
Woods, John, 35, 37, 71, 72, 218
Woodranger, 34
Woods, Richard, 118, 123
Woods Schoolhouse, 115, 171
Wood Tavern, 71, 73
Woodward, George, 228
Wool-Carding, 222
Woolen Mill, 185, 226
Woodford's Kentucky Cavalry, 62
Wool, John (Gen.), 57n
Woolsey, Israel, 87
Woman's Medical College of Philadelphia, 191
Works Progress Administration Canning Project, 250
World War I, 195, 325
World War I and II Memorials, 52
World War II, 195
Worley, Mrs. Emma, 121n
Worthy Master, 184
Wright, 101, 109
Wright, D. G., 168
Wrights Ferry, 115, 234
Wrights Ferry Road, 103
Wright, Dr. Isaac, 39, 181, 182, 234
Wright, James C., 239

Wright, Jonathan, 164
Wright, Nelson, 173
Wright, Miss Ora, 159
Wright, Willie Blount, 182
Wright, Wood, 211
Wrigley, William, 230, 272
Wrinkle, A. A., 280
Wrinkle, E. E., 280
Wrinkle, W. C., 108, 109
Wyley, James, 39, 265
Wynn, Ashley, 114

Yale College, 94
Yankee Soldiers, 60
Yates, Henry, 115
Yearout, 104, 221, 224
Yearout, Ben, 253
Yearout, Daniel, 243
Yearout, H. J., 252
Yearout, Isaac, 106
Yearout, Wm., 77
Yellow Fever Epidemic, 83
Yellow Poplar Lumber Company, 230
Yellow Springs Company, 87
Yellow Springs Place, 85
Yellow Sulphur Spring, 87, 88
Young, Ben, 89
Young, D. L., 253
Young, G. W., 131
Young, Hugh, 131
Young, Robert S., 74
Young, Sam E., 74
Young, Susie, 91n
Youngblood, Letitia, 122
Youngblood, Sarah, 122
Ypres, 68

Zeigler, I. B., 232
Zion, 114
Zoller, F. A., 191
Zoological Studies, 190
Zook, Shem, 131

www.ingramcontent.com/pod-product-compliance
Lightning Source LLC
Chambersburg PA
CBHW052338230426
43664CB00041B/2194